A History of California
and an Extended History
of Los Angeles

JAMES MILLER GUINN

JUERGEN BECK

A History of California, J.M. Guinn
Jazzybee Verlag Jürgen Beck
86450 Altenmünster, Loschberg 9
Deutschland

Printed by Createspace, North Charleston, SC, USA

ISBN: 9783849692049

www.jazzybee-verlag.de
www.facebook.com/jazzybeeverlag
admin@jazzybee-verlag.de

CONTENTS:

PREFACE

Few states of the Union have a more varied, a more interesting or a more instructive history than California, and few have done so little to preserve their history. In this statement I do not contrast California with older states of the Atlantic seaboard, but draw a parallel between our state and the more recently created states of the far west, many years younger in statehood than the Golden State of the Pacific.

When Kansas and Nebraska were uninhabited except by buffaloes and Indians, California was a populous state pouring fifty millions of gold yearly into the world's coffers. For more than a quarter of a century these states, from their public funds, have maintained state historical societies that have gathered and are preserving valuable historical material, while California, without a protest, has allowed literary pot hunters and speculative curio collectors to rob her of her historic treasures. When Washington, Montana and the two Dakotas were Indian hunting grounds, California was a state of a quarter million inhabitants; each of these states now has its State Historical Society supported by appropriations from its public funds.

California, of all the states west of the Mississippi river, spends nothing from its public funds to collect and preserve its history.

To a lover of California this is humiliating; to a student of her history exasperating. While preparing this History of California I visited all the large public libraries of the state. I found in all of them a very limited collection of books on California, and an almost entire absence of manuscripts and of the rarer books of the earlier eras. Evidently, the demand for works pertaining to California history is not very insistent. If it were, more of an effort would be put forth to procure them.

The lack of interest in our history is due largely to the fact that California was settled by one nation and developed by another. In the rapid development of the state by the conquering nation, the trials, struggles and privations of the first colonists who were of another nation have been ignored or forgotten. No forefathers' day keeps their memory green, no observance celebrates the anniversary of their landing. To many of its people the history of California begins with the discovery of gold, and all before that time is regarded as of little importance.

The race characteristics of the two peoples who have dominated California, differ widely; and from this divergence arises the lack of sympathetic unison. Perhaps no better expression for this difference can be given than is found in the popular by-words of each. The "poco tiempo" (by and by) of the Spaniard is significant of a people who are willing to wait — who would defer action till manana — tomorrow — rather than act with haste today. The "go ahead" of the American is indicative of hurry, of rush, of a strenuous existence, of a people impatient of present conditions.

In narrating the story of California, I have endeavored to deal justly with the different eras and episodes of its history; to state facts; to tell the truth without favoritism or prejudice; to give credit where credit is due and censure where it is deserved. In the preparation of this history I have endeavored to make it readable and reliable.

1

The subject matter is presented by topic and much of it in monographic form. I have deemed it better to treat fully important topics even if by so doing some minor events be excluded. The plan of the work includes first, a general history of California from its discovery by Cabrillo in the year 1342 and second, the history of Los Angeles and its Environs down to the year 1915. In gathering material for this work I have examined the collections in a number of libraries public and private, have consulted state, county and city archives and have scanned thousands of pages of newspapers and magazines.

In compiling the history of the Spanish and Mexican eras, I have taken Bancroft's History of California as the most reliable authority. I have obtained much original historical material from the Proceedings of the Ayuntamiento or Municipal Council of Los Angeles (1828 to 1850). The jurisdiction of that Ayuntamiento extended over an area now included in four of the seven counties commonly classified as Southern California. This accounts in part for the prominence of Los Angeles in the second half of this volume.

The consolidation of Los Angeles city and the cities of Wilmington, San Pedro and Hollywood has merged the recent history of these three into that of the Greater Los Angeles. The early history of these cities is given separately up to their consolidation.

Considerable space has been given to the history of San Pedro Bay and the inner harbor. Since the extension of the city limits has brought these within the jurisdiction and control of Los Angeles their early history and the efforts to develop them become important. Much of the material in the chapters on the bay and inner harbor has been obtained from perishable sources, such as articles in early newspapers, recollections of pioneers and pamphlets issued on special occasions.

From the files of The Californian. The California Star and The Alta Californian, pioneer papers of the state, I have obtained much valuable data that has not heretofore been incorporated into a volume of history. Where extracts have been made from authorities, due credit has been given in the body of the work. I have received valuable assistance from librarians, from pioneers of the state, from city and county officials, from editors and others. To all who have assisted me I return my sincere thanks. J. M. GUINN.

June 1, 1915.

CHAPTER I.
SPANISH EXPLORATIONS AND DISCOVERIES.

For centuries there had been a vague tradition of a land lying somewhere in the seemingly limitless expanse of ocean stretching westward from the shores of Europe. The poetical fancy of the Greeks had located in it the Garden of Hesperides, where grew the Golden Apples. The myths and superstitions of the middle ages had peopled it with gorgons and demons and made it the abode of lost souls.

When Columbus proved the existence of a new world beyond the Atlantic, his discovery did not altogether dispel the mysteries and superstitions that for ages had enshrouded the fabled Atlantis, the lost continent of the Hesperides. Romance and credulity had much to do with hastening the exploration of the newly discovered western world. Its interior might hold wonderful possibilities for wealth, fame and conquest to the adventurers who should penetrate its dark unknown. The dimly told traditions of the natives were translated to fit the cupidity or the credulity of adventurers, and sometimes served to promote enterprises that produced results far different from those originally intended.

The fabled fountain of youth lured Ponce de Leon over many a league in the wilds of Florida; and although he found no spring spouting forth the elixir of life, he explored a rich and fertile country, in which the Spaniards planted the first settlement ever made within the territory now held by the United States. The legend of El Dorado, the gilded man of the golden lake, stimulated adventurers to brave the horrors of the miasmatic forests of the Amazon and the Orinoco; and the search for that gold-covered hombre hastened, perhaps, by a hundred years, the exploration of the tropical regions of South America. Although the myth of Quivira that sent Coronado wandering over desert, mountain and plain, far into the interior of North America, and his quest for the seven cities of Cibola, that a romancing monk, Marcos de Niza, "led by the Holy Ghost," imagined he saw in the wilds of Pimeria, brought neither wealth nor pride of conquest to that adventurous explorer, yet these myths were the indirect cause of giving to the world an early knowledge of the vast regions to the north of Mexico.

When Cortes' lieutenant, Gonzalo de Sandoval, gave his superior officer an account of a wonderful island ten days westward from the Pacific coast of Mexico, inhabited by women only, and exceedingly rich in pearls and gold, although he no doubt derived his story from Montalvo's romance, "The Sergfas of Esplandian," a popular novel of that day, yet Cortes seems to have given credence to his subordinate's tale, and kept in view the conquest of the island.

To the energy, the enterprise and the genius of Hernan Cortes is due the early exploration of the northwest coast of North America. In 1522, eighty-five years before the English planted their first colony in America, and nearly a century before the landing of the Pilgrims on Plymouth rock, Cortes had established a shipyard at Zacatula, the most northern port on the Pacific coast of the country that he had just conquered. Here he intended to build ships to explore the upper coast of the South Sea (as the Pacific Ocean was then called), but his good fortune, that had hitherto given success to his undertakings, seemed to have deserted him, and disaster followed disaster. His warehouse, filled with material for shipbuilding, that with great labor and expense had been packed on muleback from Vera Cruz, took fire and all was destroyed. It required years to accumulate another supply. He finally, in 1527, succeeded in launching four ships. Three of these were taken possession of by the king's orders for service in the East Indies. The fourth and the smallest made a short voyage up the coast. The commander, Maldonado, returned with glowing reports of a rich country he had discovered. He imagined he had seen evidence of the existence of gold and silver, but he brought none with him.

In 1528 Cortes was unjustly deprived of the government of the country he had conquered. His successor, Nuno de Guzman, president of the royal audiencia, as the new form of government for New Spain (Mexico) was called, had pursued him for years with the malignity of a demon. Cortes returned to Spain to defend himself against the rancorous and malignant charges of his enemies. He was received at court with a show of high honors, but which in reality were hollow professions of friendship and insincere expressions of esteem. He was rewarded by the bestowal of an empty title. He was empowered to conquer and colonize countries at his own expense, for which he was to receive the twelfth part of the revenue. Cortes returned to Mexico and in 1532 he had two ships fitted out, which sailed from Acapulco, in June of that year, up the coast of Jalisco. Portions of the crews of each vessel mutinied. The mutineers were put aboard of the vessel commanded by Mazuela and the other vessels, commanded by Hurtardo, continued the voyage as far as the Yaqui country. Here, having landed in search of provisions, the natives massacred the commander and all the crew. The crew of the other vessel shared the same fate lower down the coast. The stranded vessel was afterwards plundered and dismantled by Nuno de Guzman, who was about as much of a savage as the predatory and murderous natives.

In 1533 Cortes, undismayed by his disasters, fitted out two more ships for the exploration of the northern coast of Mexico. On board one of these ships, commanded by Bercerra de Mendoza, the crew, headed by the chief pilot, Jiminez, mutinied. Mendoza was killed and all who would not join the mutineers were forced to go ashore on the coast of Jalisco. The mutineers, to escape punishment by the authorities, under the command of the pilot, Fortuno Jiminez, sailed westerly away from the coast of the main land. After several days' sailing out of sight of land, they discovered what they supposed to be an island. They landed at a place now known as La Paz, Lower California. Here Jiminez and twenty of his confederates were killed by the Indians, or their fellow mutineers, it is uncertain which. The survivors of the ill-fated expedition managed to navigate the vessel back to Jalisco, where they reported the discovery of an island rich in gold and pearls. This fabrication doubtlessly saved their necks. There is no record of their punishment for mutiny. Cortes' other ship accomplished even less than the one captured by the mutineers. Grixalvo, the commander of this vessel, discovered a desolate island, forty leagues south of Cape San Lucas, which he named Santo Tomas. But the discovery that should immortalize Grixalvo, and place him in the category with the romancing Monk, de Niza and Sandoval of the Amazonian isle, was the seeing of a merman. It swam about about the ship for a long time, playing

4

antics like a monkey for the amusement of the sailors, washing its face with its hands, combing its hair with its fingers: at last, frightened by a sea bird, it disappeared.

Cortes, having heard of Jiminez's discovery, and possibly believing it to be Sandoval's isle of the Amazons, rich with gold and pearls, set about building more ships for exploration and for the colonization of the island. He ordered the building of three ships at Tehauntepec. The royal audencia having failed to give him any redress or protection against his enemy, Nuno de Guzman, he determined to punish him himself. Collecting a considerable force of cavaliers and soldiers, he marched to Chiametla. There he found his vessel. La Concepcion, lying on her beam ends, a wreck, and plundered of everything of value. He failed to find Guzman, that worthy having taken a hasty departure before his arrival. His ships having come up from Tehauntepec, he embarked as many soldiers and settlers as his vessels would carry, and sailed away for Jiminez's island. May 3, 1535, he landed at the port where Jiminez and his fellow mutineers were killed, which he named Santa Cruz. The colonists were landed on the supposed island and the ships were sent back to Chiametla for the remainder of the settlers. His usual ill luck followed him. The vessels became separated on the gulf in a storm and the smaller of the three returned to Santa Cruz. Embarking in it, Cortes set sail to find his missing ships. He found them at the port of Guayabal, one loaded with provisions, the other dismantled and run ashore. Its sailors had deserted and those of the other ship were about to follow. Cortes stopped this, took command of the vessels and had them repaired. When the repairs were completed he set sail for his colony. But misfortune followed him. His chief pilot was killed by the falling of a spar when scarce out of sight of land. Cortes took command of the vessels himself. Then the ships encountered a terrific storm that threatened their destruction. Finally they reached their destination, Santa Cruz. There again misfortune awaited him. The colonists could obtain no sustenance from the barren soil of the desolate island. Their provisions exhausted, some of them died of starvation and the others killed themselves by over-eating when relief came.

Cortes, finding the interior of the supposed island as desolate and forbidding as the coast, and the native inhabitants degraded and brutal savages, without houses or clothing, living on vermin, insects and the scant products of the sterile land, determined to abandon his colonization scheme. Gathering together the wretched survivors of his colony, he embarked them on his ships and in the early part of 1537 landed them in the port of Acapulco.

At some time between 1535 and 1537 the name California was applied to the supposed island, but whether applied by Cortes to encourage his disappointed colonists, or whether given by them in derision, is an unsettled question. The name itself is derived from a Spanish romance, the "Sergas de Esplandian," written by Ordonez de Montalvo and published in Seville, Spain, about the year 1510. The passage in which the name California occurs is as follows: "Know that on the right hand of the Indies there is an island called California, very near the terrestrial paradise, which was peopled with black women, without any men among them, because they were accustomed to live after the fashion of Amazons. They were of strong and hardened bodies, of ardent courage and great force. The island was the strongest in the world from its steep rocks and great cliffs. Their arms were all of

5

gold and so were the caparison of the wild beasts which they rode, after having trained them, for in all the island there is no other metal." The "steep rocks and great cliffs" of Jiminez's island may have suggested to Cortes or to his colonists some fancied resemblance to the California of Montalvo's romance, but there was no other similarity.

For years Cortes had been fitting out expeditions by land and sea to explore the unknown regions northward of that portion of Mexico which he had conquered, but disaster after disaster had wrecked his hopes and impoverished his purse. The last expedition sent out by him was one commanded by Francisco Ulloa, who, in 1539, with two ships, sailed up the Gulf of California, or Sea of Cortes, on the Sonora side, to its head. Thence he proceeded down the inner coast of Lower California to the cape at its southern extremity, which he doubled, and then sailed up the outer coast to Cabo del Engano, the "Cape of Deceit." Failing to make any progress against the head winds, April 5, 1540, the two ships parted company in a storm. The smaller one, the Santa Agueda, returned safely to Santiago. The larger, La Trinidad, after vainly endeavoring to continue the voyage, turned back. The fate of Ulloa and of the vessel too, is uncertain. One authority says he was assassinated after reaching the coast of Jalisco by one of his soldiers, who, for some trivial cause, stabbed him to death; another account says that nothing is known of his fate, nor is it certainly known whether his vessel ever returned. The only thing accomplished by this voyage was to demonstrate that Lower California was a peninsula. Even this fact, although proved by Ulloa's voyage, was not fully admitted by geographers until two centuries later.

In 1540 Cortes returned to Spain to obtain, if possible, some recognition and recompense from the king for his valuable services. His declining years had been filled with bitter disappointments. Shipwreck and mutiny at sea; disaster and defeat to his forces on land; the treachery of his subordinates and the jealousy of royal officials continually thwarted his plans and wasted his substance. After expending nearly a million dollars in explorations, conquests and attempts at colonization, fretted and worried by the indifference and the ingratitude of a monarch for whom he had sacrificed so much, disappointed, disheartened, impoverished, he died at an obscure hamlet near Seville, Spain, in December, 1547

The next exploration that had something to do with the discovery of California was that of Hernando de Alarcon. With two ships he sailed from Acapulco, May 9, 1540, up the Gulf of California. His object was to co-operate with the expedition of Coronado. Coronado, with an army of four hundred men, had marched from Culiacan, April 22, 1540, to conquer the seven cities of Cibola. In the early part of 1537 Alvaro Nunez Cabeza de Vaca and three companions (the only survivors of six hundred men that Panfilo de Narvaes, ten years before, had landed in Florida for the conquest of that province) after almost incredible sufferings and hardships arrived in Culiacan on the Pacific coast. On their long journey passing from one Indian tribe to another they had seen many wondrous things and had heard of many more. Among others they had been told of seven great cities in a country called Cibola that were rich in gold and silver and precious stones.

A Franciscan friar, Marcos de Niza, having heard their wonderful stories determined to find the seven cities. Securing the service of Estevanico, a negro slave, who was one of Cabeza de Vaca's party, he set out in quest of the cities. With a number of Indian porters and Estevanico as a guide, he traveled northward a hundred leagues when he came to a desert that took four days to cross. Beyond this he found natives who told him of people four days further away who had gold in abundance. He sent the negro to investigate and that individual sent back word that Cibola was yet thirty days' journey to the northward. Following the trail of his guide, Niza travelled for two weeks crossing several deserts. The stories of the magnificence of the seven cities increased with every tribe of Indians through whose country he passed. At length, when almost to the promised land, a messenger brought the sad tidings that Estevanico had been put to death with all of his companions but two by the inhabitants of Cibola. To go forward meant death to the monk and all his party, but before turning back he climbed a high mountain and looked down upon the seven cities with their high houses and teeming populations thronging their streets. Then he returned to Culiacan to tell his wonderful stories. His tales fired the ambition and stimulated the avarice of a horde of adventurers. At the head of four hundred of these Coronado penetrated the wilds of Pimeria (now Arizona). He found seven Indian towns but no lofty houses, no great cities, no gold or silver. Cibola was a myth. Hearing of a country called Quivira far to the north, richer than Cibola, with part of his force he set out to find it. In his search he penetrated inland as far as the plains of Kansas, but Quivira proved to be as poor as Cibola, and Coronado returned disgusted. The Friar de Niza had evidently drawn on his imagination which seemed to be quite rich in cities.

Alarcon reached the head of the Gulf of California. Seeing what he supposed to be an inlet, but the water proving too shallow for his ships to enter it, he manned two boats and found his supposed inlet to be the mouth of a great river. He named it Buena Guia (Good Guide) now the Colorado. He sailed up it some distance and was probably the first white man to set foot upon the soil of Upper California. He heard of Coronado in the interior but was unable to establish communication with him. He descended the river in his boats, embarked on his vessels and returned to Mexico. The Viceroy Mendoza, who had fitted out the expedition of Alarcon, was bitterly disappointed on the return of that explorer. He had hoped to find the ships loaded with the spoils of the seven cities.

The report of the discovery of a great river did not interest his sordid soul. Alarcon found himself a disgraced man. He retired to private life and not long after died a broken hearted man.

CHAPTER II. ALTA OR NUEVA CALIFORNIA.

While Coronado was still wandering in the interior of the continent searching for Quivira and its king, Tatarrax, who wore a long beard, adored a golden cross and worshipped an image of the queen of heaven, Pedro de Alvarado, one of Cortes' former lieutenants, arrived from Guatemala, of which country he was governor, with a fleet of twelve ships. These were anchored in the harbor of Navidad. Mendoza, the viceroy, had been intriguing with Alvarado against Cortes; obtaining an interest in the fleet, he and Alvarado began preparations for an extensive scheme of exploration and conquest. Before they had perfected their plans an insurrection broke out among the Indians of Jalisco, and Pedro de Alvarado in attempting to quell it was killed. Mendoza fell heir to the fleet. The return of Coronado about this time dispelled the popular beliefs in Cibola and Quivira and put an end to further explorations of the inland regions of the northwest.

It became necessary for Mendoza to find something for his fleet to do. The Islas de Poiniente, or Isles of the Setting Sun (now the Philippines), had been discovered by Magellan. To these Mendoza dispatched five ships of the fleet under command of Lopez de Villalobos to establish trade with the natives. Two ships of the fleet, the San Salvador and the Vitoria, were placed under the command of Juan Rodriguez Cabrillo, reputed to be a Portuguese by birth and dispatched to explore the northwest coast of the Pacific. Cabrillo sailed from Navidad, June 27, 1542. Rounding the southern extremity of the peninsula of Lower California, he sailed up its outer coast. August 20 he reached Cabo del Engano, the most northerly point of Ulloa's exploration. On the 28th of September, 1542, he entered a bay which he named San Miguel (now San Diego), where he found "a land locked and very good harbor." He remained in this harbor until October 3. Continuing his voyage he sailed along the coast eighteen leagues, discovering two islands about seven leagues from the main land. These he named San Salvador and Vitoria after his ships (now Santa Catalina and San Clemente). On the 8th of October he crossed the channel between the islands and main land and anchored in a bay which he named Bahia de los Fumos y Fuegos, the Bay of Smokes and Fires (now known as the Bay of San Pedro). Heavy clouds of smoke hung over the headlands of the coast; and inland, fierce fires were raging. The Indians either through accident or design had set fire to the long dry grass that covered the plains at this season of the year.

After sailing six leagues further up the coast he anchored in a large ensenada or bight, now the Bay of Santa Monica. It is uncertain whether he landed at either place. The next day he sailed eight leagues to an Indian town which he named the Pueblo de las Canoas (the town of Canoes). This town was located on or near the present site of San Buenaventura. Sailing northwestward he passed through the Santa Barbara Channel, discovering the islands of Santa Cruz, Santa Rosa and San Miguel. Continuing up the coast he passed a long narrow point of land extending into the sea, which from its resemblance to a galley boat he named Cabo de la Galera, the Cape of the Galley (now called Point Concepcion). Baffled by head winds, the explorers slowly beat their way up the coast. On the 17th of November, they cast anchor in a large bay which they named Bahia de los Pinos, the Bay of

Pines (now the Bay of Monterey). Finding it impossible to land on account of the heavy sea, Cabrillo continued his voyage northward. After reaching a point on the coast in 40 degrees north latitude, according to his reckoning, the increasing cold and the storms becoming more frequent, he turned back and ran down the coast to the island of San Miguel, which he reached November 23. Here he decided to winter.

While on the island in October, he had broken his arm by a fall. Suffering from his broken arm he had continued in command. Exposure and unskillful surgery caused his death. He died January 3, 1543, and was buried on the island. His last resting place is supposed to be on the shore of Cuyler's harbor, on the island of San Miguel. No trace of his grave has ever been found. His companions named the island Juan Rodriguez, but he has been robbed of even this slight tribute to his memory. It would be a slight token of regard if the state would name the island Cabrillo. Saint Miguel has been well remembered in California and could spare an island.

Cabrillo on his death bed urged his successor in command, the pilot Bartolome Ferrolo, to continue the exploration. Ferrolo prosecuted the voyage of discovery with a courage and daring equal to that of Cabrillo. About the middle of February he left the harbor where he had spent most of the winter and after having made a short voyage in search of more islands he sailed up the coast. February 28, he discovered a cape which he named Mendocino in honor of the viceroy, a name it still bears. Passing the cape he encountered a fierce storm which drove him violently to the northeast, greatly endangering his ships. On March 1st, the fog partially lifting, he discovered a cape which he named Blanco, in the southern part of what is now the state of Oregon. The weather continuing stormy and the cold increasing as he sailed northward, Ferrolo reluctantly turned back. Running down the coast he reached the island of San Clemente. There in a storm the ships parted company and Ferrolo, after a search, gave up the Vitoria as lost. The ships, however, came together at Cerros island and from there, in sore distress for provisions, the explorers reached Navidad April 18, 1543. On the discoveries made by Cabrillo and Ferrolo the Spaniards claimed the territory on the Pacific coast of North America up to the forty-second degree of north latitude, a claim that they maintained for three hundred years.

The next navigator who visited California was Francis Drake, an Englishman. He was not seeking new lands, but a way to escape the vengeance of the Spaniards. Francis Drake, the "Sea King of Devon," was one of the bravest men that ever lived. Early in his maritime life he had suffered from the cruelty and injustice of the Spaniards. Throughout his subsequent career, which reads more like romance than reality, he let no opportunity slip to punish his old-time enemies. It mattered little to Drake whether his country was at peace or war with Spain; he considered a Spanish ship or a Spanish town his legitimate prey. On one of his predatory expeditions he captured a Spanish town on the isthmus of Panama named El Nombre de Dios, The Name of God. Its holy name did not protect it from Drake's rapacity. While on the isthmus he obtained information of the Spanish settlements of the South Pacific and from a high point of land saw the South sea, as the Pacific ocean was then called. On his return to England he announced his intention of fitting out a privateering expedition against the Spaniards of the South Pacific.

9

Although Spain and England were at peace, he received encouragement from the nobility, even Queen Elizabeth herself secretly contributing a thousand crown towards the venture.

Drake sailed out of Plymouth harbor, England, December 13, 1577, in command of a fleet of five small vessels, bound for the Pacific coast of South America. Some of his vessels were lost at sea and others turned back, until when he emerged from the Straits of Magellan he had but one left, the Pelican. He changed its name to the Golden Hind. It was a ship of only one hundred tons' burden. Sailing up the South Pacific coast, he spread terror and devastation among the Spanish settlements, robbing towns and capturing ships until, in the quaint language of a chronicler of the expedition, he "had loaded his vessel with a fabulous amount of fine wares of Asia, precious stones, church ornaments,gold plate and so mooch silver as did ballas the Goulden Hinde."

From one treasure ship, the Caca Fuego, he obtained thirteen chests of silver, eighty pounds weight of gold, twenty-six tons of uncoined silver, two silver drinking vessels, precious stones and a quantity of jewels; the total value of his prize amounted to three hundred and sixty thousand pesos (dollars). Having spoiled the Spaniards of treasure amounting to "eight hundred sixty-six thousand pesos of silver * * * a hundred thousand pesos of gold * * * and other things of great worth, he thought it not good to return by the streight (Magellan) * * * least the Spaniards should there waite and attend for him in great numbers and strength, whose hands, he being left but one ship, he could not possibly escape."

Surfeited with spoils and his ship loaded with plunder, it became necessary for him to find the shortest and safest route home. To return by the way he came was to invite certain destruction to his ship and death to all on board. At an island off the coast of Nicaragua he overhauled and refitted his ship. He determined to seek the Straits of Anian that were believed to connect the Atlantic and Pacific oceans. Striking boldly out on an unknown sea, he sailed more than a thousand leagues northward. Encountering contrary winds and the cold increasing as he advanced, he gave up his search for the mythical straits, and, turning, he ran down the northwest coast of North America to latitude 38°, where "hee found a harborrow for his ship." He anchored in it June 17, 1579. This "convenient and fit harborrow" is under the lee of Point Reyes and is now known as Sir Francis Drake's Bay.

Fletcher, the chronicler of Drake's voyage, in his narrative, "The World Encompassed," says: "The 3rd day following, viz., the 21st, our ship having received a leake at sea was brought to anchor neerer the shoare that her goods being landed she might be repaired; but for that we were to prevent any danger that might chance against our safety our Generall first of all landed his men with necessary provision to build tents and make a fort for defense of ourselves and goods; and that we might under the shelter of it with more safety (whatsoever should befall) end our business."

The ship was drawn upon the beach, careened on its side, caulked and refitted. While the crew were repairing the ship the natives visited them in great numbers. From some of their actions Drake inferred that they regarded himself and his men as gods. To disabuse them of this idea, Drake ordered his chaplain, Fletcher, to perform divine service according to the English Church Ritual and preach a sermon. The Indians were greatly delighted with the psalm singing, but their opinion of Fletcher's sermon is not known.

From certain ceremonial performance Drake imagined that the Indians were offering him the sovereignty of their land and themselves as subjects of the English crown. Drake gladly accepted their proffered allegiance and formally took possession of the country in the name of the English sovereign, Queen Elizabeth. He named it New Albion, "for two causes: the one in respect of the white bankes and cliffes which ly towardes the sea; and the other because it might have some affinitie with our own country in name which sometimes was so called."

Having completed the repairs to his ship, Drake made ready to depart, but before leaving "Our Generall with his company made a journey up into the land. The inland we found to be farre different from the shoare; a goodly country and fruitful soyle, stored with many blessings fit for the use of man; infinite was the company of very large and fat deere which there we saw by thousands as we supposed in a heard." They saw great numbers of small burrowing animals, which they called conies, but which were probably ground squirrels. Before departing, Drake set up a monument to show that he had taken possession of the country. To a large post firmly set in the ground he nailed a brass plate on which was engraved the name of the English Queen, the date of his arrival and the statement that the king and people of the country had voluntarily become vassals of the English crown; a new sixpence was fastened to the plate to show the Queen's likeness.

After a stay of thirty-six days, Drake took his departure, much to the regret of the Indians. He stopped at the Farallones islands for a short time to lay in a supply of seal meat; then he sailed for England by the way of the Cape of Good Hope. After encountering many perils, he arrived safely at Plymouth, the port from which he sailed nearly three years before, having "encompassed" or circumnavigated the globe. His exploits and the booty he brought back made him the most famous naval hero of his time. He was knighted by Queen Elizabeth and accorded extraordinary honors by the nation. He believed himself to be the first discoverer of the country he called New Albion. "The Spaniards never had any dealings or so much as set foote in this country; the utmost of their discoveries reaching only to many degrees southward of this place." The English founded no claim on Drake's discoveries. The land hunger that characterizes that nation now had not then been developed.

Fifty years passed after Cabrillo's visit to California before another attempt was made by the Spaniards to explore her coast. Through all these years on their return voyage far out beyond the islands the Manila galleons, freighted with the wealth of "Ormus and Ind," sailed down the coast of Las Californias from Cape Mendocino to Acapulco. Often storm-tossed and always scourged with that dread malady of the sea, the scurvy, there was no harbor of refuge for them to put into because his most Catholic Majesty, the King of Spain, had no money to spend in exploring an unknown coast where there was no return to be expected except perhaps the saving of a few sailors' lives.

In 1593, the question of a survey of the California coast for harbors to accommodate the increasing Philippine trade was agitated and Don Luis de Velasco, viceroy of New Spain, in a letter dated at Mexico, April 8, 1593, thus writes to his majesty: "In order to make the exploration or demarcation of the harbors of this main as far as the Philippine islands, as your majesty orders, money is lacking, and if it be not taken from the royal strong box it cannot be supplied, as for some time past a great deal of money has been owing to the royal treasury on account of fines forfeited to it, legal cost and the like." Don Luis fortunately discovers a way to save the contents of the royal strong box and hastens to acquaint his majesty with his plan. In a letter written to the king from the City of Mexico, April 6, 1594, he says: "I ordered the navigator who at present sails in the flag ship, who is named Sebastian Rodriguez Cermeño, and who is a man of experience in his calling, one who can be depended upon and who has means of his own, although he is a Portuguese, there being no Spaniards of his profession whose services are available, that he should make the exploration and demarcation, and I offered, if he would do this, to give him his remuneration in the way of taking on board merchandise; and I wrote to the governor (of the Philippines) that he should allow him to put on board the ship some tons of cloth that he might have the benefit of the freight-money." The result of Don Luis's economy and the outcome of attempting to explore an unknown coast in a heavily laden merchant ship are given in a paragraph taken from a letter written by a royal officer from Acapulco, February 1, 1596, to the viceroy Conde de Monterey, the successor of Velasco: "On Wednesday, the 31st of January of this year, there entered this harbor a vessel of the kind called in the Philippines a viroco, having on board Juan de Morgana, navigating officer, four Spanish sailors, five Indians and a negro, who brought tidings that the ship San Agustin, of the exploring expedition, had been lost on a coast where she struck and went to pieces, and that a barefooted friar and another person of those on board had been drowned and that the seventy men or more who embarked in this small vessel only these came in her, because the captain of said ship, Sebastian Rodriguez Cermeño, and the others went ashore at the port of Navidad, and, as they understand, have already arrived in that city (Mexico). An account of the voyage and of the loss of the ship, together with the statement made under oath by said navigating officer, Juan de Morgana, accompany this. We visited officially the vessel, finding no kind of merchandise on board, and that the men were almost naked. The vessel being so small it seems miraculous that she should have reached this country with so many people on board." A viroco was a small vessel without a deck, having one or two square sails, and propelled by sweeps. Its hull was formed from a single tree, hollowed out and having the sides built up with planks. The San Agustin was wrecked in what is now called Francis Drake's Bay, about thirty miles north of San Francisco. To make a voyage from there to Acapulco in such a vessel, with seventy men on board, and live to tell the tale, was an exploit that exceeded the most hazardous undertakings of the Argonauts of "49.

The viceroy, Conde de Monte Rey, in a letter dated at Mexico, April 19, 1596, gives the king tidings of the loss of the San Agustin. He writes: "Touching the loss of the ship, San Agustin, which was on its way from the islands of the west (the Philippines) for the purpose of making the exploration of the coast of the South Sea, in accordance with your Majesty's orders to Viceroy, Don Luis de Velasco, I wrote to Your Majesty by the second packet (mailship) what I send as duplicate with this." He then goes on to tell how he had examined the officers in regard to the loss of the vessel and that they tried to inculpate one another. The navigating officer even in the viroco tried to explore the principal bays which they crossed, but on account of the hunger and illness they experienced he was compelled to hasten the voyage. The viceroy concludes: "Thus I take it, as to this exploration the intention of Your Majesty has not been carried into effect. It is the general opinion that this enterprise should not be attempted on the return voyage from the islands and with a laden ship, but from this coast and by constantly following along it." The above account of the loss of the San Agustin is taken from Volume II, Publications of the Historical Society of Southern California, and is the only correct account published. In September, 1595, just before the viceroy, Don Luis de Velasco, was superseded by Conde de Monte Rey, he entered into a contract with certain parties of whom Sebastian Viscaino, a ship captain, was the principal, to make an expedition up the Gulf of California "for the purpose of fishing for pearls." There was also a provision in the contract empowering Viscaino to make explorations and take possession of his discoveries for the crown of Spain. The Conde de Monte Rey seems, from a letter written to the King, to have seriously doubted whether Viscaino was the right man for so important an expedition, but finally allowed him to depart. In September, 1596, Viscaino sailed up the gulf with a fleet of three vessels, the flag ship San Francisco, the San Jose and a Lancha. The flag ship was disabled and left at La Paz. With the other two vessels he sailed up the gulf to latitude 29°. He encountered severe storms. At some island he had trouble with the Indians and killed several. As the long boat was departing an Indian wounded one of the rowers with an arrow. The sailor dropped his oar, the boat careened and upset, drowning twenty of the twenty-six soldiers and sailors in it.

Viscaino returned without having procured any pearls or made any important discoveries. He proposed to continue his explorations of the Californias, but on account of his misfortunes his request was held in abeyance. He wrote a letter to the king in 1597, setting forth what supplies he required for the voyage. His inventory of the items needed is interesting, but altogether too long for insertion here. Among the items were "$35,000 in money"; "eighty arrobas of powder"; "twenty quintals of lead"; "four pipes of wine for mass and sick friars"; "vestments for the clergy and $2,000 to be invested in trifles for the Indians for the purpose of attracting them peaceably to receive the holy gospel." Viscaino's request was not granted at that time. The viceroy and the royal audiencia at one time ordered his commission revoked. Philip II died in 1598 and was succeeded by Philip III. After five years' waiting, Viscaino was allowed to proceed with his explorations. From Acapulco on the 5th of May, 1602, he writes to the king that he is ready to sail with his ships "for the discovery of harbors and bays of the coast of the South Sea as far as Cape Mendocino." "I report," he says, "merely that the said Viceroy (Conde de Monterey) has entrusted to me the accomplishment of the same in two ships, a lancha and a barcoluengo, manned with sailors and soldiers and provisioned for eleven months. To-day being Sunday, the 5th of May, I sail at five o'clock in the names of God and his blessed mother and your majesty."

Viscaino followed the same course marked out by Cabrillo sixty years before. November 10, 1602, he anchored in Cabrillo's Bay of San Miguel. Whether the faulty reckoning of Cabrillo left him in doubt of the points named by the first discoverer, or whether it was that he might receive the credit of their discovery, Viscaino changed the names given by Cabrillo to the islands, bays and headlands

13

along the California coast. Cabrillo's Bahia San Miguel became the Bay of San Diego; San Salvador and Vitoria were changed to Santa Catalina and San Clemente, and Cabrillo's Bahia de los Fumos y Fuegos appears on Viscaino's map as the Ensenada de San Andres, but in a description of the voyage compiled by the cosmographer, Cabrero Bueno, it is named San Pedro. It is not named for the Apostle St. Peter, but for St. Peter, Bishop of Alexandria, whose day in the Catholic calendar is November 26, the day of the month Viscaino anchored in the Bay of San Pedro.

Sailing up the coast, Viscaino passed through the Santa Barbara channel, which was so named by Antonio de la Ascencion, a Carmelite friar, who was chaplain of one of the ships. The expedition entered the channel December 4, which is the day in the Catholic calendar dedicated to Santa Barbara. He visited the mainland near Point Concepcion where the Indian chief of a populous rancheria offered each Spaniard who would become a resident of his town ten wives. This generous offer was rejected. December 15, 1602, he reached Point Pinos, so named by Cabrillo, and cast anchor in the bay formed by its projection. This bay he named Monterey, in honor of the viceroy, Conde de Monte Rey. Many of his men were sick with the scurvy and his provisions were becoming exhausted; so, placing the sick and disabled on the San Tomas, he sent them back to Acapulco; but few of them ever reached their destination. On the 3rd of January, 1603, with two ships, he proceeded on his search for Cape Mendocino, the northern limit of his survey. The Manila galleons on their return voyage from the Philippines sailed up the Asiatic coast to the latitude of Japan, when, taking advantage of the westerly winds and the Japan current, they crossed the Pacific, striking the North American coast in about the latitude of Cape Mendocino, and from there they ran down the coast of Las Californias and across the gulf to Acapulco. After leaving Point Reyes a storm separated his ships and drove him as far north as Cape Blanco. The smaller vessel, commanded by Martin de Aguilar, was driven north by the storm to latitude 43°, where he discovered what seemed to be the mouth of a great river; attempting to enter it, he was driven back by the swift current. Aguilar, believing he had discovered the western entrance of the Straits of Anian, sailed for New Spain to report his discovery. He, his chief pilot and most of his crew died of scurvy before the vessel reached Navidad. Viscaino, after sighting Cape Blanco, turned and sailed down the coast of California, reaching Acapulco March 21, 1603.

Viscaino, in a letter to the King of Spain, dated at the City of Mexico, May 23, 1603, grows enthusiastic over California climate and productions. It is the earliest known specimen of California boom literature. After depicting the commodiousness of Monterey Bay as a port of safety for the Philippine ships, he says: "This port is sheltered from all winds, while on the immediate shores there are pines, from which masts of any desired size can be obtained, as well as live oaks and white oaks, rosemary, the vine, the rose of Alexandria, a great variety of game, such as rabbits, hare, partridges and other sorts and species found in Spain. This land has a genial climate, its waters are good and it is fertile, judging from the varied and luxuriant growth of trees and plants; and it is thickly settled with people whom I found to be of gentle disposition, peaceable and docile. * * * Their food consists of seeds which they have in great abundance and variety, and of the flesh of game such as deer, which are larger than cows, and bear, and of neat cattle and bisons

14

and many other animals. The Indians are of good stature and fair complexion, the women being somewhat less in size than the men, and of pleasing countenance. The clothing of the people of the coast lands consists of the skins of the sea wolves (otter) abounding there, which they tan and dress better than is done in Castile; they possess also in great quantity flax like that of Castile, hemp and cotton, from which they make fishing lines and nets for rabbits and hares. They have vessels of pine wood, very well made, in which they go to sea with fourteen paddlemen of a side, with great dexterity in very stormy weather. * * * They are well acquainted with gold and silver and said that these were found in the interior."

The object of Viscaino's boom literature of three hundred years ago was the promotion of a colony scheme for the founding of a settlement on Monterey Bay. He visited Spain to obtain the consent of the king and assistance in planting a colony. After many delays, Philip III, in 1606, ordered the viceroy of New Spain to fit out immediately an expedition to be commanded by Viscaino for the occupation and settlement of the port of Monterey. Before the expedition could be gotten ready Viscaino died and his colonization scheme died with him. Had he lived to carry out his scheme, the settlement of California would have antedated that of Jamestown, Va., by one year.

CHAPTER III.
COLONIZATION OF ALTA CALIFORNIA.

Hundred and sixty years passed after the abandonment of Viscaino's colonization scheme before the Spanish crown made another attempt to utilize its vast possessions in Alta California. The Manila galleons sailed down the coast year after year for more than a century and a half, yet in all this long space of time none of them so far as we know ever entered a harbor or bay on the upper California coast. Spain still held her vast colonial possessions in America, but with a loosening grasp. As the years went by she had fallen from her high estate. Her power on sea and land had weakened. Those brave old sea kings, Drake, Hawkins and Frobisher, had destroyed her invincible Armada and burned her ships in her very harbors. The English and Dutch privateers had preyed upon her commerce on the high seas and the buccaneers had robbed her treasure ships and devastated her settlements on the islands and the Spanish main, while the freebooters of many nations had time and again captured her galleons and ravished her colonies on the Pacific coast. The energy and enterprise that had been a marked characteristic of her people in the days of Cortes and Pizarro were ebbing away. The age of luxury that began with the influx of the wealth which flowed into the mother country from her American colonies engendered intrigue and official corruption among her rulers, demoralized her army and prostrated her industries. While her kings and her nobles were reveling in luxury the poor were crying for bread. Prescriptive laws and the fear of her Holy Inquisition had driven into exile many of the most enterprising and most intelligent of her people. These baneful influences had palsied the bravery and spirit of adventure that had been marked characteristics of the Spaniards in the fifteenth and sixteenth centuries. Other nations stood ready to take advantage of her decadence. Her old-time enemy, England, which had gained in power as Spain had lost, was ever on the alert to take advantage of her weakness; and another power, Russia, almost unknown among the powers of Europe when Spain was in her prime, was threatening her possessions in Alta California. To hold this vast country it must be colonized, but her restrictions on commerce and her proscriptive laws against foreign immigrants had shut the door to her colonial possessions against colonists from all other nations. Her sparse settlements in Mexico could spare no colonists. The native inhabitants of California must be converted to Christianity and made into citizens. Poor material indeed were these degraded savages, but Spain's needs were pressing and missionary zeal was powerful. Indeed, the pristine courage and daring of the Spanish soldier seemed to have passed to her missionary priest.

The Jesuits had begun missionary work in 1697 among the degraded inhabitants of Lower California. With a perseverance that was highly commendable and a bravery that was heroic, under their devoted leaders, Salvatierra, Kino, Ugarte, Piccolo and their successors, they founded sixteen missions on the peninsula. Father Kino (or Kuhn), a German Jesuit, besides his missionary work, between 1694 and 1702, had made explorations around the head of the Gulf of California and up the Rio Colorado to the mouth of the Gila, which had clearly demonstrated that Lower California was a peninsula and not an island. Although Ulloa had sailed

16

down the inner coast and up the outer coast of Lower California and Domingo del Castillo, a Spanish pilot, had made a correct map showing it to be a peninsula, so strong was the belief in the existence of the Straits of Anian that one hundred and sixty years after Ulloa's voyage Las Californias were still believed to be islands and were sometimes called Islas Carolinas, or the Islands of Charles, named so for Charles II. of Spain. Father Kino had formed the design of establishing a chain of missions from Sonora around the head of the gulf and down the inner coast of Lower California to Cape San Lucas. He did not live to complete his ambitious project. The Jesuit missions of Baja California never grew rich in flocks and herds. The country was sterile and the few small valleys of fertile land around the missions gave the padres and the neophytes at best but a frugal return for their labors.

For years there had been, in the Catholic countries of Europe, a growing fear and distrust of the Jesuits. Portugal had declared them traitors to the government and had banished them in 1759 from her dominions. France had suppressed the order in her domains in 1764. In 1767, King Carlos III., by a pragmatic sanction or decree, ordered their expulsion from Spain and all her American colonies. So great and powerful was the influence of the order that the decree for their expulsion was kept secret until the moment of its execution. Throughout all parts of the kingdom, at a certain hour of the night, a summons came to every college, monastery or other establishment where members of the order dwelt, to assemble by command of the king in the chapel or refectory immediately. The decree of perpetual banishment was then read to them. They were hastily bundled into vehicles that were awaiting them outside and hurried to the nearest seaport, where they were shipped to Rome. During their journey to the sea-coast they were not allowed to communicate with their friends nor permitted to speak to persons they met on the way. By order of the king, any subject who should undertake to vindicate the Jesuits in writing should be deemed guilty of treason and condemned to death.

The Lower California missions were too distant and too isolated to enforce the king's decree with the same haste and secrecy that was observed in Spain and Mexico. To Governor Caspar de Portola was entrusted the enforcement of their banishment. These missions were transferred to the Franciscans, but it took time to make the substitution. He proceeded with great caution and care lest the Indians should become rebellious and demoralized. It was not until February, 1768, that all the Jesuit missionaries were assembled at La Paz; from there they were sent to Mexico and on the 13th of April, at Vera Cruz, they bade farewell to the western continent.

At the head of the Franciscan contingent that took charge of the abandoned missions of Baja California, was Father Junipero Serra, a man of indomitable will and great missionary zeal. Miguel Jose Serra was born on the island of Majorica in the year 1713. After completing his studies in the Lullian University, at the age of eighteen he became a monk and was admitted into the order of Franciscans. On taking orders he assumed the name of Junipero (Juniper). Among the disciples of St. Francis was a very zealous and devoted monk who bore the name of Junipero, of whom St. Francis once said, "Would to God, my brothers, that I had a whole forest of such Junipers." Serra's favorite study was the "Lives of the Saints," and no doubt the study of the life of the original Junipero influenced him to take that saint's name. Serra's ambition was to become a missionary, but it was not until he was nearly forty years of age that his desire was gratified. In 1749 he came to Mexico and January 1, 1750, entered the College of San Fernando. A few months later he was given charge of an Indian mission in the Sierra Gorda mountains, where, with his assistant and lifelong friend, Father Palou, he remained nine years. Under his instructions the Indians were taught agriculture and the mission became a model establishment of its kind. From this mountain mission Serra returned to the city of Mexico. He spent seven years in doing missionary work among the Spanish population of the capital and surrounding country. His success as a preacher and his great missionary zeal led to his selection as president of the missions of California, from which the Jesuits had been removed. April 2, 1768, he arrived in the port of Loreto with fifteen associates from the College of San Fernando. These were sent to the different missions of the peninsula. These missions extended over a territory seven hundred miles in length and it required several months to locate all the missionaries.

The scheme for the occupation and colonization of Alta California was to be jointly the work of church and state. The representative of the state was Jose de Galvez, visitador-general of New Spain, a man of untiring energy, great executive ability, sound business sense and, as such men are and ought to be, somewhat arbitrary. Galvez reached La Paz in July, 1768. At once he began investigating the condition of the peninsular missions and supplying their needs. This done, he turned his attention to the northern colonization. Establishing his headquarters at Santa Ana near La Paz, he summoned Father Junipero for consultation in regard to the founding of missions in Alta California. It was decided to proceed to the initial points, San Diego and Monterey, by land and sea. Three ships were to be dispatched carrying the heavier articles, such as agricultural implements, church ornaments, and a supply of provisions for the support of the soldiers and priest after their arrival in California. The expedition by land was to take along cattle and horses to stock the country. This expedition was divided into two detachments, the advance one under the command of Rivera y Moncada, who had been a long time in the country, and the second division under Governor Caspar de Portola, who was a newcomer. Captain Rivera was sent northward to collect from the missions all the live stock and supplies that could be spared and take them to Santa Maria, the most northern mission of the peninsula. Stores of all kinds were collected at La Paz. Father Serra made a tour of the missions and secured such church furniture, ornaments and vestments as could be spared.

The first vessel fitted out for the expedition by sea was the San Carlos, a ship of about two hundred tons burden, leaky and badly constructed. She sailed from La Paz January 9, 1769, under the command of Vicente Vila. In addition to the crew there were twenty-five Catalonian soldiers, commanded by Lieutenant Pages, Pedro Prat, the surgeon, a Franciscan friar, two blacksmiths, a baker, a cook and two tortilla makers. Galvez in a small vessel accompanied the San Carlos to Cape San Lucas, where he landed and set to work to fit out the San Antonio. On the 15th of February this vessel sailed from San Jose del Cabo (San Jose of the Cape), under the command of Juan Perez, an expert pilot, who had been engaged in the Philippine trade. On this vessel went two Franciscan friars, Juan Viscaino and Francisco Gomez. Captain Rivera y Moncada, who was to pioneer the way, had collected supplies and cattle at Velicata on the northern frontier. From here, with a small force of soldiers, a gang of neophytes and three muleteers, and accompanied by Padre Crespi, he began his march to San Diego on the 24th of March, 1769.

The second land expedition, commanded by Governor Caspar de Portola in person, began its march from Loreto, March 9, 1769. Father Serra, who was to have accompanied it, was detained at Loreto by a sore leg. He joined the expedition at Santa Maria, May 5, where it had been waiting for him some time. It then proceeded to Rivera's camp at Velicata, sixty miles further north, where Serra founded a mission, naming it San Fernando. Campa Coy, a friar who had accompanied the expedition thus far, was left in charge. This mission was intended as a frontier post in the travel between the peninsular missions and the Alta California settlements. On the 15th of May Portola began his 'northern march, following the trail of Rivera.

Galvez had named, by proclamation, St. Joseph is the patron saint of the California expeditions, Santa Maria was designated as the patroness of conversions.

The San Antonia, the last vessel to sail, was the first to arrive at San Diego. It anchored in the bay April 11, 1769, after a prosperous voyage of twenty-four days. There she remained at anchor, awaiting the arrival of the San Carlos, the flag ship of the expedition, which had sailed more than a month before her. On the 29th of April the San Carlos, after a disastrous voyage of one hundred and ten days, drifted into the Bay of San Diego, her crew prostrated with the scurvy, not enough able-bodied men being left to man a boat. Canvas tents were pitched and the afflicted men taken ashore. When the disease had run its course nearly all of the crew of the San Carlos, half of the soldiers who had come on her, and nine of the sailors of the San Antonio, were dead.

On the 14th of May Captain Rivera y Moncada's detachment arrived. The expedition had made the journey from Velicata in fifty-one days. On the first of July the second division, commanded by Portola, arrived. The journey had been uneventful. The four divisions of the grand expedition were now united, but its numbers had been greatly reduced. Out of two hundred and nineteen who had set out by land and sea only one hundred and twenty-six remained; death from scurvy and the desertion of the neophytes had reduced the numbers nearly one-half. The ravages of the scurvy had destroyed the crew of one of the vessels and greatly crippled that of the other, so it was impossible to proceed by sea to Monterey, the second objective point of the expedition. A council of the officers was held and it was decided to send the San Antonia back to San Bias for supplies and sailors to man the San Carlos. The San Antonia sailed on the 9th of July and after a voyage of twenty days reached her destination; but short as the voyage was, half of the crew died of the scurvy on the passage. In early American navigation the scurvy was the most dreaded scourge of the sea, more to be feared than storm and shipwreck. These might happen occasionally, but the scurvy always made its appearance on long voyages, and sometimes destroyed the whole ship's crew. Its appearance and ravages were largely due to the neglect of sanitary precautions and to the utter indifference of those in authority to provide for the comfort and health of the sailors. The intercession of the saints, novenas, fasts and penance were relied upon to protect and save the vessel and her crew, while the simplest sanitary measures were utterly disregarded. A blind, unreasoning faith that was always seeking interposition from some power without to preserve and ignoring the power within, was the bane and curse of that age of superstition.

If the mandates of King Carlos III. and the instructions of the visitador-general, Jose de Galvez, were to be carried out, the expedition for the settlement of the second point designated (Monterey) must be made by land; accordingly Governor Portola set about organizing his forces for the overland journey. On the 14th of July the expedition began its march. It consisted of Governor Portola, Padres Crespi and Gomez, Captain Rivera y Moncada, Lieutenant Pedro Pages, Engineer Miguel Constanso, soldiers, muleteers and Indian servants, numbering in all sixty-two persons.

On the 16th of July, two days after the departure of Governor Portola, Father Junipero, assisted by Padres Viscaino and Parron, founded the mission of San Diego. The site selected was in what is now Old Town, near the temporary presidio, which had been hastily constructed before the departure of Governor Portola. A hut of boughs had been constructed and in this the ceremonies of founding were held. The Indians, while interested in what was going on, manifested no desire to be converted. They were willing to receive gifts, particularly of cloth, but would not taste the food of the Spaniards, fearing that it contained poison and attributing the many deaths among the soldiers and sailors to the food. The Indians had a great liking for pieces of cloth, and their desire to obtain this led to an attack upon the people of the mission. On the 14th of August, taking advantage of the absence of Padre Parron and two soldiers, they broke into the mission and began robbing it and the beds of the sick. The four soldiers, a carpenter and a blacksmith rallied to the defense, and after several of their numbers had fallen by the guns of the soldiers, the Indians fled. A boy servant of the padres was killed and Father Viscaino wounded in the hand. After this the Indians were more cautious.

We now return to the march of Portola's expedition. As the first exploration of the main land of California was made by it, I give considerable space to the incidents of the journey. Crespi, Constanso and Pages kept journals of the march. I quote from those of Constanso and Crespi. Lieutenant Constanso thus describes the order of the march. "The setting forth was on the 14th day of June (*evidently an error, editor's note*)of the cited year of '69. The two divisions of the expedition by land marched in one, the commander so arranging because the number of horse-herd and packs was much, since of provisions and victuals alone they carried one hundred packs, which he estimated to be necessary to ration all the folk during six months; thus providing against a delay of the packets, altho' it was held to be impossible that in this interval some one of them should fail to arrive at Monterey. On the marches the following order was observed: At the head went the commandant with the officers, the six men of the Catalonia volunteers, who added themselves at San Diego, and some friendly Indians, with spades, mattocks, crowbars, axes and other implements of pioneers, to chop and open a passage whenever necessary. After them followed the pack-train, divided into four bands with the muleteers and a competent number of garrison soldiers for their escort with each band. In the rear guard with the rest of the troops and friendly Indians came the captain, Don Fernando Rivera, convoying the horse-herd and the mule herd for relays."

"It must be well considered that the marches of these troops with such a train and with such embarrassments thro' unknown lands and unused paths could not be long ones; leaving aside the other causes which obliged them to halt and camp early in the afternoon, that is to say, the necessity of exploring the land one day for the next, so as to regulate them (the marches) according to the distance of the watering-places and to take in consequence the proper precautions; setting forth again on special occasions in the evening, after having given water to the beasts in that same hour upon the sure information that in the following stretch there was no water or that the watering place was low, or the pasture scarce. The restings were measured by the necessity, every four days, more or less, according to the extraordinary fatigue occasioned by the greater roughness of the road, the toil of the pioneers, or the wandering off of the beasts which were missing from the horse herd and which it was necessary to seek by their tracks. At other times, by the necessity of humoring the sick, when there were any, and with time there were many who yielded up their strength to the continued fatigue, the excessive heat and cruel cold. In the form and according to the method related the Spaniards executed their marches; traversing immense lands more fertile and more pleasing in proportion as they penetrated more to the north. All in general are peopled with a multitude of Indians, who came out to meet them and in some parts accompanied them from one stage of the journey to the next; a folk very docile and tractable chiefly from San Diego onward."

Constanso's description of the Indians of Santa Barbara will be found in the chapter on the "Aborigines of California." "From the channel of Santa Barbara onward the lands are not so populous nor the Indians so industrious, but they are equally affable and tractable. The Spaniards pursued their voyage without opposition up to the Sierra of Santa Lucia, which they contrived to cross with much hardship. At the foot of said Sierra on the north side is to be found the port of Monterey, according to ancient reports, between the Point of Pines and that of Año Nuevo (New Year). The Spaniards caught sight of said points on the 1st of October of the year '69, and, believing they had arrived at the end of their voyage, the commandant sent the scouts forward to reconnoiter the Point of Pines; in whose near vicinity lies said Port in 36 degrees and 40 minutes North Latitude. But the scant tokens and equivocal ones which are given of it by the Pilot Cabrera Bueno, the only clue of this voyage, and the character of this Port, which rather merits the name of Bay, being spacious (in likeness to that of Cadiz), not corresponding with ideas which it is natural to form in reading the log of the aforementioned Cabrera Bueno, nor with the latitude of:37 degrees in which he located it, the scouts were persuaded that the Port must be farther to the north and they returned to the camp which our people occupied with the report that what they sought was not to be seen in those parts."

They decided that the Port was still further north and resumed their march. Seventeen of their number were sick with the scurvy, some of whom, Constanso says, seemed to be in their last extremity; these had to be carried in litters. To add to their miseries, the rains began in the latter part of October, and with them came an epidemic of diarrhea, "which spread to all without exception; and it came to be feared that this sickness which prostrated their powers and left the persons spiritless, would finish with the expedition altogether. But it turned out quite to the

21

contrary.'" Those afflicted with the scurvy began to mend and in a short time they were restored to health. Constanso thus describes the discovery of the Bay of San Francisco: "The last day of October the Expedition by land came in sight of Punta de Los Reyes and the Farallones of the Port of San Francisco, whose landmarks, compared with those related by the log of the Pilot Cabrera Bueno, were found exact. Thereupon it became of evident knowledge that the Port of Monterey had been left behind; there being few who stuck to the contrary opinion. Nevertheless the commandant resolved to send to reconnoiter the land as far as Point de los Reyes. The scouts who were commissioned for this purpose found themselves obstructed by immense estuaries, which run extraordinarily far back into the land and were obliged to make great detours to get around the heads of these. * * * Having arrived at the end of the first estuary and reconnoitered the land that would have to be followed , to arrive at the Point de Los Reyes, interrupted; with new estuaries, scant pasturage and fire-| wood and having recognized, besides this, the uncertainty of the news and the misapprehension the scouts had labored under, the commandant, with the advice of his officers, resolved upon a retreat to the Point of Pines in hopes of finding the Port of Monterey and encountering in it the Packet San Jose or the San Antonia, whose succor already was necessary; since of the provisions which had been taken in San Diego no more remained than some few sacks of flour of which a short ration was issued to each individual daily."

"On the eleventh day of November was put into execution the retreat in search of Monterey. The Spaniards reached said port and the Point of Pines on the 28th of November. They maintained themselves in this place until the 10th of December without any vessel having appeared in this time. For which reason and noting also a lack of victuals, and that the sierra of Santa Lucia was covering itself with snow, the commandant, Don Caspar de Portola, saw himself obliged to decide to continue the retreat unto San Diego, leaving it until a better occasion to return to the enterprise. On this retreat the Spaniards experienced some hardships and necessities, because they entirely lacked provisions, and because the long marches, which necessity obliged to make to reach San Diego, gave no time for seeking sustenance by the chase, nor did game abound equally everywhere. At this juncture they killed twelve mules of the pack-train on whose meat the folk nourished themselves unto San Diego, at which new establishment they arrived, all in health, on the 24th of January, 1770."

The San Jose, the third ship fitted out by visitador-General Galvez, and which Governor Portola expected to find in the Bay of Monterey, sailed from San Jose del Cabo in 2vlay, 1770, with supplies and a double crew to supply the loss of sailors on the other vessels, but nothing was ever heard of her afterwards. Provisions were running low at San Diego, no ship had arrived, and Governor Portola had decided to abandon the place and return to Loreto. Father Junipero was averse to this and prayed unceasingly for the intercession of Saint Joseph, the patron of the expedition. A novena or nine days' public prayer was instituted to terminate with a grand ceremonial on March 19th, which was the saint's own day. But on the 23rd of March, when all were ready to depart, the packet San Antonia arrived. She had sailed from San Bias the 20th of December. She encountered a storm which drove her four hundred leagues from the coast; then she made land in 35 degrees north latitude. Turning her prow southward, she ran down to Point

Concepcion, where at an anchorage in the Santa Barbara channel the captain, Perez, took on water and learned from the Indians of the return of Portola's expedition. The vessel then ran down to San Diego, where its opportune arrival prevented the abandonment of that settlement.

With an abundant supply of provisions and a vessel to carry the heavier articles needed in forming a settlement at Monterey, Portola organized a second expedition. This time he took with him only twenty soldiers and one officer, Lieutenant Pedro Pages. He set out from San Diego on the 17th of April and followed his trail made the previous year. Father Serra and the engineer, Constanso, sailed on the San Antonia, which left the port of San Diego on the 16th of April. The land expedition reached Monterey on the 23rd of May and the San Antonia on the , 31st of the same month. On the 3rd of June, 1770, the mission of San Carlos Borromeo de Monterey was formally founded with solemn church ceremonies, accompanied by the ringing of bells, the crack of musketry and the roar of cannon. Father Serra conducted the church services. Governor Portola took possession of the land in the name of King Carlos III. A presidio or fort of palisades was built and a few huts erected. Portola, having formed the nucleus of a settlement, turned over the command of the territory to Lieutenant Pages. On the 9th of July, 1770, he sailed on the San Antonia for San Bias. He never returned to Alta California.

CHAPTER IV. ABORIGINES OF CALIFORNIA.

Whether the primitive California Indian was the low and degraded being that some modern writers represent him to have been, admits of doubt. A mission training continued through three generations did not elevate him in morals at least. When freed from mission restraint and brought in contact with the white race he lapsed into a condition more degraded and more debased than that in which the missionaries found him. Whether it was the inherent fault of the Indian or the fault of his training is a question that is useless to discuss now. If we are to believe the accounts of the California Indian given by Viscaino and Constanso, who saw him before he had come in contact with civilization he was not inferior in intelligence to the nomad aborigines of the country east of the Rocky mountains.

Sebastian Viscaino thus describes the Indians he found on the shores of Monterey Bay three hundred years ago:

"The Indians are of good stature and fair complexion, the women being somewhat less in size than the men and of pleasing countenance. The clothing of the people of the coast lands consists of the skins of the sea-wolves (otter) abounding there, which they tan and dress better than is done in Castile; they possess also, in great quantity, flax like that of Castile, hemp and cotton, from which they make fishing-lines and nets for rabbits and hares. They have vessels of pine wood very well made, in which they go to sea with fourteen paddle men on a side with great dexterity, even in stormy weather."

Indians who could construct boats of pine boards that took twenty-eight paddle men to row were certainly superior in maritime craft to the birch bark canoe savages of the east. We might accuse Viscaino, who was trying to induce King Philip III. to found a colony on Monterey Bay, of exaggeration in regard to the Indian boats were not his statements confirmed by the engineer, Miguel Constanso, who accompanied Portola's expedition one hundred and sixty-seven years after Viscaino visited the coast. Constanso, writing of the Indians of the Santa Barbara Channel, says, "The dexterity and skill of these Indians is surpassing in the construction of their launches made of pine planking. They are from eight to ten varas (twenty-three to twenty-eight feet) in length, including their rake and a vara and a half (four feet three inches) beam. Into their fabric enters no iron whatever, of the use of which they know little. But they fasten the boards with firmness, one to another, working their drills just so far apart and at a distance of an inch from the edge, the holes in the upper boards corresponding with those in the lower, and through these holes they pass strong lashings of deer sinews. They pitch and calk the seams, and paint the whole in sightly colors. They handle the boats with equal cleverness, and three or four men go out to sea to fish in them, though they have capacity to carry eight or ten. They use long oars with two blades and row with unspeakable lightness and velocity. They know all the arts of fishing, and fish abound along their coasts as has been said of San Diego. They have communication and commerce with the natives of the islands, whence they get the beads of coral which are current in place of money through these lands, although they hold in more esteem the glass beads which the Spaniards gave them, and offered in exchange for these whatever they had like trays, otter skins, baskets and wooden plates. * * *

"They are likewise great hunters. To kill deer and antelope they avail themselves of an admirable ingenuity. They preserve the hide of the head and part of the neck of some one of these animals, skinned with care and leaving the horns attached to the same hide, which they stuff with grass or straw to keep its shape. They put this said shell like a cap upon the head and go forth to the woods with this rare equipage. On sighting the deer or antelope they go dragging themselves along the ground little by little with the left hand. In the right they carry the bow and four arrows. They lower and raise the head, moving it to one side and the other, and making other demonstrations so like these animals that they attract them without difficulty to the snare; and having them within a short distance, they discharge their arrows at them with certainty of hitting."

In the two chief occupations of the savage, hunting and fishing, the Indians of the Santa Barbara Channel seem to have been the equals if not the superiors of their eastern brethren. In the art of war they were inferior. Their easy conquest by the Spaniards and their tame subjection to mission rule no doubt had much to do with giving them a reputation for inferiority.

The Indians of the interior valleys and those of the coast belonged to the same general family. There were no great tribal divisions like those that existed among the Indians east of the Rocky mountains. Each rancheria was to a certain extent independent of all others, although at times they were known to combine for war or plunder. Although not warlike, they sometimes resisted the whites in battle with great bravery. Each village had its own territory in which to hunt and fish and its own section in which to gather nuts, seeds and herbs. While their mode of living was somewhat nomadic they seem to have had a fixed location for their rancherias.

The early Spanish settlers of California and the mission padres have left but very meager accounts of the manners, customs, traditions, government and religion of the aborigines. The padres were too intent upon driving out the old religious beliefs of the Indian and instilling new ones to care much what the aborigine had formerly believed or what traditions or myths he had inherited from his ancestors. They ruthlessly destroyed his fetishes and his altars wherever they found them, regarding them as inventions of the devil.

The best account that has come down to us of the primitive life of the Southern California aborigines is found in a series of letters written by Hugo Reid and published in the Los Angeles Star in 1851-52. Reid was an educated Scotchman, who came to Los Angeles in 1834. He married an Indian woman, Dona Victoria, a neophyte of the San Gabriel mission. She was the daughter of an Indian chief. It is said that Reid had been crossed in love by some high toned Spanish señorita and married the Indian woman because she had the same name as his lost love. It is generally believed that Reid was the putative father of Helen Hunt Jackson's heroine, Ramona.

From these letters, now in the possession of the Historical Society of Southern California, I briefly collate some of the leading characteristics of the Southern Indians:

Government.

"Before the Indians belonging to the greater part of this country were known to the whites they comprised, as it were, one great family under distinct chiefs; they spoke nearly the same language, with the exception of a few words, and were more to be distinguished by a local intonation of the voice than anything else. Being related by blood and marriage war was never carried on between them. When war was consequently waged against neighboring tribes of no affinity it was a common cause."

"The government of the people was invested in the hands of their chiefs, each captain commanding his own lodge. The command was hereditary in a family. If the right line of descent ran out they elected one of the same kin nearest in blood. Laws in general were made as required, with some few standing ones. Robbery was never known among them. Murder was of rare occurrence and punished with death. Incest was likewise punished with death, being held in such abhorrence that marriages between kinsfolk were not allowed. The manner of putting to death was by shooting the delinquent with arrows. If a quarrel ensued between two parties the chief of the lodge took cognizance in the case and decided according to the testimony produced. But if a quarrel occurred between parties of distinct lodges, each chief heard the witnesses produced by his own people, and then, associated with the chief of the opposite side, they passed sentence. In case they could not agree an impartial chief was called in, who heard the statements made by both and he alone decided. There was no appeal from his decision. Whipping was never resorted to as a punishment. All fines and sentences consisted in delivering shells, money, food and skins."

Religion

"They believed in one God, the Maker and Creator of all things, whose name was and is held so sacred among them as hardly ever to be used, and when used only in a low voice. That name is Qua-o-ar. When they have to use the name of the supreme being on an ordinary occasion they substitute in its stead the word Y-yo-ha-rory-nain or the Giver of Life. They have only one word to designate life and soul."

"The world was at one time in a state of chaos, until God gave it its present formation, fixing it on the shoulders of seven giants, made expressly for this end. They have their names, and when they move themselves an earthquake is the consequence. Animals were then formed, and lastly man and woman were formed, separately from earth and ordered to live together. The man's name was Tobahar and the woman's Probavit. God ascended to Heaven immediately afterward, where he receives the souls of all who die. They had no bad spirits connected with their creed, and never heard of a 'devil' or a 'heir until the coming of the Spaniards. They believed in no resurrection whatever "

26

Marriage.

"Chiefs had one, two or three wives, as their inclination dictated, the subjects only one. When a person wished to marry and had selected a suitable partner, he advertised the same to all his relatives, even to the nineteenth cousin. On a day appointed the male portion of the lodge brought in a collection of money beads. All the relations having come in with their share, they (the males) proceeded in a body to the residence of the bride, to whom timely notice had been given. All of the bride's female relations had been assembled and the money was equally divided among them, the bride receiving nothing, as it was a sort of purchase. After a few days the bride's female relations returned the compliment by taking to the bridegroom's dwelling baskets of meal made of chia, which was distributed among the male relatives. These preliminaries over, a day was fixed for the ceremony, which consisted in decking out the bride in innumerable strings of beads, paint, feathers and skins. On being ready she was taken up in the arms of one of her strongest male relatives, who carried her, dancing, towards her lover's habitation. All of her family, friends and neighbors accompanied, dancing around, throwing food and edible seeds at her feet at every step. These were collected in a scramble by the spectators as best they could. The relations of the bridegroom met them half way, and, taking the bride, carried her themselves, joining in the ceremonious walking dance. On arriving at the bridegroom's (who was sitting within his hut) she was inducted into her new residence by being placed alongside of her husband, while baskets of seeds were liberally emptied on their heads to denote blessings and plenty. This was likewise scrambled for by the spectators, who, on gathering up all the bride's seed cake, departed, leaving them to enjoy their honeymoon according to usage. A grand dance was given on the occasion, the warriors doing the dancing, the young women doing the singing. The wife never visited her relatives from that day forth, although they were at liberty to visit her."

Burials

"When a person died all the kin collected to mourn his or her loss. Each one had his own peculiar mode of crying or howling, as easily distinguished the one from the other as one song is from another. After lamenting awhile a mourning dirge was sung in a low whining tone, accompanied by a shrill whistle produced by blowing into the tube of a deer's leg bone.

Dancing can hardly be said to have formed a part of the rites, as it was merely a monotonous action of the foot on the ground. This was continued alternately until the body showed signs of decay, when it was wrapped in the covering used in life. The hands were crossed upon the breast and the body tied from head to foot. A grave having been dug in their burial ground, the body was deposited with seeds, etc., according to the means of the family. If the deceased were the head of the family or a favorite son, the hut in which he lived was burned up, as likewise were all his personal effects."

Feuds — The Song Fights.

"Animosity between persons or families was of long duration, particularly between those of different tribes. These feuds descended from father to son until it was impossible to tell of how many generations. They were, however, harmless in themselves, being merely a war of songs, composed and sung against the conflicting party, and they were all of the most obscene and indecent language imaginable. There are two families at this day (1851) whose feud commenced before the Spaniards were ever dreamed of and they still continue singing and dancing against each other. The one resides at the mission of San Gabriel and the other at San Juan Capistrano; they both lived at San Bernardino when the quarrel commenced. During the singing they continue stamping on the ground to express the pleasure they would derive from tramping on the graves of their foes. Eight days was the duration of the song fight."

Utensils.

"From the bark of nettles was manufactured thread for nets, fishing lines, etc. Needles, fishhooks, awls and many other articles were made of either bone or shell; for cutting up meat a knife of cane was invariably used. Mortars and pestles were made of granite. Sharp stones and perseverance were the only things used in their manufacture, and so skillfully did they combine the two that their work was always remarkably uniform. Their pots to cook in were made of soapstone of about an inch in thickness and procured from the Indians of Santa Catalina. Their baskets, made out of a certain species of rush, were used only for dry purposes, although they were water proof. The vessels in use for liquids were roughly made of rushes and plastered outside and in with bitumen or pitch."

Indians Of The Santa Barbara Channel.

Miguel Constanso, the engineer who accompanied Portola's expedition in 1769, gives us the best description of the Santa Barbara Indians extant.

"The Indians in whom was recognized more vivacity and industry are those that inhabit the islands and the coast of the Santa Barbara channel. They live in pueblos (villages) whose houses are of spherical form in the fashion of a half orange covered with rushes. They are up to twenty varas (fifty-five feet) in diameter. Each house contains three or four families. The hearth is in the middle and in the top of the house they leave a vent or chimney to give exit for the smoke. In nothing did these gentiles give the lie to the affability and good treatment which were experienced at their hands in other times (1602) by the Spaniards who landed upon those coasts with General Sebastian Vizcayno. They are men and women of good figure and aspect, very much given to painting and staining their faces and bodies with red ochre.

"They use great head dresses of feathers and some panderellas (small darts) which they bind up amid their hair with various trinkets and beads of coral of various colors. The men go entirely naked, but in time of cold they sport some long capes of tanned skins of nutrias (otters) and some mantles made of the same skins cut in long strips, which they twist in such a manner that all the fur remains outside; then they weave these strands one with another, forming a weft, and give it the pattern referred to.

"The women go with more decency, girt about the waist with tanned skins of deer which cover them in front and behind more than half down the leg, and with a mantelet of nutria over the body. There are some of them with good features. These are the Indian women who make the trays and vases of rushes, to which they give a thousand different forms and graceful patterns, according to the uses to which they are destined, whether it be for eating, drinking, guarding their seeds, or for other purposes; for these peoples do not know the use of earthen ware as those of San Diego use it.

"The men work handsome trays of wood, with finer inlays of coral or of bone; and some vases of much capacity, closing at the mouth, which appear to be made with a lathe — and with this machine they would not come out better hollowed nor of more perfect form. They give the whole a luster which appears the finished handiwork of a skilled artisan. The large vessels which hold water are of a very strong weave of rushes pitched within; and they give them the same form as our water jars.

"To eat the seeds which they use in place of bread they toast them first in great trays, putting among the seeds some pebbles or small stones heated until red; then they move and shake the tray so it may not burn; and getting the seed sufficiently toasted they grind it in mortars or almireses of stone. Some of these mortars were of extraordinary size, as well wrought as if they had had for the purpose the best steel tools. The constancy, attention to trifles, and labor which they employ in finishing these pieces are well worthy of admiration. The mortars are so appreciated among themselves that for those who, dying, leave behind such handiworks, they are wont to place them over the spot where they are buried, that the memory of their skill and application may not be lost.

"They inter their dead. They have their cemeteries within the very pueblo. The funerals of their captains they make with great pomp, and set up over their bodies some rods or poles, extremely tall, from which they hang a variety of utensils and chattels which were used by them. They likewise put in the same place some great planks of pine, with various paintings and figures in which without doubt they explain the exploits and prowesses of the personage.

"Plurality of wives is not lawful among these peoples. Only the captains have a right to marry two. In all their pueblos the attention was taken by a species of men who lived like the women, kept company with them, dressed in the same garb, adorned themselves with beads, pendants, necklaces and other womanish adornments, and enjoyed great consideration among the people. The lack of an interpreter did not permit us to find out what class of men they were, or to what ministry they were destined, though all suspect a defect in sex, or some abuse among those gentiles.

"In their houses the married couples have their separate beds on platforms elevated from the ground. Their mattresses are some simple petates (mats) of rushes and their pillows are of the same petates rolled up at the head of the bed. All these beds are hung about with like mats, which serve for decency and protect from the cold."

29

From the descriptions given by Viscaino and Constanso of the coast Indians they do not appear to have been the degraded creatures that some modern writers have pictured them. In mechanical ingenuity they were superior to the Indians of the Atlantic seaboard or those of the Mississippi valley. Much of the credit that has been given to the mission padres for the patient training they gave the Indians in mechanical arts should be given to the Indian himself. He was no mean mechanic when the padres took him in hand.

Bancroft says "the Northern California Indians were in every way superior to the central and southern tribes." The difference was more in climate than in race. Those of Northern California living in an invigorating climate were more active and more warlike than their sluggish brethren of the south. They gained their living by hunting larger game than those of the south whose subsistence was derived mostly from acorns, seeds, small game and fish. Those of the interior valleys of the north were of lighter complexion and had better forms and features than their southern kinsmen. They were divided into numerous small tribes or clans, like those of central and Southern California. The Spaniards never penetrated very far into the Indian country of the north and consequently knew little or nothing about the habits and customs of the aborigines there. After the discovery of gold the miners invaded their country in search of the precious metal. The Indians at first were not hostile, but ill-treatment soon made them so. When they retaliated on the whites a war of extermination was waged against them. Like the mission Indians of the south they are almost extinct.

All of the coast Indians seem to have had some idea of a supreme being. The name differed with the different tribes. According to Hugo Reid the god of the San Gabriel Indian was named Quaoar. Father Boscana, who wrote "A Historical Account of the Origin,; Customs and Traditions of the Indians" at the missionary establishment of San Juan Capistrano, published in Alfred Robinson's "Life in California," gives a lengthy account of the religion of those Indians before their conversion to Christianity. Their god was Chinigchinich. Evidently the three old men from whom Boscana derived his information mixed some of the religious teachings of the padres with their own primitive beliefs, and made up for the father a nondescript religion half heathen and half Christian. Boscana was greatly pleased to find so many allusions to Scriptural truths, evidently never suspecting that the Indians were imposing upon him.

The religious belief of the Santa Barbara Channel Indians appears to have been the most rational of any of the beliefs held by the California aborigines. Their god, Chupu, was the deification of good; and Nunaxus, their Satan, the personification of evil. Chupu the all-powerful created Nunaxus, who rebelled against his creator and tried to overthrow him; but Chupu, the almighty, punished him by creating man who, by devouring the animal and vegetable products of the earth, checked the physical growth of Nunaxus, who had hoped by liberal feeding to become like unto a mountain. Foiled in his ambition, Nunaxus ever afterwards sought to injure mankind. To secure Chupu's protection, offerings were made to him and dances were instituted in his honor. Flutes and other instruments were played to attract his attention. When Nunaxus brought calamity upon the Indians in the shape of dry years, which caused a dearth of animal and vegetable products, or sent sickness to afflict them, their old men interceded with Chupu to protect them; and to exorcise their Satan they shot arrows and threw stones in the direction in which he was supposed to be.

Of the Indian myths and traditions Hugo Reid says: "They were of incredible length and contained more metamorphoses than Ovid could have engendered in his brain had he lived a thousand years."

The Cahuilla tribes who formerly inhabited the mountain districts of the southeastern part of the state had a tradition of their creation. According to this tradition the primeval Adam and Eve were created by the Supreme Being in the waters of a northern sea. They came up out of the water upon the land, which they found to be soft and miry. They traveled southward for many moons in search of land suitable for their residence and where they could obtain sustenance from the earth. This they found at last on the mountain sides in Southern California.

Some of the Indian myths when divested of their crudities and ideas clothed in fitting language are as poetical as those of Greece or Scandinavia. The following one which Hugo Reid found among the San Gabriel Indians bears a striking resemblance to the Grecian myths of Orpheus and Eurydice but it is not at all probable that the Indians ever heard the Grecian fable. Ages ago, so runs this Indian myth, a powerful people dwelt on the banks of the Arroyo Seco and hunted over the hills and plains of what are now our modern Pasadena and the valley of San Fernando. They committed a grievous crime against the Great Spirit. A pestilence destroyed them all save a boy and girl who were saved by a foster mother possessed of supernatural powers. They grew to manhood and womanhood and became husband and wife. Their devotion to each other angered the foster mother, who fancied herself neglected. She plotted to destroy the wife. The young woman, divining her fate, told her husband that should he at any time feel a tear drop on his shoulder, he might know that she was dead. While he was away hunting the dread signal came. He hastened back to destroy the hag who had brought death to his wife, but the sorceress had escaped. Disconsolate he threw himself on the grave of his wife. For three days he neither ate nor drank. On the third day a whirlwind arose from the grave and moved toward the south. Perceiving in it the form of his wife, he hastened on until he overtook it. Then a voice came out of the cloud saying: "Whither I go, thou canst not come. Thou art of earth but I am dead to the world. Return, my husband, return!" He plead piteously to be taken with her. She consenting, he was wrapped in the cloud with her and borne across the illimitable sea that separates the abode of the living from that of the dead. When they reached the realms of ghosts a spirit voice said: "Sister, thou comest to us with an odor of earth; what dost thou bring?" Then she confessed that she had brought her living husband. "Take him away!" said a voice stern and commanding. She plead that he might remain and recounted his many virtues. To test his virtues, the spirits gave him four labors. First to bring a feather from the top of a pole so high that its summit was invisible. Next to split a hair of great length and exceeding fineness; third to make on the ground a map of the constellation of the lesser bear and locate the north star and last to slay the celestial deer that had the form of black beetles and were exceedingly swift. With the aid of his wife he accomplished all the tasks.

But no mortal was allowed to dwell in the abodes of death. "Take thou thy wife and return with her to the earth," said the spirit. "Yet remember, thou shalt not speak to her; thou shalt not touch her until three suns have passed. A penalty

31

awaits thy disobedience." He promised. They pass from the spirit land and travel to the confines of matter. By day she is invisible but by the flickering light of his camp-fire he sees the dim outline of her form. Three days pass. As the sun sinks behind the western hills he builds his camp-fire. She appears before him in all the beauty of life. He stretches forth his arms to embrace her. She is snatched from his grasp. Although invisible to him yet the upper rim of the great orb of day hung above the western verge. He had broken his promise. Like Orpheus, disconsolate, he wandered over the earth until, relenting, the spirits sent their servant Death to bring him to Tecupar (Heaven).

The following myth of the mountain Indians of the north bears a strong resemblance to the Norse fable of Gyoll the River of Death and its glittering bridge, over which the spirits of the dead pass to Hel, the land of spirits. The Indian, however, had no idea of any kind of a bridge except a foot log across a stream. The myth in a crude form was narrated to me many years ago by an old pioneer.

According to this myth when an Indian died his spirit form was conducted by an unseen guide over a mountain trail unknown and inaccessible to mortals, to the rapidly flowing river which separated the abode of the living from that of the dead. As the trail descended to the river it branched to the right and left. The right hand path led to a foot bridge made of the massive trunk of a rough barked pine which spanned the Indian styx; the left led to a slender, fresh peeled birch pole that hung high above the roaring torrent. At the parting of the trail an inexorable fate forced the bad to the left, while the spirit form of the good passed on to the right and over the rough barked pine to the happy hunting grounds, the Indian heaven. The bad reaching the river's brink and gazing longingly upon the delights beyond, essayed to cross the slippery pole — a slip, a slide, a clutch at empty space, and the ghostly spirit form was hurled into the mad torrent below, and was borne by the rushing waters into a vast lethean lake where it sunk beneath the waves and was blotted from existence forever.

San Gabriel Arcangel.

San Gabriel Arcangel was the fourth mission founded in California. Father Junipero Serra, as previously narrated, had gone north in 1770 and founded the mission of San Carlos Borromeo on Monterey Bay and the following year he established the mission of San Antonio de Padua on the Salinas river about twenty-five leagues south of Monterey. On the 6th of August, 1771, a cavalcade of soldiers and musketeers escorting Padres Somero and Cambon set out from San Diego over the trail made by Portola's expedition in 1769 (when it went north in search of Monterey Bay) to found a new mission on the River Jesus de los Temblores or to give it its full name, El Rio del Dulcisimo Nombre de Jesus de los Temblores, the river of the sweetest name of Jesus of the Earthquakes. Not finding a suitable location on that river (now the Santa Ana) they pushed on to the Rio San Miguel, also known as the Rio de los Temblores. Here they selected a site where wood and water were abundant. A stockade of poles was built inclosing a square within which a church was erected, covered with boughs.

September 8, 1771, the mission was formally founded and dedicated to the archangel Gabriel. ' The Indians who at the coming of the Spaniards were docile and friendly, a few days after the founding of the mission suddenly attacked two soldiers who were guarding the horses. One of these soldiers had outraged the wife of the chief who led the attack. The soldier who committed the crime killed the chieftain with a musket ball and the other Indians fled. The soldiers then cut off the chief's head and fastened it to a pole at the presidio gate. From all accounts the soldiers at this mission were more brutal and barbarous than the Indians and more in need of missionaries to convert them than the Indians. The progress of the mission was slow. At the end of the second year only seventy-three children and adults had been baptized. Father Serra attributed the lack of conversions to the bad conduct of the soldiers.

The first buildings at the mission Vieja were all of wood. The church was 45x18 feet, built of logs and covered with tule thatch. The church and other wooden buildings used by the padres stood within a square enclosed by pointed stakes. In 1776, five years after its founding, the mission was moved from its first location to a new site about a league distant from the old one. The old site was subject to overflow by the river. The adobe ruins pointed out to tourists as the foundations of the old mission are the debris of a building erected for a ranch house about sixty years ago. The buildings at the mission Vieja were all of wood and no trace of them remains. A chapel was first built at the new site. It was replaced by a church built of adobes one hundred and eight feet long by twenty-one feet wide. The present stone church, begun about 1794, and completed about 1806, is the fourth church erected.

The mission attained the acme of its importance in 1817, when there were seventeen hundred and one neophytes in the mission fold.

The largest grain crop raised at any mission was that harvested at San Gabriel in 1821, which amounted to 29,400 bushels. The number of cattle belonging to the mission in 1830 was 25,725. During the whole period of the mission's existence, 1.e., from 1771 to 1834, according to statistics compiled by Bancroft from mission records, the total number of baptisms was 7,854, of which 4,355 were Indian adults and 2,459 were Indian children and the remainder gente de razon or people of

35

reason. The deaths were 5,656, of which 2,916 were Indian adults and 2,363 Indian children. If all the Indian children born were baptized it would seem (if the statistics are correct) that but very few ever grew up to manhood and womanhood. In 1834, the year of its secularization, its neophyte population was 1,320.

The missionaries of San Gabriel established a station at old San Bernardino about 1820. It was not an asistencia like pala, but merely an agricultural station or ranch headquarters. The buildings were destroyed by the Indians in 1834.

San Luis Obispo De Tolosa.

On his journey southward in 1782, President Serra and Padre Cavalier, with a small escort of soldiers and a few Lower California Indians, on September 1, 1772, founded the mission of San Luis Obispo de Tolosa (St. Louis, Bishop of Tolouse). The site selected was on a creek twenty-five leagues southerly from San Antonio. The soldiers and Indians were set at work to erect buildings. Padre Cavalier was left in charge of the mission, Father Serra continuing his journey southward. This mission was never a very important one. Its greatest population was in 1803, when there were eight hundred and fifty-two neophytes within its jurisdiction. From that time to 1834 their number declined to two hundred and sixty-four. The average death rate was 7.30 per cent of the population — a lower rate than at some of the more populous missions. The adobe church built in 1793 is still in use, but has been so remodeled that it bears but little resemblance to the church of mission days.

San Francisco De Asis.

The expedition under command of Portola in 1769 failed to find Monterey Bay but it passed on and discovered the great bay of San Francisco. So far no attempt had been made to plant a mission or presidio on its shores. Early in 1775, Lieutenant Ayala was ordered to explore the bay with a view to forming a settlement near it. Rivera had previously explored the land bordering on the bay where the city now stands. Captain Anza, the discoverer of the overland route from Mexico to California via the Colorado river, had recruited an expedition of two hundred persons in Sonora for the purpose of forming a settlement at San Francisco. He set out in 1775 and reached Monterey March 10, 1776. A quarrel between him and Rivera, who was in command at Monterey, defeated for a time the purpose for which the settlers had been brought, and Anza, disgusted with the treatment he had received from Rivera, abandoned the enterprise. Anza had selected a site for a presidio at San Francisco. After his departure Rivera changed his policy of delay that had frustrated all of Anza's plans and decided at once to proceed to the establishment of a presidio. The presidio was formally founded September 17, 1776, at what is now known as Fort Point. The ship San Carlos had brought a number of persons; these with the settlers who had come up from Monterey made an assemblage of more than one hundred and fifty persons.

After the founding of the presidio Lieutenant Moraga in command of the military and Captain Quiros of the San Carlos, set vigorously at work to build a church for the mission. A wooden building having been constructed on the 9th of

October, 1776, the mission was dedicated, Father Palou conducting the service, assisted by Fathers Cambon, Nocedal and Peña. The site selected for the mission was on the Laguna de los Dolores. The lands at the mission were not very productive. The mission, however, was fairly prosperous. In 1820 it owned 11,240 cattle and the total product of wheat was 114,480 bushels. In 1820 there were 1,252 neophytes attached to it. The death rate was very heavy — the average rate being 12.4 per cent of the population. In 1832 the population had decreased to two hundred and four and at the time of secularization it had declined to one hundred and fifty. A number of neophytes had been taken to the new mission of San Francisco Solano.

San Juan Capistrano.

The revolt of the Indians at San Diego delayed the founding of San Juan Capistrano a year. October 30, 1775, the initiatory services of the founding had been held when a messenger came with the news of the uprising of the savages and the massacre of Father Jaume and others. The bells which had been hung on a tree were taken down and buried. The soldiers and the padres hastened to San Diego. November I, 1776, Fathers Serra, Mugartegui and Amurrio, with an escort of soldiers, arrived at the site formerly selected. The bells were dug up and hung on a tree, an enramada of boughs was constructed and Father Serra said mass. The first location of the mission was several miles northeasterly from the present site at the foot of the mountain. The abandoned site is still known a la Mision Vieja (the Old Mission). Just when the change of location was made is not known.

The erection of a stone church was begun in February, 1797, and completed in 1806. A master builder had been brought from Mexico and under his superintendence the neophytes did the mechanical labor. It was the largest and handsomest church in California and was the pride of mission architecture. The year 1812 was known in California as el ano de los temblores — the year of earthquakes. For months the seismic disturbance was almost continuous. On Sunday, December 8, 1812, a severe shock threw down the lofty church tower, which crashed through the vaulted roof on the congregation below. The padre who was celebrating mass escaped through the sacristy. Of the fifty persons present only five or six escaped. The church was never rebuilt. "There is not much doubt," says Bancroft, "that the disaster was due rather to faulty construction than to the violence of the temblor." The edifice was of the usual cruciform shape, about 90x180 feet on the ground, with very thick walls and arched dome-like roof all constructed of stones imbedded in mortar or cement. The stones were not hewn, but of irregular size and shape, a kind of structure evidently requiring great skill to ensure solidity. The mission reached its maximum in 1819; from that on till the date of its secularization there was a rapid decline in the numbers of its live stock and of its neophytes.

This was one of the missions in which Governor Figueroa tried his experiment of forming Indian pueblos of the neophytes. For a time the experiment was a partial success, but eventually it went the way of all the other missions. Its lands were granted to private individuals and the neophytes scattered. Its picturesque ruins are a great attraction to tourists.

Santa Clara.

The mission of Santa Clara was founded January 12, 1777. The site had been selected some time before and two missionaries designated for service at it, but the comandante of the territory, Rivera y Moncada, who was an exceedingly obstinate person, had opposed the founding on various pretexts, but positive orders coming from the viceroy Rivera did not longer delay, so on the 6th of January, 1777, a detachment of soldiers under Lieutenant Moraga, accompanied by Father Peña, was sent from San Francisco to the site selected which was about sixteen leagues south of San Francisco. Here under an enramada the services of dedication were held. The Indians were not averse to receiving a new religion and at the close of the year sixty-seven had been baptized.

The mission was quite prosperous and became one of the most important in the territory. It was located in the heart of a rich agricultural district. The total product of wheat was 175,800 bushels. In 1828 the mission flocks and herds numbered over 30,000 animals. The neophyte population in 1827 was 1,464. The death rate was high, averaging 12.63 per cent of the population. The total number of baptisms was 8,640; number of deaths 6,950. In 1834 the population had declined to 800. Secularization was effected in 1837.

San Buenaventura.

The founding of San Buenaventura had been long delayed. It was to have been among the first missions founded by Father Serra; it proved to be his last. On the 26th of March, 1782, Governor de Neve, accompanied by Father Serra (who had come down afoot from San Carlos), and Father Cambon, with a convoy of soldiers and a number of neophytes, set out from San Gabriel to found the mission. At the first camping place Governor de Neve was recalled to San Gabriel by a message from Col. Pedro Fages, informing him of the orders of the council of war to proceed against the Yumas who had the previous year destroyed the two missions on the Colorado river and massacred the missionaries.

On the 29th, the remainder of the company reached a place on the coast named by Portola in 1769, Asuncion de Nuestra Señora, which had for some time been selected for a mission site. Near it was a large Indian rancheria. On Easter Sunday, March 31st, the mission was formally founded with the usual ceremonies and dedicated to San Buenaventura (Giovanni de Fidanza of Tuscany), a follower of St. Francis, the founder of the Franciscans.

The progress of the mission was slow at first, only two adults were baptized in 1782, the year of its founding. The first buildings built of wood were destroyed by fire. The church still used for service, built of brick and adobe, was completed and dedicated, September 9, 1809. The earthquake of December 8, 1812, damaged the church to such an extent that the tower and part of the façade had to be rebuilt. After the earthquake the whole site of the mission for a time seemed to be sinking. The inhabitants, fearful of being engulfed by the sea, removed to San Joaquin y Santa Ana, where they remained several months. The mission attained its greatest prosperity in 1816, when its neophyte population numbered 1,330 and it owned 23,400 cattle.

38

Santa Barbara.

Governor Felipe de Neve founded the presidio of Santa Barbara April 21, 1782. Father Serra had hoped to found the mission at the same time, but in this he was disappointed. His death in 1784 still further delayed the founding and it was not until the latter part of 1786 that everything was in readiness for the establishing of the new mission. On the 22nd of November Father Lasuen, who had succeeded Father Serra as president of the missions, arrived at Santa Barbara, accompanied by two missionaries recently from Mexico. He selected a site about a mile distant from the presidio. The place was called Taynagan (Rocky Hill) by the Indians. There was a plentiful supply of stone on the site for building and an abundance of water for irrigation.

On the 15th of December, 1786, Father Lasuen, in a hut of boughs, celebrated the first mass; but December 4, the day that the fiesta of Santa Barbara is commemorated, is considered the date of its founding. Part of the services were held on that day. A chapel built of adobes and roofed with thatch was erected in 1787. Several other buildings of adobe were erected the same year. In 1788, tile took the place of thatch. In 1789, a second church, much larger than the first, was built. A third church of adobe was commenced in 1793 and finished in 1794. A brick portico was added in 1795 and the walls plastered.

The great earthquake of December, 1812, demolished the mission church and destroyed nearly all the buildings. The years 1813 and 1814 were spent in removing the debris of the ruined buildings and in preparing for the erection of new ones. The erection of the present mission church was begun in 1815. It was completed and dedicated September 10, 1820.

Father Caballeria, in his History of Santa Barbara, gives the dimensions of the church as follows: "Length (including walls), sixty varas; width, fourteen varas; height, ten varas (a vara is thirty-four inches)." The walls are of stone and rest on a foundation of rock and cement They are six feet thick and are further strengthened by buttresses. Notwithstanding the building has withstood the storms of four score years, it is still in an excellent state of preservation. Its exterior has not been disfigured by attempts at modernizing.

The highest neophyte population was reached at Santa Barbara in 1803, when it numbered 1,792. The largest number of cattle was 5,200 in 1809. In 1834, the year of secularization, the neophytes numbered 556, which was a decrease of 155 from the number in 1830. At such a rate of decrease it would not, even if mission rule had continued, have taken more than a dozen years to depopulate the mission.

La Purisima Concepcion.

Two missions, San Buenaventura and Santa Barbara, had been founded on the Santa Barbara channel in accordance with Neve's report of 1777, in which he recommended the founding of three missions and a presidio in that district. It was the intention of General La Croix to conduct these on a different plan from that prevailing in the older missions. The natives were not to be gathered into a missionary establishment, but were to remain in their rancherias, which were to be converted into mission pueblos. The Indians were to receive instruction in religion, industrial arts and self-government while comparatively free from restraint. The plan which no doubt originated with Governor de Neve, was a good one theoretically, and possibly might have been practically. The missionaries were bitterly opposed to it. Unfortunately it was tried first in the Colorado river missions among the fierce and treacherous Yumas. The massacre of the padres and soldiers of these missions was attributed to this innovation.

In establishing the channel missions the missionaries opposed the inauguration of this plan and by their persistence succeeded in setting it aside; and the old system was adopted. La Purisima Concepcion, or the Immaculate Conception of the Blessed Virgin, the third of the channel missions, was founded December 8, 1787. by Father Lasuen at a place called by the natives Algsacupi. Its location is about twelve miles from the ocean on the Santa Ynez river. Three years after its founding three hundred converts had been baptized but not all of them lived at the mission. The first church was a temporary structure. The second church, built of adobe and roofed with tile, was completed in 1802. December 21, 1812, an earthquake demolished the church and also about one hundred adobe houses of the neophytes. A site across the river and about four miles distant from the former one, was selected for new buildings. A temporary building for a church was erected there. A new church, built of adobe and roofed with tile, was completed and dedicated in 1818.

The Indians revolted in 1824 and damaged the building. They took possession of it and a battle lasting four hours was fought between one hundred and thirty soldiers and four hundred Indians. The neophytes cut loop holes in the church and used two old rusty cannon and a few guns they possessed; but, unused to fire arms, they were routed with the loss of several killed. During the revolt which lasted several months four white men and fifteen or twenty Indians were killed. The hostiles, most of whom fled to the Tulares, were finally subdued. The leaders were punished with imprisonment and the others returned to their missions.

This mission's population was largest in 1804, when it numbered 1,520. In 1834 there were but 407 neophytes connected with it. It was secularized in February, 1835. During mission rule from 1787 to 1834, the total number of Indian children baptized was 1,492; died 902, which was a lower death rate than at most of the southern missions.

Santa Cruz.

Santa Cruz, one of the smallest of the twenty(one missions of California, was founded September 25, 1790. The mission was never very prosperous. In 1798 many of the neophytes deserted and the same year a flood covered the planting fields and damaged the church. In 18 12 the neophytes murdered the missionary in charge. Padre Andres Quintana. They claimed that he had treated them with great cruelty. Five of those implicated in the murder received two hundred lashes each and were sentenced to work in chains from two to ten years. Only one survived the punishment. The maximum of its population was reached in 1798, when there were six hundred and forty-four Indians in the mission fold. The total number baptized from the date of its founding to 1834 was 2,466; the total number of deaths was

2,034. The average death rate was 10.93 percent of the population. At the time of its secularization in 1834 there were only two hundred and fifty Indians belonging to the mission.

La Soledad.

The mission of our Lady of Solitude was founded September 29, 1791. The site selected had borne the name Soledad (solitude) ever since the first exploration of the country. The location was thirty miles northeast of San Carlos de Monterey. La Soledad, by which name it was generally known, was unfortunate in its early missionaries. One of them. Padre Gracia, was supposed to be insane and the other. Padre Rubi, was very immoral. Rubi was later on expelled from his college for licentiousness. At the close of the century the mission had become fairly prosperous, but in 1802 an epidemic broke out and five or six deaths occurred daily. The Indians in alarm fled from the mission. The largest population of the mission was seven hundred and twenty-five in 1805. At the time of secularization its population had decreased to three hundred. The total number of baptisms during its existence was 2,222; number of deaths 1,803.

San Jose.

St. Joseph had been designated by the visitador General Galvez and Father Junipero Serra as the patron saint of the mission colonization of California. Thirteen missions had been founded and yet none had been dedicated to San Jose. Orders came from Mexico that one be established and named for him. Accordingly a detail of a corporal and five men, accompanied by Father Lasuen, president of the missions, proceeded to the site selected, which was about twelve miles northerly from the pueblo of San Jose. There, on June 11, 1797, the mission was founded. The mission was well located agriculturally and became one of the most prosperous in California. In 1820 it had a population of 1,754, the highest of any mission except San Luis Rey. The total number of baptisms from its founding to 1834 was 6,737; deaths 5,109. Secularization was effected in 1836-37. The total valuation of the mission property, not including lands or the church, was $155,000.

San Juan Bautista.

In May, 1797, Governor Borica ordered the comandante at Monterey to detail a corporal and five soldiers to proceed to a site that had been previously chosen for a mission which was about ten leagues northeast from Monterey. Here the soldiers erected of wood a church, priest's house, granary and guard house. June 24, 1797, President Lasuen, assisted by Fathers Catala and Martiari, founded the mission of San Juan Bautista (St. John the Baptist). At the close of the year, eighty-five converts had been baptized. The neighboring Indian tribes were hostile and some of them had to be killed before the others learned to behave themselves. A new church, measuring 60x160 feet, was completed and dedicated in 1812. San Juan was the only mission whose population increased between 1820 and 1830. This was due to the fact that its numbers were recruited from the eastern tribes, its location being favorable for obtaining new recruits from the gentiles. The largest population it ever reached was 1,248 in 1823. In 1834 there were but 850 neophytes at the mission.

San Miguel.

Midway between the old missions of San Antonio and San Luis Obispo, on the 25th of July, 1797, was founded the mission of San Miguel Arcangel. The two old missions contributed horses, cattle and sheep to start the new one. The mission had a propitious beginning; fifteen children were baptized on the day the mission was founded. At the close of the century the number of converts reached three hundred and eighty-five, of whom fifty-three had died. The mission population numbered 1,076 in 1814; after that it steadily declined until, in 1834, there were only 599 attached to the establishment. Total number of baptisms was 2,588; deaths 2,038. The average death rate was 6.91 per cent of the population, the lowest rate in any of the missions. The mission was secularized in 1836.

San Fernando Rey De Espana.

In the closing years of the century explorations were made for new mission sites in California. These were to be located between missions already founded. Among those selected at that time was the site of the mission San Fernando on the Encino Rancho, then occupied by Francisco Reyes. Reyes surrendered whatever right he had to the land and the padres occupied his house for a dwelling while new buildings were in the course of erection.

September 8, 1797, with the usual ceremonies, the mission was founded by President Lasuen, assisted by Father Dumetz. According to instructions from Mexico it was dedicated to San Fernando Rey de España (Fernando III., King of Spain, 1217-1251). At the end of the year 1797, fifty-five converts had been gathered into the mission fold and at the end of the century three hundred and fifty-two had been baptized.

The adobe church begun before the close of the century was completed and dedicated in December, 1806. It had a tiled roof. It was but slightly injured by the great earthquakes of December, 1812, which were so destructive to the mission buildings at San Juan Capistrano, Santa Barbara, La Purisima and Santa Ynez. This mission reached its greatest prosperity in 1819, when its neophyte population numbered 1,080. The largest number of cattle owned by it at one time was 12,800 in 1819.

Its decline was not so rapid as that of some of the other missions, but the death rate, especially among the children, was fully as high. Of the 1,367 Indian children baptized there during the existence of mission rule 965, or over seventy per cent, died in childhood. It was not strange that the fearful death rate both of children and adults at the missions sometimes frightened the neophytes into running away.

San Luis Rey De Francia.

Several explorations had been made for a mission site between San Diego and San Juan Capistrano. There was quite a large Indian population that had not been brought into the folds of either mission. In October, 1797, a new exploration of this territory was ordered and a site was finally selected, although the agricultural advantages were regarded as not satisfactory.

Governor Borica, February 28, 1798, issued orders to the comandante at San Diego to furnish a detail of soldiers to aid in erecting the necessary buildings. June 13, 1798. President Lasuen, the successor of President Serra, assisted by Fathers Peyri and Santiago, with the usual services, founded the new mission. It was named San Luis Rey de Francia (St. Louis, Kino of France). Its location was near a river on which was bestowed the name of the mission. The mission flourished from its very beginning. Its controlling power was Padre Antonio Peyri. He remained in charge of it from its founding almost to its downfall, in all thirty-three years. He was a man of great executive abilities and under his administration it became one of the largest and most prosperous missions in California. It reached its maximum in 1826, when its neophyte population numbered 2,869, the largest number at one time connected with any mission in the territory.

The asistencia or auxiliary mission of San Antonio was established at Pala, seven leagues easterly from the parent mission. A chapel was erected here and regular services held. One of the padres connected with San Luis Rey was in charge of this station. Father Peyri left California in 1831, with the exiled Governor Victoria. He went to Mexico and from there to Spain and lastly to Rome, where he died. The mission was converted into an Indian pueblo in 1834, but the pueblo was not a success. Most of the neophytes drifted to Los Angeles and San Gabriel. During the Mexican conquest American troops were stationed there. It has recently been partially repaired and is now used for a Franciscan school under charge of Father J. J. O'Keefe.

Santa Ynez.

Santa Ynez was the last mission founded in Southern California. It was established September 17, 1804. Its location is about forty miles northwesterly from Santa Barbara, on the easterly side of the Santa Ynez mountains and eighteen miles southeasterly from La Purisima. Father Tapis, president of the missions from 1803 to 1812, preached the sermon and was assisted in the ceremonies by Fathers Cipies, Calzada and Gutierrez. Carrillo, the comandante at the presidio, was present, as were also a number of neophytes from Santa Barbara and La Purisima. Some of these were transferred to the new mission.

The earthquake of December, 1812. shook down a portion of the church and destroyed a number of the neophytes' houses. In 1815, the erection of a new church was begun. It was built of adobes, lined with brick, and was completed and dedicated July 4, 1817. The Indian revolt of 1824, described in the sketch of La Purisima, broke out first at this mission. The neophytes took possession of the church. The mission guard defended themselves and the padre. At the approach of the troops from Santa Barbara the Indians fled to La Purisima.

43

San Ynez attained its greatest population, 770, in 1816. In 1834 its population had decreased to 334. From its founding in 1804 to 1834, when the decrees of secularization were put in force, 757 Indian children were baptized and 519 died, leaving only 238, or about thirty per cent of those baptized to grow up.

San Rafael.

San Rafael was the first mission established north of the Bay of San Francisco. It was founded December 14, 18 17. At first it was an asistencia or branch of San Francisco. An epidemic had broken out in the Mission Dolores and a number of the Indians were transferred to San Rafael to escape the plague. Later on it attained to the dignity of a mission. In 1828 its population was 1,140. After 1830 it began to decline and at the time of its secularization in 1834 there were not more than 500 connected with it. In the seventeen years of its existence under mission rule there were 1,873 baptisms and 698 deaths. The average death rate was 6.09 per cent of the population. The mission was secularized in 1834. All traces of the mission building have disappeared.

San Francisco Solano.

The mission of San Francisco de Asis had fallen into a rapid decline. The epidemic that had carried off a number of the neophytes and had caused the transfer of a considerable number to San Rafael had greatly reduced its population. Besides, the sterility of the soil in the vicinity of the mission necessitated going a long distance for agricultural land and pasturage for the herds and flocks. On this account and also for the reason that a number of new converts might be obtained from the gentiles living in the district north of the bay, Governor Arguello and the mission authorities decided to establish a mission in that region. Explorations were made in June and July, 1823. On the 4th of July a site was selected, a cross blessed and raised, a volley of musketry fired and mass said at a place named New San Francisco, but afterwards designated as the Mission of San Francisco Solano. On the 25th of August work was begun on the mission building and on the 4th of April, 1824, a church, 24x105 feet, built of wood, was dedicated.

It had been intended to remove the neophytes from the old mission of San Francisco to the new; but the padres of the old mission opposed its depopulation and suppression. A compromise was effected by allowing all neophytes of the old mission who so elected to go to the new. Although well located, the Mission of Solano was not prosperous. Its largest population, 996, was reached in 1832. The total number of baptisms were 1,315; deaths, 651. The average death rate was 7.8 per cent of the population. The mission was secularized in 1835, at which time there were about 550 neophytes attached to it.

The architecture of the missions was Moorish — that is, if it belonged to any school. The padres in most cases were the architects and master builders. The main feature of the buildings was massiveness. Built of adobe or rough stone, their walls were of great thickness. Most of the church buildings were narrow, their width being out of proportion to their length. This was necessitated by the difficulty of procuring joists and rafters of sufficient length for wide buildings. The padres had

44

no means or perhaps no knowledge of trussing a roof, and the width of the building had to be proportioned to the length of the timbers procurable. Some of the buildings were planned with an eye for the picturesque, others for utility only. The sites selected for the mission buildings in nearly every case commanded a fine view of the surrounding country. In their prime, their white walls looming up on the horizon could be seen at long distance and acted as beacons to guide the traveler to their hospitable shelter.

Col. J. J. Warner, who came to California in 1831, and saw the mission buildings before they had fallen into decay, thus describes their general plan: "As soon after the founding of a mission as circumstances would permit, a large pile of buildings in the form of a quadrangle, composed in part of burnt brick, but chiefly of sun-dried ones, was erected around a spacious court. A large and capacious church, which usually occupied one of the outer corners of the quadrangle, was a conspicuous part of the pile. In this massive building, covered with red tile, was the habitation of the friars, rooms for guests and for the major domos and their families. In other buildings of the quadrangle were hospital wards, storehouses and granaries, rooms for carding, spinning and weaving of woolen fabrics, shops for blacksmiths, joiners and carpenters, saddlers, shoemakers and soap boilers, and cellars for storing the product (wine and brandy) of the vineyards. Near the habitation of the friars another building of similar material was placed and used as quarters for a small number — about a corporal's guard — of soldiers under command of a non-commissioned officer, to hold the Indian neophytes in check as well as to protect the mission from the attacks of hostile Indians." The Indians, when the buildings of the establishment were complete, lived in adobe houses built in lines near the quadrangle. Some of the buildings of the square were occupied by the alcaldes or Indian bosses. When the Indians were gathered into the missions at first they lived in brush shanties constructed in the same manner as their forefathers had built them for generations. In some of the missions these huts were not replaced by adobe buildings for a generation or more. Vancouver, who visited the Mission of San Francisco in 1792, sixteen years after its founding, describes the Indian village with its brush-built huts. He says: "These miserable habitations, each of which was allotted for the residence of a whole family, were erected with some degree of uniformity about three or four feet asunder in straight rows, leaving lanes or passageways at right angles between them; but these were so abominably infested with every kind of filth and nastiness as to be rendered no less offensive than degrading to the human species."

Of the houses at Santa Clara, Vancouver says: "The habitations were not so regularly disposed nor did it (the village) contain so many as the village of San Francisco, yet the same horrid state of uncleanliness and laziness seemed to pervade the whole." Better houses were then in the course of construction at Santa Clara. "Each house would contain two rooms and a garret with a garden in the rear." Vancouver visited San Carlos de Monterey in 1792, twenty-two years after its founding. He says: "Notwithstanding these people are taught and employed from time to time in many of the occupations most useful to civil society, they had not made themselves any more comfortable habitations than those of their forefathers; nor did they seem in any respect to have benefited by the instruction they had received."

45

Captain Beechey, of the English navy, who visited San Francisco and the missions around the bay in 1828, found the Indians at San Francisco still living in their filthy hovels and grinding acorns for food. "San Jose (mission)," he says, "on the other hand, was all neatness, cleanliness and comfort." At San Carlos he found that the filthy hovels described by Vancouver had nearly all disappeared and the Indians were comfortably housed. He adds: "Sickness in general prevailed to an incredible extent in all the missions."

CHAPTER VI. PRESIDIOS OF CALIFORNIA.

The presidio was an essential feature of the Spanish colonization of America. It was usually a fortified square of brick or stone, inside of which were the barracks of the soldiers, the officers' quarters, a church, store houses for provisions and military supplies. The gates at the entrance were closed at night, and it was usually provisioned for a siege. In the colonization of California there were four presidios established, namely: San Diego, Monterey, San Francisco and Santa Barbara. Each was the headquarters of a military district and besides a body of troops kept at the presidio it furnished guards for the missions in its respective district and also for the pueblos if there were any in the district. The first presidio was founded at San Diego. As stated in a previous chapter, the two ships of the expedition by sea for the settlement of California arrived at the port of San Diego in a deplorable condition from scurvy. The San Antonia, after a voyage of fifty-nine days, arrived on April 11; the San Carlos, although she had sailed a month earlier, did not arrive until April 29, consuming one hundred and ten days in the voyage. Don Miguel Constanso, the engineer who came on this vessel, says in his report: "The scurvy had infected all without exception; in such sort that on entering San Diego already two men had died of the said sickness; most of the seamen, and half of the troops, found themselves prostrate in their beds; only four mariners remained on their feet, and attended, aided by the troops, to trimming and furling the sails and other working of the ship." "The San Antonia," says Constanso, "had the half of its crew equally affected by the scurvy, of which illness two men had likewise died." This vessel, although it had arrived at the port on the nth of April, had evidently not landed any of its sick. On the 1st of May, Don Pedro Pages, the commander of the troops, Constanso and Estorace, the second captain of the San Carlos, with twenty-five soldiers, set out to find a watering place where they could fill their barrels with fresh water. "Following the west shore of the port, after going a matter of three leagues, they arrived at the banks of a river hemmed in with a fringe of willows and cottonwoods. Its channel must have been twenty varas wide and it discharges into an estuary which at high tide could admit the launch and made it convenient for accomplishing the taking on of water." * * * "Having reconnoitered the watering place, the Spaniards betook themselves back on board the vessels and as these were found to be very far away from the estuary in which the river discharges, their captains, Vicente Vila and Don Juan Perez, resolved to approach it as closely as they could in order to give less work to the people handling the launches. These labors were accomplished with satiety of hardship; for from one day to the next the number of the sick kept increasing, along with the dying of the most aggravated cases and augmented the fatigue of the few who remained on their feet."

"Immediate to the beach on the side toward the east a scanty enclosure was constructed formed of a parapet of earth and fascines, which was garnished with two cannons. They disembarked some sails and awnings from the packets with which they made two tents capacious enough for a hospital. At one side the two officers, the missionary fathers and the surgeon put up their own tents; the sick were brought in launches to this improvised presidio and hospital." "But these diligencies," says Constanso, "were not enough to procure them health." * * * "The

47

cold made itself felt with rigor at night in the barracks and the sun by day, alternations which made the sick suffer cruelly, two or three of them dying every day. And this whole expedition, which had been composed of more than ninety men, saw itself reduced to only eight soldiers and as many mariners in a state to attend to the safeguarding of the barks, the working of the launches, custody of the camp and service of the sick."

Rivera y Moncada, the commander of the first detachment of the land expedition, arrived at San Diego May 14. It was decided by the officers to remove the camp to a point near the river. This had not been done before on account of the small force able to work and the lack of beasts of burden. Rivera's men were all in good health and after a day's rest "all were removed to a new camp, which was transferred one league further north on the right side of the river upon a hill of middling height."

Here a presidio was built, the remains of which can still be seen. It was a parapet of earth similar to that thrown up at the first camp, which, according to Bancroft, was probably within the limits of New Town and the last one in Old Town or North San Diego.

While Portola's expedition was away searching for the port of Monterey, the Indians made an attack on the camp at San Diego, killed a Spanish youth and wounded Padre Viscaino, the blacksmith, and a Lower California neophyte. The soldiers remaining at San Diego surrounded the buildings with a stockade. Constanso says, on the return of the Spaniards of Portola's expedition: "They found in good condition their humble buildings, surrounded with a palisade of trunks of trees, capable of a good defense in case of necessity."

"In 1782, the presidial force at San Diego, besides the commissioned officers, consisted of five corporals and forty-six soldiers. Six men were constantly on duty at each of the three missions of the district, San Diego, San Juan Capistrano and San Gabriel; while four served at the pueblo of Los Angeles, thus leaving a sergeant, two corporals and about twenty-five men to garrison the fort, care for the horses and a small herd of cattle, and to carry the mails, which latter duty was the hardest connected with the presidio service in time of peace. There were a carpenter and blacksmith constantly employed, besides a few servants, mostly natives. The population of the district in 1790, not including Indians, was 220."

Before the close of the century the wooden palisades had been replaced by a thick adobe wall, but even then the fort was not a very formidable defense. Vancouver, the English navigator, who visited it in 1793, describes it as "irregularly built on very uneven ground, which makes it liable to some inconveniences without the obvious appearance of any object for selecting such a spot." It then mounted three small brass cannon.

Gradually a town grew up around the presidio. Robinson, who visited San Diego in 1829, thus describes it: "On the lawn beneath the hill on which the presidio is built stood about thirty houses of rude appearance, mostly occupied by retired veterans, not so well constructed in respect either to beauty or stability as the houses at Monterey, with the exception of that belonging to our Administrator, Don Juan Bandini, whose mansion, then in an unfinished state, bid fair, when completed, to surpass any other in the country."

48

Under Spain there was attempt at least to keep the presidio in repair, but under Mexican domination it fell into decay. Dana describes it as he saw it in 1836: "The first place we went to was the old ruinous presidio, which stands on rising ground near the village which it overlooks. It is built in the form of an open square, like all the other presidios, and was in a most ruinous state, with the exception of one side, in which the comandante lived with his family. There were only two guns, one of which was spiked and the other had no carriage. Twelve half clothed and half starved looking fellows composed the garrison; and they, it was said, had not a musket apiece. The small settlement lay directly below the fort composed of about forty dark brown looking huts or houses and three or four larger ones whitewashed, which belonged to the gente de razon."

The Presidio Of Monterey.

In a previous chapter has been narrated the story of Portola's expedition in search of Monterey Bay, how the explorers, failing to recognize it, passed on to the northward and discovered the great Bay of San Francisco. On their return they set up a cross at what they supposed was the Bay of Monterey; and at the foot of the cross buried a letter giving information to any ship that might come up the coast in search of them that they had returned to San Diego. They had continually been on the lookout for the San Jose, which was to co-operate with them, but that vessel had been lost at sea with all on board. On their return to San Diego, in January, 1770, preparations were made for a return as soon as a vessel should arrive. It was not until the 16th of April that the San Antonia, the only vessel available, was ready to depart for the second objective point of settlement. On the 17th of April, Governor Portola, Lieutenant Fages, Father Crespi and nineteen soldiers took up their line of march for Monterey. They followed the trail made in 1769 and reached the point where they had set up the cross April 24. They found it decorated with feathers, bows and arrows and a string of fish. Evidently the Indians regarded it as the white man's fetish and tried to propitiate it by offerings.

The San Antonia, bearing Father Serra, Pedro Prat, the surgeon, and Miguel Constanso, the civil engineer, and supplies for the mission and presidio, arrived the last day of May. Portola was still uncertain whether this was really Monterey Bay. It was hard to discover in the open roadstead stretching out before them Viscaino's land-locked harbor, sheltered from all winds. After the arrival of the San Antonia the officers of the land and sea expedition made a reconnaissance of the bay and all concurred that at last they had reached the destined port. They located the oak under whose wide-spreading branches Padre Ascension, Viscaino's chaplain, had celebrated mass in 1602, and the springs of fresh water near by. Preparations were begun at once for the founding of mission and presidio. A shelter of boughs was constructed, an altar raised and the bells hung upon the branch of a tree. Father Serra sang mass and as they had no musical instrument, salvos of artillery and volleys of musketry furnished an accompaniment to the service. After the religious services the royal standard was raised and Governor Portola took possession of the country in the name of King Carlos III., King of Spain. The ceremony closed with the pulling of grass and the casting of stones around, significant of entire possession of the earth and its products. After the service all feasted.

Two messengers were sent by Portola with dispatches to the city of Mexico. A day's journey below San Diego they met Rivera and twenty soldiers coming with a herd of cattle and a flock of sheep to stock the mission pastures. Rivera sent back five of his soldiers with Portola's carriers. The messengers reached Todos Santos near Cape San Lucas in forty-nine days from Monterey. From there the couriers were sent to San Bias by ship, arriving at the city of Mexico August lo. There was great rejoicing at the capital. Marquis Le Croix and visitador Galvez received congratulations in the King's name for the extension of his domain.

Portola superintended the building of some rude huts for the shelter of the soldiers, the officers and the padres. Around the square containing the huts a palisade of poles was constructed. July 9, Portola having turned over the command of the troops to Lieutenant Pages, embarked on the San Antonia for San Bias; with him went the civil engineer, Constanso, from whose report I have frequently quoted. Neither of them ever returned to California.

The difficulty of reaching California by ship on account of the head winds that blow down the coast caused long delays in the arrival of vessels with supplies. This brought about a scarcity of provisions at the presidios and missions.

In 1772 the padres of San Gabriel were reduced to a milk diet and what little they could obtain from the Indians At Monterey and San Antonio the padres and the soldiers were obliged to live on vegetables. In this emergency Lieutenant Pages and a squad of soldiers went on a bear hunt. They spent three months in the summer of 1772 killing bears in the Cañada de los Osos (Bear Cañon). The soldiers and missionaries had a plentiful supply of bear meat. There were not enough cattle in the country to! admit of slaughtering any for food. The presidial walls which were substituted for the palisades were built of adobes and stone. The enclosure measured one hundred and ten yards on each side. The buildings were roofed with tiles. "On the north were the main entrance, the guard house, and the warehouses; on the west the houses of the governor comandante and other officers, some fifteen apartments in all; on the east nine houses for soldiers, and a blacksmith shop; and on the south, besides nine similar houses, was the presidio church, opposite the main gateway."

The military force at the presidio consisted of cavalry, infantry and artillery, their numbers varying from one hundred to one hundred and twenty in all. These soldiers furnished guards for the missions of San Carlos, San Antonio, San Aliguel, Soledad and San Luis Obispo. The total population of gente de razon in the district at the close of the century numbered four hundred and ninety. The rancho "del rey" or rancho of the king was located where Salinas City now stands. This rancho was managed by the soldiers of presidio and was intended to furnish the military with meat and a supply of horses for the cavalry. At the presidio a number of invalided soldiers who had served out their time were settled; these were allowed to cultivate land and raise cattle on the unoccupied lands of the public domain. A town gradually grew up around the presidio square.

Vancouver, the English navigator, visited the presidio of Monterey in 1792 and describes it as it then appeared: "The buildings of the presidio form a parallelogram or long square comprehending an area of about three hundred yards long by two hundred and fifty wide, making one entire enclosure. The external wall is of the same magnitude and built with the same materials, and except that the officers' apartments are covered with red tile made in the neighborhood, the whole presents the same lonely, uninteresting appearance as that already described at San Francisco. Like that establishment, the several buildings for the use of the officers, soldiers, and for the protection of stores and provisions are erected along the walls on the inside of the enclosure, which admits of but one entrance for carriages or persons on horseback; this, as at San Francisco, is on the side of the square fronting the church which was rebuilding with stone like that at San Carlos."

"At each corner of the square is a small kind of block house raised a little above the top of the wall where swivels might be mounted for its protection. On the outside, before the entrance into the presidio, which fronts the shores of the bay, are placed seven cannon, four nine and three three-pounders, mounted. The guns are planted on the open plain ground without breastwork or other screen for those employed in working them or the least protection from the weather."

The Presidio Of San Francisco.

In a previous chapter I have given an account of the discovery of San Francisco Bay by Portola's expedition in 1769. The discovery of that great bay seems to have been regarded as an unimportant event by the governmental officials. While there was great rejoicing at the city of Mexico over the founding of a mission for the conversion of a few naked savages, the discovery of the bay was scarcely noticed, except to construe it into some kind of a miracle. Father Serra assumed that St. Francis had concealed Monterey from the explorers and led them to the discovery of the bay in order that he (St. Francis) might have a mission named for him. Indeed, the only use to which the discovery could be put, according to Serra's ideas, was a site for a mission on its shores, dedicated to the founder of the Franciscans. Several explorations were made with this in view. In 1772, Lieutenant Fages, Father Crespi and sixteen soldiers passed up the western side of the bay and in 1774 Captain Rivera, Father Palou and a squad of soldiers passed up the eastern shore, returning by way of Monte Diablo, Amador valley and Alameda creek to the Santa Clara valley.

In the latter part of the year 1774, viceroy Bucureli ordered the founding of a mission and presidio at San Francisco. Hitherto all explorations of the bay had been made by land expeditions. No one had ventured on its waters. In 1775, Lieutenant Juan de Ayala of the royal navy was sent in the old pioneer mission ship, the San Carlos, to make a survey of it. August 5, 1775, he passed through the Golden Gate. He moored his ship at an island called by him Nuestra Señora de los Angeles, now Angel Island. He spent forty days in making explorations. His ship was the first vessel to sail upon the great Bay of San Francisco.

In 1774, Captain Juan Bautista de Anza, commander of the presidio of Tubac in Sonora, had made an exploration of a route from Sonora via the Colorado river, across the desert and through the San Gorgonia pass to San Gabriel mission. From Tubac to the Colorado river the route had been traveled before but from the Colorado westward the country was a terra incognita. He was guided over this by a lower California neophyte who had deserted from San Gabriel mission and alone had reached the rancherias on the Colorado.

After Anza's return to Sonora he was commissioned by the viceroy to recruit soldiers and settlers for San Francisco. October 23, 1775, Anza set out from Tubac with an expedition numbering two hundred and thirty-five persons, composed of soldiers and their families, colonists, musketeers and vaqueros. They brought with them large herds of horses, mules and cattle. The journey was accomplished without loss of life, but with a considerable amount of suffering. January 4, 1776, the immigrants arrived at San Gabriel mission, where they stopped to rest, but were soon compelled to move on, provisions at the mission becoming scarce. They arrived at Monterey, March 10. Here they went into camp. Anza with an escort of soldiers proceeded to San Francisco to select a presidio site. Having found a site he returned to Monterey. Rivera, the commander of the territory, had manifested a spirit of jealousy toward Anza and had endeavored to thwart him in his attempts to found a settlement. Disgusted with the action of the commander, Anza, leaving his colonists to the number of two hundred at Monterey took his departure from California. Anza in his explorations for a presidio site had fixed upon what is now Fort Point.

After his departure Rivera experienced a change of heart and instead of trying to delay the founding he did everything to hasten it. The imperative orders of the viceroy received at about this time brought about the change. He ordered Lieutenant Moraga, to whom Anza had turned over the command of his soldiers and colonists, to proceed at once to San Francisco with twenty soldiers to found the fort. The San Carlos, which had just arrived at Monterey, was ordered to proceed to San Francisco to assist in the founding. Moraga with his soldiers arrived June 27, and encamped on the Laguna de los Dolores, where the mission was a short time afterwards founded. Moraga decided to located the presidio at the site selected by Anza but awaited the arrival of the San Carlos before proceeding to build. August 18 the vessel arrived. It had been driven down the coast to the latitude of San Diego by contrary winds and then up the coast to latitude 42 degrees. On the arrival of the vessel work was begun at once on the fort. A square of ninety-two varas (two hundred and forty-seven feet) on each side was enclosed with palisades. Barracks, officers' quarters and a chapel were built inside the square. September 17, 1776, was set apart for the services of founding, that being the day of the "Sores of our seraphic father St. Francis." The royal standard was raised in front of the square and the usual ceremony of pulling grass and throwing stones was performed. Possession of the region round about was taken in the name of Carlos III., King of Spain. Over one hundred and fifty persons witnessed the ceremony. Vancouver, who visited the presidio in November, 1792, describes it as a "square area whose sides were about two hundred yards in length, enclosed by a mud wall and resembling a pound for cattle. Above this wall the thatched roofs of the low small houses just made their appearance." The wall was "about fourteen feet high and five feet in breadth and was first formed by upright and horizontal rafters of large timber, between which dried sods and moistened earth were pressed as close and hard as possible, after which the whole was cased with the earth made into a sort of mud plaster which gave it the appearance of durability."

In addition to the presidio there was another fort at Fort Point named Castillo de San Joaquin. It was completed and blessed December 8, 1794"It was of horseshoe shape, about one hundred by one hundred and twenty feet." The

52

structure rested mainly on sand; the brick-faced adobe walls crumbled at the shock whenever a salute was fired; the guns were badly mounted and for the most part worn out, only two of the thirteen twenty-four-pounders being serviceable or capable of sending a ball across the entrance of the fort.

Presidio Of Santa Barbara.

Cabrillo, in 1542, found a large Indian population inhabiting the main land of the Santa Barbara channel. Two hundred and twenty-seven years later, when Portola made his exploration, apparently there had been no decrease in the number of inhabitants. No portion of the coast offered a better field for missionary labor and Father Serra was anxious to enter it. In accordance with Governor Felipe de Neve's report of 1777, it had been decided to found three missions and a presidio on the channel. Various causes had delayed the founding and it was not until April 17, 1782, that Governor de Neve arrived at the point where he had decided to locate the presidio of Santa Barbara. The troops that were to man the fort reached San Gabriel in the fall of 1781. It was thought best for them to remain there until the rainy season was over. March 26, 1782, the governor and Father Serra, accompanied by the largest body of troops that had ever before been collected in California, set out to found the mission of San Buenaventura and the presidio. The governor, as has been stated in a former chapter, was recalled to San Gabriel. The mission was founded and the governor having rejoined the cavalcade a few weeks later proceeded to find a location for the presidio.

"On reaching a point nine leagues from San Buenaventura, the governor called a halt and in company with Father Serra at once proceeded to select a site for the presidio. The choice resulted in the adoption of the square now formed by city blocks 139, 140, 155 and 156, and bounded in common by the following streets: Figueroa, Cañon Perdido, Garden and Anacapa. A large community of Indians were residing there but orders were given to leave them undisturbed. The soldiers were at once directed to hew timbers and gather brush to erect temporary barracks which, when completed, were also used as a chapel. A large wooden cross was made that it might be planted in the center of the square and possession of the country was taken in the name of the cross, the emblem of Christianity.

April 21, 1782, the soldiers formed a square and with edifying solemnity raised the cross and secured it in the earth. Father Serra blessed and consecrated the district and preached a sermon. The royal standard of Spain was unfurled."

An enclosure, sixty varas square, was made of palisades. The Indians were friendly, and through their chief Yanoalit, who controlled thirteen rancherias, details of them were secured to assist the soldiers in the work of building. The natives were paid in food and clothing for their labor.

Irrigation works were constructed, consisting of a large reservoir made of stone and cement, with a zanja for conducting water to the presidio. The soldiers, who had families, cultivated small gardens which aided in their support. Lieutenant Ortega was in command of the presidio for two years after its founding. He was succeeded by Lieutenant Felipe de Goycoechea. After the founding of the mission in 1786, a bitter feud broke out between the padres and the comandante of the presidio. Goycoechea claimed the right to employ the Indians in the building of the presidio as he had done before the coming of the friars. This they denied. After an acrimonious controversy the dispute was finally compromised by dividing the Indians into two bands, a mission band and a presidio band.

Gradually the palisades were replaced by an adobe wall twelve feet high. It had a stone foundation and was strongly built. The plaza or enclosed square was three hundred and thirty feet on each side. On two sides of this enclosure were ranged the family houses of the soldiers, averaging in size 15x25 feet. On one side stood the officers' quarters and the church. On the remaining side were the main entrance four varas wide, the store rooms, soldiers' quarters and a guard room; and adjoining these outside the walls were the corrals for cattle and horses. A force of from fifty to sixty soldiers was kept at the post. There were bastions at two of the corners for cannon.

The presidio was completed about 1790, with the exception of the chapel, which was not finished until 1797. Many of the soldiers when they had served out their time desired to remain in the country. These were given permission to build houses outside the walls of the presidio and in course of time a village grew up around it.

At the close of the century the population of the gente de razon of the district numbered three hundred and seventy. The presidio when completed was the best in California. Vancouver, the English navigator, who visited it in November, 1793, says of it: "The buildings appeared to be regular and well constructed; the walls clean and white and the roofs of the houses were covered with a bright red tile. The presidio excels all the others in neatness, cleanliness and other smaller though essential comforts; it is placed on an elevated part of the plain and is raised some feet from the ground by a basement story which adds much to its pleasantness."

During the Spanish regime the settlement at the presidio grew in the leisurely way that all Spanish towns grew in California. There was but little immigration from Mexico and about the only source of increase was from invalid soldiers and the children of the soldiers growing up to manhood and womanhood. It was a dreary and monotonous existence that the soldiers led at the presidios. A few of them had their families with them. These when the country became more settled had their own houses adjoining the presidio and formed the nuclei of the towns that grew up around the different forts. There was but little fighting to do and the soldiers' service consisted mainly of a round of guard duty at the forts and missions. Occasionally there were conquistas into the Indian country to secure new material for converts from the gentiles. The soldiers were occasionally employed in hunting hindas or runaways from the missions. These when brought back were thoroughly flogged and compelled to wear clogs attached to their legs. Once a month the soldier couriers brought up from Loreta a budget of mail made up of official bandos and a few letters. These contained about all the news that reached them from their old homes in Mexico. But few of the soldiers returned to Mexico when their term of enlistment expired. In course of time these and their descendants formed the bulk of California's population.

CHAPTER VII. PUEBLOS.

The pueblo plan of colonization so common in Hispano-American countries did not originate with the Spanish-American colonists. It was older even than Spain herself. In early European colonization, the pueblo plan, the common square in the center of the town, the house lots grouped round it, the arable fields and the common pasture lands beyond, appears in the Aryan village, in the ancient German mark and in the old Roman presidium. The Puritans adopted this form in their first settlements in New England. Around the public square or common where stood the meeting house and the town house, they laid off their home lots and beyond these were their cultivated fields and their common pasture lands. This form of colonization was a combination of communal interests and individual ownership. Primarily, no doubt, it was adopted for protection against the hostile aborigines of the country, and secondly for social advantage. It reversed the order of our own western colonization. The town came first, it was the initial point from which the settlement radiated; while with our western pioneers the town was an afterthought, a center point for the convenience of trade.

When it had been decided to send colonists to colonize California the settlements naturally took the pueblo form. The difficulty of obtaining regular supplies for the presidios from Mexico, added to the great expense of shipping such a long distance, was the principal cause that influenced the government to establish pueblos de gente de razon. The presidios received their shipments of grain for breadstuff from San Bias by sailing vessels. The arrival of these was uncertain. Once when the vessels were unusually long in coming, the padres and the soldiers at the presidios and missions were reduced to living on milk, bear meat and what provisions they could obtain from the Indians. When Felipe de Neve was made governor of Alta or Nueva California in 1776 he was instructed by the viceroy to make observations on the agricultural possibilities of the country and the feasibility of founding pueblos where grain could be produced to supply the military establishments.

On his journey from San Diego to San Francisco in 1777 he carefully examined the country; and as a result of his observations recommended the founding of two pueblos; one on the Rio de Porciuncula in the south, and the other on the Rio de Guadalupe in the north. On the 29th of November, 1777, the Pueblo of San Jose de Guadelupe was founded. The colonists were nine of the presidio soldiers from San Francisco and Monterey, who had some knowledge of farming and five of Anza's pobladores who had come with his expedition the previous years to found the presidio of San Francisco, making with their families sixty-one persons in all. The pueblo was named for the patron saint of California, San Jose (St. Joseph), husband of Santa Maria, Queen of the Angeles.

The site selected for the town was about a mile and a quarter north of the center of the. present city. The first houses were built of palisades and the interstices plastered with mud. These huts were roofed with earth and the floor was the hard beaten ground. Each head of a family was given a suerte or sowing lot of two hundred varas square, a house lot, "ten dollars a month and a soldier's rations." Each, also, received a yoke of oxen, two cows, a mule, two sheep and two goats, together with the necessary implements and seed, all of which were to be repaid in products of the soil delivered at the royal warehouse. The first communal work done by the pobladores (colonists) was to dam the river, and construct a ditch to irrigate their sowing fields. The dam was not a success and the first sowing of grain was lost. The site selected for the houses was low and subject to overflow.

During wet winters the inhabitants were compelled to take a circuitous route of three leagues to attend church service at the mission of Santa Clara. After enduring this state of affairs through seven winters they petitioned the governor for permission to remove the pueblo further south on higher ground. The governor did not have power to grant the request. The petition was referred to the comandante-general of the Intendencia in Mexico in 1785. He seems to have studied over the matter two years and having advised with the asesor-general "finally issued a decree, June 21, 1787, to Governor Pages, authorizing the settlers to remove to the "adjacent loma (hill) selected by them as more useful and advantageous without changing or altering, for this reason, the limits and boundaries of the territory or district assigned to said settlement and to the neighboring Mission of Santa Clara, as there is no just cause why the latter should attempt to appropriate to herself that land."

Having frequently suffered from floods, it would naturally be supposed that the inhabitants, permission being granted, moved right away. They did nothing of the kind. Ten years passed and they were still located on the old marshy site, still discussing the advantages of the new site on the other side of the river. Whether the padres of the Mission of Santa Clara opposed the moving does not appear in the records, but from the last clause of the comandante-general's decree in which he says "there is not just cause why the latter (the Mission of Santa Clara) should attempt to appropriate to herself the land," it would seem that the mission padres were endeavoring to secure the new site or at least prevent its occupancy. There was a dispute between the padres and the pobladores over the boundary line between the pueblo and mission that outlived the century. After having been referred to the titled officials, civil and ecclesiastical, a boundary line was finally established, July 24, 1801, that was satisfactory to both. "According to the best evidence I have discovered," says Hall in his History of San Jose, "the removal of the pueblo took place in 1797," just twenty years after the founding. In 1798 the juzgado or town hall was built. It was located on Market street near El Dorado street.

The area of a pueblo was four square leagues (Spanish) or about twenty-seven square miles. This was sometimes granted in a square and sometimes in a rectangular form. The pueblo lands were divided into classes: Solares, house lots; suertes (chance), sowing fields, so named because they were distributed by lot; propios, municipal lands or lands the rent of which went to defray municipal expenses; ejidas, vacant suburbs or commons; dehesas, pasture where the large herds of the pueblo grazed; realenges, royal lands also used for raising revenue; these were unappropriated lands.

From various causes the founding of the second pueblo had been delayed. In the latter part of 1779, active preparations were begun for carrying out the plan of founding a presidio and three missions on the Santa Barbara Channel and a pueblo on the Rio Porciuncula to be named "Reyna de Los Angeles." The comandante-general of the Four Interior Provinces of the West (which embraced the Californias, Sonora. New Mexico and Viscaya), Don Teodoro de Croix or "El Cavallero de Croix," "The Knight of the Cross," as he usually styled himself, gave instructions to Don Fernando de Rivera y Moncada to recruit soldiers and settlers for the proposed presidio and pueblo in Nueva California. He, Rivera, crossed the gulf and began recruiting in Sonora and Sinaloa. His instructions were to secure twenty-four settlers, who were heads of families. They must be robust and well behaved, so that they might set a good example to the natives. Their families must accompany them and unmarried female relatives must be encouraged to go, with the view to marrying them to bachelor soldiers.

According to the regulations drafted by Governor Felipe de Neve, June 1, 1779, for the government of the province of California and approved by the king, in a royal order of the 24th of October, 1781, settlers in California from the older provinces were each to be granted a house lot and a tract of land for cultivation. Each poblador in addition was to receive $116.50 a year for the first two years, "the rations to be understood as comprehended in this amount, and in lieu of rations for the next three years they will receive $60 yearly."

Section 3 of Title 14 of the Reglamento provided that "To each poblador and to the community of the pueblo there shall be given under condition of repayment in horses and mules fit to be given and received, and in the payment of the other large and small cattle at the just prices, which are to be fixed by tariff, and of the tools and implements at cost, as it is ordained, two mares, two cows, and one calf, two sheep and two goats, all breeding animals, and one yoke of oxen or steers, one plow point, one hoe, one spade, one axe, one sickle, one wood knife, one musket and one leather shield, two horses and one cargo mule. To the community there shall likewise be given the males corresponding to the total number of cattle of different kinds distributed amongst all the inhabitants, one forge and anvil, six crowbars, six iron spades or shovels and the necessary tools for carpenter and cast work." For the government's assistance to the pobladores in starting their colony the settlers were required to sell to the presidios the surplus products of their lands and herds at fair prices, which were to be fixed by the government.

The terms offered to the settlers were certainly liberal, and by our own hardy pioneers, who in the closing years of the last century were making their way over the Alleghany mountains into Ohio, Kentucky and Tennessee, they would have been considered munificent; but to the indolent and energyless mixed breeds of Sonora and Sinaloa they were no inducement. After spending nearly nine months in recruiting, Rivera was able to obtain only fourteen pobladores, but little over half the number required, and two of these deserted before reaching California. The soldiers that Rivera had recruited for California, forty-two in number, with their families, were ordered to proceed overland from Alamos, in Sonora, by way of Tucson and the Colorado river to San Gabriel Mission. These were commanded by Rivera in person.

Leaving Alamos in April, 1781, they arrived in the latter part of June at the junction of the Gila and Colorado rivers. After a short delay to rest, the main company was sent on to San Gabriel Mission. Rivera, with ten or twelve soldiers, remained to recruit his live stock before crossing the desert. Two missions had been established on the California side of the Colorado the previous year. Before the arrival of Rivera the Indians had been behaving badly. Rivera's large herd of cattle and horses destroyed the mesquite trees and intruded upon the Indians' melon patches. This, with their previous quarrel with the padres, provoked the savages to an uprising. They, on July 17, attacked the two missions, massacred the padres and the Spanish settlers attached to the missions and killed Rivera and his soldiers, forty-six persons in all. The Indians burned the mission buildings. These were never rebuilt nor was there any attempt made to convert the Yumas. The hostility of the Yumas practically closed the Colorado route to California for many years.

The pobladores who had been recruited for the founding of the new pueblo, with their families and a military escort, all under the command of Lieut. Jose Zuniga, crossed the gulf from Guaymas to Loreto, in Lower California, and by the 16th of May were ready for their long journey northward. In the meantime two of the recruits had deserted and one was left behind at Loreto. On the 18th of August the eleven who had remained faithful to their contract, with their families, arrived at San Gabriel. On account of smallpox among some of the children the company was placed in quarantine about a league from the mission.

On the 26th of August, 178 1, from San Gabriel, Governor de Neve issued his instructions for the founding of Los Angeles, which gave some additional rules in regard to the distribution of lots not found in the royal reglamento previously mentioned.

On the 4th of September, 1781, the colonists, with a military escort headed by Governor Felip de Neve, took up their line of march from the Mission San Gabriel to the site selected for their pueblo on the Rio de Porciuncula. There, with religious ceremonies, the Pueblo de Nuestra Senora La Reina de Los Angeles was formally founded. A mass was said by a priest from the Mission San Gabriel, assisted by the choristers and musicians of that mission. There were salvos of musketry and a procession with a cross, candlestick, etc. At the head of the procession the soldiers bore the standard of Spain and the women followed bearing a banner with the image of our Lady the Queen of the Angels. This procession made a circuit of the plaza, the priest blessing it and the building lots. At the close of the services Governor de Neve made an address full of good advice to the colonists. Then the governor, his military escort and the priests returned to San Gabriel and the colonists were left to work out their destiny.

Few of the great cities of the land have had such humble founders as Los Angeles. Of the eleven pobladores who built their huts of poles and tule thatch around the plaza vieja one hundred and twenty-five years ago, not one could read or write. Not one could boast of an unmixed ancestry. They were mongrels in race, Caucasian, Indian and Negro mi.xed. Poor in purse, poor in blood, poor in all the sterner qualities of character that our own hardy pioneers of the west possessed, they left no impress on the city they founded; and the conquering race that possesses the land that they colonized has forgotten them. No street or landmark in the city bears the name of any one of them. No monument or tablet marks the spot where they planted the germ of their settlement. No Forefathers' day preserves the memory of their services and sacrifices. Their names, race and the number of persons in each family have been preserved in the archives of California. They are as follows:

1. Jose de Lara, a Spaniard (or reputed to be one, although it is doubtful whether he was of pure blood) had an Indian wife and three children.

2. Jose Antonio Navarro, a Mestizo, forty-two years old; wife a mulattress; three children.

3. Basilio Rosas, an Indian, sixty-eight years old, had a mulatto wife and two children.

4. Antonio Mesa, a negro, thirty-eight years old; had a mulatto wife and two children.

5. Antonio Felix Villavicencio, a Spaniard, thirty years old; had an Indian wife and one child.

6. Jose Vanegas, an Indian, twenty-eight years old; had an Indian wife and one child.

7. Alejandro Rosas, an Indian, nineteen years old, and had an Indian wife. (In the records, "wife, Coyote-Indian.")

8. Pablo Rodriguez, an Indian, twenty-five years old; had an Indian wife and one child.

9. Manuel Camero, a mulatto, thirty years old; had a mulatto wife.

10. Luis Quintero, a negro, fifty-five years old, and had a mulatto wife and five children.

11. Jose Morena, a mulatto, twenty-two years old, and had a mulatto wife.

Antonio Miranda, the twelfth person described in the padron (list) as a Chino, fifty years old and having one child, was left at Loreto when the expedition marched northward. It would have been impossible for him to have rejoined the colonists before the founding. Presumably his child remained with him, consequently there were but forty-four instead of "forty-six persons in all." Col. J. J. Warner, in his "Historical Sketch of Los Angeles," originated the fiction that one of the founders (Miranda, the Chino,) was born in China. Chino, while it does mean a Chinaman, is also applied in Spanish-American countries to persons or animals having curly hair. Miranda was probably of mixed Spanish and Negro blood, and curly haired. There is no record to show that Miranda ever came to Alta California.

When Jose de Galvez was fitting out the expedition for occupying San Diego and Monterey, he issued a proclamation naming St. Joseph as the patron saint of his California colonization scheme. Bearing this fact in mind, no doubt, Governor de Neve, when he founded San Jose, named St. Joseph its patron saint. Having named one of the two pueblos for San Jose it naturally followed that the other should be named for Santa Maria, the Queen of the Angels, wife of San Jose.

On the 1st of August, 1769, Portola's expedition, on its journey northward in search of Monterey Bay, had halted in the San Gabriel valley near where the Mission Vieja was afterwards located, to reconnoiter the country and "above all," as Father Crespi observes, "for the purpose of celebrating the jubilee of Our Lady of the Angels of Porciuncula." Next day, August 2, after traveling about three leagues (nine miles), Father Crespi, in his diary, says: "We came to a rather wide Canada having a great many Cottonwood and alder trees. Through it ran a beautiful river toward the north-northeast and curving around the point of a cliff it takes a direction to the south. Toward the north-northeast we saw another river bed which must have been a great overflow, but we found it dry. This arm unites with the river and its great floods during the rainy season are clearly demonstrated by the

59

many uprooted trees scattered along the banks." (This dry river is the Arroyo Seco.) "We stopped not very far from the river, to which we gave the name of Porciuncula." Porciuncula is the name of a hamlet in Italy near which was located the little church of Our Lady of the Angels, in which St. Francis of Assisi was praying when the jubilee was granted him. Father Crespi, speaking of the plain through which the river flows, says: "This is the best locality of all those we have yet seen for a mission, besides having all the resources required for a large town." Padre Crespi was evidently somewhat of a prophet.

The fact that this locality had for a number of years borne the name of "Our Lady of the Angels of Porciuncula" may have influenced Governor de Neve to locate his pueblo here. The full name of the town, El Pueblo de Nuestra Señora La Reyna de Los Angeles, was seldom used. It was too long for everyday use. In the earlier years of the town's history it seems to have had a variety of names. It appears in the records as El Pueblo de Nuestra Señora de Los Angeles, as El Pueblo de La Reyna de Los Angeles and as El Pueblo de Santa Maria de Los Angeles. Sometimes it was abbreviated to Santa Maria, but it was most commonly spoken of as El Pueblo, the town. At what time the name of Rio Porciuncula was changed to Rio Los Angeles is uncertain. The change no doubt was gradual.

The site selected for the pueblo of Los Angeles was picturesque and romantic. From where Alameda street now is to the eastern bank of the river the land was covered with a dense growth of willows, cottonwoods and alders; while here and there, rising above the swampy copse, towered a giant aliso (sycamore). Wild grapevines festooned the branches of the trees and wild roses bloomed in profusion. Behind the narrow shelf of mesa land where the pueblo was located rose the brown hills, and in the distance towered the lofty Sierra Madre mountains.

The last pueblo founded in California under Spanish domination was Villa de Branciforte, located on the opposite side of the river from the Mission of Santa Cruz. It was named after the Viceroy Branciforte. It was designed as a coast defense and a place to colonize discharged soldiers. The scheme was discussed for a considerable time before anything was done. Governor Borica recommended "that an adobe house be built for each settler so that the prevalent state of things in San Jose and Los Angeles, where the settlers still live in tule huts, being unable to build better dwellings without neglecting their fields, may be prevented, the houses to cost not over two hundred dollars."

The first detachment of the colonists arrived May 12, 1797, on the Concepcion in a destitute condition. Lieutenant Moraga was sent to superintend the construction of houses for the colonists. He was instructed to build temporary huts for himself and the guard, then to build some larger buildings to accommodate fifteen or twenty families each. These were to be temporary. Only nine families came and they were of a vagabond class that had a constitutional antipathy to work. The settlers received the same amount of supplies and allowance of money as the colonists of San Jose and Los Angeles. Although the colonists were called Spaniards and assumed to be of a superior race to the first settlers of the other pueblos, they made less progress and were more unruly than the mixed and mongrel inhabitants of the older pueblos.

Although at the close of the century three decades had passed since the first settlement was made in California, the colonists had made but little progress. Three pueblos of gente de razon had been founded and a few ranchos granted to ex-soldiers. Exclusive of the soldiers, the white population in the year 1800 did not exceed six hundred. The people lived in the most primitive manner. There was no commerce and no manufacturing except a little at the missions. Their houses were adobe huts roofed with tule thatch. The floor was the beaten earth and the scant furniture home-made. There was a scarcity of cloth for clothing. Padre Salazar relates that when he was at San Gabriel Mission in 1795 a man who had a thousand horses and cattle in proportion came there to beg cloth for a shirt, for none could be had at the pueblo of Los Angeles nor at the presidio of Santa Barbara.

Hermanagildo Sal, the comandante of San Francisco, writing to a friend in 1799, says, "I send you, by the wife of the pensioner Jose Barbo, one piece of cotton goods and an ounce of sewing silk. There are no combs and I have no hope of receiving any for three years." Think of waiting three years for a comb!

Eighteen missions had been founded at the close of the century. Except at a few of the older missions, the buildings were temporary structures. The neophytes for the most part were living in wigwams constructed like those they had occupied in their wild state.

CHAPTER VIII.
THE PASSING OF SPAIN'S DOMINATION.

The Spaniards were not a commercial people. Their great desire was to be let alone in their American possessions. Philip II. once promulgated a decree pronouncing death upon any foreigner who entered the Gulf of Mexico. It was easy to promulgate a decree or to pass restrictive laws against foreign trade, but quite another thing to enforce them.

After the first settlement of California seventeen years passed before a foreign vessel entered any of its ports. The first to arrive were the two vessels of the French explorer, La Perouse, who anchored in the harbor of Monterey, September 15, 1786. Being of the same faith, and France having been an ally of Spain in former times, he was well received. During his brief stay he made a study of the mission system and his observations on it are plainly given. He found a similarity in it to the slave plantations of Santo Domingo. November 14, 1792, the English navigator, Capt. George Vancouver, in the ship Discovery, entered the Bay of San Francisco. He was cordially received by the comandante of the port, Hermanagildo Sal, and the friars of the mission. On the 20th of the month, with several of his officers, he visited the Mission of Santa Clara, where he was kindly treated. He also visited the Mission of San Carlos de Monterey. He wrote an interesting account of his visit and his observations on the country. Vancouver was surprised at the backwardness of the country and the antiquated customs of the people. He says: "Instead of finding a country tolerably well inhabited, and far advanced in cultivation, if we except its natural pastures, flocks of sheep and herds of cattle, there is not an object to indicate the most remote connection with any European or other civilized nation." On a subsequent visit. Captain Vancouver met a chilly reception from the acting governor, Arrillaga. The Spaniards suspected him of spying out the weakness of their defenses. Through the English, the Spaniards became acquainted with the importance and value of the fur trade. The bays and lagoons of California abounded in sea otter. Their skins were worth in China all the way from $30 to $100 each. The trade was made a government monopoly. The skins were to be collected from the natives, soldiers and others by the missionaries, at prices ranging from $2.50 to $10 each, and turned over to the government officials appointed to receive them. All trade by private persons was prohibited. The government was sole trader. But the government failed to make the trade profitable. In the closing years of the century the American smugglers began to haunt the coast. The restrictions against trade with foreigners were proscriptive and the penalties for evasion severe, but men will trade under the most adverse circumstances. Spain was a long way off, and smuggling was not a very venal sin in the eyes of layman or churchman. Fast sailing vessels were fitted out in Boston for illicit trade on the California coast. Watching their opportunities, these vessels slipped into the bays and inlets along the coast. There was a rapid exchange of Yankee notions for sea otter skins, the most valued peltry of California, and the vessels were out to sea before the revenue officers could intercept them. If successful in escaping capture, the profits of a smuggling voyage were enormous, ranging from 500 to 1,000 per cent above cost on the goods exchanged; but the risks were great. The smuggler had no protection; he was an outlaw. He was the legitimate prey of the padres, the people and the revenue officers. The Yankee smuggler usually came out ahead. His vessel was heavily armed, and when speed or stratagem failed he was ready to fight his way out of a scrape.

Each year two ships were sent from San Bias with the memorias — mission and presidio supplies. These took back a small cargo of the products of the territory, wheat being the principal. This was all the legitimate commerce allowed California.

The fear of Russian aggression had been one of the causes that had forced Spain to attempt the colonization of California. Bering, in 1741, had discovered the strait that bears his name and had taken possession, for the Russian government, of the northwestern coast of America. Four years later, the first permanent Russian settlement, Sitka, had been made on one of the coast islands. Rumors of the Russian explorations and settlements had reached Madrid and in 1774 Captain Perez, in the San Antonia, was sent up the coast to find out what the Russians were doing.

Had Russian America contained arable land where grain and vegetables could have been grown, it is probable that the Russians and Spaniards in America would not have come in contact; for another nation, the United States, had taken possession of the intervening country, bordering the Columbia river.

The supplies of breadstuffs for the Sitka colonists had to be sent overland across Siberia or shipped around Cape Horn. Failure of supplies sometimes reduced the colonists to sore straits. In 1806, famine and diseases incident to starvation threatened the extinction of the Russian colony. Count Rezanoff, a high officer of the Russian government, had arrived at the Sitka settlement in September, 1805. The destitution prevailing there induced him to visit California with the hope of obtaining relief for the starving colonists. In the ship Juno (purchased from an American trader), with a scurvy afflicted crew, he made a perilous voyage down the stormy coast and on the 5th of April, 1806, anchored safely in the Bay of San Francisco. He had brought with him a cargo of goods for exchange but the restrictive commercial regulations of Spain prohibited trade with foreigners. Although the friars and the people needed the goods the governor could not allow the exchange. Count Rezanoff would be permitted to purchase grain for cash, but the Russian's exchequer was not plethoric and his ship was already loaded with goods. Love that laughs at locksmiths eventually unlocked the shackles that hampered commerce. Rezanoff fell in love with Dona Concepcion, the beautiful daughter of Don Jose Arguello, the comandante of San Francisco, and an old time friend of the governor, Arrillaga. The attraction was mutual. Through the influence of Dona Concepcion, the friars and Arguello, the governor was induced to sanction a plan by which cash was the supposed medium of exchange on both sides, but grain on the one side and goods on the other were the real currency.

The romance of Rezanoff and Dona Concepcion had a sad ending. On his journey through Siberia to St. Petersburg to obtain the consent of the emperor to his marriage he was killed by a fall from his horse. It was several years before the news of his death reached his affianced bride. Faithful to his memory, she never married, but dedicated her life to deeds of charity. After Rezanoff's visit the

Russians came frequently to California, partly to trade, but more often to hunt otter. While on these fur hunting expeditions they examined the coast north of San Francisco with the design of planting an agricultural colony where they could raise grain to supply the settlements in the far north. In 1812 they founded a town and built a fort on the coast north of Bodega Bay, which they named Ross. The fort mounted ten guns. They maintained a fort at Bodega Bay and also a small settlement on Russian river. The Spaniards protested against this aggression and threatened to drive the Russians out of the territory, but nothing came of their protests and they were powerless to enforce their demands. The Russian ships came to California for supplies and were welcomed by the people and the friars if not by the government officials. The Russian colony at Ross was not a success. The ignorant soldiers and the Aluets who formed the bulk of its three or four hundred inhabitants, knew little or nothing about farming and were too stupid to learn. After the decline of fur hunting the settlement became unprofitable. In 1841 the buildings and the stock were sold by the Russian governor to Capt. John A. Sutter for $30,000. The settlement was abandoned and the fort and the town are in ruins.

On the 15th of September, 1810, the patriot priest, Miguel Hidalgo, struck the first blow for Mexican independence. The revolution which began in the province of Guanajuato was at first regarded by the authorities as a mere riot of ignorant Indians that would be speedily suppressed. But the insurrection spread rapidly. Long years of oppression and cruelty had instilled into the hearts of the people an undying hatred for their Spanish oppressors. Hidalgo soon found himself at the head of a motley army, poorly armed and undisciplined, but its numbers swept away opposition. Unfortunately through over-confidence reverses came and in March, 1811, the patriots met an overwhelming defeat at the bridge of Calderon. Hidalgo was betrayed, captured and shot. Though suppressed for a time, the cause of independence was not lost. For eleven years a fratricidal war was waged — cruel, bloody and devastating. Allende, Mina, Moreles, Aldama, Rayon and other patriot leaders met death on the field of battle or were captured and shot as rebels, but "Freedom's battle" bequeathed from bleeding sire to son was won at last.

Of the political upheavals that shook Spain in the first decades of the century only the faintest rumblings reached far distant California. Notwithstanding the many changes of rulers that political revolutions and Napoleonic wars gave the mother country, the people of California remained loyal to the Spanish crown, although at times they must have been in doubt who wore the crown.

Arrillaga was governor of California when the war of Mexican independence began. Although born in Mexico he was of pure Spanish parentage and was thoroughly in sympathy with Spain in the contest. He did not live to see the end of the war. He died in 1814 and was succeeded by Pablo Vicente de Sola. Sola was Spanish born and was bitterly opposed to the revolution, even going so far as to threaten death to any one who should speak in favor of it. He had received his appointment from Viceroy Calleja, the butcher of Guanajuato, the crudest and most bloodthirsty of the vice regal governors of new Spain. The friars were to a man loyal to Spain. The success of the republic meant the downfall of their domination. They hated republican ideas and regarded their dissemination as a crime. They were the ruling power in California. The governors and the people were subservient to their wishes.

The decade between 1810 and 1820 was marked by two important events, the year of the earthquakes and the year of the insurgents.

The year 1812 was the Ano de los Temblores. The seismic disturbance that for forty years or more had shaken California seemed to concentrate in power that year and expend its force on the mission churches. The massive church of San Juan Capistrano, the pride of mission architecture, was thrown down and forty persons killed. The walls of San Gabriel Mission were cracked and some of the saints shaken out of their niches. At San Buenaventura there were three heavy shocks which injured the church so that the tower and much of the facade had to be rebuilt. The whole mission site seemed to settle and the inhabitants, fearful that they might be engulfed by the sea, moved up the valley about two miles, where they remained three months. At Santa Barbara both church and the presidio were damaged and at Santa Inez the church was shaken down. The quakes continued for several months and the people were so terrified that they abandoned their houses and lived in the open air.

The other important epoch of the decade was El Ano de los Insurgentes, the year of the insurgents. In November, 1818, Bouchard, a Frenchman in the service of Buenos Ayres and provided with letters of marque by San Martain, the president of that republic, to prey upon Spanish commerce, appeared in the port of Monterey with two ships carrying sixty-six guns and three hundred and fifty men. He attacked Monterey and after an obstinate resistance by the Californians, it was taken by the insurgents and burned. Bouchard next pillaged Ortega's rancho and burned the buildings. Then sailing down the coast he scared the Santa Barbaraños; then keeping on down he looked into San Pedro, but finding nothing there to tempt him he kept on to San Juan Capistrano. There he landed, robbed the mission of a few articles and drank the padres' wine. Then he sailed away and disappeared. He left six of his men in California, among them Joseph Chapman of Boston, the first American resident of California.

In the early part of the last century there was a limited commerce with Lima. That being a Spanish dependency, trade with it was not prohibited. Gilroy, who arrived in California in 1814, says in his reminiscences:

"The only article of export then was tallow, of which one cargo was sent annually to Callao in a Spanish ship. This tallow sold for $1.50 per hundred weight in silver or $2.00 in trade or goods. Hides, except those used for tallow bags, were thrown away. Wheat, barley and beans had no market. Nearly everything consumed by the people was produced at home. There was no foreign trade."

As the revolution in Mexico progressed times grew harder in California. The mission memorias ceased to come. No tallow ships from Callao arrived. The soldiers' pay was years in arrears and their uniforms in rags. What little wealth there was in the country was in the hands of the padres. They were supreme. "The friars," says Gilroy, "had everything their own way. The governor and the military were expected to do whatever the friars requested. The missions contained all the wealth of the country." The friars supported the government and supplied the troops with food from the products of the neophytes' labor. The crude manufacturers of the missions supplied the people with cloth for clothing and some other necessities. The needs of the common people were easily satisfied. They were not used to luxuries nor were they accustomed to what we would now consider necessities. Gilroy, in the reminiscences heretofore referred to, states that at the time of his arrival (1814) "There was not a sawmill, whip saw or spoked wheel in California. Such lumber as was used was cut with an axe. Chairs, tables and wood floors were not to be found except in the governor's house. Plates were rare unless that name could be applied to the tiles used instead. Money was a rarity. There were no stores and no merchandise to sell. There was no employment for a laborer. The neophytes did all the work and all the business of the country was in the hands of the friars."

CHAPTER IX. FROM EMPIRE TO REPUBLIC.

The condition of affairs in California steadily grew worse as the revolution in Mexico progressed. Sola had made strenuous efforts to arouse the Spanish authorities of New Spain to take some action towards benefiting the territory. After the affair with the insurgent Bouchard he had appealed to the viceroy for reinforcements. In answer to his urgent entreaties a force of one hundred men was sent from Mazatlan to garrison San Diego and an equal force from San Bias for Monterey. They reached California in August, 1819, and Sola was greatly rejoiced, but his joy was turned to deep disgust when he discovered the true character of the reinforcement and arms sent him. The only equipments of the soldiers were a few hundred old worn-out sabers that Sola declared were unfit for sickles. He ordered them returned to the comandante of San Bias, who had sent them. The troops were a worse lot than the arms sent. They had been taken out of the prisons or conscripted from the lowest class of the population of the cities. They were thieves, drunkards and vagabonds, who, as soon as landed, resorted to robberies, brawls and assassinations. Sola wrote to the viceroy that the outcasts called troops sent him from the jails of Tepic and San Bias by their vices caused continual disorders; their evil example had debauched the minds of the Indians and that the cost incurred in their collection and transportation had been worse than thrown away. He could not get rid of them, so he had to control them as best he could. Governor Sola labored faithfully to benefit the country over which he had been placed and to arouse the Spanish authorities in Mexico to do something for the advancement of California; but the government did nothing. Indeed it was in no condition to do anything. The revolution would not down. No sooner was one revolutionary leader suppressed and the rebellion apparently crushed than there was an uprising in some other part of the country under a new leader.

Ten years of intermittent warfare had been waged — one army of patriots after another had been defeated and the leaders shot; the struggle for independence was almost ended and the royalists were congratulating themselves on the triumph of the Spanish crown, when a sudden change came and the vice regal government that for three hundred years had swayed the destinies of New Spain went down forever. Agustin Iturbide, a colonel in the royal army, who in February, 1821, had been sent with a corps of five thousand men from the capital to the Sierras near Acapulco to suppress Guerrero, the last of the patriot chiefs, suddenly changed his allegiance, raised the banner of the revolution and declared for the independence of Mexico under the plan of Iguala, so named for the town where it was first proclaimed. The central ideas of the plan were "Union, civil and religious liberty."

There was a general uprising in all parts of the country and men rallied to the support of the Army of the Three Guarantees, religion, union, independence. Guerrero joined forces with Iturbide and September 21, 1821, at the head of sixteen thousand men, amid the rejoicing of the people, they entered the capital. The viceroy was compelled to recognize the independence of Mexico. A provisional government under a regency was appointed at first, but a few months later Iturbide was crowned emperor, taking the title of his most serene majesty,

Agustin I., by divine providence and by the congress of the nation, first constitutional emperor of Mexico.

Sola had heard rumors of the turn affairs were taking in Mexico, but he had kept the reports a secret and still hoped and prayed for the success of the Spanish arms. At length a vessel appeared in the harbor of Monterey floating an unknown flag, and cast anchor beyond the reach of the guns of the castillo. The soldiers were called to arms. A boat from the ship put off for shore and landed an officer, who declared himself the bearer of dispatches to Don Pablo Vicente de Sola, the governor of the province. "I demand," said he, "to be conducted to his presence in the name of my sovereign, the liberator of Mexico, General Agustin de Iturbide." There was a murmur of applause from the soldiers, greatly to the surprise of their officers, who were all loyalists. Governor Sola was bitterly disappointed. Only a few days before he had harangued the soldiers in the square of the presidio and threatened "to shoot down any one high or low without the formality of a trial who dared to say a word in favor of the traitor Iturbide."

For half a century the banner of Spain had floated from the flag staff of the presidio of Monterey. Sadly Sola ordered it lowered and in its place was hoisted the imperial flag of the Mexican Empire. A few months pass, Iturbide is forced to abdicate the throne of empire and is banished from Mexico. The imperial standard is supplanted by the tricolor of the republic. Thus the Californians, in little more than one year, have passed under three different forms of government, that of a kingdom, an empire and a republic, and Sola from the most loyal of Spanish governors in the kingdom of Spain has been transformed in a Mexican republican.

The friars, if possible, were more bitterly disappointed than the governor. They saw in the success of the republic the doom of their establishments. Republican ideas were repulsive to them. Liberty meant license to men to think for themselves. The shackles of creed and the fetters of priestcraft would be loosened by the growth of liberal ideas. It was not strange, viewing the question from their standpoint, that they refused to take the oath of allegiance to the republic. Nearly all of them were Spanish born. Spain had aided them to plant their missions, had fostered their establishments and had made them supreme in the territory. Their allegiance was due to the Spanish crown. They would not transfer it to a republic and they did not; to the last they were loyal to Spain in heart, even if they did acquiesce in the observance of the rule of the republic.

Sola had long desired to be relieved of the governorship. He was growing old and was in poor health. The condition of the country worried him. He had frequently asked to be relieved and allowed to retire from military duty. His requests were unheeded; the vice regal government of New Spain had weightier matters to attend to than requests or the complaints of the governor of a distant and unimportant province. The inauguration of the empire brought him the desired relief.

Under the empire Alta California was allowed a diputado or delegate in the imperial congress. Sola was elected delegate and took his departure for Mexico in the autumn of 1822. Luis Antonio Arguello, president of the provincial diputacion, an institution that had come into existence after the inauguration of the empire, became governor by virtue of his position as president. He was the first hijo del pais or native of the country to hold the office of governor. He was born at San

Francisco in 1784, while his father, an ensign at the presidio, was in command there. His opportunities for obtaining an education were extremely meager, but he made the best use of what he had. He entered the army at sixteen and was, at the time he became temporary governor, comandante at San Francisco.

The inauguration of a new form of government had brought no relief to California. The two Spanish ships that had annually brought los memorias del rey (the remembrances of the king) had long since ceased to come with their supplies of money and goods for the soldiers. The California ports were closed to foreign commerce. There was no sale for the products of the country. So the missions had to throw open their warehouses and relieve the necessities of the government.

The change in the form of government had made no change in the dislike of foreigners, that was a characteristic of the Spaniard. During the Spanish era very few foreigners had been allowed to remain in California. Runaway sailors and shipwrecked mariners, notwithstanding they might wish to remain in the country and become Catholics, were shipped to Mexico and returned to their own country. John Gilroy, whose real name was said to be John Cameron, was the first permanent English speaking resident of California. When a boy of eighteen he was left by the captain of a Hudson Bay company's ship at Monterey in 1814. He was sick with the scurvy and not expected to live. Nursing and a vegetable diet brought him out all right, but he could not get away. He did not like the country and every day for several years he went down to the beach and scanned the ocean for a foreign sail. When one did come he had gotten over his home-sickness, had learned the language, fallen in love, turned Catholic and married.

In 1822 William E. P. Hartnell, an Englishman, connected with a Lima business house, visited California and entered into a contract with Padre Payeras, the prefect of the missions, for the purchase of hides and tallow. Hartnell a few years later married a California lady and became a permanent resident of the territory. Other foreigners who came about the same time as Hartnell and who became prominent in California were William A. Richardson, an Englishman; Capt. John R. Cooper of Boston and William A. Gale, also of Boston. Gale had first visited California in 1810 as a fur trader. He returned in 1822 on the ship Sachem, the pioneer Boston hide drogher. The hide drogher was in a certain sense the pioneer emigrant ship of California. It brought to the coast a number of Americans who became permanent residents of the territory. California, on account of its long distance from the world's marts of trade, had but few products for exchange that would bear the cost of shipment. Its chief commodities for barter during the Mexican era were hides and tallow. The vast range of country adapted to cattle raising made that its most profitable industry. Cattle increased rapidly and required but little care or attention from their owners. As the native Californians were averse to hard labor cattle raising became almost the sole industry of the country.

After the inauguration of a republican form of government in Mexico some of the most burdensome restrictions on foreign commerce were removed. The Mexican Congress of 1824 enacted a colonization law, which was quite liberal. Under it foreigners could obtain land from the public domain. The Roman Catholic religion was the state religion and a foreigner, before he could become a permanent resident of the country, acquire property or marry, was required to be baptized and embrace the doctrines of that church. After the Mexican Congress repealed the restrictive laws against foreign commerce a profitable trade grew up between the New England ship owners and the Californians.

Vessels called hide droghers were fitted out in Boston with assorted cargoes suitable for the California trade. Making the voyage by way of Cape Horn they reached California. Stopping at the various ports along the coast they exchanged their stocks of goods and Yankee notions for hides and tallow. It took from two to three years to make a voyage to California and return to Boston, but the profits on the goods sold and on the hides received in exchange were so large that these ventures paid handsomely. The arrival of a hide drogher with its department store cargo was heralded up and down the coast. It broke the monotony of existence, gave the people something new to talk about and stirred them up as nothing else could do unless possibly a revolution.

"On the arrival of a new vessel from the United States," says Robinson in his "Life in California," "every man, woman, boy and girl took a proportionate share of interest as to the qualities of her cargo. If the first inquired for rice, sugar or tobacco, the latter asked for prints, silks and satins; and if the boy wanted a Wilson's jack knife, the girl hoped that there might be some satin ribbons for her. Thus the whole population hailed with eagerness an arrival. Even the Indian in his unsophisticated style asked for Panas Colorados and Abalaris — red handkerchiefs and beads.

"After the arrival of our trading vessel (at San Pedro) our friends came in the morning flocking on board from all quarters; and soon a busy scene commenced afloat and ashore. Boats were passing to the beach, and men, women and children partaking in the general excitement. On shore all was confusion, cattle and carts laden with hides and tallow, gente de razon and Indians busily employed in the delivery of their produce and receiving in return its value in goods. Groups of individuals seated around little bonfires upon the ground, and horsemen racing over the plains in every direction. Thus the day passed, some arriving, some departing, till long after sunset, the low white road, leading across the plains to the town (Los Angeles), appeared a living panorama."

The commerce of California during the Mexican era was principally carried on by the hide droghers. The few stores at the pueblos and presidios obtained their supplies from them and retailed their goods to customers in the intervals between the arrivals of the department store droghers.

The year 1824 was marked by a serious outbreak among the Indians of several missions. Although in the older missionary establishments many of the neophytes had spent half a century under the Christianizing influence of the padres and in these, too, a younger generation had grown from childhood to manhood under mission tutelage, yet their Christian training had not eliminated all the aboriginal savagery from their natures. The California Indians were divided into numerous small tribes, each speaking a different dialect. They had never learned, like the eastern Indians did, the advantages of uniting against a common enemy. When these numerous small tribes were gathered into the missions they were kept as far as it was possible separate and it is said the padres encouraged their feuds and tribal animosities to prevent their uniting against the missionaries. Their long residence in the missions had destroyed their tribal distinctions and merged them into one body. It had taught them, too, the value of combination.

How long the Indians had been plotting no one knew. The conspiracy began among the neophytes of Santa Ynez and La Purisima, but it spread to the missions of San Luis Obispo, Santa Barbara, San Buenaventura, San Fernando and San Gabriel. Their plan was to massacre the padres and the mission guard and having obtained arms to kill all the gente de razon and thus free themselves from mission thralldom and regain their old time freedom. The plotting had been carried on with great secrecy. Rumors had passed from mission to mission arranging the details of the uprising without the whites suspecting anything. Sunday, February 22, 1824, was the day set for beginning the slaughter. At the hour of celebrating mass, when the soldiers and the padres were within the church, the bloody work was to begin. The plot might have succeeded had not the Indians at Santa Ynez began their work prematurely. One account (Hittell's History of California) says that on Saturday afternoon before the appointed Sunday they determined to begin the work by the murder of Padre Francisco Xavier Una, who was sleeping in a chamber next the mission church. He was warned by a faithful page. Springing from his couch and rushing to a window he saw the Indians approaching. Seizing a musket from several that were in the room he shot the first Indian that reached the threshold dead. He seized a second musket and laid another Indian low. The soldiers now rallied to his assistance and the Indians were driven back; they set fire to the mission church, but a small body of troops under Sergeant Carrillo, sent from Santa Barbara to reinforce the mission guard, coming up at this time, the Indians fled to Purisima. The fire was extinguished before the church was consumed. At Purisima the Indians were more successful. The mission was defended by Corporal Tapia and five soldiers. The Indians demanded that Tapia surrender, but the corporal refused. The fight began and continued all night. The Indians set fire to the building, but all they could burn was the rafters. Tapia, by a strategic movement, succeeded in collecting all the soldiers and the women and children inside the walls of one of the largest buildings from which the roof had been burnt. From this the Indians could not dislodge him. The fight was kept up till morning, when one of the Indians, who had been a mission alcade, made a proposition to the corporal to surrender. Tapia refused to consider it, but Father Bias Ordaz interfered and insisted on a compromise. After much contention Tapia found himself overruled. The Indians agreed to spare the lives of all on condition that the whites laid down their arms. The soldiers laid down their arms and surrendered two small cannon belonging to the church. The soldiers, the women and the children were then allowed to march to Santa Ynez. While the fight was going on the Indians killed four white men, two of them, Dolores Sepulveda and Ramon Satelo, were on their way to Los Angeles and came to the mission not suspecting any danger. Seven Indians were killed in the fight and a number wounded.

The Indians at Santa Barbara began hostilities according to their prearranged plot. They made an attack upon the mission. Captain de la Guerra, who was in command at the presidio, marched to the mission and a fight of several hours ensued. The Indians sheltered themselves behind the pillars of the corridor and fought with guns and arrows. After losing several of their number they fled to the hills. Four soldiers were wounded. The report of the uprising reached Monterey and measures were taken at once to subdue the rebellious neophytes. A force of one hundred men was sent under Lieut. Jose Estrada to co-operate with Captain de

71

la Guerra against the rebels. On the 16th of March the soldiers surrounded the Indians who had taken possession of the mission church at Purisima and opened fire upon them. The Indians replied with their captured cannon, muskets and arrows. Estrada's artillery battered down the walls of the church. The Indians, unused to arms, did little execution. Driven out of the wrecked building, they attempted to make their escape by flight, but were intercepted by the cavalry which had been deployed for that purpose. Finding themselves hemmed in on all sides the neophytes surrendered. They had lost sixteen killed and a large number of wounded. Seven of the prisoners were shot for complicity in the murder of Sepulveda and the three other travelers. The four leaders in the revolt, Mariano Pacomio, Benito and Bernabe, were sentenced to ten years hard labor at the presidio and eight others to lesser terms. There were four hundred Indians engaged in the battle.

The Indians of the Santa Barbara missions and escapes from Santa Ynez and Purisima made their way over the mountains to the Tulares. A force of eighty men under command of a lieutenant was sent against these. The troops had two engagements with the rebels, whom they found at Buenavista Lake and San Emigdio. Finding his force insufficient to subdue them the lieutenant retreated to Santa Barbara. Another force of one hundred and thirty men under Captain Portilla and Lieutenant Valle was sent after the rebels. Father Ripoll had induced the governor to offer a general pardon. The padre claimed that the Indians had not harmed the friars nor committed sacrilege in the church and from his narrow view these were about the only venal sins they could commit. The troops found the fugitive neophytes encamped at San Emigdio. They now professed repentance for their misdeeds and were willing to return to mission life if they could escape punishment. Padres Ripoll and Sarria, who had accompanied the expedition, entered into negotiations with the Indians; pardon was promised them for their offenses. They then surrendered and marched back with the soldiers to their respective missions. This was the last attempt of the Indians to escape from mission rule.

CHAPTER X. FIRST DECADE OF MEXICAN RULE.

Jose Maria Echeandia, a lieutenant colonel of the Mexican army, was appointed governor of the two Californias, February 1, 1825. With his staff officers and a few soldiers he landed at Loreto June 22. After a delay of a few months at Loreto he marched overland to San Diego, where he arrived about the middle of October. He summoned Arguello to meet him there, which he did and turned over the government, October 31, 1825. Echeandia established his capital at San Diego, that town being about the center of his jurisdiction. This did not suit the people of Monterey, who became prejudiced against the new governor. Shortly after his inauguration he began an investigation of the attitude of the mission friars towards the republic of Mexico. He called padres Sanches, Zalvidea, Peyri and Martin, representatives of the four southern missions, to San Diego and demanded of them whether they would take the oath of allegiance to the supreme government. They expressed their willingness and were accordingly sworn to support the constitution of 1824. Many of the friars of the northern missions remained contumacious. Among the most stubborn of these was Padre Vicente Francisco de Sarria, former president of the missions. He had resigned the presidency to escape taking the oath of allegiance and still continued his opposition. He was put under arrest and an order issued for his expulsion by the supreme government, but the execution of the order was delayed for fear that if he were banished others of the disloyal padres would abandon their missions and secretly leave the country. The government was not ready yet to take possession of the missions. The friars could keep the neophytes in subjection and make them work. The business of the country was in the hands of the friars and any radical change would have been disastrous.

The national government in 1827 had issued a decree for the expulsion of Spaniards from Mexican territory. There were certain classes of those born in Spain who were exempt from banishment, but the friars were not among the exempts. The decree of expulsion reached California in 1828; but it was not enforced for the reason that all of the mission padres except three were Spaniards. To have sent these out of the country would have demoralized the missions. The Spanish friars were expelled from Mexico; but those in California, although some of them had boldly proclaimed their willingness to die for their king and their religion and demanded their passports to leave the country, were allowed to remain in the country. Their passports were not given them for reasons above stated. Padres Ripoll and Altimira made their escape without passports. They secretly took passage on an American brig lying at Santa Barbara. Orders were issued to seize the vessel should she put into any other harbor on the coast, but the captain, who no doubt had been liberally paid, took no chance of capture and the padres eventually reached Spain in safety. There was a suspicion that the two friars had taken with them a large amount of money from the mission funds, but nothing was proved. It was certain that they carried away something more than the bag and staff, the only property allowed them by the rules of their order.

The most bitter opponent of the new government was Father Luis Antonio Martinez of San Luis Obispo. Before the clandestine departure of Ripoll and Altimira there were rumors that he meditated a secret departure from the country.

The mysterious shipment of $6,000 in gold belonging to the mission on a vessel called the Santa Apolonia gave credence to the report of his intended flight. He had been given a passport but still remained in the territory. His outspoken disloyalty and his well known success in evading the revenue laws and smuggling goods into the country had made him particularly obnoxious to the authorities. Governor Echeandia determined to make an example of him. He was arrested in February, 1830, and confined in a room at Santa Barbara. In his trial before a council of war an attempt was made to connect him with complicity in the Solis revolution, but the evidence against him was weak. By a vote of five to one it was decided to send him out of the country. He was put on board an English vessel bound for Callao and there transferred to a vessel bound for Europe; he finally arrived safely at Madrid.

Under the empire a diputacion or provincial legislature had been established in California. Arguello in 1825 had suppressed this while he was governor. Echeandia, shortly after his arrival, ordered an election for a new diputacion. The diputacion made the general laws of the territory. It consisted of seven members called vocals. These were chosen by an electoral junta, the members of which were elected by the people. The diputacion chose a diputado or delegate to the Mexican Congress. As it was a long distance for some of the members to travel to the territorial capital a suplente or substitute was chosen for each member, so as to assure a quorum. The diputacion called by Echeandia met at Monterey, June 14, 1828. The sessions, of which there were two each week, were held in the governor's palacio. This diputacion passed a rather peculiar revenue law. It taxed domestic aguardiente (grape brandy) $5 a barrel and wine half that amount in the jurisdictions of Monterey and San Francisco; but in the jurisdictions of Santa Barbara and San Diego the rates were doubled, brandy was taxed $10 a barrel and wine $5. San Diego, Los Angeles and Santa Barbara were wine producing districts, while Monterey and San Francisco were not. As there was a larger consumption of the product in the wine producing districts than in the others the law was enacted for revenue and not for prevention of drinking.

Another peculiar freak of legislation perpetrated by this diputacion was the attempt to change the name of the territory. The supreme government was memorialized to change the name of Alta California to that of Montezuma and also that of the Pueblo de Nuestra Señora de los Angeles to that of Villa Victoria de la Reyna de los Angeles and make it the capital of the territory. A coat of arms was adopted for the territory. It consisted of an oval with the figure of an oak tree on one side, an olive tree on the other and a plumed Indian in the center with his bow and quiver, just in the act of stepping across the mythical straits of Anian. The memorial was sent to Mexico, but the supreme government paid no attention to it.

The political upheavals, revolutions and counter revolutions that followed the inauguration of a republican form of government in Mexico demoralized the people and produced a prolific crop of criminals. The jails were always full and it became a serious question what to do with them. It was proposed to make California a penal colony, similar to England's Botany Bay. Orders were issued to send criminals to California as a means of reforming their morals. The Californians protested against the sending of these undesirable immigrants, but in vain. In February, 1830, the brig Maria Ester brought eighty convicts from Acapulco to San

Diego. They were not allowed to land there and were taken to Santa Barbara. What to do with them was a serious question with the Santa Barbara authorities. The jail would not hold a tenth part of the shipment and to turn them loose in the sparsely settled country was dangerous to the peace of the community. Finally, about thirty or forty of the worst of the bad lot were shipped over to the island of Santa Cruz. They were given a supply of cattle, some fishhooks and a few tools and turned loose on the island to shift for themselves. They staid on the island until they had slaughtered and eaten the cattle, then they built a raft and drifted back to Santa Barbara, where they quartered themselves on the padres of the mission. Fifty more were sent from Mexico a few months later. These shipments of prison exiles were distributed around among the settlements. Some served out their time and returned to their native land, a few escaped over the border, others remained in the territory after their time was up and became fairly good citizens.

The colonization law passed by the Mexican Congress August 18, 1824, was the first break in the proscriptive regulations that had prevailed in Spanish-American countries since their settlement. Any foreigner of good character who should locate in the country and become a Roman Catholic could obtain a grant of public land, not exceeding eleven leagues; but no foreigner was allowed to obtain a grant within twenty leagues of the boundary of a foreign country nor within ten leagues of the sea coast. The law of April 14, 1828, allowed foreigners to become naturalized citizens. The applicant was required to have resided at least two years in the country, to be or to become a Roman Catholic, to renounce allegiance to his former country and to swear to support the constitution and laws of the Mexican republic. Quite a number of foreigners who had been residing a number of years in California took advantage of this law and became Mexican citizens by naturalization. The colonization law of November 18, 1828, prescribed a series of rules and regulations for the making of grants of land. Colonists were required to settle on and cultivate the land granted within a specified time or forfeit their grants. Any one residing outside of the republic could not retain possession of his land. The minimum size of a grant as defined by this law was two hundred varas square of irrigable land, eight hundred varas square of arable land (depending on the seasons) and twelve hundred varas square grazing land. The size of a house lot was one hundred varas square.

The Californians had grown accustomed to foreigners coming to the country by sea, but they were not prepared to have them come overland. The mountains and deserts that intervened between the United States and California were supposed to be an insurmountable barrier to foreign immigration by land. It was no doubt with feelings of dismay, mingled with anger, that Governor Echeandia received the advance guard of maldito estranjeros, who came across the continent. Echeandia hated foreigners and particularly Americans. The pioneer of overland travel from the United States to California was Capt. Jedediah S. Smith. Smith was born in Connecticut and when quite young came with his father to Ohio and located in Ashtabula county, where he grew to manhood amid the rude surroundings of pioneer life in the west. By some means he obtained a fairly good education. We have no record of when he began the life of a trapper. We first hear of him as an employee of General Ashley in 1822. He had command of a band of trappers on the waters of the Snake river in 1824. Afterwards he became a partner of Ashley under the firm name of Ashley & Smith and subsequently one of the members of the Rocky Mountain Fur Company. The latter company had about 1825 established a post and fort near Great Salt Lake. From this, August 22, 1826, Captain Smith with a band of fifteen hunters and trappers started on his first expedition to California. His object was to find some new country that had not been occupied by a fur company. Traveling in a southwesterly direction he discovered a river which he named Adams (after President John Quincy Adams) now known as the Rio Virgin. This stream he followed down to its junction with the Colorado. Traveling down the latter river he arrived at the Mojave villages, where he rested fifteen days. Here he found two wandering neophytes, who guided his party across the desert to the San Gabriel mission, where he and his men arrived safely early in December, 1826. The arrival of a party of armed Americans from across the mountains and deserts alarmed the padres and couriers were hastily dispatched to Governor Echeandia at San Diego. The Americans were placed under arrest and compelled to give up their arms. Smith was taken to San Diego to give an account of himself. He claimed that he had been compelled to enter the territory on account of the loss of horses and a scarcity of provisions. He was finally released from prison upon the endorsement of several American ship captains and supercargoes who were then at San Diego. He was allowed to return to San Gabriel, where he purchased horses and supplies. He moved his camp to San Bernardino, where he remained until February. The authorities had grown uneasy at his continued presence in the country and orders were sent to arrest him, but before this could be done he left for the Tulare country by way of Cajon Pass. He trapped on the tributaries of the San Joaquin. By the 1st of May he and his party had reached a fork of the Sacramento (near where the town of Folsom now stands). Here he established a summer camp and the river ever since has been known as the American fork from that circumstance.

Here again the presence of the Americans worried the Mexican authorities. Smith wrote a conciliatory letter to Padre Duran, president of the missions, informing him that he had "made several efforts to pass over the mountains, but the snow being so deep I could not succeed in getting over. I returned to this place, it being he only point to kill meat, to wait a few weeks until the snow melts so that I can go on." "On May 20, 1827," Smith writes, "with two men, seven horses and two mules, I started from the valley. In eight days we crossed Mount Joseph, losing two horses and one mule. After a march of twenty days eastward from Mount Joseph (the Sierra Nevadas) I reached the southwesterly corner of the Great Salt Lake. The country separating it from the mountains is arid and without game. Often we had no water for two days at a time. When we reached Salt Lake we had left only one horse and one mule, so exhausted that they could hardly carry our slight baggage. We had been forced to eat the horses that had succumbed."

Smith's route over the Sierras to Salt Lake was substantially the same as that followed by the overland emigration of later years. He discovered the Humboldt, which he named the Mary river, a name it bore until changed by Fremont in 1845. He was the first white man to cross the Sierra Nevadas. Smith left his party of trappers except the two who accompanied him in the Sacramento valley. He returned next year with reinforcements and was ordered out of the country by the governor. He traveled up the coast towards Oregon. On the Umpqua river he was attacked by the Indians. All his party except himself and two others were massacred. He lost all of his horses and furs. He reached Fort Vancouver, his clothing torn to rags and almost starved to death. In 1831, he started with a train of wagons to Santa Fe on a trading expedition. While alone searching for water near the Cimarron river he was set upon by a party of Indians and killed. Thus perished by the hands of cowardly savages in the wilds of New Mexico a man who, through almost incredible dangers and sufferings, had explored an unknown region as vast in extent as that which gave fame and immortality to the African ' explorer, Stanley; and who marked out trails over mountains and across deserts that Fremont following years afterwards won the title of "Pathfinder of the Great West." Smith led the advance guard of the fur trappers to California. Notwithstanding the fact that they were unwelcome visitors these adventurers continued to come at intervals up to 1845. They trapped on the tributaries of the San Joaquin, Sacramento and the rivers in the northern part of the territory. A few of them remained in the country and became permanent residents, but most of them sooner or later met death by the savages.

Capt. Jedediah S. Smith marked out two of the great immigrant trails by which the overland travel, after the discovery of gold, entered California, one by way of the Humboldt river over the Sierra Nevadas, the other southerly from Salt Lake, Utah Lake, the Rio Virgin, across the Colorado desert, through the Cajon Pass to Los Angeles. A third immigrant route was blazed by the Pattie party. This route led from Santa Fe, across New Mexico, down the Gila to the Colorado and from thence across the desert through the San Gorgonio Pass to Los Angeles.

This party consisted of Sylvester Pattie, James Ohio Pattie, his son, Nathaniel M. Pryor, Richard Laughlin, Jesse Furguson, Isaac Slover, William Pope and James Puter. The Patties left Kentucky in 1824 and followed trapping in New Mexico and Arizona until 1827; the elder Pattie for a time managing the copper mines of Santa Rita. In May, 1827, Pattie the elder, in command of a party of thirty trappers and hunters, set out to trap the tributaries of the Colorado. Losses by Indian hostilities, by dissensions and desertions reduced the party to eight persons. December 1st, 1827, while these were encamped on the Colorado near the mouth of the Gila, the Yuma Indians stole all their horses. They constructed rafts and floated down the Colorado, expecting to find Spanish settlements on its banks, where they hoped to procure horses to take them back to Santa Fe. They floated down the river until they encountered the flood tide from the gulf. Finding it impossible to go ahead on account of the tide or back on account of the river current, they landed, cached their furs and traps and with two days' supply of beaver meat struck out westerly across the desert. After traveling for twenty-four days and suffering almost incredible hardships they reached the old Mission of Santa Catalina near the head of the Gulf of California. Here they were detained until news of their arrival could be sent to Governor Echeandia at San Diego. A guard of sixteen soldiers was sent for them and they were conducted to San Diego, where they arrived February 27, 1828. Their arms were taken from them and they were put in prison. The elder Pattie died during their imprisonment. In September all the party except young Pattie, who was retained as a hostage, were released and permitted to go after their buried furs. They found their furs had been ruined by the overflow of the river. Two of the party, Slover and Pope, made their way back to Santa Fe; the others returned, bringing with them their beaver traps. They were again imprisoned by Governor Echeandia, but were finally released.

Three of the party, Nathaniel M. Pryor, Richard Laughlin and Jesse Furguson, became permanent residents of California. Young Pattie returned to the United States by way of Mexico. After his return, with the assistance of the Rev. Timothy Flint, he wrote an account of his adventures, which was published in Cincinnati in 1833, under the title of "Pattie's Narrative." Young Pattie was inclined to exaggeration. In his narrative he claims that with vaccine matter brought by his father from the Santa Rita mines he vaccinated twenty-two thousand people in California. In Los Angeles alone, he vaccinated twenty-five hundred, which was more than double the population of the town in 1828. He took a contract from the president of the missions to vaccinate all the neophytes in the territory. When his job was finished the president offered him in pay five hundred cattle and five hundred mules with land to pasture his stock on condition he would become a Roman Catholic and a citizen of Mexico. Pattie scorned the offer and roundly upbraided the padre for taking advantage of him. He had previously given Governor Echeandia a tongue lashing and had threatened to shoot him on sight. From his narrative he seems to have put in most of his time in California blustering and threatening to shoot somebody.

Another famous trapper of this period was "Peg Leg" Smith. His real name was Thomas L. Smith. It is said that in a fight with the Indians his leg below the knee was shattered by a bullet. He coolly amputated his leg at the knee with no other instrument than his hunting knife. He wore a wooden leg and from this came his nickname. He first came to California in 1829. He was ordered out of the country. He and his party took their departure, but with them went three or four hundred California horses. He died in a San Francisco hospital in 1866.

Ewing Young, a famous captain of trappers, made several visits to California from 1830 to 1837. In 1831 he led a party of thirty hunters and trappers, among those of his party who remained in California was Col. J. J. Warner, who became prominent in the territory and state. In 1837 Ewing Young with a party of sixteen men came down from Oregon, where he finally located, to purchase cattle for the new settlements on the Willamette river. They bought seven hundred cattle at $3 per head from the government and drove them overland to Oregon, reaching there after a toilsome journey of four months with six hundred. Young died in Oregon in 1841.

From the downfall of Spanish domination in 1822, to the close of that decade there had been but few political disturbances in California. The only one of any consequence was Soils' and Herrera's attempt to revolutionize the territory and seize the government. Jose Maria Herrera had come to California as a commissioner of the commissary department, but after a short term of service had been removed from office for fraud. Joaquin Solis was a convict who was serving a ten years sentence of banishment from Mexico. The ex-official and the exile with others of damaged character combined to overturn the government.

On the night of November 12, 1829, Solis, with a band of soldiers that he had induced to join his standard, seized the principal government officials at Monterey and put them in prison. At Solis' solicitation Herrera drew up a pronunciamiento. It followed the usual line of such documents. It began by deploring the evils that had come upon the territory through Echeandia's misgovernment and closed with

78

promises of reformation if the revolutionists should obtain control of the government. To obtain the sinews of war the rebels seized $3,000 of the public funds. This was distributed among the soldiers and proved a great attraction to the rebel cause. Solis with twenty men went to San Francisco and the soldiers there joined his standard. Next he marched against Santa Barbara with an army of one hundred and fifty men. Echeandia on hearing of the revolt had marched northward with all the soldiers he could enlist. The two armies met at Santa Ynez. Solis opened fire on the governor's army. The fire was returned. Solis' men began to break away and soon the army and its valiant leader were in rapid flight. Pacheco's cavalry captured the leaders of the revolt. Herrara, Solis and thirteen others were shipped to Mexico under arrest to be tried for their crimes. The Mexican authorities, always lenient to California revolutionists, probably from a fellow feeling, turned them all loose and Herrera was sent back to fill his former office.

Near the close of his term Governor Echeandia formulated a plan for converting the mission into pueblos. To ascertain the fitness of the neophytes for citizenship he made an investigation to find out how many could read and write. He found so very few that he ordered schools opened at the missions. A pretense was made of establishing schools, but very little was accomplished. The padres were opposed to educating the natives for the same reason that the southern slave-holders were opposed to educating the negro, namely, that an ignorant people were more easily kept in subjection. Echeandia's plan of secularization was quite elaborate and dealt fairly with the neophytes. It received the sanction of the diputacion when that body met in July, 1830, but before anything could be done towards enforcing it another governor was appointed. Echeandia was thoroughly hated by the mission friars and their adherents. Robinson in his "Life in California" calls him a man of vice and makes a number of damaging assertions about his character and conduct, which are not in accordance with the facts. It was during Echeandia's term as governor that the motto of Mexico, Dios y Libertad (God and Liberty), was adopted. It became immensely popular and was used on all public documents and often in private correspondence.

A romantic episode that has furnished a theme for fiction writers occurred in the last year of Echeandia's rule. It was the elopement of Henry D. Fitch with Doha Josefa, daughter of Joaquin Carrillo of San Diego. Fitch was a native of New Bedford, Mass. He came to California in 1826 as master of the Maria Ester. He fell in love with Dofia Josefa. There were legal obstructions to their marriage. Fitch was a foreigner and a Protestant. The latter objection was easily removed by Fitch becoming a Catholic. The Dominican friar who was to perform the marriage service, fearful that he might incur the wrath of the authorities, civil and clerical, refused to perform the ceremony, but suggested that there were other countries where the laws were less strict and offered to go beyond the limits of California and marry them. It is said that at this point Dofia Josefa said: "Why don't you carry me off, Don Enrique?" The suggestion was quickly acted upon. The next night the lady, mounted on a steed with her cousin, Pio Pico, as an escort, was secretly taken to a point on the bay shore where a boat was waiting for her. The boat put off to the Vulture, where Captain Fitch received her on board and the vessel sailed for Valparaiso, where the couple were married. A year later Captain Fitch returned to California with his wife and infant son. At Monterey Fitch was arrested on an order of Padre Sanchez of San Gabriel and put in prison. His wife was also placed under arrest at the house of Captain Cooper. Fitch was taken to San Gabriel for trial, "his offenses being most heinous." At her intercession, Governor Echeandia released Mrs. Fitch and allowed her to go to San Gabriel, where her husband was imprisoned in one of the rooms of the mission. This act of clemency greatly enraged the friar and his fiscal, Palomares, and they seriously considered the question of arresting the governor. The trial dragged along for nearly a month. Many witnesses were examined and many learned points of clerical law discussed. Vicar Sanchez finally gave his decision that the marriage at Valparaiso, though not legitimate, was not null and void, but valid. The couple were condemned to do penance by "presenting themselves in church with lighted candles in their hands to hear high mass for three feast days and recite together for thirty days one-third of the rosary of the holy virgin." In addition to these joint penances the vicar inflicted an additional penalty on Fitch in these words: "Yet considering the great scandal which Don Enrique has caused in this province I condemn him to give as penance and reparation a bell of at least fifty pounds in weight for the church at Los Angeles, which barely has a borrowed one." Fitch and his wife no doubt performed the joint penance imposed upon them, but the church at Los Angeles had to get along with its borrowed bell. Don Enrique never gave it one of fifty pounds or any other weight.

CHAPTER XI.
REVOLUTIONS — THE HIJAR COLONISTS.

Manuel Victoria was appointed governor in March, 1830, but did not reach California until the last month of the year. Victoria very soon became unpopular. He undertook to overturn the civil authority and substitute military rule. He recommended the abolition of the ayuntamientos and refused to call together the territorial diputacion. He exiled Don Abel Stearns and Jose Antonio Carrillo; and at different times, on trumped-up charges, had half a hundred of the leading citizens of Los Angeles incarcerated in the pueblo jail. Alcalde Vicente Sanchez was the petty despot of the pueblo, who carried out the tyrannical decrees of his master, Victoria. Among others who were imprisoned in the cuartel was Jose Maria Avila. Avila was proud, haughty and overbearing. He had incurred the hatred of both Victoria and Sanchez. Sanchez, under orders from Victoria, placed Avila in prison, and to humiliate him put him in irons. Avila brooded over the indignities inflicted upon him and vowed to be revenged.

Victoria's persecutions became so unbearable that Pio Pico, Juan Bandini and Jose Antonio Carrillo raised the standard of revolt at San Diego and issued a pronunciamento, in which they set forth the reasons why they felt themselves obliged to rise against the tyrant, Victoria. Pablo de Portilla, comandante of the presidio of San Diego, and his officers, with a force of fifty soldiers, joined the revolutionists and marched to Los Angeles. Sanchez's prisoners were released and he was chained up in the pueblo jail. Here Portilla's force was recruited to two hundred men. Avila and a number of the other released prisoners joined the revolutionists, and all marched forth to meet Victoria, who was moving southward with an armed force to suppress the insurrection. The two forces met on the plains of Cahuenga, west of the pueblo, at a place known as the Lomitas de la Canada de Breita. The sight of his persecutor so infuriated Avila that alone he rushed upon him to run him through with his lance. Captain Pacheco, of Victoria's staff, parried the lance thrust. Avila shot him dead with one of his pistols and again attacked the governor and succeeded in wounding him, when he himself received a pistol ball that unhorsed him. After a desperate struggle (in which he seized Victoria by the foot and dragged him from his horse) he was shot by one of Victoria's soldiers. Portilla's army fell back in a panic to Los Angeles and Victoria's men carried the wounded governor to the Mission San Gabriel, where his wounds were dressed by Joseph Chapman, who, to his many other accomplishments, added that of amateur surgeon. Some citizens who had taken no part in the fight brought the bodies of Avila and Pacheco to the town. "They were taken to the same house, the same hands rendered them the last sad rites, and they were laid side by side. Side by side knelt their widows and mingled their tears, while sympathizing countrymen chanted the solemn prayers of the church for the repose of the souls of these untimely dead. Side by side beneath the orange and the olive in the little churchyard upon the plaza sleep the slayer and the slain."

Next day, Victoria, supposing himself mortally wounded, abdicated and turned over the governorship of the territory to Echeandia. He resigned the office December 9, 1831, having been governor a little over ten months. When Victoria was able to travel he was sent to San Diego, from where he was deported to Mexico, San Diego borrowing $125 from the ayuntamiento of Los Angeles to pay the expense of shipping him out of the country. Several years afterwards the money had not been repaid, and the town council began proceedings to recover it, but there is no record in the archives to show that it was ever paid. And thus it was that California got rid of a bad governor and Los Angeles incurred a bad debt.

January 10, 1832, the territorial legislature met at Los Angeles to choose a "gefe politico," or governor, for the territory. Echeandia was invited to preside but replied from San Juan Capistrano that he was busy getting Victoria out of the country. The diputacion, after waiting some time and receiving no satisfaction from Echeandia whether he wanted the office or not, declared Pio Pico, by virtue of his office of senior vocal, "gefe politico."

No sooner had Pico been sworn into office than Echeandia discovered that he wanted the office and wanted it badly. He protested against the action of the diputacion and intrigued against Pico. Another revolution was threatened. Los Angeles favored Echeandia, although all the other towns in the territory had accepted Pico. (Pico at that time was a resident of .San Diego.) A mass meeting was called on February 12, 1832, at Los Angeles, to discuss the question whether it should be Pico or Echeandia. I give the report of the meeting in the quaint language of the pueblo archives:

"The town, acting in accord with the Most Illustrious Ayuntamiento, answered in a loud voice, saying they would not admit Citizen Pio Pico as 'gefe politico,' but desired that Lieut. Col. Citizen Jose Maria Echeandia be retained in office until the supreme government appoint. Then the president of the meeting, seeing the determination of the people, asked the motive or reason of refusing Citizen Pio Pico, who was of unblemished character. To this the people responded that while it was true that Citizen Pio Pico was to some extent qualified, yet they preferred Lieut.-Col. Citizen Jose M. Echeandia. The president of the meeting then asked the people whether they had been bribed, or was it merely insubordination that they opposed the resolution of the Most Excellent Diputacion? Whereupon the people answered that they had not been bribed, nor were they insubordinate, but that they opposed the proposed 'gefe politico' because he had not been named by the supreme government."

At a public meeting February 19 the matter was again brought up. Again the people cried out "they would not recognize or obey any other gefe politico than Echeandia." The Most Illustrious Ayuntamiento opposed Pio Pico for two reasons: "First, because his name appeared first on the plan to oust Gefe Politico Citizen Manuel Victoria," and "Second, because he, Pico, had not sufficient capacity to fulfill the duties of the office." Then Jose Perez and Jose Antonio Carrillo withdrew from the meeting, saying they would not recognize Echeandia as "gefe politico." Pico, after holding the office for twenty days, resigned for the sake of peace. And this was the length of Pico's first term as governor.

Echeandia, by obstinacy and intrigue, had obtained the coveted office, "gefe politico," but he did not long enjoy it in peace. News came from Monterey that Capt. Agustin V. Zamorano had declared himself governor and was gathering a force to invade the south and enforce his authority. Echeandia began at once marshaling his forces to oppose him. Ybarra, Zamarano's military chief, with a force of one hundred men, by a forced march, reached Paso de Bartolo, on the San Gabriel river, where, fifteen years later, Stockton fought the Mexican troops under Flores. Here Ybarra found Captain Borroso posted with a piece of artillery and fourteen men. He did not dare to attack him. Echeandia and Borroso gathered a force of a thousand neophytes at Paso de Bartolo, where they drilled them in military evolutions. Ybarra's troops had fallen back to Santa Barbara, where he was joined by Zamorano with reinforcements. Ybarra's force was largely made up of ex-convicts and other undesirable characters, who took what they needed, asking no questions of the owners. The Angelenos, fearing those marauders, gave their adhesion to Zamorano's plan and recognized him as military chief of the territory. Captain Borroso, Echeandia's faithful adherent, disgusted with the fickleness of the Angelenos, at the head of a thousand mounted Indians, threatened to invade the recalcitrant pueblo, but at the intercession of the frightened inhabitants this modern Coriolanus turned aside and regaled his neophyte retainers on the fat bullocks of the Mission San Gabriel, much to the disgust of the padres. The neophyte warriors were disbanded and sent to their respective missions.

A peace was patched up between Zamorano and Echeandia. Alta California was divided into two territories. Echeandia was given jurisdiction over all south of San Gabriel and Zamorano all north of San Fernando. This division apparently left a neutral district, or "no man's land," between. Whether Los Angeles was in this neutral territory the records do not show.

If it was, it is probable that neither of the governors wanted the job of governing the rebellious pueblo.

In January, 1833, Governor Figueroa arrived in California. Echeandia and Zamorano each surrendered his half of the divided territory to the newly appointed governor, and California was united and at peace. Figueroa proved to be the right man for the times. He conciliated the factions and brought order out of chaos. The two most important events in Figueroa's term of office were the arrival of the Hijar Colony in California and the secularization of the missions. These events were most potent factors in the evolution of the territory.

In 1833 the first California colonization scheme was inaugurated in Mexico. At the head of this was Jose Maria Hijar, a Mexican gentleman of wealth and influence. He was assisted in its promulgation by Jose M. Padres, an adventurer, who had been banished from California by Governor Victoria. Padres, like some of our modern real estate boomers, pictured the country as an earthly paradise — an improved and enlarged Garden of Eden. Among other inducements held out to the colonists, it is said, was the promise of a division among them of the mission property and a distribution of the neophytes for servants.

Headquarters were established at the city of Mexico and two hundred and fifty colonists enlisted. Each family received a bonus of $10, and all were to receive free transportation to California and rations while on the journey. Each head of a family was promised a farm from the public domain, live stock and farming implements; these advances to be paid for on the installment plan. The original plan was to found a colony somewhere north of San Francisco bay, but this was not carried out. Two vessels were dispatched with the colonists — the Morelos and the Natalia. The latter was compelled to put into San Diego on account of sickness on board. She reached that port September I, 1834. A part of the colonists on board her were sent to San Pedro and from there they were taken to Los Angeles and San Gabriel. The Morelos reached Monterey September 25. Hijar had been appointed governor of California by President Farias, but after the sailing of the expedition, Santa Ana, who had succeeded Farias, dispatched a courier overland with a countermanding order. By one of the famous rides of history, Amador, the courier, made the journey from the city of Mexico to Monterey in forty days and delivered his message to Governor Figueroa. When Hijar arrived he found to his dismay that he was only a private citizen of the territory instead of its governor. The colonization scheme was abandoned and the immigrants distributed themselves throughout the territory. Generally they were a good class of citizens, and many of them became prominent in California affairs.

That storm center of political disturbances, Los Angeles, produced but one small revolution during Figueroa's term as governor. A party of fifty or sixty Sonorans, some of whom were Hijar colonists who were living either in the town or its immediate neighborhood, assembled at Los Nietos on the night of March 7, 1835. They formulated a pronunciamiento against Don Jose Figueroa, in which they first vigorously arraigned him for sins of omission and commission and then laid down their plan of government of the territory. Armed with this formidable document and a few muskets and lances, these patriots, headed by Juan Gallado, a cobbler, and Felipe Castillo, a cigar maker, in the gray light of the morning, rode into the pueblo, took possession of the town hall and the big cannon and the ammunition that had been stored there when the Indians of San Luis Rey had threatened hostilities. The slumbering inhabitants were aroused from their dreams of peace by the drum beat of war. The terrified citizens rallied to the juzgado, the ayuntamiento met, the cobbler statesman, Gallado, presented his plan; it was discussed and rejected. The revolutionists, after holding possession of the pueblo throughout the day, tired, hungry and disappointed in not receiving their pay for saving the country, surrendered to the legal authorities the real leaders of the revolution and disbanded. The leaders proved to be Torres, a clerk, and Apalategui, a doctor, both supposed to be emissaries of Hijar. They were imprisoned at San Gabriel. When news of the revolt reached Figueroa he had Hijar and Padres arrested for complicity in the outbreak. Hijar, with half a dozen of his adherents, was shipped back to Mexico. And thus the man who the year before had landed in California with a commission as governor and authority to take possession of all the property belonging to the missions returned to his native land an exile. His grand colonization scheme and his "Compania Cosmopolitana" that was to revolutionize California commerce were both disastrous failures.

Governor Jose Figueroa died at Monterey on the 29th of September, 1835. He is generally regarded as the best of the Mexican governors sent to California. He was of Aztec extraction and took a great deal of pride in his Indian blood.

CHAPTER XII.
THE DECLINE AND FALL OF THE MISSIONS.

The Franciscan Missions of Aha California have of late been a prolific theme for a certain class of writers and especially have they dwelt upon the secularization of these establishments. Their productions have added little or nothing to our previous knowledge of these institutions. Carried away by sentiment these writers draw pictures of mission life that are unreal, that are purely imaginary, and aroused to indignation at the injustice they fancy was done to their ideal institutions they deal out denunciations against the authorities that brought about secularization as unjust as they are undeserved. Such expressions as "the robber hand of secularization," and "the brutal and thievish disestablishment of the missions," emanate from writers who seem to be ignorant of the purpose for which the missions were founded, and who ignore, or who do not know, the causes which brought about their secularization.

It is an historical fact known to all acquainted with California history that these establishments were not intended by the Crown of Spain to become permanent institutions. The purpose for which the Spanish government fostered and protected them was to Christianize the Indians and make of them self-supporting citizens. Very early in its history, Governor Borica, Pages and other intelligent Spanish officers in California discovered the weakness of the mission system. Governor Borica, writing in 1796, said: "According to the laws the natives are to be free from tutelage at the end of ten years, the missions then becoming doctrinairs, but those of New California, at the rate they are advancing, will not reach the goal in ten centuries; the reason God knows, and men, too, know something about it."

The tenure by which the mission friars held their lands is admirably set forth in William Carey Jones' "Report on Land Titles in California," made in 1850. He says, "It had been supposed that the lands they (the missions) occupied were grants held as the property of the church or of the mission establishments as corporations. Such, however, was not the case; all the missions in Upper California were established under the direction and mainly at the expense of the government, and the missionaries there had never any other right than to the occupation and use of the lands for the purpose of the missions and at the pleasure of the government. This is shown by the history and principles of their foundation, by the laws in relation to them, by the constant practice of the government toward them and, in fact, by the rules of the Franciscan order, which forbid its members to possess property."

With the downfall of Spanish domination in Mexico came the beginning of the end of missionary rule in California. The majority of the mission padres were Spanish born. In the war of Mexican independence their sympathies were with their mother country, Spain. After Mexico attained her independence, some of them refused to acknowledge allegiance to the republic. The Mexican authorities feared and distrusted them. In this, in part, they found a pretext for the disestablishment of the missions and the confiscation of the mission estates. There was another cause or reason for secularization more potent than the loyalty of the padres to Spain. Few forms of land monopoly have ever exceeded that in vogue under the mission system of California. From San Diego to San Francisco bay the twenty missions established under Spanish rule monopolized the greater part of the fertile land between the coast range and the sea. The limits of one mission were said to cover the intervening space to the limits of the next. There was but little left for other settlers. A settler could not obtain a grant of land if the padres of the nearest mission objected.

The twenty-four ranchos owned by the Mission San Gabriel contained about a million and a half acres and extended from the sea to the San Bernardino mountains. The greatest neophyte population of San Gabriel was in 1817, when it reached 1,701. Its yearly average for the first three decades of the present century did not exceed 1,500. It took a thousand acres of fertile land under the mission system to support an Indian, even the smallest papoose of the mission flock. It is not strange that the people clamored for a subdivision of the mission estates; and secularization became a public necessity. The most enthusiastic admirer of the missions to-day, had he lived in California seventy years ago, would no doubt have been among the loudest in his wail against the mission system.

The abuse heaped upon the Mexican authorities for their secularization of these institutions is as unjust as it is unmerited. The act of the Mexican Congress of August 17, 1833, was not the initiative movement towards their disestablishment. Indeed in their foundation their secularization, their subdivision into pueblos, was provided for and the local authorities were never without lawful authority over them. 'In the very beginning of missionary work in Alta California the process of secularizing the mission establishments was mapped out in the following "Instructions given by Viceroy Bucarili August 17, 1773, to the comandante of the new establishments of San Diego and Monterey.

Article 15, when it shall happen that a mission is to be formed into a pueblo or village the comandante will proceed to reduce it to the civil and economical government, which, according to the laws, is observed by other villages of this kingdom; their giving it a name and declaring for its patron the saint under whose memory and protection the mission was founded."

The purpose for which the mission was founded was to aid in the settlement of the country, and to convert the natives to Christianity. "These objects accomplished the missionary's labor was considered fulfilled and the establishment subject to dissolution. This view of their purpose and destiny fully appears in the tenor of the decree of the Spanish Cortes of September 13, 1813. It was passed in consequence of a complaint by the Bishop of Guiana of the evils that affected that province on account of the Indian settlements in charge of missions not being delivered to the ecclesiastical ordinary, although thirty, forty and fifty years had passed since the reduction and conversion of the Indians."

The Cortes decreed 1st, that all the new reduciones y doctrinairs (settlements of newly converted Indians) not yet formed into parishes of the province beyond the sea which were in charge of missionary monks and had been ten years subjected should be delivered immediately to the respective ecclesiastical ordinaries (bishops) without resort to any excuse or pretext conformably to the laws and cedulas in that respect. Section 2nd, provided that the secular clergy should attend to the spiritual wants of these curacies. Section 3rd, the missionary monks relieved from the converted settlements shall proceed to the conversion of other heathen."

The decree of the Mexican Congress, passed November 20, 1833, for the secularization of the missions of Upper and Lower California, was very similar in its provisions to the decree of the Spanish Cortes of September, 1813. The Mexican government simply followed the example of Spain and in the conversion of the missions into pueblos was attempting to enforce a principle inherent in the foundation of the missionary establishments. That secularization resulted disastrously to the Indians was not the fault of the Mexican government so much as it was the defect in the industrial and intellectual training of the neophytes. Except in the case of those who were trained for choir services in the churches there was no attempt made to teach the Indians to read or write. The padres generally entertained a poor opinion of the neophytes' intellectual ability. The reglamento governing the secularization of the missions, published by Governor Echeandia in 1830, but not enforced, and that formulated by the diputacion under Governor Figueroa in 1834, approved by the Mexican Congress and finally enforced in 1834-5-6, were humane measures. These regulations provided for the colonization of the neophytes into pueblos or villages. A portion of the personal property and a part of the lands held by the missions were to be distributed among the Indians as follows:

"Article 5 — To each head of a family and all who are more than twenty years old, although without families, will be given from the lands of the mission, whether temporal (lands dependent on the seasons) or watered, a lot of ground not to contain more than four hundred varas (yards) in length, and as many in breadth not less than one hundred. Sufficient land for watering the cattle will be given in common. The outlets or roads shall be marked out by each village, and at the proper time the corporation lands shall be designated." This colonization of the neophytes into pueblos would have m thrown large bodies of the land held by the missions open to settlement by white settlers. The personal property of missionary establishments was to have been divided among their neophyte retainers thus: "Article 6. Among the said individuals will be distributed, ratably and justly, according to the discretion of the political chief, the half of the movable property, taking as a basis the last inventory which the missionaries have presented of all descriptions of cattle. Article 7. One-half or less of the implements and seeds indispensable for agriculture shall be allotted to them.

The political government of the Indian pueblos was to be organized in accordance with existing laws of the territory governing other towns. The neophyte could not sell, mortgage or dispose of the land granted him; nor could he sell his cattle. The regulations provided that "Religious missionaries shall be relieved from the administration of temporalities and shall only exercise the duties of their ministry so far as they relate to spiritual matters." The nunneries or the houses where the Indian girls were kept under the charge of a duena until they were of marriageable age were to be abolished and the children restored to their parents. Rule 7 provided that "What is called the 'priesthood' shall immediately cease, female children whom they have in charge being handed over to their fathers, explaining to them the care they should take of them, and pointing out their obligations as parents. The same shall be done with the male children."

Commissioners were to be appointed to take charge of the mission property and superintend its subdivision among the neophytes. The conversion of ten of the missionary establishments into pueblos was to begin in August, 1835. That of the others was to follow as soon as possible. San Gabriel, San Fernando and San Juan Capistrano were among the ten that were to be secularized first. For years secularization had threatened the missions, but hitherto something had occurred at the critical time to avert it. The missionaries had used their influence against it, had urged that the neophytes were unfitted for self-support, had argued that the emancipation of the natives from mission rule would result in disaster to them. Through all the agitation of the question in previous years the padres had labored on in the preservation and upbuilding of their establishments; but with the issuing of the secularization decree by the Mexican Congress, August 17, 1833, the organization of the Hijar Colony in Mexico and the instructions of acting president Farias to Hijar to occupy all the property of the missions and subdivide it among the colonists on their arrival in California, convinced the missionaries that the blow could no longer be averted. The revocation of Hijar's appointment as governor and the controversy which followed between him and Governor Figueroa and the diputacion for a time delayed the enforcement of the decree.

In the meantime, with the energy born of despair, eager at any cost to outwit those who sought to profit by their ruin, the mission fathers hastened to destroy that which through more than half a century thousands of human beings had spent their lives to accumulate. The wealth of the missions lay in their herds of cattle. The only marketable products of these were the hides and tallow. Heretofore a certain number of cattle had been slaughtered each week to feed the neophytes and sometimes when the ranges were in danger of becoming overstocked cattle were killed for their hides and tallow, and the meat left to the coyotes and the carrion crows. The mission fathers knew that if they allowed the possession of their herds to pass to other hands neither they nor the neophytes would obtain any reward for years of labor. The blow was liable to fall at any time. Haste was required. The mission butchers could not slaughter the animals fast enough. Contracts were made with the rancheros to kill on shares. The work of destruction began at the missions. The country became a mighty shambles. The matansas were no longer used. An animal was lassoed on the plain, thrown, its throat cut and while yet writhing in death agony, its hide was stripped and pegged upon the ground to dry. There were no vessels to contain the tallow and this was run into pits in the ground to be taken out when there was more time to spare and less cattle to be killed. The work of destruction went on as long as there were cattle to kill. So great was the stench from rotting carcasses of the cattle on the plains that a pestilence was threatened. The ayuntamiento of Los Angeles, November 15, 1833, passed an ordinance compelling all persons slaughtering cattle for the hides and tallow to cremate the carcasses. Some of the rancheros laid the foundations of their future wealth by appropriating herds of young cattle from the mission ranges.

Hugo Reid, in the letters previously referred to in this volume, says of this period at San Gabriel, "These facts (the decree of secularization and the distribution of the mission property) being known to Padre Tomas (Estenaga), he, in all probability, by order of his superior, commenced a work of destruction. The back buildings were unroofed and the timber converted into fire wood. Cattle were killed on the halves by people who took a lion's share. Utensils were disposed of and goods and other articles distributed in profusion among the neophytes. The vineyards were ordered to be cut down, which, however, the Indians refused to do." After the mission was placed in charge of an administrator, Padre Tomas remained as minister of the church at a stipend of $1,500 per annum, derived from the pious fund.

Hugo Reid says of him, "As a wrong impression of his character may be produced from the preceding remarks, in justice to his memory, be it stated that he was a truly good man, a sincere Christian and a despiser of hypocrisy. He had a kind, unsophisticated heart, so that he believed every word told him. There has never been a purer priest in California. Reduced in circumstances, annoyed on many occasions by the petulancy of administrators, he fulfilled his duties according to his conscience, with benevolence and good humor. The nuns, who, when the secular movement came into operation, had been set free, were again gathered together under his supervision and maintained at his expense, as were also a number of old men and women."

The experiment of colonizing the Indians in pueblos was a failure and they were gathered back into the mission, or as many of them as could be got back, and placed in charge of administrators. "The Indians," says Reid, "were made happy at this time in being permitted to enjoy once more the luxury of a tule dwelling, from which the greater part had been debarred for so long; they could now breathe freely again." (The close adobe buildings in which they had been housed in mission days were no doubt one of the causes of the great mortality among them.)

"Administrator followed administrator until the mission could support no more, when the system was broken up." * * * "The Indians during this period were continually running off. Scantily clothed and still more scantily supplied with food, it was not to be wondered at. Nearly all the Gabrielinos went north, while those of San Diego, San Luis and San Juan overrun this country, filling the Angeles and surrounding ranchos with more servants than were required. Labor, in consequence, was very cheap. The different missions, however, had alcaldes continually on the move, hunting them up and carrying them back, but to no purpose; it was labor in vain."

"Even under the dominion of the church in mission days," Reid says, "the neophytes were addicted both to drinking and gaming, with an inclination to steal;" but after their emancipation they went from bad to worse. Those attached to the ranchos and those located in the town were virtually slaves. They had bosses or owners and when they ran away were captured and returned to their master. The account book for 1840 of the sindico of Los Angeles contains this item. "For the delivery of two Indians to their boss $12."

In all the large towns there was an Indian village known as the pueblito or little town. These were the sink holes of crime and the favorite resorts of dissolute characters, both white and red. The Indian village at Los Angeles between what is now Aliso and First street became such an intolerable nuisance that on petition of the citizens it was removed across the river to the "Spring of the Abilas," but its removal did not improve its morals. Vicente Guerrero, the sindico, discussing the Indian question before the ayuntamiento said, "The Indians are so utterly depraved that no matter where they may settle down their conduct would be the same, since they look upon death even with indifference, provided they can indulge in their pleasures and vices." This was their condition in less than a decade after they were freed from mission control.

What did six decades of mission rule accomplish for the Indian? In all the older missions between their founding and their secularization three generations of adults had come under the influence of mission life and training' — first, the adult converts made soon after the founding; second, their children born at the missions, and third, the children of these who had grown to manhood before the fall of the missions. How great an improvement had the neophytes of the third generation made over those of the first? They had to a great extent lost their original language and had acquired a speaking knowledge of Spanish. They had abandoned or forgotten their primitive religious belief, but their new religion exercised but little influence on their lives. After their emancipation they went from bad to worse. Some of the more daring escaped to the mountains and joining the wild tribes there became the leaders in frequent predatory excursions on the horses and cattle of the settlers in the valleys. They were hunted down and shot like wild beasts.

What became of the mission estates? As the cattle were killed off the different ranchos of the mission domains, settlers petitioned the ayuntamiento for grants. If upon investigation it was found that the land asked for was vacant the petition was referred to the governor for his approval. In this way the vast mission domains passed into private hands. The country improved more in wealth and population between 1836 and 1846 than in the previous fifty years. Secularization was destruction to the mission and death to the Indian, but it was beneficial to the country at large. The decline of the missions and the passing of the neophyte had begun long before the decrees of secularization were enforced. Nearly all the missions passed their zenith in population during the second decade of the century. Even had the missionary establishments not been secularized they would eventually have been depopulated. At no time during the mission rule were the number of births equal to the number of deaths. When recruits could no longer be obtained from the Gentiles or wild Indians the decline became more rapid. The mission annals show that from 1769 to 1834, when secularization was enforced — an interval of sixty-five years — 79,000 converts were baptized and 62,000 deaths recorded. The death rate among the neophytes was about twice that of the negro in this country and four times that of the white race. The extinction of the neophyte or mission Indian was due to the enforcement of that inexorable law or decree of nature, the Survival of the Fittest. Where a stronger race comes in contact with a weaker, there can be but one termination of the contest — the extermination of the weaker.

CHAPTER XIII. THE FREE AND SOVEREIGN STATE OF ALTA CALIFORNIA.

Governor Figueroa on his deathbed turned over the civil command of the territory to Jose Castro, who thereby became "gefe politico ad interem." The military command was given to Lieut.-Col. Nicolas Gutierrez with the rank of comandante general. The separation of the two commands was in accordance with the national law of May 6, 1822.

Castro was a member of the diputacion, but was not senior vocal or president. Jose Antonio Carrillo, who held that position, was diputado or delegate to congress and was at that time in the city of Mexico. It was he who secured the decree from the Mexican Congress May 23, 1835, making Los Angeles the capital of California, and elevating it to the rank of a city. The second vocal, Jose Antonio Estudillo, was sick at his home in San Diego. Jose Castro ranked third. He was the only one of the diputacion at the capital and at the previous meeting of the diputacion he had acted as presiding officer. Gutierrez, who was at San Gabriel when appointed to the military command, hastened to Monterey, but did not reach there until after the death of Figueroa. Castro, on assuming command, sent a notification of his appointment to the civil authorities of the different jurisdictions. All responded favorably except San Diego and Los Angeles. San Diego claimed the office for Estudillo, second vocal, and Los Angeles declared against Castro because he was only third vocal and demanded that the diputacion should meet at the legal capital (Los Angeles) of the territory. This was the beginning of the capital war that lasted ten years and increased in bitterness as it increased in age. The diputacion met at Monterey. It decided in favor of Castro and against removing the capital to Los Angeles.

Castro executed the civil functions of gefe politico four months and then, in accordance with orders from the supreme government, he turned over his part of the governorship to Comandante General Gutierrez and again the two commands were united in one person. Gutierrez filled the office of "gobernador interno" from January 2, 1836, to the arrival of his successor, Mariano Chico. Chico had been appointed governor by President Barragan, December 16, 1835, but did not arrive in California until April, 1836. Thus California had four governors within nine months. They changed so rapidly there was not time to foment a revolution. Chico began his administration by a series of petty tyrannies. Just before his arrival in California a vigilance committee at Los Angeles shot to death Gervacio Alispaz and his paramour, Maria del Rosaria Villa, for the murder of the woman's husband, Domingo Feliz. Alispaz was a countryman of Chico. Chico had the leaders arrested and came down to Los Angeles with the avowed purpose of executing Prudon, Arzaga and Aranjo, the president, secretary and military commander, respectively, of the Defenders of Public Security, as the vigilantes called themselves. He announced his intention of arresting and punishing every man who had taken part in the banishment of Governor Victoria. He summoned Don Abel Stearns to Monterey and threatened to have him shot for some imaginary offense. He fulminated a fierce pronunciamento against foreigners, that incurred their wrath, and made himself so odious that he was hated by all, native or foreigner. He was a centralist and opposed to popular rights. Exasperated beyond endurance by his scandalous conduct and unseemly exhibitions of temper the people of Monterey rose en masse against him, and so terrified him that he took passage on board a brig that was lying in the harbor and sailed for Mexico with the threat that he would return with an armed force to punish the rebellious Californians, but he never came back again.

With the enforced departure of Chico, the civil command of the territory devolved upon Nicolas Gutierrez, who still held the military command. He was of Spanish birth and a centralist or anti-federalist in politics. Although a mild mannered man he seemed to be impressed with the idea that he must carry out the arbitrary measures of his predecessor. Centralism was his nemesis. Like Chico, he was opposed to popular rights and at one time gave orders to disperse the diputacion by force. He was not long in making himself unpopular by attempting to enforce the centralist decrees of the Mexican Congress.

He quarreled with Juan Bautista Alvarado, the ablest of the native Californians. Alvarado and Jose Castro raised the standard of revolt. They gathered together a small army of rancheros and an auxiliary force of twenty-five American hunters and trappers under Graham, a backwoodsman from Tennessee. By a strategic movement they captured the Castillo or fort which commanded the presidio, where Gutierrez and the Mexican army officials were stationed. The patriots demanded the surrender of the presidio and the arms. The governor refused. The revolutionists had been able to find but a single cannon ball in the Castillo, but this was sufficient to do the business. A well-directed shot tore through the roof of the governor's house, covering him and his staff with the debris of broken tiles; that and the desertion of most of his soldiers to the patriots brought him to terms. On the 5th of November, 1836, he surrendered the presidio and resigned his authority as governor. He and about seventy of his adherents were sent aboard a vessel lying in the harbor and shipped out of the country.

With the Mexican governor and his officers out of the country, the next move of Castro and Alvarado was to call a meeting of the diputacion or territorial congress. A plan for the independence of California was adopted. This, which was known afterwards as the Monterey plan, consisted of six sections, the most important of which were as follows: "First, Alta California hereby declares itself independent from Mexico until the Federal System of 1824 is restored. Second, the same California is hereby declared a free and sovereign state; establishing a congress to enact the special laws of the country and the other necessary supreme powers. Third, the Roman Apostolic Catholic religion shall prevail; no other creed shall be allowed, but the government shall not molest anyone on account of his private opinions." The diputacion issued a declaration of independence that arraigned the mother country, Mexico, and her officials very much in the style that our own Declaration gives it to King George III. and England.

Castro issued a pronunciamiento, ending with Viva La Federacion! Viva La Libertad! Viva el Estado Libre y Soberano de Alta California! Thus amid vivas and proclamations, with the beating of drums and the booming of cannon, El Estado Libre de Alta California (The Free State of Alta California) was launched on the political sea. But it was rough sailing for the little craft. Her ship of state struck a rock and for a time shipwreck was threatened.

For years there had been a growing jealousy between Northern and Southern California. Los Angeles, as has been stated before, had by a decree of the Mexican congress been made the capital of the territory. Monterey had persistently refused to give up the governor and the archives. In the movement to make Alta California a free and independent state, the Angeleños recognized an attempt on the part of the people of the north to deprive them of the capital. Although as bitterly opposed to Mexican governors, and as active in fomenting revolutions against them as the people of Monterey, the Angeleños chose to profess loyalty to the mother country. They opposed the plan of government adopted by the congress at Monterey and promulgated a plan of their own, in which they declared California was not free; that the "Roman Catholic Apostolic religion shall prevail in this jurisdiction, and any person publicly professing any other shall be prosecuted by law as heretofore." A mass meeting was called to take measures "to prevent the spreading of the Monterey revolution, so that the progress of the nation may not be paralyzed," and to appoint a person to take military command of the department.

San Diego and San Luis Rey took the part of Los Angeles in the quarrel, Sonoma and San Jose joined Monterey, while Santa Barbara, always conservative, was undecided, but finally issued a plan of her own. Alvarado and Castro determined to suppress the revolutionary Angeleños. They collected a force of one hundred men, made up of natives, with Graham's contingent of twenty-five American riflemen. With this army they prepared to move against the recalcitrant sureños.

The ayuntamiento of Los Angeles began preparations to resist the invaders. An army of two hundred and seventy men was enrolled, a part of which was made up of neophytes. To secure the sinews of war Jose Sepulveda, second alcalde, was sent to the Mission San Fernando to secure what money there was in the hands of the major domo. He returned with two packages, which, when counted, were found to contain $2,000.

Scouts patrolled the Santa Barbara road as far as San Buenaventura to give warning of the approach of the enemy, and pickets guarded the Pass of Cahuenga and the Rodeo de Las Aguas to prevent northern spies from entering and southern traitors from getting out of the pueblo. The southern army was stationed at San Fernando under the command of Alierez (Lieut.) Rocha. Alvarado and Castro, pushing down the coast, reached Santa Barbara, where they were kindly received and their force recruited to one hundred and twenty men with two pieces of artillery. Jose Sepulveda at San Fernando sent to Los Angeles for the cannon at the town house and $200 of the mission money to pay his men.

On the 16th of January, 1837, Alvarado from San Buenaventura dispatched a communication to the ayuntamiento of Los Angeles and the citizens, telling them what military resources he had, which he would use against them if it became necessary, but he was willing to confer upon a plan of settlement. Sepulveda and Antonio M. Osio were appointed commissioners and sent to confer with the governor, armed with several propositions, the substance of which was that California shall not be free and the Catholic religion must prevail with the privilege to prosecute any other religion, "according to law as heretofore." The commissioners met Alvarado on "neutral ground," between San Fernando and San

Buenaventura. A long discussion followed without either coming to the point. Alvarado, by a coup d'état, brought it to an end. In the language of the commissioners' report to the ayuntamiento: "While we were a certain distance from our own forces with only four unarmed men and were on the point of coming to an agreement with Juan B. Alvarado, we saw the Monterey division advancing upon us and we were forced to deliver up the instructions of this illustrious body through fear of being attacked." They delivered up not only the instructions, but the Mission San Fernando. The southern army was compelled to surrender it and fall back on the pueblo, Rocha swearing worse than "our army in Flanders" because he was not allowed to fight. The southern soldiers had a wholesome dread of Graham's riflemen. These fellows, armed with long Kentucky rifles, shot to kill, and a battle once begun somebody would have died for his country and it would not have been Alvarado's riflemen.

The day after the surrender of the mission, January 21, 1837, the ayuntamiento held a session and the members were as obdurate and belligerent as ever. They resolved that it was only in the interests of humanity that the mission had been surrendered and their army forced to retire. "This ayuntamiento, considering the commissioners were forced to comply, annuls all action of the commissioners and does not recognize this territory as a free and sovereign state nor Juan B. Alvarado as its governor, and declares itself in favor of the Supreme Government of Mexico." A few days later Alvarado entered the city without opposition, the Angeleñian soldiers retiring to San Gabriel and from there scattering to their homes.

On the 26th of January an extraordinary session of the most illustrious ayuntamiento was held. Alvarado was present and made a lengthy speech, in which he said, "The native sons were subjected to ridicule by the Mexican mandarins sent here, and knowing our rights we ought to shake off the ominous yoke of bondage." Then he produced and read the six articles of the Monterey plan, the council also produced a plan and a treaty of amity was effected. Alvarado was recognized as governor pro tem. and peace reigned. The belligerent sureños vied with each other in expressing their admiration for the new order of things. Pio Pico wished to express the pleasure it gave him to see a "hijo del pais" in office. And Antonio Osio, the most belligerent of the sureños, declared "that sooner than again submit to a Mexican dictator as governor, he would flee to the forest and be devoured by wild beasts." The ayuntamiento was asked to provide a building for the government, "this being the capital of the state." The hatchet apparently was buried. Peace reigned in El Estado Libre. At the meeting of the town council, on the 30th of January, Alvarado made another speech, but it was neither conciliatory nor complimentary. He arraigned the "traitors who were working against the peace of the country" and urged the members to take measures "to liberate the city from the hidden hands that will tangle them m their own ruin." The pay of his troops who were ordered here for the welfare of California is due "and it is an honorable and preferred debt, therefore the ayuntamiento will deliver to the government the San Fernando money," said he. With a wry face, very much such as a boy wears when he is told that he has been spanked for his own good, the alcalde turned over the balance of the mission money to Juan Bautista, and the governor took his departure for Monterey, leaving, however. Col. Jose Castro with part of his army stationed at Mission San Gabriel, ostensibly "to support the city's authority," but in reality to keep a close watch on the city authorities.

Los Angeles was subjugated, peace reigned and El Estado Libre de Alta California took her place among the nations of the earth. But peace's reign was brief. At the meeting of the ayuntamiento May 27, 1838, Juan Bandini and Santiago E. Arguello of San Diego, appeared with a pronunciamiento and a plan, San Diego's plan of government. Monterey, Santa Barbara and Los Angeles had each formulated a plan of government for the territory, and now it was San Diego's turn. Agustin V. Zamorano, who had been exiled with Governor Gutierrez, had crossed the frontier and was made comandante-general and territorial political chief ad interim by the San Diego revolutionists. The plan restored California to obedience to the supreme government; all acts of the diputacion and the Monterey plan were annulled and the northern rebels were to be arraigned and tried for their part in the revolution; and so on through twenty articles.

On the plea of an Indian outbreak near San Diego, in which the redmen, it was said, "were to make an end of the white race," the big cannon and a number of men were secured at Los Angeles to assist in suppressing the Indians, but in reality to reinforce the army of the San Diego revolutionists. With a force of one hundred and twenty-five men under Zamorano and Portilla, "the army of the supreme government" moved against Castro at Los Angeles. Castro retreated to Santa Barbara and Portilla's army took position at San Fernando.

The civil and military officials of Los Angeles took the oath to support the Mexican constitution of 1836 and, in their opinion, this absolved them from all allegiance to Juan Bautista and his Monterey plan. Alvarado hurried reinforcements to Castro at Santa Barbara, and Portilla called loudly for "men, arms and horses," to march against the northern rebels. But neither military chieftain advanced, and the summer wore away without a battle. There were rumors that ^Mexico was preparing to send an army of one thousand men to subjugate the rebellious Californians. In October came the news that Jose Antonio Carrillo, the Machiavelli of California politics, had persuaded President Bustamente to appoint Carlos Carrillo, Jose's brother, governor of Alta California.

Then consternation seized the arribeños (uppers) of the north and the abajeños (lowers) of Los Angeles went wild with joy. It was not that they loved Carlos Carrillo, for he was a Santa Barbara man and had opposed them in the late unpleasantness, but they saw in his appointment an opportunity to get revenge on Juan Bautista for the way he had humiliated them. They sent congratulatory messages to Carrillo and invited him to make Los Angeles the seat of his government. Carrillo was flattered by their attentions and consented. The 6th of December, 1837, was set for his inauguration, and great preparations were made for the event. The big cannon was brought over from San Gabriel to fire salutes and the city was ordered illuminated on the nights of the 6th, 7th and 8th of December. Cards of invitation were issued and the people from the city and country were invited to attend the inauguration ceremonies, "dressed as decent as possible," so read the invitations.

The widow Josefa Alvarado's house, the finest in the city, was secured for the governor's palacio (palace). The largest hall in the city was secured for the services and decorated as well as it was possible. The city treasury, being in its usual state of

95

collapse, a subscription for defraying the expenses was opened and horses, hides and tallow, the current coin of the pueblo, were liberally contributed.

On the appointed day, "the most illustrious ayuntamiento and the citizens of the neighborhood (so the old archives read) met his excellency, the governor, Don Carlos Carrillo, who made his appearance with a magnificent accompaniment." The secretary, Narciso Botello, "read in a loud, clear and intelligible voice, the oath, and the governor repeated it after him." At the moment the oath was completed, the artillery thundered forth a salute and the bells rang out a merry peal. The governor made a speech, when all adjourned to the church, where a mass was said and a solemn Te Deum sung; after which all repaired to the house of his excellency, where the southern patriots drank his health in bumpers of wine and shouted themselves hoarse in vivas to the new government. An inauguration ball was held — the "beauty and the chivalry of the south were gathered there." Outside the tallow dips flared and flickered from the porticos of the house, bonfires blazed in the streets and cannon boomed salvos from the old plaza. Los Angeles was the capital at last and had a governor all to herself, for Santa Barbara refused to recognize Carrillo, although he belonged within its jurisdiction.

The Angeleños determined to subjugate the Barbarenos. An army of two hundred men, under Castenada, was sent to capture the city. After a few futile demonstrations, Castenada's forces fell back to San Buenaventura.

Then Alvarado determined to subjugate the Angeleños. He and Castro, gathering together an army of two hundred men, by forced marches reached San Buenaventura, and by a strategic movement captured all of Castenada's horses and drove his army into the mission church. For two days the battle raged and, "cannon to the right of them," and "cannon in front of them volleyed and thundered." One man was killed on the northern side and the blood of several mustangs watered the soil of their native land — died for their country. The southerners slipped out of the church at night and fled up the valley on foot. Castro's caballeros captured about seventy prisoners. Pio Pico, with reinforcements, met the remnant of Castenada's army at the Santa Clara river, and together all fell back to Los Angeles. Then there was wailing in the old pueblo, where so lately there had been rejoicing. Gov. Carlos Carrillo gathered together what men he could get to go with him and retreated to San Diego. Alvarado's army took possession of the southern capital and some of the leading conspirators were sent as prisoners to the castillo at Sonoma.

Carrillo, at San Diego, received a small reinforcement from Mexico, under a Captain Tobar. Tobar was made general and given command of the southern army. Carrillo, having recovered from his fright, sent an order to the northern rebels to surrender within fifteen days under penalty of being shot as traitors if they refused. In the meantime Los Angeles was held by the enemy. The second alcalde (the first, Louis Aranas, was a prisoner) called a meeting to devise some means "to have his excellency, Don Carlos Carrillo, return to this capital, as his presence is very much desired by the citizens to protect their lives and property " A committee was appointed to locate Don Carlos.

Instead of surrendering, Castro and Alvarado, with a force of two hundred men, advanced against Carrillo. The two armies met at Campo de Las Flores. General Tobar had fortified a cattle corral with rawhides, carretas and Cottonwood poles. A few shots from Alvarado's artillery scattered Tobar's rawhide fortifications. Carrillo surrendered. Tobar and a few of the leaders escaped to Mexico. Alvarado ordered the misguided Angeleñian soldiers to go home and behave themselves. He brought the captive governor back with him and left him with his (Carrillo's) wife at Santa Barbara, who became surety for the deposed ruler. Not content with his unfortunate attempts to rule, he again claimed the governorship on the plea that he had been appointed by the supreme government. But the Angeleños had had enough of him. Disgusted with his incompetency, Juan Gallardo, at the session of May 14, 1838, presented a petition praying that this ayuntamiento do not recognize Carlos Carrillo as governor, and setting forth the reasons why we, the petitioners, "should declare ourselves subject to the northern governor" and why they opposed Carrillo.

"First. In having compromised the people from San Buenaventura south into a declaration of war, the incalculable calamities of which will never be forgotten, not even by the most ignorant.

"Second. Not satisfied with the unfortunate event of San Buenaventura, he repeated the same at Campo de Las Flores, which, only through a divine dispensation, California is not to-day in mourning." Seventy citizens signed the petition, but the city attorney, who had done time in Vallejo's castillo, decided the petition illegal because it was written on common paper when paper with the proper seal could be obtained.

Next day Gallardo returned with his petition on legal paper. The ayuntamiento decided to sound the "public alarm" and call the people together to give them "public speech." The public alarm was sounded. The people assembled at the city hall; speeches were made on both sides; and when the vote was taken twenty-two were in favor of the northern governor, five in favor of whatever the ayuntamiento decides, and Serbulo Vareles alone voted for Don Carlos Carrillo. So the council decided to recognize Don Juan Bautista Alvarado as governor and leave the supreme government to settle the contest between him and Carrillo.

Notwithstanding this apparent burying of the hatchet, there were rumors of plots and intrigues in Los Angeles and San Diego against Alvarado. At length, aggravated beyond endurance, the governor sent word to the sureños that if they did not behave themselves he would shoot ten of the leading men of the south. As he had about that number locked up in the Castillo at Sonoma, his was no idle threat. One by one Alvarado's prisoners of state were released from Vallejo's bastile at Sonoma and returned to Los Angeles, sadder if not wiser men. At the session of the ayuntamiento October 20, 1838, the president announced that Senior Regidor Jose Palomares had returned from Sonoma, where he had been compelled to go by reason of "political differences," and that he should be allowed his seat in the council. The request was granted unanimously.

At the next meeting Narciso Botello, its former secretary, after five and a half months' imprisonment at Sonoma, put in an appearance and claimed his office and his pay. Although others had filled the office in the interim the illustrious ayuntamiento, "ignoring for what offense he was incarcerated, could not suspend his salary." But his salary was suspended. The treasury was empty. The last horse and the last hide had been paid out to defray the expense of the inauguration festivities of Carlos, the Pretender, and the civil war that followed. Indeed there was a treasury deficit of whole caballadas of horses, and bales of hides. Narciso's back pay was a preferred claim that outlasted El Estado Libre.

The sureños of Los Angeles and San Diego, finding that in Alvarado they had a man of courage and determination to deal with, ceased from troubling him and submitted to the inevitable. At the meeting of the ayuntamiento, October 5, 1839, a notification was received, stating that the supreme government of Mexico had appointed Juan Bautista Alvarado governor of the department. There was no grumbling or dissent. On the contrary, the records say, "This illustrious body acknowledges receipt of the communication and congratulated his excellency. It will announce the same to the citizens to-morrow (Sunday), will raise the national colors, salute the same with the required number of volleys, and will invite the people to illuminate their houses for a better display in rejoicing at such a happy appointment." With his appointment by the supreme government the "free and sovereign state of Alta California" became a dream of the past — a dead nation. Indeed, months before Alvarado had abandoned his idea of founding an independent state and had taken the oath of allegiance to the constitution of 1836. The loyal sureños received no thanks from the supreme government for all their professions of loyalty, whilst the rebellious arribeños of the north obtained all the rewards — the governor, the capital and the offices. The supreme government gave the deposed governor, Carlos Carrillo, a grant of the island of Santa Rosa, in the Santa Barbara Channel, but whether it was given him as a salve to his wounded dignity or as an Elba or St. Helena, where, in the event of his stirring up another revolution, he might be banished a la Napoleon, the records do not inform us.

CHAPTER XIV.
DECLINE AND FALL OF MEXICAN DOMINATION.

While the revolution begun by Alvarado and Castro had not established California's independence, it had effectually rid the territory of Mexican dictators. A native son was governor of the department of the Californians (by the constitution of 1836 Upper and Lower California had been united into a department); another native son was comandante of its military forces. The membership of the departmental junta, which had taken the place of the diputacion, was largely made up of sons of the soil, and natives filled the minor offices. In their zeal to rid themselves of Mexican office-holders they had invoked the assistance of another element that was ultimately to be their undoing.

During the revolutionary era just passed the foreign population had largely increased. Not only had the foreigners come by sea, but they had come by land. Capt. Jedediah S. Smith, a New England-born trapper and hunter, was the first man to enter California by the overland route. A number of trappers and hunters came in the early '30s from New Mexico by way of the old Spanish trail. This immigration was largely American, and was made up of a bold, adventurous class of men, some of them not the most desirable immigrants. Of this latter class were some of Graham's followers.

By invoking Graham's aid to put him in power, Alvarado had fastened upon his shoulders an old Man of the Sea. It was easy enough to enlist the services of Graham's riflemen, but altogether another matter to get rid of them. Now that he was firmly established in power, Alvarado would, no doubt, have been glad to be rid entirely of his recent allies, but Graham and his adherents were not backward in giving him to understand that he owed his position to them, and they were inclined to put themselves on an equality with him. This did not comport with his ideas of the dignity of his office. To be hailed by some rough buckskin-clad trapper with "Ho! Bautista; come here, I want to speak with you," was an affront to his pride that the governor of the two Californias could not quietly pass over, and, besides, like all of his countrymen, he disliked foreigners.

There were rumors of another revolution, and it was not difficult to persuade Alvarado that the foreigners were plotting to revolutionize California. Mexico had recently lost Texas, and the same class of "malditos extranjeros" (wicked strangers) were invading California, and would ultimately possess themselves of the country. Accordingly, secret orders were sent throughout the department to arrest and imprison all foreigners. Over one hundred men of different nationalities were arrested, principally Americans and English. Of these forty-seven were shipped to San Blas, and from there marched overland to Tepic, where they were imprisoned for several months. Through the efforts of the British consul, Barron, they were released. Castro, who had accompanied the prisoners to Mexico to prefer charges against them, was placed under arrest and afterwards tried by court-martial, but was acquitted. He had been acting under orders from his superiors. After an absence of over a year twenty of the exiles landed at Monterey on their return from Mexico. Robinson, who saw them land, says: "They returned neatly dressed, armed with rifles and swords, and looking in much better condition than when they were sent away, or probably than they had ever looked in their lives before." The Mexican government had been compelled to pay them damages for their arrest and imprisonment and to return them to California. Graham, the reputed leader of the foreigners, was the owner of a distillery near Santa Cruz, and had gathered a number of hard characters around him. It would have been no loss had he never returned.

The only other event of importance during Alvarado's term as governor was the capture of Monterey by Commodore Ap Catesby Jones, of the United States navy. This event happened after Alvarado's successor, Micheltorena, had landed in California, but before the government had been formally turned over to him.

The following extract from the diary of a pioneer, who was an eye-witness of the affair, gives a good description of the capture:

"Monterey, Oct. 19, 1842. — At 2 p. m. the United States man-of-war United States, Commodore Ap Catesby Jones, came to anchor close alongside and in-shore of all the ships in port. About 3 p. m. Capt. Armstrong came ashore, accompanied by an interpreter, and went direct to the governor's house, where he had a private conversation with him, which proved to be a demand for the surrender of the entire coast of California, upper and lower, to the United States government. When he was about to go on board he gave three or four copies of a proclamation to the inhabitants of the two Californias, assuring them of the protection of their lives, persons and property. In his notice to the governor (Alvarado) he gave him only until the following morning at 9 a. m. to decide. If he received no answer, then he would fire upon the town."

"I remained on shore that night and went down to the governor's with Mr. Larkin and Mr. Eagle. The governor had had some idea of running away and leaving Monterey to its fate, but was told by Mr. Spence that he should not go, and finally he resolved to await the result. At 12 at night some persons were sent on board the United States who had been appointed by the governor to meet the commodore and arrange the terms of the surrender. Next I morning at half-past ten o'clock about one hundred sailors and fifty marines disembarked. The sailors marched up from the shore and took possession of the fort. The American colors were hoisted. The United States fired a salute of thirteen guns; it was returned by the fort, which fired; twenty-six guns. The marines in the meantime had marched up to the government house. The officers and soldiers of the California government were discharged and their guns and other arms taken possession of and carried to the fort. The stars and stripes now wave over us. Long may they wave here in California!"

"Oct. 21, 4 p. m. — Flags were again changed, the vessels were released, and all was quiet again. The commodore had received later news by some Mexican newspapers."

Commodore Jones had been stationed at Callao with a squadron of four vessels. An English fleet was also there, and a French fleet was cruising in the Pacific. Both these were supposed to have designs on California. Jones learned that the English admiral had received orders to sail next day. Surmising that his destination might be California, he slipped out of the harbor the night before and crowded all sail to reach California before the English admiral. The loss of Texas, and the constant influx of immigrants and adventurers from the United States into

California, had embittered the Mexican government more and more against foreigners. Manuel Micheltorena, who had served under Santa Anna in the Texas war, was appointed January 19, 1842, comandante-general inspector and gobernador propietario of the Californias.

Santa Anna was president of the Mexican republic. His experience with Americans in Texas during the Texan war of independence, in 1836-37, had decided him to use every effort to prevent California from sharing the fate of Texas.

Micheltorena, the newly-appointed governor, was instructed to take with him sufficient force to check the ingress of Americans. He recruited a force of three hundred and fifty men, principally convicts enlisted from the prisons of Mexico. His army of thieves and ragamuffins landed at San Diego in August, 1842.

Robinson, who was at San Diego when one of the vessels conveying Micheltorena's cholos (convicts) landed, thus describes them: "Five days afterward the brig Chato arrived with ninety soldiers and their families. I saw them land, and to me they presented a state of wretchedness and misery unequaled. Not one individual among them possessed a jacket or pantaloons, but, naked, and like the savage Indians, they concealed their nudity with dirty miserable blankets. The females were not much better off, for the scantiness of their mean apparel was too apparent for modest observers. They appeared like convicts, and, indeed, the greater portion of them had been charged with crime, either of murder or theft."

Micheltorena drilled his Falstaffian army at San Diego for several weeks and then began his march northward; Los Angeles made great preparations to receive the new governor. Seven years had passed since she had been decreed the capital of the territory, and in all these years she had been denied her rights by Monterey. A favorable impression on the new governor might induce him to make the ciudad his capital. The national fiesta of September 16 was postponed until the arrival of the governor. The best house in the town was secured for him and his staff. A grand ball was projected and the city illuminated the night of his arrival. A camp was established down by the river and the cholos, who in the meantime had been given white linen uniforms, were put through the drill and the manual of arms. They were incorrigible thieves, and stole for the very pleasure of stealing. They robbed the hen roosts, the orchards, the vineyards and the vegetable gardens of the citizens. To the Angeleños the glory of their city as the capital of the territory faded in the presence of their empty chicken coops and plundered orchards. They longed to speed the departure of their now unwelcome guests. After a stay of a month in the city Micheltorena and his army took up their line of march northward. He reached a point about twenty miles north of San Fernando, when, on the night of the 24th of October, a messenger aroused him from his slumbers with the news that the capital had been captured by the Americans. Micheltorena seized the occasion to make political capital for himself with the home government. He spent the remainder of the night in fulminating proclamations against the invaders fiercer than the thunderbolts of Jove, copies of which were dispatched post haste to Mexico. He even wished himself a thunderbolt "that he might fly over intervening space and annihilate the invaders," Then, with his own courage and doubtless that of his brave cholos aroused to the highest pitch, instead of rushing on the invaders, he and his army fled back to San Fernando, where, afraid to advance or retreat, he halted until news reached him that Commodore Jones had restored Monterey to the Californians. Then his valor reached the boiling point. He boldly marched to Los Angeles, established his headquarters in the city and awaited the coming of Commodore Jones and his officers from Monterey.

On the 19th of January, 1843, Commodore Jones and his staff came to Los Angeles to meet the governor. At the famous conference in the Palacio de Don Abel, Micheltorena presented his articles of convention. Among other ridiculous demands were the following: "Article VI. Thomas Ap C. Jones will deliver fifteen hundred complete infantry uniforms to replace those of nearly one-half of the Mexican force, which have been ruined in the violent march and the continued rains while they were on their way to recover the port thus invaded." "Article VII. Jones to pay $15,000 into the national treasury for expenses incurred from the general alarm; also a complete set of musical instruments in place of those ruined on this occasion." Judging from Robinson's description of the dress of Micheltorena's cholos it is doubtful whether there was an entire uniform among them.

"The commodore's first impulse," writes a member of his staff, "was to return the papers without comment and to refuse further communication with a man who could have the effrontery to trump up such charges as those for which indemnification was claimed." The commodore on reflection put aside his personal feelings, and met the governor at the grand ball in Sanchez hall, held in honor of the occasion. The ball was a brilliant affair, "the dancing ceased only with the rising of the sun next morning." The commodore returned the articles without his signature. The governor did not again refer to his demands. Next morning, January 21, 1843, Jones and his officers took their departure from the city "amidst the beating of drums, the firing of cannon and the ringing of bells, saluted by the general and his wife from the door of their quarters. On the 31st of December, Micheltorena had taken the oath of office in Sanchez' hall, which stood on the east side of the plaza. Salutes were fired, the bells were rung and the city was illuminated for three evenings. For the second time a governor had been inaugurated in Los Angeles.

Micheltorena and his cholo army remained in Los Angeles about eight months. The Angeleños had all the capital they cared for. They were perfectly willing to have the governor and his army take up their residence in Monterey. The cholos had devoured the country like an army of chapules (locusts) and were willing to move on. Monterey would no doubt have gladly transferred what right she had to the capital if at the same time she could have transferred to her old rival, Los Angeles, Micheltorena's cholos. Their pilfering was largely enforced by their necessities. They received little or no pay, and they often had to steal or starve. The leading native Californians still entertained their old dislike to "Mexican dictators" and the retinue of three hundred chicken thieves accompanying the last dictator intensified their hatred.

Micheltorena, while not a model governor, had many good qualities and was generally liked by the better class of foreign residents. He made an earnest effort to establish a system of public education in the territory. Schools were established in all the principal towns, and territorial aid from the public funds to the amount of $500 each was given them. The school at Los Angeles had over one hundred pupils in attendance. His worst fault was a disposition to meddle in local affairs. He was unreliable and not careful to keep his agreements. He might have succeeded in giving California a stable government had it not been for the antipathy to his soldiers and the old feud between the "hijos del pais" and the Mexican dictators.

These proved his undoing. The native sons under Alvarado and Castro rose in rebellion. In November, 1844, a revolution was inaugurated at Santa Clara. The governor marched with an army of one hundred and fifty men against the rebel forces, numbering about two hundred. They met at a place called the Laguna de Alvires. A treaty was signed in which Micheltorena agreed to ship his cholos back to Mexico.

This treaty the governor deliberately broke. He then intrigued with Capt. John A. Sutter of New Helvetia and Isaac Graham to obtain assistance to crush the rebels. January 9, 1845, Micheltorena and Sutter formed a junction of their forces at Salinas — their united commands numbering about five hundred men. They marched against the rebels to crush them. But the rebels did not wait to be crushed. Alvarado and Castro, with about ninety men, started for Los Angeles, and those left behind scattered to their homes. Alvarado and his men reached Los Angeles on the night of January 20, 1845. The garrison stationed at the curate's house was surprised and captured. One man was killed and several wounded. Lieutenant Medina, of Micheltorena's army, was the commander of the pueblo troops. Alvarado's army encamped on the plaza and he and Castro set to work to revolutionize the old pueblo. The leading Angelenos had no great love for Juan Bautista, and did not readily fall into his schemes. They had not forgotten their enforced detention in Vallejo's bastile during the Civil war. An extraordinary session of the ayuntamiento was called January 21. Alvarado and Castro were present and made eloquent appeals. The records say: "The ayuntamiento listened, and after a short interval of silence and meditation decided to notify the senior member of the department assembly of Don Alvarado and Castros' wishes."

They were more successful with the Pico brothers. Pio Pico was senior vocal, and in case Micheltorena was disposed he, by virtue of his office, would become governor. Through the influence of the Picos the revolution gained ground. The most potent influence in spreading the revolt was the fear of Micheltorena's army of chicken thieves. Should the town be captured by them it certainly would be looted. The department assembly was called together. A peace commission was sent to meet Micheltorena, who was leisurely marching southward, and intercede with him to give up his proposed invasion of the south. He refused. Then the assembly pronounced him a traitor, deposed him by vote and appointed Pio Pico governor. Recruiting went on rapidly. Hundreds of saddle horses were contributed, "old rusty guns were repaired, hacked swords sharpened, rude lances manufactured" and cartridges made for the cannon. Some fifty foreigners of the south joined Alvarado's army; not that they had much interest in the revolution, but to protect their property against the rapacious invaders — the cholos — and Sutter's Indians,[*] who were as much dreaded as the cholos. On the 19th of February, Micheltorena reached the Encinos, and the Angeleñian army marched out through Cahuenga Pass to meet him. On the 20th the two armies met on the southern edge of the San Fernando valley, about fifteen miles from Los Angeles. Each army numbered about four hundred men. Micheltorena had three pieces of artillery and Castro two. They opened on each other at long range and seem to have fought the battle throughout at very long range. A mustang or a mule (authorities differ) was killed.

Wilson, Workman and McKinley of Castro's army decided to induce the Americans on the other side, many of whom were their personal friends, to abandon Micheltorena. Passing up a ravine, they succeeded in attracting the attention of some of them by means of a white flag. Gantt, Hensley and Bidwell joined them in the ravine. The situation was discussed and the Americans of Micheltorena's army agreed to desert him if Pico would protect them in their land grants. Wilson, in his account of the battle, says: "I knew, and so did Pico, that these land questions were the point with those young Americans. Before I started on my journey or embassy, Pico was sent for; on his arrival among us I, in a few words, explained to him what the party had advanced. 'Gentlemen,' said he, 'are any of you citizens of Mexico?' They answered 'No.' 'Then your title deeds given you by Micheltorena are not worth the paper they are written on, and he knew it well when he gave them to you; but if you will abandon his cause I will give you my word of honor as a gentleman, and Don Benito Wilson and Don Juan Workman to carry out what I promise, that I will protect each one of you in the land that you now hold, and when you become citizens of Mexico I will issue you the proper titles.' They said that was all they asked, and promised not to fire a gun against us. They also asked not to be required to fight on our side,' which was agreed to.

"Micheltorena discovered (how, I do not know) that his Americans had abandoned him. About an hour afterwards he raised his camp and flanked us by going further into the valley towards San Fernando, then marching as though he intended to come around the bend of the river to the city. The Californians and we foreigners at once broke up our camp and came back through the Cahuenga Pass, marched through the gap into the Feliz ranch, on the Los Angeles River, till we came into close proximity to Micheltorena's camp. It was now night, as it was dark when we broke up our camp. Here we waited for daylight, and some f of our men commenced maneuvering for a fight with the enemy. A few cannon shots were I fired, when a white flag was discovered flying from Micheltorena's front. The whole matter then went into the hands of negotiators appointed by both parties and the terms of surrender were agreed upon, one of which was that Micheltorena and his obnoxious officers and men were to march back up the river to the Cahuenga Pass, then down on the plain to the west of Los Angeles, the most direct line to San Pedro, and embark at that point on a vessel then anchored there to carry them back to Mexico." Sutter was taken prisoner, and his Indians, after being corralled for a time, were sent back to the Sacramento,

The roar of the battle of Cahuenga, or the Alamo, as it is sometimes called, could be distinctly heard in Los Angeles, and the people remaining in the city were greatly alarmed. William Heath Davis, in his Sixty Years in California, thus describes the alarm in the town: "Directly to the north of the town was a high hill" (now known as Mt. Lookout). "As soon as firing was heard all the people remaining in the town, men, women and children, ran to the top of this hill. As the wind was blowing from the north, the firing was distinctly heard, five leagues away, on the battle-field throughout the day. All business places in town were closed. The scene on the hill was a remarkable one, women and children, with crosses in their hands, kneeling and praying to the saints for the safety of their fathers, brothers, sons, husbands, lovers, cousins, that they might not be killed in the battle; indifferent to their personal appearance, tears streaming from their eyes, and their hair blown about by the wind, which had increased to quite a breeze. Don Abel Stearns, myself and others tried to calm and pacify them, assuring them that there was probably no danger; somewhat against our convictions, it is true, judging from what we heard of the firing and from our knowledge of Micheltorena's disciplined force, his battery, and the riflemen he had with him. During the day the scene on the hill continued. The night that followed was a gloomy one, caused by the lamentations of the women and children."

Davis, who was supercargo on the Don Quixote, the vessel on which Micheltorena and his soldiers were shipped to Mexico, claims that the general "had ordered his command not to injure the Californians in the force opposed to him, but to fire over their heads, as he had no desire to kill them."

Another Mexican-born governor had been deposed and deported, gone to join his fellows, Victoria, Chico and Gutierrez. In accordance with the treaty of Cahuenga and by virtue of his rank as senior member of the departmental assembly, Pio Pico became governor. The hijos del pais were once more in the ascendency. Jose Castro was made comandante-general. Alvarado was given charge of the custom house at Monterey, and Jose Antonio Carrillo was appointed commander of the military district of the south. Los Angeles was made the capital, although the archives and the treasury remained in Monterey. The revolution apparently had been a success. In the proceedings of the Los Angeles ayuntamiento, March 1, 1845, appears this record: "The agreements entered into at Cahuenga between Gen. Emanuel Micheltorena and Lieut.-Col. Jose Castro were then read, and as they contain a happy termination of affairs in favor of the government, this Illustrious Body listened with satisfaction and so answered the communication."

The people joined with the ayuntamiento in expressing their "satisfaction" that a "happy termination" had been reached of the political disturbances which had distracted the country. But the end was not yet. Pico did his best to conciliate the conflicting elements, but the old sectional jealousies that had divided the people of the territory would crop out. Jose Antonio Carrillo, the Machiavel of the south, hated Castro and Alvarado and was jealous of Pico's good fortune. He was the superior of any of them in ability, but made himself unpopular by his intrigues and his sarcastic speech. When Castro and Alvarado came south to raise the standard of revolt they tried to win him over. He did assist them. He was willing enough to plot against Micheltorena, but after the overthrow of the Mexican he was equally ready to plot against Pico and Castro. In the summer of 1845 he was implicated in a plot to depose Pico, who, by the way, was his brother-in-law. Pico placed him and two of his fellow conspirators, Serbulo and Hilario Varela, under arrest. Carrillo and Hilario Varela were shipped to Mazatlan to be tried for their misdeed. Serbulo Varela made his escape from prison. The two exiles returned early in 1846 unpunished and ready for new plots.

Pico was appointed gobernador proprietario, or constitutional governor of California, September 3, 1845, by President Herrera. The supreme government of Mexico never seemed to lake offense or harbor resentment against the Californians for deposing and sending home a governor. As the officials of the supreme government usually obtained office by revolution, they no doubt had a fellow feeling for the revolting Californians. When Micheltorena returned to Mexico he was coldly received and a commissioner was sent to Pico with dispatches virtually approving all that had been done.

Castro, too, gave Pico a great deal of uneasiness. He ignored the governor and managed the military affairs of the territory to suit himself. His headquarters were at Monterey and doubtless he had the sympathy if not the encouragement of the people of the north in his course. But the cause of the greatest uneasiness was the increasing immigration from the United States. A stream of emigrants from the western states, increasing each year, poured down the Sierra Nevadas and spread over the rich valleys of California. The Californians recognized that through the advent of these "foreign adventurers," as they called them, the "manifest destiny" of California was to be absorbed by the United States. Alvarado had appealed to Mexico for men and arms and had been answered by the arrival of Micheltorena and his cholos. Pico appealed and for a time the Californians were cheered by the prospect of aid.

In the summer of 1845, a force of six hundred veteran soldiers, under command of Colonel Iniestra, reached Acapulco, where ships were lying to take them to California, but a revolution broke out in Mexico and the troops destined for the defense of California were used to overthrow President Herrera and to seat Paredes. California was left to work out her own destiny unaided or drift with the tide — and she drifted. In the early months of 1846 there was a rapid succession of important events in her history, each in passing bearing her near and nearer to a manifest destiny — the downfall of Mexican domination in California. These will be presented fully in the chapter on the Acquisition of California by the United States. But before taking up these we will turn aside to review life in California in the olden time under Spanish and Mexican rule.

CHAPTER XV. MUNICIPAL GOVERNMENT— HOMES AND HOME-LIFE OF THE CALIFORNIANS.

Under Spain the government of California was semi-military and semi-clerical. The governors were military officers and had command of the troops in the territory, and looked after affairs at the pueblos; the friars were supreme at the missions. The municipal government of the pueblos was vested in ayuntamientos. The decree of the Spanish Cortes passed May 23, 1812, regulated the membership of the ayuntamiento according to the population of the town — "there shall be one alcalde (mayor), two regidores (councilmen), and one procurador-syndico (treasurer) in all towns which do not have more than two hundred inhabitants; one alcalde, four regidores and one syndico in those the population of which exceeds two hundred, but does not exceed five hundred." When the population of a town exceeded one thousand it was allowed two alcaldes, eight regidores and two syndicos. Over the members of the ayuntamiento in the early years of Spanish rule was a quasi-military officer called a comisionado, a sort of petty dictator or military despot, who, when occasion required or inclination moved him, embodied within himself all three departments of government, judiciary, legislative and executive. After Mexico became a republic the office of comisionado was abolished. The alcalde acted as president of the ayuntamiento, as mayor and as judge of the court of first instance. The second alcalde took his place when that officer was ill or absent. The syndico was a general utility man. He acted as city or town attorney, tax collector and treasurer. The secretary was an important officer; he kept the records, acted as clerk of the alcalde's court and was the only municipal officer who received pay, except the syndico, who received a commission on his collections.

In 1837 the Mexican Congress passed a decree abolishing ayuntamientos in capitals of departments having a population of less than four thousand and in interior towns of less than eight thousand. In 1830 Governor Alvarado reported to the Departmental Assembly that no town in California had the requisite population. The ayuntamientos all closed January 1, 1840. They were re-established in 1844. During their abolition the towns were governed by prefects and justices of the peace, and the special laws or ordinances were enacted by the departmental assembly.

The jurisdiction of the ayuntamiento often extended over a large area of country beyond the town limits. That of Los Angeles, after the secularization of the missions, extended over a country as large as the state of Massachusetts. The authority of the ayuntamiento was as extensive as its jurisdiction. It granted town lots and recommended to the governor grants of land from the public domain. In addition to passing ordinances its members sometimes acted as executive officers to enforce them. It exercised the powers of a board of health, a board of education, a police commission and a street department. During the civil war between Northern and Southern California, in 1837-38, the ayuntamiento of Los Angeles raised and equipped an army and assumed the right to govern the southern half of the territory.

The ayuntamiento was spoken of as Muy Ilustre (Most Illustrious), in the same sense that we speak of the honorable city council, but it was a much more dignified body than a city council. The members were required to attend their public functions "attired in black apparel, so as to add solemnity to the meetings." They served without pay, but if a member was absent from a meeting without a good excuse he was liable to a fine. As there was no pay in the office and its duties were numerous and onerous, there was not a large crop of aspirants for councilmen in those days, and the office usually sought the man. It might be added that when it caught the right man it was loath to let go of him.

The misfortunes that beset Francisco Pantoja aptly illustrate the difficulty of resigning in the days when office sought the man, not man the office. Pantoja was elected fourth regidor of the ayuntamiento of Los Angeles in 1837. In those days wild horses were very numerous. When the pasture in the foothills was exhausted they came down into the valleys and ate up the feed needed for the cattle. On this account, and because most of these wild horses were worthless, the rancheros slaughtered them. A corral was built with wings extending out on the right and left from the main entrance. When the corral was completed a day was set for a wild horse drive. The bands were rounded up and driven into the corral. The pick of the caballados were lassoed and taken out to be broken to the saddle and the refuse of the drive killed. The Vejars had obtained permission from the ayuntamiento to build a corral between the Cerritos and the Salinas for the purpose of corralling wild horses. Pantoja, being something of a sport, petitioned his fellow regidores for a twenty days' leave of absence to join in the wild horse chase. A wild horse chase was wild sport and dangerous, too. Somebody was sure to get hurt, and Pantoja in this one was one of the unfortunates. When his twenty days' leave of absence was up he did not return to his duties of regidor, but instead sent his resignation on plea of illness. His resignation was not accepted and the president of the ayuntamiento appointed a committee to investigate his physical condition. There were no physicians in Los Angeles in those days, so the committee took along Santiago McKinley, a canny Scotch merchant, who was reputed to have some knowledge of surgery. The committee and the improvised surgeon held an ante-mortem inquest on what remained of Pantoja. The committee reported to the council that he was a physical wreck; that he could not mount a horse nor ride one when mounted. A native Californian who had reached such a state of physical dilapidation that he could not mount a horse might well be excused from official duties. To excuse him might establish a dangerous precedent. The ayuntamiento heard the report, pondered over it and then sent it and the resignation to the governor. The governor took them under advisement. In the meantime a revolution broke out and before peace was restored and the governor had time to pass upon the case Pantoja's term had expired by limitation.

That modern fad of reform legislation, the referendum, was in full force and effect in California three-quarters of a century ago. When some question of great importance to the community was before the ayuntamiento and the regidores were divided in opinion, the alarma publica or public alarm was sounded by the beating of the long roll on the drum and all the citizens were summoned to the hall of sessions. Any one hearing the alarm and not heeding it was fined $3. When the citizens were convened the president of the ayuntamiento, speaking in a loud voice, stated the question and the people were given "public speech." The question was debated by all who wished to speak. When all had had their say it was decided by a show of hands.

The ayuntamientos regulated the social functions of the pueblos as well as the civic. Ordinance 5, ayuntamiento proceedings of Los Angeles, reads: "All individuals serenading promiscuously around the street of the city at night without first having obtained permission from the alcalde will be fined $1.50 for the first offense, $3 for the second offense, and for the third punished according to law." Ordinance 4, adopted by the ayuntamiento of Los Angeles, January 28, 1838, reads: "Every person not having any apparent occupation in this city or its jurisdiction is hereby ordered to look for work within three days, counting from the day this ordinance is published; if not complied with, he will be fined $2 for the first offense, $4 for the second offense, and will be given compulsory work for the third." From the reading of the ordinance it would seem if the tramp kept looking for work, but was careful not to find it, there could be no offense and consequently no fines or compulsory work.

Some of the enactments of the old regidores would fade the azure out of the blue laws of Connecticut in severity. In the plan of government adopted by the sureños in the rebellion of 1837 appears this article: "Article 3, The Roman Catholic Apostolic religion shall prevail throughout this jurisdiction; and any person professing publicly any other religion shall be prosecuted."

Here is a blue law of Monterey, enacted March 23, 1816: "All persons must attend mass and respond in a loud voice, and if any persons should fail to do so without good cause they will be put in the stocks for three hours."

The architecture of the Spanish and Mexican eras of California was homely almost to ugliness. There was no external ornamentation to the dwellings and no internal conveniences. There was but little attempt at variety and the houses were mostly of one style, square walled, tile covered, or flat roofed with pitch, and usually but one story high. Some of the mission churches were massive, grand and ornamental, while others were devoid of beauty and travesties on the rules of architecture. Every man was his own architect and master builder. He had no choice of material, or, rather, with his ease-loving disposition, he chose to use that which was most convenient, and that was adobe clay, made into sun-dried brick. The Indian was the brickmaker, and he toiled for his taskmasters, like the Hebrew of old for the Egyptian, making bricks without straw and without pay. There were no labor strikes in the building trades then. The Indian was the builder, and he did not know how to strike for higher wages, because he received no wages, high or low. The adobe bricks were moulded into form and set up to dry. Through the long summer days they baked in the hot sun, first on one side, then on the other; and when dried through they were laid in the wall with mud mortar. Then the walls had to dry and dry perhaps through another summer before the house was habitable. Time was the essence of building contracts then.

There was but little wood used in house construction then. It was only the aristocrats who could indulge in the luxury of wooden floors. Most of the houses had floors of the beaten earth. Such floors were cheap and durable. Gilroy says, when he came to Monterey in 1814, only the governor's house had a wooden floor. A door of rawhide shut out intruders and wooden-barred windows admitted sunshine and air.

The legendry of the hearthstone and the fireside which fills so large a place in the home life and literature of the Anglo-Saxon had no part in the domestic system of the old-time Californian. He had no hearthstone and no fireside, nor could that pleasing fiction of Santa Claus coming down the chimney with toys on Christmas eve that so delights the children of to-day have been understood by the youthful Californian of long ago. There were no chimneys in California. The only means of warming the houses by artificial heat was a pan (or brasero) of coals set on the floor. The people lived out of doors in the open air and invigorating sunshine; and they were healthy and long-lived. Their houses were places to sleep in or shelters from rain.

The furniture was meager and mostly homemade. A few benches or rawhide-bottomed chairs to sit on; a rough table; a chest or two to keep the family finery in; a few cheap prints of saints on the walls — these formed the furnishings and the decorations of the living rooms of the common people. The bed was the pride and the ambition of the housewife. Even in humble dwellings, sometimes, a snowy counterpane and lace-trimmed pillows decorated a couch whose base was a dried bullock's hide stretched on a rough frame of wood. A shrine dedicated to the patron saint of the household was a very essential part of a well-regulated home.

Fashions in dress did not change with the seasons. A man could wear his grandfather's hat and his coat, too, and not be out of the fashion. Robinson, writing of California in 1829, says: "The people were still adhering to the costumes of the past century." It was not until after 1834, when the Hijar colonists brought the latest fashions from the City of Mexico, that the style of dress for men and women began to change. The next change took place after the American conquest. Only two changes in half a century, a garment had to be very durable to become unfashionable.

The few wealthy people in the territory dressed well, even extravagantly. Robinson describes the dress of Tomas Yorba, a wealthy ranchero of the Upper Santa Ana, as he saw him in 1829: "Upon his head he wore a black silk handkerchief, the four corners of which hung down his neck behind. An embroidered shirt; a cravat of white jaconet, tastefully tied; a blue damask vest; short clothes of crimson velvet; a bright green cloth jacket, with large silver buttons, and shoes of embroidered deerskin composed his dress. I was afterwards informed by Don Manuel (Dominguez) that on some occasions, such as some particular feast day or festival, his entire display often exceeded in value a thousand dollars."

"The dress worn by the middle class of females is a chemise, with short embroidered sleeves, richly trimmed with lace; a muslin petticoat, flounced with scarlet and secured at the waist by a silk band of the same color; shoes of velvet or blue satin; a cotton reboso or scarf; pearl necklace and earrings; with hair falling in broad plaits down the back."* After 1834 the men generally adopted calzoneras instead of the knee breeches or short clothes of the last century.

"The calzoneras were pantaloons with the exterior seam open throughout its length. On the upper edge was a strip of cloth, red, blue or black, in which were buttonholes. On the other edge were eyelet holes for buttons. In some cases the calzonera was sewn from hip to the middle of the thigh; in others, buttoned. From the middle of the thigh downward the leg was covered by the bota or leggins, used by every one, whatever his dress." The short jacket, with silver or bronze buttons, and the silken sash that served as a connecting link between the calzoneras and the jacket, and also supplied the place of what the Californians did not wear, suspenders, this constituted a picturesque costume, that continued in vogue until the conquest, and with many of the natives for years after. "After 1834 the fashionable women of California exchanged their narrow for more flowing garments and abandoned the braided hair for the coil and the large combs till then in use for smaller combs. "

For outer wraps the serapa for men and the rebosa for women were universally worn. The texture of these marked the social standing of the wearer. It ranged from cheap cotton and coarse serge to the costliest silk and the finest French broadcloth. The costume of the neophyte changed but once in centuries, and that was when he divested himself of his coat of mud and smear of paint and put on the mission shirt and breech clout. Shoes he did not wear and in time his feet became as hard as the hoofs of an animal. The dress of the mission women consisted of a chemise and a skirt; the dress of the children was a shirt and sometimes even this was dispensed.

Filial obedience and respect for parental authority were early impressed upon the minds of the children. The commandment, "Honor thy father and mother," was observed with an oriental devotion. A child was never too old or too large to be exempt from punishment. Stephen C. Foster used to relate an amusing story of a case of parental disciplining he once saw at Los Angeles. An old lady, a grandmother, was belaboring, with a barrel stave, her son, a man thirty years of age. The son had done something of which the mother did not approve. She sent for him to come over to the maternal home to receive his punishment. He came. She took him out to the metaphorical woodshed, which, in this case, was the portico of her house, where she stood him up and proceeded to administer corporal punishment. With the resounding thwacks of the stave, she would exclaim, "I'll teach you to behave yourself." "I'll mend your manners, sir." "Now you'll be good, won't you?" The big man took his punishment without a thought of resisting or rebelling. In fact, he seemed to enjoy it. It brought back feelingly and forcibly a memory of his boyhood days.

In the earlier years of the republic, before revolutionary ideas had perverted the usages of the Californians, great respect was shown to those in authority, and the authorities were strict in requiring deference from their constituents. In the Los Angeles archives of 1828 are the records of an impeachment trial of Don Antonio Maria Lugo, held to depose him from the office of judge of the plains. The principal duty of such a judge was to decide cases of disputed ownership of horses and cattle. Lugo seems to have had an exalted idea of the dignity of his office. Among the complaints presented at the trial was one from young Pedro Sanchez, in which he testified that Lugo had tried to ride his horse over him in the street because he, Sanchez, would not take off his hat to the juez del campo and remain standing uncovered while the judge rode past. Another complainant at the same trial related how at a rodeo Lugo adjudged a neighbor's boy guilty of contempt of court because the boy gave him an impertinent answer, and then he proceeded to give the boy an unmerciful whipping. So heinous was the offense in the estimation of the judge that the complainant said, "had not Lugo fallen over a chair he would have been beating the boy yet."

111

Under Mexican domination in California there was no tax levied on land and improvements. The municipal funds of the pueblos were obtained from revenue on wine and brandy; from the licenses of saloons and other business houses; from the tariff on imports; from permits to give balls or dances; from the fines of transgressors, and from the tax on bull rings and cock pits. Then men's pleasures and vices paid the cost of governing. In the early '40s the city of Los Angeles claimed a population of two thousand, yet the municipal revenues rarely exceeded $1,000 a year. With this small amount the authorities ran a city government and kept out of debt. It did not cost much to run a city government then. There was no army of high-salaried officials with a horde of political heelers quartered on the municipality and fed from the public crib at the expense of the taxpayer. Politicians may have been no more honest then than now, but where there was nothing to steal there was no stealing. The alcaldes and regidores put no temptation in the way of the politicians, and thus they kept them reasonably honest, or at least they kept them from plundering the taxpayers by the simple expedient of having no taxpayers.

The functions of the various departments of the municipal governments were economically administered. Street cleaning and lighting were performed at individual expense instead of public. There was an ordinance in force in Los Angeles and Santa Barbara and probably in other municipalities that required each owner of a house every Saturday to sweep and clean in front of his premises to the middle of the street. His neighbor on the opposite side met him half way, and the street was swept without expense to the pueblo. There was another ordinance that required each owner of a house of more that two rooms on a main street to hang a lighted lantern in front of his door from twilight to eight o'clock in winter and to nine in summer. There were fines for neglect of these duties. There was no fire department in the pueblos. The adobe houses with their clay walls, earthen floors, tiled roofs and rawhide doors were as nearly fireproof as any human habitation could 1»R made. The cooking was done in detached kitchens and in beehive-shaped ovens without flues. The houses were without chimneys, so the danger from fire was reduced to a minimum. A general conflagration was something unknown in the old pueblo days of California.

There was no paid police department. Every able-bodied young man was subject to military duty. A volunteer guard or patrol was kept on duty at the cuartels or guard houses. The guards policed the pueblos, but they were not paid. Each young man had to take his turn at guard duty.

CHAPTER XVI.
TERRITORIAL EXPANSION BY CONQUEST.

The Mexican war marked the beginning by the United States of territorial expansion by conquest. "It was," says General Grant, "an instance of a republic following the bad example of European monarchies in not considering justice in their desire to acquire additional territory." The "additional territory" was needed for the creation of slave states. The southern politicians of the extreme pro-slavery school saw in the rapid settlement of the northwestern states the downfall of their domination and the doom of their beloved institution, slavery. Their peculiar institution could not expand northward and on the south it had reached the Mexican boundary. The only way of acquiring new territory for the extension of slavery on the south was to take it by force from the weak Republic of Mexico. The annexation of Texas brought with it a disputed boundary line. The claim to a strip of country between the Rio Nueces and the Rio Grande furnished a convenient pretext to force Mexico to hostilities. Texas as an independent state had never exercised jurisdiction over the disputed territory. As a state of the Union after annexation she could not rightfully lay claim to what she never possessed, but the army of occupation took possession of it as United States property, and the war was on. In the end we acquired a large slice of Mexican territory, but the irony of fate decreed that not an acre of its soil should be tilled by slave labor.

The causes that led to the acquisition of California antedated the annexation of Texas and the invasion of Mexico. After the adoption of liberal colonization laws by the Mexican government in 1824, there set in a steady drift of Americans to California. At first they came by sea, but after the opening of the overland route in 1841 they came in great numbers by land. It was a settled conviction in the minds of these adventurous nomads that the manifest destiny of California was to become a part of the United States, and they were only too willing to aid destiny when an opportunity offered. The opportunity came and it found them ready for it.

Capt. John C. Fremont, an engineer and explorer in the services of the United States, appeared at Monterey in January, 1846, and applied to General Castro, the military comandante, for permission to buy supplies for his party of sixty-two men who were encamped in the San Joaquin valley, in what is now Kern county. Permission was given him. There seems to have been a tacit agreement between Castro and Fremont that the exploring party should not enter the settlements, but early in March the whole force was encamped in the Salinas valley. Castro regarded the marching of a body of armed men through the country as an act of hostility, and ordered them out of the country. Instead of leaving, Fremont entrenched himself on an eminence known as Gabilian Peak (about thirty miles from Monterey), raised the stars and stripes over his barricade, and defied Castro. Castro maneuvered his troops on the plain below, but did not attack Fremont. After two days' waiting Fremont abandoned his position and began his march northward. On May 9, when near the Oregon line, he was overtaken by Lieutenant Gillespie, of the United States navy, with a dispatch from the president. Gillespie had left the United States in November, 1845, and, disguised, had crossed Mexico from Vera Cruz to Mazatlan, and from there had reached Monterey. The exact nature of the dispatches to Fremont is not known, but presumably they related to the impending war between Mexico and the United States, and the necessity for a prompt seizure of the country to prevent it from falling into the hands of England. Fremont returned to the Sacramento, where he encamped.

On the 14th of June, 1846, a body of American settlers from the Napa and Sacramento valleys, thirty-three in number, of which Ide, Semple, Grigsby and Merritt seem to have been the leaders, after a night's march, took possession of the old Castillo or fort at Sonoma, with its rusty muskets and unused cannon, and made Gen. M. G. Vallejo, Lieut.-Col. Prudon, Capt. Salvador Vallejo and Jacob P. Leese, a brother-in-law of the Vallejos, prisoners. There seems to have been no privates at the Castillo, all officers. Exactly what was the object of the American settlers in taking General Vallejo prisoner is not evident. General Vallejo was one of the few eminent Californians who favored the annexation of California to the United States. He is said to have made a speech favoring such a movement in the junta at Monterey a few months before. Castro regarded him with suspicion. The prisoners were sent under an armed escort to Fremont's camp. William B. Ide was elected captain of the revolutionists who remained at Sonoma, to "hold the fort." He issued a pronunciamiento in which he declared California a free and independent government, under the name of the California Republic. A nation must have a flag of its own, so one was improvised. It was made of a piece of cotton cloth, or manta, a yard wide and five feet long. Strips of red flannel torn from the shirt of one of the men were stitched on the bottom of the flag for stripes. With a blacking brush, or, as another authority says, the end of a chewed stick for a brush, and red paint, William L. Todd painted the figure of a grizzly bear passant on the field of the flag. The natives called Todd's bear "cochino," a pig; it resembled that animal more than a bear. A five-pointed star in the left upper corner, painted with the same coloring matter, and the words "California republic" printed on it in ink, completed the famous bear flag.

The California republic was ushered into existence June 14, 1846, attained the acme of its power July 4, when Ide and his fellow patriots burnt a quantity of powder in salutes, and fired off oratorical pyrotechnics in honor of the new republic. It utterly collapsed on the 9th of July, after an existence of twenty-five days, when news reached Sonoma that Commodore Sloat had raised the stars and stripes at Monterey and taken possession of California in the name of the United States. Lieutenant Revere arrived at Sonoma on the 9th and he it was who lowered the bear flag from the Mexican flagstaff, where it had floated through the brief existence of the California republic, and raised in its place the banner of the United States.

Commodore Sloat, who had anchored in Monterey Bay July 2, 1846, was for a time undecided whether to take possession of the country. He had no official information that war had been declared between the United States and Mexico; but, acting on the supposition that Captain Fremont had received definite instructions, on the 7th of July he raised the flag and took possession of the custom-house and government buildings at Monterey. Captain Montgomery, on the 9th, raised it at San Francisco, and on the same day the bear flag gave place to the stars and stripes at Sonoma.

General Castro was holding Santa Clara and San Jose when he received Commodore Sloat's proclamation informing him that the commodore had taken possession of Monterey. Castro, after reading the proclamation, which was written in Spanish, formed his men in line, and addressing them, said: "Monterey is taken by the Americans. What can I do with a handful of men against the United States? I am going to Mexico. All of you who wish to follow me, 'About face!' All that wish to remain can go to their homes."* A very small part of his force followed him.

Commodore Sloat was superseded by Commodore Stockton, who set about organizing an expedition to subjugate the southern part of the territory which remained loyal to Mexico. Fremont's exploring party, recruited to a battalion of one hundred and twenty men, had marched to Monterey, and from there was sent by vessel to San Diego to procure horses and prepare to act as cavalry.

While these stirring events were transpiring in the north, what was the condition in the south where the capital, Los Angeles, and the bulk of the population of the territory were located? Pio Pico had entered upon the duties of the governorship with a desire to bring peace and harmony to the distracted country. He appointed Juan Bandini, one of the ablest statesmen of the south, his secretary. After Bandini resigned he chose J. M. Covarrubias, and later Jose M. Moreno filled the office.

The principal offices of the territory had been divided equally between the politicians of the north and the south. While Los Angeles became the capital, and the departmental assembly met there, the military headquarters, the archives and the treasury remained at Monterey. But, notwithstanding this division of the spoils of office, the old feud between the arribeños and the abajeños would not down, and soon the old-time quarrel was on with all its bitterness. Castro, as military comandante, ignored the governor, and Alvarado was regarded by the sureños as an emissary of Castro's. The departmental assembly met at Los Angeles, in March, 1846. Pico presided, and in his opening message set forth the unfortunate condition of affairs in the department. Education was neglected; justice was not administered; the missions were so burdened by debt that but few of them could be rented; the army was disorganized and the treasury empty.

Not even the danger of war with the Americans could make the warring factions forget their fratricidal strife. Castro's proclamation against Fremont was construed by the sureños into a scheme to inveigle the governor to the north so that the comandante-general could depose him and seize the office for himself. Castro's preparations to resist by force the encroachments of the Americans were believed by Pico and the Angeleñians to be fitting out of an army to attack Los Angeles and overthrow the government.

On the 16th of June, Pico left Los Angeles for Monterey with a military force of a hundred men. The object of the expedition was to oppose, and, if possible, to depose Castro. He left the capital under the care of the ayuntamiento. On the 20th of June, Alcalde Gallardo reported to the ayuntamiento that he had positive information "that Don Castro had left Monterey and would arrive here in three days with a military force for the purpose of capturing this city." (Castro had left Monterey with a force of seventy men, but he had gone north to San Jose.) The sub-prefect, Don Abel Stearns, was authorized to enlist troops to preserve order. On the 23rd of June three companies were organized, an artillery company under

Miguel Pryor, a company of riflemen under Benito Wilson, and a cavalry company under Gorge Palomares. Pico, with his army at San Luis Obispo, was preparing to march against Monterey, when the news reached him of the capture of Sonoma by the Americans, and next day, July 12th, the news reached Los Angeles just as the council had decided on a plan of defense against Castro, who was five hundred miles away. Pico, on the impulse of the moment, issued a proclamation, in which he arraigned the United States for perfidy and treachery, and the gang of "North American adventurers," who captured Sonoma "with the blackest treason the spirit of evil can invent." His arraignment of the "North American nation" was so severe that some of his American friends in Los Angeles took umbrage at his pronunciamento. He afterwards tried to recall it, but it was too late; it had been published.

Castro, finding the "foreign adventurers" too numerous and too aggressive in the northern part of the territory, determined, with what men he could induce to go with him, to retreat to the south; but before so doing he sent a mediator to Pico to negotiate a treaty of peace and amity between the factions. On the 12th of July the two armies met at Santa Margarita, near San Luis Obispo. Castro brought the news that Commodore Sloat had hoisted the United States flag at Monterey and taken possession of the country for his government. The meeting of the governor and the comandante-general was not very cordial, but in the presence of the impending danger to the territory they concealed their mutual dislike and decided to do their best to defend the country they both loved.

Sorrowfully they began their retreat to the capital; but even threatened disaster to their common country could not wholly unite the north and the south. The respective armies, Castro's numbering about one hundred and fifty men, and Pico's one hundred and twenty, kept about a day's march apart. They reached Los Angeles, and preparations were begun to resist the invasion of the Americans. Pico issued a proclamation ordering all able-bodied men between fifteen and sixty years of age, native and naturalized, to take up arms to defend the country; any able-bodied Mexican refusing was to be treated as a traitor. There was no enthusiasm for the cause. The old factional jealousy and distrust was as potent as ever. The militia of the south would obey none but their own officers; Castro's troops, who considered themselves regulars, ridiculed the raw recruits of the sureños, while the naturalized foreigners of American extraction secretly sympathized with their own people.

Pico, to counteract the malign influence of his Santa Barbara proclamation and enlist the sympathy and more ready adhesion of the foreign element of Los Angeles, issued the following circular: (This circular or proclamation has never before found its way into print. I find no allusion to it in Bancroft's or Hittell's Histories. A copy, probably the only one in existence, was donated some years since to the Historical Society of Southern California.)

Seal Of Gobierno Del Dep. De Californias.
"Circular. — As Owing To The Unfortunate Condition Of Things That Now Prevails In This Department In Consequence Of The War Into Which The United States Has Provoked The Mexican Nation, Some Ill Feeling Might Spring Up Between The Citizens Of The Two Countries, Out Of Which Unfortunate Occurrences Might Grow, And As This Government

Desires To Remove Every Cause Of Friction, It Has Seen Fit, In The Use Of Its Power, To Issue The Present Circular.

"The Government Of The Department Of California Declares In The Most Solemn Manner That All The Citizens Of The United States That Have Come Lawfully Into Its Territory, Relying Upon The Honest Administration Of The Laws And The Observance Of The Prevailing Treaties, Shall Not Be Molested In The Least, And Their Lives And Property Shall Remain In Perfect Safety Under The Protection Of The Mexican Laws And Authorities Legally Constituted.

"Therefore, In The Name Of The Supreme Government Of The Nation, And By Virtue Of The Authority Vested Upon Me, I Enjoin Upon All The Inhabitants Of California To Observe Towards The Citizens Of The United States That Have Lawfully Come Among Us, The Kindest And Most Cordial Conduct, And To Abstain From All Acts Of Violence Against Their Persons Or Property; Provided They Remain Neutral, As Heretofore, And Take No Part In The Invasion Effected By The Armies Of Their Nation.

"The Authorities Of The Various Municipalities And Corporations Will Be Held Strictly Responsible For The Faithful Fulfillment Of This Order, And Shall, As Soon As Possible, Take The Necessary Measures To Bring It To The Knowledge Of The People. God And Liberty.

"Pio Pico.

"Jose Matias Mareno, Secretary Pro Tem."

Angeles, July 27, 1846.

When we consider the conditions existing in California at the time this circular was issued, its sentiments reflect great credit on Pico for his humanity and forbearance. A little over a month before, a party of Americans seized General Vallejo and several other prominent Californians in their homes and incarcerated them in prison at Sutter's Fort. Nor was this outrage mitigated when the stars and stripes were raised. The perpetrators of the outrage were not punished. These native Californians were kept in prison nearly two months without any charge against them. Besides, Governor Pico and the leading Californians very well knew that the Americans whose lives and property this proclamation was designed to protect would not remain neutral when their countrymen invaded the territory. Pio Pico deserved better treatment from the Americans than he received. He was robbed of his landed possessions by unscrupulous land sharks, and his character defamed by irresponsible historical scribblers.

Pico made strenuous efforts to raise men and means to resist the threatened invasion. He had mortgaged the government house to de Celis for $2,000, the mortgage to be paid "as soon as order shall be established in the department." This loan was really negotiated to fit out the expedition against Castro, but a part of it was expended after his return to Los Angeles in procuring supplies while preparing to meet the American army. The government had but little credit. The moneyed men of the pueblo were averse to putting money into what was almost sure to prove a lost cause. The bickerings and jealousies between the factions neutralized to a considerable degree the efforts of Pico and Castro to mobilize the army.

Castro established his camp on the mesa east of the river. Here he and Andres Pico undertook to drill the somewhat incongruous collection of hombres in

117

military maneuvering. Their entire force at no time exceeded three hundred men. These were poorly armed and lacking in discipline.

We left Stockton at Monterey preparing an expedition against Castro at Los Angeles. On taking command of the Pacific squadron, July 29, he issued a proclamation. It was as bombastic as the pronunciamiento of a Mexican governor. Bancroft says: "The paper was made up of falsehood, of irrelevant issues and bombastic ranting in about equal parts, the tone being offensive and impolitic even in those inconsiderable portions which were true and legitimate." His only object in taking possession of the country was "to save from destruction the lives and property of the foreign residents and citizens of the territory who had invoked his protection." In view of Pico's humane circular and the uniform kind treatment that the Californians accorded the American residents, there was very little need of Stockton's interference on that score. Commodore Sloat did not approve of Stockton's proclamation or of his policy.

On the 6th of August, Stockton reached San Pedro and landed three hundred and sixty sailors and marines. These were drilled in military movements on land and prepared for the march to Los Angeles.

Castro sent two commissioners, Pablo de La Guerra and Jose M. Flores, to Stockton, asking for a conference and a cessation of hostilities while negotiations were pending. They asked that the United States forces remain at San Pedro while the terms of the treaty were under discussion. These requests Commodore Stockton peremptorily refused, and the commissioners returned to Los Angeles without stating the terms on which they proposed to treat.

In several so-called histories, I find a very dramatic account of this interview. On the arrival of the commissioners they were marched up to the mouth of an immense mortar, shrouded in skins save its huge aperture. Their terror and discomfiture were plainly discernible. Stockton received them with a stern and forbidding countenance, harshly demanding their mission, which they disclosed in great confusion. They bore a letter from Castro proposing a truce, each party to hold its own possessions until a general pacification should be had. This proposal Stockton rejected with contempt, and dismissed the commissioners with the assurance that only an immediate disbandment of his forces and an unconditional surrender would shield Castro from the vengeance of an incensed foe. The messengers remounted their horses in dismay and fled back to Castro." The mortar story, it is needless to say, is pure fabrication, yet it runs through a number of so-called histories of California. Castro, on the 9th of August, held a council of war with his officers at the Campo en La Mesa. He announced his intention of leaving the country for the purpose of reporting to the supreme government, and of returning at some future day to punish the usurpers. He wrote to Pico: "I can count only one hundred men, badly armed, worse supplied and discontented by reason of the miseries they suffer; so that I have reason to fear that not even these men will fight when the necessity arises." And this is the force that some imaginative historians estimate at eight hundred to one thousand men.

Pico and Castro left Los Angeles on the night of August 10, for Mexico; Castro going by the Colorado River route to Sonora, and Pico, after being concealed for a time by his brother-in-law, Juan Froster, at the Santa Margarita and narrowly escaping capture by Fremont's men, finally reached Lower California and later on crossed the Gulf to Sonora.

Stockton began his march on Los Angeles August II. He took with him a battery of four guns. The guns were mounted on carretas, and each gun drawn by four oxen. He had with him a good brass band.

Major Fremont, who had been sent to San Diego with his battalion of one hundred and seventy men, had, after considerable skirmishing among the ranchos, secured enough horses to move, and on the 8th of August had begun his march to join Stockton. He took with him one hundred and twenty men, leaving about fifty to garrison San Diego.

Stockton consumed three days on the march. Fremont's troops joined him just south of the city, and at 4 p. m. of the 13th the combined force, numbering nearly five hundred men, entered the town without opposition, "our entry," says Major Fremont, "having more the effect of a parade of home guards than of an enemy taking possession of a conquered town." Stockton reported finding at Castro's abandoned camp ten pieces of artillery, four of them spiked. Fremont says he (Castro) "had buried part of his guns." Castro's troops that he had brought down with him took their departure for their northern homes soon after their general left, breaking up into small squads as they advanced. The southern troops that Pico had recruited dispersed to their homes before the arrival of the Americans. Squads of Fremont's battalion were sent out to scour the country and bring in any of the Californian officers or leading men whom they could find. These, when found, were paroled.

Another of those historical myths, like the mortar story previously mentioned, which is palmed off on credulous readers as genuine history, runs as follows: "Stockton, while en route from San Pedro to Los Angeles, was informed by a courier from Castro 'that if he marched upon the town he would find it the grave of himself and men.' 'Then,' answered the commodore, 'tell the general to have the bells ready to toll at eight o'clock, as I shall be there by that time.' " As Castro left Los Angeles the day before Stockton began his march from San Pedro, and when the commodore entered the city the Mexican general was probably two hundred miles away, the bell tolling myth goes to join its kindred myths in the category of history as it should not be written.

On the 17th of August, Stockton issued a second proclamation, in which he signs himself commander-in-chief and governor of the territory of California. It was milder in tone and more dignified than the first. He informed the people that their country now belonged to the United States. For the present it would be governed by martial law. They were invited to elect their local officers if those now in office refused to serve.

Four days after the capture of Los Angeles, The Warren, Captain Hull, commander, anchored at San Pedro. She brought official notice of the declaration of war between the United States and Mexico. Then for the first time Stockton learned that there had been an official declaration of war between the two countries. United States officers had waged war and had taken possession of California upon the strength of a rumor that hostilities existed between the countries.

119

The conquest, if conquest it can be called, was accomplished without the loss of a life, if we except the two Americans, Fowler and Cowie, of the Bear Flag party, who were brutally murdered by a band of Californians under Padillo, and the equally brutal shooting of Beryessa and the two de Haro boys by the Americans at San Rafael. These three men were shot as spies, but there was no proof that they were such, and they were not tried. These murders occurred before Commodore Sloat raised the stars and stripes at Monterey.

On the 15th of August, 1846, just thirty-seven days after the raising of the stars and stripes at Monterey, the first newspaper ever published in California made its appearance. It was published at Monterey by Semple and Colton and named The Californian. Rev. Walter Colton was a chaplain in the United States navy and came to California on the Congress with Commodore Stockton. He was made alcalde of Monterey and built, by the labor of the chain gang and from contributions and fines, the first schoolhouse in California, named for him Colton Hall. Colton thus describes the other member of the firm, Dr. Robert Semple: "My partner is an emigrant from Kentucky, who stands six feet eight in his stockings. He is in a buckskin dress, a foxskin cap; is true with his rifle, ready with his pen and quick at the type case." Semple came to California in 1845, with the Hastings party, and was one of the leaders in the Bear Flag revolution. The type and press used were brought to California by Augustin V. Zamorano in 1834, and by him sold to the territorial government, and had been used for printing bandos and pronunciamentos. The only paper the publishers of The Californian could procure was that used in the manufacture of cigarettes, which came in sheets a little larger than foolscap. The font of type was short of w's, so two v's were substituted for that letter, and when these ran out two u's were used. The paper was moved to San Francisco in 1848 and later on consolidated with the California Star.

CHAPTER XVII. REVOLT OF THE CALIFORNIANS.

Hostilities had ceased in all parts of the territory. The leaders of the Californians had escaped to Mexico, and Stockton, regarding the conquest as completed, set about organizing a government for the conquered territory. Fremont was to be appointed military governor. Detachments from his battalion were to be detailed to garrison different towns, while Stockton, with what recruits he could gather in California, and his sailors and marines, was to undertake a naval expedition against the west coast of Mexico, land his forces at Mazatlan or Acapulco and march overland to "shake hands with General Taylor at the gates of Mexico." Captain Gillespie was made military commandant of the southern department, with headquarters at Los Angeles, and assigned a garrison of fifty men. Commodore Stockton left Los Angeles for the north September 2. Fremont, with the remainder of his battalion, took up his line of march for Monterey a few days later. Gillespie's orders were to place the city under martial law, but not to enforce the more burdensome restrictions upon quiet and well-disposed citizens. A conciliatory policy in accordance with instructions of the secretary of the navy was to be adopted and the people were to be encouraged to "neutrality, self-government and friendship."

Nearly all historians who have written upon this subject lay the blame for the subsequent uprising of the Californians and their revolt against the rule of the military commandant, Gillespie, to his petty tyrannies. Col. J. J. Warner, in his Historical Sketch of Los Angeles County, says: "Gillespie attempted by a coercive system to effect a moral and social change in the habits, diversions and pastimes of the people and to reduce them to his standard of propriety." Warner was not an impartial judge. He had a grievance against Gillespie which embittered him against the captain. Gillespie may have been lacking in tact, and his schooling in the navy under the tyrannical regime of the quarterdeck of sixty years ago was not the best training to fit him for government, but it is hardly probable that in two weeks' time he undertook to enforce a "coercive system" looking toward an entire change in the moral and social habits of the people. Los Angeles under Mexican domination was a hotbed of revolutions. It had a turbulent and restless element among its inhabitants that was never happier than when fomenting strife and conspiring to overthrow those in power. Of this class Colton, writing in 1846, says: "They drift about like Arabs. If the tide of fortune turns against them they disband and scatter to the four winds. They never become martyrs to any cause. They are too numerous to be brought to punishment by any of their governors, and thus escape justice." There was a conservative class in the territory, made up principally of the large landed proprietors, both native and foreign-born, but these exerted small influence in controlling the turbulent. While Los Angeles had a monopoly of this turbulent and revolutionary element, other settlements in the territory furnished their full quota of that class of political knight errants whose chief pastime was revolution, and whose capital consisted of a gaily caparisoned steed, a riata, a lance, a dagger and possibly a pair of horse pistols. These were the fellows whose "habits, diversions and pastimes" Gillespie undertook to reduce "to his standard of propriety." I That Commodore Stockton should have left Gillespie so small a garrison to hold the city and surrounding country in subjection shows that either he was ignorant of the character of the people, or that he placed too great reliance in the completeness of their subjection. With Castro's men in the city or dispersed among the neighboring ranchos, many of them still retaining their arms, and all of them ready to rally at a moment's notice to the call of their leaders; with no reinforcements nearer than five hundred miles to come to the aid of Gillespie in case of an uprising, it was foolhardiness in Stockton to entrust the holding of the most important place in California to a mere handful of men, half disciplined and poorly equipped, without fortifications for defense or supplies to hold out in case of a siege.

Scarcely had Stockton and Fremont, with their men, left the city before trouble began. The turbulent element of the city fomented strife and seized every occasion to annoy and harass the military commandant and his men. While his "petty tyrannies," so called, which were probably nothing more than the enforcement of martial law, may have been somewhat provocative, the real cause was more deep seated. The Californians, without provocation on their part and without really knowing the cause why, found their country invaded, their property taken from them and their government in the hands of an alien race, foreign to them in customs and religion. They would have been a tame and spiritless people indeed, had they neglected the opportunity that Stockton's blundering gave them to regain their liberties. They did not waste much time. Within two weeks from the time Stockton sailed from San Pedro hostilities had begun and the city was in a state of siege.

Gillespie, writing in the Sacramento Statesman in 1858, thus describes the first attack: "On the 22nd of September, at three o'clock in the morning, a party of sixty-five Californians and Sonorenos made an attack upon my small command quartered in the government house. We were not wholly surprised, and with twenty-one rifles we beat them back without loss to ourselves, killing and wounding three of their number. When daylight came, Lieutenant Hensley, with a few men, took several prisoners and drove the Californians from the town. This party was merely the nucleus of a revolution commenced and known to Colonel Fremont before he left Los Angeles. In twenty-four hours, six hundred well-mounted horsemen, armed with escopetas (shotguns), lances and one fine brass piece of light artillery, surrounded Los Angeles and summoned me to surrender. There were three old honey-combed iron guns (spiked) in the corral of my quarters, which we at once cleared and mounted upon the axles of carts."

Serbulo Varela, a young man of some ability, but of a turbulent and reckless character, had been the leader at first, but as the uprising assumed the character of a revolution, Castro's old officers came to the front. Capt. Jose Maria Flores was chosen comandante-general; Jose Antonio Carrillo, major-general; and Andres Pico, comandante de escuadron. The main camp of the insurgents was located on the mesa, east of the river, at a place called Paredon Blanco (White Bluff).

On the 24th of September, from the camp at White Bluff, was issued the famous Pronunciamiento de Barelas y otros Californias contra Los Americanos (The Proclamation of Barelas and other Californians against the Americans). It was signed by Serbulo Varela (spelled Barelas), Leonardo Cota and over three hundred others. Although this proclamation is generally credited to Flores, there is no evidence to show that he had anything to do with framing it. He promulgated it over his signature October I. It is probable that it was written by Varela and Cota. It has been the custom of American writers to sneer at this production as florid and bombastic. In fiery invective and fierce denunciation it is the equal of Patrick Henry's famous "Give me liberty or give me death!" Its recital of wrongs is brief, but to the point. "And shall we be capable of permitting ourselves to be subjugated and to accept in silence the heavy chains of slavery? Shall we lose the soil inherited from our fathers, which cost them so much blood? Shall we leave our families victims of the most barbarous servitude? Shall we wait to see our wives outraged, our innocent children beaten by American whips, our property sacked, our temples profaned, to drag out a life full of shame and disgrace? No! a thousand times no! Compatriots, death rather than that! Who of you does not feel his heart beat and his blood boil on contemplating our situation? Who will be the Mexican that will not be indignant and rise in arms to destroy our oppressors? We believe there will be not one so vile and cowardly!"

Gillespie had left the government house (located on what is now the site of the St. Charles Hotel) and taken a position on Fort Hill, where he had erected a temporary barricade of sacks filled with earth and had mounted his cannon there. The Americans had been summoned to surrender, but had refused. They were besieged by the Californians. There was but little firing between the combatants, an occasional sortie and a volley of rifle balls by the Americans when the Californians approached too near. The Californians were well mounted, but poorly armed, their weapons being principally muskets, shotguns, pistols, lances and riatas; while the Americans were armed with long-range rifles, of which the Californians had a wholesome dread. The fear of these arms and his cannon doubtless saved Gillespie and his men from capture.

On the 24th Gillespie dispatched a messenger to find Stockton at Monterey, or at San Francisco if he had left Monterey, and apprise him of the perilous situation of the Americans at Los Angeles. Gillespie's dispatch bearer, John Brown, better known by his California nickname, Juan Flaco or Lean John, made one of the most wonderful rides in history. Gillespie furnished Juan Flaco with a package of cigarettes, the paper of each bearing the inscription, "Believe the bearer;" these were stamped with Gillespie's seal. Brown started from Los Angeles at 8 p. m., September 24, and claimed to have reached Yerba Buena at 8 p. m. of the 28th, a ride of six hundred and thirty miles in four days. This is incorrect. Colton, who was alcalde of Monterey at that time, notes Brown's arrival at that place on the evening of the 29th. Colton, in his "Three Years in California," says that Brown rode the whole distance (Los Angeles to Monterey) of four hundred and sixty miles in fifty-two hours, during which time he had not slept. His intelligence was for Commodore Stockton and, in the nature of the case, was not committed to paper, except a few words rolled in a cigar fastened in his hair. But the commodore had sailed for San Francisco and it was necessary he should go one hundred and forty miles further. He was quite exhausted and was allowed to sleep three hours. Before day he was up and away on his journey. Gillespie, in a letter published in the Los Angeles Star, May 28, 1858, describing Juan Flaco's ride says: "Before sunrise of the 29th he was lying in the bushes at San Francisco, in front of the Congress frigate, waiting for the early market boat to come on shore, and he delivered my dispatches to Commodore Stockton before 7 o'clock."

In trying to steal through the picket line of the Mexicans at Los Angeles, he was discovered and pursued by a squad of them. A hot race ensued. Finding the enemy gaining on him he forced his horse to leap a wide ravine. A shot from one of his pursuers mortally wounded his horse, which, after running a short distance, fell dead. Flaco, carrying his spurs and riata, made his way on foot in the darkness to Las Virgines, a distance of twenty-seven miles. Here he secured another mount and again set off on his perilous journey. The trail over which Flaco held his way was not like "the road from Winchester town, a good, broad highway leading down," but instead a Camino de heradura, bridle path, now winding up through rocky cañons, skirting along the edge of precipitous cliffs, then zigzagging down chaparral covered mountains; now over the sands of the sea beach and again across long stretches of brown mesa, winding through narrow valleys and out onto the rolling hills — a trail as nature made it, unchanged by the hand of man. Such was the highway over which Flaco's steeds "stretched away with utmost speed." Harassed and pursued by the enemy, facing death night and day, with scarcely a stop or a stay to eat or sleep, Juan Flaco rode six hundred miles.

> *"Of All The Rides Since The Birth Of Time,*
> *Told In Story Or Sung In Rhyme.*
> *The Fleetest Ride That Ever Was Sped,"*

was Juan Flaco's ride from Los Angeles to San Francisco. Longfellow has immortalized the "Ride of Paul Revere," Robert Browning tells in stirring verse of the riders who brought the good news from Ghent to Aix, and Buchanan Read thrills us with the heroic measures of Sheridan's Ride. No poet has sung of Juan Flaco's wonderful ride, fleeter, longer and more perilous than any of these. Flaco rode six hundred miles through the enemy's country, to bring aid to a besieged garrison, while Revere and Jorris and Sheridan were in the country of friends or protected by an army from enemies.

Gillespie's situation was growing more and more desperate each day. B. D. Wilson, who with a company of riflemen had been on an expedition against the Indians, had been ordered by Gillespie to join him. They reached the Chino ranch, where a fight took place between them and the Californians. Wilson's men being " out of ammunition were compelled to surrender. In the charge upon the adobe, where Wilson and his men had taken refuge, Carlos Ballestaros had been killed and several Californians wounded. This and Gillespie's stubborn resistance had embittered the Californians against him and his men. The Chino prisoners had been saved from massacre after their surrender by the firmness and bravery of Varela. If Gillespie continued to hold the town his obstinacy might bring down the vengeance of the Californians not only upon him and his men, but upon many of the American residents of the south, who had favored their countrymen.

Finally Flores issued his ultimatum to the Americans, surrender within twenty-four hours or take the consequences of an onslaught by the Californians, which might result in the massacre of the entire garrison. In the meantime he kept his cavalry deployed on the hills, completely investing the Americans. Despairing of assistance from Stockton, on the advice of Wilson, who had been permitted by Flores to intercede with Gillespie, articles of capitulation were drawn up and signed by Gillespie and the leaders of the Californians. On the 30th of September the Americans marched out of the city with all the honors of war, drums beating, colors flying, and two pieces of artillery mounted on carts, drawn by oxen. They arrived at San Pedro without molestation and four or five days later embarked on the merchant ship Vandalia, which remained at anchor in the bay. Gillespie in his march was accompanied by a few of the American residents and probably a dozen of the Chino prisoners, who had been exchanged for the same number of Californians, whom he had held under arrest most likely as hostages.

Gillespie took two cannon with him when he evacuated the city, leaving two spiked and broken on Fort Hill. There seems to have been a proviso in the articles of capitulation requiring him to deliver the guns to Flores on reaching the embarcadero. If there was such a stipulation Gillespie violated it. He spiked the guns, broke off the trunnions and rolled one of them into the bay.

CHAPTER XVIII.
THE DEFEAT AND RETREAT OF MERVINE'S MEN.

The revolt of the Californians at Los Angeles was followed by similar uprisings in the different centers of population where American garrisons were stationed. Upon the receipt of Gillespie's message Commodore Stockton ordered Captain Mervine to proceed at once to San Pedro to regain, if possible, the lost territory. Juan Flaco had delivered his message to Stockton on September 30. Early on the morning of October 1st, Captain Mervine got under way for San Pedro. "He went ashore at Sausalito," says Gillespie, "on some trivial excuse, and a dense fog coming on he was compelled to remain there until the 4th."

Of the notable events occurring during the conquest of California there are few others of which there are so contradictory accounts as that known as the battle of Dominguez Ranch, where Mervine was defeated and compelled to retreat to San Pedro. Historians differ widely in the number engaged and in the number killed. The following account of Mervine's expedition I take from a log book kept by Midshipman and Acting Lieut. Robert C. Duvall of the Savannah. He commanded a company during the battle. This book was donated to the Historical Society of Southern California by Dr. J. E. Cowles of Los Angeles, a nephew of Lieutenant Duvall. The account given by Lieutenant Duvall is one of the fullest and most accurate in existence.

"At 9.30 a. m." (October 1, 1846), says Lieutenant Duvall, "we commenced working out of the harbor of San Francisco on the ebb tide. The ship anchored at Sausalito, where, on account of a dense fog, it remained until the 4th, when it put to sea. On the 7th the ship entered the harbor of San Pedro. At 6:30 p. m., as we were standing in for anchorage, we made out the American merchant ship Vandalia, having on her decks a body of men. On passing she saluted with two guns, which was repeated with three cheers, which we returned. * * * * Brevet Capt. Archibald Gillespie came on board and reported that he had evacuated the Pueblo de Los Angeles on account of the overpowering force of the enemy and had retired with his men on board the Vandalia after having spiked his guns, one of which he threw into the water. He also reported that the whole of California below the pueblo had risen in arms against our authorities, headed by Flores, a Mexican captain on furlough in this country, who had but a few days ago given his parole of honor not to take up arms against the United States. We made preparations to land a force to march to the pueblo at daylight.

"October 8, at 6 a. m., all the boats left the ship for the purpose of landing the forces, numbering in all two hundred and ninety-nine men, including the volunteers under command of Captain Gillespie. At 6:30 all were landed without opposition, the enemy in small detachments retreating toward the pueblo. From their movements we apprehended that their whole force was near. Captain Mervine sent on board ship for a reinforcement of eighty men, under command of Lieut. R. B. Hitchcock. At 8 a. m. the several companies, all under command of Capt William Mervine, took up the line of march for the purpose of retaking the pueblo. The

126

enemy retreated as our forces advanced. (On landing, William A. Smith, first cabin boy, was killed by the accidental discharge of a Colt's pistol.) The reinforcements under the command of Lieut. R. B. Hitchcock returned on board ship. For the first four miles our march was through hills and ravines, which the enemy might have taken advantage of, but preferred to occupy as spectators only, until our approach. A few shots from our flankers (who were the volunteer riflemen) would start them off; they returned the compliment before going. The remainder of our march was performed over a continuous plain overgrown with wild mustard, rising in places to six or eight feet in height. The ground was excessively dry, the clouds of dust were suffocating and there was not a breath of wind in motion. There was no water on our line of march for ten or twelve miles and we suffered greatly from thirst.

"At 2:30 p. m. we reached our camping ground. The enemy appeared in considerable numbers. Their numbers continued to increase until sundown, when they formed on a hill near us, gradually inclining towards our camp. They were admirably formed for a cavalry charge. We drew up our forces to meet them, but finding they were disposed to remain stationary, the marines, under command of Captain Marston, the Colt's riflemen, under command of Lieut. I. B. Carter and myself, and the volunteers, under command of Capt. A. Gillespie, were ordered to charge on them, which we did. They stood their ground until our shots commenced 'telling' on them, when they took to flight in every direction. They continued to annoy us by firing into our camp through the night. About 2 a. m. they brought a piece of artillery and fired into our camp, the shot striking the ground near us. The marines, riflemen and volunteers were sent in pursuit of the gun, but could see or hear nothing of it.

"We left our camp the next morning at 6 o'clock. Our plan of march was in column by platoon. We had not proceeded far before the enemy appeared before us drawn up on each side of the road, mounted on fine horses, each man armed with a lance and carbine. They also had a field piece (a four-pounder), to which were hitched eight or ten horses, placed on the road ahead of us.

"Captain Mervine, thinking it was the enemy's intention to throw us into confusion by using their gun on us loaded with round shot and copper grape shot and then charge us with their cavalry, ordered us to form a square — which was the order of march throughout the battle. When within about four hundred yards of them the enemy opened on us with their artillery. We made frequent charges, driving them before us, and at one time causing them to leave some of their cannon balls and cartridges; but owing to the rapidity with which they could carry off the gun, using their lassos on every part, enabled them to choose their own distance, entirely out of all range of our muskets. Their horsemen kept out of danger, apparently content to let the gun do the fighting. They kept up a constant fire with their carbines, but these did no harm. The enemy numbered between one hundred and seventy-five and two hundred strong.

"Finding it impossible to capture the gun, the retreat was sounded. The captain consulted with his officers on the best steps to be taken. It was decided unanimously to return on board ship. To continue the march would sacrifice a number of lives to no purpose, for, admitting we could have reached the pueblo, all communications would be cut off with the ship, and we would further be constantly annoyed by their artillery without the least chance of capturing it. It was reported that the enemy were between five and six hundred strong at the city and it was thought he had more artillery. On retreating they got the gun planted on a hill ahead of us.

"The captain made us an address, saying to the troops that it was his intention to march straight ahead in the same orderly manner in which we had advanced, and that sooner than he would surrender to such an enemy, he would sacrifice himself and every other man in his command. The enemy fired into us four times on the retreat, the fourth shot falling short, the report of the gun indicating a small quantity of powder, after which they remained stationary and manifested no further disposition to molest us. We proceeded quietly on our march to the landing, where we found a body of men under command of Lieutenant Hitchcock with two nine-pounder cannon gotten from the Vandalia to render us assistance in case we should need it.

"We presented truly a pitiable condition, many being barely able to drag one foot after the other from excessive fatigue, having gone through the exertions and excitement in battle and afterwards performing a march of eighteen or twenty miles without rest. This is the first battle I have ever been engaged in, and, having taken particular notice of those around me, I can assert that no men could have acted more bravely. Even when their shipmates were falling by their sides, I saw but one impulse and that was to push forward, and when retreat was ordered I noticed a general reluctance to turn their backs to the enemy.

"The following is a list of the killed and wounded: Michael Hoey, ordinary seaman, killed; David Johnson, ordinary seaman, killed; William H. Berry, ordinary seaman, mortally wounded; Charles Sommers, musician, mortally wounded; John Tyre, seaman, severely wounded; John Anderson, seaman, severely wounded; recovery doubtful. The following named were slightly wounded: William Conland, marine; Hiram Rockvill, marine; H. Linland, marine; James Smith, marine.

"On the following morning we buried the bodies of William A. Smith, Charles Sommers, David Johnson and Michael Hoey on an island in the harbor.

"At II a. m. the captain called a council of commissioned officers regarding the proper course to adopt in the present crisis, which decided that no force should be landed, and that the ship remain here until further orders from the commodore, who is daily expected."

Entry in the log for Sunday, nth: "William H. Berry, ordinary seaman, departed this life from the effect of wounds received in battle. Sent his body for interment to Dead Man's Island, so named by us. Mustered the command at quarters, after which performed divine service."

From this account it will be seen that the number killed and died of wounds received in battle was four; number wounded six, and one accidentally killed before the battle. On October 22nd, Henry Lewis died and was buried on the island. Lewis' name does not appear in the list of wounded. It is presumable that he died of disease. Six of the crew of the Savannah were buried on Dead Man's Island, four of whom were killed in battle. Lieutenant Duvall gives the following list of the officers in the "Expedition on the march to retake Pueblo de Los Angeles:" Capt. William Mervine, commanding; Capt. Ward Marston, commanding marines; Brevet Capt. A. H. Gillespie, commanding volunteers; Lieut. Henry W. Queen, adjutant; Lieut. B. F. Pinckney, commanding first company; Lieut. W. Rinckindoff, commanding second company; Lieut. I. B. Carter, Colt's riflemen; Midshipman R. D. Minor, acting lieutenant second company; Midshipman S. P. Griffin, acting lieutenant first company; Midshipman P. G. Walmough, acting lieutenant second company; Midshipman R. C. Duvall, acting lieutenant Colt's riflemen; Captain Clark and Captain Goodsall, commanding pikemen; Lieutenant Hensley, first lieutenant volunteers; Lieutenant Russeau, second lieutenant volunteers.

The piece of artillery that did such deadly execution on the Americans was the famous Old Woman's gun. It was a bronze four-pounder, or pedrero (swivel-gun) that for a number of years had stood on the plaza in front of the church, and was used for firing salutes on feast days and other occasions. When on the approach of Stockton's and Fremont's forces Castro abandoned his artillery and fled, an old lady, Dona Clara Cota de Reyes, declared that the gringos should not have the church's gun; so, with the assistance of her daughters, she buried it in a cane patch near her residence, which stood on the east side of Alameda street, near First. When the Californians revolted against Gillespie's rule the gun was unearthed and used against him. The Historical Society of Southern California has in its possession a brass grapeshot, one of a charge that was fired into the face of Fort Hill at Gillespie's men when they were posted on the hill. This gun was in the exhibit of trophies at the New Orleans Exposition in 1885. The label on it read: "Trophy 53, No. 63, Class 7. Used by Mexico against the United States at the battle of Dominguez' Ranch, October 9, 1846; at San Gabriel and the Mesa, January 8 and 9, 1847; used by the United States forces against Mexico at Mazatlan, November II, 1847; Urios (crew all killed or wounded), Palos Prietos, December 13, 1847, and Lower California, at San Jose, February 15, 1848."

Before the battle the old gun had been mounted on forward axle of a Jersey wagon, which a man by the name of Hunt had brought across the plains the year before. It was lashed to the axle by means of rawhide thongs, and was drawn by riatas, as described by Lieutenant Duvall. The range was obtained by raising or lowering the pole of the wagon. Ignacio Aguilar acted as gunner, and having neither lanyard or pent-stock to fire it, he touched off the gun with the lighted end of a cigarette. Never before or since, perhaps, was a battle won with such crude artillery. Jose Antonio Carrillo was in command of the Californians. During the skirmishing of the first day he had between eighty and ninety men. During the night of the 8th Flores joined him with a force of sixty men. Next morning Flores returned to Los Angeles, taking with him twenty men. Carrillo's force in the battle numbered about one hundred and twenty men. Had Mervine known that the Californians had fired their last shot (their powder being exhausted) he could have pushed on and captured the pueblo.

The expulsion of Gillespie's garrison from Los Angeles and the defeat of Mervine's force raised the spirits of the Californians, and there was great rejoicing at the pueblo. Detachments of Flores' army were kept at Sepulveda's rancho, the Palos Verdes, and at Temple's rancho of the Cerritos, to watch the Savannah and report any attempt at landing. The leaders of the revolt were not so sanguine of success as the rank and file. They were without means to procure arms and supplies. There was a scarcity of ammunition, too. An inferior article of gunpowder was manufactured in limited quantities at San Gabriel. The only uniformity in weapons was in lances. These were rough, home-made affairs, the blade beaten out of a rasp or file, and the shaft a willow pole about eight feet long. These weapons were formidable in a charge against infantry, but easily parried by a swordsman in a cavalry charge.

After the defeat of Mervine, Flores set about reorganizing the territorial government. He called together the departmental assembly. It met at the capital (Los Angeles) October 26th. The members present, Figueroa, Botello, Guerra and Olvera, were all from the south. The assembly decided to fill the place of governor, vacated by Pico, and that of comandante-general, left vacant by the flight of Castro.

Jose Maria Flores, who was now recognized as the leader of the revolt against American rule, was chosen to fill both offices, and the two offices, as had formerly been the custom, were united in one person. He chose Narciso Botello for his secretary. Flores, who was Mexican born, was an intelligent and patriotic officer. He used every means in his power to prepare his forces for the coming conflict with the Americans, but with little success. The old jealousy of the hijos del pais against the Mexican would crop out, and it neutralized his efforts. There were bickerings and complaints in the ranks and among the officers. The natives claimed that a Californian ought to be chief in command.

The feeling of jealousy against Flores at length culminated in open revolt. Flores had decided to send the prisoners taken at the Chino fight to Mexico. His object was twofold — first, to enhance his own glory with the Mexican government, and, secondly, by showing what the Californians had already accomplished to obtain aid in the coming conflict. As most of these men were married to California wives, and by marriage related to many of the leading California families of the south, there was at once a family uproar and fierce denunciations of Flores. But as the Chino prisoners were foreigners, and had been taken while fighting against the Mexican government, it was necessary to disguise the hostility to Flores under some other pretext. He was charged with the design of running away to Sonora with the public funds. On the night of December 3, Francisco Rico, at the head of a party of Californians, took possession of the cuartel, or guard house, and arrested Flores. A special session of the assembly was called to investigate the charges.

Flores expressed his willingness to give up his purpose of sending the Chino prisoners to Mexico, and the assembly found no foundation to the charge of his design of running away with the public funds, nor did they find any funds to run away with. Flores was liberated, and Rico imprisoned in turn.

Flores was really the last Mexican governor of California. Like Pico, he was elected by the territorial legislature, but he was not confirmed by the Mexican congress. Generals Scott and Taylor were keeping President Santa Anna and his congress on the move so rapidly they had no time to spare for California affairs.

Flores was governor from October 26, 1846, to January 8, 1847.

With a threatened invasion by the Americans and a divided people within, it was hard times in the old pueblo. The town had to supply the army with provisions. The few who possessed money hid it away and all business was suspended except preparations to meet the invaders.

CHAPTER XIX.
THE FINAL CONQUEST OF CALIFORNIA.

Commodore Stockton, convinced that the revolt of the Californians was a serious affair, ordered Fremont's battalion, which had been recruited to one hundred and sixty men, to proceed to the south to co-operate with him in quelling the rebellion. The battalion sailed on the Sterling, but shortly after putting to sea, meeting the Vandalia, Fremont learned of Mervine's defeat and also that no horses could be procured in the lower country; the vessel was put about and the battalion landed at Monterey, October 28. It was decided to recruit the battalion to a regiment and mounting it to march down the coast. Recruiting was actively begun among the newly arrived immigrants. Horses and saddles were procured by giving receipts on the government, payable after the close of the war or by confiscation if it brought returns quicker than receipts.

The report of the revolt in the south quickly spread among the Californians in the north and they made haste to resist their spoilers. Manuel Castro was made comandante of the military forces of the north, headquarters at San Luis Obispo. Castro collected a force of about one hundred men, well mounted but poorly armed. His purpose was to carry on a sort of guerrilla warfare, capturing men and horses from the enemy whenever an opportunity offered.

Fremont, now raised to the rank of lieutenant-colonel in the regular army with headquarters at Monterey, was rapidly mobilizing his motley collection of recruits into a formidable force. Officers and men were scouring the country for recruits, horses, accouterments and supplies. Two of these recruiting squads encountered the enemy in considerable force and an engagement known as the battle of Natividad ensued. Capt. Charles Burroughs with thirty-four men and two hundred horses, recruited at Sacramento, arrived at San Juan Bautista, November 15, on his way to Monterey on the same day Captain Thompson, with about the same number of men recruited at San Jose, reached San Juan. The Californians, with the design of capturing the horses, made a night march from their camp on the Salinas. At Gomez rancho they took prisoner Thomas O. Larkin, the American consul, who was on his way from Monterey to San Francisco on official business. On the morning of the 16th the Americans began their march for Monterey. At Gomez rancho their advance learned of the presence of the enemy and of the capture of Larkin. A squad of six or eight scouts was sent out to find the Californians. The scouts encountered a detachment of Castro's force at Encinalitos (Little Oaks) and a fight ensued. The main body of the enemy came up and surrounded the grove of oaks. The scouts, though greatly outnumbered, were well armed with long range rifles and held the enemy at bay, until Captains Burroughs and Thompson brought up their companies. Burroughs, who seems to have been the ranking officer, hesitated to charge the Californians, who had the superior force, and besides he was fearful of losing his horses and thus delaying Fremont's movements. But, taunted with cowardice and urged on by Thompson, a fire eater, who was making loud protestations of his bravery, Burroughs ordered a charge. The Americans, badly mounted, were soon strung out in an irregular line. The Californians, who had made a feint of retreating, turned and attacked with vigor, Captain Burroughs and four or five others were killed. The straggling line fell back on the main body and the Californians, having expended their ammunition, retreated. The loss in killed and wounded amounted to twelve or fifteen on each side.

The only other engagement in the north was the bloodless battle of Santa Clara. Fremont's methods of procuring horses, cattle and other supplies was to take them and give in payment demands on the government, payable after the close of the war. After his departure the same method was continued by the officers of the garrisons at San Francisco, San Jose and Monterey. Indeed, it was their only method of procuring supplies. The quartermasters were without money and the government without credit. On the 8th of December, Lieutenant Bartlett, also alcalde of Yerba Buena, with a squad of five men started down the peninsula toward San Jose to purchase supplies. Francisco Sanchez, a rancher, whose horse and cattle corrals had been raided by former purchasers, with a band of Californians waylaid and captured Bartlett and his men. Other California rancheros who had lost their stock in similar raids rallied to the support of Sanchez and soon he found himself at the head of one hundred men. The object of their organization was rather to protect their property than to fight. The news soon spread that the Californians had revolted and were preparing to massacre the Americans. Captain Weber of San Jose had a company of thirty-three men organized for defense. There was also a company of twenty men under command of Captain Aram stationed at the ex-mission of Santa Clara. On the 29th of December, Capt. Ward Marston with a detachment of thirty-four men and a field piece in charge of Master de Long and ten sailors was sent to Santa Clara. The entire force collected at the seat of war numbered one hundred and one men. On January 2 the American force encountered the Californians, one hundred strong, on the plains of Santa Clara. Firing at long range began and continued for an hour or more. Sanchez sent in a flag of truce asking an; armistice preparatory to the settlement of difficulties. January 3, Captain Maddox arrived from Monterey with fifty-nine mounted men, and on the 7th Lieutenant Grayson came with fifteen men. On the 8th a treaty of peace was concluded, by which the enemy surrendered Lieutenant Bartlett and all the other prisoners, as well as their arms, including a small field piece and were permitted to go to their homes. Upon "reliable authority" four Californians were reported killed, but their graves have never been discovered nor did their living relatives, so far as known, mourn their loss.

Stockton with his flagship, the Congress, arrived at San Pedro on the 23rd of October, 1846. The Savannah was still lying at anchor in the harbor. The commodore had now at San Pedro a force of about eight hundred men; but, notwithstanding the contemptuous opinion he held of the Californian soldiers, he did not march against the pueblo. Stockton in his report says: "Elated by this transient success (Mervine's defeat), which the enemy with his usual want of veracity magnified into a great victory, they collected in large bodies on all the adjacent hills and would not permit a hoof except their own horses to be within fifty miles of San Pedro." But "in the face of their boasting insolence" Stockton landed and again hoisted "the glorious stars and stripes in the presence of their horse covered hills." "The enemy had driven off every animal, man and beast from that section of the country; and it was not possible by any means in our power to carry provisions for our march to the city." The city was only thirty miles away and

American soldiers have been known to carry rations in their haversacks for a march of one hundred miles. The "transient success" of the insolent enemy had evidently made an impression on Stockton. He estimated the California force in the vicinity of the landing at eight hundred men, which was just seven hundred too high. He determined to approach Los Angeles by way of San Diego, and on the last day of October he sailed for that port. B. D. Wilson, Stephen C. Foster and others attribute Stockton's abandonment of an attack on Los Angeles from San Pedro to a trick played on him by Jose Antonio Carrillo. Carrillo was in command of the detachment stationed at the Cerritos and the Palos Verdes. Carrillo was anxious to obtain an interview with Stockton and if possible secure a cessation of hostilities until the war then progressing in Mexico should be decided, thus settling the fate of California. B. D. Wilson, one of the Chino prisoners, was sent with a Mexican sergeant to raise a white flag as the boats of the Congress approached the landing and present Carrillo's proposition for a truce. Carrillo, with the intention of giving Stockton an exaggerated idea of the number of his troops and thus obtaining more favorable terms in the proposed treaty, collected droves of wild horses from the plains; these his caballeros kept in motion, passing and repassing through a gap in the hills, which was in plain view from Stockton's vessel. Owing to the dust raised by the cavalcade it was impossible to discover that most of the horses were riderless. The troops were signaled to return to the vessel, and the commodore shortly afterwards sailed to San Diego. Carrillo always regretted that he made too much demonstration.

As an illustration of the literary trash that has been palmed off for California history, I give an extract from Frost's Pictorial History of California, a book written the year after the close of the Mexican war by Prof. John Frost, a noted compiler of histories, who writes LL. D. after his name. It relates to Stockton's exploits at San Pedro. "At the Rancho Sepulveda (the Palos Verdes) a large force of Californians were posted. Commodore Stockton sent one hundred men forward to receive the fire of the enemy and then fall back on the main body without returning it. The main body of Stockton's army was formed in a triangle with the guns hid by the men. By the retreat of the advance party the enemy were decoyed close to the main force, when the wings (of the triangle) were extended and a deadly fire from the artillery opened upon the astonished Californians. More than one hundred were killed, the same number wounded and one hundred prisoners taken." The mathematical accuracy of Stockton's artillerists was truly astonishing. They killed a man for every one wounded and took a prisoner for every man they killed. As Flores' army never amounted to more than three hundred, if we are to believe Frost, Stockton had all the enemy "present or accounted for." This silly fabrication of Frost's runs through a number of so-called histories of California. Stockton was a brave man and a very energetic commander, but he would boast of his achievements, and his reports are unreliable.

As previously mentioned, Fremont after his return to Monterey proceeded to recruit a force to move against Los Angeles by land from Monterey. His recruits were principally obtained from the recently arrived immigrants. Each man was furnished with a horse and was to receive $25 a month. A force of about four hundred and fifty was obtained. Fremont left Monterey November 17 and rendezvoused at San Juan Bautista, where he remained to the 29th of the month organizing his battalion. On the 29th of November he began his march southward to co-operate with Stockton against Flores.

After the expulsion of Gillespie and his men from Los Angeles, detachments from Flores' army were sent to Santa Barbara and San Diego to recapture these places. At Santa Barbara Fremont had left nine men of his battalion under Lieut. Theodore Talbot to garrison the town. A demand was made on the garrison to surrender by Colonel Garfias of Flores' army. Two hours were given the Americans to decide. Instead of surrendering they fell back into the hills, where they remained three or four days, hoping that reinforcements might be sent them from Monterey. Their only subsistence was the flesh of an old gray mare of Daniel Hill's that they captured, brought into camp and killed. They secured one of Micheltorena's cholos that had remained in the country and was living in a canon among the hills for a guide. He furnished them a horse to carry their blankets and conducted them through the mountains to the San Joaquin valley. Here the guide left them with the Indians, he returning to Santa Barbara. The Indians fed them on chia (wild flaxseed), mush and acorn bread. They traveled down the San Joaquin valley. On their journey they lived on the flesh of wild horses, seventeen of which they killed. After many hardships they reached Monterey on the 8th of November, where they joined Fremont's battalion.

Captain Merritt, of Fremont's battalion, had been left at San Diego with forty men to hold the town when the battalion marched north to co-operate with Stockton against Los Angeles. Immediately after Gillespie's retreat, Francisco Rico was sent with fifty men to capture the place. He was joined by recruits at San Diego. Merritt being in no condition to stand a siege, took refuge on board the American whale ship Stonington, which was lying at anchor. After remaining on board the Stonington ten days, taking advantage of the laxity of discipline among the Californians, he stole a march on them, recapturing the town and one piece of artillery. He sent Don Miguel de Pedrorena, who was one of his allies, in a whale boat with four sailors to San Pedro to obtain supplies and assistance. Pedrorena arrived at San Pedro on the 13th of October with Merritt's dispatches. Captain Mervine chartered the whale ship Magnolia, which was lying in the San Pedro harbor, and dispatched Lieutenant Minor, Midshipman Duvall and Morgan with thirty-three sailors and fifteen of Gillespie's volunteers to reinforce Merritt. They reached San Diego on the 16th. The combined forces of Minor and Merritt, numbering about ninety men, put in the greater part of the next two weeks in dragging cannon from the old fort and mounting them at their barracks, which were located on the hill at the edge of the plain on the west side of the town, convenient to water. They succeeded in mounting six brass nine-pounders and building two bastions of adobes, taken from an old house. There was constant skirmishing between the hostile parties, but few fatalities. The Americans claimed to have killed three of the enemy, and one American was ambushed and killed.

The Californians kept well out of range, but prevented the Americans from obtaining supplies. Their provisions were nearly exhausted, and when reduced to almost the last extreme they made a successful foraging expedition and procured a supply of mutton. Midshipman Duvall thus describes the adventure: "We had with us an Indian (chief of a numerous tribe) who, from his knowledge of the country, we thought could avoid the enemy; and getting news of a number of sheep about thirty-five miles to the south on the coast, we determined to send him and his companion to drive them onto an island which at low tide connected with the mainland. In a few days a signal was made on the island, and the boats of the whale ship Stonington, stationed off the island, were sent to it. Our good old Indian had managed, through his cunning and by keeping concealed in ravines, to drive onto the island about six hundred sheep, but his companion had been caught and killed by the enemy. I shall never forget his famished appearance, but pride in his Indian triumph could be seen playing in his dark eyes.

"For thirty or forty days we were constantly expecting, from the movements of the enemy, an attack, soldiers and officers sleeping on their arms and ready for action. About the 1st of November, Commodore Stockton arrived, and, after landing Captain Gillespie with his company and about forty-three marines, he suddenly disappeared, leaving Lieutenant Minor governor of the place and Captain Gillespie commandant."

Foraging continued, the whale ship Stonington, which had been impressed into the government service, being used to take parties down the coast, who made raids inland and brought back with them catties and horses.

It was probably on one of these excursions that the flag-making episode occurred, of which there are more versions than Homer had birthplaces. The correct version of the story is as follows: A party had been sent under command of Lieutenant Hensley to Juan Bandini's rancho in Lower California to bring up bands of cattle and horses. Bandini was an adherent of the American cause. He and his family returned with the cavalcade to San Diego. At their last camping place before reaching the town, Hensley, in a conversation with Bandini, regretted they had no flag with them to display on their entry into the town. Senora Bandini volunteered to make one, which she did from red, white and blue dresses of her children. This flag, fastened to a staff, was carried at the head of the cavalcade when it made its triumphal entry into San Diego. The Mexican government confiscated Bandini's ranchos in Lower California on account of his friendship to the Americans during the war.

Skirmishing continued almost daily. Jose Antonio Carrillo was now in command of the Californians, their force numbering about one hundred men. Commodore Stockton returned and decided to fortify. Midshipman Duvall, in the Log Book referred to in the previous chapter, thus describes the fort: "The commodore now commenced to fortify the hill which overlooked the town by building a fort, constructed by placing three hundred gallon casks full of sand close together. The enclosure was twenty by thirty yards. A bank of earth and small gravel was thrown up in front as high as the top of the casks and a ditch dug around on the outside. Inside a ball-proof vault of ketch was built out of plank and lined on the inside with adobes, on top of which a swivel was mounted. The entrance was guarded by a strong gate, with a drawbridge in front across the ditch or moat. The whole fortification was completed and the guns mounted on it in about three weeks. Our men working on the fort were on short allowance of beef and wheat, and for a time without bread, tea, sugar or coffee, many of them being destitute of shoes, but there were few complaints.

"About the 1st of December, information having been received that General Kearny was at Warner's Pass, about eighty miles distant, with one hundred dragoons on his march to San Diego, Commodore Stockton immediately sent an escort of fifty men under command of Captain Gillespie, accompanied by Past Midshipmen Beale and Duncan, having with them one piece of artillery. They reached General Kearny without molestation. On the march the combined force was surprised by about ninety-three Californians at San Pasqual, under command of Andres Pico, who had been sent to that part of the country to drive off all the cattle and horses to prevent us from getting them. In the battle that ensued General Kearny lost in killed Captains Johnston and Moore and Lieutenant Hammond, and fifteen dragoons. Seventeen dragoons were severely wounded. The enemy captured one piece of artillery. General Kearny and Captains Gillespie and Gibson were severely wounded; also one of the engineer officers. Some of the dragoons have since died." * * *

"After the engagement General Kearny took position on a hill covered with large rocks. It was well suited for defense. Lieutenant Godey of Gillespie's volunteers, the night after the battle, escaped through the enemy's line of sentries and came in with a letter from Captain Turner to the commodore. Whilst among the rocks, Past Midshipman Beale and Kit Carson managed, under cover of night, to pass out through the enemy's ranks, and after three days' and nights' hard marching through the mountains without water, succeeded in getting safely into San Diego, completely famished. Soon after arriving Lieutenant Beale fainted away, and for some days entirely lost his reason."

On the night of Beale's arrival, December 9, about 9 p. m., detachments of two hundred sailors and marines from the Congress and Portsmouth, under the immediate command of Captain Zeilin, assisted by Lieutenants Gray, Hunter, Renshaw, Parrish, Thompson and Tilghman and Midshipmen Duvall and Morgan, each man carrying a blanket, three pounds of jerked beef and the same of hardtack, began their march to relieve General Kearny. They marched all night and camped on a chaparral covered mountain during the day. At 4 p. m. of the second night's march they reached Kearny's camp, surprising him. Godey, who had been sent ahead to inform Kearny that assistance was coming, had been captured by the enemy. General Kearny had burnt and destroyed all his baggage and camp equipage, saddles, bridles, clothing, etc., preparatory to forcing his way through the enemy's line. Burdened with his wounded, it is doubtful whether he could have escaped. Midshipman Duvall says: "It would not be a hazard of opinion to say he would have been overpowered and compelled to surrender." The enemy disappeared on the arrival of reinforcements. The relief expedition, with Kearny's men, reached San Diego after two days' march.

A brief explanation of the reason why Kearny was at San Pasqual may be necessary. In June, 1846, Gen. Stephen W. Kearny, commander of the Army of the West, as his command was designated, left Fort Leavenworth with a force of regulars and volunteers to take possession of New Mexico. The conquest of that territory was accomplished without a battle. Under orders from the war department, Kearny began his march to California with a part of his force to co-operate with the naval forces there. October 6, near Socorro, N. M., he met Kit Carson with an escort of fifteen men en route from Los Angeles to Washington, bearing dispatches from Stockton, giving the report of the conquest of California. Kearny required Carson to turn back and act as his guide. Carson was very unwilling to do so, as he was within a few days' journey of his home and family, from whom he had been separated for nearly two years. He had been guide for Fremont on his exploring expedition. He, however, obeyed Kearny's orders.

General Kearny sent back about three hundred of his men, taking with him one hundred and twenty. After a toilsome march by way of the Pima villages, Tucson, the Gila and across the Colorado desert, they reached the Indian village of San Pasqual (about forty miles from San Diego), where the battle was fought. It was the bloodiest battle of the conquest; Kearny's men, at daybreak, riding on broken down mules and half broken horses, in an irregular and disorderly line, charged the Californians. While the American line was stretched out over the plain Capt. Andres Pico, who was in command, wheeled his column and charged the Americans. A fierce hand to hand fight ensued, the Californians using their lances and lariats, the Americans clubbed guns and sabers. Of Kearny's command eighteen men were killed and nineteen wounded; three of the wounded died. Only one, Capt. Abraham R. Johnston (a relative of the author's), was killed by a gunshot; all the others were lanced. The mules to one of the howitzers became unmanageable and ran into the enemy's lines. The driver was killed and the gun captured. One Californian was captured and several slightly wounded; none were killed. Less than half of Kearny's one hundred and seventy men took part in the battle. His loss in killed and wounded was fifty per cent of those engaged. Dr. John S. Griffin, for many years a leading physician of Los Angeles, was the surgeon of the command.

The foraging expeditions in Lower California having been quite successful in bringing in cattle, horses and mules. Commodore Stockton hastened his preparation for marching against Los Angeles. The enemy obtained information of the projected movement and left for the pueblo.

"The Cyane having arrived," says Duvall, "our force was increased to about six hundred men, most of whom, understanding the drill, performed the evolutions like regular soldiers. Everything being ready for our departure, the commodore left Captain Montgomery and officers in command of the town, and on the 29th of December took up his line of march for Los Angeles. General Kearny was second in command and having the immediate arrangement of the forces, reserving for himself the prerogative which his rank necessarily imposed upon him. Owing to the weak state of our oxen we had not crossed the dry bed of the river San Diego before they began breaking down, and the carts, which were thirty or forty in number, had to be dragged by the men. The general urged on the commodore that it was useless to commence such a march as was before us with our present means of transportation, but the commodore insisted on performing at least one day's march even if we should have to return the next day. We succeeded in reaching the valley of the Soledad that night by dragging our carts. Next day the commodore proposed to go six miles farther, which we accomplished, and then continued six miles farther. Having obtained some fresh oxen, by assisting the carts up hill we made ten or twelve miles a day. At San Luis Rey we secured men, carts and oxen, and after that our days' marches ranged from fifteen to twenty-two miles a day.

"The third day out from San Luis Rey a white flag was seen ahead, the bearer of which had a communication from Flores, signing himself 'Commander-in-Chief and Governor of California,' asking for a conference for the purpose of coming to

137

terms, which would be alike 'honorable to both countries.' The commodore refused to answer him in writing, saying to the bearer of the truce that his answer was, 'he knew no such person as Governor Flores; that he himself was the only governor in California; that he knew a rebel by that name, a man who had given his parole of honor not to take up arms against the government of the United States, who, if the people of California now in arms against the forces of the United States would deliver up, he (Stockton) would treat with them on condition that they surrender their arms and retire peaceably to their homes and he would grant them, as citizens of the United States, protection from further molestation.' This the embassy refused to entertain, saying 'they would prefer to die with Flores than to surrender on such terms.' " * * *

"On the 8th of January, 1847, they met us on the banks of the river San Gabriel with between five and six hundred men mounted on good horses and armed with lances and carbines, having also four pieces of artillery planted on the heights about three hundred and fifty yards distant from the river. Owing to circumstances which have occurred since the surrender of the enemy, I prefer not mentioning the particulars of this day's battle and also that of the day following, or of referring to individuals concerned in the successful management of our forces." (The circumstance to which Lieutenant Duvall refers was undoubtedly the quarrel between Stockton and Kearny after the capture of Los Angeles.) "It is sufficient to say that on the 8th of January we succeeded in crossing the river and driving the enemy from the heights. Having resisted all their charges, dismounted one of their pieces and put them to flight in every direction, we encamped on the ground they had occupied during the fight.

"The next day the Californians met us on the plains of the mesa. For a time the fighting was carried on by both sides with artillery, but that proving too hot for them they concentrated their whole force in a line ahead of us and at a given signal divided from the center and came down on us like a tornado, charging us on all sides at the same time; but they were effectually defeated and fled in every direction in the utmost confusion. Many of their horses were left dead on the field. Their loss in the two battles, as given by Andres Pico, second in command, was eighty-three killed and wounded; our loss, three killed (one accidentally), and fifteen or twenty wounded, none dangerously. The enemy abandoned two pieces of artillery in an Indian village near by."

I have given at considerable length Midshipman Duvall's account of Stockton's march from San Diego and of the two battles fought, not because it is the fullest account of those events, but because it is original historical matter, never having appeared in print before, and also because it is the observations of a participant written at the time the events occurred. In it the losses of the enemy are greatly exaggerated, but that was a fault of his superior officers as well. Commodore Stockton, in his official reports of the two battles, gives the enemy's loss in killed and wounded "between seventy and eighty." And General Kearny, in his report of the battle of San Pasqual, claimed it as a victory, and states that the enemy left six dead on the field. The actual loss of the Californians in the two battles (San Gabriel river and La Mesa) was three killed and ten or twelve wounded.

While the events recorded in this chapter were transpiring at San Diego and its vicinity, what was the state of affairs in the capital, Los Angeles? After the exultation and rejoicing over the expulsion of Gillespie's garrison, Mervine's defeat and the victory over Kearny at San Pasqual there came a reaction. Dissension continued between the leaders. There was lack of arms and laxity of discipline. The army was but little better than a mob. Obedience to orders of a superior was foreign to the nature of a Californian. His wild, free life in the saddle made him impatient of all restraint. Then the impossibility of successful resistance against the Americans became more and more apparent as the final conflict approached. Fremont's army was moving down on the doomed city from the north, and Stockton's was coming up from the south. Either one of these, in numbers, exceeded the force that Flores could bring into action; combined they would crush him out of existence. The California troops were greatly discouraged and it was with great difficulty that the officers kept their men together. There was another and more potent element of disintegration. Many of the wealthier natives and all the foreigners, regarding the contest as hopeless, secretly favored the American cause, and it was only through fear of loss of property that they furnished Flores and his officers any supplies for the army.

During the latter part of December and the first days of January Flores' army was stationed at the San Fernando Mission, on the lookout for Fremont's battalion; but the more rapid advance of Stockton's army compelled a change of base. On the 6th and 7th of January Flores moved his army back secretly through the Cahuenga Pass, and, passing to the southward of the city, took position where La Jaboneria (the soap factory) road crosses the San Gabriel river. Here his men were stationed in the thick willows to give Stockton a surprise. Stockton received information of the trap set for him and after leaving the Los Coyotes swung off to the right until he struck the Upper Santa Ana road. The Californians had barely time to effect a change of base and get their cannon planted when the Americans arrived at the crossing.

Stockton called the engagement there the battle of San Gabriel river; the Californians call it the battle of Paso de Bartolo, which is the better name. The place where the battle was fought is on bluff just south of the Upper Santa Ana road, near where the Southern California railroad crosses the old San Gabriel river. (The ford or crossing was formerly known as Pico's Crossing.) There was, at the time of the battle, but one San Gabriel river. The new river channel was made in the great flood of 1868. What Stockton, Emory, Duvall and other American officers call the battle of the Plains of the Mesa the Californians call the battle of La Mesa, which is most decidedly a better name than the "Plains of the Plain." It was fought at a ravine, the Canada de Los Alisos, near the southeastern corner of the Los Angeles city boundary. In these battles the Californians had four pieces of artillery, two iron nine-pounders, the old woman's gun and the howitzer captured from Kearny. Their powder was very poor. It was made at San Gabriel. It was owing to this that they did so little execution in the fight. That the Californians escaped with so little punishment was probably due to the wretched marksmanship of Stockton's sailors and marines.

CHAPTER XX.
CAPTURE AND OCCUPATION OF THE CAPITAL.

After the battle of La Mesa, the Americans, keeping to the south, crossed the Los Angeles river at about the point where the south boundary line of the city crosses it and camped on the right bank. Here, under a willow tree, those killed in battle were buried. Lieutenant Emory, in his "Notes of a Military Reconnaissance," says: "The town, known to contain great quantities of wine and aguardiente, was four miles distant (four miles from the battlefield). From previous experience of the difficulty of controlling men when entering towns, it was determined to cross the river San Fernando (Los Angeles), halt there for the night and enter the town in the morning, with the whole day before us.

"After we had pitched our camp, the enemy came down from the hills, and four hundred horsemen with four pieces of artillery drew off towards the town, in order and regularity, whilst about sixty made a movement down the river on our rear and left flank. This led us to suppose they were not yet whipped, as we thought, and that we should have a night attack.

"January 10 (1847) — Just as we had raised our camp, a flag of truce, borne by Mr. Cells, a Castilian; Mr. Workman, an Englishman, and Alvarado, the owner of the rancho at the Alisos, was brought into camp. They proposed, on behalf of the Californians, to surrender their dear City of the Angels provided we would respect property and persons. This was agreed to, but not altogether trusting to the honesty of General Flores, who had once broken his parole, we moved into the town in the same order we should have done if expecting an attack. It was a wise precaution, for the streets were full of desperate and drunken fellows, who brandished their arms and saluted us with every term of reproach. The crest, overlooking the town, in rifle range, was covered with horsemen engaged in the same hospitable manner.

"Our men marched steadily on, until crossing the ravine leading into the public square (plaza), when a fight took place amongst the Californians on the hill; one became disarmed and to avoid death rolled down the hill towards us, his adversary pursuing and lancing him in the most cold-blooded manner. The man tumbling down the hill was supposed to be one of our vaqueros, and the cry of 'rescue him' was raised. The crew of the Cyane, nearest the scene, at once and without any orders, halted and gave the man that was lancing him a volley; strange to say, he did not fall. The general gave the jack tars a cursing, not so much for the firing without orders, as for their bad marksmanship."

Shortly after the above episode, the Californians did open fire from the hill on the vaqueros in charge of the cattle. (These vaqueros were Californians in the employ of the Americans and were regarded by their countrymen as traitors.) A company of riflemen was ordered to clear the hill. A single volley effected this, killing two of the enemy. This was the last bloodshed in the war; and the second conquest of California was completed as the first had been by the capture of Los Angeles. Two hundred men, with two pieces of artillery, were stationed on the hill.

The Angeleños did not exactly welcome the invaders with "bloody hands to inhospitable graves," but they did their best to let them know they were not wanted. The better class of the native inhabitants closed their houses and took refuge with foreign residents or went to the ranchos of their friends in the country. The fellows of the baser sort, who were in possession of the city, exhausted their vocabularies of abuse on the invading gringos. There was one paisano who excelled all his countrymen in this species of warfare. It is a pity his name has not been preserved in history with that of other famous scolds and kickers. He rode by the side of the advancing column up Main street, firing volleys of invective and denunciation at the hated gringos. At certain points of his tirade he worked himself to such a pitch of indignation that language failed him; then he would solemnly go through the motions of "Make ready, take aim!" with an old shotgun he carried, but when it came to the order "Fire!" discretion got the better of his valor; he lowered his gun and began again, firing invective at the gringo soldiers; his mouth would go off if his gun would not.

Commodore Stockton's headquarters were in the Abila house, the second house on Olvera street, north of the plaza. The building is still standing, but has undergone many changes in fifty years. A rather amusing account was recently given me by an old pioneer of the manner in which Commodore Stockton got possession of the house. The widow Abila and her daughters, at the approach of the American army, had abandoned their house and taken refuge with Don Luis Vignes of the Aliso. Vignes was a Frenchman and friendly to both sides. The widow left a young Californian in charge of her house (which was finely furnished), with strict orders to keep it closed. Stockton had with him a fine brass band, something new in California. When the troops halted on the plaza, the band began to play. The boyish guardian of the Abila casa could not resist the temptation to open the door and look out. The enchanting music drew him to the plaza. Stockton and his staff, hunting for a place suitable for headquarters, passing by, found the door invitingly open, entered, and, finding the house deserted, took possession. The recreant guardian returned to find himself dispossessed and the house in possession of the enemy. "And the band played on."

It is a fact not generally known that there were two forts planned and partially built on Fort Hill during the war for the conquest of California. The first was planned by Lieut. William H. Emory, topographical engineer of General Kearny's staff, and work was begun on it by Commodore Stockton's sailors and marines. The second was planned by Lieut. J. W. Davidson, of the First United States Dragoons, and built by the Mormon battalion. The first was not completed and not named. The second was named Fort Moore. Their location seems to have been identical. The first was designed to hold one hundred men. The second was much larger. Flores' army was supposed to be in the neighborhood of the city ready to make a dash into it, so Stockton decided to fortify.

"On January 11th," Lieutenant Emory writes, "I was ordered to select a site and place a fort capable of containing a hundred men. With this in view a rapid reconnaissance of the town was made and the plan of a fort sketched, so placed as to enable a small garrison to command the town and the principal avenues to it, the plan was approved."

"January 12. I laid off the work and before night broke the first ground. The population of the town and its dependencies is about three thousand; that of the town itself about fifteen hundred. * * * Here all the revolutions have had their origin, and it is the point upon which any Mexican force from Sonora would be directed. It was therefore desirable to establish a fort which, in case of trouble, should enable a small garrison to hold out till aid might come from San Diego, San Francisco or Monterey, places which are destined to become centers of American settlements."

"January 13. It rained steadily all day and nothing was done on the work. At night I worked on the details of the fort."

"January 15. The details to work on the fort were by companies. I sent to Captain Tilghman, who commanded on the hill, to detach one of the companies under his command to commence the work. He furnished, on the 16th, a company of artillery (seamen from the Congress) for the day's work, which was performed bravely, and gave me great hopes of success."

On the 18th Lieutenant Emory took his departure with General Kearny for San Diego. From there he was sent with dispatches, via Panama, to the war department. In his book he says: "Subsequent to my departure the entire plan of the fort was changed, and I am not the projector of the work finally adopted for defense of that town."

As previously stated, Fremont's battalion began its march down the coast on the 29th of November, 1846. The winter rains set in with great severity. The volunteers were scantily provided with clothing and the horses were in poor condition. Many of the horses died of starvation and hard usage. The battalion encountered no opposition from the enemy on its march and did no fighting. On the nth of January, a few miles above San Fernando, Colonel Fremont received a message from General Kearny informing him of the defeat of the enemy and the capture of Los Angeles. That night the battalion encamped in the mission buildings at San Fernando. From the mission that evening Jesus Pico, a cousin of Gen. Andres Pico, set out to find the Californian army and open negotiations with its leaders. Jesus Pico, better known as Tortoi, had been arrested at his home near San Luis Obispo, tried by court-martial and sentenced to be shot for breaking his parole. Fremont, moved by the pleadings of Pico's wife and children, pardoned him. He became a warm admirer and devoted friend of Fremont's.

He found the advance guard of the Californians encamped at Verdugas. He was detained here, and the leading officers of the army were summoned to a council. Pico informed them of Fremont's arrival and the number of his men. With the combined forces of Fremont and Stockton against them, their cause was hopeless. He urged them to surrender to Fremont, as they could obtain better terms from him than from Stockton.

General Flores, who held a commission in the Mexican army, and who had been appointed by the territorial assembly governor and comandante-general by virtue of his rank, appointed Andres Pico general and gave him command of the army. The same night he took his departure for Mexico, by way of San Gorgonio Pass, accompanied by Colonel Garfias, Diego Sepulveda, Manuel Castro, Segura, and about thirty privates. General Pico, on assuming command, appointed Francisco Rico and Francisco de La Guerra to go with Jesus Pico to confer with

Colonel Fremont. Fremont appointed as commissioners to negotiate a treaty. Major P. B. Reading, Major William H. Russell and Capt. Louis M'Clane. On the return of Guerra and Rico to the Californian camp, Gen. Andres Pico appointed as commissioners, Jose Antonio Carrillo, commander of the cavalry squadron, and Agustin Olvera, diputado of the assembly, and moved his army near the river at Cahuenga. On the 13th Fremont moved his camp to the Cahuenga. The commissioners met in the deserted ranch-house, and the treaty was drawn up and signed.

The principal conditions of the treaty or capitulation of "Cahuenga," as it was termed, were that the Californians, on delivering up their artillery and public arms, and promising not again to take arms during the war, and conforming to the laws and regulations of the United States, shall be allowed peaceably to return to their homes. They were to be allowed the same rights and privileges as are allowed to citizens of the United States, and were not to be compelled to take an oath of allegiance until a treaty of peace was signed between the United States and Mexico, and were given the privilege of leaving the country if they wished to. An additional section was added to the treaty on the 16th at Los Angeles releasing the officers from their paroles. Two cannon were surrendered, the howitzer captured from General Kearny at San Pasqual and the woman's gun that won the battle of Dominguez. On the 14th, Fremont's battalion marched through the Cahuenga Pass to Los Angeles in a pouring rainstorm, and entered it four days after its surrender to Stockton. The conquest of California) was completed. Stockton approved the treaty, although it was not altogether satisfactory to him. On the 16th he appointed Colonel Fremont governor of the territory, and William H. Russell, of the battalion, secretary of state.

This precipitated a quarrel between Stockton and Kearny, which had been brewing for some time. General Kearny claimed that under his instructions from the government he should be recognized as governor. As he had directly under his command but the one company of dragoons that he brought across the plain with him, he was unable to enforce his authority. He left on the 18th for San Diego, taking with him the officers of his staff. On the 20th Commodore Stockton, with his sailors and marines, marched to San Pedro, where they all embarked on a man-of-war for San Diego to rejoin their ships. Shortly afterwards Commodore Stockton was superseded in the command of the Pacific squadron by Commodore Shubrick.

CHAPTER XXI.
TRANSITION AND TRANSFORMATION.

The capitulation of Gen. Andres Pico at Cahuenga put an end to the war in California. The instructions from the secretary of war were to pursue a policy of conciliation towards the Californians with the ultimate design of transforming them into American citizens. Colonel Fremont was left in command at Los Angeles. He established his headquarters on the second floor of the Bell block (corner of Los Angeles and Aliso streets), then the best building in the city. One company of his battalion was retained in the city; the others, under command of Captain Owens, were quartered at the Mission San Gabriel.

The Mormons had been driven out of Illinois and Missouri. A sentiment of antagonism had been engendered against them and they had begun their migration to the far west, presumably to California. They were encamped on the Missouri river at Kanesville, now Council Bluffs, preparatory to crossing the plains, when hostilities broke out between the United States and Mexico, in April, 1846. A proposition was made by President Polk to their leaders to raise a battalion of five hundred men to serve as United States volunteers for twelve months. These volunteers, under command of regular army officers, were to march to Santa Fe, or, if necessary, to California, where, at the expiration of their term of enlistment, they were to be discharged and allowed to retain their arms. Through the influence of Brigham Young and other leaders, the battalion was recruited and General Kearny, commanding the Army of the West, detailed Capt. James Allen, of the First United States Dragoons, to muster them into the service and take command of the battalion. On the 16th of July, at Council Bluffs, the battalion was mustered into service and on the 14th of August it began its long and weary march. About eighty women and children, wives and families of the officers and some of the enlisted men, accompanied the battalion on its march. Shortly after the beginning of the march, Allen, who had been promoted to lieutenant-colonel, fell sick and died. The battalion was placed temporarily under the command of Lieut. A. J. Smith, of the regular army. At Santa Fe Lieut.-Col. Philip St. George Cooke took command under orders from General Kearny. The battalion was detailed to open a wagon road by the Gila route to California. About sixty of the soldiers who had become unfit for duty and all the women except five were sent back and the remainder of the force, after a toilsome journey, reached San Luis Rey, Cal., January 29, 1847, where it remained until ordered to Los Angeles, which place it reached March 17.

Captain Owens, in command of Fremont's battalion, had moved all the artillery, ten pieces, from Los Angeles to San Gabriel, probably with the design of preventing it falling into the hands of Colonel Cooke, who was an adherent of General Kearny. General Kearny, under additional instructions from the general government, brought by Colonel Mason from the war department, had established himself as governor at Monterey. With a governor in the north and one in the south, antagonistic to each other, California had fallen back to its normal condition under Mexican rule. Colonel Cooke, shortly after his arrival in the territory, thus describes the condition prevailing: "General Kearny is supreme somewhere up the coast. Colonel Fremont is supreme at Pueblo de Los Angeles; Colonel Stockton is commander-in-chief at San Diego; Commodore Shubrick the same at Monterey; and I at San Luis Rey; and we are all supremely poor, the government having no money and no credit, and we hold the territory because Mexico is the poorest of all."

Col. R. B. Mason was appointed inspector of the troops in California and made an official visit to Los Angeles. In a misunderstanding about some official matters he used insulting language to Colonel Fremont. Fremont promptly challenged him to fight a duel. The challenge was accepted; double-barreled shotguns were chosen as the weapons and the Rancho Rosa del Castillo as the place of meeting. Mason was summoned north and the duel was postponed until his return. General Kearny, hearing of the proposed affair of honor, put a stop to further proceedings by the duelists.

Col. Philip St. George Cooke, of the Mormon battalion, was made commander of the military district of the south with headquarters at Los Angeles. Fremont's battalion was mustered out of service. The Mormon soldiers and the two companies of United States Dragoons who came with General Kearny were stationed at Los Angeles to do guard duty and prevent any uprising of the natives.

Colonel Fremont's appointment as governor of California had never been recognized by General Kearny. So when the general had made himself supreme at Monterey he ordered Fremont to report to him at the capital and turn over the papers of his governorship. Fremont did so and passed out of office. He was nominally governor of the territory about two months. His appointment was made by Commodore Stockton, but was never confirmed by the president or secretary of war. His jurisdiction did not extend beyond Los Angeles. He left Los Angeles May 12 for Monterey. From that place, in company with General Kearny, on May 31, he took his departure for the states. The relations between the two were strained. While ostensibly traveling as one company, each officer, with his staff and escort, made separate camps. At Fort Leavenworth General Kearny placed Fremont under arrest and preferred charges against him for disobedience of orders. He was tried by court-martial at Washington and was ably defended by his father-in-law. Colonel Benton, and his brother-in-law, William Carey Jones. The court found him guilty and fixed the penalty, dismissal from the service. President Polk remitted the penalty and ordered Colonel Fremont to resume his sword and report for duty. He did so, but shortly afterward resigned his commission and left the army.

While Colonel Cooke was in command of the southern district rumors reached Los Angeles that the Mexican general, Bustamente, with a force of fifteen hundred men, was preparing to reconquer California. "Positive information," writes Colonel Cooke, under date of April 20, 1847, "has been received that the Mexican government has appropriated $600,000 towards fitting out this force." It was also reported that cannon and military stores had been landed at San Vicente, in Lower California. Rumors of an approaching army came thick and fast. The natives were supposed to be in league with Bustamente and to be secretly preparing for an uprising. Precautions were taken against a surprise. A troop of cavalry was sent to Warner's ranch to patrol the Sonora road as far as the desert. The construction of a fort on the hill fully commanding the town, which had previously been determined upon, was begun and a company of infantry posted on the hill.

On the 23rd of April, three months after work had ceased on Emory's fort, the construction of the second fort was begun and pushed vigorously. Rumors continued to come of the approach of the enemy. May 3, Colonel Cooke writes: "A report was received through the most available sources of information that General Bustamente had crossed the Gulf of California near its head, in boats of the pearl fishers, and at last information was at a rancho on the western road, seventy leagues below San Diego." Colonel Stevenson's regiment of New York volunteers had recently arrived in California. Two companies of that regiment had been sent to Los Angeles and two to San Diego. The report that Colonel Cooke had received reinforcement and that Los Angeles was being fortified was supposed to have frightened Bustamente into abandoning his invasion of California. Bustamente's invading army was largely the creation of somebody's fertile imagination. The scare, however, had the effect of hurrying up work on the fort. May 13, Colonel Cooke resigned and Col. J. B. Stevenson succeeded him in the command of the southern military district.

Colonel Stevenson continued work on the fort and on the 1st of July work had progressed so far that he decided to dedicate and name it on the 4th. He issued an official order for the celebration of the anniversary of the birthday of American independence at this port, as he called Los Angeles. "At sunrise a Federal salute will be fired from the field work on the hill which commands this town and for the first time from this point the American standard will be displayed. At II o'clock all the troops of the district, consisting of the Mormon battalion, the two companies of dragoons and two companies of the New York volunteers, were formed in a hollow square at the fort. The Declaration of Independence was read in English by Captain Stuart Taylor and in Spanish by Stephen C. Foster. The native Californians, seated on their horses in rear of the soldiers, listened to Don Esteban as he rolled out in sonorous Spanish the Declaration's arraignment of King George III., and smiled. They had probably never heard of King George or the Declaration of Independence, either, but they knew a pronunciamiento when they heard it, and after a pronunciamiento in their governmental system came a revolution, therefore they smiled at the prospect of a gringo revolution. "At the close of this ceremony (reading of the Declaration) the field work will be dedicated and appropriately named; and at 12 o'clock a national salute will be fired. The field work at this post having been planned and the work conducted entirely by Lieutenant Davidson of the First Dragoons, he is requested to hoist upon it for the first time on the morning of the 4th the American standard." * * * The commander directs that from and after the 4th instant the fort shall bear the name of Moore. Benjamin D. Moore, after whom the fort was named, was captain of Company A, First United States Dragoons. He was killed by a lance thrust in the disastrous charge at the battle of San Pasqual. This fort was located on what is now called Fort Hill, near the geographical center of Los Angeles. It was a breastwork about four hundred feet long with bastions and embrasures for cannon. The principal embrasure commanded the church and the plaza, two places most likely to be the rallying points in a rebellion. It was built more for the suppression of a revolt than to resist an invasion. It was in a commanding position; two hundred men, about its capacity, could have defended it against a thousand if the attack came from the front; but as it was never completed, in an attack from the rear it could easily have been captured with an equal force.

Col. Richard B. Mason succeeded General Kearny as commander-in-chief of the troops and military governor of California. Col. Philip St. George Cooke resigned command of the military district of the south May 13, joined General Kearny at Monterey and went east with him. As previously stated. Col. J. D. Stevenson, of the New York volunteers, succeeded him. His regiment, the First New York, but really the Seventh, had been recruited in the eastern part of the state of New York in the summer of 1846, for the double purpose of conquest and colonization. The United States government had no intention of giving up California once it was conquered, and therefore this regiment came to the coast well provided with provisions and implements of husbandry. It came to California via Cape Horn in three transports. The first ship, the Perkins, arrived at San Francisco, March 6, 1847; the second, the Drew, March 19; and the third, the Loo Choo, March 26. Hostilities had ceased in California before their arrival. Two companies, A and B, under command of Lieutenant-Colonel Burton, were sent to Lower California, where they saw hard service and took part in several engagements. The other companies of the regiment were sent to different towns in Alta California to do garrison duty.

Another military organization that reached California after the conquest was Company F of the Third United States Artillery. It landed at Monterey January 28, 1847. It was commanded by Capt. C. Q. Thompkins. With it came Lieuts. K O. C. Ord, William T. Sherman and H. W. Halleck, all of whom became prominent in California affairs and attained national reputation during the Civil war. The Mormon battalion was mustered out in July, 1847. One company under command of Captain Hunt re-enlisted. The others made their way to Utah, where they joined their brethren who the year before had crossed the plains and founded the City of Salt Lake. The New York volunteers were discharged in August, 1848. After the treaty of peace, in 1848, four companies of United States Dragoons, under command of Major L. P. Graham, marched from Chihuahua, by way of Tucson, to California. Major Graham was the last military commander of the south.

Commodore W. Branford Shubrick succeeded Commodore Stockton in command of the naval forces of the north Pacific coast. Jointly with General Kearny he issued a circular or proclamation to the people of California, printed in English and Spanish, setting forth "That the president of the United States, desirous to give and secure to the people of California a share of the good government and happy civil organization enjoyed by the people of the United States, and to protect them at the same time from the attacks of foreign foes and from internal commotions, has invested the undersigned with separate and distinct powers, civil and military; a cordial cooperation in the exercise of which, it is hoped and believed, will have the happy results desired.

"To the commander-in-chief of the naval forces the president has assigned the regulation of the import trade, the conditions on which vessels of all nations, our own as well as foreign, may be admitted into the ports of the territory, and the establishment of all port regulations. To the commanding military officer the president has assigned the direction of the operations on land and has invested him with administrative functions of government over the people and territory occupied by the forces of the United States.

"Done at Monterey, capital of California, this 1st day of March, A. D. 1847. W. Branford Shubrick, commander-in-chief of the naval forces. S. W. Kearny, Brig.-Gen. United States Army, and Governor of California."

Under the administration of Col. Richard B. Mason, the successor of General Kearny as military governor, the reconstruction, or, more appropriately, the transformation period began. The orders from the general government were to conciliate the people and to make no radical changes in the form of government. The Mexican laws were continued in force. Just what these laws were, it was difficult to find out. No code commissioner had codified the laws and it sometimes happened that the judge made the law to suit the case. Under the old regime the alcalde was often law-giver, judge, jury and executioner, all in one. Occasionally there was friction between the military and civil powers, and there were rumors of insurrections and invasions, but nothing came of them. The Californians, with easy good nature so characteristic of them, made the best of the situation. "A thousand things," says Judge Hays, "combined to smooth the asperities of war. Fremont had been courteous and gay; Mason was just and firm. The natural good temper of the population favored a speedy and perfect conciliation. The American officers at once found themselves happy in every circle. In suppers, balls, visiting in town and country, the hours glided away with pleasant reflections."

There were, however, a few individuals who were not happy unless they could stir up dissensions and cause trouble. One of the chief of these was Serbulo Varela, agitator and revolutionist. Varela, for some offense not specified in the records, had been committed to prison by the second alcalde of Los Angeles. Colonel Stevenson turned him out of jail, and Varela gave the judge a tongue lashing in refuse Castilian. The judge's official dignity was hurt. He sent a communication to the ayuntamiento saying: "Owing to personal abuse which I received at the hands of a private individual and from the present military commander, I tender my resignation."

The ayuntamiento sent a communication to Colonel Stevenson asking why he had turned Varela out of jail and why he had insulted the judge. The colonel curtly replied that the military would not act as jailers over persons guilty of trifling offenses while the city had plenty of persons to do guard duty at the jail. As to the abuse of the judge, he was not aware that any abuse had been given, and would take no further notice of him unless he stated the nature of the insult offered him. The council decided to notify the governor of the outrage perpetrated by the military commander, and the second alcalde said since he could get no satisfaction for insults to his authority from the military despot, he would resign; but the council would not accept his resignation, so he refused to act, and the city had to worry along with one alcalde.

Although foreigners had been coming to California ever since 1814, their numbers had not increased very rapidly. Nearly all of these had found their way there by sea. Those who had become permanent residents had married native Californian women and adopted the customs of the country. Capt. Jedediah S. Smith, in 1827, crossed the Sierra Nevada mountains from California and by way of the Humboldt, or, as he named it, the Mary River, had reached the Great Salt Lake.

From there through the South Pass of the Rocky mountains the route had been traveled for several years by the fur trappers. This latter became the great emigrant route to California a few years later. A southern route by way of Santa Fe had been marked out and the Pattee party had found their way to the Colorado by the Gila route, but so far no emigrant trains had come from the States to California with women and children. The first of these mixed trains was organized in western Missouri in May, 1841. The party consisted of sixty-nine persons, including men, women and children. This party divided at Soda Springs, half going to Oregon and the others keeping on their way to California. They reached the San Joaquin valley in November, 1841, after a toilsome journey of six months. The first settlement they found was Dr. Marsh's ranch in what is now called Contra Costa county. Marsh gave them a cordial reception at first, but afterwards treated them meanly.

Fourteen of the party started for the Pueblo de San Jose. At the Mission of San Jose, twelve miles from the Pueblo, they were all arrested by order of General Vallejo. One of the men was sent to Dr. Marsh to have him come forthwith and explain why an armed force of his countrymen were roaming around the country without passports. Marsh secured their release and passports for all the party. On his return home he charged the men who had remained at his ranch $5 each for a passport, although the passports had cost him nothing. As there was no money in the party, each had to put up some equivalent from his scanty possessions. Marsh had taken this course to reimburse himself for the meal he had given the half-starved emigrants the first night of their arrival at his ranch.

In marked contrast with the meanness of Marsh was the liberality of Captain Sutter. Sutter had built a fort at the junction of the American river and the Sacramento in 1839 and had obtained extensive land grants. His fort was the frontier post for the overland emigration. Gen. John Bidwell, who came with the first emigrant train to California, in a description of "Life in California Before the Gold Discovery," says: "Nearly everybody who came to California then made it a point to reach Sutter's Fort. Sutter was one of the most liberal and hospitable of men. Everybody was welcome, one man or a hundred, it was all the same."

Another emigrant train, known as the Workman-Rowland party, numbering forty-five persons, came from Santa Fe by the Gila route to Los Angeles. About twenty-five of this party were persons who had arrived too late at Westport, Mo., to join the northern emigrant party, so they went with the annual caravan of St. Louis traders to Santa Fe and from there, with traders and trappers, continued their journey to California. From 1841 to the American conquest immigrant trains came across the plains every year.

One of the most noted of these, on account of the tragic fate that befell it, was the Donner party. The nucleus of this party, George and Jacob Donner and James K. Reed, with their families, started from Springfield, Ill., in the spring of 1846. By accretions and combinations, when it reached Fort Bridger, July 25, it had increased to eighty-seven persons — thirty-six men, twenty-one women and thirty children, under the command of George Donner. A new route called the Hastings Cut-Off, had just been opened by Lansford W. Hastings. This route passed to the south of Great Salt Lake and struck the old Fort Hall emigrant road on the Humboldt. It was claimed that the "cut-off" shortened the distance three hundred miles. The Donner party, by misrepresentations, were induced to take this route.

The cut-off proved to be almost impassable. They started on the cut-off the last day of July, and it was the end of September when they struck the old emigrant trail on the Humboldt. They had lost most of their cattle and were nearly out of provisions. From this on, unmerciful disaster followed them fast and faster. In an altercation. Reed, one of the best men of the party, killed Snyder. He was banished from the train and compelled to leave his wife and children behind. An old Belgian named Hardcoop and Wolfinger, a German, unable to keep up, were abandoned to die on the road. Pike was accidentally shot by Foster. The Indians stole a number of their cattle, and one calamity after another delayed them. In the latter part of October they had reached the Truckee. Here they encountered a heavy snow storm, which blocked all further progress. They wasted their strength in trying to ascend the mountains in the deep snow that had fallen. Finally, finding this impossible, they turned back and built cabins at a lake since known as Donner Lake, and prepared to pass the winter. Most of their oxen had strayed away during the storm and perished. Those still alive they killed and preserved the meat. A party of fifteen, ten men and five women, known as the "Forlorn Hope," started, December 16, on snowshoes to cross the Sierras. They had provisions for six days, but the journey consumed thirty-two days. Eight of the ten men perished, and among them the noble Stanton, who had brought relief to the emigrants from Sutter's Fort before the snows began to fall. The five women survived. Upon the arrival of the wretched survivors of the "Forlorn Hope," the terrible sufferings of the snow-bound immigrants were made known at Sutter's Fort, and the first relief party was organized, and on the 5th of February started for the lake. Seven of the thirteen who started succeeded in reaching the lake. On the 19th they started back with twenty-one of the immigrants, three of whom died on the way. A second relief, under Reed and McCutchen, was organized. Reed had gone to Yerba Buena to seek assistance. A public meeting was called and $1,500 subscribed. The second relief started from Johnston's Ranch, the nearest point to the mountains, on the 23rd of February and reached the camp on March 1st. They brought out seventeen. Two others were organized and reached Donner Lake, the last on the 17th of April. The only survivor then was Keseburg, a German, who was hated by all the company. There was a strong suspicion that he had killed Mrs. Donner, who had refused to leave her husband (who was too weak to travel) with the previous relief. There were threats of hanging him. Keseburg had saved his life by eating the bodies of the dead. Of the original party of eighty-seven, a total of thirty-nine perished from starvation. Most of the survivors were compelled to resort to cannabalism. They were not to blame if they did.

CHAPTER XXII.
MEXICAN LAWS AND AMERICAN OFFICIALS.

Upon the departure of General Kearny, May 31, 1847, Col. Richard B. Mason became governor and commander-in-chief of the United States forces in California by order of the president. Stockton, Kearny and Fremont had taken their departure, the dissensions that had existed since the conquest of the territory among the conquerors ceased, and peace reigned.

There were reports of Mexican invasions and suspicions of secret plottings against gringo rule, but the invaders came not and the plottings never produced even the mildest form of a Mexican revolution. Mexican laws were administered for the most part by military officers. The municipal authorities were encouraged to continue in power and perform their governmental functions, but they were indifferent and sometimes rebelled. Lender Mexican rule there was no trial by jury. The alcalde acted as judge and in criminal cases a council of war settled the fate of the criminal. The Rev. Walter Colton, while acting as alcalde of Monterey, in 1846-47, impaneled the first jury ever summoned in California. "The plaintiff and defendant," he writes, "are among the principal citizens of the country. The case was one involving property on the one side and integrity of character on the other. Its merits had been pretty widely discussed, and had called forth an unusual interest. One-third of the jury were Mexicans, one-third Californians and the other third Americans. This mixture may have the better answered the ends of justice, but I was apprehensive at one time it would embarrass the proceedings; for the plaintiff spoke in English, the defendant in French; the jury, save the Americans, Spanish, and the witnesses, all the languages known to California. By the tact of Mr. Hartnell, who acted as interpreter, and the absence of young lawyers, we got along very well.

"The examination of witnesses lasted five or six hours. I then gave the case to the jury, stating the questions of fact upon which they were to render their verdict. They retired for an hour and then returned, when the foreman handed in their verdict, which was clear and explicit, though the case itself was rather complicated. To this verdict both parties bowed without a word of dissent. The inhabitants who witnessed the trial said it was what they liked, that there could be no bribery in it, that the opinion of twelve honest men should set the case forever at rest. And so it did, though neither party completely triumphed in the issue. One recovered his property, which had been taken from him by mistake, the other his character, which had been slandered by design."

The process of Americanizing the people was no easy undertaking. The population of the country and its laws were in a chaotic condition. It was an arduous task that Colonel Mason and the military commanders at the various pueblos had to perform, that of evolving order out of the chaos that had been brought about by the change in nations. The native population neither understood the language nor the customs of their new rulers, and the newcomers among the Americans had very little toleration for the slow-going Mexican ways and methods they found prevailing. To keep peace between the factions required more tact than knowledge of law, military or civil, in the commanders.

Los Angeles, under Mexican domination, had been the storm center of revolutions, and here under the new regime the most difficulty was encountered in transforming the quondam revolutionists into law-abiding and peaceful American citizens. The ayuntamiento was convened in 1847, after the conquest, and continued in power until the close of the year. When the time came round for the election of a new ayuntamiento there was trouble. Stephen C. Foster, Colonel Stevenson's interpreter, submitted a paper to the council stating that the government had authorized him to get up a register of voters. The ayuntamiento voted to return the paper just as it was received. Then the colonel made a demand of the council to assist Stephen in compiling a register of voters. Regidor Chavez took the floor and said such a register should not be gotten up under the auspices of the military, but, since the government had so disposed, thereby outraging this honorable body, no attention should be paid to said communication. But the council decided that the matter did not amount to much, so they granted the request, much to the disgust of Chavez. The election was held and a new ayuntamiento elected. At the last meeting of the old council, December 29, 1847, Colonel Stevenson addressed a note to it requesting that Stephen C. Foster be recognized as first alcalde and judge of the first instance. The council decided to turn the whole business over to its successor, to deal with as it sees fit.

Colonel Stevenson's request was made in accordance with the wish of Governor Mason that a part of the civil offices be filled by Americans. The new ayuntamiento resented the interference. How the matter terminated is best told in Stephen C. Foster's own words: "Colonel Stevenson was determined to have our inauguration done in style. So on the day appointed, January 1, 1848, he. together with myself and colleague, escorted by a guard of soldiers, proceeded from the colonel's quarters to the alcalde's office. There we found the retiring ayuntamiento and the new one awaiting our arrival. The oath of office was administered by the retiring first alcalde. We knelt to take the oath, when we found they had changed their minds, and the alcalde told us that if two of their number were to be kicked out they would all go. So they all marched out and left us in possession. Here was a dilemma, but Colonel Stevenson was equal to the emergency. He said he could give us a swear as well as the alcalde. So we stood up and he administered to us an oath to support the constitution of the United States and administer justice in accordance with Mexican law. I then knew as much about Mexican law as I did about Chinese, and my colleague knew as much as I did. Guerrero gathered up the books that pertained to his office and took them to his house, where he established his office, and I took the archives and records across the street to a house I had rented, and there I was duly installed for the next seventeen months, the first American alcalde and carpet-bagger in Los Angeles."

Colonel Stevenson issued a call for the election of a new ayuntamiento, but the people stayed at home and no votes were cast. At the close of the year the voters had gotten over their pet and when a call was made a council was elected, but only Californians (hijos del pais) were returned. The ayuntamientos continued to be the governing power in the pueblos until superseded by city and county governments in 1850.

The most difficult problem that General Kearny in his short term had to confront and, unsolved, he handed down to his successor. Colonel Mason, was the

152

authority and jurisdiction of the alcaldes. Under the Mexican regime these officers were supreme in the pueblo over which they ruled. For the Spanish transgressor fines of various degrees were the usual penalty; for the mission neophyte, the lash, well laid on, and labor in the chain gang. There was no written code that defined the amount of punishment; the alcalde meted out justice and sometimes injustice, as suited his humor. Kearny appointed John H. Nash alcalde of Sonoma. Nash was a rather erratic individual, who had taken part in the Bear Flag revolution. When the offices of the prospective California Republic were divided among the revolutionists, he was to be the chief justice. After the collapse of that short-lived republic, Nash was elected alcalde. His rule was so arbitrary and his decisions so biased by favoritism or prejudice that the American settlers soon protested and General Kearny removed him or tried to. He appointed L. W. Boggs, a recently arrived immigrant, to the office. Nash refused to surrender the books and papers of the office. Lieut. W. T. Sherman was detailed by Colonel Mason, after his succession to the office of governor, to proceed to Sonoma and arrest Nash. Sherman quietly arrested him at night and before the bellicose alcalde's friends (for he had quite a following) were aware of what was going on, marched him off to San Francisco. He was put on board the Dale and sent to Monterey. Finding that it was useless for him to resist the authority of the United States, its army and navy as well, Nash expressed his willingness to submit to the inevitable, and surrendered his office. He was released and ceased from troubling. Another strenuous alcalde was William Blackburn, of Santa Cruz. He came to the country in 1845, and before his elevation to the honorable position of a judge of the first instance he had been engaged in making shingles in the redwoods. He had no knowledge of law and but little acquaintance with books of any kind. His decisions were always on the side of justice, although some of the penalties imposed were somewhat irregular.

In Alcalde Blackburn's docket for August 14, 1847, appears this entry: "Pedro Gomez was tried for the murder of his wife, Barbara Gomez, and found guilty. The sentence of the court is that the prisoner be conducted back to prison, there to remain until Monday, the 16th of August, and then be taken out and shot." August 17, sentence carried into effect on the 16th accordingly. William Blackburn, Alcalde.

It does not appear in the records that Blackburn was the executioner. He proceeded to dispose of the two orphaned children of the murderer. The older daughter he indentured to Jacinto Castro "to raise until she is twenty-one years of age, unless sooner married, said Jacinto Castro, obligating himself to give her a good education, three cows and calves at her marriage or when of age." The younger daughter was disposed of on similar terms to A. Rodriguez. Colonel Mason severely reprimanded Blackburn, but the alcalde replied that there was no use making a fuss over it; the man was guilty, he had a fair trial before a jury and deserved to die. Another case in his court illustrates the versatility of the judge. A Spanish boy, out of revenge, sheared the mane and tail of a neighbor's horse. The offense was proved, but the judge was sorely perplexed when he came to sentence the culprit. He could find no law in his law books to fit the case. After pondering over the question a while, he gave this decision: "I find no law in any of the statutes to fit this case, except in the law of Moses, 'An eye for an eye and a tooth for a tooth.' Let the prisoner be taken out in front of this office and there sheared close." The sentence was immediately executed.

Another story is told of Blackburn, which may or may not be true. A mission Indian who had committed murder took the right of sanctuary in the church, and the padre refused to give him up. Blackburn wrote to the governor, stating the case. The Indian, considering himself safe while with the padre, left the church in company with the priest. Blackburn seized him, tried him and hung him. He then reported to the governor: "I received your order to suspend the execution of the condemned man, but I had hung him. When I see you I will explain the affair."

Some of the military commanders of the presidios and pueblos gave Governor Mason as much trouble as the alcaldes. These, for the most part, were officers of the volunteers who had arrived after the conquest. They were unused to "war's alarms," and, being new to the country and ignorant of the Spanish language, they regarded the natives with suspicion. They were on the lookout for plots and revolutions. Sometimes they found these incubating and undertook to crush them, only to discover that the affair was a hoax or a practical joke. The Canon Perdido (lost cañon) of Santa Barbara episode is a good illustration of the trouble one "finicky" man can make when entrusted with military power.

In the winter of 1847-48 the American bark Elisabeth was wrecked on the Santa Barbara coast. Among the flotsam of the wreck was a brass cannon of uncertain caliber; it might have been a six, a nine or a twelve pounder. What the capacity of its bore matters not, for the gun unloaded made more noise in Santa Barbara than it ever did when it belched forth shot and shell in battle. The gun, after its rescue from a watery grave, lay for some time on the beach, devoid of carriage and useless, apparently, for offense or defense.

One dark night a little squad of native Californians stole down to the beach, loaded the gun in an ox cart, hauled it to the estero and hid it in the sands. What was their object in taking the gun no one knows. Perhaps they did not know themselves. It might come handy in a revolution, or maybe they only intended to play a practical joke on the gringos. Whatever their object, the outcome of their prank must have astonished them. There was a company (F) of Stevenson's New York volunteers stationed at Santa Barbara, under command of Captain Lippett. Lippett was a fussy, nervous individual who lost his head when anything unusual occurred. In the theft of the cannon he thought he had discovered a California revolution in the formative stages, and he determined to crush it in its infancy. He sent post haste a courier to Governor Mason at Monterey, informing him of the prospective uprising of the natives and the possible destruction of the troops at Santa Barbara by the terrible gun the enemy had stolen.

Colonel Mason, relying on Captain Lippett's report, determined to give the natives a lesson that would teach them to let guns and revolutions alone. He issued an order from headquarters at Monterey, in which he said that ample time having been allowed for the return of the gun, and the citizens having failed to produce it, he ordered that the town be laid under a contribution of $500, assessed in the following manner: A capitation tax of $2 on all males over twenty years of age; the balance to be paid by the heads of families and property-holders in the proportion of the value of their respective real and personal estate in the town of Santa Barbara and vicinity. Col. J. D. Stevenson was appointed to direct the appraisement

154

of the property and the collection of the assessment. If any failed to pay his capitation, enough of his property was to be seized and sold to pay his enforced contribution.

The promulgation of the order at Santa Barbara raised a storm of indignation at the old pueblo. Colonel Stevenson came up from Los Angeles and had an interview with Don Pablo de La Guerra, a leading citizen of Santa Barbara. Don Pablo was wrathfully indignant at the insult put upon his people, but after talking over the affair with Colonel Stevenson, he became somewhat mollified. He invited Colonel Stevenson to make Santa Barbara his headquarters and inquired about the brass band at the lower pueblo. Stevenson took the hint and ordered up the band from Los Angeles. July 4th had been fixed upon as the day for the payment of the fines, doubtless with the idea of giving the Californians a little celebration that would remind them hereafter of Liberty's natal day. Colonel Stevenson contrived to have the band reach Santa Barbara on the night of the 3rd. The band astonished Don Pablo and his family with a serenade. The Don was so delighted that he hugged the colonel in the most approved style. The band serenaded all the Dons of note in town and tooted until long after midnight, then started in next morning and kept it up till ten o'clock, the time set for each man to contribute his "dos pesos" to the common fund. By that time every hombre on the list was so filled with wine, music and patriotism that the greater portion of the fine was handed over without protest. The day closed with a grand ball. The beauty and the chivalry of Santa Barbara danced to the music of a gringo brass band and the brass cannon for the nonce was forgotten.

But the memory of the city's ransom rankled, and although an American band played Spanish airs, American injustice was still remembered. When the city's survey was made in 1850 the nomenclature of three streets, Cañon Perdido (Lost Cannon street), Quinientos (Five Hundred street) and Mason street kept the cannon episode green in the memory of the Barbareños. When the pueblo, by legislative act, became a ciudad, the municipal authorities selected this device for a seal: In the center a cannon emblazoned, encircled with these words, Vale Quinientos Pesos — Worth $500, or, more liberally translated. Good-bye, $500, which, by the way, as the sequel of the story will show, is the better translation. This seal was used from the incorporation of the city in 1850 to 1860, when another design was chosen.

After peace was declared, Colonel Mason sent the $500 to the prefect at Santa Barbara, with instructions to use it in building a city jail; and although there was pressing need for a jail, the jail was not built. The prefect's needs were pressing, too. Several years passed; then the city council demanded that the prefect turn the money into the city treasury. He replied that the money was entrusted to him for a specific purpose, and he would trust no city treasurer with it. The fact was that long before he had lost it in a game of monte.

Ten years passed, and the episode of the lost cannon was but a dimly remembered story of the olden time. The old gun reposed peacefully in its grave of sand and those who buried it had forgotten the place of its interment. One stormy night in December, 1858, the estero (creek) cut a new channel to the ocean. In the morning, as some Barbareños were surveying the changes caused by the flood, they saw the muzzle of a large gun protruding from the cut in the bank. They unearthed it, cleaned off the sand and discovered that it was El Canon Perdido, the lost cannon. It was hauled up State street to Canon Perdido, where it was mounted on an improvised carriage. But the sight of it was a reminder of an unpleasant incident. The finders sold it to a merchant for $80. He shipped it to San Francisco and sold it at a handsome profit for old brass.

Governor Pio Pico returned from Mexico to California, arriving at San Gabriel July 17, 1848. Although the treaty of peace between the United States and Mexico had been signed and proclaimed, the news had not reached California. Pico, from San Fernando, addressed letters to Colonel Stevenson at Los Angeles and Governor Mason at Monterey, stating that as Mexican governor of California he had come back to the country with the object of carrying out the armistice which then existed between the United States and Mexico. He further stated that he had no desire to impede the establishment of peace between the two countries; and that he wished to see the Mexicans and Americans treat each other in a spirit of fraternity. Mason did not like Pico's assumption of the title of Mexican governor of California, although it is not probable that Pico intended to assert any claim to his former position. Governor Mason sent a special courier to Los Angeles with orders to Colonel Stevenson to arrest the ex-governor, who was then at his Santa Margarita rancho, and send him to Monterey, but the news of the ratification of the treaty of Guadalupe Hidalgo reached Los Angeles before the arrest was made, and Pico was spared this humiliation.

The treaty of peace between the United States and Mexico was signed at Guadalupe Hidalgo, a hamlet a few miles from the City of Mexico, February 2, 1848; ratifications were exchanged at Queretaro, May 30 following, and a proclamation that peace had been established between the two countries was published July 4, 1848. Under this treaty the United States assumed the payment of the claims of American citizens against Mexico, and paid, in addition, $15,000,000 to Mexico for Texas, New Mexico and Alta California. Out of what was the Mexican territory of Alta California there has been carved all of California, all of Nevada, Utah and Arizona and part of Colorado and Wyoming. The territory acquired by the treaty of Guadalupe Hidalgo was nearly equal to the aggregated area of the thirteen original states at the time of the Revolutionary war.

The news of the treaty of peace reached California August 6, 1848. On the 7th Governor Mason issued a proclamation announcing the ratification of the treaty. He announced that all residents of California, who wished to become citizens of the United States, were absolved from their allegiance to Mexico. Those who desired to retain their Mexican citizenship could do so, provided they signified such intention within one year from May 30, 1848. Those who wished to go to Mexico were at liberty to do so without passports. Six months before. Governor Mason had issued a proclamation prohibiting any citizen of Sonora from entering California except on official business, and then only under flag of truce. He also required all Sonorans in the country to report themselves either at Los Angeles or Monterey.

The war was over; and the treaty of peace had made all who so elected, native or foreign born, American citizens. Strict military rule was relaxed and the people henceforth were to be self-governing. American and Californian were one people and were to enjoy the same rights and to be subject to the same penalties. The war

156

ended, the troops were no longer needed. Orders were issued to muster out the volunteers. These all belonged to Stevenson's New York regiment. The last company of the Mormon battalion had been discharged in April.

The New York volunteers were scattered all along the coast from Sonoma to Cape St. Lucas, doing garrison duty. They were collected at different points and mustered out. Although those stationed in Alta California had done no fighting, they had performed arduous service in keeping peace in the conquered territory. Most of them remained in California after their discharge and rendered a good account of themselves as citizens.

CHAPTER XXIII. GOLD! GOLD! GOLD!

Sebastian Viscaino, from the bay of Monterey, writing to the King of Spain three hundred years ago, says of the Indians of California: "They are well acquainted with gold and silver, and said that these were found in the interior." Viscaino was endeavoring to make a good impression on the mind of the king in regard to his discoveries, and the remark about the existence of gold and silver in California was thrown to excite the cupidity of his Catholic majesty. The traditions of the existence of gold in California before any was discovered are legion. Most of these have been evolved since gold was actually found. Col. J. J. Warner, a pioneer of 1831, in his Historical Sketch of Los Angeles County, briefly and very effectually disposes of these rumored discoveries. He says: "While statements respecting the existence of gold in the earth of California and its procurement therefrom have been made and published as historical facts, carrying back the date of the knowledge of the auriferous character of this state as far as the time of the visit of Sir Francis Drake to this coast, there is no evidence to be found in the written or oral history of the missions, the acts and correspondence of the civil or military officers, or in the unwritten and traditional history of Upper California that the existence of gold, either with ores or in its virgin state, was ever suspected by any inhabitant of California previous to 1841, and, furthermore, there is conclusive testimony that the first known grain of native gold dust was found upon or near the San Francisco ranch, about forty-five miles north-westerly from Los Angeles City, in the month of June, 1841. This discovery consisted of grain gold fields (known as placer mines), and the auriferous fields discovered in that year embraced the greater part of the country drained by the Santa Clara river from a point some fifteen or twenty miles from its mouth to its source, and easterly beyond Mount San Bernardino."

The story of the discovery as told by Warner and by Don Abel Stearns agrees in the main facts, but differs materially in the date. Stearns says gold was first discovered by Francisco Lopez, a native of California, in the month of March, 1842, at a place called San Francisquito, about thirty-five miles northwest from this city (Los Angeles). The circumstances of the discovery by Lopez, as related by himself, are as follows: "Lopez, with a companion, was out in search of some stray horses, and about midday they stopped under some trees and tied their horses out to feed, they resting under the shade, when Lopez, with his sheath-knife, dug up some wild onions, and in the dirt discovered a piece of gold, and, searching further, found some more. He brought these to town, and showed them to his friends, who at once declared there must be a placer of gold. This news being circulated, numbers of the citizens went to the place, and commenced prospecting in the neighborhood, and found it to be a fact that there was a placer of gold."

Colonel Warner says: "The news of this discovery soon spread among the inhabitants from Santa Barbara to Los Angeles, and in a few weeks hundreds of people were engaged in washing and winnowing the sands and earth of these gold fields."

Warner visited the mines a few weeks after their discovery. He says: "From these mines was obtained the first parcel of California gold dust received at the

United States mint in Philadelphia, and which was sent with Alfred Robinson, and went in a merchant ship around Cape Horn." This shipment of gold was 18.34 ounces before and 18.1 ounces after melting; fineness, •925; value, $344.75, or over $19 to the ounce. a very superior quality of gold dust. It was deposited in the mint July 8, 1843.

It may be regarded as a settled historical fact that the first authenticated discovery of gold in Aha California was made on the San Francisco rancho in the San Feliciano Cañon, Los Angeles county. This cañon is about ten miles northwest of Newhall station on the Southern Pacific railroad, and about forty miles northwest of Los Angeles.

The date of the discovery is in doubt. A petition to the governor (Alvarado) asking permission to work the placers, signed by Francisco Lopez, Manuel Cota and Domingo Bermudez is on file in the California archives. It recites: "That as Divine Providence was pleased to give us a placer of gold on the 9th of last March in the locality of San Francisco rancho, that belongs to the late Don Antonio del Valle." This petition fixes the day of the month the discovery was made, but unfortunately omits all other dates. The evidence is about equally divided between the years 1841 and 1842.

It is impossible to obtain definite information in regard to the yield of the San Fernando placers, as these mines are generally called. William Heath Davis, in his "Sixty Years in California," states that from $80,000 to $100,000 was taken out for the first two years after their discovery. He says that Melius at one time shipped $5,000 of dust on the ship Alert. Bancroft says: "That by December, 1843, two thousand ounces of gold had been taken from the San Fernando mines." Don Antonio Coronel informed the author that he, with the assistance of three Indian laborers, in 1842, took out $600 worth of dust in two months. De Moiras, in his book, states that Carlos Baric, a Frenchman, in 1842, was obtaining an ounce a day of pure gold from his placer.

These mines were worked continuously from the time of their discovery until the American conquest, principally by Sonorians. The discovery of gold at Coloma, January 24, 1848, drew away the miners, and no work was done on these mines between 1848 and 1854. After the latter dates work was resumed, and in 1855, Francisco Garcia, working a gang of Indians, is reported to have taken out $65,000 in one season. The mines are not exhausted, but the scarcity of water prevents working them profitably.

It is rather a singular coincidence that the exact dates of both the first and second authenticated discoveries of gold in California are still among the undecided questions of history. In the first, we know the day but not the year; in the second, we know the year but not the day of the month on which Marshall picked up the first nuggets in the millrace at Coloma. For a number of years after the anniversary of Marshall's discovery began to be observed the 19th of January was celebrated. Of late years January 24 has been fixed upon as the correct date, but the Associated Pioneers of the Territorial Days of California, an association made up of men who were in the territory at the time of Marshall's discovery or came here before it became a state, object to the change. For nearly thirty years they have held their annual dinners on January 18, "the anniversary of the discovery of gold at Sutter's sawmill, Coloma, Cal." This society has its headquarters in New York City. In a

159

circular recently issued, disapproving of the change of date from the 18th to the 24th, the trustees of that society say: "Upon the organization of this society, February 11, 1875, it was decided to hold its annual dinners on the anniversary of the discovery of gold at Sutter's sawmill, Coloma, Cal. Through the Hon. Newton Booth, of the United States Senate, this information was sought, with the result of a communication from the secretary of the state of California to the effect 'that the archives of the state of California recorded the date as of January 18, 1848. Some years ago this date was changed by the society at San Francisco to that of January 24, and that date has been adopted by other similar societies located upon the Pacific and Atlantic coasts. This society took the matter under advisement, with the result that the new evidence upon which it was proposed to change the date was not deemed sufficient to justify this society in ignoring its past records, founded on the authority of the state of California; therefore it has never accepted the new date."

Marshall himself was uncertain about the exact date. At various times he gave three different dates — the 18th, 19th and 20th, but never moved it along as far as the 24th. In the past thirty years three different dates — the 18th, 19th and 24th of January — have been celebrated as the anniversary of Marshall's gold discovery.

The evidence upon which the date was changed to the 24th is found in an entry in a diary kept by H. W. Bigler, a Mormon, who was working for Marshall on the millrace at the time gold was discovered. The entry reads: "January 24. This day some kind of metal that looks like gold was found in the tailrace." On this authority about ten years ago the California Pioneers adopted the 24th as the correct date of Marshall's discovery.

While written records, especially if made at the time of the occurrence of the event, are more reliable than oral testimony given long after, yet when we take into consideration the conflicting stories of Sutter, Marshall, the Winners and others who were immediately concerned in some way with the discovery, we must concede that the Territorial Pioneers have good reasons to hesitate about making a change in the date of their anniversary. In Dr. Trywhitt Brook's "Four Months Among the Gold Finders," a book published in London in 1849, and long since out of print, we have Sutter's version of Marshall's discovery given only three months after that discovery was made. Dr. Brooks visited Sutter's Fort early in May, 1848, and received from Sutter himself the story of the find. Sutter stated that he was sitting in his room at the fort, one afternoon, when Marshall, whom he supposed to be at the mill, forty miles up the American river, suddenly burst in upon him. Marshall was so wildly excited that Sutter, suspecting that he was crazy, looked to see whether his rifle was in reach. Marshall declared that he had made a discovery that would give them both millions and millions of dollars. Then he drew his sack and poured out a handful of nuggets on the table. Sutter, when he had tested the metal and found that it was gold, became almost as excited as Marshall. He eagerly asked if the workmen at the mill knew of the discovery. Marshall declared that he had not spoken to a single person about it. They both agreed to keep it secret. Next day Sutter and Marshall arrived at the sawmill. The day after their arrival, they prospected the bars of the river and the channels of some of the dry creeks and found gold in all.

"On our return to the mill," says Sutter, "we were astonished by the work-people coming up to us in a body and showing us some flakes of gold similar to those we had ourselves procured. Marshall tried to laugh the matter off with them, and to persuade them that what they had found was only some shining mineral of trifling value; but one of the Indians, who had worked at a gold mine in the neighborhood of La Paz, Lower California, cried out: 'Oral Oral' (gold! gold!), and the secret was out."

Captain Sutter continues: "I heard afterward that one of them, a sly Kentuckian, had dogged us about and, that, looking on the ground to see if he could discover what we were in search of, he lighted on some of the flakes himself."

If this account is correct, Bigler's entry in his diary was made on the day that the workmen found gold, which was five or six days after Marshall's first find, and consequently the 24th is that much too late for the true date of the discovery. The story of the discovery given in the "Life and Adventures of James W. Marshall," by George Frederick Parsons, differs materially from Sutter's account. The date of the discovery given in that book is January 19, 1848. On the morning of that day Marshall, after shutting off the water, walked down the tailrace to see what sand and gravel had been removed during the night. (The water was turned into the tailrace during the night to cut it deeper.) While examining a mass of debris, "his eye caught the glitter of something that lay lodged in a crevice on a riffle of soft granite some six inches under water." Picking up the nugget and examining it, he became satisfied that it must be one of three substances — mica, sulphurets of copper, or gold. Its weight satisfied him that it was not mica. Knowing that gold was malleable, he placed the specimen on a flat rock and struck it with another; it bent, but did not crack or break. He was satisfied that it was gold. He showed the nugget to his men. In the course of a few days he had collected several ounces of precious metal. "Some four days after the discovery it became necessary for him to go below, for Sutter had failed to send a supply of provisions to the mill, and the men were on short commons. While on his way down he discovered gold in a ravine at a place afterwards known as Mormon island. Arrived at the fort, he interviewed Sutter in his private office and showed him about three ounces of gold nuggets. Sutter did not believe it to be gold, but after weighing it in scales against $3.25 worth of silver, all the coin they could raise at the fort, and testing it with nitric acid obtained from the gun shop, Sutter became convinced and returned to the mill with Marshall. So little did the workmen at the mill value the discovery that they continued to work for Sutter until the mill was completed, March 11, six weeks after the nuggets were found in the tailrace. The news of the discovery spread slowly. It was I two months in reaching San Francisco, although the distance is not over one hundred and twenty-five miles. The great rush to the mines from San Francisco did not begin until the middle of May, nearly four months after the discovery. On the 10th of May, Dr. Brooks, who was in San Francisco, writes: "A number of people have actually started off with shovels, mattocks and pans to dig the gold themselves. It is not likely, however, that this will be allowed, for Captain Folsom has already written to Colonel Mason about taking possession of the mine on behalf of the government, it being, he says, on public land."

As the people began to realize the richness and extent of the discovery, the excitement increased rapidly. May 17, Dr. Brooks writes: "This place (San

Francisco) is now in a perfect furore of excitement; all the workpeople have struck. Walking through the town to-day, I observed that laborers were employed only upon about half a dozen of the fifty new buildings which were in course of being run up. The majority of the mechanics at this place are making preparations for moving off to the mines, and several people of all classes — lawyers, storekeepers, merchants, etc., are smitten with the fever; in fact, there is a regular gold mania springing up. I counted no less than eighteen houses which were closed, the owners having left. If Colonel Mason is moving a force to the American Fork, as is reported here, their journey will be in vain."

Colonel Mason's soldiers moved without orders — they nearly all deserted, and ran off to the mines.

The first newspaper announcement of the discovery appeared in The Californian of March 15, 1848, nearly two months after the discovery. But little attention was paid to it. In the issue of April 19, another discovery is reported. The item reads: "New gold mine. It is stated that a new gold mine has been discovered on the American Fork of the Sacramento, supposed to be on the land of W. A. Leidesdorff, of this place. A specimen of the gold has been exhibited, and is represented to be very pure." On the 29th of May, The Californian had suspended publication. "Othello's occupation is gone," wails the editor. "The majority of our subscribers and many of our advertising patrons have closed their doors and places of business and left town, and we have received one order after another conveying the pleasant request that the printer will please stop my paper or my ad, as I am about leaving for Sacramento."

The editor of the other paper, The California Star, made a pilgrimage to the mines in the latter part of April, but gave them no extended write-up. "Great country, fine climate," he wrote on his return. "Full flowing streams, mighty timber, large crops, luxuriant clover, fragrant flowers, gold and silver," were his comments on what he saw. The policy of both papers seems to have been to ignore as much as possible the gold discovery. To give it publicity was for a time, at least, to lose their occupation.

In The Star of May 20, 1848, its eccentric editor, E. C. Kemble, under the caption "El Dorado Anew," discourses in a dubious manner upon the effects of the discovery and the extent of the gold fields: "A terrible visitant we have had of late. A fever which has well-nigh depopulated a town, a town hard pressing upon a thousand souls, and but for the gracious interposition of the elements, perhaps not a goose would have been spared to furnish a quill to pen the melancholy fate of the remainder. It has preyed upon defenseless old age, subdued the elasticity of careless youth and attacked indiscriminately sex and class, from town councilman to tow-frocked cartman, from tailor to tippler, of which, thank its pestilential powers, it has beneficially drained (of tipplers, we mean) every villainous pulperia in the place.

"And this is the gold fever, the only form of that popular southerner, yellow jack, with which we can be alarmingly threatened. The insatiate maw of the monster, not appeased by the easy conquest of the rough-fisted yeomanry of the north, must needs ravage a healthy, prosperous place beyond his dominion and turn the town topsy-turvy in a twinkling.

"A fleet of launches left this place on Sunday and Monday last bound up the Sacramento river, close stowed with human beings, led by love of filthy lucre to the perennial yielding gold mines of the north. When any man can find two ounces a day and two thousand men can find their hands full, of work, was there ever anything so superlatively silly!

"Honestly, though, we are inclined to believe the reputed wealth of that section of country, thirty miles in extent, all sham, a superb take-in as was ever got up to guzzle the gullible. But it is not improbable that this mine, or, properly, placer of gold can be traced as far south as the city of Los Angeles, where the precious metal has been found for a number of years in the bed of a stream issuing from its mountains, said to be a continuation of this gold chain which courses southward from the base of the snowy mountains. But our best information respecting the metal and the quantity in which it is gathered varies much from many reports current, yet it is beyond a question that no richer mines of gold have ever been discovered upon this continent.

"Should there be no paper forthcoming on Saturday next, our readers may assure themselves it will not be the fault of us individually. To make the matter public, already our devil has rebelled, our pressman (poor fellow) last seen was in search of a pickaxe, and we feel like Mr. Hamlet, we shall never again look upon the likes of him. Then, too, our compositors have, in defiance, sworn terrible oaths against type-sticking as vulgar and unfashionable. Hope has not yet fled us, but really, in the phraseology of the day, 'things is getting curious.' "

And things kept getting more and more curious. The rush increased. The next issue of The Star (May 27) announces that the Sacramento, a first-class craft, left here Thursday last thronged with passengers for the gold mines, a motley assemblage, composed of lawyers, merchants, grocers, carpenters, cartmen and cooks, all possessed with the desire of becoming rich. The latest accounts from the gold country are highly flattering. Over three hundred men are engaged in washing gold, and numbers are continually arriving from every part of the country. Then the editor closes with a wail: "Persons recently arrived from the country speak of ranches deserted and crops neglected and suffered to waste. The unhappy consequence of this state of affairs is easily foreseen. One more twinkle, and The Star disappeared in the gloom. On June 14 appeared a single sheet, the size of foolscap. The editor announced: "In fewer words than are usually employed in the announcement of similar events, we appear before the remnant of a reading community on this occasion with the material or immaterial information that we have stopped the paper, that its publication ceased with the last regular issue (June 7). On the approach of autumn, we shall again appear to announce The Star's redivus. We have done. Let our parting word be hasta luego." Star and Californian reappeared November 14, 1848. The Star had absorbed The Californian. E. C. Kemble was its editor and proprietor.)

Although there was no paper in existence on the coast to spread the news from the gold fields, it found its way out of California, and the rush from abroad began. It did not acquire great force in 1848, but in 1849 the immigration to California exceeded all previous migrations in the history of the race.

Among the first foreigners to rush to the mines were the Mexicans of Sonora. Many of these had had some experience in placer mining in their native country, and the report of rich placers in California, where gold could be had for the picking up, aroused them from their lazy self-content and stimulated them to go in search of it. Traveling in squads of from fifty to one hundred, they came by the old Auza trail across the Colorado desert, through the San Gorgonio Pass, then up the coast and on to the mines. They were a job lot of immigrants, poor in purse and poor in brain. They were despised by the native Californians and maltreated by the Americans. Their knowledge of mining came in play, and the more provident among them soon managed to pick up a few thousand dollars, and then returned to their homes, plutocrats. The improvident gambled away their earnings and remained in the country to add to its criminal element. The Oregonians came in force, and all the towns in California were almost depopulated of their male population. By the close of 1848, there were ten thousand men at work in the mines.

The first official report of the discovery was sent to Washington by Thomas O. Larkin, June 1, and reached its destination about the middle of September. Lieutenant Beale, by way of Mexico, brought dispatches dated a month later, which arrived about the same time as Larkin's report. These accounts were published in the eastern papers, and the excitement began.

In the early part of December, Lieutenant Loeser arrived at Washington with Governor Mason's report of his observations in the mines made in August. But the most positive evidence was a tea caddy of gold dust containing about two hundred and thirty ounces that Governor Mason had caused to be purchased in the mines with money from the civil service fund. This the lieutenant had brought with him. It was placed on exhibition al the war office. Here was tangible evidence of the existence of gold in California, the doubters were silenced and the excitement was on and the rush began.

By the 1st of January, 1849, vessels were fitting out in every seaport on the Atlantic coast' and the Gulf of Mexico. Sixty ships were announced to sail from New York in February and seventy from Philadelphia and Boston. All kinds of crafts were pressed into the service, some to go by way of Cape Horn, others to land their passengers at Vera Cruz, Greytown and Chagres, the voyagers to take their chances on the Pacific side for a passage on some unknown vessel.

With opening of spring, the overland travel began. Forty thousand men gathered at different points on the Missouri river, but principally at St. Joseph and Independence. Horses, mules, oxen and cows were used for the propelling power of the various forms of vehicles that were to convey the provisions and other impedimenta of the army of gold seekers. By the 1st of May the grass was grown enough on the plains to furnish feed for the stock, and the vanguard of the grand army of gold hunters started. For two months, company after company left the rendezvous and joined the procession until for one thousand miles there was an almost unbroken line of wagons and pack trains. The first half of the journey was made with little inconvenience, but on the last part there was great suffering and loss of life. The cholera broke out among them, and it is estimated that five thousand died on the plains. The alkali desert of the Humboldt was the place where the immigrants suffered most. Exhausted by the long journey and weakened by lack of food, many succumbed under the hardship of the desert journey and died. The crossing of the Sierras was attended with great hardships. From the loss of their horses and oxen, many were compelled to cross the mountain on foot. Their provisions exhausted, they would have perished but for relief sent out from California. The greatest sufferers were the woman and children, who in considerable numbers made the perilous journey.

The overland immigration of 1850 exceeded that of 1849. According to record kept at Fort Laramie, there passed that station during the season thirty-nine thousand men, two thousand five hundred women and six hundred children, making a total of forty-two thousand one hundred persons. These immigrants had with them when passing Fort Laramie twenty-three thousand horses, eight thousand mules, three thousand six hundred oxen, seven thousand cows and nine thousand wagons.

Besides those coming by the northern route, that is by the South Pass and the Humboldt river, at least ten thousand found their way to the land of gold by the old Spanish trail, by the Gila route and by Texas, Coahuila and Chihuahua into Arizona, and thence across the Colorado desert to Los Angeles, and from there by the coast route or the San Joaquin valley to the mines.

The Pacific Mail Steamship Company had been organized before the discovery of gold in California. March 3, 1847, an act of Congress was passed authorizing the secretary of the navy to advertise for bids to carry the United States mails by one line of steamers between New York and Chagres, and by another line between Panama and Astoria, Ore. On the Atlantic side the contract called for five ships of one thousand five hundred tons burden, on the Pacific side two of one thousand tons each, and one of six hundred tons. These were deemed sufficient for the trade and travel between the Atlantic and Pacific coasts of the United States. The Pacific Mail Steamship Company was incorporated April 12, 1848, with a capital stock of $500,000. October 6, 1848, the California, the first steamer for the Pacific, sailed from New York, and was followed in the two succeeding months by the Oregon and the Panama. The California sailed before the news of the gold discovery had reached New York, and she had taken no passengers. When she arrived at Panama, January 30, 1849, she encountered a rush of fifteen hundred gold hunters, clamorous for a passage. These had reached Chagres on sailing vessels, and ascended the Chagres river in bongos or dugouts to Gorgona, and from thence by land to Panama. The California had accommodations for only one hundred, but four hundred managed to find some place to stow themselves away. The price of tickets rose to a fabulous sum, as high as $1,000 having been paid for a steerage passage. The California entered the bay of San Francisco February 28, 1849, and was greeted by the boom of cannon and the cheers of thousands of people lining the shores of the bay. The other two steamers arrived on time, and the Pacific Mail Steamship Company became the predominant factor in California travel for twenty years, or up to the completion of the first transcontinental railroad in 1869. The charges for fare on these steamers in the early '50s were prohibitory to men of small means. From New York to Chagres in the saloon the fare was $150, in the cabin $120. From Panama to San Francisco in the saloon, $250; cabin, $200. Add to these the expense of crossing the isthmus, and the argonaut was out a goodly sum when he reached the land of the golden fleece, indeed, he was often fleeced of his last dollar before he entered the Golden Gate.

The first effect of the gold discovery on San Francisco, as we have seen, was to depopulate it, and of necessity suspend all building operations. In less than three months the reaction began, and the city experienced one of the most magical booms in history. Real estate doubled in some instances in twenty-four hours. The Californian of September 3, 1848, says: "The vacant lot on the corner of

Montgomery and Washington streets was offered the day previous for $5,000 and next day sold readily for $10,000." Lumber went up in value until it was sold at a dollar per square foot. Wages kept pace with the general advance. Sixteen dollars a day was mechanic's wages, and the labor market was not overstocked even at these high rates. With the approach of winter, the gold seekers came flocking back to the city to find shelter and to spend their suddenly acquired wealth. The latter was easily accomplished, but the former was more difficult. Any kind of a shelter that would keep out the rain was utilized for a dwelling. Rows of tents that circled around the business portion, shanties patched together from pieces of packing boxes and sheds thatched with brush from the chaparral-covered hills constituted the principal dwellings at that time of the future metropolis of California. The yield of the mines for 1848 has been estimated at ten million dollars. This was the result of only a few months' labor of not to exceed at any time ten thousand men. The rush of miners did not reach the mines until July, and mining operations were mainly suspended by the middle of October.

New discoveries had followed in quick succession Marshall's find at Coloma until by the close of 1848 gold placers had been located on all the principal tributaries of the Sacramento and San Joaquin rivers. Some of the richest yields were obtained from what was known as "Dry Diggins." These were dry ravines from which pay dirt had to be packed to water for washing or the gold separated by dry washing, tossing the earth into the air until it was blown away by the wind, the gold, on account of its weight, remaining in the pan.

A correspondent of the Californian, writing August 15, 1848, from what he designates as "Dry Diggins," gives this account of the richness of that gold field: "At the lower mines (Mormon Island) the miners count the success of the day in dollars; at the upper mines near the mill (Coloma), in ounces, and here in pounds. The only instrument used at first was a butcher knife, and the demand for that article was so great that $40 has been refused for one.

"The earth is taken out of the ravines which make out of the mountains and is carried in wagons or packed on horses from one to three miles to water and washed. Four hundred dollars is the average to the cart load. In one instance five loads yielded $16,000. Instances are known here where men have carried the earth on their backs and collected from $800 to $1,500 a day."

The rapidity with which the country was explored by prospectors was truly remarkable. The editor of the Californian, who had suspended the publication of his paper on May 29 to visit the mines, returned and resumed it on July 15 (1848). In an editorial in that issue he gives his observations: "The country from the Ajuba (Yuba) to the San Joaquin rivers, a distance of one hundred and twenty miles, and from the base toward the summit of the mountains as far as Snow Hill, about seventy miles, has been explored, and gold found in every part. There are probably three thousand men, including Indians, engaged in collecting gold. The amount collected by each man who works ranges from $10 to $350 per day. The publisher of this paper, while on a tour alone to the mining district, collected, with the aid of a shovel, pick and pan, from $44 to $128 a day, averaging about $100. The largest piece of gold known to be found weighed four pounds." Among other remarkable yields the Californian reports these: "One man dug $12,000 in six days, and three others obtained thirty-six pounds of pure metal in one day."

166

CHAPTER XXIV. MAKING A STATE.

Col. R. B. Mason, who had been the military governor of California since the departure of General Kearny in May, 1847, had grown weary of his task. He had been in the military service of his country thirty years and wished to be relieved. His request was granted, and on the 12th of April, 1849, Brevet Brigadier General Bennett Riley, his successor, arrived at Monterey and the next day entered upon his duties as civil governor. Gen. Persifer F. Smith, who had been appointed commander of the Pacific division of the United States army, arrived at San Francisco February 26, 1849, and relieved Colonel Mason of his military command. A brigade of troops six hundred and fifty strong had been sent to California for military service on the border and to maintain order. Most of these promptly deserted as soon as an opportunity offered and found their way to the mines.

Colonel Mason, who under the most trying circumstances had faithfully served his government and administered justice to the people of California, took his departure May 1, 1849. The same year he died at St. Louis of cholera. A year had passed since the treaty of peace with Mexico had been signed, which made California United States territory, but Congress had done nothing toward giving it a government. The anomalous condition existed of citizens of the United States, living in the United States, being governed by Mexican laws administered by a mixed constituency of Mexican-born and American-born officials. The proslavery element in Congress was determined to foist the curse of human slavery on a portion of the territory acquired from Mexico, but the discovery of gold and the consequent rush of freemen to the territory had disarranged the plans of the slave-holding faction in Congress, and as a consequence all legislation was at a standstill.

The people were becoming restive at the long delay. The Americanized Mexican laws and forms of government were unpopular and it was humiliating to the conqueror to be governed by the laws of the people conquered. The question of calling a convention to form a provisional government was agitated by the newspapers and met a hearty response from the people. Meetings were held at San Jose, December II, 1848; at San Francisco, December 21, and at Sacramento, January 6, 1849, to consider the question of establishing a provisional government. It was recommended by the San Jose meeting that a convention be held at that place on the second Monday of January. The San Francisco convention recommended the 5th of March; this the Monterey committee considered too early as it would take the delegates from below fifteen days to reach the pueblo of San Jose. There was no regular mail and the roads in February (when the delegates would have to start) were impassable. The committee recommended May 1 as the earliest date for the meeting to consider the question of calling of a convention. Sonoma, without waiting, took the initiative and elected ten delegates to a provisional government convention. There was no unanimity in regard to the time of meeting or as to what could be done if the convention met. It was finally agreed to postpone the time of meeting to the first Monday of August, when, if Congress had done nothing towards giving California some form of government better than that existing, the convention should meet and organize a provisional government.

The local government of San Francisco had become so entangled and mixed up by various councils that it was doubtful whether it had any legal legislative body. When the term of the first council, which had been authorized by Colonel Mason in 1848, was about to expire an election was held December 27, to choose their successors. Seven new councilmen were chosen. The old council declared the election fraudulent and ordered a new one. An election was held, notwithstanding the protest of a number of the best citizens, and another council chosen. So the city was blessed or cursed with three separate and distinct councils. The old council voted itself out of existence and then there were but two, but that was one too many. Then the people, disgusted with the condition of affairs, called a public meeting, at which it was decided to elect a legislative assembly of fifteen members, who should be empowered to make the necessary laws for the government of the city. An election was held on the 21st of February, 1849, and a legislative assembly and justices elected. Then Alcalde Levenworth refused to turn over the city records to the Chief Magistrate-elect Norton. On the 22nd of March the legislative assembly abolished the office of alcalde, but Levenworth still held on to the records. He was finally compelled by public opinion and a writ of replevin to surrender the official records to Judge Norton. The confusion constantly arising from the attempt to carry on a government that was semi-military and semi-Mexican induced Governor Riley to order an election to be held August 1st, to elect delegates to a convention to meet in Monterey September 1st, 1849, to form a state constitution or territorial organization to be ratified by the people and submitted to Congress for its approval. Judges, prefects and alcaldes were to be elected at the same time in the principal municipal districts. The constitutional convention was to consist of thirty-seven delegates, apportioned as follows: San Diego two, Los Angeles four, Santa Barbara two, San Luis Obispo two, Monterey five, San Jose five, San Francisco five, Sonoma four, Sacramento four, and San Joaquin four. Instead of thirty-seven delegates as provided for in the call, forty-eight were elected and seated.

The convention met September 1, 1849, at Monterey in Colton Hall. This was a stone building erected by Alcalde Walter Colton for a town hall and school house. The money to build it was derived partly from fines and partly from subscriptions, the prisoners doing the greater part of the work. It was the most commodious public building at that time in the territory.

Of the forty-eight delegates elected twenty-two were natives of the northern states; fifteen of the slave states; four were of foreign birth, and seven were native Californians. Several of the latter neither spoke nor understood the English language and William E. P. Hartnell was appointed interpreter. Dr. Robert Semple of Bear Flag fame was elected president, William G. Marcy and J. Ross Browne reporters.

Early in the session the slavery question was disposed of by the adoption of a section declaring that neither slavery or involuntary servitude, unless for the punishment of crimes, shall ever be tolerated in this state. The question of fixing the boundaries of the future state excited the most discussion. The pro-slavery faction was led by William M. Gwin, who had a few months before migrated from Mississippi to California with the avowed purpose of representing the new state in the United States senate. The scheme of Gwin and his southern associates was to make the Rocky mountains the eastern boundary. This would create a state with an era of about four hundred thousand square miles. They reasoned that when the admission of the state came before congress the southern members would oppose the admission of so large an area under a free state constitution and that ultimately a compromise might be effected. California would be split in two from east to west, the old dividing line, the parallel of 36° 30', would be established and Southern California come into the Union as a. slave state. There were at that time fifteen free and fifteen slave states. If two states, one free and one slave, could be made out of California, the equilibrium between the opposing factions would be maintained. The Rocky mountain boundary was at one time during the session adopted, but in the closing days of the session the free state men discovered Gwin's scheme and it was defeated. The present boundaries were established by a majority of two.

A committee had been appointed to receive propositions and designs for a state seal. Only one design was offered. It was presented by Caleb Lyon of Lyondale, as he usually signed his name, but was drawn by Major Robert S. Garnett, an army officer. It contained a figure of Minerva in the foreground, a grizzly bear feeding on a bunch of grapes; a miner with an uplifted pick; a gold rocker and pan; a view of the Golden Gate with ships riding at anchor in the Bay of San Francisco; the peaks of the Sierra Nevadas in the distance; a sheaf of wheat; thirty-one stars and above all the word "Eureka" (I have found it), which might apply either to the miner or the bear. The design seems to have been an attempt to advertise the resources of the state. General Vallejo wanted the bear taken out of the design, or if allowed to remain, that he be made fast by a lasso in the hands of a vaquero. This amendment was rejected, as was also one submitted by O. M. Wozencraft to strike out the figures of the gold digger and the bear and introduce instead bales of merchandise and bags of gold. The original design was adopted with the addition of the words, "The Great Seal of the State of California." The convention voted to give Lyon $1,000 as full compensation for engraving the seal and furnishing the press and all appendages.

Garnett, the designer of the seal, was a Virginian by birth. He graduated from West Point in 1841, served through the Mexican war and through several of the Indian wars on the Pacific coast. At the breaking out of the rebellion in 1861 he joined the Confederates and was made a brigadier general. He was killed at the battle of Carrick's Ford July 15, 1861.

The constitution was completed on the nth of October and an election was called by Governor Riley to be held on the 13th of November to vote upon the adoption of the constitution and to elect state officers, a legislature and members of congress.

At the election Peter H. Burnett, recently from Oregon territory, who had been quite active in urging the organization of a state government, was chosen governor; John McDougall, lieutenant governor, and George W. Wright and Edward Gilbert members of congress. San Jose had been designated by the constitutional convention the capital of the state pro tem.

The people of San Jose had pledged themselves to provide a suitable building for the meeting of the legislature in hopes that their town might be made the permanent capital. They were unable to complete the building designed for a state capital in time for the meeting. The uncomfortable quarters furnished created a great deal of dissatisfaction. The legislature consisted of sixteen senators and thirty-six assemblymen. There being no county organization, the members were elected by districts. The representation was not equally distributed; San Joaquin district had more senators than San Francisco. The senate and assembly were organized on the 17th of December. E. K. Chamberlain of San Diego was elected president pro tem. of the senate and Thomas J. White of Sacramento speaker of the assembly. The governor and lieutenant-governor were sworn in on the 20th. The state government being organized the legislature proceeded to the election of United States senators. The candidates were T. Butler King, John C. Fremont, William M. Gwin, Thomas J. Henly, John W. Geary, Robert Semple and H. W. Halleck. Fremont received twenty-nine out of forty-six votes on the first ballot and was declared elected. Of the aspirants, T. Butler King and William M. Gwin represented the ultra pro-slavery element. King was a crossroads politician from down in Georgia, who had been sent to the coast as a confidential agent of the government. The officers of the army and navy were enjoined to "in all matters aid and assist him in carrying out the views of the government and be guided by his advice and council in the conduct of all proper measures within the scope of those instructions." He made a tour of the mines, accompanied by General Smith and his staff; Commodore Ap Catesby Jones and staff and a cavalry escort under Lieutenant Stoneman. He wore a black stovepipe hat and a dress coat. He made himself the laughing stock of the miners and by traveling in the heat of the day contracted a fever that very nearly terminated his existence. He had been active so far as his influence went in trying to bring California into the Union with the hope of representing it in the senate. Gwin had come a few months before from Mississippi with the same object in view. Although the free state men were in the majority in the legislature they recognized the fact that to elect two senators opposed to the extension of slavery would result in arraying the pro-slavery faction in congress against the admission of the state into the Union. Of the two representatives of the south, Gwin was the least objectionable and on the second ballot he was elected. On the 21st Governor Burnett delivered his message. It was a wordy document, but not marked by any very brilliant ideas or valuable suggestions. Burnett was a southerner from Missouri. He was hobbled on the subject of the exclusion of free negroes. The African, free to earn his own living unrestrained by a master, was, in his opinion, a menace to the perpetuity of the commonwealth.

On the 22nd the legislature elected the remaining state officers, viz.: Richard Roman, treasurer; John I. Houston, controller; E. J. C. Kewen, attorney general; Charles J. Whiting, surveyor-general; S. C. Hastings, chief justice; Henry Lyons and Nathaniel Bennett, associate justices. The legislature continued in session until April 22, 1850. Although it was nicknamed the "Legislature of a thousand drinks," it did a vast amount of work and did most of it well. It was not made up of hard drinkers. The majority of its members were above the average legislator in intelligence, temperance and patriotism. The members were not there for pay or for political preferment. They were there for the good of their adopted state and labored conscientiously for its benefit. The opprobrious nickname is said to have originated thus: A roistering individual by the name of Green had been elected to the senate from Sacramento as a joke. He regarded the whole proceedings as a huge joke. He kept a supply of liquors on hand at his quarters and when the legislature adjourned he was in the habit of calling: "Come, boys, let us take a thousand drinks."

The state had set up housekeeping without a cent on hand to defray expenses. There was not a quire of paper, a pen, nor an inkstand belonging to the state and no money to buy supplies. After wrestling with the financial problem some time an act authorizing a loan of $200,000 for current expenses was passed. Later on in the session another act was passed authorizing the bonding of the state for $300,000 with interest at the rate of three per cent a month. The legislature divided the state into twenty-seven counties, created nine judicial districts, passed laws for the collection of revenue, taxing all real and personal property and imposing a poll tax of $5 on all male inhabitants over twenty-one and under fifty years of age.

California was a self-constituted state. It had organized a state government and put it into successful operation without the sanction of congress. Officials, state, county and town, had been elected and had sworn to support the constitution of the state of California and yet there was really no state of California. It had not been admitted into the Union. It was only a state de facto and it continued in that condition nine months before it became a state de jure.

When the question of admitting California into the Union came before congress it evoked a bitter controversy. The senate was equally divided, thirty senators from the slave states and the same number from the free. There were among the southern senators some broad minded and patriotic men, willing to do what was right, but they were handicapped by an ultra pro-slavery faction, extremists, who would willingly sacrifice the Union if by that they could extend and perpetuate that sum of all villainies, human slavery. This faction in the long controversy resorted to every known parliamentary device to prevent the admission of California under a free state constitution. To admit two senators from a free state would destroy the balance of power. That gone, it could never be regained by the south. The north was; increasing in power and population, while the south, under the blighting influence of slavery, was retrograding.

Henry Clay, the man of compromises, undertook to bridge over the difficulty by a set of resolutions known as the Omnibus bill. These were largely concessions to the slave holding faction for the loss of the territory acquired by the Mexican war. Among others was this, that provision should be made by law for the restitution of fugitive slaves in any state or territory of the Union. This afterward was embodied into what was known as the fugitive slave law and did more perhaps than any other cause to destroy the south's beloved institution.

These resolutions were debated through many months and were so amended and changed that their author could scarcely recognize them. Most of them were adopted in some form and effected a temporary compromise.

On August 13th the bill for the admission of California finally came to a vote. It passed the senate, thirty-four ayes to eighteen noes. Even then the opposition did not cease. Ten of the southern pro-slavery extremists, led by Jefferson Davis, joined in a protest against the action of the majority, the language of which was an insult to the senate and treason to the government. In the house the bill passed by a vote of one hundred and fifty ayes to fifty-six ultra southern noes. It was approved and signed by President Fillmore September 9, 1850. On the nth of September the

171

California senators and congressmen presented themselves to be sworn in. The slave holding faction in the senate, headed by Jefferson Davis, who had been one of the most bitter opponents to the admission, objected. But their protest availed them nothing. Their ascendency was gone. We might sympathize with them had their fight been made for a noble principle, but it was not. From that day on until the attempt was made in 1861 these men schemed to destroy the Union. The admission of California as a free state was the beginning of the movement to destroy the Union of States.

The news of the admission of California reached San Francisco on the morning of October 18, by the mail steamer Oregon, nearly six weeks after congress had admitted it. Business was at once suspended, the courts were adjourned and the people went wild with excitement. Messengers, mounted on fleet steeds, spread the news throughout the state. Newspapers from the states containing an account of the proceedings of congress at the time of admission sold for $5 each. It was decided to hold a formal celebration of the event on the 29th and preparations were begun for a grand demonstration. Neither labor nor money was spared to make the procession a success. The parade was cosmopolitan in the fullest meaning of that word. There were people in it from almost every nation under the sun. The Chinese made quite an imposing spectacle in the parade. Dressed in rich native costumes, each carrying a gaudily painted fan, they marched under command of their own marshals. Ah He and Ah Sing. At their head proudly marched a color bearer carrying a large blue silk banner, inscribed the "China boys." Following them came a triumphal car, in which was seated thirty boys in black trousers and white shirts, representing the thirty states. In the center of this group, seated on a raised platform, was a young girl robed in white with gold and silver gauze floating about her and supporting a breast plate, upon which was inscribed "California, the Union, it must and shall be preserved." The California pioneers carried a banner on which was represented a New Englander in the act of stepping ashore and facing a native Californian with lasso and serape. In the center the state seal and the inscription, "Far west. Eureka 1846, California pioneers, organized August, 1850." Army and navy officers, soldiers, sailors and marines, veterans of the Mexican war, municipal officers, the fire department, secret and benevolent societies and associations, with a company of mounted native Californians bearing a banner with thirty-one stars on a blue satin ground with the inscription in gold letters, California, E Pluribus Unum, all these various organizations and orders with their marshals and aids mounted on gaily caparisoned steeds and decked out with their gold and silver trimmed scarves, made an imposing display that has seldom if ever been equaled since in the metropolis of California.

At the plaza a flag of thirty-one stars was raised to the mast head. An oration was delivered by Judge Nathaniel Bennett and Mrs. Wills recited an original ode of her own composition. The rejoicing over, the people settled down to business. Their unprecedented action in organizing a state government and putting it into operation without the sanction of congress had been approved and legalized by that body.

Like the Goddess Minerva, represented on its great seal, who sprung full grown from the brain of Jupiter, California was born a fully matured state. She passed through no territorial probation. No state had such a phenomenal growth in its

172

infancy. No state before or since has met with such bitter opposition when it sought admission into the family of states. Never before was there such a medley of nationalities — Yankees, Mexicans, English, Germans, French, Spaniards, Peruvians, Polynesians. Mongolians — organized into a state and made a part of the body politic nolens volens.

The constitutional convention of 1849 did not definitely fix the state capital. San Jose was designated as the place of meeting for the legislature and the organization of the state government. San Jose had offered to donate a square of thirty-two acres, valued at $60,000, for capitol grounds and provide a suitable building for the legislature and state officers. The offer was accepted, but when the legislature met there December 15, 1849, the building was unfinished and for a time the meetings of the legislature were held at a private residence. There was a great deal of complaining and dissatisfaction. The first capitol of the state was a two-story adobe building 40x60, which had been intended for a hotel. It was destroyed by fire April 29, 1853. The accommodations at San Jose were so unsatisfactory that the legislature decided to locate the capital at some other point. Propositions were received from Monterey, from Reed of San Jose, from Stevenson & Parker of New York of the Pacific and from Gen. M. G. Vallejo. Vallejo's proposition was accepted. He offered to donate one hundred and fifty-six acres of land in a new town that he proposed to lay out on the straits of Carquinez (now Vallejo) for a capital site and within two years to give $370,000 in money for the erection of public buildings. He asked that his proposition be submitted to a vote of the people at the next general election. His proposition was accepted by the legislature. At the general election, October 7, 1850, Vallejo received seventy-four hundred and seventy-seven votes; San Jose twelve hundred and ninety-two, and Monterey three hundred and ninety-nine. The second legislature convened at San Jose. General Vallejo exerted himself to have the change made in accordance with the previous proposition. The citizens of San Jose made an effort to retain the capital, but a bill was passed making Vallejo the permanent seat of government after the close of the session, provided General Vallejo should give bonds to carry out his proposals. In June Governor McDougal caused the governmental archives to be removed from San Jose to Vallejo.

When the members of the third legislature met at the new capital January 2, 1852, they found a large unfurnished and partly unfinished wooden building for their reception. Hotel accommodations could not be obtained and there was even a scarcity of food to feed the hungry lawmakers. Sacramento offered its new court house and on the 16th of January the legislature convened in that city. The great flood of March, 1852, inundated the city and the lawmakers were forced to reach the halls of legislation in boats and again there was dissatisfaction. Then Benicia came to the front with an offer of her new city hall, which was above high water mark. General Vallejo had become financially embarrassed and could not carry out his contract with the state, so it was annulled. The offer of Benicia was accepted and on May 18, 1853, that town was declared the permanent capital.

In the legislature of 1854 the capital question again became an issue. Offers were made by several aspiring cities, but Sacramento won with the proffer of her court house and a block of land between I and J, Ninth and Tenth streets. Then the question of the location of the capital got into the courts. The supreme court decided in favor of Sacramento. Before the legislature met again the court house that had been offered to the state burned down. A new and more commodious one was erected and rented to the state at $12,000 a year. Oakland made an unsuccessful effort to obtain the capital. Finally a bill was passed authorizing the erection of a capitol building in Sacramento at a cost not to exceed $500,000. Work was begun on the foundation in October, 1860. The great flood of 1861-62 inundated the city and ruined the foundations of the capitol. San Francisco made a vigorous effort to get the capital removed to that city, but was unsuccessful. Work was resumed on the building, the plans were changed, the edifice enlarged, and, finally, after many delays, it was ready for occupancy in December, 1869. From the original limit of half a million dollars its cost when completed had reached a million and a half. The amount expended on the building and grounds to date foots up $2,600,000.

CHAPTER XXV. THE ARGONAUTS.

When or by whom the name argonaut was first applied to the early California gold seekers I have not been able to ascertain. The earliest allusion to the similarity of Jason's voyage after the Golden Fleece and the miners' rush to the gold fields of California is found in a caricature published in the London Punch in 1849. On the shore of an island is a guide board bearing the inscription "California;" near it is a miner digging gold and presumably singing at his work. In a boat near the shore is a fat individual, a typical "Johnny Bull." He is struggling desperately with two individuals who are holding him back from leaping into the water, so fascinated is he by the song of the miner. Under the drawing are the words, "The Song of the Sirens."

If we include among the argonauts all who traveled by land or voyaged by sea in search of the golden fleece in the days of '49 we will have a motley mixture. The tales of the fabulous richness of the gold fields of California spread rapidly throughout the civilized world and drew to the territory all classes and conditions of men, the bad as well as the good, the indolent as well as the industrious, the vicious as well as the virtuous. They came from Europe, from South America and from Mexico. From Australia and Tasmania came the ex-convict and the ticket-of-leave man; from the isles of the sea came the Polynesian, and from Asia the Hindu and the "Heathen Chinese."

The means of reaching the land of gold were as varied as the character of the people who came. Almost every form of vehicle was pressed into service on land. One individual, if not more, made the trip trundling his impedimenta in a wheelbarrow. Others started out in carriages, intent on making the journey in comfort and ease, but finished on foot, weary, worn and ragged. When the great rush came, old sailing vessels that had long been deemed unseaworthy were fitted out for the voyage to California. It must have been the providence that protects fools which prevented these from going to the bottom of the ocean. With the desperate chances that the argonauts took on these old tubs, it is singular that there were so few shipwrecks and so little loss of life. Some of these were such slow sailers that it took them the greater part of a year to round Cape Horn and reach their destination. On one of these some passengers, exasperated at its slowness, landed near Cape St. Lucas and made the long journey up the peninsula of Lower California and on to San Francisco on foot, arriving there a month before their vessel. Another party undertook to make the voyage from Nicaragua in a whale boat and actually did accomplish seven hundred miles of it before they were picked up in the last extremities by a sailing vessel.

The Sierra Nevada region, in which gold was first found, comprised a strip about thirty miles wide and two hundred miles long from north to south in the basins of the Feather, Yuba, Bear, American, Cosumne, Mokolumne, Stanislaus, Tuolumne and Merced rivers, between the elevations of one thousand and five thousand feet. In all these streams miners washed gold in 1848. The placer mines on the Upper Sacramento and in the Shasta region were discovered and worked late in the fall of 1848. The Klamath mines were discovered later.

The southern mines, those on the San Joaquin, Fresno, Kern and San Gabriel rivers, were located between 1851 and 1855. Gold was found in some of the ravines and creeks of San Diego county. Practically the gold belt of California extends from the Mexican line to Oregon, but at some points it is rather thin. The first gold digging was done with butcher knives, the gold hunter scratching in the sand and crevices of the rock to find nuggets. Next the gold pan came into use and the miners became experts in twirling the pan in a pool of water, so as to wash out the sand and gravel and leave the gold dust in the pan. Isaac Humphreys, who had mined gold in Georgia, was the first person to use a rocker or gold cradle in California. Although a very simple piece of machinery those who reached the mines early found it quite an expensive one. Dr. Brooks in his diary, under date of June ii, 1848, writes: "On Tuesday we set to work upon our cradle. We resolved upon the construction of two and for this purpose went down to the store in a body to see about the boards. We found timber extravagantly dear, being asked $40 a hundred feet. The next question was as to whether we should hire a carpenter. We were told there was one or two in the diggings, who might be hired, though at a very extravagant rate. Accordingly Bradley and I proceeded to see one of these gentlemen, and found him washing away with a hollow log and a willow branch sieve. He offered to help us at the rate of $35 a day, we finding provisions and tools, and could not be brought to charge less. We thought this by far too extravagant and left him, determined to undertake the work ourselves. After two days' work of seven men they produced two rough cradles and found that three men with a cradle or rocker could wash out as much gold in a day as six could with pans in the same time."

A rocker or gold cradle had some resemblance to a child's cradle with similar rockers and was rocked by means of a perpendicular handle fastened to the cradle box. The cradle box consisted of a wooden trough about twenty inches wide and forty inches long with sides four or five inches high. The lower end was left open. On the upper end sat the hopper, a box twenty inches square with sides four inches high and a bottom of sheet iron or zinc pierced with holes one-half inch in diameter. Where zinc or iron could not be obtained a sieve of willow rods was used. Under the hopper was an apron of canvas, which sloped down from the lower end of the hopper to the upper end of the cradle box. A wooden riffle bar an inch square was nailed across the bottom of the cradle box about its middle, and another at its lower end. Under the cradle box were nailed rockers, and near the middle an upright handle by which motion was imparted. If water and pay dirt were convenient two men were sufficient to operate the machine. Seated on a stool or rock the operator rocked with one hand, while with a long handled dipper he dipped water from a pool and poured it on the sand and gravel in the hopper. When the sand and earth had been washed through the holes in the sieve the rocks were emptied and the hopper filled again from the buckets of pay dirt supplied by the other partner. The gold was caught on the canvas apron by the riffle bars, while the thin mud and sand were washed out of the machine by the water.

In the dry diggings a method of separating the gold from the earth was resorted to principally by Sonorans. The pay dirt was dug and dried in the sun, then pulverized by pounding into fine dust. With a batea or bowl-shaped Indian basket filled with this dust, held in both hands, the Mexican skillfully tossed the earth in the air, allowing the wind to blow away the dust and catching the heavier particles and the gold in the basket, repeating the process until there was little left but the gold.

The Long Tom was a single sluice with a sieve and a box underneath at the end and riffle bars to stop the gold. The pay dirt was shoveled in at the upper end and a rapid current of water washed away the sand and earth, the gold falling into the receptacle below. Ground sluicing was resorted to where a current of water from a ditch could be directed against a bank of earth or hill with a sloping bedrock. The stream of water washing against the upper side of the bank caved it down and carried the loose earth through a string of sluices, depositing the gold in the riffle bars in the bottom of the sluices.

In the creeks and gulches where there was not much fall, sluice mining was commonly resorted to. A string of sluice boxes was laid, each fitting into the upper end of the one below, and in the lower ones riffle bars were placed to stop the gold. The sluice boxes were placed on trestles four feet from the ground and given an incline of five or six inches to the rod. The gravel from the bedrock up as far as there was any pay dirt was shoveled into the upper boxes and a rapid current of water flowing through the boxes carried away the gravel and rocks, the gold remaining in the riffles. Quicksilver was placed between the riffles to catch the fine gold. The gold amalgamated with quicksilver was cleaned out of the boxes at the end of the day's work and separated from the quicksilver in a retort. These were the principal methods of mining used by the argonauts. The machinery and appliances were simple and inexpensive. Hydraulic mining came in later, when larger capital was required and the mines had fallen into the hands of corporations.

When the news spread throughout the states of the wonderful "finds" of gold in California, the crudest ideas prevailed in regard to how the precious metal was to be extracted from the earth. Gold mining was an almost unknown industry in the United States. Only in a few obscure districts of North Carolina and Georgia had gold been found, and but very few people outside of these districts had ever visited the mines. Not one in ten thousand of those who joined the rush to California in 1849 had ever seen a grain of virgin gold. The idea prevailed among the gold seekers that the gold being found in grains it could be winnowed from the sand and earth in which it was found like wheat is separated from chaff. Imbued with this idea Yankee ingenuity set to work to invent labor-saving machines that would accomplish the work quickly and enrich the miner proportionally. The ships that bore the argonauts from their native land carried out a variety of these gold machines, all guaranteed to wrest from the most secret recesses the auriferous deposits in nature's treasure vaults. These machines were of all varieties and patterns. They were made of copper, iron, zinc and brass. Some were operated by means of a crank, others had two cranks, while others were worked with a treadle. Some required that the operator should stand, others allowed the miner to sit in an arm chair and work in comfort.

Haskins, in his "Argonauts of California," describes one of these machines that was brought around the Horn in the ship he came on: "It was in the shape of a huge fanning mill, with sieves properly arranged for sorting the gold ready for bottling. All chunks too large for the bottle would be consigned to the pork barrel." (The question of bringing home the gold in bottles or barrels had been seriously discussed and decided in favor of barrels because these could be rolled and thus save cost of transportation from the mines.)

"This immense machine which, during our passage, excited the envy and jealousy of all who had not the means and opportunity of securing a similar one required, of course, the services of a hired man to turn the crank, whilst the proprietor would be busily engaged is shoveling in pay dirt and pumping water; the greater portion of the time, however, being required, as was firmly believed, in corking the bottles and fitting the heads in the barrels. This machine was owned by a Mr. Allen of Cambridge, Mass., who had brought with him a colored servant to manage and control the crank portion of the invaluable institution.

"Upon landing we found lying on the sand and half buried in the mud hundreds of similar machines, bearing silent witness at once to the value of our gold saving machines without the necessity of a trial."

Nor was it the argonaut alone who came by sea that brought these machines. Some of these wonderful inventions were hauled across the plains in wagons, their owners often sacrificing the necessities of life to save the prized machine. And, when, after infinite toil and trouble, they had landed their prize in the mines, they were chagrined to find it the subject of jest and ridicule by those who had some experience in mining.

The gold rush came early in the history of California placer mining. The story of a rich strike would often depopulate a mining camp in a few hours. Even a bare rumor of rich diggings in some indefinite locality would send scores of miners tramping off on a wild goose chase into the mountains. Some of these rushes originated through fake stories circulated for sinister purpose; others were caused by exaggerated stories of real discoveries.

One of the most famous fakes of early days was the Gold Lake rush of 1850. This wonderful lake was supposed to be located about two hundred miles northeast of Marysville, on the divide between the Feather and the Yuba rivers. The Sacramento Transcript of June 19, 1850, says: "We are informed by a gentleman from Marysville that it is currently reported there that the Indians upon this lake use gold for their commonest purposes; that they have a ready way of knocking out square blocks, which they use for seats and couches upon which to place their beds, which are simply bundles of wild oats, which grow so profusely in all sections of the state. According to report also they use for fishhooks crooked pieces of gold and kill their game with arrows made of the same material. They are reported to be thunderstruck at the movements of the whites and their eagerness to collect and hoard the materials of the very ground upon which they tread.

"A story is current that a man at Gold Lake saw a large piece of gold floating on the lake which he succeeded in getting ashore. So clear are the waters that another man saw a rock of gold on the bottom. After many efforts he succeeded in lassoing the rock. Three days afterward he was seen standing holding on to his rope."

The Placer Times of Marysville reports that the specimens brought into Marysville are of a value from $1,500 down. Ten ounces is reported as no unusual yield to the pan. The first party of sixty which started out under guidance of one who had returned successful were assured that they would not get less than $500 each per day. We were told that two hundred had left town with a full supply of provisions and four hundred mules. Mules and horses have doubled in value. Many places of business are closed. The diggings at the lake are probably the best ever discovered." The Times of June 19 says: "It is reported that up to last Thursday two thousand persons had taken up their journey. Many who were working good claims deserted them for the new discovery. Mules and horses were about impossible to obtain. Although the truth of the report rests on the authority of but two or three who have returned from Gold Lake, yet few are found who doubt the marvelous revelations. A party of Kanakas are said to have wintered at Gold Lake, subsisting chiefly on the flesh of their animals. They are said to have taken out $75,000 the first week. When a conviction takes such complete possession of a whole community, who are fully conversant with all the exaggerations that have had their day, it is scarcely prudent to utter even a qualified dissent from what is universally believed."

The denouement of the Gold Lake romance may be found in the Transcript of July 1, 1850. "The Gold Lake excitement, so much talked of and acted upon of late, has almost subsided. A crazy man comes in for a share of the responsibility. Another report is that they have found one of the pretended discoverers at Marysville and are about to lynch him. Indeed, we are told that a demonstration against the town is feared by many. People who have returned after traveling some one hundred and fifty to two hundred miles say that they left vast numbers of people roaming between the sources of the Yuba and the Feather rivers."

Scarcely had the deluded argonauts returned from a bootless search for the lake of gold when another rumored discovery of gold fields of fabulous richness sent them rushing off toward the sea coast. Now it was Gold Bluff that lured them away. On the northwest coast of California, near the mouth of the Klamath river, precipitous bluffs four hundred feet high mark the coast line of the ocean. A party of prospectors in the fall of 1850, who had been up in the Del Norte country, were making their way down to the little trading and trapping station of Trinidad to procure provisions. On reaching the bluffs, thirty miles above Trinidad, they were astonished to find stretching out before them a beach glittering with golden sands. They could not stop to gather gold; they were starving. So, scraping up a few handfuls of the glittering sands, they hastened on. In due time they reached San Francisco, where they exhibited their sand, which proved to be nearly half gold. The report of the wonderful find was spread by the newspapers and the excitement began. Companies were formed and claims located at long range. One company of nine locators sent an expert to examine their claims. He, by a careful mathematical calculation, ascertained that the claim would yield forty-three million dollars to each partner. As there were fifteen miles of gold beach, the amount of gold in the sands was sufficient to demonetize the precious metal. A laudable desire to benefit the human race possessed some of the claim owners. They formed joint stock companies with shares at $100 each. Gold Bluff mining stock went off like the proverbial hot cakes and prospectors went off as rapidly. Within two days after the expert's wonderful story was spread abroad nine ships were fitted out for Gold Bluff. The first to arrive off the Bluff was the vessel containing a party of the original discoverers. In attempting to land in a boat, the boat was upset in the breakers and five of the six occupants were drowned, Bertram, the leader of the party making the discovery, alone escaping. The vessel put back to Trinidad and the gold hunters made their way up the coast to the Bluff. But alas for their golden

179

dreams! Where they had hoped to gather gold by the ship load no gold was found. Old ocean had gathered it back into his treasure vaults.

The bubble burst as suddenly as it had expanded. And yet there was gold at Gold Bluff and there is gold there yet. If the ocean could be drained or coffer dammed for two hundred miles along the gold coast of northern California and Oregon, all the wealth of Alaska would be but the panning out of a prospect hole compared to the richness that lies hidden in the sands of Gold Beach. For years after the bursting of the Gold Bluff bubble, when the tide was low, the sands along Gold Beach were mined with profit.

The Kern river excitement in the spring of 1855 surpassed everything that had preceded it. Seven years of mining had skimmed the richness of the placers. The northern and central gold fields of California had been thoroughly prospected. The miners who had been accustomed to the rich strikes of early years could not content themselves with moderate returns. They were on the qui vive for a rich strike and ready for a rush upon the first report of one. The first discoveries on the Kern river were made in the summer of 1854, but no excitement followed immediately. During the fall and winter rumors were set afloat of rich strikes on the head waters of that stream. The stories grew as they traveled. One that had a wide circulation and was readily accepted ran about as follows: "A Mexican doctor had appeared in Mariposa loaded down with gold nuggets. He reported that he and four companions had found a region paved with gold. The very hills were yellow with outcroppings. While gloating over their wealth and loading it into sacks the Indians attacked them and killed his four companions. He escaped with one sack of gold. He proposed to organize a company large enough to exterminate the Indians and then bring out the gold on pack mules." This as well as other stories as improbable were spread broadcast throughout the state. Many of the reports of wonderful strikes were purposely magnified by merchants and dealers in mining supplies who were overstocked with unsalable goods; and by transportation companies with whom business was slack. Their purpose was accomplished and the rush was on. It began in January, 1855. Every steamer down the coast to Los Angeles was loaded to the guards with adventurers for the mines. The sleepy old metropolis of the cow counties waked up to find itself suddenly transformed into a bustling mining camp. The Southern Californian of February 8, 1855, thus describes the situation: "The road from our valley is literally thronged with people on their way to the mines. Hundreds of people have been leaving not only the city, but every portion of the county. Every description of vehicle and animal has been brought into requisition to take the exultant seekers after wealth to the goal of their hopes. Immense ten-mule wagons strung out one after another: long trains of pack mules and men mounted and on foot, with picks and shovels; boarding-house keepers with their tents; merchants with their stocks of miners' necessaries and gamblers with their 'papers' are constantly leaving for the Kern river mines. The wildest stories are afloat. If the mines turn out $10 a day to the man everybody ought to be satisfied. The opening of these mines has been a godsend to all of us, as the business of the entire country was on the point of taking to a tree. The great scarcity of money is seen in the present exorbitant rates of interest which it commands; 8, 10 and even 15 per cent a month is freely paid and the supply even at these rates is too meager to meet the demands." As the rush increased our editor grows more jubilant. In his

180

issue of March 7, he throws out these headlines: "Stop the Press! Glorious News from Kern River! Bring Out the Big Gun! There are a thousand gulches rich with gold and room for ten thousand miners. Miners averaged $50 a day. One man with his own hands took out $160 in a day. Five men in ten days took out $4,500."

Another stream of miners and adventurers was pouring into the mines by way of the San Joaquin valley. From Stockton to the Kern river, a distance of three hundred miles, the road was crowded with men on foot, on stages, on horseback and on every form of conveyance that would take them to the new El Dorado. In four months five or six thousand men had found their way into the Kern river basin. There was gold there, but not enough to go around. A few struck it rich, the many struck nothing but "hard luck" and the rush out began. Those who had ridden into the valley footed it out, and those who had footed it in on sole leather footed it out on their natural soles.

After the wild frenzy of Kern river, the press of the state congratulated the public with the assurance that the era of wild rushes was past — "what had been lost in money had been gained in experience." As if prospectors ever profited by experience! Scarcely had the victims of Kern river resumed work in the old creeks and cañons they had deserted to join in the rush when a rumor came, faint at first, but gathering strength at each repetition, that rich diggings had been struck in the far north. This time it is Frazer river. True, Frazer river is in the British possessions, but what of that? There are enough miners in California to seize the country and hold it until the cream of the mines has been skimmed. Rumors of the richness of mines increased with every arrival of a steamer from the north. Captains, pursers, mates, cooks and waiters all confirmed the stories of rich strikes. Doubters asserted that the dust and nuggets exhibited had made the trip from San Francisco to Victoria and back. But they were silenced by the assurance that the transportation company was preparing to double the number of its vessels on that route. Commodore Wright was too smart to run his steamers on fake reports, and thus the very thing that should have caused suspicion was used to confirm the truth of the rumors. The doubters doubted no more, but packed their outfits for Frazer river. California was played out. Where could an honest miner pan out $100 a day in California now? He could do it every day in Frazer; the papers said so. The first notice of the mines was published in March, 1858. The rush began the latter part of April and in four months thirty thousand men, one-sixth of the voting population of the state, had rushed to the mines.

The effect of the craze was disastrous to business in California. Farms were abandoned and crops lost for want of hands to harvest them. Rich claims in old diggings were sold for a trifle of their value. Lots on Montgomery street that a few years later were worth $1,500 a front foot were sold for $100. Real estate in the interior towns was sacrificed at 50 to 75 per cent less than it was worth before the rush began. But a halt was called in the mad rush. The returns were not coming in satisfactorily. By the middle of July less than $100,000 in dust had reached San Francisco, only about $3 for each man who had gone to the diggings. There was gold there and plenty of it, so those interested in keeping up the excitement said: "The Frazer river is high; wait till it subsides." But it did not subside, and it has not subsided since. If the Frazer did not subside the excitement did, and that suddenly. Those who had money enough or could borrow from their friends got away at once. Those who had none hung around Victoria and New Westminster until they were shipped back at the government's expense. The Frazer river craze was the last of the mad, unreasoning "gold rushes." The Washoe excitement of '59 and the "Ho! for Idaho of 1863-64" had some of the characteristics of the early gold rushes, but they soon settled down to steady business and the yield from these fairly recompensed those who were frugal and industrious.

Never before perhaps among civilized people was there witnessed such a universal leveling as occurred in the first years of the mining excitement in California. "As the labor required was physical instead of mental, the usual superiority of head workers over hand workers disappeared entirely. Men who had been governors and legislators and judges in the old states worked by the side of outlaws and convicts; scholars and students by the side of men who could not read or write; those who had been masters by the side of those who had been slaves; old social distinctions were obliterated; everybody did business on his own account, and not one man in ten was the employee and much less the servant of another. Social distinctions appeared to be entirely obliterated and no man was considered inferior to another. The hard-fisted, unshaven and patch-covered miner was on terms of perfect equality with the well-dressed lawyer, surgeon or merchant; and in general conferences, discussions and even conversations the most weather-beaten and strongly marked face, or, in other words, the man who had seen and experienced the most, notwithstanding his wild and tattered attire, was listened to with more attention and respectful consideration than the man of polished speech and striking antithesis. One reason of this was that in those days the roughest-looking man not infrequently knew more than anybody else of what was wanted to be known, and the raggedest man ' not infrequently was the most influential and sometimes the richest man in the locality."

This independent spirit was characteristic of the men of '48 and '49. Then nearly everybody was honest and theft was almost unknown. With the advent of the criminal element in 1850 and later there came a change. Before that a pan of gold dust could be left in an open tent unguarded, but with the coming of the Sydney ducks from Australia and men of their class it became necessary to guard property with sedulous care.

CHAPTER XXVI. SAN FRANCISCO.

In 1835, Capt. William A. Richardson built the first house on the Yerba Buena cove. It was a shanty of rough board, which he replaced a year later with an adobe building. He was granted a lot in 1836 and his building stood near what is now the corner of Dupont and Clay streets. Richardson had settled at Sausalito in 1822. He was an Englishman by birth and was one of the first foreigners to settle in California.

Jacob P. Leese, an American, in partnership with Spear & Hinckley, obtained a lot in 1836 and built a house and store near that of Captain Richardson. There is a tradition that Mr. Leese began his store building on the first of July and finished it at ten o'clock on the morning of July 4, and for a house warming celebrated the glorious Fourth in a style that astonished the natives up and down the coast. The house was sixty feet long and twenty-five broad, and, if completed in three days, Mr. Leese certainly deserves the credit of having eclipsed some of the remarkable feats in house building that were performed after the great fires of San Francisco in the early '50s. Mr. Leese and his neighbor, Captain Richardson, invited all the high-toned Spanish families for a hundred miles around to the celebration. The Mexican and American flags floated over the building and two six-pounders fired salutes. At five o'clock the guests sat down to a sumptuous dinner which lasted, toasts and all, till 10 o'clock, and then came dancing; and, as Mr. Leese remarks in his diary: "Our Fourth ended on the evening of the fifth." Mr. Leese was an energetic person. He built a house in three days, gave a Fourth of July celebration that lasted two days, and inside of a week had a store opened and was doing a thriving business with his late guests. He fell in love with the same energy that he did business. Among the guests at his 4th of July celebration were the Vallejos, the nabobs of Sonoma. Leese courted one of the girls and in a few months after the celebration married her. Their daughter, Rosalie Leese, was the first child born in Yerba Buena. Such was the beginning of San Francisco.

This settlement was on a crescent-shaped cove that lay between Clark's Point and the Rincon. The locality was known as Yerba Buena (good herb), a species of mint to which the native Californians attributed many medicinal virtues. The peninsula still bore the name that had been applied to it when the mission and presidio were founded, San Francisco. Yerba Buena was a local appellation and applied only to the little hamlet that had grown up on the cove. This settlement, although under the Mexican government, was not a Mexican town. The foreign element, the American predominating, had always been in the ascendency. At the time of the conquest, among its two hundred inhabitants, were representatives of almost every civilized nation on the globe. It was a cosmopolitan town. In a very short time after the conquest it began to take on a new growth and was recognized as the coming metropolis of California. The curving beach of the cove at one point (Jackson street) crossed the present line of Montgomery street.

Richardson and Leese had built their stores and warehouses back from the beach because of a Mexican law that prohibited the building of a house on the beach where no custom house existed. All houses had to be built back a certain number of varas from high-water mark. This regulation was made to prevent smuggling. Between the shore line of the cove and anchorage there was a long stretch of shallow water. This made transportation of goods from ship to shore very inconvenient and expensive. With the advent of the Americans and the inauguration of a more progressive era it became necessary for the convenient landing of ships and for the discharging and receiving of their cargoes that the beach front of the town should be improved by building wharves and docks. The difficulty was to find the means to do this. The general government of the United States could not undertake it. The war with Mexico was still in progress. The only available way was to sell off beach lots to private parties, but who was to give title was the question. Edwin Bryant, February 22, 1847, had succeeded Washington Bartlett as alcalde. Bryant was a progressive man, and, recognizing the necessity of improvement in the shipping facilities of the town, he urged General Kearny, the acting governor, to relinquish, on the part of the general government, its claim to the beach lands in ' front of the town in favor of the municipality under certain conditions. General Kearny really had no authority to relinquish the claim of the general government to the land, for the simple reason that the general government had not perfected a claim. The country was held as conquered territory. Mexico had made no concession of the land by treaty. It was not certain that California would be ceded to the United States. Under Mexican law the governor of the territory, under certain conditions, had the right to make grants, and General Kearny, assuming the power given a Mexican governor, issued the following decree: "I, Brig.Gen. S. W. Kearny, Governor of California, by virtue of authority in me vested by the President of the United States of America, do hereby grant, convey, and release unto the Town of San Francisco, the people or corporate authorities thereof, all the right, title and interest of the Government of the United States and of the Territory of California in and to the Beach and Water Lots on the East front of said Town of San Francisco included between the points known as the Rincon and Fort Montgomery, excepting such lots as may be selected for the use of the United States Government by the senior officers of the army and navy now there; provided, the said ground hereby ceded shall be divided into lots and sold by public auction to the highest bidder, after three months' notice previously given; the proceeds of said sale to be for the benefit of the town of San Francisco. Given at Monterey, capital of California, this 10th day of March, 1847, and the seventy-first year of the independence of the United States."

S. W. Kearny,

Brig.-Gen'l & Gov. of California.

In pursuance of this decree, Alcalde Bryant advertised in the Californian that the ground described in the decree, known as Water Lots, would be surveyed and divided into convenient building lots and sold to the highest bidder on the 29th of June (1847). He then proceeds in the advertisement to boom the town. "The site of the town of San Francisco is known by all navigators and mercantile men acquainted with the subject to be the most commanding commercial position on the entire western coast of the Pacific ocean, and the Town itself is no doubt destined to become the commercial emporium of the western side of the North American continent.'" The alcaldes' assertions must have seemed rather extravagant

184

to the dwellers in the little burgh on the cove of Yerba Buena. But Bryant was a far-seeing man and proved himself in this instance to be a prophet.

It will be noticed that both General Kearny and Alcalde Bryant call the town San Francisco. Alcalde Bartlett, the predecessor in office of Alcalde Bryant, had changed its name just before he was recalled to his ship. He did not like the name Yerba Buena, so he summarily changed it. He issued a proclamation setting forth that hereafter the town should be known as San Francisco. Having proclaimed a change of name, he proceeded to give his reasons: Yerba Buena was a paltry cognomen for a certain kind of mint found on an island in the bay; it was a merely local name, unknown beyond the district, while San Francisco had long been familiar on the maps. "Therefore it is hereby ordained, etc." Bartlett built better than he knew. It would have been a sad mistake for the city to have carried the "outlandish name which Americans would mangle in pronouncing," as the alcalde said.

The change was made in the latter part of January, 1847, but it was some time before the new name was generally adopted.

The California Star, Sam Brannan's paper, which had begun to shine January 9, 1847, in its issue of March 20, alluding to the change, says: "We acquiesce in it, though we prefer the old name. When the change was first attempted we viewed it as a mere assumption of authority, without law of precedent, and therefore we adhered to the old name — Yerba Buena."

"It was asserted by the late alcalde, Washington Bartlett, that the place was called San Francisco in some old Spanish paper which he professed to have in his possession; but how could we believe a man even about that which it is said 'there is nothing in it,' who had so often evinced a total disregard for his own honor and character and the honor of the country which gave him birth and the rights of his fellow citizens in the district?" Evidently the editor had a grievance and was anxious to get even with the alcalde. Bartlett demanded an investigation of some charges made against his administration. He was cleared of all blame. He deserves the thanks of all Californians in summarily suppressing Yerba Buena and preventing it from being fastened on the chief city of the state.

There was at that time (on paper) a city of Francisca. The city fathers of this budding metropolis were T. O. Larkin and Robert Semple. In a half-column advertisement in the Californian of April 20, 1847, and several subsequent issues, headed "Great Sale of City Lots," they set forth the many advantages and merits of Francisca. The streets are eighty feet wide, the alleys twenty feet wide, and the lots fifty yards front and forty yards back. The whole city comprises five square miles."

"Francisca is situated on the Straits of Carquinez, on the north side of the Bay of San Francisco, about thirty miles from the mouth of the bay and at the head of ship navigation. In front of the city is a commodious bay, large enough for two hundred ships to ride at anchor, safe from any wind." * * * "The entire trade of the great Sacramento and San Joaquin valleys, a fertile country of great width and near seven hundred miles long from north to south, must of necessity pass through the narrow channel of Carquinez and the bay and country is so situated that every person who passes from one side of the bay to the other will find the nearest and best way by Francisca." Francisca, with its manifold natural advantages, ought to have been a great city, the metropolis of California, but the Fates were against it.

Alcalde Bartlett, probably without any design of doing so, dealt it a fearful blow when he dubbed the town of the good herb, San Francisco. Two cities with names so nearly alike could not live and thrive in the same state. Francisca became Benicia. The population of San Francisco (or Yerba Buena, as it was then called) at the time that Captain Montgomery raised the stars and stripes and took possession of it probably did not exceed two hundred. Its change of masters accelerated its growth. The Californian of September 4, 1847 (fourteen months after it came under the flag of the United States), gives the following statistics of its population and progress: Total white male population, 247; female, 123; Indians, male, 26; female, 8; South Sea Islanders, male, 39; female 1; negroes, male, 9; female 1; total population, 454.

Nearly every country on the globe had representatives in its population, and the various vocations by which men earn a living were well represented. Minister, one; doctors, three; lawyers, three; surveyors, two; agriculturists, eleven; bakers, seven; blacksmiths, six; brewer, one; butchers, seven; cabinetmakers, two; carpenters, twenty-six; cigarmaker, one; coopers, three; clerks, thirteen; gardener, one; grocers, five; gunsmiths, two; hotel-keepers, three; laborers, twenty; masons, four; merchants, eleven; miner, one; morocco case maker, one; navigators (inland), six; navigator (ocean), one; painter, one; printer, one; soldier, one; shoemakers, four; silversmith, one; tailors, four; tanners, two; watchmaker, one; weaver, one. Previous to April 1, 1847, according to the Californian, there had been erected in the town seventy-nine buildings, classified as follows: Shanties, twenty-two; frame buildings, thirty-one; adobe buildings, twenty-six. Since April I, seventy-eight buildings have been erected, viz.: Shanties, twenty; frame buildings, forty-seven; adobe buildings, eleven. "Within five months last past," triumphantly adds the editor of the Californian, "as many buildings have been built as were erected in all the previous years of the town's existence."

The town continued to grow with wonderful rapidity throughout the year 1847, considering that peace had not yet been declared and the destiny of California was uncertain. According to a school census taken in March, 1848, by the Board of Trustees, the population was: Males, five hundred and seventy-five; females, one hundred and seventy-seven; and "children of age to attend school," sixty, a total of eight hundred and twelve. Building kept pace with the increase of population until the "gold fever" became epidemic. Dr. Brooks, writing in his diary May 17, says: "Walking through the town to-day, I observed that laborers were employed only upon about half a dozen of the fifty new buildings which were in the course of being run up."

The first survey of lots in the town had been made by a Frenchman named Vioget. No names had been given to the streets. This survey was made before the conquest. In 1847, Jasper O'Farrell surveyed and platted the district extending about half a mile in the different directions from the plaza. The streets were named, and, with a very few changes, still retain the names then given. In September the council appointed a committee to report upon the building of a wharf. It was decided to construct two wharves, one from the foot of Clay street and the other from the foot of Broadway. Money was appropriated to build them and they had been extended some distance seaward when the rush to the mines suspended operations. After considerable agitation by the two newspapers and canvassing for funds, the first schoolhouse was built. It was completed December 4, 1847, but, for lack of funds, or, as the Star says, for lack of energy in the council, school was not opened on the completion of the house. In March the council appropriated $400 and April 1, 1848, Thomas Douglas, a graduate of Yale College, took charge of the school. San Francisco was rapidly developing into a progressive American city. Unlike the older towns of California, it had but a small Mexican population. Even had not gold been discovered, it would have grown into a commercial city of considerable size.

The first effect of the gold discovery and the consequent rush to the mines was to bring everything to a standstill. As Kemble, of the Star, puts it, it was "as if a curse had arrested our onward course of enterprise; everything wears a desolate and somber look; everywhere all is dull, monotonous, dead." The return of the inhabitants in a few months and the influx of new arrivals gave the town a boom in the fall of 1848. Building was only limited by the lack of material, and every kind of a makeshift was resorted to to provide shelter against winter rains. From the many attempts at describing the town at this stage of its development, I select this from "Sights in the Gold Regions," a book long since out of print. Its author, T. T. Johnson, arrived at San Francisco April 1, 1849. "Proceeding on our survey, we found the streets, or, properly, the roads, laid out regularly, those parallel with the water being a succession of terraces, and these ascending the hills or along their sides being in some instances cut down ten or twelve feet below the surface. Except a portion of the streets fronting upon the cove, they are all of hard-beaten, sandy clay, as solid as if macadamized. About three hundred houses, stores, shanties and sheds, with a great many tents, composed the town at that period. The houses were mostly built of rough boards and unpainted; brown cottons or calico nailed against the beams and joists answered for wall and ceiling of the better class of tenements. With the exception of the brick warehouse of Howard and Melius, the establishments of the commercial houses of which we had heard so much were inferior to the outhouses of the country seats on the Hudson; and yet it would puzzle the New York Exchange to produce merchant princes of equal importance." * * * "We strolled among the tents in the outskirts of the town. Here was 'confusion worse confounded,' chiefly among Mexicans, Peruvians and Chileans. Every kind, size, color and shape of tent pitched helter-skelter and in the most awkward manner were stowed full of everything under the sun."

In the first six months of 1849 fifteen thousand souls were added to the population of San Francisco; in the latter half of that year about four thousand arrived every month by sea alone. At first the immigrants were from Mexico, Chile, Peru and the South American ports generally; but early in the spring the Americans began to arrive, coming by way of Panama and Cape Horn, and later across the plains. Europe sent its contingent by sea via Cape Horn; and China, Australia and the Hawaiian Islands added to the city's population an undesirable element. A large majority of those who came by sea made their way to the mines, but many soon returned to San Francisco, some to take their departure for home, others to become residents. At the end of the year San Francisco had a population of twenty-five thousand. The following graphic description of life in San Francisco in the fall of '49 and spring of '50 I take from a paper, "Pioneer Days in San Francisco," written by John Williamson Palmer, and published in the Century Magazine (1890):

"And how did they all live? In frame houses of one story, more commonly in board shanties and canvas tents, pitched in the midst of sand or mud and various rubbish and strange filth and fleas; and they slept on rude cots or on soft planks, under horse blankets, on tables, counters, floors, on trucks in the open air, in bunks braced against the weather-boarding, forty of them in one loft; and so they tossed and scratched and swore and laughed and sang and skylarked, those who were not tired or drunk enough to sleep. And in the working hours they bustled, and jostled, and tugged, and sweated, and made money, always made money. They labored and they lugged; they worked on lighters, drove trucks, packed mules, rang bells, carried messages, 'waited' in restaurants, 'marked' for billiard tables, served drinks in bar rooms, 'faked' on the plaza, 'cried' at auctions, toted lumber for houses, ran a game of faro or roulette in the El Dorado or the Bella Union, or manipulated three-card monte on the head of a barrel in front of the Parker House; they speculated, and, as a rule, gambled.

"Clerks in stores and offices had munificent salaries. Five dollars a day was about the smallest stipend even in the custom house, and one Baptist preacher was paid $10,000 a year. Laborers received $1 an hour; a pick or a shovel was worth $10; a tin pan or a wooden bowl $5, and a butcher knife $30. At one time carpenters who were getting $12 a day struck for $16. Lumber rose to $500 per thousand feet, and every brick in a house cost a dollar one way or another. Wheat, flour and salt pork sold at $40 a barrel; a small loaf of bread was fifty cents and a hard-boiled egg a dollar. You paid $3 to get into the circus and $55 for a private box at the theater. Forty dollars was the price for ordinary coarse boots, and a pair that came above the knees and would carry you gallantly through the quagmires brought a round hundred. When a shirt became very dirty the wearer threw it away and bought a new one. Washing cost $15 a dozen in 1849.

"Rents were simply monstrous; $3,000 a month in advance for a 'store' hurriedly built of rough boards. Wright & Co. paid $75,000 for the wretched little place on the corner of the plaza that they called the Miners' Bank, and $36,000 was asked for the use of the Old Adobe as a custom-house. The Parker House paid $120,000 a year in rents, nearly one-half of that amount being collected from gamblers who held the second floor; and the canvas tent next door used as a gambling saloon, and called the El Dorado, was good for $40,000 a year. From 10 to 15 per cent a month was paid in advance for the use of money borrowed on substantial security. The prices of real estate went up among the stars; $8,000 for a fifty-vara lot that had been bought in 1849 for $20. A lot purchased two years before for a barrel of aguardiente sold for $18,000. Yet, for all that, everybody made money.

"The aspect of the streets of San Francisco at this time was such as one may imagine of an unsightly waste of sand and mud churned by the continual grinding of heavy wagons and trucks and the tugging and floundering of horses, mules and oxen; thoroughfares irregular and uneven, ungraded, unpaved, unplanked, obstructed by lumber and goods, alternate humps and holes, the actual dumping-places of the town, handy receptacles for the general sweepings and rubbish and indescribable offal and filth, the refuse of an indiscriminate population 'pigging' together in shanties and tents. And these conditions extended beyond the actual settlement into the chaparral and underbrush that covered the sand hills on the north and west.

"The flooding rains of winter transformed what should have been thoroughfares into treacherous quagmires set with holes and traps fit to smother horse and man. Loads of brushwood and branches of trees cut from the hills were thrown into these swamps; but they served no more than a temporary purpose and the inmates of tents and houses made such bridges and crossings as they could with boards, boxes and barrels. Men waded through the slough and thought themselves lucky when they sank no deeper than their waists."

It is said that two horses mired down in the mud of Montgomery street were left to die of starvation, and that three drunken men were suffocated between Washington and Jackson streets. It was during the winter of '49 that the famous sidewalk of flour sacks, cooking stoves and tobacco boxes was built. It extended from Simmons, Hutchinson & Co.'s store to Adams Express office, a distance of about seventy-five yards. The first portion was built of Chilean flour in one hundred pound sacks, next came the cooking stoves in a long row, and then followed a double row of tobacco boxes of large size, and a yawning gap of the walk was bridged by a piano. Chile flour, cooking stoves, tobacco and pianos were cheaper material for building walks, owing to the excessive supply of these, than lumber at $600 a thousand.

In the summer of '49 there were more than three hundred sailing vessels lying in the harbor of San Francisco, from which the sailors had deserted to go to the mines. Some of these vessels rotted where they were moored. Some were hauled up in the sand or mud flats and used for store houses, lodging houses and saloons. As the water lots were filled in and built upon, these ships sometimes formed part of the line of buildings on the street. The brig Euphemia was the first jail owned by the city; the store ship Apollo was converted into a lodging house and saloon, and the Niantic Hotel at the corner of Sansome and Clay streets was built on the hull of the ship Niantic. As the wharves were extended out into the bay the space between was filled in from the sand hills and houses built along the wharves. In this way the cove was gradually filled in. The high price of lumber and the great scarcity of houses brought about the importation from New York, Boston, Philadelphia and London of houses ready framed to set up. For a time immense profits were made in this, but an excessive shipment like that of the articles of which the famous sidewalk was made brought down the price below cost, and the business ceased.

The first of the great fires that devastated San Francisco occurred on Christmas eve, 1849. It started in Denison's Exchange, a gambling house on the east side of the plaza. It burned the greater part of the block between Washington and Clay streets and Kearny and Montgomery streets. The loss was estimated at a million and a quarter dollars. The second great fire occurred on May 4, 1850. It burned over the three blocks between Montgomery and Dupont streets, bounded by Jackson and Clay streets, and the north and east sides of Portsmouth square. The loss was estimated at $4,000,000. It started in the United States Exchange, a gambling den, at four o'clock in the morning, and burned for seven hours. The fire was believed to be of incendiary origin and several suspicious characters were arrested, but nothing could be proved against them. A number of the lookers-on refused to assist in arresting the progress of the flames unless paid for their labor; and $3 an hour was demanded and paid to some who did.

On the 14th of June, 1850, a fire broke out in the Sacramento House, on the east side of Kearny street, between Clay and Sacramento. The entire district from Kearny street between Clay and California to the water front was burned over, causing a loss of $3,000,000. Over three hundred houses were destroyed. The fourth great fire of the fateful year of 1850 occurred September 17. It started on Jackson street and destroyed the greater part of the blocks between Dupont and Montgomery streets from Washington to Pacific streets. The loss in this was not so great from the fact that the district contained mostly one-story houses. It was estimated at half a million dollars. December 14 of the same year a fire occurred on Sacramento street below Montgomery. Although the district burned over was not extensive, the loss was heavy. The buildings were of corrugated iron, supposed to be fireproof, and were filled with valuable merchandise. The loss amounted to $1,000,000. After each fire, building was resumed almost before the embers of the fire that consumed the former buildings were extinguished. After each fire better buildings were constructed. A period of six months" exemption had encouraged the inhabitants of the fire-afflicted city to believe that on account of the better class of buildings constructed the danger of great conflagrations was past, but the worst was yet to come. At 11 p. m. May 3, 1851, a fire, started by incendiaries, broke out on the south side of the plaza. A strong northwest wind swept across Kearny street in broad sheets of flame, first southeastward, then, the wind changing, the flames veered to the north and east. All efforts to arrest them were useless; houses were blown up and torn down in attempts to cut off communication, but the engines were driven back step by step, while some of the brave firemen fell victims to the fire fiend. The flames, rising aloft in whirling volumes, swept away the frame houses and crumbled up with intense heat the supposed fireproof structures. After ten hours, when, the fire abated for want of material to burn, all that remained of the city were the sparsely settled outskirts. All of the business district between Pine and Pacific streets, from Kearny to the Battery on the water front, was in ruins. Over one thousand houses had been burned. The loss of property was estimated at $10,000,000, an amount greater than the aggregate of all the preceding fires. A number of lives were lost. During the progress of the fire large quantities of goods were stolen by bands of thieves. The sixth and last of the great conflagrations that devastated the city occurred on the 22nd of June, 1851. The fire started in a building on Powell street and ravaged the district between Clay and Broadway, from Powell to Sansome. Four hundred and fifty houses were burned, involving a loss of $2,500,000. An improved fire department, more stringent building regulations and a better water supply combined to put an end to the era of great fires.

After the great fires of 1851 had swept over the city there was practically nothing left of the old metropolis of the early gold rush. The hastily constructed wooden shanties were gone; the corrugated iron building imported from New York and London, and warranted to be fireproof, had proved to be worthless to withstand great heat; the historic buildings had disappeared; the new city that. Phoenix-like, arose from the ashes of the old was a very different city from its predecessor that had been wiped from the earth by successive conflagrations. Stone and brick buildings covered the former site of wooden structures. The unsightly mud flats between the wharves were filled in from the sand hills and some of the streets paved. The year 1853 was memorable for the rapid progress of the city. Assessed property values increased from $18,000,000 to $28,000,000. Real estate values went soaring upward and the city was on the high tide of prosperity; but a reaction came in 1855. The rush to the mines had ceased, immigration had fallen off, and men had begun to retrench and settle down to steady business habits. Home productions had replaced imports, and the people were abandoning mining for farms. The transition from gold mining to grain growing had begun. All these affected the city and real estate declined. Lots that sold for $8,000 to $10,000 in 1853 could be bought for half that amount in 1855. Out of one thousand business houses, three hundred were vacant. Another influence that helped to bring about a depression was the growing political corruption and the increased taxation from peculations of dishonest officials.

The defalcations and forgeries of Harry Meigs, which occurred in 1854, were a terrible blow to the city. Meigs was one of its most trusted citizens. He was regarded as the embodiment of integrity, the stern, incorruptible man, the watch-dog of the treasury. By his upright conduct he had earned the sobriquet of Honest Harry Meigs. Over-speculation and reaction from the boom of 1853 embarrassed him. He forged a large amount of city scrip and hypothecated it to raise money. His forgeries were suspected, but before the truth was known he made his escape on the barque America to Costa Rica and from there he made his way to Peru. His forgeries amounted to $1,500,000, of which $1,000,000 was in comptroller's warrants, to which he forged the names of Mayor Garrison and Controller Harris. The vigilance committee of 1856 cleared the political atmosphere by clearing the city, by means of hemp and deportation, of a number of bad characters. The city was just beginning to regain its former prosperity when the Frazer river excitement brought about a temporary depression. The wild rush carried away about one sixth of its population. These all came back again, poorer and perhaps wiser; at least, their necessities compelled them to go to work and weaned them somewhat of their extravagant habits and their disinclination to work except for the large returns of earlier days. Since 1857 the growth of the city has been steady, unmarked by real estate booms; nor has it been retarded by long periods of financial depression.

CHAPTER XXVII. CRIME, CRIMINALS AND VIGILANCE COMMITTEES.

There was but little crime in California among its white inhabitants during the Spanish and Mexican eras of its history. The conditions were not conducive to the development of a criminal element. The inhabitants were a pastoral people, pursuing an outdoor vocation, and there were no large towns or cities where the viciously inclined could congregate and find a place of refuge from justice. "From 1819 to 1846, that is, during the entire period of Mexican domination under the Republic," says Bancroft, "there were but six murders among the whites in all California." There were no lynchings, no mobs, unless some of the revolutionary uprisings might be called such, and but one vigilance committee.

San Francisco is credited with the origin of that form of popular tribunal known as the vigilance committee. The name "vigilance committee" originated with the uprising, in 1851, of the people of that city against the criminal element; but, years before there was a city of San Francisco, Los Angeles had originated a tribunal of the people, had taken criminals from the lawfully constituted authorities and had tried and executed them. The causes which called into existence the first vigilance committee in California were similar to those that created the later ones, namely, laxity in the administration of the laws and distrust in the integrity of those chosen to administer them. During the "decade of revolutions," that is, between 1830 and 1840, the frequent change of rulers and the struggles of the different factions for power engendered in the masses a disregard, not only for their rulers, but for law and order as well. Criminals escaped punishment through the law's delays. No court in California had power to pass sentence of death on a civilian until its findings had been approved by the superior tribunal of Mexico. In the slow and tedious processes of the different courts, a criminal stood a good show of dying of old age before his case reached final adjudication. The first committee of vigilance in California was organized at Los Angeles, in the house of Juan Temple, April 7, 1836. It was called "Junta Defensora de La Seguridad Publica," United Defenders of the Public Security (or safety). Its motto, which appears in the heading of its "acta," and is there credited as a quotation from Montesquieu's Exposition of the Laws, Book 26, Chapter 23, was, "Salus populi suprema lex est" (The safety of the people is the supreme law). There is a marked similarity between the proceedings of the Junta Defensora of 1836 and the San Francisco vigilance committee of 1856; it is not probable, however, that any of the actors in the latter committee participated in the former. Although there is quite a full account of the proceedings of the Junta Defensora in the Los Angeles city archives, no historian heretofore except Bancroft seems to have found it.

The circumstances which brought about the organization of the Junta Defensora are as follows: The wife of Domingo Feliz (part owner of the Los Feliz Rancho), who bore the poetical name of Maria del Rosario Villa, became infatuated with a handsome but disreputable Sonoran vaquero, Gervacio Alispaz by name. She abandoned her husband and lived with Alispaz as his mistress at San Gabriel. Feliz sought to reclaim his erring wife, but was met by insults and abuse from her paramour, whom he once wounded in a personal altercation. Feliz finally invoked the aid of the authorities. The woman was arrested and brought to town. A reconciliation was effected between the husband and wife. Two days later they left town for the rancho, both riding one horse. On the way they were met by Alispaz, and in a personal encounter Feliz was stabbed to death by the wife's paramour. The body was dragged into a ravine and covered with brush and leaves. Next day, March 29, the body was found and brought to the city. The murderer and the woman were arrested and imprisoned. The people were filled with horror and indignation, and there were threats of summary vengeance, but better counsel prevailed.

On the 30th the funeral of Feliz took place, and, like that of James King of William, twenty years later, was the occasion for the renewal of the outcry for vengeance. The attitude of the people became so threatening that on the 1st of April an extraordinary session of the ayuntamiento was held. A call was made upon the citizens to form an organization to preserve the peace. A considerable number responded and were formed into military patrols under the command of Don Juan B. Leandry. The illustrious ayuntamiento resolved "that whomsoever shall disturb the public tranquility shall be punished according to law." The excitement apparently died out, but it was only the calm that precedes the storm. The beginning of the Easter ceremonies was at hand, and it was deemed a sacrilege to execute the assassins in holy week, so all further attempts at punishment were deferred until April 7, the Monday after Easter, when at dawn, by previous understanding, a number of the better class of citizens gathered at the house of Juan Temple, which stood on the site of the new post office. An organization was effected. Victor Prudon, a native of Breton, France, but a naturalized citizen of California, was elected president; Manuel Arzaga, a native of California, w-as elected secretary, and Francisco Araujo, a retired army officer, was placed in command of the armed force. Speeches were made by Prudon, and by the military commandant and others, setting forth the necessity of their organization and justifying their actions. It was unanimously decided that both the man and the woman should be shot; their guilt being evident, no trial was deemed necessary.

An address to the authorities and the people was formulated. A copy of this is preserved in the city archives. It abounds in metaphors. It is too long for insertion here. I make a few extracts: "* * * Believing that immorality has reached such an extreme that public security is menaced and will be lost if the dike of a solemn example is not opposed to the torrent of atrocious perfidy, we demand of you that you execute or deliver to us for immediate execution the assassin, Gervacio Alispaz, and the unfaithful Maria del Rosario Villa, his accomplice. * * * Nature trembles at the sight of these venomous reptiles and the soil turns barren in its refusal to support their detestable existence. Let the infernal pair perish! It is the will of the people. We will not lay down our arms until our petition is granted and the murderers are executed. The proof of their guilt is so clear that justice needs no investigation. Public vengeance demands an example and it must be given. The blood of the Alvarez, of the Patinos, of the Jenkins, is not yet cold — they, too, being the unfortunate victims of the brutal passions of their murderers. Their bloody ghosts shriek for vengeance. Their terrible voices re-echo from their graves. The afflicted widow, the forsaken orphan, the aged father, the brother in mourning, the inconsolable mother, the public — all demand speedy punishment of the guilty.

We swear that outraged justice shall be avenged to-day or we shall die in the attempt. The blood of the murderers shall be shed to-day or ours will be to the last drop. It will be published throughout the world that judges in Los Angeles tolerate murderers, but that there are virtuous citizens who sacrifice their lives in order to preserve those of their countrymen."

"A committee will deliver to the First Constitutional Alcalde a copy of these resolutions, that he may decide whatever he finds most convenient, and one hour's time will be given him in which to do so. If in that time no answer has been received, then the judge will be responsible before God and man for what will follow. Death to the murderers!

"God and liberty. Angeles, April 7, 1836."

Fifty-five signatures are attached to this document; fourteen of these are those of naturalized foreigners and the remainder those of native Californians. The junta was made up of the best citizens, native and foreign. An extraordinary session of the ayuntamiento was called. The members of the junta, fully armed, marched to the city hall to await the decision of the authorities. The petition was discussed in the council, and, in the language of the archives: "This Illustrious Body decided to call said Breton Prudon to appear before it and to compel him to retire with the armed citizens so that this Illustrious Body may deliberate at liberty."

"This was done, but he declined to appear before this body, as he and the armed citizens were determined to obtain Gervacio Alispaz and Maria del Rosario Villa. The ayuntamiento decided that as it had not sufficient force to compel the armed citizens to disband, they being in large numbers and composed of the best and most respectable men of the town, to send an answer saying that the judges could not accede to the demand of the armed citizens."

The members of the Junta Defensora then marched in a body to the jail and demanded the keys of the guard. These were refused. The keys were secured by force and Gervacio Alispaz taken out and shot. The following demand was then sent to the first alcalde, Manuel Requena:

"It is absolutely necessary that you deliver to this junta the key of the apartment where Maria del Rosario Villa is kept.

"God and liberty.

"Victor Prudon, President.

"Manuel Arzaga, Secretary."

To this the alcalde replied: "Maria del Rosario Villa is incarcerated at a private dwelling, whose owner has the key, with instructions not to deliver the same to any one. The prisoner is left there at the disposition of the law only.

"God and liberty.

"Manuel Requena, Alcalde."

The key was obtained. The wretched Maria was taken to the place of execution on a carreta and shot. The bodies of the guilty pair were brought back to the jail and the following communication sent to the alcalde:

"Junta of the Defenders of Public Safety.

"To the 1st Constitutional Alcalde: "The dead bodies of Gervacio Alispaz and Maria del Rosario Villa are at your disposal. We also forward you the jail keys that you may deliver them to whomsoever is on guard. In case you are in need of men to serve as guards, we are all at your disposal.

194

"God and liberty.

Angeles, April 7, 1836.

"Victor Prudon, Pres.

"Manuel Arzaga, Sec."

A few days later the Junta Defensora de La Seguridad Publica disbanded; and so ended the only instance in the seventy-five years of Spanish and Mexican rule in California, of the people, by popular tribunal, taking the administration of justice out of the hands of the legally constituted authorities.

The tales of the fabulous richness of the gold fields of California were quickly spread throughout the world and drew to the territory all classes and conditions of men, the bad as well as the good, the vicious as well as the virtuous; the indolent, the profligate and the criminal came to prey upon the industrious. These conglomerate elements of society found the Land of Gold practically without law, and the vicious among them were not long in making it a land without order. With that inherent trait, which makes the Anglo-Saxon wherever he may be an organizer, the American element of the gold seekers soon adjusted a form of government to suit the exigencies of the land and the people. There may have been too much lynching, too much vigilance committee in it and too little respect for lawfully constituted authorities, but it was effective and was suited to the social conditions existing.

In 1851 the criminal element became so dominant as to seriously threaten the existence of the chief city, San Francisco. Terrible conflagrations had swept over the city in May and June of that year and destroyed the greater part of the business portion. The fires were known to be of incendiary origin. The bold and defiant attitude of the vicious classes led to the organization by the better element, of that form of popular tribunal called a committee of vigilance. The law abiding element among the citizens disregarding the legally constituted authorities, who were either too weak or too corrupt to control the law-defying, took the power in their own hands, organized a vigilance committee and tried and executed by hanging four notorious criminals, namely: Jenkins, Stuart, Whitaker and McKenzie.

During the proceedings of the vigilance committee a case of mistaken identity came near costing an innocent man his life. About 8 o'clock in the evening of February 18, two men entered the store of a Mr. Jansen on Montgomery street and asked to see some blankets. As the merchant stooped to get the blankets one of the men struck him with a sling shot and both of them beat him into insensibility. They then opened his desk and carried away all the gold they could find, about $2,000. The police arrested two men on suspicion of being the robbers. One of the men was identified as James Stuart, a noted criminal, who had murdered Sheriff Moore at Auburn. He gave the name of Thomas Burdue, but this was believed to be one of Stuart's numerous aliases. The men were identified by Mr. Jansen as his assailants. They were put on trial. When the court adjourned over to the next day a determined effort was made by the crowd to seize the men and hang them. They were finally taken out of the hands of the officers and given a trial by a jury selected by a committee of citizens. The jury failed to agree, three of the jury being convinced that the men were not Jansen's assailants. Then the mob made a rush to hang the jury, but were kept back by a show of revolvers. The prisoners were turned over to the court. One of them, Wildred, broke jail and escaped. Burdue was

195

tried, convicted and sentenced to fourteen years' imprisonment. Before the sentence of the court was executed he was taken to Marysville and arraigned for the murder of Sheriff Moore. A number of witnesses swore positively that the man was Stuart; others swore even more positively that he was not. A close examination revealed that the prisoner bore every distinguishing mark on his person by which Stuart could be identified. He was convicted and sentenced to be hanged in thirty days. In the meantime the vigilance committee of 1856 was organized and the real Stuart accidentally fell into the hands of the vigilantes at San Francisco. He was arrested for a theft he had not committed and recognized by one of the committee's guards that he had formerly employed in the mines. By adroit questioning he was forced to confess that he was the real Stuart, the murderer of Sheriff Moore and the assailant of Jansen. His confederate in the robbery was Whitaker, one of the four hanged by the committee. Burdue was finally released, after having twice stood under the shadow of the gallows for the crimes of his double. The confessions of Stuart and Whitaker implicated a number of their pals. Some of these were convicted and sent to prison and others fled the country; about thirty were banished. Nearly all of the criminals were ex-convicts from Australia and Tasmania.

The vigorous measures adopted by the committee purified the city of the vicious class that had preyed upon it. Several of the smaller towns and some of the mining camps organized vigilance committees and a number of the knaves who had fled from San Francisco met a deserved fate in other places.

In the early '50s the better elements of San Francisco's population were so engrossed in business that they had no time to spare to look after its political affairs; and its government gradually drifted into the hands of vicious and corrupt men. Many of the city authorities had obtained their offices by fraud and ballot stuffing and "instead of protecting the community against scoundrels they protected the scoundrels against the community." James King of William, an ex-banker and a man of great courage and persistence, started a small paper called the Daily Evening Bulletin. He vigorously assailed the criminal elements and the city and county officials. His denunciations aroused public sentiment. The murder of United States Marshal Richardson by a gambler named Cora still further inflamed the public mind. It was feared that by the connivance of some of the corrupt county officials Cora would escape punishment. His trial resulted in a hung jury. " There was a suspicion that some of the jurymen were bribed. King continued through the Bulletin to hurl his most bitter invectives against the corrupt officials. They determined to silence him. He published the fact that James Casey, a supervisor from the twelfth ward, was an ex-convict of Sing Sing prison. Casey waylaid King at the corner of Montgomery and Washington streets and in a cowardly manner shot him down. The shooting occurred on the 14th of May, 1856. Casey immediately surrendered himself to a deputy sheriff, Lafayete M. Byrne, who was near. King was not killed, but an examination of the wound by the physicians decided that there was no hopes of his recovery. Casey was conducted to the city prison and as a mob began to gather, for greater safety he was taken to the county jail. A crowd pursued him crying, "Hang him," "kill him." At the jail the mob was stopped by an array of deputy sheriffs, police officers and a number of Casey's friends, all armed. The excitement spread throughout the city. The old vigilance

196

committee of 1851, or rather a new organization out of the remnant of the old, was formed. Five thousand men were enrolled in a few days. Arms were procured and headquarters established on Sacramento street between Davis and Front. The men were divided into companies. William T. Coleman, chairman of the vigilance committee of 1851, was made president or No. 1, and Isaac Bluxome, Jr., the secretary, was No. 33. Each man was known by number. Charles Doane was elected chief marshal of the military division.

The San Francisco Herald (edited by John Nugent), then the leading paper of the city, came out with a scathing editorial denouncing the vigilance committee. The merchants at once withdrew their advertising patronage. Next morning the paper appeared reduced from forty columns to a single page, but still hostile to the committee. It finally died for want of patronage.

On Sunday, May 18, 1856, the military division was ready to storm the jail if necessary to obtain possession of the prisoners, Casey and Cora. The different companies, marching from their headquarters by certain prescribed routes, all reached the jail at the same time and completely invested it. They had with them two pieces of artillery. One of these guns was planted so as to command the door of the jail. There were fifteen hundred vigilantes under arms. A demand was made on Sheriff Scannell for the prisoners, Cora and Casey. The prison guard made no resistance, the prisoners were surrendered and taken at once to the vigilantes' headquarters.

On the 20th of May the murderers were put on trial; while the trial was in progress the death of King was announced. Both men were convicted and sentenced to be hanged. King's funeral, the largest and most imposing ever seen in San Francisco, took place on the 23rd. While the funeral cortege was passing through the streets Casey and Cora were hanged in front of the windows of the vigilance headquarters. About an hour before his execution Cora was married to a notorious courtesan, Arabella Ryan, but commonly called Belle Cora. A Catholic priest, Father Accolti, performed the ceremony.

Governor J. Neely Johnson, who at first seemed inclined not to interfere with the vigilantes, afterwards acting under the advice of David S. Terry, Volney E. Howard and others of "the law and order faction," issued a proclamation commanding the committee to disband, to which no attention was paid. The governor then appointed William T. Sherman major-general. Sherman called for recruits to suppress the uprising. Seventy-five or a hundred, mostly gamblers, responded to his call. General Wool, in command of the troops in the department of the Pacific, refused to loan Governor Johnson arms to equip his "law and order" recruits and General Sherman resigned. Volney E. Howard was then appointed major-general. His principal military service consisted in proclaiming what he would do to the "pork merchants" who constituted the committee. He did nothing except to bluster. A squad of the vigilance police attempted to arrest a man named Maloney. Maloney was at the time in the company of David S. Terry (then chief justice of the state) and several other members of the "law and order" party. They resisted the police and in the melee Terry stabbed the sergeant of the squad, Sterling A. Hopkins, and then he and his associates made their escape to the armory of the San Francisco Blues, one of their strongholds.

When the report of the stabbing reached headquarters the great bell sounded the alarm and the vigilantes in a very brief space of time surrounded the armory building and had their cannon planted to batter it down. Terry, Maloney, and the others of their party in the building, considering discretion the better part of valor, surrendered and were at once taken to Fort Gunnybags, the vigilantes' headquarters. The arms of the "law and order" party at their various rendezvous were surrendered to the vigilantes and the companies disbanded.

Terry was closely confined in a cell at the headquarters of the committee; Hopkins, after lingering some time between life and death, finally recovered. Terry was tried for assault on Hopkins and upon several other persons, was found guilty, but, after being held as a prisoner for some time, was finally released. He at once joined Johnson and Howard at Sacramento, where he felt much safer than in San Francisco. He gave the vigilantes no more trouble.

On the 29th of July, Hethrington and Brace were hanged from a gallows erected on Davis street, between Sacramento and Commercial. Both of these men had committed murder. These were the last executions by the committee. The committee transported from the state thirty disreputable characters and a number deported themselves. A few, and among them the notorious Ned McGowan, managed to keep concealed until the storm was over. A few of the expatriated returned after the committee dissolved and brought suit for damages, but failed to recover anything. The committee had paid the fare of the exiles. It was only the high toned rascals who were given a cabin passage that brought the suits. The committee finished its labors and dissolved with a grand parade on the 18th of August (1856). It did a good work. For several years after, San Francisco from being one of the worst, became one of the best governed cities in the United States. The committee was made up of men from the northern and western states. The so-called "law and order" party was mostly composed of the proslavery office-holding faction that ruled the state at that time.

When the vigilance committees between 1851 and 1856 drove disreputable characters from San Francisco and the northern mines, many of them drifted southward and found a lodgment for a time in the southern cities and towns. Los Angeles was not far from the Mexican line, and any one who desired to escape from justice, fleet mounted, could speedily put himself beyond the reach of his pursuers. All these causes and influences combined to produce a saturnalia of crime that disgraced that city in the early '50s.

Gen. J. H. Bean, a prominent citizen of Southern California, while returning to Los Angeles from his place of business at San Gabriel late one evening in November, 1852, was attacked by two men, who had been lying in wait for him. One seized the bridle of his horse and jerked the animal back on his haunches; the other seized the general and pulled him from the saddle. Bean made a desperate resistance, but was overpowered and stabbed to death. The assassination of General Bean resulted in the organization of a vigilance committee and an effort was made to rid the country of desperadoes. A number of arrests were made. Three suspects were tried by the committee for various crimes. One, Cipiano Sandoval, a poor cobbler of San Gabriel, was charged with complicity in the murder of General Bean. He strenuously maintained that he was innocent. He, with the other two, were sentenced to be hanged. On the following Sunday morning the doomed men were conducted to the top of Fort Hill, where the gallows stood. Sandoval made a brief speech, again declaring his innocence. The others awaited their doom in silence. The trap fell and all were launched into eternity. Years afterward one of the real murderers on his deathbed revealed the truth and confessed his part in the crime. The poor cobbler was innocent.

In 1854 drunkenness, gambling, murder and all forms of immorality and crime were rampant in Los Angeles. The violent deaths, it is said, averaged one for every day in the year. It was a common question at the breakfast table, "Well, how many were killed last night?" Little or no attention was paid to the killing of an Indian or a half breed; it was only when a gente de razon was the victim that the community was aroused to action.

The Kern river gold rush, in the winter of 1854-55, brought from the northern mines fresh relays of gamblers and desperadoes and crime increased. The Southern Californian of March 7, 1855, commenting on the general lawlessness prevailing, says: "Last Sunday night was a brisk night for killing. Four men were shot and killed and several wounded in shooting affrays."

A worthless fellow by the name of David Brown, who had, without provocation, killed a companion named Clifford, was tried and sentenced to be hanged with one Felipe Alvitre, a Mexican, who had murdered an American named Ellington, at El Monte. There was a feeling among the people that Brown, through quibbles of law, would escape the death penalty, and there was talk of lynching. Stephen C. Foster, the mayor, promised that if justice was not legally meted out to Brown by the law, then he would resign his office and head the lynching party. January 10, 1855, an order was received from Judge Murray, of the supreme court, staying the execution of Brown, but leaving Alvitre to his fate. January 12 Alvitre was hanged by the sheriff in the jail yard in the presence of an immense crowd. The gallows were taken down and the guards dismissed. The crowd gathered outside the jail yard. Speeches were made. The mayor resigned his office and headed the mob. The doors of the jail were broken down; Brown was taken across Spring street to a large gateway opening into a corral and hanged from the crossbeam. Foster was re-elected by an almost unanimous vote at a special election. The city marshal, who had opposed the action of the vigilantes, was compelled to resign.

During 1855 and 1856 lawlessness increased. There was an organized band of about one hundred Mexicans, who patrolled the highways, robbing and murdering. They threatened the extermination of the Americans and there were fears of a race war, for many who were not members of the gang sympathized with them. In 1856 a vigilance committee was organized with Myron Norton as president and H. N. Alexander as secretary. A number of disreputable characters were forced to leave town. The banditti, under their leaders, Pancho Daniel and Juan Flores, were plundering and committing outrages in the neighborhood of San Juan Capistrano.

On the night of January 22, 1857, Sheriff James R. Barton left Los Angeles with a posse, consisting of William H. Little, Charles K. Baker, Charles F. Daley, Alfred Hardy and Frank Alexander with the intention of capturing some of the robbers. At Sepulveda's ranch next morning the sheriff's party was warned that the robbers were some fifty strong, well armed and mounted, and would probably attack them. Twelve miles further the sheriff and his men encountered a detachment of the banditti. A short, sharp engagement took place. Barton, Baker, Little and Daley were killed. Hardy and Alexander made their escape by the fleetness of their horses. When the news reached Los Angeles the excitement became intense. A public meeting was held to devise plans to rid the community not only of the roving gang of murderers, but also of the criminal classes in the city, who were known to be in sympathy with the banditti. All suspicious houses were searched and some fifty persons arrested. Several companies were organized; the infantry to guard the city and the mounted men to scour the country. Companies were also formed at San Bernardino and El Monte, while the military authorities at Fort Tejon and San Diego dispatched soldiers to aid in the good work of exterminating crime and criminals.

The robbers were pursued into the mountains and nearly all captured. Gen. Andres Pico, with a company of native Californians, was most efficient in the pursuit. He captured Silvas and Ardillero, two of the most noted of the gang, and hanged them where they were captured. Fifty-two were lodged in the city jail. Of these, eleven were hanged for various crimes and the remainder set free. Juan Flores, one of the leaders, was condemned by popular vote and on February 14, 1857, was hanged near the top of Fort Hill in the presence of nearly the entire population of the town. He was only twenty-one years of age. Pancho Daniel, another of the leaders, was captured on the 19th of January, 1858, near San Jose. He was found by the sheriff, concealed in a haystack. After his arrest he was part of the time in jail and part of the time out on bail. He had been tried three times, but through law quibbles had escaped conviction. A change of venue to Santa Barbara had been granted. The people determined to take the law in their own hands. On the morning of November 30, 1858, the body of Pancho was hanging from a beam across the gateway of the jail yard. Four of the banditti were executed by the people of San Gabriel, and Leonardo Lopez, under sentence of the court, was hanged by the sheriff. The gang was broken up and the moral atmosphere of Los Angeles somewhat purified.

November 17, 1862, John Rains of Cucamonga ranch was murdered near Azusa. December 9, 1863, the sheriff was taking Manuel Cerradel to San Quentin to serve a ten years' sentence. When the sheriff went aboard the tug boat Cricket at Wilmington, to proceed to the Senator, quite a number of other persons took passage. On the way down the harbor, the prisoner was seized by the passengers, who were vigilantes, and hanged to the rigging; after hanging twenty minutes the body was taken down, stones tied to the feet and it was thrown overboard. Cerradel was implicated in the murder of Rains.

In the fall of 1863 lawlessness had again become rampant in Los Angeles; one of the chiefs of the criminal class was a desperado by the name of Boston Daimwood. He was suspected of the' murder of a miner on the desert and was loud in his threats against the lives of various citizens. He and four other well-known criminals, Wood, Chase, Ybarra and Olivas, all of whom were either murderers or horse thieves, were lodged in jail. On the 21st of November two hundred armed citizens battered down the doors of the jail, took the five wretches out and hanged them to the portico of the old court house on Spring street, which stood on the present site of the Phillips block.

On the 24th of October, 1871, occurred in Los Angeles a most disgraceful affair, known as the Chinese massacre. It grew out of one of those interminable feuds between rival tongs of highbinders, over a woman. Desultory firing had been kept up between the rival factions throughout the day. About 5:30 p. m. Policeman Bilderrain visited the seat of war, an old adobe house on the corner of Arcadia street and "Nigger alley," known as the Coronel building. Finding himself unable to quell the disturbance he called for help. Robert Thompson, an old resident of the city, was among the first to reach the porch of the house in answer to the police call for help. He received a mortal wound from a bullet fired through the door of a Chinese store. He died an hour later in Wollweber's drug store. The Chinese in the meantime barricaded the doors and windows of the old adobe and prepared for battle. The news of the fight and of the killing of Thompson spread throughout the city and an immense crowd gathered in the streets around the building with the intention of wreaking vengeance on the Chinese.

The first attempt by the mob to dislodge the Chinamen was by cutting holes through the flat brea covered roof and firing pistol shots into the interior of the building. One of the besieged crawled out of the building and attempted to escape, but was shot down before half way across Negro alley. Another attempted to escape into Los Angeles street; he was seized, dragged to the gate of Tomlinson's corral on New High street, and hanged.

About 9 o'clock a part of the mob had succeeded in battering a hole in the eastern end of the building; through this the rioters, with demoniac howlings, rushed in, firing pistols to the right and left. Huddled in corners and hidden behind boxes they found eight terror-stricken Chinamen, who begged piteously for their lives. These were brutally dragged out and turned over to the fiendish mob. One was dragged to death by a rope around his neck; three, more dead than alive from kicking and beating, were hanged to a wagon on Los Angeles street; and four were hanged to the gateway of Tomlinson's corral. Two of the victims were mere boys. While the shootings and hangings were going on thieves were looting the other houses in the Chinese quarters. The houses were broken into, trunks, boxes and other receptacles rifled of their contents, and any Chinamen found in the buildings were dragged forth to slaughter. Among the victims was a doctor, Gene Tung, a quiet, inoffensive old man. He pleaded for his life in good English, offering his captors all his money, some $2,000 to $3,000. He was hanged, his money stolen and one of his fingers cut off to obtain a ring he wore. The amount of money stolen by the mob from the Chinese quarters was variously estimated at from $40,000 to $50,000.

About 9:30 p. m. the law abiding citizens, under the leadership of Henry Hazard, R. M. Widney, H. C. Austin, Sheriff Burns and others, had rallied in sufficient force to make an attempt to quell the mob. Proceeding to Chinatown they rescued several Chinamen from the rioters. The mob finding armed opposition quickly dispersed.

The results of the mob's murderous work were ten men hanged on Los Angeles street, some to wagons and some to awnings: five hanged at Tomlinson's corral and four shot to death in Negro alley, nineteen in all. Of all the Chinamen murdered, the only one known to be implicated in the highbinder war was Ah Choy. All the other leaders escaped to the country before the attack was made by the mob. The grand jury, after weeks of investigation, found indictments against one hundred and fifty persons alleged to have been actively engaged in the massacre. The jury's report severely censured "the officers of this county, as well as of this city, whose duty it is to preserve peace," and declared that they "were deplorably inefficient in the performance of their duty during the scenes of confusion and bloodshed which disgraced our city, and has cast a reproach upon the people of Los Angeles county." Of all those indicted but six were convicted. These were sentenced to from four to six years in the state's prison, but through some legal technicality they were all released after serving a part of their sentence.

The last execution in Los Angeles by a vigilance committee was that of Michael Lachenias, a French desperado, who had killed five or six men. The offense for which he was hanged was the murder of Jacob Bell, a little inoffensive man, who owned a small farm near that of Lachenias, south of the city. There had been a slight difference between them in regard to the use of water from a zanja. Lachenias, without a word of warning, rode up to Bell, where he was at work in his field, drew a revolver and shot him dead. The murderer then rode into town and boastingly informed the people of what he had done and told them where they would find Bell's body. He then surrendered himself to the officers and was locked up in jail.

Public indignation was aroused. A meeting was held in Stearns' hall on Los Angeles street. A vigilance committee was formed and the details of the execution planned. On the morning of the 17th of December, 1870, a body of three hundred armed men marched to the jail, took Lachenias out and proceeded with him to Tomlinson's corral on Temple and New High streets, and hanged him. The crowd then quietly dispersed.

A strange metamorphosis took place in the character of the lower classes of the native Californians after the conquest. (The better classes were not changed in character by the changed conditions of the country, but throughout were true gentlemen and most worthy and honorable citizens.) Before the conquest by the Americans they were a peaceful and contented people. There were no organized bands of outlaws among them. After the discovery of gold the evolution of a banditti began and they produced some of the boldest robbers and most daring highwaymen the world has seen.

The injustice of their conquerors had much to do with producing this change. The Americans not only took possession of their country and its government, but in many cases they despoiled them of their ancestral acres and their personal property. Injustice rankles; and it is not strange that the more lawless among the native population sought revenge and retaliation. They were often treated by the rougher American element as aliens and intruders, who had no right in the land of their birth. Such treatment embittered them more than loss of property. There were those, however, among the natives, who, once entered upon a career of crime, found robbery and murder congenial occupations. The plea of injustice was no extenuation for their crimes.

Joaquin Murieta was the most noted of the Mexican and Californian desperadoes of the early '50s. He was born in Sonora of good family and received some education. He came to California with the Sonoran migration of 1849, and secured a rich claim on the Stanislaus. He was dispossessed of this by half a dozen American desperadoes, his wife abused and both driven from the diggings. He next took up a ranch on the Calaveras, but from this he was driven by two Americans.

202

He next tried mining in the Murphy diggings, but was unsuccessful. His next occupation was that of a monte player. While riding into town on a horse borrowed from his half-brother he was stopped by an American, who claimed that the horse was stolen from him. Joaquin protested that the horse was a borrowed one from his half-brother and offered to procure witnesses to prove it. He was dragged from the saddle amid cries of "hang the greaser." He was taken to the ranch of his brother. The brother was hanged to the limb of a tree, no other proof of his crime being needed than the assertion of the American that the horse was his. Joaquin was stripped, bound to the same tree and flogged. The demon was aroused within him, and no wonder, he vowed revenge on the men who had murdered his brother and beaten him. Faithfully he carried out his vow of vengeance. Had he doomed only these to slaughter it would have been but little loss, but the implacable foe of every American, he made the innocent suffer with the guilty. He was soon at the head of a band of desperadoes, varying in numbers from twenty to forty. For three years he and his band were the terror of the state. From the northern mines to the Mexican border they committed robberies and murders. Claudio and some of his subordinates were killed, but the robber chief seemed to bear a charmed life. Large rewards were offered for him dead or alive and numerous attempts were made to take him. Capt. Harry Love at the head of a band of rangers August, 1853, came upon Joaquin and six of his gang in a camp near the Tejon Pass. In the fight that ensued Joaquin and Three Fingered Jack were killed. With the loss of their leaders the organization was broken up.

The last organized band of robbers which terrorized the southern part of the state was that of Vasquez. Tiburcio Vasquez was born in Monterey county, of Mexican parents, in 1837. Early in life he began a career of crime. After committing a number of robberies and thefts he was captured and sent to San Quentin for horse stealing. He was discharged in 1863, but continued his disreputable career. He united with Procopio and Soto, two noted bandits. Soto was killed by Sheriff Morse of Alameda county in a desperate encounter. Vasquez and his gang of outlaws committed robberies throughout the southern part of the state, ranging from Santa Clara and Alameda counties to the Mexican line. Early in May, 1874, Sheriff William Rowland of Los Angeles county, who had repeatedly tried to capture Vasquez, but whose plans had been foiled by the bandit's spies, learned that the robber chief was making his headquarters at the house of Greek George, about ten miles due west of Los Angeles, toward Santa Monica, in a cañon of the Cahuenga mountains. The morning of May 15 was set for the attack. To avert suspicion Sheriff Rowland remained in the city. The attacking force, eight in number, were under command of Under-Sheriff Albert Johnson, the other members of the force were Major H. M. Mitchell, attorney-at-law; J. S. Bryant, city con' stable; E. Harris, policeman; W. E. Rogers, citizen; B. F. Hartley, chief of police; and D. K. Smith, citizen, all of Los Angeles, and a Mr. Beers, of San Francisco, special correspondent of the San Francisco Chronicle.

At 4 a. m. on the morning of the 15th of May the posse reached Major Mitchell's bee ranch in a small canon not far from Greek George's. From this point the party reconnoitered the bandit's hiding place and planned an attack. As the deputy sheriff and his men were about to move against the house a high box wagon drove up the canon from the direction of Greek George's place. In this were two natives; the sheriff's party climbed into the high wagon box and, lying down, compelled the driver to drive up to the back of Greek George's house, threatening him and his companion with death on the least sign of treachery. Reaching the house they surrounded it and burst in the door, Vasquez, who had been eating his breakfast, attempted to escape through a small window. The party opened fire on him. Being wounded and finding himself surrounded on all sides, he surrendered. He was taken to the Los Angeles jail. His injuries proved to be mere flesh wounds. He received a great deal of maudlin sympathy from silly women, who magnified him into a hero. He was taken to San Jose, tried for murder, found guilty and hanged, March 19, 1875. His band was thereupon broken up and dispersed.

CHAPTER XXVIII.
FILIBUSTERS AND FILIBUSTERING.

The rush of immigration to California in the early '50s had brought to the state a class of adventurers who were too lazy or too proud to work. They were ready to engage in almost any lawless undertaking that promised plunder and adventure. The defeat of the pro-slavery politicians in their attempts to fasten their "peculiar institution" upon any part of the territory acquired from Mexico had embittered them. The more unscrupulous among them began to look around for new fields, over which slavery might be extended. As it could be made profitable only in southern lands, Cuba, Mexico and Central America became the arenas for enacting that form of piracy called "filibustering." The object of these forays, when organized by Americans, was to seize upon territory as had been done in Texas and erect it into an independent government that ultimately would be annexed to the United States and become slave territory. Although the armed invasion of countries with which the United States was at peace was a direct violation of its neutrality laws, yet the federal office-holders in the southern states and in California, all of whom belonged to the proslavery faction, not only made no attempt to prevent these invasions, but secretly aided them or at least sympathized with them to the extent of allowing them to recruit men and depart without molestation. There was a glamour of romance about these expeditions that influenced unthinking young men of no fixed principles to join them; these were to be pitied. But the leaders of them and their abettors were cold, selfish, scheming politicians, willing, if need be, to overthrow the government of the nation and build on its ruins an oligarchy of slave holders. The first to organize a filibuster expedition in California was a Frenchman. Race prejudices were strong in early mining days. The United States had recently been at war with Mexico. The easy conquest of that country had bred a contempt for its peoples. The Sonoran migration, that begun soon after the discovery of gold in California, brought a very undesirable class of immigrants to the state. Sailing vessels had brought from the west coast of South America another despised class of mongrel Spanish. It exasperated the Americans to see these people digging gold and carrying it out of the country. This antagonism extended, more or less, to all foreigners, but was strongest against men of the Latin races. Many Frenchmen, through emigration schemes gotten up in Paris, had been induced to come to California. Some of these were men of education and good standing, but they fell under the ban of prejudices and by petty persecutions were driven out of the mines and forced to earn a precarious living in the cities. There was a great deal of dissatisfaction among the Frenchmen with existing conditions in California, and they were ready to embark in any scheme that promised greater rewards. Among the French population of San Francisco was a man of noble family. Count Gaston Roaul de Raousset-Boulbon. He had lost his ancestral lands and was in reduced circumstances. He was a man of education and ability, but visionary. He conceived the idea of establishing a French colony on the Sonora border and opening the mines that had been abandoned on account of Apache depredations. By colonizing the border he hoped to put a stop to American encroachments. He divulged his scheme to the French consul, Dillon, at San

Francisco, who entered heartily into it. Raousset was sent to the City of Mexico, where he obtained from President Arista the desired concession of land and the promise of financial assistance from a leading banking house there on condition that he proceed at once to Sonora with an armed company of Frenchmen. Returning to San Francisco he quickly recruited from among the French residents two hundred and fifty men and with these he sailed for Guaymas, where he arrived early in June, 1852. He was well received at first, but soon found himself regarded with suspicion. He was required by the authorities to remain at Guaymas. After a month's detention he was allowed to proceed through Hermosilla to the Arizona border.

When about one hundred miles from Arispe he received an order from General Blanco, then at Hermosilla, to report to him. While halting at El Caric to consider his next move he received a reinforcement of about eighty French colonists, who had come to the country the year before under command of Pindray. Pindray had met his death in a mysterious manner. It was supposed that he was poisoned. The colonist had remained in the country. Raousset sent one of his men, Gamier, to interview Blanco. General Blanco gave his ultimatum — First, that the Frenchmen should become naturalized citizens of Mexico; or, secondly, they should wait until letters of security could be procured from the capital, when they might proceed to Arizona and take possession of any mines they found; or, lastly, they might put themselves under the leadership of a Mexican officer and then proceed. Raousset and his followers refused to accede to any of these propositions. Blanco began collecting men and munitions of war to oppose the French. Raousset raised the flag of revolt and invited the inhabitants to join him in gaining the independence of Sonora. After drilling his men a few weeks and preparing for hostilities he began his march against Hermosilla, distant one hundred and fifty miles. He met with no opposition, the people along his route welcoming the French. General Blanco had twelve hundred men to defend the city. But instead of preparing to resist the advancing army he sent delegates to Raousset to offer him money to let the city alone. Raousset sent back word that at 8 o'clock he would begin the attack; and at II would be master of the city. He was as good as his word. The Frenchmen charged the Mexicans and although the opposing force numbered four to one of the assailants, Raousset's men captured the town and drove Blanco's troops out of it. The Mexican loss was two hundred killed and wounded. The French loss seventeen killed and twenty-three wounded Raousset's men were mere adventurers and were in the country without any definite purpose. Could he have relied on them, he might have captured all of Sonora.

He abandoned Hermosilla. Blanco, glad to get rid of the filibusters on any terms, raised $11,000 and chartered a vessel to carry them back to San Francisco. A few elected to remain. Raousset went to Mazatlan and a few months later he reached San Francisco, where he was lionized as a hero. Upon an invitation from Santa Ana, who had succeeded Arista as president, he again visited the Mexican capital in June, 1853. Santa Ana was profuse in promises. He wanted Raousset to recruit five hundred Frenchmen to protect the Sonora frontier against the Indians, promising ample remuneration and good pay for their services. Raousset, finding that Santa Ana's promises could not be relied upon, and that the wily schemer was about to have him arrested, made his escape to Acapulco, riding several horses to death to reach there ahead of his pursuers. He embarked immediately for San Francisco.

In the meantime another filibuster, William Walker, with forty-one followers had landed at La Paz November 3, 1853, and proclaimed a new nation, the Republic of Lower California. Santa Ana, frightened by this new invasion, began making overtures through the Mexican consul, Luis del Valle, at San Francisco to secure French recruits for military service on the Mexican frontier. Del Valle applied to the French consul, Dillon, and Dillon applied to Raousset. Raousset soon secured eight hundred recruits and chartered the British ship Challenge to take them to Guaymas. Then the pro-slavery federal officials at San Francisco were aroused to action. The neutrality laws were being violated. It was not that they cared for the laws, but they feared that this new filibustering scheme might interfere with their pet, Walker, who had, in addition to the Republic of Lower California, founded another nation, the Republic of Sonora, in both of which he had decreed slavery. The ship was seized, but after a short detention was allowed to sail with three hundred Frenchmen.

Del Valle was vigorously prosecuted by the federal authorities for violation of a section of the neutrality laws, which forbade the enlistment within the United States of soldiers to serve under a foreign power. Dillon, the French consul, was implicated and on his refusal to testify in court he was arrested. He fell back on his dignity and asserted that his nation had been insulted through him and closed his consulate. For a time there were fears of international trouble.

Del Valle was found guilty of violating the neutrality laws, but was never punished. The pro-slavery pet, Walker, and his gang were driven out of Mexico and the federal officials had no more interest in enforcing neutrality laws. Meanwhile Raousset, after great difficulties, had joined the three hundred Frenchmen at Guaymas. A strip of northern Sonora had been sold under what is known as the Gadsden purchase to the United States. There was no longer any opportunity to secure mines there from Mexico, but Raousset thought he could erect a barrier to any further encroachments of the United States and eventually secure Mexico for France. His first orders on reaching Guaymas to the commander of the French, Desmaris, was to attack the Mexican troops and capture the city. His order did not reach Desmaris. His messenger was arrested and the Mexican authorities begun collecting forces to oppose Raousset. Having failed to receive reinforcements, and his condition becoming unendurable, he made an attack on the Mexican forces, twelve hundred strong. After a brave assault he was defeated. He surrendered to the French consul on the assurance that his life and that of his men would be spared. He was treacherously surrendered by the French consul to the Mexican general. He was tried by a court-martial, found guilty and sentenced to be shot. On the morning of August 12, 1854, he was executed. His misguided followers were shipped back to San Francisco. So ended the first California filibuster.

The first American born filibuster who organized one of these piratical expeditions was William Walker, a native of Tennessee. He came to California with the rush of 1850. He had started out in life to be a doctor, had studied law and finally drifted into journalism. He belonged to the extreme pro-slavery faction. He located in San Francisco and found employment on the Herald. His bitter invective against the courts for their laxity in punishing crime raised the ire of Judge Levi

Parsons, who fined Walker $500 for contempt of court and ordered him imprisoned until the fine was paid. Walker refused to pay the fine and went to jail. He at once bounded into notoriety. He was a martyr to the freedom of the press. A public indignation meeting was called. An immense crowd of sympathizers called on Walker in jail. A writ of habeas corpus was sued out and he was released from jail and discharged. In the legislature of 1852 he tried to have Parson impeached, but failed. He next opened a law office in Marysville.

The success of Raousset-Boulbon in his first expedition to Sonora had aroused the ambition of Walker to become the founder of a new government. His first efforts were directed towards procuring from Mexico a grant on the Sonora border; this was to be colonized with Americans, who would protect the Mexican frontier from Apache incursion. This was a mere subterfuge and the Mexican authorities were not deceived by it — he got no grant. To forestall Raousset-Boulbon, who was again in the field with his revolutionary scheme, Walker opened a recruiting office. Each man was to receive a square league of land and plunder galore. The bait took, meetings were held, scrip sold and recruits flocked to Walker. The brig Arrow was chartered to carry the liberators to their destination. The pro-slavery officials, who held all the offices, winked at this violation of the neutrality laws. There was but one man, General Hitchcock, who dared to do his duty. He seized the vessel; it was released, and Hitchcock removed from command. Jefferson Davis was secretary of war and Hitchcock was made to feel his wrath for interfering with one of Davis' pet projects, the extension of slavery. Walker sailed in another vessel, the Caroline, taking with him forty-one of his followers, well armed with rifles and revolvers to develop the resources of the country.

The vessel with Walker and his gang sneaked into La Paz under cover of a Mexican flag. He seized the unsuspecting governor and other officials and then proclaimed the Republic of Lower California. He appointed from his following a number of officials with high sounding titles. He adopted the code of Louisiana as the law of the land. This, as far as he was able, introduced into the country human slavery, which indeed was about the sole purpose of his filibustering schemes. Fearing that the Mexican government might send an expedition across the gulf to stop his marauding, he slipped out of the harbor and sailed up to Todas Santos, so as to be near the United States in case the Mexican government should make it uncomfortable for him. With this as headquarters he began preparations for an invasion of Sonora. His delectable followers appropriated to their own use whatever they could find in the poverty-stricken country. The news of the great victory at La Paz reached San Francisco and created great enthusiasm among Walker's sympathizers. His vice-president, Watkins, enrolled three hundred recruits and sent them to him, "greatly to the relief of the criminal calendar."

Walker began to drill his recruits for the conquest of Sonora. These patriots, who had rallied to the support of the new republic, under the promise of rich churches to pillage and well stocked ranches to plunder, did not take kindly ' to a diet of jerked beef and beans and hard drilling under a torrid sun. Some rebelled and it became necessary for Walker to use the lash and even to shoot two of them for the good of the cause. The natives rebelled when they found their cattle and frijoles disappearing and the so-called battle of La Gualla was fought between the natives and a detachment of Walker's foragers, several of whom were killed. The news of this battle reached San Francisco and was magnified into a great victory. The new republic had been baptized in the blood of its martyrs.

After three months spent in drilling. Walker began his march to Sonora with but one hundred men, and a small herd of cattle for food. Most of the others had deserted. In his journey across the desert the Indians stole some of his cattle and more of his men deserted. On reaching the Colorado river about half of his force abandoned the expedition and marched to Fort Yuma, where Major Heintzelman relieved their necessities. Walker with thirty-five men had started back for Santa Tomas. They brought up at Tia Juana, where they crossed the American line, surrendered and gave their paroles to Major McKinstry of the United States army. When Walker and his Falstaffian army reached San Francisco they were lionized as heroes. All they had done was to kill a few inoffensive natives on the peninsula and steal their cattle. Their valiant leader had proclaimed two republics and decreed (on paper) that slavery should prevail in them. He had had several of his dupes whipped and two of them shot, which was probably the most commendable thing he had done. His proclamations were ridiculous and his officers with their high sounding titles had returned from their burlesque conquest with scarcely rags enough on them to cover their nakedness. Yet, despite all this, the attempt to enlarge the area of slave territory covered him with glory and his rooms were the resort of all the pro-slavery officials of California.

The federal officials made a show of prosecuting the filibusters. Watkins, the vice-president of the Republic of Lower California and Sonora, was put on trial in the United States district court. The evidence was so plain and the proof so convincing that the judge was compelled to convict against his will. This delightful specimen of a pro-slavery justice expressed from the bench his sympathy for "those spirited men who had gone forth to upbuild the broken altars and rekindle the extinguished fires of liberty in Mexico and Lower California." With such men to enforce the laws, it was not strange that vigilance committees were needed in California. Watkins and Emory, the so-called secretary of state, were fined each $1,500. The fines were never paid and no effort was ever made to compel their payment. The secretary of war and the secretary of the navy were put on trial and acquitted. This ended the shameful farce.

Walker's next expedition was to Nicaragua in 1855. A revolution was in progress there. He joined forces with the Democratic party or anti-legitimists. He took but fifty-six men with him. These were called the American phalanx. His first engagement was an attack upon the fortified town of Rivas. Although his men fought bravely, they were defeated and two of his best officers, Kewen and Crocker, killed. His next fight was the battle of Virgin Bay, in which, with fifty Americans and one hundred and twenty natives, he defeated six hundred legitimists. He received reinforcements from California and reorganized his force. He seized the Accessory Transit Company's lake steamer La Virgin against the protest of the company, embarked his troops on board of it and by an adroit movement captured the capital city, Granada. His exploits were heralded abroad and recruits flocked to his support. The legitimist had fired upon a steamer bringing passengers up the San Juan river and killed several. Walker in retaliation ordered Mateo Mazorga, the legitimist secretary of state, whom he had taken prisoner at Granada, shot. Peace was declared between .the two parties and Patrico

Rivas made president. Rivas was president only in name; Walker was the real head of the government and virtually dictator.

He was now at the zenith of his power. By a series of arbitrary acts he confiscated the Accessory Transit Company's vessels and charter. This company had become a power in California travel and had secured the exclusive transit of passengers by the Nicaragua route, then the most popular route to California.

By this action he incurred the enmity of Vanderbilt, who henceforth worked for his downfall. The confiscation of the transit company's right destroyed confidence in the route, and travel virtually ceased by it. This was a blow to the prosperity of the country. To add to Walker's misfortunes, the other Central American states combined to drive the hated foreigners out of the country. He had gotten rid of Rivas and had secured the presidency for himself. He had secured the repeal of the Nicaragua laws against slavery and thus paved the way for the introduction of his revered institution. His army now amounted to about twelve hundred men, mostly recruited from California and the slave states. The cholera broke out among his forces and in the armies of the allies and numbers died. His cause was rapidly waning. Many of his dupes deserted. A series of disasters arising from his blundering and incapacity, resulted in his overthrow. He and sixteen of his officers were taken out of the country on the United States sloop of war, St. Mary's. The governor of Panama refused to allow him to land in that city. He was sent across the isthmus under guard to Aspinwall and from there with his staff took passage to New Orleans. His misguided followers were transported to Panama and found their way back to the United States.

Upon arriving at New Orleans he began recruiting for a new expedition. One hundred and fifty of his "emigrants" sailed from Mobile; the pro-slavery federal officials allowing them to depart. They were wrecked on Glover's reef, about seventy miles from Balize. They were rescued by a British vessel and returned to Mobile. Walker, with one hundred and thirty-two armed emigrants, landed at Punta Arenas, November 25, 1857, and hoisted his Nicaraguan flag and called himself commander-in-chief of the army of Nicaragua. He and his men began a career of plunder; seized the fort or Castillo on the San Juan river; captured steamers, killed several inhabitants and made prisoners of others. Commander Paulding, of the United States flagship Wabash, then on that coast, regarded these acts as rapine and murder, and Walker and his men as outlaws and pirates. He broke up their camp, disarmed Walker and his emigrants and sent them to the United States for trial. But instead of Walker and his followers being tried for piracy their pro-slavery abettors made heroes of them.

Walker's last effort to regain his lost prestige in Nicaragua was made in 1860. With two hundred men, recruited in New Orleans, he landed near Truxillo, in Honduras. His intention was to make his way by land to Nicaragua. He very soon found armed opposition. His new recruits were not inclined to sacrifice themselves to make him dictator of some country that they had no interest in. So they refused to stand up against the heavy odds they encountered in every fight. Finding his situation growing desperate, he was induced to surrender himself to the captain of the British man-of-war Icarus. The authorities of Honduras made a demand on the captain for Walker. That British officer promptly turned the filibuster over to them. He was tried by a court-martial, hastily convened, found guilty of the offenses charged, and condemned to die. September 25, 1860, he was marched out and, in accordance with his sentence, shot to death.

Walker's career is an anomaly in the history of mankind. Devoid of all the characteristics of a great leader, without a commanding presence, puny in size, homely to the point of ugliness, in disposition, cold, cruel, selfish, heartless, stolidly indifferent to the suffering of others, living only to gratify the cravings of his inordinate ambition — it is strange that such a man could attract thousands to offer their lives for his aggrandizement and sacrifice themselves for a cause of which he was the exponent, a cause the most ignoble, the extension of human slavery, that for such a man and for such a cause thousands did offer up their lives is a sad commentary on the political morality of that time. It is said that over ten thousand men joined Walker in his filibustering schemes and that fifty-seven hundred of these found graves in Nicaragua. Of the number of natives killed in battle or who died of disease, there is no record, but it greatly exceeded Walker's losses.

While Walker was attaining some success in Nicaragua, another California filibuster entered the arena. This was Henry A. Crabb, a Stockton lawyer. Like Walker, he was a native of Tennessee, and, like him, too, he was a rabid pro-slavery advocate. He had served in the assembly and one term in the state senate. It is said he was the author of a bill to allow slaveholders who brought their slaves into California before its admission to take their human chattels back into bondage. He was originally a Whig, but had joined the Know-Nothing party and was a candidate of that party for United States senator in 1856; but his extreme southern principles prevented his election. He had married a Spanish wife, who had numerous and influential relatives in Sonora. It was claimed that Crabb had received an invitation from some of these to bring down an armed force of Americans to overthrow the government and make himself master of the country. Whether he did or did not receive such an invitation, he did recruit a body of men for some kind of service in Sonora. With a force of one hundred men, well armed with rifles and revolvers, he sailed, in January, 1857, on the steamer Sea Bird, from San Francisco to San Pedro and from there marched overland. As usual, no attempt was made by the federal authorities to prevent him from invading a neighboring country with an armed force.

He entered Sonora at Sonita, a small town one hundred miles from Yuma. His men helped themselves to what they could find. When approaching the town of Cavorca they were fired upon by a force of men lying in ambush. The fire was kept up from all quarters. They made a rush and gained the shelter of the houses. In the charge two of their men had been killed and eighteen wounded. In the house they had taken possession of they were exposed to shots from a church. Crabb and fifteen of his men attempted to blow open the doors of the church with gunpowder, but in the attempt, which failed, five of the men were killed, and seven, including Crabb, wounded. After holding out for five days they surrendered to the Mexicans, Gabilondo, the Mexican commander, promising to spare their lives. Next morning they were marched out in squads of five to ten and shot. Crabb was tied to a post and a hundred balls fired into him; his head was cut off and placed in a jar of mescal. The only one spared was a boy of fifteen, Charles E. Evans. A party of sixteen men whom Crabb had left at Sonita was surprised and all massacred. The boy Evans was the only one left to tell the fate of the ill-starred expedition. This put an end to filibustering expeditions into Sonora.

These armed forays on the neighboring countries to the south of the United States ceased with the beginning of the war of secession. They had all been made for the purpose of acquiring slave territory. The leaders of them were southern men and the rank and file were mostly recruited from natives of the slave states. Bancroft truthfully says of these filibustering expeditions: "They were foul robberies, covered by the flimsiest of political and social pretenses, gilded by false aphorisms and profane distortion of sacred formulae. Liberty dragged in the mud for purposes of theft and human enslavement; the cause of humanity bandied in filthy mouths to promote atrocious butcheries; peaceful, blooming valleys given over to devastation and ruin; happy families torn asunder, and widows and orphans cast adrift to nurse affliction; and finally, the peace of nations imperiled, and the morality of right insulted. The thought of such results should obliterate all romance, and turn pride to shame. They remain an ineffaceable stain upon the government of the most progressive of nations, and veil in dismal irony the dream of manifest destiny."

CHAPTER XXIX.
FROM GOLD TO GRAIN AND FRUITS.

Under the Spanish and Mexican jurisdictions there was but little cultivation of the soil in California. While the gardens of some of the missions, and particularly those of Santa Barbara and San Buenaventura, presented a most appetizing display of fruit and vegetables, at the ranchos there were but meager products. Gilroy says that when he came to the country, in 1814, potatoes were not cultivated and it was a rare thing outside of the mission gardens to find any onions or cabbages. A few acres of wheat and a small patch of maize or corn furnished bread, or, rather, tortillas for a family. At the missions a thick soup made of boiled wheat or maize and meat was the standard article of diet for the neophytes. This was portioned out to them in the quantity of about three pints to each person. Langsdorff, who witnessed the distribution of soup rations to the Indians at Santa Clara, says: "It appeared incomprehensible how any one could three times a day eat so large a portion of such nourishing food." The neophytes evidently had healthy appetites. Frijoles (beans) were the staple vegetable dish in Spanish families. These were served up at almost every meal. The bill of fare for a native Californian family was very simple.

A considerable amount of wheat was raised at the more favorably located missions. It was not raised for export, but to feed the neophytes. The wheat fields had to be fenced in, or perhaps it would be more in accordance with the facts to say that the cattle had to be fenced out. As timber was scarce, adobe brick did duty for fencing as well as for house building. Sometimes the low adobe walls were made high and safe by placing on top of them a row of the skulls of Spanish cattle with the long, curving horns attached to them pointing outward. These were brought from the matanzas or slaughter corrals where there were thousands of them lying around. It was almost impossible for man or beast to scale such a fence.

The agricultural implements of the early Californians were few and simple. The Mexican plow was a forked stick with an iron point fastened to the fork or branch that penetrated the ground. It turned no furrow, but merely scratched the surface of the ground. After sowing it was a race between the weeds and the grain. It depended on the season which won. If the season was cold and backward, so that the seed did not sprout readily, the weeds got the start and won out easily. And yet with such primitive cultivation the yield was sometimes astonishing. At the Mission San Diego the crop of wheat one year produced one hundred and ninety-five fold. As the agriculturist had a large area from which to select his arable land, only the richest soils were chosen. Before the discovery of gold there was little or no market for grain, and each ranchero raised only enough for his own use. For a time there was some trade with the Russians in grain to supply their settlements in Alaska, but this did not continue long.

When some of the Americans who came in the gold rush began to turn their attention to agriculture they greatly underrated the productiveness of the country. To men raised where the summer rains were needed to raise a crop it seemed impossible to produce a crop in a country that was rainless for six or eight months of the year. All attempts at agriculture hitherto had been along the rivers, and it was generally believed that the plains back from the water courses could never be used for any other purpose than cattle raising.

The mining rush of '49 found California without vegetables and fresh fruit. The distance was too great for the slow transportation of that day to ship these into the country. Those who first turned their attention to market gardening made fortunes. The story is told of an old German named Schwartz who had a small ranch a few miles below Sacramento. In 1848, when everybody was rushing to the mines, he remained on his farm, unmoved by the stories of the wonderful finds of gold. Anticipating a greater rush in 1849, he planted several acres in watermelons. As they ripened he took them up to the city and disposed of them at prices ranging from $1 to $5, according to size. He realized that season from his melons alone $30,000. The first field of cabbages was grown by George H. Peck and a partner in 1850. From defective seed or some other cause the cabbage failed to come to a head. Supposing that the defect was in the climate and not in the cabbage, the honest rancher marketed his crop in San Francisco, carrying a cabbage in each hand along the streets until he found a customer. To the query why there were no heads to them the reply was, "That's the way cabbages grow in California." He got rid of his crop at the rate of $1 apiece for each headless cabbage. But all the vegetable growing experiments were not a financial success. The high price of potatoes in 1849 started a tuber-growing epidemic in 1850. Hundreds of acres were planted to "spuds" in the counties contiguous to San Francisco, the agriculturists paying as high as fifteen cents per pound for seed. The yield was enormous and the market was soon overstocked. The growers who could not dispose of their potatoes stacked them up in huge piles in the fields; and there they rotted, filling the country around with their effluvia. The next year nobody planted potatoes, and prices went up to the figures of '49 and the spring of '50.

The size to which vegetables grew astonished the amateur agriculturists. Beets, when allowed to grow to maturity, resembled the trunks of trees; onions looked like squash, while a patch of pumpkins resembled a tented field; and corn grew so tall that the stalks had to be felled to get at the ears. Onions were a favorite vegetable in the mining camps on account of their anti-scorbutic properties as a preventive of scurvy. The honest miner was not fastidious about the aroma. They were a profitable crop, too. One ranchero in the Napa valley was reported to have cleared $8,000 off two acres of onions.

With the decline of gold mining, wheat became the staple product of central California. The nearness to shipping ports and the large yields made wheat growing very profitable. In the years immediately following the Civil war the price ranged high and a fortune was sometimes made from the products of a single field. It may be necessary to explain that the field might contain anywhere from five hundred to a thousand acres. The grain area was largely extended by the discovery that land in the upper mesas, which had been regarded as only fit for pasture land, was good for cereals. The land in the southern part of the state, which was held in large grants, continued to be devoted to cattle raising for at least two decades after the American conquest. After the discovery of gold, cattle raising became immensely profitable. Under the Mexican regime a steer was worth what his hide and tallow would bring or about $2 or $3. The rush of immigration in 1849 sent the price of cattle up until a fat bullock sold for from $30 to $35. The profit to a ranchero who had a thousand or more marketable cattle was a fortune. A good, well-stocked cattle ranch was more valuable than a gold mine.

The enormous profits in cattle raising dazed the Californians. Had they been thrifty and economical, they might have grown rich. But the sudden influx of wealth engendered extravagant habits and when the price of cattle fell, as it did in a few years, the spendthrift customs were continued. When the cattle market was dull it was easy to raise money by mortgaging the ranch. With interest at the rate of 5 per cent per month, compounded monthly, it did not take long for land and cattle both to change hands. It is related of the former owner of the Santa Gertrudes rancho that he borrowed $500 from a money lender, at 5 per cent a month, to beat a poker game, but did not succeed. Then he borrowed more money to pay the interest on the first and kept on doing so until interest and principal amounted to $100,000; then the mortgage was foreclosed and property to-day worth $1,000,000 was lost for a paltry $500 staked on a poker game.

Gold mining continued to be the prevailing industry of northern California. The gold production reached its acme in 1853, when the total yield was $65,000,000. From that time there was a gradual decline in production and in the number of men employed. Many had given up the hopes of striking it rich and quit the business for something more certain and less illusive. The production of gold in 1852 was $60,000,000, yet the average yield to each man of the one hundred thousand engaged in it was only about $600, or a little over $2 per day to the man. scarcely living wages as prices were then. It has been claimed that the cost of producing the gold, counting all expenditures, was three times the value of that produced. Even if it did, the development of the country and impulse given to trade throughout the world would more than counterbalance the loss.

At the time of the discovery of gold nearly all of the fruit raised in California was produced at Santa Barbara and Los Angeles. In Spanish and Mexican days, Los Angeles had been the principal wine-producing district of California. Although wine, as well as other spirituous liquors, were in demand, the vineyardists found it more profitable to ship their grapes to San Francisco than to manufacture them into wine. Grapes retailed in the city of San Francisco at from twelve and one-half to twenty-five cents a pound. The vineyards were as profitable as the cattle ranches. The mission Indians did the labor in the vineyards and were paid in aguardiente on Saturday night. By Sunday morning they were all drunk; then they were gathered up and put into a corral. On Monday morning they were sold to pay the cost of their dissipation. It did not take many years to kill off the Indians. The city has grown over the former sites of the vineyards.

The first orange trees were planted at the Mission San Gabriel about the year 1815 and a few at Los Angeles about the same time. But little attention was given to the industry by the Californians. The first extensive grove was planted by William Wolfskill in 1840. The impression then prevailed that oranges could be grown only on the low lands near the river. The idea of attempting to grow them on the mesa lands was scouted at by the Californians and the Americans. The success that attended the Riverside experiment demonstrated that they could be grown on the mesas, and that the fruit produced was superior to that grown on the river bottoms. This gave such an impetus to the industry in the south that it has distanced all others. The yearly shipment to the eastern markets is twenty thousand car loads. The citrus belt is extending every year.

The Californians paid but little attention to the quality of the fruit they raised. The seed fell in the ground and sprouted. If the twig survived and grew to be a tree, they ate the fruit, asking no question whether the quality might be improved. The pears grown at the missions and at some of the ranch houses were hard and tasteless. It was said they never ripened. A small black fig was cultivated in a few places, but the quantity of fruit grown outside of the mission gardens was very small.

The high price of all kinds of fruit in the early '50S induced the importation of apple, peach, pear, plum and prune trees. These thrived and soon supplied the demand. Before the advent of the railroads and the shipment east the quantity of deciduous fruit produced had outgrown the demand, and there was no profit in its production. All this has been changed by eastern shipment.

Sheep were brought to the country with the first missionary expeditions. The Indian in his primitive condition did not use clothing. A coat of mud was his only garment and he was not at all particular about the fit of that. After his conversion the missionaries put clothing on him, or, rather, on part of him. He was given a shirt, which was a shirt of Nessus, being made of the coarse woolen cloth manufactured at the mission. It was irritating to the skin and compelled the poor wretches to keep up a continual scratching; at least, that is what Hugo Reid tells us. During the Civil war and for several years after, the sheep industry was very profitable. The subdivision of the great ranchos and the absorption of the land for grain growing and fruit culture have contracted the sheep ranges until there is but little left for pasture except the foothills that are too rough for cultivation.

Up to 1863 the great Spanish grants that covered the southern part of the state had, with a few exceptions, been held intact and cattle raising had continued to be the principal industry. For several seasons previous to the famine years of 1863 and 1864 there had been heavy rainfalls and consequently feed was abundant. With the price of cattle declining, the rancheros overstocked their ranges to make up by quantity for decrease in value. When the dry year of 1863 set in, the feed on ranches was soon exhausted and the cattle starving. The second famine year following, the cattle industry was virtually wiped out of existence and the cattle owners ruined. In Santa Barbara, where the cattle barons held almost imperial sway. and, with their army of retainers, controlled the political affairs of the county, of the two hundred thousand cattle listed on the assessment roll of 1862, only five thousand were alive when grass grew in 1865. On the Stearns' ranchos in Los Angeles county, one hundred thousand head of cattle and horses perished, and the owner of a quarter million acres and a large amount of city property could not raise money enough to pay his taxes.

Many of the rancheros were in debt when the hard times came, and others mortgaged their land at usurious rates of interest to carry them through the famine years. Their cattle dead, they had no income to meet the interest on the cancerous mortgage that was eating up their patrimony. The result was that they were compelled either to sell their land or the mortgage was foreclosed and they lost it. This led to the subdivision of the large grants into small holdings, the new proprietors finding that there was more profit in selling them off in small tracts

216

than in large ones. This brought in an intelligent and progressive population, and in a few years entirely revolutionized the agricultural conditions of the south. Grain growing and fruit raising became the prevailing industries. The adobe ranch house with its matanzas and its Golgotha of cattle skulls and bones gave place to the tasty farm house with its flower garden, lawn and orange grove.

The Californians paid but little attention to improving the breed of their cattle. When the only value in an animal was the hide and tallow, it did not pay to improve the breed. The hide of a long-horned, mouse-colored Spanish steer would sell for as much as that of a high-bred Durham or Holstein, and, besides, the first could exist where the latter would starve to death. After the conquest there was for some time but little improvement. Cattle were brought across the plains, but for the most part these were the mongrel breeds of the western states and were but little improvement on the Spanish stock. It was not until the famine years virtually exterminated the Spanish cattle that better breeds were introduced.

As with cattle, so also it was with horses. Little attention was given to improving the breed. While there were a few fine race horses and saddle horses in the country before its American occupation, the prevailing equine was the mustang. He was a vicious beast, nor was it strange that his temper was bad. He had to endure starvation and abuse that would have killed a more aristocratic animal. He took care of himself, subsisted on what he could pick up and to the best of his ability resented ill treatment. Horses during the Mexican regime were used only for riding. Oxen were the draft animals. The mustang had one inherent trait that did not endear him to an American, and that was his propensity to "buck." With his nose between his knees, his back arched and his legs stiffened, by a series of short, quick jumps, he could dismount an inexperienced rider with neatness and dispatch. The Californian took delight in urging the bronco to "buck" so that he (the rider) might exhibit his skillful horsemanship. The mustang had some commendable traits as well. He was sure-footed as a goat and could climb the steep hillsides almost equal to that animal. He had an easy gait under the saddle and could measure off mile after mile without a halt. His power of endurance was wonderful. He could live off the country when apparently there was nothing to subsist on except the bare ground. He owed mankind a debt of ingratitude which he always stood ready to pay when an opportunity offered. The passing of the mustang began with the advent of the American farmer.

The founding of agricultural colonies began in the '50s. One of the first, if not the first, was the German colony of Anaheim, located thirty miles south of Los Angeles. A company of Germans organized in San Francisco in 1857 for the purpose of buying land for the cultivation of the wine grape and the manufacture of wine. The organization was a stock company. Eleven hundred acres were purchased in a Spanish grant. This was subdivided into twenty and forty acre tracts; an irrigating ditch brought in from the Santa Ana river. A portion of each subdivision was planted in vines and these were cultivated by the company until they came into bearing, when the tracts were divided among the stockholders by lot, a certain valuation being fixed on each tract. The man obtaining a choice lot paid into the fund a certain amount and the one receiving an inferior tract received a certain amount, so that each received the same value in the distribution. The colony proved quite a success, and for thirty years Anaheim was one of the largest wine-producing districts in the United States. In 1887 a mysterious disease destroyed all the vines and the vineyardists turned their attention to the cultivation of oranges and English walnuts.

The Riverside colony, then in San Bernardino county, now in Riverside county, was founded in 1870. The projectors of the colony were eastern gentlemen. At the head of the organization was Judge J. W. North. They purchased four thousand acres of the Roubidoux or Jurupa rancho and fourteen hundred and sixty acres of government land from the California Silk Center Association. This association had been organized in 1869 for the purpose of founding a colony to cultivate mulberry trees and manufacture silk. It had met with reverses, first in the death of its president, Louis Prevost, a man skilled in the silk business, next in the revocation by the legislature of the bounty for mulberry plantations, and lastly in the subsidence of the sericulture craze. To encourage silk culture in California, the legislature, in 1866, passed an act authorizing the payment of a bounty of $250 for every plantation of five thousand mulberry trees two years old. This greatly stimulated the planting of mulberry trees, if it did not greatly increase the production of silk. In 1869 it was estimated that in the central and southern portions of the state there were ten millions of mulberry trees in various stages of growth. Demands for the bounty poured in upon the commissioners in such numbers that the state treasury was threatened with bankruptcy. The revocation of the bounty killed the silk worms and the mulberry trees; and those who had been attacked with the sericulture craze quickly recovered. The Silk Center Association, having fallen into hard lines, offered its lands for sale at advantageous terms, and in September, 1870, they were purchased by the Southern California Colony Association. The land was bought at $3.50 per acre. It was mesa or table land that had never been cultivated. It was considered by old-timers indifferent sheep pasture, and Roubidoux, it is said, had it struck from the tax roll because it was not worth taxing.

The company had the land subdivided and laid off a town which was first named Jurupa, but afterwards the name was changed to Riverside. The river, the Santa Ana, did not flow past the town, but the colonists hoped to make a goodly portion of its waters do so. The lands were put on sale at reasonable prices, a ditch at a cost of $50,000 was constructed. Experiments were made with oranges, raisin grapes and deciduous fruits, but the colony finally settled down to orange producing. In 1873 the introduction of the Bahia or navel orange gave an additional impetus to orange growing in the colony, the fruit of that species being greatly superior to any other. This fruit was propagated by budding from two trees received from Washington, D. C, by J. A. Tibbetts, of Riverside.

The Indiana colony, which later became Pasadena, was founded in 1873 by some gentlemen from Indiana. Its purpose was the growing of citrus fruits and raisin grapes, but it has grown into a city, and the orange groves, once the pride of the colony, have given place to business blocks and stately residences.

During the early '70s a number of agricultural colonies were founded in Fresno county. These were all fruit-growing and raisin-producing enterprises. They proved successful and Fresno has become the largest raisin-producing district in the state.

CHAPTER XXX.
THE CIVIL WAR-LOYALTY AND DISLOYALTY.

The admission of California into the Union as a free state did not, in the opinion of the ultra pro-slavery faction, preclude the possibility of securing a part of its territory for the "peculiar institution" of the south. The question of state division which had come up in the constitutional convention was again agitated. The advocates of division hoped to cut off from the southern part, territory enough for a new state. The ostensible purpose of division was kept concealed. The plea of unjust taxation was made prominent. The native Californians who under Mexican rule paid no taxes on their land were given to understand that they were bearing an undue proportion of the cost of government, while the mining counties, paying less tax, had the greater representation. The native Californians were opposed to slavery, an open advocacy of the real purpose would defeat the division scheme.

The leading men in the southern part of the state were from the slave states. If the state were divided, the influence of these men would carry the new state into the Union with a constitution authorizing slave-holding and thus the south would gain two senators. The division question came up in some form in nearly every session of the legislature for a decade after California became a state.

In the legislature of 1854-55, Jefferson Hunt, of San Bernardino county, introduced a bill in the assembly to create and establish, "out of the territory embraced within the limits of the state of California, a new state, to be called the state of Columbia." The territory embraced within the counties of Santa Cruz, Santa Clara, San Joaquin, Calaveras, Amador, Tuolumne, Stanislaus, Mariposa, Tulare, Monterey, Santa Barbara, San Luis Obispo, Los Angeles, San Bernardino and San Diego, with the islands on the coast, were to constitute the new state. "The people residing within the above mentioned territory shall be and they are hereby authorized, so soon as the consent of the congress of the United States shall be obtained thereto, to proceed to organize a state government under such rules as are prescribed by the constitution of the United States." The bill was referred to a select committee of thirteen members representing different sections of the state. This committee reported as a substitute, "An Act to create three states out of the territory of California," and also drafted an address to the people of California advocating the passage of the act. The eastern boundary line of California was to be moved over the mountains to the one hundred and nineteenth degree of longitude west of Greenwich, which would have taken about half of the present state of Nevada. The northern state was to be called Shasta, the central state California and the southern Colorado.

The southern boundary of the state of Shasta began at the mouth of Maron's river; thence easterly along the boundary line between Yerba and Butte counties and between Sierra and Plumas to the summit of the Sierra Nevadas and thence easterly to the newly established state line.

219

The northern boundary of the state of Colorado began at the mouth of the Pajara river, running up that river to the summit of the Coast Range; thence in a straight line to the mouth of the Merced river, thence up that river to the summits of the Sierra Nevadas and then due east to the newly established state line.

The territory not embraced in the states of Colorado and Shasta was to constitute the state of California.

The taxable property of Shasta for the year 1854 was $7,000,000 and the revenue $100,000; that of Colorado $9,764,000 and the revenue $186,000. These amounts the committee considered sufficient to support the state governments. The bill died on the files.

The legislature of 1859 was intensely pro-slavery. The divisionists saw in it an opportunity to carry out their long-deferred scheme. The so-called Pico law, an act granting the consent of the legislature to the formation of a different government for the southern counties of this state, was introduced early in the session, passed in both houses and approved by the governor April 18, 1859. The boundaries of the proposed state were as follows: "All of that part or portion of the present territory of this state lying all south of a line drawn eastward from the west boundary of the state along the sixth standard parallel south of the Mount Diablo meridian, east to the summit of the coast range; thence southerly following said summit to the seventh standard parallel; thence due east on said standard, parallel to its intersection with the northwest boundary of Los Angeles county; thence northeast along said boundary to the eastern boundary of the state, including the counties of San Luis Obispo, Santa Barbara, Los Angeles, San Diego, San Bernardino and a part of Buena Vista, shall be segregated from the remaining portion of the state for the purpose of the formation by congress, with the concurrent action of said portion (the consent for the segregation of which is hereby granted), of a territorial or other government under the name of the "Territory of Colorado," or such other name as may be deemed meet and proper."

Section second provided for the submitting the question of "For a Territory" or "Against a Territory" to the people of the portion sought to be segregated at the next general election; "and in case two-thirds of the whole number of voters voting thereon shall vote for a change of government, the consent hereby given shall be deemed consummated." In case the vote was favorable the secretary of state was to send a certified copy of the result of the election and a copy of the act annexed to the president of the United States and to the senators and representatives of California in congress. At the general election in September, 1859, the question was submitted to a vote of the people of the southern counties, with the following result:

	For	vs.	Against.
Los Angeles county	1,407	vs.	441
San Bernardino	441	vs.	29
San Diego	207	vs.	24
San Luis Obispo	10	vs.	283
Santa Barbara	395	vs.	51
Tulare	17	vs.	0.
Total	2,477	vs.	828

The bill to create the county of Buena Vista from the southern portion of Tulare failed to pass the legislature, hence the name of that county does not appear in the returns. The result of the vote showed that considerably more than two-thirds were in favor of a new state. The results of this movement for division and the act were sent to the president and to congress, but nothing came of it. The pro-slavery faction which with the assistance of its coadjutors of the north had so long dominated congress had lost its power. The southern senators and congressmen were preparing for secession and had weightier matters to think of than the division of the state of California. Of late years, a few feeble attempts have been made to stir up the old question of state division and even to resurrect the old "Pico law."

For more than a decade after its admission into the Union, California was a Democratic state and controlled by the pro-slavery wing of that party. John C. Fremont and William H. Gwin, its first senators, were southern born, Fremont in South Carolina and Gwin in Tennessee. Politics had not entered into their election, but the lines were soon drawn. Fremont drew the short term and his services in the senate were very brief. He confidently expected a re-election, but in this he was doomed to disappointment. The legislature of 1851, after balloting one hundred and forty-two times, adjourned without electing, leaving California with but one senator in the session of 1850-51. In the legislature of 1852 John B. Wilier was elected. He was a northern man with southern principles. His chief opponent for the place was David Colbert Broderick, a man destined to fill an important place in the political history of California. He was an Irishman by birth, but had come to America in his boyhood. He had learned the stone cutters' trade with his father. His early associations were with the rougher element of New York City. Aspiring to a higher position than that of a stone cutter he entered the political field and soon arose to prominence. At the age of 26 he was nominated for Congress, but was defeated by a small majority through a split in the party. In 1849 he came to California, where he arrived sick and penniless. With F. D. Kohler, an assayer, he engaged in coining gold. The profit from buying gold dust at $14 an ounce and making it into $5 and $10 pieces put him in affluent circumstances.

His first entry into politics in California was his election to fill a vacancy in the senate of the first legislature. In 1851 he became president of the senate. He studied law, history and literature and was admitted to the bar. He was appointed clerk of the supreme court and had aspirations for still higher positions. Although Senator Gwin was a Democrat, he had managed to control all the federal appointments of Fillmore, the Whig president, and he had filled the offices with pro-slavery Democrats.

No other free state in the Union had such odious laws against negroes as had California. The legislature of 1852 enacted a law "respecting fugitives from labor and slaves brought to this state prior to her admission to the Union." "Under this law a colored man or woman could be brought before a magistrate, claimed as a slave, and the person so seized not being permitted to testify, the judge had no alternative but to issue a certificate to the claimant, which certificate was conclusive of the right of the person or persons in whose favor granted, and prevented all molestation of such person or persons, by any process issued by any court, judge, justice or magistrate or other person whomsoever." Anyone who rendered assistance to a fugitive was liable to a fine of $500 or imprisonment for two months. Slaves who had been brought into California by their masters before it became a state, but who were freed by the adoption of a constitution prohibiting slavery, were held to be fugitives and were liable to arrest, although they had been free for several years and some of them had accumulated considerable property. By limitation the law should have become inoperative in 1853, but the legislature of that year re-enacted it, and the succeeding legislatures of 1854 and 1855 continued it in force. The intention of the legislators who enacted the law was to legalize the kidnapping of free negroes, as well as the arrest of fugitives. Broderick vigorously opposed the prosecution of the colored people and by so doing called down upon his head the wrath of the pro-slavery chivalry. From that time on he was an object of their hatred. While successive legislatures were passing laws to punish black men for daring to assert their freedom and their right to the products of their honest toil, white villains were rewarded with political preferment, provided always that they belonged to the dominant wing of the Democratic party. The Whig party was but little better than the other, for the same element ruled in both. The finances of the state were in a deplorable condition and continually growing worse. The people's money was recklessly squandered. Incompetency was the rule in office and honesty the exception. Ballot box stuffing had been reduced to a mechanical science, jury bribing was one of the fine arts and suborning perjury was a recognized profession. During one election in San Francisco it was estimated that $1,500,000 was spent in one way or another to influence voters. Such was the state of affairs just preceding the uprising of the people that evolved in San Francisco the vigilance committee of 1856.

At the state election in the fall of 1855 the Know Nothings carried the state. The native American or Know Nothing party was a party of few principles. Opposition to Catholics and foreigners was about the only plank in its platform. There was a strong opposition to foreign miners in the mining districts and the pro-slavery faction saw in the increased foreign immigration danger to the extension of their beloved institution into new territory. The most potent cause of the success of the new party in California was the hope that it might bring reform to relieve the tax burdened people. But in this they were disappointed. It was made up from the same element that had so long misgoverned the state.

The leaders of the party were either proslavery men of the south or northern men with southern principles. Of the latter class was J. Neely Johnson, the governor-elect. In the legislature of 1855 the contest between Gwin and Broderick, which had been waged at the polls the previous year, culminated after thirty-eight ballots in no choice and Gwin's place in the senate became vacant at the expiration of his term. In the legislature of 1856 the Know Nothings had a majority in both houses. It was supposed that they would elect a senator to succeed Gwin. There were three aspirants: H. A. Crabb, formerly a Whig; E. C. Marshall and Henry S. Foote, formerly Democrats. All were southerners and were in the new party for office. The Gwin and Broderick influence was strong enough to prevent the Know Nothing legislature from electing a senator and California was left with but one representative in the upper house of Congress.

The Know Nothing party was short lived. At the general election in 1856 the Democrats swept the state. Broderick, by his ability in organizing and his superior

222

leadership, had secured a majority in the legislature and was in a position to dictate terms to his opponents. Weller's senatorial term would soon expire and Gwin's already two years vacant left two places to be filled. Broderick, who had heretofore been contending for Gwin's place, changed his tactics and aspired to fill the long term. According to established custom, the filling of the ' vacancy would come up first, but Broderick, by superior finesse, succeeded in having the caucus nominate the successor to Weller first. Ex-Congressman Latham's friends were induced to favor the arrangement on the expectation that their candidate would be given the short term. Broderick was elected to the long term on the first ballot, January 9, 1857, and his commission was immediately made out and signed by the governor. For years he had bent his energies to securing the senatorship and at last he had obtained the coveted honor. But he was not satisfied yet. He aspired to control the federal patronage of the state; in this way he could reward his friends. He could dictate the election of his colleague for the short term. Both Gwin and Latham were willing to concede to him that privilege for the sake of an election. Latham tried to make a few reservations for some of his friends to whom he had promised places. Gwin offered to surrender it all without reservation. He had had enough of it. Gwin was elected and next day published an address, announcing his obligation to Broderick and renouncing any claim to the distribution of the federal patronage.

Then a wail long and loud went up from the chivalry, who for years had monopolized all the offices. That they, southern gentlemen of aristocratic antecedents, should be compelled to ask favors of a mudsill of the north was too humiliating to be borne. Latham, too, was indignant and Broderick found that his triumph was but a hollow mockery. But the worst was to come. He who had done so much to unite the warring Democracy and give the party a glorious victory in California at the presidential election of 1856 fully expected the approbation of President Buchanan, but when he called on that old gentleman he was received coldly and during Buchanan's administration he was ignored and Gwin's advice taken and followed in making federal appointments. He returned to California in April, 1857, to secure the nomination of his friends on the state ticket, but in this he was disappointed. The Gwin element was in the ascendency and John B. Weller received the nomination for governor. He was regarded as a martyr, having been tricked out of a re-election to the senate by Broderick. There were other martyrs of the Democracy, who received balm for their wounds and sympathy for their sufferings at that convention. In discussing a resolution denouncing the vigilance committee, O'Meara in his "History of Early Politics in California," says: "Col. Joseph P. Hoge, the acknowledged leader of the convention, stated that the committee had hanged four men, banished twenty-eight and arrested two hundred and eighty; and that these were nearly all Democrats.

On Broderick's return to the senate in the session of 1857-58, he cast his lot with Senator Douglas and opposed the admission of Kansas under the infamous Lecompton constitution. This cut him loose from the administration wing of the party.

In the state campaign of 1859 Broderick rallied his followers under the Anti-Lecompton standard and Gwin his in support of the Buchanan administration. The party was hopelessly divided. Two Democratic tickets were placed in the field. The Broderick ticket, with John Currey as governor, and the Gwin, with Milton Latham, the campaign was bitter. Broderick took the stump and although not an orator his denunciations of Gwin were scathing and merciless and in his fearful earnestness he became almost eloquent. Gwin in turn loosed the vials of his wrath upon Broderick and criminations and recriminations flew thick and fast during the campaign. It was a campaign of vituperation, but the first aggressor was Gwin.

Judge Terry, in a speech before the Lecompton convention at Sacramento in June, 1859, after flinging out sneers at the Republican party, characterized Broderick's party as sailing "under the flag of Douglas, but it is the banner of the black Douglass, whose name is Frederick, not Stephen." This taunt was intended to arouse the wrath of Broderick. He read Terry's speech while seated at breakfast in the International hotel at San Francisco. Broderick denounced Terry's utterance in forcible language and closed by saying: "I have hitherto spoken of him as an honest man, as the only honest man on the bench of a miserable, corrupt supreme court, but now I find I was mistaken. I take it all back." A lawyer by the name of Perley, a friend of Terry's, to whom the remark was directed, to obtain a little reputation, challenged Broderick. Broderick refused to consider Parley's challenge on the ground that he was not his (Broderick's) equal in standing and beside that he had declared himself a few days before a British subject. Perley did not stand very high in the community. Terry had acted as a second for him in a duel a few years before.

Broderick, in his reply to Perley, said; "I have determined to take no notice of attacks from any source during the canvass. If I were to accept your challenge, there are probably many other gentlemen who would seek similar opportunities for hostile meetings for the purpose of accomplishing a political object or to obtain public notoriety. I cannot afford at the present time to descend to a violation of the Constitution and state laws to subserve either their or your purposes."

Terry a few days after the close of the campaign sent a letter to Broderick demanding a retraction of the offensive remarks. Broderick, well knowing that he would have to fight some representative of the chivalry if not several of them in succession, did not retract his remarks. He had for several years, in expectation of such a result in a contest with them, practiced himself in the use of fire arms until he had become quite expert.

A challenge followed, a meeting was arranged to take place in San Mateo county, ten miles from San Francisco, on the 12th of September. Chief of Police Burke appeared on the scene and arrested the principals. They were released by the court, no crime having been committed. They met next morning at the same place; ex-Congressman McKibben and David D. Colton were Broderick's seconds. Calhoun Benham and Thomas Hayes were Terry's. The pistols selected belonged to a friend of Terry's. Broderick was ill, weak and nervous, and it was said that his pistol was quicker on the trigger than Terry's. When the word was given it was discharged before it reached a level and the ball struck the earth, nine feet from where he stood. Terry fired, striking Broderick in the breast. He sank to the earth mortally wounded and died three days afterwards. Broderick dead was a greater man than Broderick living. For years he had waged a contest against the representatives of the slave oligarchy in California and the great mass of the people had looked on with indifference, even urging on his pursuers to the tragic end. Now that he was killed, the cry went up for vengeance on his murderers. Terry was arrested and admitted to bail in the sum of $10,000. The trial was put off on some pretext and some ten months later he obtained a change of venue to Marin county on the plea that he could not obtain a fair and impartial trial in San Francisco. His case was afterwards dismissed without trial by a pro-slavery judge named Hardy. Although freed by the courts he was found guilty and condemned by public opinion. He went south and joined the Confederates at the breaking out of the Civil war. He some time after the close of the war returned to California. In 1880 he was a presidential elector on the Democratic ticket. His colleagues on the ticket were elected, but he was defeated. He was killed at Lathrop by a deputy United States marshal while attempting an assault on United States Supreme Judge Field.

In the hue and cry that was raised on the death of Broderick, the chivalry read the doom of their ascendency. Gwin, as he was about to take the steamer on his return to Washington, "had flaunted in his face a large canvas frame, on which was painted a portrait of Broderick and this: 'It is the will of the people that the murderers of Broderick do not return again to California;' and below were also these words attributed to Mr. Broderick: 'They have killed me because I was opposed to the extension of slavery, and a corrupt administration.' "

Throughout his political career Broderick was a consistent anti-slavery man and a friend of the common people. Of all the politicians of the ante-bellum period, that is, before the Civil war, he stands to-day the highest in the estimation of the people of California. Like Lincoln, he was a self-made man. From a humble origin, unaided, he had fought his way up to a lofty position. Had he been living during the war against the perpetuity of human slavery, he would have been a power in the senate or possibly a commander on the field of battle. As it was, during that struggle in his adopted state, his name became a synonym of patriotism and love for the Union.

Milton S. Latham, who succeeded John B. Weller as governor in 1860, was, like his predecessor, a northern man with southern principles. Almost from the date of his arrival in California he had been an office-holder. He was a man of mediocre ability. He was a state divisionist and would have aided in that scheme by advocating in the senate of the United States (to which body he had been elected three days after his inauguration) the segregation of the southern counties and their formation into a new state with the hopes of restoring the equilibrium between the north and the south. But the time had passed for such projects. The lieutenant-governor, John G. Downey, succeeded Latham. Downey gained great popularity by his veto of the "bulkhead bill." This was a scheme of the San Francisco Dock and Wharf Company to build a stone bulkhead around the city water front in consideration of having the exclusive privilege of collecting wharfage and tolls for fifty years. Downey lost much of his popularity, particularly with the Union men, during the Civil war on account of his sympathy with the Confederates.

At the state election in September, 1861, Leland Stanford was chosen governor. He was the first Republican chosen to that office. He received fifty-six thousand votes. Two years before he had been a candidate for that office and received only ten thousand votes, so rapidly had public sentiment changed. The news of the firing upon Fort Sumter reached San Francisco April 24, twelve days after its occurrence. It came by pony express. The beginning of hostilities between the north and the south stirred up a strong Union sentiment. The great Union mass meeting held in San Francisco May II, 1861, was the largest and most enthusiastic

225

public demonstration ever held on the Pacific coast. The lines were sharply drawn between the friends of the government and its enemies. Former political alliances were forgotten. Most of the Anti-Lecompton or Douglas Democrats arrayed themselves on the side of the Union. The chivalry wing of the Democratic party were either open or secret sympathizers with the Confederates. Some of them were bold and outspoken in their disloyalty. The speech of Edmund Randolph at the Democratic convention July 24, 1861, is a sample of such utterances. * * * "To me it seems a waste of time to talk. For God's sake, tell me of battles fought and won. Tell me of usurpers overthrown; that Missouri is again a free state, no longer crushed under the armed heel of a reckless and odious despot. Tell me that the state of Maryland lives again; and, oh! gentlemen, let us read, let us hear, at the first moment, that not one hostile foot now treads the soil of Virginia! (Applause and cheers.) If this be rebellion, I am a rebel. Do you want a traitor, then I am a traitor. For God's sake, speed the ball; may the lead go quick to his heart, and may our country be free from the despot usurper that now claims the name of the president of the United States." (Cheers.) Some of the chivalry Democrats, most of whom had been holding office in California for years, went south at the breaking out of the war to fight in the armies of the Confederacy, and among these was Gen. Albert Sidney Johnston, who had been superseded in the command of the Pacific Department by Gen. Edwin V. Sumner. Johnston, with a number of fellow sympathizers, went south by the overland route and was killed a year later, at the battle of Shiloh, while in command of the Confederate army.

One form of disloyalty among the class known as "copperheads" (northern men with southern principles) was the advocacy of a Pacific republic. Most prominent among these was ex-Governor John B. Weller. The movement was a thinly disguised method of aiding the southern Confederacy. The flag of the inchoate Pacific republic was raised in Stockton January 16, 1861. It is thus described by the Stockton Argus: "The flag is of silk of the medium size of the national ensign and with the exception of the Union (evidently a misnomer in this case) which contains a lone star upon a blue ground, is covered by a painting representing a wild mountain scene, a huge grizzly bear standing in the foreground and the words 'Pacific Republic' near the upper border." The flag raising was not a success. At first it was intended to raise it in the city. But as it became evident this would not be allowed, it was raised to the mast head of a vessel in the slough. It was not allowed to float there long. The halyards were cut and a boy was sent up the mast to pull it down. The owner of the flag was convinced that it was not safe to trifle with the loyal sentiment of the people.

At the gubernatorial election in September, 1863, Frederick F. Low, Republican, was chosen over John G. Downey, Democrat, by a majority of over twenty thousand. In some parts of the state Confederate sympathizers were largely in the majority. This was the case in Los Angeles and in some places in the San Joaquin valley. Several of the most outspoken were arrested and sent to Fort Alcatraz, where they soon became convinced of the error of their ways and took the oath of allegiance. When the news of the assassination of Lincoln reached San Francisco, a mob destroyed the newspaper plants of the Democratic Press, edited by Beriah Brown; the Occidental, edited by Zach. Montgomery; the News Letter, edited by F. Marriott, and the Monitor, a Catholic paper, edited by Thomas A.

226

Brady. These were virulent copperhead sheets that had heaped abuse upon the martyred president. Had the proprietors of these journals been found the mob would, in the excitement that prevailed, have treated them with violence. After this demonstration Confederate sympathizers kept silent.

CHAPTER XXXI.
TRADE, TRAVEL AND TRANSPORTATION.

The beginning of the ocean commerce of California was the two mission transport ships that came every year to bring supplies for the missions and presidios and take back what few products there were to send. The government fixed a price upon each and every article of import and export. There was no cornering the market, no bulls or bears in the wheat pit, no rise or fall in prices except when ordered by royal authority. An Arancel de Precios (fixed rate of prices) was issued at certain intervals, and all buying and selling was governed accordingly. These arancels included everything in the range of human needs — physical, spiritual or mental. According to a tariff of prices promulgated by Governor Pages in 1788, which had been approved by the audencia and had received the royal sanction, the price of a Holy Christ in California was fixed at $1.75, a wooden spoon six cents, a horse $9, a deerskin twenty-five cents, red pepper eighteen cents a pound, a dozen of quail twenty-five cents, brandy seventy-five cents per pint, and so on throughout the list.

In 1785 an attempt was made to open up trade between California and China, the commodities for exchange being seal and otter skins for quicksilver. The trade in peltries was to be a government monopoly. The skins were to be collected from the natives by the mission friars, who were to sell them to a government agent at prices ranging from $2.50 to $10 each. The neophytes must give up to the friars all the skins in their possession. All trade by citizens or soldiers was prohibited and anyone attempting to deal in peltries otherwise than the regularly ordained authorities was liable, if found out, to have his goods confiscated. Spain's attempt to engage in the fur trade was not a success. The blighting monopoly of church and state nipped it in the bud. It died out, and the government bought quicksilver, on which also it had a monopoly, with coin instead of otter skins.

After the government abandoned the fur trade the American smugglers began to gather up the peltries, and the California producer received better prices for his furs than the missionaries paid.

The Yankee smuggler had no arancel of prices fixed by royal edict. His price list varied according to circumstances. As his trade was illicit and his vessel and her cargo were in danger of confiscation if he was caught, his scale of prices ranged high. But he paid a higher price for the peltries than the government, and that was a consolation to the seller. The commerce with the Russian settlements of the northwest in the early years of the century furnished a limited market for the grain produced at some of the missions, but the Russians helped themselves to the otter and the seal of California without saying "By your leave" and they were not welcome visitors.

During the Mexican revolution, as has been previously mentioned, trade sprang up between Lima and California in tallow, but it was of short duration. During the Spanish era it can hardly be said that California had any commerce. Foreign vessels were not allowed to enter her ports except when in distress, and their stay was limited to the shortest time possible required to make repairs and take on supplies.

It was not until Mexico gained her independence and removed the prescriptive regulations with which Spain had hampered commerce that the hide droghers opened up trade between New England and California. This trade, which began in 1822, grew to considerable proportions. The hide droghers were emigrant ships as well as mercantile vessels. By these came most of the Americans who settled in California previous to 1840. The hide and tallow trade, the most important item of commerce in the Mexican era, reached its maximum in 1834, when the great mission herds were, by order of the padres, slaughtered to prevent them from falling into the hands of the government commissioners. Thirty-two vessels came to the coast that year, nearly all of which were engaged in the hide and tallow trade.

During the year 1845, the last of Mexican rule, sixty vessels visited the coast. These were not all trading vessels; eight were men-of-war, twelve were whalers and thirteen came on miscellaneous business. The total amount received at the custom house for revenue during that year was $140,000. The majority of the vessels trading on the California coast during the Mexican era sailed under the stars and stripes. Mexico was kinder to California than Spain, and under her administration commercial relations were established to a limited extent with foreign nations. Her commerce at best was feeble and uncertain. The revenue laws and their administration were frequently changed, and the shipping merchant was never sure what kind of a reception his cargo would receive from the custom house officers. The duties on imports from foreign countries were exorbitant and there was always more or less smuggling carried on. The people and the padres, when they were a power, gladly welcomed the arrival of a trading vessel on the coast and were not averse to buying goods that had escaped the tariff if they could do so with safety. As there was no land tax, the revenue on goods supported the expenses of the government.

Never in the world's history did any country develop an ocean commerce so quickly as did California after the discovery of gold. When the news spread abroad, the first ships to arrive came from Peru, Chile and the South Sea islands. The earliest published notice of the gold discovery appeared in the Baltimore Sun, September 20, 1848, eight months after it was made. At first the story was ridiculed, but as confirmatory reports came thick and fast, preparations began for a grand rush for the gold mines. Vessels of all kinds, seaworthy and unseaworthy, were overhauled and fitted out for California. The American trade with California had gone by way of Cape Horn or the Straits of Magellan, and this was the route that was taken by the pioneers. Then there were short cuts by the way of the Isthmus of Panama, across Mexico and by Nicaragua. The first vessels left the Atlantic seaports in November, 1848. By the middle of the winter one hundred vessels had sailed from Atlantic and Gulf seaports, and by spring one hundred and fifty more had taken their departure, all of them loaded with human freight and with supplies of every description. Five hundred and forty-nine vessels arrived in San Francisco in nine months, forty-five reaching that port in one day.

April 12, 1848, before the treaty of peace with Mexico had been proclaimed by the President, the Pacific Mail Steamship Company was incorporated with a capital of $500,000. Astoria, Ore., was to have been the Pacific terminus of the company's line, but it never got there. The discovery of gold in California made San Francisco the end of its route. The contract with the government gave the company a subsidy of $200,000 for maintaining three steamers on the Pacific side between Panama and Astoria. The first of these vessels, the California, sailed from New York October 6, 1848, for San Francisco and Astoria via Cape Horn. She was followed in the two succeeding months by the Oregon and the Panama. On the Atlantic side the vessels of the line for several years were the Ohio, Illinois and Georgia. The vessels on the Atlantic side were fifteen hundred tons burden, while those on the Pacific were a thousand tons. Freight and passengers by the Panama route were transported across the isthmus by boats up the Chagres river to Gorgona, and then by mule-back to Panama. In 1855 the Panama railroad was completed. This greatly facilitated travel and transportation. The Atlantic terminus of the road was Aspinwall, now called Colon.

Another line of travel and commerce between the states and California in early days was the Nicaragua route. By that route passengers on the Atlantic side landed at San Juan del Norte or Greytown. From there they took a river steamer and ascended the Rio San Juan to Lake Nicaragua, then in a larger vessel they crossed the lake to La Virgin. From there a distance of about twelve miles was made on foot or on mule-back to San Juan del Sur, where they reembarked on board the ocean steamer for San Francisco.

The necessity for the speedy shipment of merchandise to California before the days of transcontinental railroads at a minimum cost evolved the clipper ship. These vessels entered quite early into the California trade and soon displaced the short, clumsy vessels of a few hundred tons burden that took from six to ten months to make a voyage around the Horn. The clipper ship Flying Cloud, which arrived at San Francisco in August, 1851, made the voyage from New York in eighty-nine days. These vessels were built long and narrow and carried heavy sail. Their capacity ranged from one to two thousand tons burden. The overland railroads took away a large amount of their business.

Capt. Jedediah S. Smith, as previously stated, was the real pathfinder of the western mountains and plains. He marked out the route from Salt Lake by way of the Rio Virgin, the Colorado and the Cajon Pass to Los Angeles in 1826. This route was extensively traveled by the belated immigrants of the early '50s. Those reaching Salt Lake City too late in the season to cross the Sierra Nevadas turned southward and entered California by Smith's trail.

The early immigration to California came by way of Fort Hall. From there it turned southerly. At Fort Hall the Oregon and California immigrants separated. The disasters that befell the Donner party were brought upon them by their taking the Hastings cut-off, which was represented to them as saving two hundred and fifty miles. It was shorter, but the time spent in making a wagon road through a rough country delayed them until they were caught by the snows in the mountains. Lassen's cut-off was another route that brought disaster and delays to many of the immigrants who were induced to take it. The route up the Platte through the South Pass of the Rocky mountains and down the Humboldt received by far the larger amount of travel.

The old Santa Fe trail from Independence to Santa Fe, and from there by the old Spanish trail around the north bank of the Colorado across the Rio Virgin down the Mojave river and through the Cajon Pass to Los Angeles, was next in importance. Another route by which much of the southern emigration came was what was known as the Gila route. It started at Fort Smith, Ark., thence via El Paso and Tucson and down the Gila to Yuma, thence across the desert through the San Gorgono Pass to Los Angeles. In 1852 it was estimated one thousand wagons came by this route. There was another route still further south than this which passed through the northern states of Mexico, but it was not popular on account of the hostility of the Mexicans and the Apaches.

The first overland stage line was established in 1857. The route extended from San Antonio de Bexar, Tex., to San Diego, via El Paso, Messillo, Tucson and Colorado City (now Yuma). The service was twice a month. The contract was let to James E. Burch, the Postal Department reserving "the right to curtail or discontinue the service should any route subsequently put under contract cover the whole or any portion of the route." The San Diego Herald, August 12, 1857, thus notes the departure of the first mail by that route: "'The pioneer mail train from San Diego to San Antonio, Tex., under the contract entered into by the government with Mr. James Burch, left here on the 9th inst. (August 9, 1857) at an early hour in the morning, and is now pushing its way for the east at a rapid rate. The mail was of course carried on pack animals, as will be the case until wagons which are being pushed across will have been put on the line. * * * The first mail from the other side has not yet arrived, although somewhat overdue, and conjecture is rife as to the cause of the delay." The eastern mail arrived a few days later.

The service continued to improve, and the fifth trip from, the eastern terminus to San Diego "was made in the extraordinary short time of twenty-six days and twelve hours," and the San Diego Herald on this arrival, October 6, 1857, rushed out an extra "announcing the very gratifying fact of the complete triumph of the southern route notwithstanding the croakings of many of the opponents of the administration in this state." But the "triumph of the southern route" was of short duration. In September, 1858, the stages of the Butterfield line began making their semi-weekly trips. This route from its western terminus, San Francisco, came down the coast to Gilroy, thence through Pacheco Pass to the San Joaquin valley, up the valley and by way of Fort Tejon to Los Angeles; from there eastward by Temecula and Warner's to Yuma, thence following very nearly what is now the route of the Southern Pacific Railroad through Arizona and New Mexico to El Paso, thence turning northward to Fort Smith, Ark. There the route divided, one branch going to St. Louis and the other to Memphis. The mail route from San Antonio to San Diego was discontinued.

The Butterfield stage line was one of the longest continuous lines ever organized. Its length was two thousand eight hundred and eighty miles. It began operation in September, 1858. The first stage from the east reached Los Angeles October 7 and San Francisco October 10. A mass-meeting was held at San Francisco the evening of October 11 "for the purpose of expressing the sense entertained by the people of the city of the great benefits she is to receive from the establishment of the overland mail." Col. J. B. Crocket acted as president and Frank M. Pixley as secretary. The speaker of the evening in his enthusiasm said: "In my opinion one of the greatest blessings that could befall California would be to discontinue at once all communication by steamer between San Francisco and New York. On yesterday we received advices from New York, New Orleans and St.

Louis in less than twenty-four days via El Paso. Next to the discovery of gold this is the most important fact yet developed in the history of California." W. L. Ormsby, special correspondent of the New York Herald, the first and only through passenger by the overland mail coming in three hours less than twenty-four days, was introduced to the audience and was greeted with terrific applause. He gave a description of the route and some incidents of the journey.

The government gave the Butterfield company a subsidy of $600,000 a year for a service of two mail coaches each way a week. In 1859 the postal revenue from this route was only $27,000, leaving Uncle Sam more than half a million dollars out of pocket. At the breaking out of the Civil war the southern overland mail route was discontinued and a contract was made with Butterfield for a six-times-a-week mail by the central route via Salt Lake City, with a branch line to Denver. The eastern terminus was at first St. Joseph, but on account of the war it was changed to Omaha. The western terminus was Placerville, Cal., time twenty days for eight months, and twenty-three days for the remaining four months. The contract was for three years at an annual subsidy of $1,000,000. The last overland stage contract for carrying the mails was awarded to Wells, Fargo & Co., October 1, 1868, for $1,750,000 per annum, with deductions for carriage by railway. The railway was rapidly reducing the distance of stage travel.

The only inland commerce during the Mexican era was a few bands of mules sold to New Mexican traders and driven overland to Santa Fe by the old Spanish trail and one band of cattle sold to the Oregon settlers in 1837 and driven by the coast route to Oregon City. The Californians had no desire to open up an inland trade with their neighbors and the traders and trappers who came overland were not welcome.

After the discovery of gold, freighting to the mines became an important business. Supplies had to be taken by pack trains and wagons. Freight charges were excessively high at first. In 1848, "it cost $5 to carry a hundred pounds of goods from Sutter's Fort to the lower mines, a distance of twenty miles, and $10 per hundred weight for freight to the upper mines, a distance of forty miles. Two horses can draw one thousand five hundred pounds." In December, 1849, the roads were almost impassable and teamsters were charging from $40 to $50 a hundred pounds for hauling freight from Sacramento to Mormon Island.

In 1855 an inland trade was opened up between Los Angeles and Salt Lake City. The first shipment was made by Banning and Alexander. The wagon train consisted of fifteen ten-mule teams heavily freighted with merchandise. The venture was a success financially. The train left Los Angeles in May and returned in September, consuming four months in the journey. The trade increased and became quite an important factor in the business of the southern part of the state. In 1859 sixty wagons were loaded for Salt Lake in the month of January, and in March of the same year one hundred and fifty loaded with goods were sent to the Mormon capital. In 1865 and 1866 there was a considerable shipment of goods from Los Angeles to Idaho and Montana by wagon trains. These trains went by way of Salt Lake. This trade was carried on during the winter months when the roads over the Sierras and the Rocky mountains were blocked with snow.

Freighting by wagon train to Washoe formed a very important part of the inland commerce of California between 1859 and 1869. The immense freight wagons called "prairie schooners" carried almost as much as a freight car. The old-time teamster, like the old-time stage driver, was a unique character. Both have disappeared. Their occupation is gone. We shall never look on their like again.

The pony express rider came early in the history of California. Away back in 1775, when the continental congress made Benjamin Franklin postmaster-general of the United Colonies, on the Pacific coast soldier couriers, fleet mounted, were carrying their monthly budgets of mail between Monterey in Alta California, and Loreto, near the southern extremity of the peninsula of Lower California, a distance of one thousand five hundred miles.

In the winter of 1859-60 a Wall street lobby was in Washington trying to get an appropriation of $5,000,000 for carrying the mails one year between New York and San Francisco. William H. Russell, of the firm of Russell, Majors & Waddell, then engaged in running a daily stage line between the Missouri river and Salt Lake City, hearing of the lobby's efforts, offered to bet $200,000 that he could put on a mail line between San Francisco and St. Joseph that could make the distance, one thousand nine hundred and fifty miles, in ten days. The wager was accepted. Russell and his business manager, A. B. Miller, an old plains man, bought the fleetest horses they could find in the west and employed one hundred and twenty-five riders selected with reference to their light weight and courage. It was essential that the horses should be loaded as lightly as possible. The horses were stationed from ten to twenty miles apart and each rider was required to ride seventy-five miles. For change of horses and mail bag two minutes were allowed, at each station. One man took care of the two horses kept there. Everything being arranged a start was made from St. Joseph, April 3, 1860. The bet was to be decided on the race eastward. At meridian on April 3, 1860, a signal gun on a steamer at Sacramento proclaimed the hour of starting. At that signal Mr. Miller's private saddle horse, Border Ruffian, with his rider bounded away toward the foothills of the Sierra Nevadas. The first twenty miles were covered in forty-nine minutes. All went well till the Platte river was reached. The river was swollen by recent rain. Rider and horse plunged boldly into it, but the horse mired in the quicksands and was drowned. The rider carrying the mail bag footed it ten miles to the next relay station. When the courier arrived at the sixty mile station out from St. Joseph he was one hour behind time. The last one had just three hours and thirty minutes in which to make the sixty miles and win the race. A heavy rain was falling and the roads were slippery, but with six horses to make the distance he won with five minutes and a fraction to spare. And thus was finished the longest race for the largest stake ever run in America.

The pony express required to do its work nearly five hundred horses, about one hundred and ninety stations, two hundred station keepers and over a hundred riders. Each rider usually rode the horses on about seventy-five miles, but sometimes much greater distances were made. Robert H. Haslam, Pony Bob, made on one occasion a continuous ride of three hundred and eighty miles and William F. Cody, now famous as Buffalo Bill, in one continuous trip rode three hundred and eighty-four miles, stopping only for meals, and to change horses.

The pony express was a semi-weekly service. Fifteen pounds was the limit of the weight of the waterproof mail bag and its contents. The postage or charge was $5 on a letter of half an ounce. The limit was two hundred letters, but sometimes there were not more than twenty in a bag. The line never paid. The shortest time ever made by the pony express was seven days and seventeen hours. This was in March, 1861, when it carried President Lincoln's message. At first telegraphic messages were received at St. Joseph up to five o'clock p. m. of the day of starting and sent to San Francisco on the express, arriving at Placerville, which was then the eastern terminus of the line. The pony express was suspended October 2^, 1861, on the completion of the telegraph.

The first stage line was established between Sacramento and Mormon Island in September, 1849, fare $16 to $32, according to times. Sacramento was the great distributing point for the mines and was also the center from which radiated numerous stage lines. In 1853 a dozen lines were owned there and the total capital invested in staging was estimated at $335,000. There were lines running to Coloma, Nevada, Placerville, Georgetown, Yankee Jim's, Jackson, Stockton, Shasta and Auburn. In 1851 Stockton had seven daily stages. The first stage line between San Francisco and San Jose was established in April, 1850, fare $32. A number of lines were consolidated. In 1860 the California stage company controlled eight lines northward, the longest extending seven hundred and ten miles to Portland with sixty stations, thirty-five drivers and five hundred horses, eleven drivers and one hundred and fifty horses pertaining to the rest. There were seven independent lines covering four hundred and sixty-four miles, chiefly east and south, the longest to Virginia City. These lines disappeared with the advent of the railroad.

The pack train was a characteristic feature of early mining days. Many of the mountain camps were inaccessible to wagons and the only means of shipping in goods was by pack tram. A pack train consisted of from ten to twenty mules each, laden with from two hundred to four hundred pounds. The load was fastened on the animal by means of a pack saddle which was held in its place by a cinch tightly laced around the animal's body. The sure-footed mules could climb steep grades and wind round narrow trails on the side of steep mountains without slipping or tumbling over the cliffs. Mexicans were the most expert packers.

The scheme to utilize camels and dromedaries as beasts of burden on the arid plains of the southwest was agitated in the early fifties. The chief promoter if not the originator of the project was Jefferson Davis, afterwards president of the Southern Confederacy. During the last days of the congress of 1851, Mr. Davis offered an amendment to the army appropriation bill appropriating $30,000 for the purchase of thirty camels and twenty dromedaries. The bill was defeated. When Davis was secretary of war in 1854, congress appropriated $30,000 for the purchase and importation of camels and in December of that year Major C. Wayne was sent to Egypt and Arabia to buy seventy-five. He secured the required number and shipped them on the naval store ship Supply. They were landed at Indianola, Tex., February 10, 1857. Three had died on the voyage. About half of the herd were taken to Albuquerque, where an expedition was fitted out under the command of Lieutenant Beale for Fort Tejon, Cal.; the other half was employed in packing on the plains of Texas and in the Gadsen Purchase, as Southern Arizona was then called.

It very soon became evident that the camel experiment would not be a success. The American teamster could not be converted into an Arabian camel driver. From the very first meeting there was a mutual antipathy between the American mule whacker and the beast of the prophet. The teamsters when transformed into camel drivers deserted and the troopers refused to have anything to do with the misshapen beasts. So because there was no one to load and navigate these ships of the desert their voyages became less and less frequent, until finally they ceased altogether; and these desert ships were anchored at the different forts in the southwest. After the breaking out of the Civil war the camels at the forts in Texas and New Mexico were turned loose to shift for themselves. Those in Arizona and California were condemned and sold by the government to two Frenchmen who used them for packing, first in Nevada and later in Arizona, but tiring of the animals they turned them out on the desert. Some of these camels or possibly their descendants are still roaming over the arid plains of southern Arizona and Sonora.

The first telegraph was completed September II, 1853. It extended from the business quarter of San Francisco to the Golden Gate and was used for signaling vessels. The first long line connected Marysville, Sacramento, Stockton and San Jose. This was completed October 24, 1853. Another line about the same time was built from San Francisco to Placerville by way of Sacramento. A line was built southward from San Jose along the Butterfield overland mail route to Los Angeles in 1860. The Overland Telegraph, begun in 1858, was completed November 7, 1861.

The first express for the States was sent under the auspices of the California Star (newspaper). The Star of March 1, 1848, contained the announcement that "We are about to send letters by express to the States at fifty cents each, papers twelve and a half cents; to start April 15; any mail arriving after that time will be returned to the writers. The Star refused to send copies of its rival, The Californian, in its express.

The first local express was started by Charles L. Cady in August, 1847. It left San Francisco every Monday and Fort Sacramento, its other terminus, every Thursday. Letters twenty-five cents. Its route was by way of Saucelito, Napa and Petaluma to Sacramento. Weld & Co.'s express was established in October, 1849. This express ran from San Francisco to Marysville, having its principal offices in San Francisco, Benicia and Sacramento. It was the first express of any consequence established in California. Its name was changed to Hawley & Co.'s express. The first trip was made in the Mint, a sailing vessel, and took six days. Afterward it was transferred to the steamers Hartford and McKim. The company paid these boats $800 per month for the use of one state room; later for the same accommodation it paid $1,500 per month. The Alta California of January 7, 1850, says: "There are so many new express companies daily starting that we can scarcely keep the run of them."

The following named were the principal companies at that time: Hawley & Co., Angel, Young & Co., Todd, Bryan, Stockton Express, Henly, McKnight & Co., Brown, Knowlton & Co. The business of these express companies consisted largely in carrying letters to the mines. The letters came through the post office in San Francisco, but the parties to whom they were addressed were in the mines. While the miner would gladly give an ounce to hear from home he could not make the trip to the Bay at a loss of several hundred dollars in time and money. The express companies obviated this difficulty. The Alta of July 27, 1850, says: "We scarcely know what we should do if it were not for the various express lines established which enable us to hold communication with the mines. With the present defective mail communication we should scarcely ever be able to hear from the towns throughout California or from the remote portions of the Placers north or south. Hawley & Co., Todd & Bryan and Besford & Co. are three lines holding communication with different sections of the country. Adams & Co. occupy the whole of a large building on Montgomery street."

Adams & Co., established in 1850, soon became the leading express company of the coast. It absorbed a number of minor companies. It established relays of the fastest horses to carry the express to the mining towns. As early as 1852 the company's lines had penetrated the remote mining camps. Some of its riders performed feats in riding that exceeded the famous pony express riders. Isaac W. Elwell made the trip between Placerville and Sacramento in two hours and fifty minutes, distance sixty-four miles; Frank Ryan made seventy-five miles in four hours and twenty minutes. On his favorite horse, Colonel, he made twenty miles in fifty-five minutes. Adams & Co. carried on a banking business and had branch banks in all the leading mining towns. They also became a political power. In the great financial crash of 1855 they failed and in their failure ruined thousands of their depositors. Wells, Fargo & Co. express was organized in 1851. It weathered the financial storm that carried down Adams & Co. It gained the confidence of the people of the Pacific coast and has never betrayed it. Its business has grown to immense proportions. It is one of the leading express companies of the world.

CHAPTER XXXII. RAILROADS.

The agitation of the Pacific railroad question began only two years after the first passenger railway was put in operation in the United States. The originator of the scheme to secure the commerce of Asia by a transcontinental railway from the Atlantic to the Pacific was Hartwell Carver, grandson of the famous explorer, Jonathan Carver. He published articles in the New York Courier and Inquirer in 1832 elaborating his idea, and memorialized congress on the subject. The western terminus was to be on the Columbia river. His road was to be made of stone. There were to be sleeping cars and dining cars attached to each train. In 1836, John Plumbe, then a resident of Dubuque, Iowa, advocated the building of a railroad from Lake Michigan to Oregon. At a public meeting held in Dubuque, March 26, 1838, which Plumbe addressed, a memorial to congress was drafted "praying for an appropriation to defray the expense of the survey and location of the first link in the great Atlantic and Pacific railroad, namely, from the lakes to the Mississippi." Their application was favorably received and an appropriation being made the same year, which was expended under the direction of the secretary of war, the report being of a very favorable character.

Plumbe received the endorsement of the Wisconsin legislature of 1839-40 and a memorial was drafted to congress urging the continuance of the work. Plumbe went to Washington to urge his project. But the times were out of joint for great undertakings. The financial panic of 1837 had left the government revenues in a demoralized condition. Plumbe's plan was to issue stock to the amount of $100,000,000 divided in shares of $5 each. The government was to appropriate alternate sections of the public lands along the line of the road. Five million dollars were to be called in for the first installment. After this was expended in building, the receipts from the sale of the lands was to continue the building of the road. One hundred miles were to be built each year and twenty years was the time set for the completion of the road. A bill granting the subsidy and authorizing the building of the road was introduced in congress, but was defeated by the southern members who feared that it would foster the growth of free states.

The man best known in connection with the early agitation of the Pacific railroad scheme was Asa Whitney, of New York. For a time he acted with Carver in promulgating the project, but took up a plan of his own. Whitney wanted a strip of land sixty miles wide along the whole length of the road, which would have given about one hundred million acres of the public domain. Whitney's scheme called forth a great deal of discussion. It was feared by some timorous souls that such a monopoly would endanger the government and by others that it would bankrupt the public treasury. The agitation was kept up for several years. The acquisition of California and New Mexico threw the project into politics. The question of depleting the treasury or giving away the public domain no longer worried the pro-slavery politicians in congress. The question that agitated them now was how far south could the road be deflected so that it would enhance the value of the lands over which they hoped to spread their pet institution — human slavery.

Another question that agitated the members of congress was whether the road should be built by the government — should be a national road. The route which the road should take was fought over year after year in congress. The south would not permit the north to have the road for fear that freemen would absorb the public lands and build up free states. It was the old dog-in-the-manger policy so characteristic of the southern proslavery politicians.

The California newspapers early took up the discussion and routes were thick as leaves in Valambrosa. In the Star of May 13, 1848, Dr. John Marsh outlines a route which was among the best proposed: "From the highest point on the Bay of San Francisco to which seagoing vessels can ascend; thence up the valley of the San Joaquin two hundred and fifty miles; thence through a low pass (Walker's) to the valley of the Colorado and thence through Arizona and New Mexico by the Santa Fe trail to Independence, Mo."

Routes were surveyed and the reports of the engineers laid before congress; memorials were received from the people of California praying for a road; bills were introduced and discussed, but the years passed and the Pacific railroad was not begun. Slavery, that "sum of all villainies," was an obstruction more impassable than the mountains and deserts that intervened between the Missouri and the Pacific. Southern politicians, aided and abetted by Gwin of California neutralized every attempt.

One of the first of several local railroad projects that resulted in something more than resolutions, public meetings and the election of a board of directors that never directed anything was the building of a railroad from San Francisco to San Jose. The agitation was begun early in 1850 and by February, 1851, $100,000 had been subscribed. September 6 of that year a company was organized and the projected road given the high sounding title of the Pacific & Atlantic railroad. Attempts were made to secure subscriptions for its stock in New York and in Europe, but without success. Congress was appealed to, but gave no assistance and all that there was to the road for ten years was its name. In 1859 a new organization was effected under the name of the San Francisco & San Jose railroad company. An attempt was made to secure a subsidy of $900,000 from the three counties through which the road was to pass, but this failed and the corporation dissolved. Another organization, the fourth, was effected with a capital stock of $2,000,000. The construction of the road was begun in October, 1860, and completed to San Jose January 16, 1864.

The first railroad completed and put into successful operation in California was the Sacramento Valley road. It was originally intended to extend the road from Sacramento through Placer and Sutter counties to Mountain City, in Yuba county, a distance of about forty miles. It came to a final stop at a little over half that distance. Like the San Jose road the question of building was agitated several years before anything was really done. In 1853 the company was reorganized under the railroad act of that year. Under the previous organization subscriptions had been obtained. The Sacramento Union of September 19, 1852, says: "The books of the Sacramento Valley railroad company were to have been opened in San Francisco Wednesday. Upwards of $200,000 of the necessary stock has been subscribed from here." The Union of September 24 announces, "That over $600,000 had already been subscribed at San Francisco and Sacramento." Under the reorganization a new board was elected November 12, 1853. C. L. Wilson was made president; F. W. Page, treasurer, and W. H. Watson, secretary. Theodore D. Judah, afterwards famous in California railroad building, was employed as engineer and the construction of the road began in February, 1855. It was completed to Folsom a, distance of twenty-two miles from Sacramento and the formal opening of the road for business took place February 22, 1856. According to the secretary's report for 1857 the earnings of that year averaged $18,000 per month. The total earnings for the year amounted to $216,000; the expenses $84,000, leaving a profit of $132,000. The cost of the road and its equipment was estimated at $700,000. From this showing it would seem that California's first railroad ought to have been a paying investment, but it was not. Money then was worth 5 per cent a month and the dividends from the road about 18 per cent a year. The difference between one and a half per cent and 5 per cent a month brought the road to a standstill.

Ten years had passed since California had become a state and had its representatives in congress. In all these years the question of a railroad had come up in some form in that body, yet the railroad seemingly was as far from a consummation as it had been a decade before. In 1859 the silver mines of the Washoe were discovered and in the winter of 1859-60 the great silver rush began. An almost continuous stream of wagons, pack trains, horsemen and footmen poured over the Sierra Nevadas into Carson Valley and up the slopes of Mount Davidson to Virginia City. The main line of travel was by way of Placerville, through Johnson's Pass to Carson City. An expensive toll road was built over the mountains and monster freight wagons hauled great loads of merchandise and mill machinery to the mines. "In 1863 the tolls on the new road amounted to $300,000 and the freight bills on mills and merchandise summed up $13,000,000."

The rush to Washoe gave a new impetus to railroad projecting. A convention of the whole coast had been held at San Francisco in September, 1859, but nothing came of it beyond propositions and resolutions. Early in 1861, Theodore P. Judah called a railroad meeting at the St. Charles hotel in Sacramento. The feasibility of a road over the mountains, the large amount of business that would come to that road from the Washoe mines and the necessity of Sacramento moving at once to secure that trade were pointed out. This road would be the beginning of a transcontinental line and Sacramento had the opportunity of becoming its terminus. Judah urged upon some of the leading business men the project of organizing a company to begin the building of a transcontinental road. The Washoe trade and travel would be a very important item in the business of the road.

On the 28th of June, 1861, the Central Pacific Railroad company was organized under the general incorporation law of the state. Leland Stanford was chosen president, C. P. Huntington, vice-president, Mark Hopkins, treasurer, James Bailey, secretary, and T. D. Judah, chief engineer. The directors were those just named and E. B. Crocker, John F. Morse, D. W. Strong and Charles Marsh. The capital stock of the company was $8,500,000 divided into eighty-five thousand shares of $100 each. The shares taken by individuals were few, Stanford, Huntington, Hopkins, Judah and Charles Crocker subscribing for one hundred and fifty each; Glidden & Williams, one hundred and twenty-five shares; Charles A. Lombard and Orville D. Lombard, three hundred and twenty shares; Samuel Hooper, Benjamin J. Reed, Samuel P. Shaw, fifty shares each; R. O. Ives, twenty-five shares; Edwin B. Crocker, ten shares; Samuel Brannan, two hundred shares; cash subscriptions of which 10 per cent was required by law to be paid down realizing but a few thousand dollars with which to begin so important a work as a railroad across the Sierra Nevada.

The total amount subscribed was $158,000, scarcely enough to build five miles of road on the level plains if it had all been paid up. None of the men in the enterprise was rich. Indeed, as fortunes go now, none of them had more than a competence. Charles Crocker, who was one of the best off, in his sworn statement, placed the value of his property at $25,000; C. P. Huntington placed the value of his individual possessions at $7,222, while Leland Stanford and his brother together owned property worth $32,950. The incubus that so long had prevented building a Pacific railroad was removed. The war of secession had begun. The southern senators and representatives were no longer in congress to obstruct legislation. The thirty-second and the thirty-fifth parallel roads southern schemes, were out of the way or rather the termini of these roads were inside the confederate lines.

A bill "to aid in the construction of a railroad and telegraph line from the Missouri river to the Pacific ocean and to secure to the government the use of the same for postal, military and other purposes passed both houses and became a law July 1, 1862. The bill provided for the building of the road by two companies. The Union Pacific (which was to be a union of several roads already projected) was given the construction of the road to the eastern boundary of California, where it would connect with the Central Pacific. Government bonds were to be given to the companies to the amount of $16,000 per mile to the foot of the mountains and $48,000 per mile through the mountains when forty miles of road had been built and approved by the government commissioners. In addition to the bonds the companies were to receive "every alternate section of public land designated by odd numbers to the amount of five alternate sections per mile on each side of the railroad on the line thereof and within the limits of ten miles on each side of the road not sold, reserved or otherwise disposed of by the United States." Mineral lands were exempted and any lands unsold three years after the completion of the entire road were subject to a preemption like other public lands at a price not exceeding $1.25 per acre, payable to the company.

The government bonds were a first mortgage on the road. The ceremony of breaking ground for the beginning of the enterprise took place at Sacramento, February 22, 1863, Governor Stanford throwing the first shovelful of earth, and work was begun on the first eighteen miles of the road which was let by contract to be finished by August, 1863. The Central Pacific company was in hard lines. Its means were not sufficient to build forty miles which must be completed before the subsidy could be received. In October, 1863, Judah who had been instrumental in securing the first favorable legislation set out a second time for Washington to ask further assistance from congress. At New York he was stricken with a fever and died there. To him more than any other man is due the credit of securing for the Pacific coast its first transcontinental railroad. In July, 1864, an amended act was passed increasing the land grant from six thousand four hundred acres to twelve thousand eight hundred per mile and reducing the number of miles to be built annually from fifty to twenty-five. The company was allowed to bond its road to the same amount per mile as the government subsidy.

The Western Pacific, which was virtually a continuation of the Central Pacific, was organized in December, 1862, for the purpose of building a railroad from

240

Sacramento via Stockton to San Jose. A branch of this line was constructed from Niles to Oakland, which was made the terminus of the Central Pacific. The Union Pacific did not begin construction until 1865, while the Central Pacific had forty-four miles constructed. In 1867 the Central Pacific had reached the state line. It had met with many obstacles in the shape of lawsuits and unfavorable comments by the press. From the state line it pushed out through Nevada and on the 28th of April, 1869, the two companies met with their completed roads at Promontory Point in Utah, fifty-three miles west of Ogden. The ceremony of joining the two roads took place May 10. The last tie, a handsomely finished piece of California laurel, was laid and Governor Stanford with a silver hammer drove a golden spike. The two locomotives, one from the east and one from the west, bumped noses and the first transcontinental railroad was completed.

The Southern Pacific Railroad company of California was incorporated in December, 1865. It was incorporated to build a railroad from some point on the bay of San Francisco through the counties of Santa Clara, Monterey, San Luis Obispo, Tulare, Los Angeles to San Diego and thence easterly through San Diego to the eastern boundary of the state there to connect with a railroad from the Mississippi river.

"In July, 1866, congress granted to the Atlantic and Pacific Railroad company to aid in the construction of its road and telegraph line from Springfield, Mo., by the most eligible route to Albuquerque in New Mexico and thence by the thirty-fifth parallel route to the Pacific, an amount of land equal to that granted to the Central Pacific. By this act the Southern Pacific Railroad was authorized to connect with the Atlantic and Pacific near the boundary line of California, at such point as should be deemed most suitable by the companies and should have therefore the same amount of land per mile as the Atlantic and Pacific."

In 1867 the Southern Pacific company decided to change its route and instead of building down through the coast counties to go eastward from Gilroy through Pacheco's pass into the upper San Joaquin valley through Fresno, Kern and San Bernardino to the Colorado river near Fort Mojave. This contemplated change left the lower coast counties out in the cold and caused considerable dissatisfaction, and an attempt was made to prevent it from getting a land subsidy. Congress, however, authorized the change, as did the California legislature of 1870, and the road secured the land.

The San Francisco and San Jose Railroad came into possession of the Southern Pacific company, San Francisco donating three thousand shares of stock in that road on condition that the Southern Pacific company, after it secured the San Jose road, should extend it to the southeastern boundary of the state. In 1869 a proposition was made to the supervisors of San Francisco to donate $1,000,000 in bonds of the city to the Southern Pacific company, on condition that it build two hundred miles south from Gilroy, the bonds to be delivered on the completion and stocking of each section of fifty miles of road. The bonds were voted by the people of the city. The road was built to Soledad, seventy miles from Gilroy, and then stopped. The different branch roads in the San Jose and Salinas valley were all consolidated under the name of the Southern Pacific. The Central Pacific and the Southern Pacific, although apparently different organizations, were really one company.

The Southern Pacific built southward from Lathrop, a station on the Central Pacific's line, a railroad up the valley by way of Tehachapi Pass to Los Angeles. While this road was in course of construction in 1872 a proposition was made to the people of Los Angeles through the county board of supervisors to vote a subsidy equal to 5 per cent of the entire amount of the taxable property of the county on condition that the Southern Pacific build fifty miles of its main line to Yuma in the county. Part of the subsidy was to be paid in bonds of the Los Angeles & San Pedro Railroad, amounting to $377,000 and sixty acres of land for depot purposes. The total amount of subsidy to be given was $610,000. The proposition was accepted by the people, the railroad company in addition to its original offer agreeing to build a branch road twenty-seven miles long to Anaheim. This was done to head off the Tom Scott road which had made a proposition to build a branch road from San Diego to Los Angeles to connect with the Texas Pacific road which the year before had been granted a right of way from Marshall, Tex., to San Diego, and was preparing to build its road. The Southern Pacific completed its road to Los Angeles in September, 1876, and reached the Colorado river on its way east in April, 1877. It obtained the old franchise of the Texas Pacific and continued its road eastward to El Paso, Tex., where it made connections with roads to New Orleans and other points south and east, thus giving California its second transcontinental railroad. This road was completed to El Paso in 1881.

The Atlantic & Pacific road with which the Southern Pacific was to connect originally, suffered from the financial crash of 1873 and suspended operations for a time. Later it entered into a combination with the Atchison, Topeka & Santa Fe and St. Louis & San Francisco railroad companies. This gave the Atchison road a half interest in the charter of the Atlantic & Pacific. The two companies built a main line jointly from Albuquerque (where the Atchison road ended) west to the Colorado river at the Needles. Their intention was to continue the road to Los Angeles and San Francisco.

The California Southern and the California Southern Extension companies were organized to extend the Atlantic & Pacific from Barstow to San Diego. These companies consolidated and completed a road from San Diego to San Bernardino September 13, 1883. The Southern Pacific interfered. It attempted to prevent the California Southern from crossing its tracks at Colton by placing a heavy engine at the point of crossing, but was compelled to move the engine to save it from demolition. It built a branch from Mojave station to connect with the Atlantic & Pacific in which it had an interest. This gave connection for the Atlantic & Pacific over the Southern Pacific lines with both Los Angeles and San Francisco. This was a serious blow to the California Southern, but disasters never come singly. The great flood of January, 1884, swept down through the Temecula Cañon and carried about thirty miles of its track out to sea. It was doubtful under the circumstances whether it would pay to rebuild it. Finally the Southern Pacific agreed to sell its extension from Barstow to the Needles to the California Southern, reserving its road from Barstow to Mojave. Construction was begun at once on the California Southern line from Barstow to San Bernardino and in November, 1885, the road was completed from Barstow to San Diego. In October, 1886, the road passed under control of the Atchison, Topeka & Santa Fe. In the spring of 1887 the road

242

was extended westerly from San Bernardino to meet the San Gabriel valley road which had been built eastward from Los Angeles through Pasadena. The completed line reached Los Angeles in May, 1887, thus giving California a third transcontinental line.

After many delays the gap in the Southern Pacific coast line was closed and the first trains from the north and the south passed over its entire length between Los Angeles and San Francisco on the 31st of March, 1901, nearly thirty years after the first section of the road was built.

The Oregon & California and the Central Pacific were consolidated in 1870. The two ends of the road were united at Ashland, Ore., in 1887. The entire line is now controlled by the Southern Pacific, and, in connection with the Northern Pacific and the Oregon Railway & Navigation Road at Portland, forms a fourth transcontinental line for California.

CHAPTER XXXIII. THE INDIAN QUESTION.

It is quite the fashion now with a certain school of writers, who take their history of California from "Ramona" and their information on the "Indian question" under the rule of the mission padres from sources equally fictitious, to draw invidious comparisons between the treatment of the Indian by Spain and Mexico when mission rule was dominant in California and his treatment by the United States after the conquest.

That the Indian was brutally treated and unmercifully slaughtered by the American miners and rancheros in the early '50s none will deny; that he had fared but little better under the rule of Spain and Mexico is equally true. The tame and submissive Indians of the sea coast with whom the mission had to deal were a very different people from the mountain tribes with whom the Americans came in conflict.

We know but little of the conquistas or gentile hunts that were occasionally sent out from the mission to capture subjects for conversion. The history of these was not recorded. From "The narrative of a voyage to the Pacific and Berings strait with the Polar expedition; performed in his majesty's ship Blossom, under command of Capt. F. W. Beechey, R. N., in the years 1825-26-27-28, we have the story of one of these conquistas or convert raids. Captain Beechey visited California in 1828. While in California he studied the missions, or at least those he visited, and after his return to England published his observations. His observations have great value. He was a disinterested observer and gave a plain, straightforward, truthful account of what he saw, without prejudice or partiality. His narrative dispels much of the romance that some modern writers throw around mission life. This conquista set out from the Mission San Jose.

"At a particular period of the year also, when the Indians can be spared from agricultural concerns of the establishment, many are permitted to take the launch of the mission and make excursions to the Indian territory. All are anxious to go on such occasions. Some to visit friends, some to procure the manufactures of their barbarian countrymen (which, by the by, are often better than their own) and some with a secret determination never to return. On these occasions the padres desire them to induce as many of their unconverted brethren as possible to accompany them back to the mission: of course, implying that this is to be done only by persuasion; but the boat being furnished with a cannon and musketry and in every respect equipped for war, it too often happens that the neophytes and the gente de razon, who superintend the direction of the boat, avail themselves of their superiority with the desire of ingratiating themselves with their master and receiving a reward. There are besides repeated acts of aggression, which it is necessary to punish, all of which furnish proselytes. Women and children are generally the first objects of capture, as their husbands and parents sometimes voluntarily follow them into captivity. These misunderstandings and captivities keep up a perpetual enmity amongst the tribes whose thirst for revenge is insatiable."

We had an opportunity of witnessing the tragical issue of one of these holyday excursions of the neophytes of the Mission San Jose. The launch was armed, as usual, and placed under the superintendence of an alcalde of the mission, who appears from one statement (for there are several), converted the party of pleasure either into an attack for procuring proselytes or of revenge upon a particular tribe for some aggression in which they were concerned. They proceeded up the Rio San Joachin until they came to the territory of a particular tribe named Consemenes, when they disembarked with the gun and encamped for the night near the village of Los Gentiles, intending to make an attack upon them next morning, but before they were prepared the gentiles, who had been apprised of their intention and had collected a large body of their friends, became the assailants and pressed so hard upon the party that, notwithstanding they dealt death in every direction with their cannon and musketry and were inspired with confidence by the contempt in which they held the valor and tactics of their unconverted countrymen, they were overpowered by numbers and obliged to seek their safety in flight and to leave the gun in the woods. Some regained the launch and were saved and others found their way overland to the mission, but thirty-four of the party never returned to tell their tale.

"There were other accounts of the unfortunate affair, one of which accused the padre of authorizing the attack. The padre was greatly displeased at the result of the excursion, as the loss of so many Indians to the mission was of great consequence and the confidence with which the victory would inspire the Indians was equally alarming.

"He therefore joined with the converted Indians in a determination to chastise and strike terror into the victorious tribe and in concert with the governor planned an expedition against them. The mission furnished money, arms, Indians and horses and the presidio troops, headed by Alferez Sanches, a veteran, who had been frequently engaged with the Indians and was acquainted with that part of the country. The expedition set out November 19 and we heard nothing of it until the 27th, but two days after the troops had taken to the field some immense columns of smoke rising above the mountains in the direction of the Cosemmes bespoke the conflagration of the village of the persecuted gentiles; and on the day above mentioned the veteran Sanches made a triumphant entry into the Mission of San Jose, escorting forty miserable women and children. The gun which had been lost in the first battle was retaken and other trophies captured.

"This victory, so glorious according to the ideas of the conquerors, was achieved with the loss of only one man on the part of the Christians, who was mortally wounded by the bursting of his own gun; but on the part of the enemy it was considerable, as Sanches the morning after the battle counted forty-one men, women and children dead. It is remarkable that none of the prisoners was wounded and it is greatly to be feared that the Christians, who could scarcely be prevented from revenging the death of their relatives upon those who were brought to the mission, glutted their brutal passions on all who fell into their hands.

"The prisoners they had captured were immediately enrolled in the list of the mission, except a nice little boy whose mother was shot while running away with him in her arms, and he was sent to the presidio and, as I heard, given to the Alferez as a reward for his services. The poor little orphan had received a slight wound in his forehead; he wept bitterly at first and refused to eat, but in time became reconciled to his fate.

"Those who were taken to the mission were immediately converted and were daily taught by the neophytes to repeat the Lord's prayer and certain hymns in the Spanish language. I happened to visit the mission about this time and saw these unfortunate beings under tuition. They were clothed in blankets and arranged in a row before a blind Indian, who understood their dialect and was assisted by an alcalde to keep order. Their tutor began by desiring them to kneel, informing them that he was going to teach them the names of the persons composing the trinity and they were to repeat in Spanish what he dictated. The neophytes being arranged, the speaker began: 'Santisima Trinidad, Dios, Jesu Christo, Espiritu Santo,' pausing between each name to listen if the simple Indians, who had never before spoken a word of Spanish, pronounced it correctly or anything near the mark. After they had repeated these names satisfactorily, their blind tutor, after a pause, added 'Santos' and recapitulated the names of a great many saints, which finished the morning's lesson.

"They did not appear to me to pay much attention to what was going forward and I observed to the padre that I thought their teachers had an arduous task, but he said they had never found any difficulty; that the Indians were accustomed to change their own gods and that their conversion was in a measure habitual to them.

"The expenses of the late expedition fell heavily upon the mission and I was glad to find the padre thought it was paying very dear for so few converts, as in all probability it will lessen his desire to undertake another expedition and the poor Indians will be spared the horrors of being butchered by their own countrymen or dragged from their homes into captivity."

This conquista and the results that followed were very similar to some of the so-called Indian wars that took place after the American occupation. The Indians were provoked to hostilities by outrage and injustice. Then the military came down on them and wiped them out of existence.

The unsanitary condition of the Indian villages at some of the missions was as fatal as an Indian war. The Indian was naturally filthy, but in his native state he had the whole country to roam over. If his village became too filthy and the vermin in it too aggressive, he purified it by fire — burned up his wigwam. The adobe houses that took the place of the brush hovel, which made up the early mission villages, could not be burned to purify them. No doubt the heavy death rate at the missions was due largely to the uncleanly habits of the neophytes. The statistics given in the chapter on the Franciscan missions show that in all the missionary establishments a steady decline, a gradual extinction of the neophyte population, had been in progress for two to three decades before the missions were secularized. Had secularization been delayed or had it not taken place in the course of a few decades, at the rate the neophytes were dying off the missions would have become depopulated. The death rate was greater than the birth rate in all of them and the mortality among the children was greater even than among the adults. After secularization the neophytes drifted to the cities and towns where they could more readily gratify their passion for strong drink. Their mission training and their Christianity had no restraining influence upon them. Their vicious habits, which were about the only thing they had acquired by their contact with the whites, soon put an end to them.

During the Spanish and Mexican eras Northern California remained practically a terra incognita. Two missions, San Rafael and San Francisco Solano, and the castillo at Sonora, had been established as a sort of protection to the northern frontier. A few armed incursions had been made into the country beyond these to punish Indian horse and cattle thieves. General Vallejo, who was in command of the troops on the frontera del norte, had always endeavored to cultivate friendly relations with the gentiles, but the padres disliked to have these near the missions on account of their influence on the neophytes. Near the Mission San Rafael, in 1833, occurred one of those Indian massacres not uncommon under Spanish and Mexican rule. A body of gentiles from the rancherias of Pulia, encouraged by Figueroa and Vallejo, came to the Mission San Rafael with a view to establishing friendly relations. The padre put off the interview until next day. During the night a theft was committed, which was charged to the gentiles. Fifteen of them were seized and sent as prisoners to San Francisco. Padre Mercado, fearing that their countrymen might retaliate, sent out his major doma Molina with thirty-seven armed neophytes, who surprised the gentiles in their rancheria, killed twenty-one, wounded many more and captured twenty men, women and children. Vallejo was indignant at the shameful violation of his promises of protection to the Indians. He released the prisoners at San Francisco and the captives at the mission and tried to pacify the wrathful gentiles. Padre Mercado was suspended from his ministry for a short time, but was afterward freed and returned to San Rafael.

There was a system of Indian slavery in existence in California under the rule of Spain and Mexico. Most of the wealthier Spanish and Mexican families had Indian servants. In the raids upon the gentiles the children taken by the soldiers were sometimes sold or disposed of to families for servants. Expeditions were gotten up upon false pretexts, while the main purpose was to steal Indian children and sell them to families for servants. This practice was carried on by the Americans, too, after the conquest.

For a time after the discovery of gold the Indians and the miners got along amicably. The first miners were mainly old Californians, used to the Indians, but with the rush of 49 came many rough characters who, by their injustice, soon stirred up trouble. Sutter had employed a large number of Indians on his ranches and in various capacities. These were faithful and honest. Some of them were employed at his mill in Coloma and in the diggings. In the spring of '49 a band of desperadoes known as the Mountain Hounds murdered eight of these at the mill. Marshall, in trying to defend them, came near being lynched by the drunken brutes.

The injustice done the Indians soon brought on a number of so-called Indian wars. These were costly affairs to the state and in less than two years had plunged the young commonwealth into a debt of nearly $1,000,000. In a copy of the Los Angeles Star for February 28, 1852, I find this enumeration of the wars and the estimated cost of each: The Morehead expedition, $120,000; General Bean's first expedition, $66,000; General Bean's second expedition, $50,000; the Mariposa war, $230,000; the El Dorado war, $300,000. The Morehead war originated out of an injustice done the Yuma Indians. These Indians, in the summer of 1849, had obtained an old scow and established a ferry across the Colorado river below the mouth of the Gila, and were making quite a paying business out of it by ferrying emigrants across the river. A Dr. A. L. Lincoln, from Illinois, had established a

247

ferry at the mouth of the Gila early in 1850. Being short handed he employed eight men of a party of immigrants, and their leader, Jack Glanton, who seems to have been a desperado. Glanton insulted a Yuma chief and the Indians charged him with destroying their boat and killing an Irishman they had employed.

Watching their chance the Yumas killed eleven of the ferrymen, including Lincoln and Glanton. Governor Burnett ordered Major-General Bean to march against the Yumas. Bean sent his quartermaster-general, Joseph C. Morehead. Morehead, on Bean's orders, provided necessaries for a three months' campaign at most extravagant prices, paying for them in drafts on the state treasury. Morehead started out from Los Angeles with forty men, but by the time he reached the Colorado river he had recruited his force to one hundred and twenty-five men. The liquid supplies taken along doubtless stimulated recruiting. They reached the Colorado in the summer of 1850, and camped at the ferry. The Indians at their approach fled up the river. After two months' services they were disbanded. William Carr, one of the three ferrymen who escaped, was wounded and came to Los Angeles for treatment. The doctor who treated him charged the state $500. The man who boarded him put in a bill of $120; and the patriot who housed him wanted $45 for house rent. Bean's first and second expeditions were very similar in results to the Morehead campaign. The El Dorado expedition or Rogers' war, as it was sometimes called, was another of Governor Burnett's fiascos. He ordered William Rogers, sheriff of El Dorado county, to call out two hundred men at the state's expense to punish the Indians for killing some whites who had, in all probability, been the aggressors and the Indians had retaliated. It was well known that there were men in that part of the country who had wantonly killed Indians for the pleasure of boasting of their exploits.

Nor were the whites always the aggressors. There were bad Indians, savages, who killed without provocation and stole whenever an opportunity offered. In their attempts at retaliation the Indians slaughtered indiscriminately and the innocent more often were their victims than the guilty. On the side of the whites it was a war of extermination waged in many instances without regard to age or sex; on the part of the Indian it was a war of retaliation waged with as little distinction.

The extermination of the aborigines was fearfully rapid. Of over ten thousand Indians in Yuba, Placer, Nevada and Sierra counties in 1849 not more than thirty-eight hundred remained in 1854. Much of this decrease had been brought about by dissipation and disease engendered by contact with the whites. Reservations were established in various parts of the state, where Indians abounded, but the large salaries paid to agents and the numerous opportunities for peculation made these positions attractive to politicians, who were both incompetent and dishonest. The Indians, badly treated at the reservations, deserted them whenever an opportunity offered.

A recital of the atrocities committed upon each other in the northwestern part of the state during a period of nearly twenty years would fill a volume. The Indian with all his fiendishness was often outmatched in cruelty by his pale faced brother. The Indian Island massacre was scarcely ever equaled in the annals of Indian cruelties. Indian Island lies nearly opposite the city of Eureka in Humboldt Bay. On this island, fifty years ago, was a large rancheria of inoffensive Indians, who lived chiefly by fishing. They had not been implicated in any of the wars or raids that had disturbed that part of the country. They maintained many of their old customs and had an annual gathering, at which they performed various rites and ceremonies, accompanied by dancing. A number of the Indians from the mainland joined them at these times. Near midnight of February 25, 1860, a number of boats filled with white men sped silently out to the island. The whites landed and quietly surrounded the Indians, who were resting after their orgies, and began the slaughter with axes, knives and clubs, splitting skulls, knocking out brains and cutting the throats of men, women and children. Of the two hundred Indians on the island only four or five men escaped by swimming to the mainland. The same night a rancheria at the entrance of Humboldt Bay and another at the mouth of Eel river were attacked and about one hundred Indians slaughtered. The fiends who committed these atrocities belonged to a secret organization. No rigid investigation was ever made to find out who they were. The grand jury mildly condemned the outrage and there the matter ended.

The Indians kept up hostilities, rendering travel and traffic unsafe on the borders of Humboldt, Klamath and Trinity counties. Governor Stanford in 1863 issued a proclamation for the enlistment of six companies of volunteers from the six northwestern counties of the state. These recruits were organized into what was known as the Mountaineer battalion with Lieut. Col. Stephen G. Whipple in command. A number of Indian tribes united and a desultory warfare began. The Indians were worsted in nearly every engagement. Their power was broken and in February, 1865, fragments of the different tribes were gathered into the Hoopa Valley reservation. The Mountaineer battalion in what was known as the "Two Years' War" settled the Indian question from Shasta to the sea for all time.

The Modoc war was the last of the Indian disturbances in the state. The Modocs inhabited the country about Rhett Lake and Lost river in the northeast part of the state, bordering on Oregon. Their history begins with the massacre of an immigrant train of sixty-five persons, men, women and children, on their way from Oregon to California. This brought upon them a reprisal by the whites in which forty-one out of forty-six Indians who had been invited by Benjamin Wright to a pow wow after they had laid aside their arms were set upon by Wright and his companions with revolvers and all killed but five. In 1864 a treaty had been made with the Modocs by which they were to reside on the Klamath reservation. But tiring of reservation life, under their leader. Captain Jack, they returned to their old homes on Lost river. A company of United States troops and several volunteers who went along to see the fun were sent to bring them back to the reservation. They refused to go and a fight ensued in which four of the volunteers and one of the regulars were killed, and the troops retreated. The Modocs after killing several settlers gathered at the lava beds near Rhett Lake and prepared for war.

Lieutenant-Colonel Wheaton with about four hundred men attacked the Indians in the lava beds January 17, 1873. Captain Jack had but fifty-one men. When Wheaton retreated he had lost thirty-five men killed and a number wounded, but not an Indian had been hurt. A few days after the battle a peace commission was proposed at Washington. A. B. Meacham, Jesse Applegate and Samuel Case were appointed. Elijah Steele of Yreka, who was on friendly terms with the Indians, was sent for. He visited the lava beds with the interpreter, Fairchild, and had a big talk. He proposed to them to surrender and they would be sent to Angel Island

249

near San Francisco, fed and cared for and allowed to select any reservation they wished. Steele, on his return to camp, reported that the Indians accepted the terms, but Fairchild said they had not and next day on his return Steele found out his mistake and barely escaped with his life. Interviews continued without obtaining any definite results, some of the commission became disgusted and returned home. General Canby, commanding the department, had arrived and taken charge of affairs. Commissioner Case resigned and Judge Rosborough was appointed in his place and the Rev. E. Thomas, a doctor of divinity in the Methodist church, was added to the commission. A man by the name of Riddle and his wife Toby, a Modoc, acted as go-betweens and negotiations continued.

A pow wow was arranged at the council tent at which all parties were to meet unarmed, but Toby was secretly informed that it was the intention of the Modocs to massacre the commissioners as had been done to the Indian commissioners twenty years before by Benjamin Wright and his gang. On April 10, while Meacham and Dyer, the superintendent of the Klamath reservation, who had joined the commissioners, were away from camp, the Rev. Dr. Thomas made an agreement with a delegation from Captain Jack for the commission and General Canby to meet the Indians at the council tent. Meacham on his return opposed the arrangement, fearing treachery. The doctor insisted that God had done a wonderful work in the Modoc camp, but Meacham shocked the pious doctor by saying "God had not been in the Modoc camp this winter."

Two of the Indian leaders, Boston Charley and Bogus Charley, came to headquarters to accompany the commission. Riddle and his wife, Toby, bitterly opposed the commissioners' going, telling them they would be killed, and Toby going so far as to seize Meacham's horse to prevent him from going, telling him, "You get kill." Canby and the doctor insisted upon going, despite all protests, the doctor saying, "Let us go as we agreed and trust in God." Meacham and Dyer secured derringers in their side pockets before going. When the commissioners, the interpreters, Riddle and his wife, reached the council tent they found Captain Jack, Schonchin John, Black Jim, Shancknasty Jim, Ellen's Man and Hooker Jim sitting around a fire at the council tent. Concealed behind some rocks a short distance away were two young Indians with a number of rifles. The two Charleys, Bogus and Boston, who had come with the commissioners from headquarters, informed the Indians that the commissioners were not armed. The interview began. The Indians were very insolent. Suddenly, at a given signal, the Indians uttered a war whoop, and Captain Jack drew a revolver from under his coat and shot General Canby. Boston Charley shot Dr. Thomas, who fell, rose again, but was shot down while begging for his life. The young Indians had brought up the rifles and a fusillade was begun upon the others. All escaped without injury except Meacham, who, after running some distance, was felled by a bullet fired by Hooker Jim, and left for dead. He was saved from being scalped by the bravery of Toby. He recovered, however, although badly disfigured. While this was going on, Curly Haired Doctor and several other Modocs, with a white flag, inveigled Lieutenants Boyle and Sherwood beyond the lines. Seeing the Indians were armed, the officers turned to flee, when Curly Haired Jack fired and broke Lieutenant Sherwood's thigh. He died a few days later. The troops were called to arms when the firing began, but the Indians escaped to the lava beds. After a few days' preparation.

Colonel Gillem, who was in command, began an attack on the Indian stronghold. Their position was shelled by mountain howitzers. In the fighting, which lasted four days, sixteen soldiers were killed and thirteen wounded. In a reconnaissance under Captain Thomas a few days later, a body of seventy troops and fourteen Warm Spring Indians ran into an ambush of the Indians and thirteen soldiers, including Thomas, were killed. Gen. Jefferson C. Davis was placed in command. The Indians were forced out of the lava beds, their water supply having been cut off. They quarreled among themselves, broke up into parties, were chased down and all captured. Captain Jack and Schonchin John, the two leaders, were shackled together. General Davis made preparations to hang these and six or eight others, but orders from Washington stopped him. The leading Indians were tried by court-martial. Captain Jack, Schonchin John, Black Jim and Boston Charley were hung, two others were sentenced to imprisonment for life. The other Modocs, men, women and children, were sent to a fort in Nebraska and afterwards transferred to the Quaw Paw Agency in Indian Territory. This ended the Modoc war and virtually put an end to the Modoc Indians.

CHAPTER XXXIV. SOME POLITICAL HISTORY.

The first Chinese emigrants to California arrived in the brig Eagle, from Hong Kong, in the month of February, 1848. They were two men and one woman. This was before the discovery of gold was known abroad. What brought these waifs from the Flowery Kingdom to California does not appear in the record. February 1, 1849, there were fifty-four Chinamen and one Chinawoman in the territory. January 1, 1850, seven hundred and eighty-nine men and two women had arrived. January 1, 1851, four thousand and eighteen men and seven women; a year later their numbers had increased to eight thousand one hundred and twenty-one men and eight women; May 7, 1852, eleven thousand seven hundred and eighty men and seven women had found their way to the land of gold. The Alta California, from which I take these figures, estimated that between seven and ten thousand more would arrive in the state before January 1, 1853. The editor sagely remarks: "No one fears danger or misfortune from their excessive numbers." There was no opposition to their coming; on the contrary, they were welcomed and almost lionized. The Alta of April 27, 1851, remarks: "An American barque yesterday brought eighty worshippers of the sun, moon and many stars. These Celestials make excellent citizens and we are pleased to notice their daily arrival in large numbers." The Alta describes a Great Chinese meeting on Portsmouth Square, which took place in 1851. It seems to have been held for the purpose of welcoming the Chinese to California and at the same time doing missionary work and distributing religious tracts among' them. The report says: "A large assemblage of citizens and several ladies collected on the plaza to witness the ceremonies. Ah Hee assembled his division and Ah Sing marched his into Kearny street, where the two divisions united and then marched to the square. Many carried fans. There were several peculiar looking Chinamen among them. One, a very tall, old Celestial with an extensive tail, excited universal attention. He had a huge pair of spectacles upon his nose, the glasses of which were about the size of a telescope lens. He also had a singularly colored fur mantle or cape upon his shoulders and a long sort of robe. We presume he must be a mandarin at least.

"Vice Consul F. A. Woodworth, His Honor, Major J. W. Geary, Rev. Albert Williams, Rev. A. Fitch and Rev. F. D. Hunt were present. Ah Hee acted as interpreter. The Rev. Hunt gave them some orthodox instruction in which they were informed of the existence of a country where the China boys would never die; this made them laugh quite heartily. Tracts, scriptural documents, astronomical works, almanacs and other useful religious and instructive documents printed in Chinese characters were distributed among them."

I give the report of another meeting of "The Chinese residents of San Francisco," taken from the Alta of December 10, 1849. I quote it to show how the Chinese were regarded when they first came to California and how they were flattered and complimented by the presence of distinguished citizens at their meetings. Their treatment a few years later, when they were; mobbed and beaten in the streets for no fault of theirs except for coming to a Christian country, must have given them a very poor opinion of the white man's consistency. "A public meeting of the Chinese residents of the town was held on the evening of Monday,

November 19, at the Canton Restaurant on Jackson street. The following preamble and resolutions were presented and adopted:

" 'Whereas, It becomes necessary for us, strangers as we are in a strange land, unacquainted with the language and customs of our adopted country, to have some recognized counselor and advisor to whom we may all appeal with confidence for wholesome instruction, and,

" 'Whereas, We should be at a loss as to what course of action might be necessary for us to pursue therefore,

" 'Resolved, That a committee of four be appointed to wait upon Selim E. Woodworth, Esq., and request him in behalf of the Chinese residents of San Francisco to act in the capacity of arbiter and advisor for them.'

"Mr. Woodworth was waited upon by Ah Hee, Jon Ling, Ah Ting and Ah Toon and kindly consented to act. The whole affair passed off in the happiest manner. Many distinguished guests were present, Hon. J. W. Geary, alcalde; E. H. Harrison, ex-collector of the port, and others."

At the celebration of the admission of California into the Union the "China Boys" were a prominent feature. One report says: "The Celestials had a banner of crimson satin on which were some Chinese characters and the inscription 'China Boys.' They numbered about fifty and were arrayed in the richest stuff and commanded by their chief, Ah Sing."

While the "China Boys" were feted and flattered in San Francisco they were not so enthusiastically welcomed by the miners. The legislature in 1850 passed a law fixing the rate of license for a foreign miner at $20 per month. This was intended to drive out and keep out of the mines all foreigners, but the rate was so excessively high that it practically nullified the enforcement of the law and it was repealed in1 851. As the Chinese were only allowed peaceable possession of mines that would not pay white man's wages they did not make fortunes in the diggings. If by chance the Asiatics should happen to strike it rich in ground abandoned by white men there was a class among the white miners who did not hesitate to rob the Chinamen of their ground.

As a result of their persecution in the mines the Chinese flocked to San Francisco and it was not long until that city had more "China Boys" than it needed in its business. The legislature of 1855 enacted a law that masters, owners or consignors of vessels bringing to California persons incompetent to become citizens under the laws of the state should pay a fine of $50 for every such person landed. A suit was brought to test the validity of the act; it was declared unconstitutional. In 1858 the foreign miner's tax was $10 per month and as most of the other foreigners who had arrived in California in the early '50s had by this time become citizens by naturalization the foreigners upon whom the tax bore most heavily were the Chinese who could not become citizens. As a consequence many of them were driven out of the mines and this again decreased the revenue of the mining counties, a large part of which was made up of poll tax and license.

The classes most bitterly opposed to the Chinese in the mines were the saloon-keepers, the gamblers and their constituents. While the Chinaman himself is a most inveterate gambler and not averse to strong drink he did not divest himself of his frugal earnings in the white man's saloon or gambling den, and the gentry who kept these institutions were the first, like Bill Nye in Bret Harte's poem, to raise the cry,

"We are ruined by Chinese cheap labor." While the southern politicians who were the rulers of the state before the Civil war were opposed to the Chinese and legislated against them, it was not done in the interest of the white laborer. An act to establish a coolie system of servile labor was introduced in the pro-slavery legislature of 1854. It was intended as a substitute for negro slavery. Senator Roach, a free state man, exposed its iniquity. It was defeated. The most intolerant and the most bitter opponents of the Chinese then and later when opposition had intensified were certain servile classes of Europeans who in their native countries had always been kept in a state of servility to the aristocracy, but when raised to the dignity of American citizens by naturalization proceeded to celebrate their release from their former serfdom by persecuting the Chinese, whom they regarded as their inferiors. The outcry these people made influenced politicians, who pandered to them for the sake of their votes to make laws and ordinances that were often burlesques on legislation.

In 1870 the legislature enacted a law imposing a penalty of not less than $1,000 nor more than $5,000 or imprisonment upon any one bringing to California any subject of China or Japan without first presenting evidence of his or her good character to the commissioner of immigration. The supreme court decided the law unconstitutional. Laws were passed prohibiting the employment of Chinese on the public works; prohibiting them from owning real estate and from obtaining licenses for certain kinds of business. The supervisors of San Francisco passed an ordinance requiring that the hair of any male prisoner convicted of an offense should be cut within one inch of his head. This, of course, was aimed at Chinese convicts and intended to deprive them of their queues and degrade them in the estimation of their people. It was known as the Pig Tail Ordinance; the mayor vetoed it. Another piece of class legislation by the San Francisco supervisors imposed a license of $15 a quarter on laundries using no horses, while a laundry using a one-horse wagon paid but $2 per quarter. The Chinese at this time (1876) did not use horses in their laundry business. The courts decided against this ordinance.

Notwithstanding the laws and ordinances against them the Chinese continued to come and they found employment of some kind to keep them from starving. They were industrious and economical; there were no Chinese tramps. Although they filled a want in the state, cheap and reliable labor, at the beginning of its railroad and agricultural development, they were not desirable citizens. Their habits and morals were bad. Their quarters in the cities reeked with filth and immorality. They maintained their Asiatic customs and despised the "white devils" among whom they lived, which, by the way, was not strange considering the mobbing and maltreatment they received from the other aliens. They made merchandise of their women and carried on a revolting system of female slavery.

The Burlingame treaty guaranteed mutual protection to the citizens of China and the United States on each other's soil; to freedom in religious opinions; to the right to reside in either country at will and other privileges accorded to civilized nations. Under this treaty the Chinese could not be kept out of California and agitation was begun for the modification or entire abrogation of the treaty.

For a number of years there had been a steady decline in the price of labor. Various causes had contributed to this. The productiveness of the mines had decreased; railroad communication with the east had brought in a number of workmen and increased competition; the efforts of the labor unions to decrease the hours of labor and still keep up the wages at the old standard had resulted in closing up some of the manufacturing establishments, the proprietors finding it impossible to compete with eastern factories. All these and other causes brought about a depression in business and brought on in 1877-78 a labor agitation that shook the foundations of our social fabric. The hard times and decline in wages was charged against the Chinese. No doubt the presence of the Mongolians in California had considerable to do with it and particularly in the lower grades of employment but the depression was mainly caused from over-production and the financial crisis of 1873, which had affected the whole United States. Another cause local to California was the wild mania for stock gambling that had prevailed in California for a number of years. The bonanza kings of the Washoe by getting up corners in stocks running up fraudulent values and then unloading on outside buyers had impoverished thousands of people of small means and enriched themselves without any return to their dupes.

Hard times always brings to the front a class of noisy demagogues who with no remedy to prescribe increase the discontent by vituperative abuse of everybody outside of their sympathizers. The first of the famous sand lot mass meetings of San Francisco was held July 23, 1877, on a vacant lot on the Market street side of the city hall. Harangues were made and resolutions passed denouncing capitalists, declaring against subsidies to steamship and railroad lines, declaring that the reduction of wages was part of a conspiracy for the destruction of the republic and that the military should not be employed against strikers. An anti-coolie club was formed and on that and the two succeeding evenings a number of Chinese laundries were destroyed. In a fight between the police (aided by the committee of safety) and the rioters several of the latter were killed. Threats were made to destroy the railroad property and burn the vessels of the Pacific Mail Steamship Company unless the Chinese in their employ were immediately discharged.

Among the agitators that this ebullition of discontent threw to the front was an Irish drayman named Dennis Kearney. He was shrewd enough to see that some notoriety and political capital could be made by the organization of a Workingmen's party.

On the 5th of October a permanent organization of the Workingmen's party of California was effected. Dennis Kearney was chosen president, J. G. Day, vice-president, and H. L. Knight, secretary. The principles of the party were the condensed essence of selfishness. The working classes were to be elevated at the expense of every other. "We propose to elect none but competent workingmen and their friends to any office whatever." "The rich have ruled us till they have ruined us." "The republic must and shall be preserved, and only workingmen will do it." "This party will exhaust all peaceable means of attaining its ends, but it will not be denied justice when it has the power to enforce it." "It will encourage no riot or outrage, but it will not volunteer to repress or put down or arrest, or prosecute the hungry and impatient who manifest their hatred of the Chinamen by a crusade against John or those who employ him." These and others as irrelevant and immaterial were the principles of the Workingmen's party that was to bring the millennium. The movement spread rapidly, clubs were formed in every ward in San Francisco and there were organizations in all the cities of the state. The original leaders were all of foreign birth, but when the movement became popular native born demagogues, perceiving in it an opportunity to obtain office, abandoned the old parties and joined the new.

Kearney now devoted his whole time to agitation, and the applause he received from his followers pampered his inordinate conceit. His language was highly incendiary. He advised every workingman to own a musket and one hundred rounds of ammunition and urged the formation of military companies. He posed as a reformer and even hoped for martyrdom. In one of his harangues he said: 'If I don't get killed I will do more than any reformer in the history of the world. I hope I will be assassinated, for the success of the movement depends on that." The incendiary rant of Kearney and his fellows became alarming. It was a tame meeting, at which no "thieving millionaire, scoundrelly official or extortionate railroad magnate" escaped lynching by the tongues of laborite reformers. The charitable people of the city had raised by subscription $20,000 to alleviate the prevailing distress among the poor. It was not comforting to a rich man to hear himself doomed to "hemp! hemp! hemp!" simply because by industry, economy and enterprise he had made a fortune. It became evident that if Kearney and his associates were allowed to talk of hanging men and burning the city some of their dupes would put in practice the teachings of their leaders. The supervisors, urged on by the better class of citizens, passed an ordinance called by the sand-lotters "Gibbs' gag law." On the 29th of October, Kearney and his fellow agitators, with a mob of two or three thousand followers, held a meeting on Nob Hill, where Stanford, Crocker, Hopkins and other railroad magnates had built palatial residences. He roundly denounced as thieves the nabobs of Nob Hill and declared that they would soon feel the power of the workingmen. When his party was thoroughly organized they would march through the city and compel the thieves to give up their plunder; that he would lead them to the city hall, clear out the police, hang the prosecuting attorney, burn every book that had a particle of law in it, and then enact new laws for the workingmen. These and other utterances equally inflammatory caused his arrest while addressing a meeting on the borders of the Barbary coast. Trouble was expected, but he quietly submitted and was taken to jail and a few days later Day, Knight, C. C. O'Dormell and Charles E. Pickett were arrested on charges of inciting riot and taken to jail. A few days in jail cooled them off and they began to "squeal." They addressed a letter to the mayor, saying their utterances had been incorrectly reported by the press and that if released they were willing to submit to any wise measure to allay the excitement. They were turned loose after two weeks' imprisonment and their release was celebrated on Thanksgiving Day, November 29, by a grand demonstration of sand letters — seven thousand of whom paraded the streets.

It was not long before Kearney and his fellows were back on the sand lots hurling out threats of lynching, burning and blowing up. On January 5 the grand jury presented indictments against Kearney, Wellock, Knight, O'Donnell and Pickett. They were all released on the rulings of the judge of the criminal court on the grounds that no actual riot had taken place.

The first victory of the so-called Workingmen's party was the election of a state senator in Alameda county to fill a vacancy caused by the death of Senator Porter. An individual by the name of John W. Bones was elected. On account of his being long and lean he was known as Barebones and sometimes Praise God Barebones. His only services in the senate were the perpetration of some doggerel verses and a speech or two on Kearney's theme, "The Chinese Must Go." At the election held June 19, 1878, to choose delegates to a constitutional convention of the one hundred and fifty-two delegates the Workingmen elected fifty-seven, thirty-one of whom were from San Francisco. The convention met at Sacramento, September 28, 1878, and continued to sit in all one hundred and fifty-seven days. It was a mi.xed assemblage. There were some of the ablest men in the state in it, and there were some of the most narrow minded and intolerant bigots there. The Workingmen flocked by themselves, while the non-partisans, the Republicans and Democrats, for the most part, acted in unison. Opposition to the Chinese, which was a fundamental principle of the Workingmen's creed, was not confined to them alone; some of the non-partisans were as bitter in their hatred of the Mongolians as the Kearneyites. Some of the crudities proposed for insertion in the new constitution were laughable for their absurdity. One sand lotter proposed to amend the bill of rights, that all men are by nature free and independent, to read, "All men who are capable of becoming citizens of the United States are by nature free and independent." One non-partisan wanted to incorporate into the fundamental law of the state Kearney's slogan, "The Chinese Must Go."

After months of discussion the convention evolved a constitution that the ablest men in that body repudiated, some of them going so far as to take the stump against it. But at the election it carried by a large majority. Kearney continued his sand lot harangues. In the summer of 1879 he made a trip through the southern counties of the state, delivering his diatribes against the railroad magnates, the land monopolists and the Chinese. At the town of Santa Ana, now the county seat of Orange county, in his harangue he made a vituperative attack upon the McFadden Brothers, who a year or two before had built a steamer and run it in opposition to the regular coast line steamers until forced to sell it on account of losses incurred by the competition. Kearney made a number of false and libelous statements in regard to the transaction. While he was waiting for the stage to San Diego in front of the hotel he was confronted by Rule, an employee of the McFadden's, with an imperious demand for the name of Kearney's informant. Kearney turned white with fear and blubbered out something about not giving away his friends. Rule struck him a blow that sent him reeling against the building. Gathering himself together he made a rush into the hotel, drawing a pistol as he ran. Rule pursued him through the dining room and out across a vacant lot and into a drug store, where he downed him and, holding him down with his knee on his breast, demanded the name of his informer. One of the slandered men pulled Rule off the "martyr" and Kearney, with a face resembling a beefsteak, took his departure to San Diego. From that day on he ceased his vituperative attacks on individuals. He had met the only argument that could convince him of the error of his ways. He lost caste with his fellows. This braggadocio, who had boasted of leading armies to conquer the enemies of the Workingmen, with a pistol in his hand had ignominiously fled from an unarmed man and had taken a humiliating punishment without a show of resistance. His following began to desert him and Kearney went if the Chinese did not. The Workingmen's party put up a state ticket in 1879, but it was beaten at the polls and went to pieces. In 1880 James Angell of Michigan, John

F. Swift of California, and William H. Trescott of South Carolina were appointed commissioners to proceed to China for the purpose of forming new treaties. An agreement was reached with the Chinese authorities by which laborers could be debarred for a certain period from entering the United States. Those in the country were all allowed the rights that aliens of other countries had. The senate ratified the treaty May 5th, 1881.

The following is a list of the governors of California, Spanish, Mexican and American, with date of appointment or election: Spanish: Caspar de Portola, 1767; Felipe Barri, 1771; Felipe de Neve, 1774; Pedro Fages, 1790; Jose Antonio Romeu, 1790; Jose Joaquin de Arrillaga, 1792; Diego de Borica, 1794; Jose Joaquin de Arrillaga, 1800; Jose Arguello, 1814: Pablo Vicente de Sola, 1815. Mexican governors: Pablo Vicente de Sola, 1822; Luis Arguello, 1823; Jose Maria Echeandia, 1825; Manuel Victoria, 1831; Pio Pico, 1832; Jose Maria Echeandia, Agustin Zamorano, 1832; Jose Figueroa, 1833; Jose Castro, 1835; Nicolas Gutierrez, 1836; Mariano Chico, 1836; Nicolas Gutierrez, 1836; Juan B. Alvarado, 1836; Manuel Micheltorena, 1842; Pio Pico, 1845. American military governors: Commodore Robert F. Stockton, 1846; Col. John C. Fremont, January, 1847; Gen. Stephen W. Kearny, March I, 1847; Col. Richard B. Mason, May 31, 1847: Gen. Bennet Riley, April 13, 1849. American governors elected: Peter H. Burnett, 1849. John McDougal, Lieutenant-governor, became governor on resignation of P. H. Burnett in January, 1851: John Bigler, 1851; John Bigler, 1853; J. Neely Johnson, 1855; John B. Weller, 1857; M. S. Latham, 1859; John G. Downey, lieutenant-governor, became governor in 1859 by election of Latham to United States senate; Leland Stanford, 1861; Frederick F. Low, 1863; Henry H. Haight, 1867; Newton Booth, 1871; Romualdo Pacheco, lieutenant governor, became governor February, 1875, on election of Booth to the United States senate; William Irwin, 1875; George C. Perkins, 1879; George Stoneman, 1882; Washington Bartlett, 1886; Robert W. Waterman, lieutenant-governor, became governor September 12, 1887, upon the death of Governor Bartlett; H. H. Markham, 1890; James H. Budd, 1894; Henry T. Gage, 1898; George C. Pardee, 1902; James H. Gillett, 1906.

CHAPTER XXXV. EDUCATION AND EDUCATIONAL INSTITUTIONS.

The Franciscans, unlike the Jesuits, were not the patrons of education. They bent all their energies towards proselyting. Their object was to fit their converts for the next world. An ignorant soul might be as happy in paradise as the most learned. Why educate the neophyte? He was converted, and then instructed in the work assigned him at the mission. There were no public schools at the missions. A few of the brightest of the neophytes, who were trained to sing in the church choirs, were taught to read, but the great mass of them, even those of the third generation, born and reared at the missions, were as ignorant of book learning as were their great-grandfathers, who ran naked among the oak trees of the mesas and fed on acorns.

Nor was there much attention paid to education among the gente de razon of the presidios and pueblos. But few of the common people could read and write. Their ancestors had made their way in the world without book learning. Why should the child know more than the parent? And trained to have great filial regard for his parent, it was not often that the progeny aspired to rise higher in the scale of intelligence than his progenitor. Of the eleven heads of families who founded Los Angeles, not one could sign his name to the title deed of his house lot. Nor were these an exceptionally ignorant collection of hombres. Out of fifty men comprising the Monterey company in 1785, but fourteen could write. In the company stationed at San Francisco in 1794 not a soldier among them could read or write; and forty years later of one hundred men at Sonoma not one could write his name.

The first community want the American pioneers supplied was the school house. Wherever the immigrants from the New England and the middle states planted a settlement, there, at the same time, they planted a school house. The first community want that the Spanish pabladores (colonists) supplied was a church. The school house was not wanted or if wanted it was a long felt want that was rarely or never satisfied. At the time of the acquisition of California by the Americans, seventy-seven years from the date of its first settlement, there was not a public school house owned by any presidio, pueblo or city in all its territory.

The first public school in California was opened in San Jose in December, 1794, seventeen years after the founding of that pueblo. The pioneer teacher of California was Manuel de Vargas, a retired sergeant of infantry. The school was opened in the public granary. Vargas, in 1795, was offered $250 to open a school in San Diego. As this was higher wages than he was receiving he accepted the offer. Jose Manuel Toca, a gamute or ship boy, arrived on a Spanish transport in 1795 and the same year was employed at Santa Barbara as schoolmaster at a yearly salary of $125. Thus the army and the navy pioneered education in California.

Governor Borica, the founder of public schools in California, resigned in 1800 and was succeeded by Arrillaga. Governor Arrillaga, if not opposed to, was at least indifferent to the education of the common people. He took life easy and the schools took long vacations; indeed, it was nearly all vacation during his term. Governor Sola, the successor of Arrillaga, made an effort to establish public schools, but the indifference of the people discouraged him. In the lower pueblo,

Los Angeles, the first school was opened in 1817, thirty-six years after the founding of the town. The first teacher there was Maximo Piña, an invalid soldier. He received $140 a year for his services as schoolmaster. If the records are correct, his was the only school taught in Los Angeles during the Spanish regime. One year of schooling to forty years of vacation, there was no educational cramming in those days. The schoolmasters of the Spanish era were invalid soldiers, possessed of that dangerous thing, a "little learning;" and it was very little indeed. About all they could teach was reading, writing and the doctrina Christiana. They were brutal tyrants and their school government a military despotism. They did not spare the rod or the child, either. The rod was too mild an instrument of punishment. Their implement of torture was a cat-o'-nine-tails, made of hempen cords with iron points. To fail in learning the doctrina Christiana was an unpardonable sin. For this, for laughing aloud, playing truant or other offenses no more heinous, the guilty boy "was stretched face downward upon a bench with a handkerchief thrust into his mouth as a gag and lashed with a dozen or more blows until the blood ran down his little lacerated back." If he could not imbibe the Christian doctrine in any other way, it was injected into him with the points of the lash.

Mexico did better for education in California than Spain. The school terms were lengthened and the vacation shortened proportionally. Governor Echeandia, a man hated by the friars, was an enthusiastic friend of education. "He believed in the gratuitous and compulsory education of rich and poor, Indians and gente de razon alike." He held that learning was the corner-stone of a people's wealth and it was the duty of the government to foster education. When the friars heard of his views "they called upon God to pardon the unfortunate ruler unable to comprehend how vastly superior a religious education was to one merely secular. Echeandia made a brave attempt to establish a public school system in the territory. He demanded of the friars that they establish a school at each mission for the neophytes; they promised, but, with the intention of evading, a show was made of opening schools. Soon it was reported that the funds were exhausted and the schools had to close for want of means to support them. Nor was Echeandia more successful with the people. He issued an order to the commanding officers at the presidios to compel parents to send their children to school. The school at Monterey was opened, the alcalde acting as schoolmaster. The school furniture consisted of one table and the school books were one arithmetic and four primers. The school funds were as meager as the school furniture. Echeandia, unable to contend against the enmity of the friars, the indifference of the parents and the lack of funds, reluctantly abandoned his futile fight against ignorance.

One of the most active and earnest friends of the public schools during the Mexican era was the much abused Governor Micheltorena. He made an earnest effort to establish a public school system in California. Through his efforts schools were established in all the principal towns and a guarantee of $500 from the territorial funds promised to each school. Micheltorena promulgated what might be called the first school law of California. It was a decree issued May 1, 1844, and consisted of ten articles, which prescribed what should be taught in the schools, school hours, school age of the pupils and other regulations. Article 10 named the most holy virgin of Guadalupe as patroness of the schools. Her image was to be placed in each school. But, like all his predecessors, Micheltorena failed; the funds were soon exhausted and the schools closed.

Even had the people been able to read there would have been nothing for them to read but religious books. The friars kept vigilant watch that no interdicted books were brought into the country. If any were found they were seized and publicly burned. Castro, Alvarado and Vallejo were at one time excommunicated for reading Rousseau's works, Telemachus and other books on the prohibited list. Alvarado having declined to pay Father Duran some money he owed him because it was a sin to have anything to do with an excommunicated person, and therefore it would be a sin for the father to take money from him, the padre annulled the sentence, received the money and gave Alvarado permission to read anything he wished.

During the war for the conquest of California and for some time afterwards the schools were all closed. The wild rush to the gold mines in 1848 carried away the male population. No one would stay at home and teach school for the paltry pay given a schoolmaster. The ayuntamiento of Los Angeles in the winter of 1849-50 appointed a committee to establish a school. After a three months' hunt the committee reported "that an individual had just presented himself who, although he did not speak English, yet could he teach the children many useful things; and besides the same person had managed to get the refusal of Mrs. Pollerena's house for school purpose." At the next meeting of the ayuntamiento the committee reported that the individual who had offered to teach had left for the mines and neither a school house nor a schoolmaster could be found.

In June, 1850, the ayuntamiento entered into a contract with Francisco Bustamente, an ex-soldier, "to teach to the children first, second and third lessons and likewise to read script, to write and count and so much as I may be competent to teach them orthography and good morals." Bustamente was to receive $60 per month and $20 for house rent. This was the first school opened in Los Angeles after the conquest.

"The first American school in San Francisco and, we believe, in California, was a merely private enterprise. It was opened by a Mr. Marston from one of the Atlantic states in April, 1847, in a small shanty which stood on the block between Broadway and Pacific streets, west of Dupont street. There he collected some twenty or thirty pupils, whom he continued to teach for almost a whole year, his patrons paying for tuition."

In the fall of 1847 a school house was built on the southwest corner of Portsmouth square, fronting on Clay street. The money to build it was raised by subscription. It was a very modest structure — box shaped with a door and two windows in the front and two windows in each end. It served a variety of purposes besides that of a school house. It was a public hall for all kinds of meetings. Churches held service in it. The first public amusements were given in it. At one time it was used for a court room. The first meeting to form a state government was held in it. It was finally degraded to a police office and a station house. For some time after it was built no school was kept in it for want of funds.

On the 21st of February, 1848, a town meeting was called for the election of a board of school trustees and Dr. F. Fourguard, Dr. J. Townsend, C. L. Ross, J. Serrini and William H. Davis were chosen. On the 3rd of April following these trustees opened a school in the school house under the charge of Thomas Douglas, A. M., a graduate of Yale College and an experienced teacher of high reputation. The board pledged him a salary of $1,000 per annum and fixed a tariff of tuition to aid towards its payment; and the town council, afterwards, to make up any deficiency, appropriated to the payment of the teacher of the public school in this place $200 at the expiration of twelve months from the commencement of the school. "Soon after this Mr. Marston discontinued his private school and Mr. Douglas collected some forty pupils."

The school flourished for eight or ten weeks. Gold had been discovered and rumors were coming thick and fast of fortunes made in a day. A thousand dollars a year looked large to Mr. Douglas when the contract was made, but in the light of recent events it looked rather small. A man in the diggings might dig out $1,000 in a week. So the schoolmaster laid down the pedagogical birch, shouldered his pick and hied himself away to the diggings. In the rush for gold, education was forgotten. December 12,1848, Charles W. H. Christian reopened the school, charging tuition at the rate of $10. Evidently he did not teach longer than it took him to earn money to reach the mines. April 23, 1849, the Rev. Albert Williams, pastor of the First Presbyterian church, obtained the use of the school house and opened a private school, charging tuition. He gave up school teaching to attend to his ministerial duties. In the fall of '49 John C. Pelton, a Massachusetts schoolmaster, arrived in San Francisco and December 26 opened a school with three pupils in the Baptist church on Washington street. He fitted up the church with writing tables and benches at his own expense, depending on voluntary contributions for his support. In the spring of 1850 he applied to the city council for relief and for his services and that of his wife he received $500 a month till the summer of 1851, when he closed his school.

Col. T. J. Nevins, in June, 1850, obtained rent free the use of a building near the present intersection of Mission and Second streets for school purposes. He employed a Mr. Samuel Newton as teacher. The school was opened July 13. The school passed under the supervision of several teachers. The attendance was small at first and the school was supported by contributions, but later the council voted an appropriation. The school was closed in 1851. Colonel Nevins, in January, 1851, secured a fifty-vara lot at Spring Valley on the Presidio road and built principally by subscription a large school building, employed a teacher and opened a free school, supported by contributions. The building was afterwards leased to the city to be used for a free school, the term of the lease running ninety-nine years. This was the first school building in which the city had an ownership. Colonel Nevins prepared an ordinance for the establishment, regulation and support of free common schools in the city. The ordinance was adopted by the city council September 25, 1851, and was the first ordinance establishing free schools and providing for their maintenance in San Francisco.

A bill to provide for a public school system was introduced in the legislature of 1850, but the committee on education reported that it would be two or three years before any means would become available from the liberal provisions of the constitution; in the meantime the persons who had children to educate could do it out of their own pockets. So all action was postponed and the people who had children paid for their tuition or let them run without schooling.

The first school law was passed in 1851. It was drafted mainly by G. B. Lingley, John C. Pelton and the superintendent of public instruction, J. G. Marvin. It was revised and amended by the legislatures of 1852 and 1853. The state school fund then was derived from the sale and rental of five hundred thousand acres of state land: the estates of deceased persons escheated to the state; state poll tax and a state tax of five cents on each $100 of assessed property. Congress in 1853 granted to California the 16th and 36th sections of the public lands for school purposes. The total amount of this grant was six million seven hundred and sixty-five thousand five hundred and four acres, of which forty-six thousand and eighty acres were to be deducted for the founding of a state university or college and six thousand four hundred acres for public buildings.

The first apportionment of state funds was made in 1854. The amount of state funds for that year was $52,961. The county and municipal school taxes amounted to $157,702. These amounts were supplemented by rate bills to the amount of $42,557. In 1856 the state fund had increased to $69,961, while rate bills had decreased to $28,619. That year there were thirty thousand and thirty-nine children of school age in the state, of these only about fifteen thousand were enrolled in the schools.

In the earlier years, following the American conquest, the schools were confined almost entirely to the cities. The population in the country districts was too sparse to maintain a school. The first school house in Sacramento was built in 1849. It was located on I street. C. H. T. Palmer opened school in it in August. It was supported by rate bills and donations. He gathered together about a dozen pupils. The school was soon discontinued. Several other parties in succession tried school keeping in Sacramento, but did not make a success of it. It was not until 1851 that a permanent school was established. A public school was taught in Monterey in 1849 by Rev. Willey. The school was kept in Colton Hall. The first public school house in Los Angeles was built in 1854. Hugh Overns taught the first free school there in 1850.

The amount paid for teachers' salaries in 1854 was $85,860; in 1906 it reached $5,666,045. The total expenditures in 1854 for school purposes amounted to $275,606; in 1906 to $8,727,008. The first high school in the state was established, in San Francisco in 1856. In 1906 there were one hundred and ninety high schools, with an attendance of eighteen thousand eight hundred and seventy-nine students. Four millions of dollars were invested in high school buildings, furniture and grounds, and one thousand teachers were employed in these schools.

The University Of The Pacific.

This institution was chartered in August, 1851, as the California Wesleyan College, which name was afterwards changed by act of the legislature to that it now bears. The charter was obtained under the general law of the state as it then was, and on the basis of a subscription of $27,500 and a donation of some ten acres of land adjacent to the village of Santa Clara. A school building was erected in which the preparatory department was opened in May, 1852, under the charge of Rev. E. Banister as principal, aided by two assistant teachers, and before the end of the first session had over sixty pupils. Near the close of the following year another edifice

263

was so far completed that the male pupils were transferred to it, and the Female Collegiate Institute, with its special course of study, was organized and continued in the original building. In 1854 the classes of the college proper were formed and the requisite arrangement with respect to president, faculty, and course of study made. In 1858 two young men, constituting the first class, received the degree of A. B., they being the first to receive that honor from any college in California. In 1865 the board of trustees purchased the Stockton rancho, a large body of land adjoining the town of Santa Clara. This was subdivided into lots and small tracts and sold at a profit. By this means an endowment was secured and an excellent site for new college building obtained.

The College Of California.

The question of founding a college or university in California had been discussed early in 1849, before the assembling of the constitutional convention at San Jose. The originator of the idea was the Rev. Samuel H. Willey, D. D., of the Presbyterian church. At that time he was stationed at Monterey. The first legislature passed a bill providing for the granting of college charters. The bill required that application should be made to the supreme court, which was to determine whether the property possessed by the proposed college was worth $20,000, and whether in other respects a charter should be granted. A body of land for a college site had been offered by James Stokes and Kimball H. Dimmick to be selected from a large tract they owned on the Guadalupe river, near San Jose. When application was made for a college charter the supreme court refused to give a charter to the applicants on the plea that the land was unsurveyed and the title not fully determined.

The Rev. Henry Durant, who had at one time been a tutor in Yale College, came to California in 1853 to engage in teaching. At a meeting of the presbytery of San Francisco and the Congregational Association of California held in Nevada City in May, 1853, which Mr. Durant attended, it was decided to establish an academy at Oakland. There were but few houses in Oakland then and the only communication with San Francisco was by means of a little steamer that crossed the bay two or three times a day. A house was obtained at the corner of Broadway and Fifth street and the academy opened with three pupils. A site was selected for the school, which, when the streets were opened, proved to be four blocks, located between Twelfth and Fourteenth, Franklin and Harrison streets. The site of Oakland at that time was covered with live oaks and the sand was knee deep. Added to other discouragements, titles were in dispute and squatters were seizing upon the vacant lots. A building was begun for the school, the money ran out and the property was in danger of seizure on a mechanics' lieu, but was rescued by the bravery and resourcefulness of Dr. Durant.

In 1855 the College of California was chartered and a search begun for a permanent site. A number were offered at various places in the state. The trustees finally selected the Berkeley site, a tract of one hundred and sixty acres on Strawberry creek near Oakland, opposite the Golden Gate. The college school in Oakland was flourishing. A new building. Academy Hall, was erected in 1858. A college faculty was organized. The Rev. Henry Durant and the Rev. Martin Kellogg were chosen professors and the first college class was organized in June, 1860. The college classes were taught in the buildings of the college school, which were usually called the College of California. The college classes were small and the endowment smaller. The faculty met with many discouragements. It became evident that the institution could never become a prominent one in the educational field with the limited means of support it could command. In 1863 the idea of a state university began to be agitated. A bill was passed by the state legislature in 1866, devoting to the support of a narrow polytechnical school, the federal land grants to California for the support of agricultural schools and a college of mechanics. The trustees of the College of California proposed in 1867 to transfer to the state the college site at Berkeley, opposite the Golden Gate, together with all the other assets remaining after the debts were paid, on condition that the state would build a University of California on the site at Berkeley, which should be a classical and technological college.

University Of California.

A bill for the establishing of a state university was introduced in the legislature March 5, 1868, by Hon. John W. Dwinelle of Alameda county. After some amendments it was finally passed, March 21, and on the 27th of the same month a bill was passed making an appropriation for the support of the institution.

The board of regents of the university was organized June 9, 1868, and the same day Gen. George B. McClellan was elected president of the university, but at that time being engaged in building Stevens Battery at New York he declined the honor. September 2^, 1869, the scholastic exercises of the university were begun in the buildings of the College of California in Oakland and the first university class was graduated in June, 1873. The new buildings of the university at Berkeley were occupied in September, 1873. Prof. John Le Conte was acting president for the first year. Dr. Henry Durant was chosen to fill that position and was succeeded by D. C. Gilman in 1872. The cornerstone of the Agricultural College, called the South Hall, was laid in August, 1872, and that of the North Hall in the spring of 1873.

The university, as now constituted, consists of Colleges of Letters, Social Science, Agriculture, Mechanics, Mining, Civil Engineering, Chemistry and Commerce, located at Berkeley; the Lick Astronomical Department at Mount Hamilton; and the professional and affiliated colleges in San Francisco, namely, the Hastings College of Law, the Medical Department, the Post-Graduate Medical Department, the College of Dentistry and Pharmacy, the Veterinary Department and the Mark Hopkins Institute of Art. The total value of the property belonging to the university at this time is about $5,000,000 and the endowment funds nearly $3,000,000. The total income in 1900 was $475,254.

Leland Stanford Junior University.

"When the intention of Senator Stanford to found a university in memory of his lamented son was first announced, it was expected from the broad and comprehensive views which he was known to entertain upon the subject, that his plans, when formed, would result in no ordinary college endowment or educational scheme, but when these plans were laid before the people their magnitude was so far beyond the most extravagant of public anticipation that all were astonished at the magnificence of their aggregate, the wide scope of their detail and the absolute grandeur of their munificence. The brief history of California as an American state comprises much that is noble and great, but nothing in that history will compare in grandeur with this act of one of her leading citizens. The records of history may be searched in vain for a parallel to this gift of Senator Stanford to the state of his adoption. * * * By this act Senator Stanford will not only immortalize the memory of his son, but will erect for himself a monument more enduring than brass or marble, for it will be enshrined in the hearts of succeeding generations for all time to come."

Senator Stanford, to protect the endowments he proposed to make, prepared a bill, which was passed by the legislature, approved by the governor and became a law March 9, 1885. It is entitled "An act to advance learning, the arts and sciences and to promote the public welfare, by providing for the conveyance, holding and protection of property, and the creation of trusts for the founding, endowment, erection and maintenance within this state of universities, colleges, schools, seminaries of learning, mechanical institutes, museums and galleries of art."

Section 2 specifies how a grant for the above purposes may be made: "Any person desiring in his lifetime to promote the public welfare by founding, endowing and having maintained within this state a university, college, school, seminary of learning, mechanical institute, museum or gallery of art or any or all thereof, may, to that end, and for such purpose, by grant in writing, convey to a trustee, or any number of trustees named in such grant (and their successors), any property, real or personal, belonging to such person, and situated or being within this state; provided, that if any such person be married and the property be community property, then both husband and wife must join in such grant." The act contains twelve sections. After the passage of the act twenty-four trustees were appointed. Among them were judges of the supreme and superior courts, a United States senator and business men in various lines.

Among the lands deeded to the university by Senator Stanford and his wife were the Palo Alto estate, containing seventy-two hundred acres. This ranch had been devoted principally to the breeding and rearing of thoroughbred horses. On this the college buildings were to be erected. The site selected was near the town of Palo Alto, which is thirty-four miles south from San Francisco on the railroad to San Jose, in Santa Clara county.

Another property donated was the Vina rancho, situated at the junction of Deer creek with the Sacramento river in Tehama county. It consisted of fifty-five thousand acres, of which thirty-six thousand were planted to vines and orchard and the remainder used for grain growing and pasture.

The third rancho given to the support of the university was the Gridley ranch, containing about twenty-one thousand acres. This was situated in Butte county and included within its limits some of the richest wheat growing lands in the state. At the time it was donated its assessed value was $1,000,000. The total amount of land conveyed to the university by deed of trust was eighty-three thousand two hundred acres.

The name selected for the institution was Leland Stanford Junior University. The cornerstone of the university was laid May 14, 1887, by Senator and Mrs. Leland Stanford. The site of the college buildings is about one mile west from Palo Alto.

State Normal Schools

California supports eight State Normal Schools for the education and training of teachers for her public schools. The order and the date of the establishment of these schools are as follows: San Jose (first located in San Francisco), 1862; Los Angeles, 1881; Chico, 1889; San Diego. 1897; San Francisco, 1899; Santa Barbara, 1909; Fresno, 1911; Areata, 1913. The first Normal for the training of teachers was a private institution conducted by Prof. George W. Minns. It was established at San Francisco in 1857. It was discontinued in 1863, at the organization of the first State Normal, Minns becoming principal.

The Legislature of 1862 passed an act authorizing the establishment of a State Normal School "at San Francisco or such other place as the Legislature may hereafter direct." The school was opened in San Francisco in 1863 with an enrollment of five students and a course of study of only one year beyond the grade of the grammar schools. In 1871 the school was removed to San Jose, where a site had been donated. The first building was destroyed by fire. A new site was secured and a large and commodious building erected.

The second Normal School in the state was established by the Legislature at Los Angeles in 1881. An appropriation of $50,000 was made on condition the city donated a site. Several sites were offered. The trustees chose a five-acre orange grove at the head of West Fifth street, for which $7,500, raised by subscription, was paid, the seller reserving the orange crop. At that time the western limit of the settlement of the hill portion of the city ended at Hope street. The corner stone of the building was laid December 17, 1881, Lieutenant Governor Mansfield presiding, and the oration was delivered by Hon. R. F. Del Valle, who had been active in the Legislature in securing the appropriation. A building was erected on Charity street, now Grand avenue.

The school was opened in August, 1882, with an enrollment of sixty-one students — forty-eight women and thirteen men. Vice-Principal C. J. Flatt, Miss Emma L. Hawks and J. Redway constituted the faculty.

In 1884 Prof. Ira More was appointed principal and in 1887 the school was made independent of the parent institution at San Jose and given a board of trustees of its own. An additional building was erected in the rear of the first, more than doubling the capacity of the school buildings. In 1893 Principal Ira More retired and was succeeded by Prof. Edward T. Pierce. With the growth of the city and the contiguous country the number of students increased beyond the capacity of the buildings. Agitation was begun for more buildings, but the little orange grove that thirty years before was deemed ample was now too small for the buildings needed. In 1904 President Edward T. Pierce retired after eleven years' service and was succeeded by President Jesse F. Millspaugh, now head of the institution.

In 1907 the board of trustees was authorized by the Legislature to sell the buildings and grounds for $500,000 and from the proceeds purchase a new site and erect new buildings. In 1911 the Legislature amended the act of 1907 and appropriated $100,000 for the purchase of a new site. October 1, 1912, the old site and buildings were sold to a syndicate for $600,000, the property ultimately to be conveyed to the city of Los Angeles. A site of twenty-five acres was purchased at the corner of Vermont and Willowbrook avenues, at a cost of $110,000, the Legislature having added $10,000 to the original appropriation. The firm of Allison & Allison drew the plans for the buildings and a contract was let to the Alta Planing Mill Company for their erection. The cornerstone of the administration building was laid November 18, 1913. The group of ten buildings was completed in August, 1914, and the school moved into its new quarters in .September following. The buildings are classified as follows: Administration, Library, Domestic Science, Fine Arts, Gymnasium, Training School, Cafeteria, Manual Arts, Science and Kindergarten.

The number of students enrolled in the Normal Department May 1, 1915. was 1,804; in Training School same date was 449. Its faculty numbers eighty-five persons. It is the largest Normal School in the state.

The Santa Barbara Normal is a special school devoted to training in manual arts, home economics and domestic science.

LOS ANGELES AND THE COUNTY

INTRODUCTORY

Under the rule of Spain and Mexico there was no form of municipal government in California corresponding to our county government. The ayuntamientos of the cities and towns exercised jurisdiction over the inhabitants of the adjacent ranches, but there were no lines drawn to define the area of an ayuntamiento's domains. There was no tax on land in those days; the revenue to support the municipal government was derived from fines of offenders against the law, from licenses of pulperias, cock pits, bull fights, dances and so forth. Men's vices and pleasures paid the cost of governing; consequently inhabitants were of more value for income than acres.

During the interregnum that lasted from the downfall of Mexican domination in California to the inauguration of a state government — a period of three years and a half — Mexican laws were continued in force. Alcaldes and regidores administered the ordinances in force before the conquest or made new ones to suit the changed conditions of the country.

The territorial government was semi-military and semi-civil; a form exceedingly unsatisfactory to the American immigrants who had flocked to the country after the discovery of gold. Although the conquerors had adopted the codes and forms of government they found in the country partly to conciliate the conquered, yet the natives were dissatisfied. Military commanders interfered in the administration of law by the alcaldes and regidores and there was friction between the native Californian and the newly arrived gringo.

For three years the people waited for Congress to establish some American form of government for the territory, but none was given them. The admission of California into the Union was a bone of contention between the proslavery and anti-slavery politicians in Congress. At that time the two factions were equally balanced in the senate. To admit it either as a free or a slave state destroyed the political equilibrium, and to the politicians the necessity of maintaining a balance of power was of more importance than the welfare of California. Tired of waiting and driven to desperation by the inchoate condition of affairs in the territory the people organized and put in force a state government without asking authority from Congress. For almost one year California had a de facto state government before it was admitted into the Union.

The first legislature met at San Jose, December 15, 1849. Among the first acts passed by it was one dividing the inchoate state into twenty-seven counties and another providing a form of county government. A large portion of California at that time was a terra incognita. There were no good maps existing. Many of the legislators were recent arrivals in the state and they had vague ideas of the territory they were subdividing. As a result some of the county boundaries were erratic and uncertain.

CHAPTER XXXVI LOS ANGELES COUNTY

The county of Los Angeles, as created by the act of February 18, 1850, did not extend to the Colorado river. For some reason not known the legislature gave San Diego all the desert, making that county "L" shaped. The county of Los Angeles, as created by the act of February 18, 1850, did not contain all of what is now San Bernardino county. The original boundaries of Los Angeles county were defined as follows:

"County of Los Angeles. — Beginning on the coast of the Pacific at the southern boundary of the farm called Trumfo, and running thence along the summit of the ridge of hills called Santa Susana to the northwestern boundary of the farm called San Francisco; thence along the northern and northeastern boundary of said farm of San Francisco to the farm called Piro; thence in a line running due northeast to the summit of the Coast Range; thence along the summit of said range to the western boundary of San Diego county; thence in a due southerly direction along said boundary to the source of the creek San Mateo; thence down said creek San Mateo to the coast and three English miles into the sea; thence in a northwesterly direction parallel with the coast to a point three miles from land and opposite to the southern boundary of the farm called Trumfo; and thence to the shore at said boundary, which was the point of beginning, including the islands of Santa Catalina and San Clemente. The seat of justice shall be Los Angeles."

These boundaries were very indefinite, some portions of the area being included in both counties instead of one, and some of the territory was in no county. No conflict of authority arose. A large portion of both counties was a "terra incognita" — a land where the foot of white man had never trod. The Indians, who inhabited these regions, were of the class that are "not taxed," and any conflict of authority with them was settled by bullets and not by boundary lines.

This act was repealed by an act of the second legislature, passed April 25, 1851, which defined the boundaries of Los Angeles county as follows:

"Section 3, County of Los Angeles. — Beginning on the coast of the Pacific, at a point parallel with the northern boundary of the rancho called Malaga; thence in a direction so as to include said rancho, to the northwest corner of the rancho, known as Trumfo, running on the northerly line of the same to the northeast corner; thence to the summit of the ridge of hills called Santa Susana; thence in a direct line to the rancho Casteyne (Castaic) and Jejon (El Tejon), and along their northern line to the northeastern corners; and thence in a northeast line to the eastern boundary of the state, and along said boundary line to the junction of the northern boundary of San Diego county with the Colorado; thence following said line to the Pacific ocean and three miles therein; thence in a northwesterly direction parallel with the coast to a point three miles from land, and opposite to the southern boundary of the rancho called Malaga, and thence east to the place of beginning; including the islands of Santa Catalina and San Clemente. The seat of justice shall be at Los Angeles."

These boundaries included all the territory that was afterwards included in the county of San Bernardino. In 1851 a colony of Mormons from Salt Lake located where now the city of San Bernardino stands, on a tract of land bought from the Lugos. They were reinforced by other immigrants from Salt Lake and by some non-Mormon families. The settlement grew quite rapidly. These settlers petitioned the legislature of 1853 to create a new county out of the eastern portion of Los Angeles county. By an act entitled, "An Act for dividing the county of Los Angeles and making a new county therefrom to be called San Bernardino county," approved April 26, 1853, it was provided:

"Section 3. The county of Los Angeles is hereby divided as follows: Beginning at a point where a due south line drawn from the highest peak of the Sierra de Santiago intercepts the northern boundary of San Diego county; thence running along the summit of said Sierra to the Santa Ana river, between the rancho of Sierra and the residence of Bernardino Yorba; thence across the Santa Ana river along the summit of the range of hills that lie between the Coyotes and Chino (leaving the ranchos of Ontiveras and Ybarra to the west of this line), to the southeast corner of the rancho of San Jose; thence along the eastern boundaries of said rancho and of San Antonio, and the western and northern boundaries of Cucamonga ranch to the ravine of Cucamonga; thence up said ravine to its source in the Coast Range; thence due north to the northern boundary of Los Angeles county; thence northeast to the state line; thence along the state line to the northern boundary line of San Diego county, thence westerly along the northern boundary of San Diego to the place of beginning.

"Section 4. The eastern portion of Los Angeles county, so cut off, shall be called San Bernardino county and the seat of justice thereof shall be at such a place as a majority of voters shall determine at the first county election, hereinafter provided to be held in said county and shall remain at the place designated until changed by the people, as provided by law."

The county of Los Angeles, before the creation of San Bernardino county, was an empire in itself. It extended from the Pacific ocean on the west to the Colorado river on the east, an extreme length of 270 miles, and from San Diego county on the south to Santa Barbara and Mariposa counties on the north. Its average breadth was 150 miles. Its area was about 34,000 square miles, over one-fifth of the area of the entire state. Excepting Maine it was equal in area to all the New England states. In its vast area it embraced the most diversified scenery, soil and climate of any other county in the United States. Within its limits were the barren sands and torrid heat of the desert; the perpetual ice and snow of the lofty mountain tops; the genial sunshine and fragrant perfume of the orange groves of the valleys, and the unvarying temperature of the sea coast.

The formation of San Bernardino county cut off from Los Angeles 24,000 square miles, leaving her 10,000. For the second time she was cut off from all claim to a portion of the Colorado desert, but still retained her interest in the Mojave.

In 1866, the county of Kern was formed from portions of Tulare and Los Angeles counties. From 1855 to 1860 there had appeared in the legislature proceedings a spectral county called Buena Vista. In 1855 and again in 1859 it had been made a part of the proposed new state of Colorado, which was to include all the country south of San Luis Obispo. The county was never officially created and the territory included in the proposed county remained part of Los Angeles and Tulare counties until the creation of Kern county in 1866. This county took from

Los Angeles about 5,000 square miles, but as this territory was mostly mountains and desert there was no opposition to the segregation.

In 1869 began the struggle to cut off a portion from the southeastern part to form a new county. This movement the people of Los Angeles resisted. The contest over county division lasted for twenty years. It ended in 1889 with the formation of Orange county. The story of this long-drawn-out contest is told in full in the history of Orange county.

After the formation of Orange county Los Angeles had an area of 3,980 square miles. In 1891 an effort was made to cut a slice off the eastern side to form with territory taken from San Bernardino the county of Pomona. Fortunately the scheme failed.

Organization Of The County Government.

The transition from the Mexican form of government in California to that of the United States was very gradual. Los Angeles, the last Mexican stronghold, surrendered January 10, 1847. It was not until June 24, 1850, that the American municipal form of government by county officers superseded the ayuntamientos, alcaldes, prefects and sindicos of Spain and Mexico. The legislature had passed a county government act, February 18, 1850, and had provided for an election of county officers to be held the first Monday of April. The election was held April 1, 377 votes were cast in the county and the following named officers elected:

County judge, Agustin Olvera.
County attorney, Benjamin Hays.
County clerk, B. D. Wilson.
Sheriff, G. Thompson Burrill.
Treasurer, Manuel Garfias.
Assessor, Antonio F. Coronel.
Recorder, Ignacio del Valle.
Surveyor, J. R. Conway.
Coroner, Charles B. Cullen.

Court Of Sessions.

The court of sessions, which consisted of the county judge and two justices of the peace, constituted the legislative body of the county governments of the state up to 1853, when the civil business of the counties was turned over to a board of supervisors, created by an act of the legislature. The court of sessions had jurisdiction over the criminal business, the impaneling of juries and filling vacancies in office up to 1865, when it was legislated out of office.

The court of sessions was the motive power that set the county machinery in operation. The first meeting of the court in Los Angeles was held June 24, 1850. Hon. Agustin Olvera was the presiding judge; the associate justices were Jonathan R. Scott and Luis Robideau. Antonio F. Coronel, assessor-elect, and Charles B. Cullen, coroner-elect, were cited before the court to qualify and file their official bonds. Coronel appeared next day and qualified, but Cullen declined to serve.

At the meeting of the court, June 26, Jailer Samuel Whiting was allowed $7 per day salary, out of which he was to employ a competent assistant. He was allowed "for feeding the prisoners, fifty cents each; that each prisoner shall have per day an amount of bread to the value of twelve and one-half cents or an equivalent in rice or beans; balance of the allowance in good meat."

A. P. Hodges, M. D., was appointed coroner (during his term as coroner he also served as the first mayor of the city). The county judge could not speak English and at least one associate judge spoke no Spanish, so G. Thompson Burrill was appointed county interpreter for the court at a salary of $50 per month. He was also sheriff.

At the session of July 11, 1850. it was ordered that the town council be permitted to work the county prisoners by paying the daily expense of each one's keeping — fifty cents — a master stroke of economy. Some one has sneeringly said that the first public buildings the Americans built in California after it came into their possession, were jails. This was true of Los Angeles, and in fact of all the counties of Southern California.

July II, 1850, commissioners were appointed by the city and county to select a site for a jail. Lots Nos. I, 2, 3, 7, 8 and 9 in square No. 34 (north of the Plaza church) were selected for a jail site. The city council was asked to donate said lots to the county and the city was requested to loan the county $2,000, to be used in building said jail, the city council to have permission to use said jail until the loan is refunded. The city fathers did not take kindly to these requests of the judges; so the county had to worry along two years longer before a jail was built and then it was not built on the site selected by the joint commission.

Judges Of The Plains.

There was one Hispano-American institution that long survived the fall of Mexican domination in California; and that was the office of jueces del campo, judge of the plains. A judge of the plains was a very important functionary.

It was his duty to be present at the annual rodeos (round-ups of cattle) and recojedas (gathering up of horses). His seat of justice was in the saddle, his court room the mesa, and from his decision there was no appeal. All disputes about ownership of stock came before him. The code of his court was unwritten, or mostly so, which was fortunate, for many of the judges could not read. This hap-hazard way of administering justice did not suit American ideas, so, at a meeting of the court of sessions, July 23, 1850, the county attorney was ordered "to collect the various bandos and reglamentos heretofore made up in this district respecting the jueces del campo and give his opinion upon the same at the next term of this court." At the next session of the court, August 22, the county attorney reported a number of regulations, some written, others established by custom. The court added several new regulations to those already existing, the most important of which (to the jueces) was a salary of $100 a year to each judge, payable out of the county treasury. Under Mexican rule the plains judge took his pay in honor. As there were a round dozen of these officials in the county in 1850, their aggregate pay exceeded the entire expense of the municipal government of the district during the last year of the Mexican rule. After jails the next innovation the Americans introduced was taxes.

Fees And Salaries.

The first fee and salary bill of California was based upon prices ruling in the mining counties, where a sheriff's fees amounted to more than the salary of the president of the United States. The liberal fees allowed for official services soon bankrupted the treasuries of the cow counties, and in 1851 they were petitioning the legislature for a reduction of fees. It cost $100 to hold an inquest on a dead Indian and as violent deaths were of almost daily or nightly occurrence, the coroner's office was quite lucrative. Some of the verdicts of the coroner's juries showed remarkable familiarity with the decrees of the Almighty. On a native Californian named Gamico, found dead in the street, the verdict was "Death by the visitation of God." Of a dead Indian, found near the zanja, the Los Angeles Star says: "Justice Dryden and a jury sat on the body. The verdict was 'Death from intoxication or by the visitation of God.' Bacilio was a Christian Indian and was confessed by the reverend padre yesterday afternoon." The jurors were paid $10 each for sitting on a body. Coroner Hodges made the champion record on inquests. October 20, 1851, he held eleven inquests in one day. These were held on Irving's band of horse thieves and robbers, who were killed by the Coahuilla Indians in the San Bernardino mountains.

The criminal element had been steadily increasing in Los Angeles. In 1851 a military company was organized to aid the sheriff in keeping order. November 24, 1851, the court of sessions ordered that the sheriff cause fifty good lances to be made for the use of the volunteer company. The pioneer blacksmith, John Goller, made the lances and was paid $87.50 for the job. Goller also made a branding iron for the county. The county brand consisted of the letters "L. A.," three inches long. In January, 1852, the house occupied by Benjamin Hays, under lease from Felipe Garcia, was sub-let by him to the county for a court house for the balance of his term, expiring November 16, 1853. The sum of $650 was appropriated by order of the court of sessions to pay the rent for the agreed term. The first building used for a court house was the old government house that Pio Pico bought from Isaac Williams for the capitol. Pico had resided in it during his term as governor. After the conquest two companies of United States Dragoons were quartered in it. A contract was let, July 8, 1851, to build a jail and John G. Nichols appointed at $6 a day to superintend the job, but some misunderstanding with the city arising, the building was not erected, and September 13, 1851, the court ordered the sheriff to sell the adobes now on hand for use of jail at the highest market price and turn the money over to the clerk of the court.

The first county jail was the adobe building on the hill back of the present post office site used by the troops for a guard house. There were no cells in it. Staples were driven into a heavy pine log that reached across the building, and short chains attached to the staples were fastened to the handcuffs of the prisoners. Solitary confinement was out of the question then. Indian culprits were chained to logs outside of the jail so that they could more fully enjoy the glorious climate of California. In 1853 the city and county built a jail on die present site of the Phillips block, northwest corner of Spring and Franklin streets. It was the first public building erected in the county.

The legislature of 1852 created the office of county supervisor. The first election for supervisors of the county was held June 14, 1852, and the following named persons elected: Jefferson Hunt, Julian Chavis, Francisco P. Temple, Manuel Requena and Samuel Arbuckle. The board held its first meeting on the first Monday of July, 1852. Arbuckle was elected chairman. The supervisors transacted the civil business of the county.

The machinery of the county's government was now in full working order. We will turn our attention to other phases of its development.

Spanish And Mexican Land Grants.

In what comprised the original county of Los Angeles there were during the Spanish and Mexican regimes sixty grants of land made. These varied in size from a grant of 44.36 acres to the Mission of San Juan Capistrano to the Rancho ex-Mission of San Fernando, granted to Eulogio de Cells, containing 121,619.24 acres.

At the time of the conquest about all the land fit for pasturage had been sequestered from the public domain in the form of grants. The oldest grants made within what is now the county of Los Angeles are the Nietos and the San Rafael. According to Col. J. J. Warner's historical sketch, "The Nietos tract, embracing all the land between the Santa Ana and San Gabriel and from the sea to and including some of the hill land on its northeastern frontier, was granted by Governor Pedro Fages to Manuel Nietos in 1784.

"The San Rafael tract, lying on the left bank of the Los Angeles river and extending to the Arroyo Seco, was granted by Governor Pedro Fages, October 20, 1784, and the grant was reaffirmed by Governor Borica, January 12, 1798, to Jose Maria Verdugo." If as Colonel Warner claims, the "Nietos tract" embraced all the land between the Santa Ana and the San Gabriel rivers, from the sea to the hills, Nietos' heirs did not hold it. Subsequently, there was a number of grants made in that territory. The Mission San Gabriel, previous to 1830, had possession of several subdivisions of this tract such as Las Bolsas, Alamitos, Los Coyotes, Puente and others. After the secularization of the missions all the lands held by the padres, except small tracts in the immediate neighborhood of the mission buildings, were granted to private owners.

Shortly after the admission of California to the Union the long-drawn-out legal contests over the confirmation of the Spanish and Mexican grants began. These contests, in some cases, were waged for years before the United States claims commission, the various courts and the land commissioner at Washington, before they were settled. Litigation often ruined both the contesting parties, and when the case was finally decided the litigants, like in "Jarndyce vs. Jarndyce," had nothing left but their bundles of legal documents. Even when a claimant did win and the decisions of courts and commissions gave him undisputed possession of his broad acres, it often happened that a cancerous mortgage, the result of litigation, was eating away his patrimony. The land grants in Los Angeles have all been confirmed and it is to be hoped that they will remain so. No greater blight can fall on a community than an attack upon the validity of its title to its lands.

275

In early times the county officials followed the Mexican plan of designating districts and legal subdivision by ranchos. August 7, 1851, the court of sessions "ordered that the county of Los Angeles be divided into six townships named as follows, and to comprehend the ranchos and places as follows to each appropriated": The first of these was the township of Los Angeles. There are few now living who could trace from the description given in the records the boundaries of Los Angeles township fifty-five years ago. Here is the description:

Township of Los Angeles. "The city of Los Angeles and the following ranchos, to-wit: Los Corralitos, Feliz, Verdugos, Cahunga, Tujunga, San Fernando, ex-Mission, San Francisco, Piro, Camulos, Cañada de los Alamos, La Liebre, El Tejon, Trumfo, Las Vergenes, Escorpion, Los Cuervos, San Antonio de la Mesa, Los Alamitos, Vicente Lugo, Arroyo Seco, Encino, Maligo, Santa Monico, San Vicente, Buenos Ayres, La Bayona, Rincon de los Buey, Rodeo de Las Aguas, La Cienega, La Centinela, Sausal Redondo, Palos Verdes, San Pedro, Los Dominguez, Rancho Nuevo, Paredon Blanco, Los Cerritos. La Jaboneria, Rosa de Castilla."

"The residence of the authorities shall be in Los Angeles city."

Immigrants And Immigrant Routes.

The Sonorese or Sonoran migration began in 1848, as soon as the news of the discovery of gold in California reached Mexico. While these gold-seekers were called Sonorese or Sonorans, they came from the different states of northern Mexico, but in greater numbers from Sonora. The trail from Mexico by way of Aristo, Tucson, the Pima villages, across the desert and through the San Gorgonio Pass had been traveled for three-quarters of a century. Another branch of this trail crossed the desert from Yuma to Warner's ranch; and then by way of Temecula, Jurupa and the Chino, reached Los Angeles. Along these trails from 1848 to 1852 came the Sonorese migration. The extent of this migration was much greater than historians usually consider it. When Dr. Lincoln and ten of his ferrymen were massacred at the Yuma crossing of the Colorado river, one of the ferrymen who escaped stated in his deposition taken by Alcalde Stearns that Lincoln had $50,000 in silver and between $20,000 and $30,000 in gold. This was the proceeds of the ferry secured in less than four months almost entirely from the Sonoran immigrants. The charge for ferrying was $1 for a man, $1 for an animal and the same for a pack or mule cargo. The influx of these people in 1848, 1849 and 1850 must have reached 25.000 a year. These pilgrims to the shrine of Mammon were for the most part a hard lot. They were poor and ignorant and not noted for good morals. From Los Angeles northward, they invariably traveled by the coast route, and in squads of from 50 to 100. Some of them brought their women and children with them. With their few possessions packed on donkeys and mules they tramped their weary way from Mexico to the mines. They were not welcomed to the land of gold. The Americans disliked them and the native Californians treated them with contempt. The men wore cotton shirts, white pantaloons, sandals and sombreros. Their apparel, like the laws of the Medes and Persians, "changed not," nor did they change it as long as a shred of it held together. The native Californians nick-named them "calzonares blancos" (white breeches), and imposed upon them when an opportunity offered. The story is told of a native Californian alcalde or justice of the peace who had his office near the old mission church of San Luis Obispo. When a band of these Sonoran pilgrims came along the highway which led past the old mission, they invariably stopped at the church to make the sign of the cross and to implore the protection of the saints. This gave the alcalde his opportunity. Stationing his alguaciles or constables on the road to bar their progress, he proceeded to collect fifty cents toll off each pilgrim. If word was passed back to the squads behind and they attempted to avoid the toll-gatherer by a detour to the right or left, the alcalde sent out his mounted constables and rounded up the poor Sonorans like so many cattle at a rodeo, then he and his alguaciles committed highway robbery on a small scale. Retributive justice overtook this unjust judge. The vigilantes hanged him, not, however, for tithing the Sonorese, but for horse stealing.

The Sonoran migration began to decline after 1850, and entirely ceased a year or two later. The foreign miner's tax and their persecution by the Americans convinced the Sonorans that there was no place like home. So they went home and stayed there.

A route by which a number of immigrants from Texas and some of the other gulf states came in 1849 through the northern states of Mexico until it intercepted the Sonora trail and then by that to Los Angeles.

The old Santa Fe trail to New Mexico, then across Arizona, following the Gila to the Colorado river, was another southern route by which a great deal of overland travel reached Southern California. In 1854, from actual count, it was ascertained that 9,075 persons came by that route. About one-fourth of the 61,000 overland immigrants who came to the state that year reached it by the southern routes. But the route by which the majority of the Argonauts of '49 and the early '50s reached Southern California led south from Salt Lake City until it intercepted the great Spanish trail from Los Angeles to Santa Fe at the southern end of Utah Lake. Immigrants by this route, crossing the Colorado desert, reached the San Bernardino valley through the Cajon pass. Capt. Jedediah S. Smith, in 1826, was the first white man to reach Los Angeles by this trail. There was considerable trade and travel between Santa Fe and Los Angeles over the old Spanish trail before the conquest of California. The early immigration from New Mexico came by this route. By it came J. J. Warner, William Wolfskill, the Rowland-Workman party, numbering forty-four persons; B. D. Wilson, D. W. Alexander, John Reed, Dr. John Marsh and many other pioneers. For several years before the conquest, on account of the hostility of the Indians, this trail had been little used, and to the great many of the Argonauts who crossed the plains in 1849 it was unknown. The belated immigrants of that year who reached Salt Lake too late to cross the Sierra Nevadas had the alternative presented them of wintering with the Saints or of finding a southern route into California and thus evading the fate that befell the Donner party in the snows of the Sierras. These delayed Argonauts found a Mormon captain, Jefferson Hunt, late captain of Company A of the Mormon Battalion, who had recently arrived in Salt Lake by this southern route. He was engaged as a guide. A train of about 500 wagons started in November, 1849, for Southern California. After several weeks' travel, a number of the immigrants having become dissatisfied with Hunt's leadership, and hearing that there was a shorter route to the settlements than the train was pursuing, seceded from the main body and struck out westward across the desert. After traveling for several days together, they disagreed. Some returned to the main body; the others broke up into small parties and took different directions.

One of these parties, numbering eleven persons, penetrated Death valley and all perished. Another, after incredible hardships and after losing several of their number on the desert, reached Los Angeles by the Soledad pass. Another company, after weeks of wandering and suffering, reached the Tulare valley, where they were relieved by the Indians. The main body, with but little inconvenience, arrived in San Bernardino valley the last of January, 1850.

After the establishment of the Mormon colony at San Bernardino, in June, 1851, the Salt Lake route became a well-traveled road, over which, up to the completion of the Union Pacific Railroad in 1869, a large amount of freight and travel passed between the City of the Saints and the City of the Angels. By this route came a number of the pioneer American families of Los Angeles. Among others may be named the Macys, Andersons, Workmans, Ulyards, Hazards, Montagues.

Ox Carts, Stages And Steamers.

San Pedro was, in 1850, as it had been for more than half a century before, the entrepot through which the commerce of the Los Angeles district passed. It was, next to San Francisco, the principal seaport of the coast. In the early '50s all the trade and travel up and down the coast came and went by sea. No stage lines had been established in the lower coast counties. In 1848, and for several years after, the only means of getting to the city from the port and vice versa was on horseback. A caballada (band) of horses was kept in pasture on the Palos Verdes for this purpose.

In 1849 Temple & Alexander had a general merchandise store at San Pedro, and did about all the forwarding business of the port. Goods were freighted to Los Angeles in carts drawn by two yoke of oxen yoked by the horns. The carts were similar to the Mexican carretas, except that they had spoked and tired wheels instead of solid ones. A regular freight train was composed of ten carts and forty oxen. Freight charges were $20 a ton. In 1852 stages were put on the route by Banning & Alexander. Tomlinson put on an opposition line, and in 1853 B. A. Townsend was running an accommodation line between the city and the port and advertising in the Star, "Good coaches and teams as the county will afford." The stage fare was at first $10, then $7.50, dropped to $5, and as opposition increased went down to $1, and as the rivalry grew keener passengers were carried free.

The first steamer that ever entered the bay of San Pedro was the Gold Hunter, which anchored in the port in 1849. She was a side-wheel vessel which had made the voyage from San Francisco to Mazatlan, stopping at way ports.

The Gold Hunter was followed by the steamers Ohio, Southerner, Sea Bird and Goliah in 1850 and 1851. In 1853 the Sea Bird was making three trips a month between San Francisco and San Diego, touching at Monterey, Santa Barbara and San Pedro. The price of a first-class passage from San Pedro to San Francisco m the early '50s was $55. The bill of fare consisted of salt beef, hard bread, potatoes and coffee without milk or sugar. Freight charges were $25 a ton. It cost $10 to

278

transport a barrel of flour from San Francisco to Los Angeles. The trip occupied four days. The way ports were Santa Barbara, San Luis Obispo and Monterey. There were no wharves or lighters on the route; passengers and freight were landed in the steamer's boats. If the sea was very rough the passengers were carried to San Francisco and brought back on the return trip. Sometimes, when the tide was low, they had to be carried from the boat to the shore on the sailors' backs. The sailor, like the bronco, sometimes bucked, and the passenger waded ashore. Both man and beast were somewhat uncertain "in the days of gold — the days of '49."

The imports by sea greatly exceeded the exports. Cattle and horses, the principal products of the county, transported themselves to market. The vineyards along the river, principally within the city limits, were immensely profitable in the early '50s. There was but little fresh fruit in the country. Grapes, in San Francisco, retailed all the way from twenty-five to fifty cents a pound. The vineyards were cultivated by Indian labor. About all that it cost the vineyardist for labor was the amount of aguardiente that it took to give the Indian his regular Saturday night drunk. So the grape crop was about all profit.

FIRST STATE census.

The first state census of California was taken in 1852: According to this census the county had a total population of 7,831, divided as follows:

Whites.

Males	.2,496
Females	1,597
Total	4,093

Domesticated Indians.

Males	.2,278
Females	.1,415
Total	.3,693

The cattle numbered 113,475; horses, 12,173; wheat produced, 34,230 bushels; barley, 12,120 bushels; corn, 6,934 bushels. Number of acres under cultivation, 5,587; grape vines, 450;000, of which 400,000 were within the city. This was before any portion of the county had been segregated

Its limits extended from San Juan Capistrano on the south to the Tulares on the north, and from the sea to the Colorado river; of its 34,000 square miles, less than nine square miles were cultivated, and yet it had been settled for three-quarters of a century. During the '50s the county grew slowly. Land was held in large tracts and cattle-raising continued to-be the principal industry. At the El Monte several families from the southwestern states had formed a. small settlement and were raising grain, principally com. The Mormons, at San Bernardino, were raising corn, wheat, barley and vegetables, and selling them at a good price. One season they received as high as $5 a bushel for their wheat.

279

CHAPTER XXXVII. GROWTH OF LOS ANGELES COUNTY AND CITY IN WEALTH AND POPULATION.

Under the rule of Spain and Mexico there was no assessment of real estate and personal property for the purpose of taxation. Tariff on goods imported, fines for drunkenness and other vices, licenses for dances, for saloons, for stores, for cock pits, bull rings and such afforded the revenues for municipal expenses. Men's pleasures and vices paid for the cost of governing. The pueblo's expenses were light. The only salaried officials in the old pueblo days were the secretary of the ayuntamiento, or town council, and the schoolmaster. The highest salary paid the secretary was $40 per month. The schoolmaster's pay was fixed at $15 per month. If he asked for more he lost his job. The largest municipal revenue collected in one year by the syndico of the pueblo was $1,000. The syndico and the alcalde received fees for their services. All this was changed when the Americans took possession of the offices; and they were not backward in coming forward when there were offices to fill. In the first list of county officers the names of only two native Californians appear — Don Agustin Olvera, county judge, and Don Antonio F. Coronel, county assessor. Coronel was elected assessor at the first county election, held April 1, 1850. As nine-tenths of the residents of the newly created county of Los Angeles understood the Spanish language only, it was highly necessary to have some one who spoke their language to explain to them the new system of taxation introduced by the conquerors.

If Don Antonio made an assessment for the year 1850 I have been unable to find any record of it. The first report of the amount of the county assessment that I have found is that for 1851, in which the wealth of the county is estimated at $2,882,949. The first county assessment roll in existence is one made by Don Antonio F. Coronel in 1852. It is written on unruled sheets of Spanish foolscap pasted together into leaves two feet long and stitched into a book of 34 pages, covered with blue calico. This one book constituted the entire assessment roll for that year. The following are the principal items of that assessment:

Number of acres assessed 1,505,180
Value of real estate $748,606
Value of improvements 301,947
Value of personal property 1,183,898
Total $2,234,451

The county at that time contained over thirty million acres and only one in twenty was assessed. The average value was less than fifty cents per acre. The county then extended from San Juan Capistrano on the south to Tehachapi on the north, and from the Pacific ocean to the Colorado river. Don Antonio's district exceeded in extent the aggregate area of five New England states. By far the larger part of its inhabitants were "Indians not taxed." It is not probable that Don Antonio traveled over the vast territory of the thinly populated county. Los Angeles was the only city in the county and doubtless the inhabitants, like those in the days of old, when Herod was reducing the infant population of Judea, "went up to the city to be taxed." The assessment roll for 1853 footed up $3,030,131, which showed a rapid rise in values or that Don Antonio was becoming more expert in finding property. The assessor's report for the fiscal year ending November 29, 1856, is the first one in which the city valuation is segregated from the county: Total number of acres in the county

assessed 1,003,930
Value of county real estate $ 402,219
Value of county improvements 230,336
Value of city real estate 187,582
Value of city improvements 457.535
Value of personal property 1,213,079
Total $2,490,751

San Bernardino county had been cut off from Los Angeles at this time and had evidently taken away half a million acres of assessable land from the parent county. The value of county real estate had dropped to forty cents per acre. The assessment for 1S66 was as follows:

Total value of real estate and improvements $1,149,267
Total value of personal property 1,204,125
Total $2,353,392

Comparing the assessment of 1866 with that of 1856 it will be seen that not only was there no increase in the property values of the county in ten years, but actually a falling off of over $140,000. This is accounted for by the great loss of stock during the famine years of 1863-64.

The county assessment for 1864 was $1,622,370, about two millions less than the assessment of 1862. This represents the loss in cattle, horses and sheep during the great drought of two years when the rainfall was not sufficient to sprout the grass seeds. The greatest financial depression the county has ever known occurred during these years. The people after the loss of their stock had nothing that they could sell. Land had no value. A judgment for $4,070 on account of delinquent taxes of 1863 was entered up against the richest man in the county and all his real estate and personal property advertised for sale at public auction December 12, 1864. The magnificent Rancho de Los Alamitos, containing over 26,000 acres, was advertised for sale on account of unpaid taxes, amounting in all to $152. The Bolsas Chico, containing nearly 9,000 acres "on which there is due and unpaid the sum of $27.34, I have this day levied on and shall sell all the right, title and interest of the defendant for cash, to the highest bidder in gold and silver coin of the United States," so said the sheriff's advertisement. But, of all the vast possessions of the great cattle barons advertised for sale on account of unpaid taxes forty-two years ago, the least valued parcel then is the most valuable now. This consisted of four Ord survey lots, 120x165 foot each, located respectively on the northwest and southwest corners of Main and Fifth, the southwest corner of Spring and the southeast corner of Fort street, now Broadway, and Fourth street. These magnificent business corners, worth to-day two million dollars, were offered at sheriff's sale December 12, 1864, for the beggarly sum of $2.52 unpaid taxes and there were no takers. The tax on each lot was sixty-three cents and the assessed value about twenty-five cents a front foot or $30 a lot. "

The county recovered slowly from the great disaster of the famine years. It was six years before the county assessments equaled the amount of that of the years preceding the great drought. The subdivision of the great ranchos which induced immigration was largely instrumental in causing the return of prosperity to the financially depressed county. Sheep husbandry succeeded the cattle industry and in the closing years of the '60s was very profitable. The second great drought which occurred in 1877 put a check upon this industry from which it never recovered. The loss to the shepherd kings of the county was over a million dollars. Some of the great land holders who had held their ranchos intact subdivided them after the last great drought. For thirty years the growth of the county in population and wealth has been uninterrupted by any great disaster. During the great real estate boom of 1887-88 property values increased $62,000,000 in two years. The county assessment made in March, 1886, before inflation began, gave the wealth of the county at $40,091,820; that of March, 1888, made before reaction commenced, was $102,701,629. Never in the world's history did people grow rich so rapidly. In 1890, when financial depression had reached its deepest depth, adding the value of the property taken from the roll by the segregation of Orange county the assessment showed that the county was still worth $82,000,000, a contraction of $20,000,000 in values in two years.

From 1890 to the close of the century there was a slow but steady increase in wealth averaging about two millions a year. The assessment is not an infallible index of true values. Assessors are sometimes incompetent and state boards of equalization are not always impartial in equalizing the burthens of taxation.

The most rapid permanent increase in values has been during the beginning years of the present century. The county assessment, as will be seen by the accompanying table, has increased from $100,000,000 in 1900 to $305,000,000 in 1906. An increase of over three hundred percent. This is largely due to the rapid growth of the cities and towns in the county. Thousands of acres of farming land have been cut up into city lots and selling value advanced in some cases a thousand per cent. During the years of the present century, judging from the county assessment returns, the people have grown rich almost as rapidly as they did in the booming days of the later '80s. In the March, 1900, assessment the county's wealth was estimated at $100,136,070. Five years later, March, 1905, it footed up $232,610,753, an increase of 132 per cent in half a decade. The assessment for March, 1906, is $305,302,995, an increase of over 30 per cent in one year. A study of the annexed table will show fairly well the periods of prosperity and adversity through which Los Angeles has passed in the fifty-five years since the county was created. In some instances, however, the sudden rise in the assessed valuation is not due to a rapid increase in the county's wealth, but to the incompetency of the individual or individuals making the assessment. For instance, the assessment of 1896 showed an increase of $15,000,000 over that of 1905, while the assessment of 1897 showed a loss of $7,000,000 as compared with 1896. No such fluctuation

282

really occurred. The following table gives the county assessment at different periods from 1851 to 1906, both inclusive:

Total County Assessment (incl. railroad)

1851	$ 2,282,949
1852	2,234,451
1853	3,030,131
1856	2,490,750
1858	2,370,523
1860	3,650,330
1864	1,622,370
1867	2,556,083
1868	3,764,045
1869	5,797,171
1870	6,918,074
1871	6,358,022
1872	9,147,073
1873	9,845,593
1874	12,085,110
1875	14,890,765
1876	14,844,322
1878	1 5,700,000
1880	18,503,773
1882	20,916,835
1883	26,138,117
1884	30,922,290
1885	35,344,483
1886	40,091,820
1887	89,833,506
1888	102,701,629
1889	93,647,086
1890	69,475,025
1891	82,616,577
1892	82,839,924
1893	77,244,050
1894	79,495,921
1895	84,797,196
1896	99,520,611
1897	92,580,978
1898	93,256,089
1899	98,391,783
1900	100,136,070
1901	103,328,904
1902	1 13,976,897
1903	169,226,936
1904	201,509,786
1905	232,610,753

1906 305,302,995
1907 375,719,358

City Assessments.

Up to 1860 the city assessments seem to have been included in the county. The assessed value of the city's real estate and improvements were segregated, but the values of the personal property were "lumped" on the roll.

During the fiscal year of 1863-64, when calamities were affecting the city in the shape of a dry year and a fearful epidemic of small-pox, there seems to have been no city assessment made, as there was almost no value in real estate and it was impossible to collect delinquent taxes by selling land, for the reason that nobody wanted any. The city fathers, no doubt, considered it a stroke of economy to get along without an assessment.

The following gives the city assessments from 1860 to 1906, both inclusive:
Total Assessment for Each Fiscal Year.

1860-61 . . . .$1,425,648
1861-62 1,299,719
1862-63 1,098,469
1863-64 . . . .
1864-65 878,718
1865-66 989,413
1866-67 . . . .
1867-68 1,271,290
1868-69 . . . .
1869-70 2,108,061
1870-71 . . . .
1871-72 2,134,093
1872-73 4,191,996
1873-74 3,816,679
1874-75 4,589,746
1875-76 5,935,219
1876-77 5,291,148
1877-78 5,871,881
1878-79 5,947,580
1879-80 6,871,913
1880-81 7,259,598
1881-82 7,574,926
1882-83 9,294,074
1883-84 12,232,353
1884-85 14,781,865
1885-86 16,273,535
1886-87 18,448,535
1887-88 27,803,924
1888-89 . . . . 39.476,712
1889-90 46,997,101

284

```
1890-91 . . . . . . . . . . . . . . . . . . . . . 49,320,670
1891-92 . . . . . . . . . . . . . . . . . . . . . 45,953,704
1892-93 . . . . . . . . . . . . . . . . . . . . . 45,310,807
1893-94 . . . . . . . . . . . . . . . . . . . . . 47,281,778
1894-95 . . . . . . . . . . . . . . . . . . . . . 47,396,165
1895-96 . . . . . . . . . . . . . . . . . . . . . 48,814,145
1896-97 . . . . . . . . . . . . . . . . . . . . . 52,242,302
1897-98 . . . . . . . . . . . . . . . . . . . . . 52,140,293
1898-99 . . . . . . . . . . . . . . . . . . . . . 60,930,266
1899-1900 . . . . . . . . . . . . . . . . . . . . 64,915,326
1900-01 . . . . . . . . . . . . . . . . . . . . . 67,576,047
1901-02 . . . . . . . . . . . . . . . . . . . . . 70,562,307
1902-03 . . . . . . . . . . . . . . . . . . . . . 86,416,735
1903-04 . . . . . . . . . . . . . . . . . . . . . 1o9,983,823
1904-05 . . . . . . . . . . . . . . . . . . . . . 126,126,563
1905-06 . . . . . . . . . . . . . . . . . . . . . 156,661,566
1906-07 . . . . . . . . . . . . . . . . . . . . . 205,767,729
```

Banks Of Los Angeles City.

The first bank in Los Angeles city and county was organized early in 1868 by Alvinza Hayward of San Francisco and John G. Downey of Los Angeles under the firm name of Hayward & Company, capital, $100,000. The banking rooms were in the old Downey block recently demolished to give place to the new post office. Later in the same year the banking house of Hellman, Temple & Co. was established. Hellman afterwards became associated with Downey in the former bank, which took the name of The Farmers & Merchants' Bank. The latter bank was reorganized as the Temple & Workman Bank. Its banking house was in the then newly erected three-story building at the junction of North Spring and Main streets. It was a very popular bank and carried large deposits. In the crisis of 1875, when nearly every bank in the state closed its doors for a time, the Temple & Workman Bank temporarily suspended. It made an attempt to resume business, but a short run upon it closed it forever. Its failure was a terrible disaster to the southern country. Its creditors lost all their deposits. So complete was its collapse that $300,000 of its assets were sold by the receiver under an order of Judge Hoffman of the United States Court for $30. The bank had been woefully mismanaged.

The second bank in point of age is the First National, organized as the Commercial Bank in 1875. It recently absorbed the Los Angeles National and the Southwestern National. To give a history of all the banking institutions of Los Angeles would occupy more space than I have at my command. At the close of the year 1906 Los Angeles had an even half hundred banking institutions. Of these nine operate under national charter, fourteen under state charter, five are trust companies and thirteen savings banks. There are several commercial corporations doing a banking business. The paid-in capital stock of all the banks of Los Angeles city at the close of the year 1906 was estimated at $11,183,133, the deposits exceeded $100,000,000. The remarkable growth of Los Angeles in recent years in

285

population, business and commercial importance is well illustrated by a comparison of the yearly totals of exchanges.

The following are the clearing house totals for the past ten years:

1897 . . . . $63,663,969
1898 74,413,508
1899 90,261,931
1900 122,692,555
1901 161,466,671
1902 245,516,094
1903 307,316,530
1904 345,343,956
1905 479,985,298
1906 578,635,517

Population Of Los Angeles City.

1781 (founded) . . . . Official 44
1790 . . . ." 141
1800 . . . ." 315
1810 . . . ." 415
1820 . . . ." 650
1830 . . . . .estimated. 770
1840 . . . . " 1,250
1850 . . . . Official 1,610
1860 . . . . " 4,399
1870 . . . ." 5,614
1880 . . . ."11,183
1890 . . . ."150,395
1900 . . . ."102,479
1910 . . . ."319,198

CHAPTER XXXVIII.
MINING RUSHES AND REAL ESTATE BOOMS.

To the Argonauts of '49 and the early '50s Los Angeles was known as a cow county. Few, if any, of these seekers after the golden fleece who entered the land of gold by the southern routes knew that the first gold discovered in California was found within the limits of the despised cow county, that the first gold rush took place there and that many of its mountain cañons were rich in the precious metal. The pilgrims to the shrine of Mammon saw the hills and plains covered with thousands of cattle. They found the inhabitants calmly indifferent to the wild rush to the mines. To the gold seekers such a country had no attractions. Its climate might be salubrious, but they were not seeking climate; its soil might be rich and productive, but they had no use for a soil unmixed with gold dust. They hurried on over the Tehachapi range or up the Coast route to the northern mines. The first discovery of gold in California was made by Francisco Lopes in the San Feliciano cañon of the San Fernando mountains, March 9, 1841: A full account of this discovery is given in Chapter XXIII of this volume.

The famous Kern river gold rush of 1855 brought an influx of population. Some of that population was very undesirable. The gold rush made business lively for a time, but when the reaction came it left a number of wrecks financially stranded. This mining excitement had one good effect: it called the attention of the Angeleños to the mineral resources of their own county and indirectly brought about their development.

The Kern river gold rush brought a number of experienced miners to the county. Some of these disappointed in the Kern river mines turned their attention to prospecting in the mountains of Los Angeles county. A party of prospectors in April, 1855, entering the mountains by way of the Cajon pass, penetrated to the headwaters of the San Gabriel river and found good prospects. Captain Hammager with a company of prospectors the same year went up the canon and discovered diggings that panned out $5 to $6 a day.

The Santa Anita placers, about fifteen miles from the city, were discovered in 1856. The discoverers attempted to conceal their find and these mines were known as the "Secret Diggings," but the secret was found out. These mines paid from $6 to $10 a day.

Work was actively resumed in the San Fernando diggings. Francisco Garcia, working a gang of Indians, in 1855 took out $65,000. It is said that one nugget worth $1,900 was found in these mines. In 1858 the Santa Anita Mining Company was organized, D. Marchessault, president; V. Beaudry, treasurer; capital, $50000. A ditch four miles long was cut around the foot of the mountain and hydraulic works constructed. Upon the completion of these works, February 15, 1859, the company gave a dinner to invited guests from the city. The success of the enterprise was toasted and wine and wit flowed as freely as the water in the hydraulic pipes. The mines returned a handsome compensation on the outlay.

During the year 1859 the cañon of the San Gabriel was prospected for forty miles and some rich placer claims located. On some of the bars as high as $8 to the pan were obtained. The correspondent of the Los Angeles Star reports these strikes: "From a hill claim four men took out $80 in one day." "Two Mexicans, with a common wooden bowl or batea, panned out $90 in two days." "Two hydraulic companies are taking out $1,000 a week." In July, 1859, 300 men were at work in the cañon and all reported doing well. A stage line ran from the city to the mines. Three stores at Eldoradoville, the chief mining camp of the cañon, supplied the miners with the necessaries of life, and several saloons furnished liquid refreshment and excitement.

The editor of the Star, in the issue of December 3, 1859, grows enthusiastic over the mining prospects of Los Angeles. He says: "Gold placers are now being worked from Fort Tejon to San Bernardino. Rich deposits have been discovered in the northern part of the county. The San Gabriel mines have been worked very successfully this season. The Santa Anita placers are giving forth their golden harvest. Miners are at work in the San Fernando hills rolling out the gold and in the hills beyond discoveries have been made which prove the whole district to be one grand placer." Next day it rained and it kept at it continuously for three days and nights. It was reported that twelve inches of water fell in the mountains during the storm. In the narrow cañon of the San Gabriel river the water rose to an unprecedented height and swept everything before it. The miners' wheels, sluices, long toms, wing dams, coffer dams, and all other dams, went floating off toward the sea.

The year 1860 was a prosperous one for the San Gabriel miners, notwithstanding the disastrous flood of December, 1859. The increased water supply afforded facilities for working dry claims. Some of the strikes of that season in the cañon have the sound of the flush days of '49: "Baker & Smith realized from their claim $800 in eight days;" "Driver & Co. washed out $350 of dust in two hours."

In the spring of 1862, Wells, Fargo & Co. were shipping to San Francisco from their Los Angeles office, $12,000 of gold dust a month by steamer and probably as much more was sent by other shippers or taken by private parties; all this was produced from the San Fernando, San Gabriel and Santa Anita placers. In the past forty years a large amount of gold has been taken out of the San Gabriel placers — how much it is impossible to say. As late as 1876 there were two hydraulic companies working in the cañon. One company reported a yield of $1,365 for a run of twenty-six days, working five men — an average of $10.50 a day to the man. Placer mining is still carried on in a desultory way every winter in the San Fernando and San Gabriel mines. But a limited amount of capital has at any time been employed in these mines, and the methods of working them have been unsystematic and wasteful. With more abundant capital, with improved appliances and cheaper methods of working, these mines could be made to yield rich returns.

In the winter of 1862-63 placer mines were discovered on the Colorado river and a rush followed. Los Angeles profited by it while it lasted, but it was soon over.

In 1863 there was a mining boom on the island of Santa Catalina. Some rich specimens of gold and silver quartz rock were found and the boom began. The first location was made in April, 1863, by Martin M. Kimberly and Daniel E. Way. At a miners' meeting held on the island April 20, 1863, the San Pedro Mining District was formed and a code of mining laws formulated "for the government of locators of veins or lodes of quartz, or other rock containing precious metals and ores (gold, silver, copper, galena or other minerals or mines) that may be discovered, taken up or located in Los Angeles county, San Pedro district, state of California." The boundaries of San Pedro district were somewhat indefinite; it included "all the islands of Los Angeles county and the Coast Range of mountains between the northern and southern boundaries of said county."

The first discoveries were made near the isthmus on the northwestern part of the island. The principal claims were located in Fourth of July valley, Cherry valley and Mineral hill.

A site for a city was located on Wilson Harbor. Lots were staked off and Queen City promised to become the metropolis of the mining district of Catalina.

Numerous discoveries were made. Within nine months from the first location notices of claims to over a hundred thousand feet of leads, lodes or veins, with their dips, spurs and angles, were recorded in the recorder's office of Los Angeles county and probably three times that number of claims were located that were either recorded in the district records on the island or were not recorded at all. Assays were made of gold and silver bearing rock, that ranged from $150 to $800 a ton. Stock companies were formed with capital bordering on millions— indeed, a company that had not "millions in it" was not worth organizing in those days. It is needless to say that the capital stock was not paid up in full nor in part either. The miners believed implicitly in the wealth of their mines, but they had no money to develop their claims nor could they induce capitalists to aid them. The times were out of joint for great enterprises. Washoe stocks had flooded the local mining market and the doubtful practices of mining sharks had brought discredit on feet and stocks. Capital from abroad could not be induced to seek investment in mines on an island in the far Pacific. The nation was engaged in a death struggle with the Southern Confederacy and there was more money in fat government contracts than in prospect holes.

The boom collapsed unexpectedly — burst by "military despotism." There were rumors that this mining rush was a blind to conceal a plot to seize the island and make it a rendezvous for Confederate privateers, from which they could fit out and prey upon the commerce of the coast. Many of the miners were southern sympathizers, but whether such a plot was seriously contemplated is doubtful. If such was incubating, the government crushed it before it was hatched. A military force was placed on the island and the following order issued:

Headquarters, Santa Catalina Island,
February 5th, 1864. Special Order No. 7.
No Person Or Persons Other Than Owners Of Stock Or Incorporated Companies'
Employees Will Be Allowed To Remain On The Island On Or After This Date; Nor Will
Any Person Be Allowed To Land Until Further Instructions Are Received From Washington. I
Hereby Notify Miners Prospecting Or Other Persons To Leave Immediately. By Order.
B. R. West, Captain Fourth California Infantry Commanding Post.

After such an invitation to leave the miners stood not on the order of their going — they went — those whose sympathies were with the Confederacy breathing curses against the tyrant Lincoln and his blue-coated minions. After the withdrawal of the troops, September 15, 1864, a few of the miners returned, but work was not resumed, the excitement was over — the boom had burst.

The Great Real Estate Boom Of 1887.

The following account of the real-estate boom of 1887 is compiled from a paper written by the author of this history and published in the Annual of the Southern California Historical Society for 1890. The writer describes what he saw and heard:

"In the history of nearly every great American city there is an epoch which marks a turning point in its civic life. The great epoch in the civic life of Los Angeles is that which is always spoken of as 'The Boom.' An event is referred to as occurring 'before the boom,' 'during the boom,' or 'after the boom.'

"By the 'boom' is meant the great real-estate bubble of 1887. Boom, in the sense we use it, is intended to express a sudden inflation of values; and on the western side of our continent it has superseded the older used and more expressive word, bubble. Boom, 'to rush with violence,' is better suited to the dash, the impetuosity and the recklessness of western speculators than the more effeminate term, bubble. Boom has come into our literature to stay, however unstable it may be in other places.

"Communities and nations as well are subject, at times, to financial booms — periods when the mania for money-making seems to become epidemic. The South Sea Bubble; the Darien Colonization Scheme; the Mississippi Scheme of John Law; the Northern Pacific Railroad Bubble of Jay Cooke — have each been followed by financial panics and Black Fridays, but the experience of one generation is lost on the succeeding. Experience as schoolmaster is too often a failure.

"There were no booms in Los Angeles under Spanish or under Mexican rule. Then all vacant lands belonged to the pueblo. If a man needed a building lot he petitioned the comisionado, or, later on, the ayuntamiento, for a grant of a lot. If he failed to use the lot it was taken from him. Under such conditions neither real-estate booms nor real-estate agents could flourish.

"After the discovery of gold in California, Los Angeles experienced its first real-estate boom. In 1849 the Ord survey lots were put on the market and a number of them sold.

There was a great demand for houses. Buildings framed and ready for putting together were shipped around Cape Horn from Boston, New York, London and Liverpool.

"As the gold excitement decreased the city gradually sank into a comatose state — took a Rip Van Winkle sleep for twenty years or thereabouts. Times were hard, money scarce and real-estate low. Markets were distant, transportation was high and most of the agricultural lands were held in large tracts. These conditions began to change about 1868. The Stearns ranchos, containing about 200,000 acres, were subdivided. Settlers from the New England and northwestern states began to come in and the push and energy of these began to work a transformation in the sleepy old ciudad and the country around. Between 1868 and 1875 a number of the large ranchos were subdivided, several colonies were promoted and new towns founded.

"From 1875 to 1881 was a period of financial depression. The Temple-Workman Bank failure, a succession of dry years that ruined the sheep industry, overproduction, high freight rates and a poor market for our products brought the country to the verge of bankruptcy. The building of the Southern Pacific Railroad eastward gave us a new and better market for our products in the mining regions of Arizona and New Mexico. The completion of this road in 1881 gave us a new transcontinental route and immigrants began to arrive from the eastern states. The price of land steadily advanced and gradually we recovered from our financial depression.

"Up till 1886 the growth of our cities and towns had kept pace with the growth and development of the surrounding country, the crying need for new cities and towns had not been heard. The merits of the country had been well advertised in the eastern states. Excursion agents, real-estate dealers, and the newspapers of Southern California had depicted in glowing colors the salubrity of our climate, the variety of our production, the fertility of our soil and the immense profits to be made from the cultivation of semi-tropical fruits. The last link of the Santa Fe Railroad system was approaching completion. In the spring of 1886 a rate war was precipitated between the two transcontinental lines. Tickets from the Missouri river points to Los Angeles were sold all the way from $1 to $15.

"Visitors and immigrants poured in by the thousands. The country was looking its loveliest. Leaving the ice and snows of Minnesota, Iowa and Kansas, in three or four days they found themselves in a land of orange groves, green fields and flower-covered hills. In the new land they found everybody prosperous, and these visitors returned to their homes to sell their possessions and come to the promised land.

"The immediate causes that precipitated our great real-estate boom of 1887 may be briefly enumerated as follows:

"First. The completion of a competing continental railroad, with its western terminus at Los Angeles, and an era of active local railroad building and railroad projecting in Southern California.

"Second. High prices for all our products, an easy money market and employment, at high wages, for all who wished it.

"Third. An immense immigration, part of it induced to come on account of a better climate and greater rewards for labor, and part of it attracted by reports of the large profits to be made by speculating in real estate.

"Lastly. The arrival among us of a horde of boomers from western cities and towns — patriots, many of them, who had exiled themselves from their former places of abode between two days — fellows who had left their consciences (that is, if they had any to leave) on the other side of the Rockies. These professionals had learned the tricks of their trade in the boom cities of the west when that great wave of immigration which began moving after the close of the war was sweeping westward from the Mississippi river to the shores of the Pacific. These boomers came here not to build up the country, but to make money, honestly if they could not make it any other way. It is needless to say they made it the other way.

"During 1884-5-6 a number of lots were put on the market, but these were made mostly by subdivisions of acreage within or of additions immediately joining the older established cities and towns. Very few new town sites had been laid off previous to 1887. As the last section of the Santa Fe Railway system approached completion the creation of new towns began, and the rapidity with which they were created was truly astonishing. During the months of March, April and May, 1887, no less than thirteen town sites were platted on the line of this road between Los Angeles and San Bernardino and the lots thrown upon the market. Before the close of 1887, between the eastern limits of Los Angeles and San Bernardino county line, a distance by way of the Santa Fe Railroad of thirty-six miles, there were twenty-five cities and towns located, an average of one to each mile and a half of the road. Paralleling the Santa Fe on the line of the Southern Pacific Railroad, eight more towns claimed the attention of lot buyers, with three more thrown in between the roads, making a grand total of thirty-six cities and towns in the San Gabriel valley. The area of some of these was quite extensive. 'No pent-up Utica contracted the powers' of their founders. The only limit to the greatness of a city was the boundary lines of the adjoining cities. The corporate limits of the city of Monrovia were eight square miles; Pasadena, with its additions, the same; Lordsburg spread over eight hundred acres; Chicago Park numbered nearly three thousand lots, located in the wash of the San Gabriel river. The city of Azusa, with its house lots and suburban farm lots, covered an area of four thousand acres.

"The craze to secure lots in some of these towns is well exemplified in the first sale of lots in Azusa. The founding of the city of Azusa was intended to satisfy a long-felt want. The rich valley of the Azusa de Duarte had no commercial metropolis. Azusa city was recognized by real-estate speculators as the coming commercial center of trade for the valley, and they thought there was money in the first pick of lots. The lots were to be put on sale on a certain day. Through the long hours of the night previous and until nine o'clock of the day of sale a line of hungry and weary lot buyers stood in front of the office where the lots were to be sold.

Number two claimed to have been offered $1,000 for his place in the line; number three sold out for $500; number fifty-four loudly proclaimed that he would not take a cent less than a cool hundred for his chance. Number one was deaf to all offers; and through the weary hours of the night he clung to the 'handle of the big front door,' securing at last the coveted prize — the first choice. Two hundred and eighty thousand dollars worth of lots were sold the first day. The sale continued three days. Not one in ten of the purchasers had seen the town site, not one in a hundred expected to occupy the land purchased.

"Even this performance was surpassed later on in the boom. The sale of lots in a certain town was to begin Wednesday morning at the agent's office in the city. On Sunday evening a line of prospective purchasers began to form The agent, as an advertising dodge, hired a large hall for the display of his would-be investors. At stated intervals the line formed, the roll was called and woe to the unfortunate who failed to answer to his number; his place in the line was forfeited and he was compelled to go down to the foot. Financially, the agent's scheme was a failure. The crowd was made up principally of impecunious speculators and tramps who had hoped to sell out their places in the line.

"An aristocratic and euphonious name was desideratum to a new-born town, although, as in the following case, it sometimes failed to boom the prospective city. An enterprising newspaper man found a piece of unoccupied land on the line of the Santa Fe Railroad — that is, a piece not occupied by a town site— and founded the city of Gladstone. An advertisement prolific in promises of the future greatness of the city, and tropical in its luxuriance of descriptive adjectives, proclaimed among other inducements to buy that a lot had been deeded to the premier of all England, and it was left to be inferred that the 'grand old man' might build a princely residence on his lot and become one of the attractions to draw dwellers to the new city. In olden times, when a conqueror wished to destroy a rival city, he razed it to the ground, caused the plowshare to pass over its ruins and sowed the site with salt. The city of Gladstone was prevented from rising above the ground by the caustic criticisms of a rival newspaper man, the plowshare has passed many times over its ruins and its site has been sown in barley. The enterprising newspaper man lost his land (he held it by contract to purchase only), the surveyor who platted the town lost his pay and Gladstone lost his lot.

"Of the phantom cities of the boom, cities that have faded from mortal view, cities that have become specters that rise out of the mists of the past to haunt the dupes who invested their money in them, of these Carlton is a good illustration. It was located on the slope of the Santa Ana mountains, east of Anaheim. It is described as commanding a beautiful view of the valley of the Santa Ana, with a glimpse of the Pacific ocean m the distance. View was its chief resource — the only commodity other than town lots it had to offer. The promises of its projectors were unbounded, and the credulity of its investors seemed to be unlimited. Railroads were to center there. There manufactories were to rear their lofty chimneys, and the ever-present hotel in the course of erection was to be a palace of luxury for the tourist and a health-restoring sanitarium to the one-lunged consumptive.

"Promises were cheap and plentiful, and so were the lots. They started at $25 each for a lot twenty-five feet front; rose to $35; jumped to $50, and choice corners changed hands all the way from $100 to $500.

"One enterprising agent sold three thousand, and many others did their best to supply a long felt want — cheap lots. Capitalists, speculators, mechanics, merchants, day laborers, clerks and servant girls crowded and jostled one another in their eagerness to secure choice lots in the coming metropolis. Business blocks, hotels, restaurants and dwelling houses lined the streets on paper. A bank building, with a costly vault, was in course of construction, and it continued in that course to the end. A railroad was surveyed to the city and a few ties and rails scattered at intervals along the line. A number of cheap houses were built, and a population of three or four hundred congregated there at the height of the boom, and for a time managed to subsist in a semi-cannibalistic way on the dupes who came there to buy lots. The site of the city was on the mountain side above the zanja (ditch), and the water supply of the inhabitants had to be hauled up hill in water carts. The productive land lay far below in the valley, and the cities of the plain absorbed all the trade. When the excursionist and lot-buyer ceased to come, 'Picturesque Carlton,' 'Nature's Rendezvous,' as its poetic founder styled it, was abandoned, and now the jack-rabbit nibbles the grass in its deserted streets and the howl of the coyote and the hoot of the boding owl echo amid its ruins — that is, if there are enough ruins to make an echo.

"Of the purely paper cities of the boom, Border City and Manchester are the best illustrations. An unprincipled speculator by the name of Simon Homberg secured two quarter-sections of government land situated respectively forty and forty-three miles northeast of Los Angeles. These were the sites of Homberg's famous or rather infamous twin cities. Border City was appropriately named. It was located on the border of the Mojave desert, on the northeastern slope of the Sierra Madre mountains. (It was named Border City because it was located on the eastern border of Los Angeles county.) It was most easily accessible by means of a balloon, and was as secure from hostile invasion as the homes of the cliff dwellers. Its principal resource, like Carlton, was view — a view of the Mojave desert. The founder did not go to the expense of having the site surveyed and the lots staked off. Indeed, about the only way it could be surveyed was through a field glass. He platted it by blocks and recorded his map. The streets were forty feet wide and the lots twenty-five feet front by one hundred deep. The quarter-section made nineteen hundred and twenty lots, an average of twelve to the acre. Such width of street Homberg found to be a waste of land, and in laying out the city of Manchester he was more economical. Out of the quarter section on which that city was located he carved two thousand three hundred and four lots, or about fourteen to the acre. All streets running east and west were 27 2-13 feet wide, and all running north and south were 34 2-7 feet wide. The lots were twenty-five feet front by ninety-five deep. Manchester was a city of greater resources than Border City. Being located higher up the mountain, it had a more extended view of the desert.

"These lots were not offered for sale in Southern California, nor to those who might investigate and expose the fraud, but were extensively advertised in Northern California, in Oregon, in the eastern states, and even in Europe. It would seem almost incredible that Homberg could have found dupes enough to buy such property unsight, unseen; yet, judging from the records, he sold about all of his four thousand lots, and his profits must have footed up in the neighborhood of $50,000. Sc many of his deeds were filed for record that the county recorder had a book of records containing three hundred and sixty pages, especially prepared with printed forms, of Homberg's deeds, so that when one was filed for record, all that was necessary to engross it was to fill in the name of the purchaser and the number of the lot and block.

"The lots cost Homberg about an average of ten cents each, and were sold at all prices, from $1 up to $250 each, the prices varying according to the means or the gullibility of the purchaser. One buyer would pay $250 for a single lot; the next investor might get ten or a dozen for that sum. One enthusiast in San Jose invested $1,000 in a bunch of forty-eight lots, securing at one fell swoop four business blocks in the center of Border City. Nearly every state in the Union had its victims of misplaced confidence in the future of Homberg's twin cities. Nor were his operations confined to the United States alone. England, Germany, Holland, Denmark and Sweden furnished him dupes as well.

"The magnitude of our great boom can be measured more accurately by a money standard than any other. The total of the considerations named in the instruments filed for record during the year 1887 reached the enormous sum of $98,084,162. But even this does not tell half the story. By far the larger number of lots and blocks in the various tracts and town sites that were thrown on the market were sold on contract, the terms of payment being one-third or one-fourth cash, balance in installments payable in six, twelve or eighteen months, a deed to be given when the final payment was made. But few of the agreements were recorded. Frequently property bought on agreement to convey was resold from one to half a dozen times, and each time at an advance; yet the consideration named in the deed, when given, would be the sum named in the original agreement. Deeds to the great bulk of property sold on contract in 1887 did not go on record until the following year, and many of them not then. Thousands of contracts were forfeited and never appeared of record. It is safe to estimate that the considerations in the real-estate transactions during 1887 in Los Angeles county alone reached $200,000,000.

"So sudden and so great an inflation of land values was perhaps never equaled in the world's history. When unimproved land in John Law's Mississippi Colony sold for 30,000 livres ($5,550) a square league, all Europe was amazed and historians still quote the Mississippi bubble as a marvel of inflation. To have bought a square league of land in the neighborhood of some of our cities in the booming days of 1887 would have taken an amount of money equal to the capital of the national bank of France, in the days of John Law. Unimproved lands adjoining the city of Los Angeles sold as high as $2,500 per acre or at the rate of $14,400,000 a square league. Land that sold at $100 an acre in 1886, changed hands in 1887 at $1,500 per acre; and city lots bought in 1886 at $500 each, a year later were rated at $5,000.

"The great booms of former times measured by the money standard, dwarf into insignificance when compared with ours. The capital stock of John Law's National Bank of France, with his Mississippi grants thrown in, figured up less than $15,000,000, an amount about equal to our real-estate transactions for one month; yet, the bursting of John Law's Mississippi bubble very nearly bankrupted the French Empire. The relative proportions of the South Sea bubble of 1700 to our real estate boom are as a soap bubble is to a mammoth balloon. The amount of capital invested in the Darien Colonization scheme, a scheme which bankrupted Scotland and came near plunging all Europe into war, was only 220,000 pounds sterling, a sum about equal to our real-estate transfers for one day.

"From a report compiled for the Los Angeles County Board of Equalization in July, 1889, I find the area included in sixty towns, all of which were laid out since January 1, 1887, estimated at 79,350 acres. The total population of these sixty towns at that time was placed at 3,350. Some of the largest of these on paper were without inhabitants. Carlton, containing 4,060 lots, was an unpeopled waste; Nadeau, 4,470 lots, had no inhabitants; Manchester, 2,304 lots, no inhabitants; Santiago 2,110 lots, was a deserted village. Others still contained a small remnant of their former population. Chicago Park, containing 2,289 lots, had one inhabitant, the watchman who took care of its leading hotel; Sunset, 2,014 lots, one inhabitant, watchman of an expensive hotel which was in the course of construction when the boom burst. (The building was burned a few years since.)

"The sites of a majority of the boom cities of twenty years ago have been returned to acreage, the plowshare has passed over their ruins and barley grows in the deserted streets.

"The methods of advertising the attractions of the various tracts, subdivisions and town sites thrown on the market, and the devices resorted to to inveigle purchasers into investing were various, often ingenious and sometimes infamous. Brass bands, street processions, free excursions and free lunches, columns of advertisements rich in description and profuse in promises that were never intended to be fulfilled, pictures of massive hotels in the course of erection, lithographs of colleges about to materialize, lotteries, the prizes in which were handsome residences or family hotels, railroads that began and ended in the imaginations of the projectors — such were a few of the many devices resorted to to attract purchasers and induce them to invest their coin.

"Few, if any, of the inhabitants to the manor born, or those of permanent residence and reputable character engaged in these doubtful practices and disreputable methods of booming. The men who blew the bubble to greatest inflation were new importations — fellows of the baser sort who knew little or nothing about the resources or characteristics of the country and cared less. They were here to make money. When the bubble burst they disappeared — those who got away with their gains, chuckling over ill-gotten wealth; those who lost, abusing the country and vilifying the people they had duped. Retributive justice overtook a few of the more unprincipled boomers and they have since done some service to the country in striped uniforms.

"The collapse of our real-estate boom was not the sudden bursting of a financial bubble, like the South Sea bubble or John Law's Mississippi bubble, nor did it end in a financial crash like the monetary panics of 1837 and 1857, or like Black Friday in Wall street. Its collapse was more like the steady contraction of a balloon from the pressure of the heavier atmosphere on the outside. It gradually shriveled up. The considerations named in the recorded transfers of the first three months of 1888 exceeded $20,000,000. After that they decreased rapidly."

CHAPTER XXXIX. LOS ANGELES CITY.

From Pueblo To Ciudad.
(From Town To City.)

For fifty-five years after its founding Los Angeles was officially a pueblo. In 1835, as narrated in a previous chapter, the Mexican congress raised it to the rank of a city. It was only in official records and communications that it was accorded the dignity of a "ciudad" (city). The people spoke of it as el pueblo — the town. American writers of the decade previous to the American conquest all speak of it as the pueblo, and one of them, Hastings, who came to California overland in 1843 and wrote a book describing the country and telling how to get there, seems not to have heard its real name, but designated it "Poablo below," and San Jose "Poablo above." Los Angeles was often spoken of as El Pueblo abajo, the town below; and San Jose, El Pueblo, the town above. Hastings, with his imperfect knowledge of Spanish, seems to have taken these as the real names of the towns.

Its elevation to a ciudad by the Mexican congress made no change in its form of government. The ayuntamiento was still the ruling power, and the number of its members was not increased. The ayuntamiento was abolished at the beginning of the year 1840. The Mexican congress had enacted a law allowing ayuntamientos only to cities with a population of four thousand and upwards. The ayuntamiento of Los Angeles was re-established in 1844, and continued the governing body of the city until superseded by the common council July 3, 1850.

In the beginning Los Angeles was symmetrical. The pueblo contained four square leagues (Spanish). In the center was the plaza, 75x100 varas. It was the geographical center of the settlement. One league toward each wind you reached the pueblo's boundary lines. The narrow streets went out from the plaza at right angles to its sides. The houses faced inward upon it. As the town grew it wandered off from its old center and became demoralized. The streets crooked to suit the convenience of house builders. The houses stood at different angles to the streets and the house lots were of all geometrical shapes. No man had a written title to his land. Possession was ten points of the law. Indeed, it was all the law he had to protect his title. If he ceased to use his land he might lose it. Anyone was at liberty to denounce unused land, and the ayuntamiento, on proof being made that it was unused, declared the possession forfeited.

With the fall of the missions a spasm of territorial expansion seized the colonists. In 1834 the territorial legislature, by an enactment, fixed the boundaries of the pueblo of Los Angeles at "two leagues to each of the four winds, measuring from the center of the plaza." This gave the pueblo an area of sixteen square leagues, or over one hundred square miles. Next year (1835) Los Angeles was made the capital of Alta California by the Mexican congress and raised to the dignity of a city; and then its first real estate boom was on. There was an increased demand for lots and lands, but there were no maps or plats to grant by and no additions or subdivisions of the pueblo lands on the market. All the unoccupied lands belonged to the municipality, and when a citizen wanted a house lot to build on he petitioned the ayuntamiento for a lot, and if the piece asked for was vacant he was granted a lot — large or small, deep or shallow, on the street or off it, just as it happened.

With the growth of the town the confusion and irregularity increased. The disputes arising from overlapping grants, conflicting property lines and indefinite descriptions induced the ayuntamiento of 1836 to appoint a commission to investigate and report upon the manner of granting house lots and agricultural lands. The commissioners reported "that they had consulted with several of the founders and with old settlers, who declared that from the founding of the town the concession of lots and lands had been made verbally without any other formality than locating and measuring the extent of the land the fortunate one should occupy."

"In order to present a fuller report your commission obtained an 'Instruction' signed by Don Jose Francisco de Ortega, dated at San Gabriel, February 2, 1782, and we noted that articles 3, 4 and 17 of said 'Instruction' provides that concession of said agricultural lands and house lots must be made by the government, which shall issue the respective titles to the grantees. According to the opinion of the city's advisers, said 'Instruction,' or at least the three articles referred to, have not been observed, as there is no property owner who can show a legal title to his property.

"The commissioners cannot do otherwise but call attention of the Alost Illustrious Ayuntamiento to the evil consequences which may result by reason of said abuses, and recommend that some means may be devised that they may be avoided. God and Liberty." "Angeles, March 8, 1836.

"Abel Stearns, "Bacilio Valdez, "Jose M. Herrerras, "Commissioners."

Acting on the report of the commissioners, the ayuntamiento required all holders of property to apply for written titles. But the poco tiempo ways of the pobladores could not be altogether overcome. We find from the records that in 1847 the land of Mrs. Carmen Navarro, one of the founders of the town, was denounced (filed on) because she could not show a written title to it. The ayuntamiento decided "that as she had always been allowed to hold it, her claim should be respected because she was one of the founders," "which makes her entitled to a lot on which to live."

March 17, 1836, "a commission on streets, plazas and alleys was appointed to report a plan for repairing the monstrous irregularity of the streets brought about by ceding house lots and erecting houses in this pueblo."

The commission reported in favor of "formulating a plat of the city as it actually exists, on which shall be marked the names of the streets, alleys and plazas, also the house lots and common lands of the pueblo." But nothing came of the report, no plat was made, and the ayuntamiento went on in the same old way, granting lots of all shapes and forms.

In March, 1846, another commission was appointed to locate the bounds of the pueblo lands. All that was done was to measure two leagues "in the direction of the four winds from the plaza church," and set stakes to mark the boundary lines. Then came the American conquest of California, and the days of poco tiempo were numbered. In 1847, after the conquest, another attempt was made to straighten and widen the streets. Some of the Yankee spirit of fixing up things seems to have pervaded the ayuntamiento. A street commission was appointed to try to bring order out of the chaos into which the streets had fallen. The commissioners reported July 22, 1847, ^s follows: "Your commissioners could not but be amazed seeing the disorder and the manner how the streets run. More particularly the street which leads to the cemetery, whose width is out of proportion to its length, and whose aspect offends the sense of the beautiful which should prevail in the city." When discussing this state of affairs with the sindico (city attorney) he informed us that on receiving his instructions from the ayuntamiento he was ordered to give the streets a width of fifteen varas (about forty-one feet). This he found to be in conflict with the statutes. The law referred to is in Book IV, Chapter 7, Statute 10 (probably a compilation of the "laws of the Indies," two or three centuries old, and brought from Spain). The law reads: "In cold countries the streets shall be wide, and in warm countries narrow; and when there are horses it would be convenient to have wide streets for purpose of an occasional defense or to widen them in the form above mentioned, care being taken that nothing is done to spoil the looks of the buildings, weaken the points of defense or encroach upon the comfort of the people."

"The instructions given the sindico by the ayuntamiento are absolutely opposed to this law, and therefore illegal." It probably never occurred to the commission to question the wisdom of so senseless a law; it had been a law in Spanish America for centuries and therefore must be venerated for its antiquity. A blind, unreasoning faith in the wisdom of church and state has been the undoing of the Spanish people. Apparently the commission did nothing more than report. California being a warm country, the streets perforce must be narrow.

The same year a commission was appointed to "square the plaza." Through carelessness some of the houses fronting on the square had been allowed to encroach upon it; others were set back so that the boundary lines of the plaza zigzagged back and forth like a Virginia rail fence. The neighborhood of the plaza was the aristocratic residence quarter of the city then, and a plaza front was considered high-toned. The commission found the squaring of the plaza as difficult a problem as the squaring of a circle. After many trials and tribulations the commissioners succeeded in overcoming most of the irregularities by reducing the area of the plaza. The houses that intruded were not torn down, but the property line was moved forward. The north, south and west lines were each fixed at 134 varas and the east line 112 varas. The ayuntamiento attempted to open a street from the plaza north of the church, but Pedro Cabrera, who had been granted a lot which fell in the line of the street, refused to give up his plaza front for a better lot without that aristocratic appendage which the council offered him. Then the city authorities offered him as compensation for the difference a certain number of days' labor of the chain gang (the treasury was in the usual state of collapse"), but Pedro could not be traded out of his plaza front, so the street took a twist around Pedro's lot — a twist that sixty years has not straightened out. The irregularities in granting portions of the unapportioned city lands still continued and the confusion of titles increased.

In May, 1849, the territorial governor. General Bennett Riley, sent a request to the ayuntamiento for a city map and information in regard to the manner of granting lots. The ayuntamiento replied that there was no map of the city in existence and no surveyor here who could make one. The governor was asked to send a surveyor to make a plan or plat of the city. He was also informed that in making land grants within "the perimeter of two leagues square the city acted in the belief that it is entitled to that much land as a pueblo."

Lieut. E. O. C. Ord, of the United States army, was sent down by the governor to plat the city. On the 18th of July, 1849, he submitted this proposition to the ayuntamiento: "He would make a map of the city, marking boundary lines and points of the municipal lands for $1,500, coin, ten lots selected from among the defined lots on the map and vacant lands to the extent of 1,coo varas to be selected in sections of 200 varas wherever he may choose it, or he would make a map for $3,000 in coin."

The ayuntamiento chose the last proposition — the president prophetically remarking that the time might come in the future when the lots alone would be worth $3,000. The money to pay for the survey was borrowed from Juan Temple, at the rate of one per cent a month, and lots pledged as security for payment. The time has come and passed when a single front foot of an Ord survey has sold for .$3,000.

The ayuntamiento also decided that there should be embodied in the map a plan of all the lands actually under cultivation, from the principal dam down to the last cultivated field below. "As to the lots that should be shown on the map, they should begin at the cemetery and end with the house of Botiller (near Ninth street). As to the commonalty lands of this city, the surveyor should determine the four points of the compass, and, taking the parish church for a center, measure two leagues in each cardinal direction. These lines will bisect the four sides of a square within which the lands of the municipality will be contained, the area of the same being sixteen square leagues, and each side of the square measuring four leagues." (The claims commission reduced the city's area in 1856 to just one-fourth these dimensions.)

Lieutenant Ord, assisted by William R. Hutton, completed his Plan de la Ciudad de Los Angeles, August 29, 1849. He divided into blocks all that portion of the city bounded north by First street, and the base of the first line of hills, east by Main street, south by Twelfth street, and west by Pearl street (now Figueroa), and into lots all of the above to Eighth street; also into lots and blocks that portion of the city north of Short street and west of Upper Main (San Fernando) to the base of the hills. On the "plan" the lands between Main street and the river are designated as "plough grounds, gardens, corn and vine lands." The streets in the older portion of the city are marked on the map, but not named. The blocks, except the tier between First and Second streets, are each 600 feet in length, and are divided into ten lots, each 120 feet by 165 feet deep. Ord took his compass course for the line of Main street, south 24° 45' west, from the corner opposite Jose Antonio Carrillo's house, which stood where the Pico house or National hotel now stands. On his map Main, Spring and Fort (now Broadway) streets ran in parallel straight lines southerly to Twelfth street.

The names of the streets on Ord's plan are given in both Spanish and English. Beginning with Main street, they are as follows: Calle Principal. Main street; Calle Primavera, Spring street (named for the season spring); Calle Fortin, Fort street (so named because the street extended would pass through the old fort on the hill); Calle Loma, Hill street; Calle Accytuna,. Olive street; Calle de Caridad, the street of charity (now Grand avenue); Calle de Las Esperanzas, the street of hopes; Calle de Las Flores, the street of flowers; Calle de Los Chapules, the street of grasshoppers (now South Figueroa street).

Above the plaza church the north and south streets were the Calle de Eternidad (Eternity street, so named because it had neither beginning nor end, or, rather, because each end terminated in the hills); Calle del Toro (street of the bull, so named because the upper end of the street terminated at the Carrida de Toro — the bull ring, where bull-fights were held); Calle de Las Avispas (street of the hornets or wasps, a very lively street at times); Calle de Los Adobes, Adobe street. The east and west streets were: Calle Corta, Short street; Calle Alta, High street; Calle de Las Virgines (street of virgins); Calle del Colegio (street of the college, the only street north of the church that retains its primitive name). Spring street was known as Calle de Caridad (the street of charity) at the time of the American conquest. The town then was centered around the plaza, and Spring street was well out in the suburbs. Its inhabitants in early times were of the poorer classes, who were largely dependent on the charity of their wealthier neighbors around the plaza. It is part of an old road made more than a century ago. On Ord's "plan" this road is traced northwestward from the junction of Spring and Main. It follows the present line of North Spring street to First street, then crosses the blocks bounded by Spring, Broadway, First and Third street diagonally to the corner of Third street and Broadway. It intersects Hill at Fourth street and Olive at Fifth street; skirting the hills, it passes out of the city near Ninth street to the Brea Springs, from which the colonists obtained the roofing material for their adobe houses. This road was used for many years after the American occupation, and was recognized as a street in conveyances. Ord evidently transferred Spring street's original name, "La Caridad," to one of his western streets which was a portion of the old road.

1 Main street, from the junction south, in 1846 was known as Calle de la Allegria — Junction street; Los Angeles street was the Calle Principal, or Main street. Whether the name had been transferred to the present Main street before Ord's survey I have not been able to ascertain. In the early years of the century Los Angeles street was known as the Calle de la Zanja (Ditch street). Later on it was sometimes called Calle de Los Vifias (Vineyard street), and with its continuation the Calle de Los Huertos (Orchard street) — now San Pedro — formed the principal highway running southward to the embarcadero of San Pedro.

Of the historic streets of Los Angeles that have disappeared before the march of improvements none perhaps was so widely known in early days as the one called Calle de Los Negros in Castilian Spanish, but Nigger alley in vulgar United States. Whether its ill-omened name was given from the dark hue of the dwellers on it or from the blackness of the deeds done in it the records do not tell. Before the American conquest it was a respectable street, and some of the wealthy rancheros dwelt on it, but it was not then known as Nigger alley. It gained its unsavory reputation and name in the flush days of gold mining, between 1849 and 1856. It was a short, narrow street or alley, extending from the upper end of Los Angeles street at Arcadia to the plaza. It was at that time the only street except Main entering the plaza from the south. In length it did not exceed 500 feet, but in wickedness it was unlimited. On either side it was lined with saloons, gambling hells, dance houses and disreputable dives. It was a cosmopolitan street.

Representatives of different races and many nations frequented it. Here the ignoble red man, crazed with aguardiente, fought his battles, the swarthy Sonoran plied his stealthy dagger and the click of the revolver mingled with the clink of gold at the gaming table when some chivalric American felt that his word of "honah" has been impugned.

The Calle de Los Negros in the early '50s, when the deaths from violence in Los Angeles were of almost daily occurrence, was the central point from which the wickedness of the city radiated.

With the decadence of gold mining the character of the street changed, but its morals were not improved by the change. It ceased to be the rendezvous of the gambler and the desperado and became the center of the Chinese quarter of the city. Carlyle says the eighteenth century blew its brains out in the French Revolution. Nigger alley might be said to have blown its brains out, if it had any, in the Chinese massacre of 1871. That dark tragedy of our city's history, in which eighteen Chinamen were hanged by a mob, occurred on this street. It was the last of the many tragedies of the Calle de Los Negros; the extension of Los Angeles street, in 1886, wiped it out of existence, or so nearly that there is not enough of it left to be wicked.

The Calle del Toro was another historic street with a mixed reputation. Adjoining this street, near where the French hospital now stands, was located the Plaza de Los Toros. Here on fete days the sport-loving inhabitants of Los Angeles and the neighborhood round about gathered to witness that national amusement of Mexico and old Spain — the corida de toros (bull fights). And here, too, when a grizzly bear could be obtained from the neighboring mountains, were witnessed those combats so greatly enjoyed by the native Californians — ^bull and bear baiting. There were no humanitarian societies in those days to prohibit this cruel pastime. Macauley says the Puritans hated bear-baiting, not because it gave pain to the bear, but because of the pleasure it gave the spectators — all pleasure, from their ascetic standpoint, being considered sinful. The bear had no friends among the Californians to take his part from any motive. It was death to poor bruin, whether he was victor or vanquished: but the bull sometimes made it uncomfortable for his tormentors. The Los Angeles Star of December 18, 1858, describes this occurrence at one of these bull fights on the Calle del Toro: "An infuriated bull broke through the enclosure and rushed at the affrighted spectators. A wild panic ensued. Don Felipe Lugo spurred his horse in front of the furious bull. The long horns of the maddened animal were plunged into the horse. The gallant steed and his daring rider went down in the dust. The horse was instantly killed, but the rider escaped unhurt. Before the bull could rally for another charge half a dozen bullets from the ready revolvers of the spectators put an end to his existence."

The Plaza de Los Toros has long since been obliterated, and Bull street became Castelar more than a third of a century ago.

Previous to 1S47 there was but one street opening out from the plaza to the northward, and that was the narrow street known to old residents as Bath street, since widened and extended, and now called North Main street. The committee that had charge of the "squaring of the plaza" projected the opening of another street to the north. It was the street known as Upper Main, now called San

Fernando. This street was cut through the old cuartel or guardhouse, built in 1785, which stood on the southeastern side of the Plaza vieja, or old Plaza, laid out by Governor Felipe de Neve when he founded the pueblo. Upper Main street opened into the Calle Real, or Main street, which was one of de Neve's original streets opening out from the old plaza to the northeast.

Ord's survey or plan left some of the houses in the old parts of the city in the middle of the streets and others were cut off from frontage. The city council labored long to adjust property lines to the new order of things. Finally, in 1854, an ordinance was passed allowing property owners to claim frontages to the streets nearest their houses.

Under Mexican domination the transition of Los Angeles from a pueblo to a ciudad had made no change in the laws and customs of its people. For three years and a half following the American conquest the new rulers of California continued the old forms of government, but a change was coming to the old pueblo. The legislature of California had made it a city and had provided for it a new form of government. The common council was to supplant the ayuntamiento. For nearly three score years and ten under the rule of Spain and her daughter Mexico the ayuntamiento had been the lawmaker of the pueblo. Generations had grown to manhood and had passed out of existence under its domination. Monarchy, empire and republic had ruled the territory, had loosened their hold and lost their power, but through all the ayuntamiento had held its sway. Now, too, it must go. Well might the old-time Angeleño heave a sigh of regret at the downfall of that bulwark of his liberty, "muy illustre ayuntamiento."

The following is a copy of the act of incorporation passed by the state legislature April 4, 1850:

AN ACT To Incorporate The City Of Los Angeles.
The People Of The State Of California, Represented In Senate And Assembly, Do Enact
As Follows:
Section 1. All That Tract Of Land Included Within The Limits Of The Pueblo De Los
Angeles, As Heretofore Known And Acknowledged, Shall Henceforth Be Known As The City
Of Los Angeles, And The Said City Is Hereby Declared To Be Incorporated According To The
Provisions Of The Act Entitled "An Act To Provide For The Incorporation Of Cities,"
Approved March 18, 1850. Provided, However, That If Such Limits Include More Than Four
Square Miles, The Council Shall, Within Three Months After They Are Elected And
Qualified, Fix By Ordinance The Limits Of The City, Not To Include More Than Said
Quantity Of Land, And The Boundaries So Determined Shall Thenceforth Be The Boundaries
Of The City.
Section 2. The Number Of Councilmen Shall Be Seven; The First Election Of City Officers
Shall Be Held On The Second Monday Of May Next.
Section 3. The Corporation Created By This Act Shall Succeed To All The Rights, Claims,
And Powers Of The Pueblo De Los Angeles In Regard To Property, And Shall Be Subject To
All The Liabilities Incurred And Obligations Created By The Ayuntamiento Of Said Pueblo.

303

CHAPTER XL.
LOS ANGELES CITY— CONTINUED.

The Evolution Of A Metropolis.

IN the previous chapter I have quoted in full the act to incorporate Los Angeles as a city. It will be noticed that the act provides that "all that tract of land included within the Pueblo de Los Angeles as heretofore known and acknowledged shall henceforth be known as the City of Los Angeles." Section 3 of an "Act to provide for the incorporation of cities," passed March 11, 1850, limited the area of a city to four square miles. Evidently the legislators of the fall of '49 and spring of '50 did not take into consideration the possibilities of the growth of California cities.

The Pueblo of Los Angeles had begun business in 1781 with four square leagues, or about twenty-seven square miles, and, as previously stated, the year (1834) before it was raised to the dignity of a ciudad by the Mexican Congress, the Departmental Assembly had expanded its boundaries to include sixteen square leagues, or over one hundred square miles. A provision in the act of incorporation of 1850 gave the council three months in which to pare down the limits of the city to the standard fixed by the legislature — four square miles.

Two nations by legislative decrees had made a city of Los Angeles. Yet it was not much of a city after all. Within its bounds there was not a graded street, a sidewalk, a water pipe or a public building of any kind belonging to the municipality.

The first city election under its American incorporation was held July 1, 1850. The officers elected were: A. P. Hodges, mayor (who also held the office of county coroner); Francisco Figueroa, treasurer; A. F. Coronel, city assessor (also county assessor); Samuel Whiting, city marshal (also county jailer).

The first common council met July 3, 1850, and the first record of its doings reads thus:

"Messrs. David W. Alexander, Alexander Bell, Manuel Requena, Juan Temple, Morris L. Goodman, Cristobal Aguilar and Julian Chavez took the oath of office in conformity with Section 3, Article XI, of the state constitution, before Jonathan R. Scott (justice of the peace), and entered upon the discharge of their duties as members of the common council of this city, to which office they had been elected by the people on the first day of this month." David W. Alexander was elected president and Vicente del Campo secretary. The members had been sworn to support the constitution of the State of California, and yet there was no state. California had not been admitted as a state of the Union. It had taken upon itself the function of a state. The legislature had made counties and cities and provided for their organization and government, and a governor elected by the people had approved the acts of the legislature. The state government was a political nondescript. It had sloughed off its territorial condition, but it could not become a state until congress admitted it into the Union and the slave-holding faction of that body would not let it in.

The first common council of the city was a patriotic and self-denying body. The first resolution passed was as follows: "It having been observed that in other places the council members were drawing a salary, it was unanimously resolved that the members of this council shall receive neither salary nor fees of whatsoever nature for discharging their duties as such." But some of them wearied of serving an ungrateful public and taking their pay in honor. Before sixty days had passed two had resigned, and at the end of the year only two of the original members, David W. Alexander and Manuel Requena, were left. There had been six resignations in eight months; and the first council had thirteen different members during its short existence.

The seven members elected to the first council, with the exception of Alexander Bell, had been either native born or naturalized citizens of Mexico, but the treaty of Guadalupe Hidalgo made them citizens of the United States. The council re-enacted many of the ordinances of the old ayuntamiento and enacted some new ones to suit the conditions then existing in the city. I append a few to illustrate the issues with which our first legislators had to contend when Los Angeles became an American city:

Art. 1st. The city's prisoners shall be formed in a chain-gang and occupied in public works.

Art. 2nd. All city prisoners must be sentenced within two days.

Art. 3rd. When the city has no work in which to employ the chain-gang the recorder shall, by means of notices conspicuously posted, notify the public that such and such a number of prisoners will be turned over to the highest bidder for private service, and in that manner they shall be disposed of for a sum which shall not be less than the amount of their fine and for double the time which they were to serve out at hard labor.

Art. 6th. Every citizen of the corporation shall as a duty, sweep in front of his habitation on Saturdays, as far as the middle of the street, or at least eight varas.

Art. 7th. No filth shall be thrown into zanjas (canals) carrying water for common use, nor into the streets of the city, nor shall any cattle be slaughtered in the same.

Art. 9th. Every owner of a store or tavern, and every person that lives in a house of more than two rooms facing to the street shall put a light at the door of said house during the first two hours of every dark night.

Art. 10th. Every shop or tavern shall close in winter at eight o'clock and in summer at nine o'clock at night.

Art. 12th. The washing of clothes in the zanjas which furnish water for common use is prohibited.

Art. 13th. Whosoever shall walk the streets in a scandalous attire or molest the neighbors with yells or in any other manner, shall be taken to jail, if the hour be late for business or the offender be intoxicated, and afterwards at the proper hour, or when again sober, the recorder shall impose a fine of not less than ten dollars, nor more than twenty-five, which must be paid on the spot, otherwise the offender shall be sent to the chain-gang, for the space of from ten to twenty-five days.

Art. 14th. The same penalty shall be imposed for playing cards in the street, regardless of the kind of game, likewise for playing any other game of the kind played in houses that are paying a tax for the privilege. If he be an Indian he shall pay a fine of three to five dollars or be imprisoned eight days in the chain-gang.

In the original draft of the ordinance. Article 2 prohibited "the carrying of firearms or blank arms" within the city limits, and Article 3 prohibited the discharge of the same, "except in defense of home and property." At a subsequent meeting the committee on police reported that it found "that the second and third articles, although they were useful, were difficult to enforce; it has withdrawn the same and today submits in lieu thereof others which it deems more expedient." These are Articles 1 and 2, quoted above, and relate to the sentencing of prisoners and their sale to the highest bidder. The police evidently found it healthier and more lucrative to capture and sell drunken Indians for revenue than to capture white desperadoes for carrying guns or collect fines from them for shooting up the town.

The following "Ordinance Relative to Public Washing," adopted March 27, 1852, illustrates a phase of domestic economy in early days that has long since disappeared. In the early '50s there was no system of water distribution except the Indian and his water buckets. To have carried enough water from the river to do the family washing would have been a stupendous undertaking for the lazy Indian. So the "wash" instead was carried to the canal that runs from the "little river."

"All persons," so reads the ordinance, "who may find it necessary to wash articles of any kind near the habitable portions of the city will do it in the water canal that runs from the little river, but will be bound to place their board or washer on the outer edge of the border of the canal, by which means, although they use the water, yet the washings from the dirty articles are not permitted, under any pretence, to again mix with the water intended for drinking purposes.

"The infraction of this ordinance will subject the delinquent to a fine which shall not pass three dollars, at the discretion of the mayor.

"B. D. Wilson,

"Manuel Requena, Mayor.

"(Pres. of the Common Council.)"

At the time this ordinance was adopted there was an island of considerable size in the river between the old Aliso road and First street. The portion of the river channel running on the western side of the island was known as the "little river."

The most difficult task the members of that first common council had before them was the Americanizing of the people of the old ciudad. The population of the town and the laws were in a chaotic state. It was an arduous and thankless task that these old-time municipal legislators had to perform — that of evolving order out of the chaos that had been brought about by the change of nations as rulers. The native population neither understood the language, the laws nor the customs of their rulers, and the newcomers among the Americans had very little toleration for the slow-going Mexican ways and methods they found prevailing in the city. To keep peace between the various factions required more tact than knowledge of law or lawmaking in the legislator. Fortunately, the first council was made up of level-headed men.

The Indian was one of the disturbing elements that worried the city fathers; not the wild ones of the mountains who raided the ranches and stole the rancheros' horses and cattle and were shot on sight, but the ex-neophytes of the missions. The mission Indians constituted the labor element of the city and country. When sober they were harmless and were fairly good laborers, but in their drunken orgies they became veritable fiends, and the usual result of their Saturday night revels was a dead Indian or two on Sunday morning; and all the others, old and young, male and female, were dead drunk. They were gathered up on Sunday after their carousal and carted of? to a corral. On Monday they were sentenced to hard labor for varying terms. At first they worked in the city chain gang on the streets, but the supply became too great and the council passed an ordinance (given elsewhere in this chapter), authorizing the auctioning of them off to private parties for double the amount of their fine. Evidently auctioning Indians to the highest bidders paid the city quite a revenue, for at a subsequent meeting, after the passing of the above-named ordinance, the recorder or police judge was authorized to pay the Indian alcaldes or chiefs the sum of one real (twelve and a half cents) out of every fine collected from Indians the said alcaldes may bring to the recorder for trial. A month or so later the recorder presented a bill of $15, the amount of money he had paid the alcaldes out of fines. At the rate of eight Indians to the dollar the alcaldes had evidently gathered up a hundred and twenty poor Los.!

The whipping post was used to instill lessons ^ of honesty and morality into the Indian. One court record reads: "Chino Valencia (Indian) was fined $50 and twenty-five lashes for stealing a pair of shears; the latter fine (the lashes) was paid in full; for the former he stands committed to the chain-gang for two months." At the same session of the court Vicente Guero, a white man, was fined $30 for selling liquor to the Indians – "fine paid and defendant discharged." Drunkenness, immorality and epidemics, civilization's gift to the aborigines, settled the Indian question in the old pueblo — settled it by exterminating the Indian.

When the United States land commission in 1852 began its herculean task of adjudicating the Mexican land grants in California, the city of Los Angeles laid claim to sixteen square leagues of land. In 1853 Henry Hancock surveyed the pueblo land lying beyond Ord's survey into thirty-five acre lots. The blocks of this survey contained eight lots of thirty-five acres each. Hancock's survey extended south of the city limits to Los Cuervos rancho, a distance of about three miles below the old pueblo boundary. It extended west to La Cienega, a distance of about two miles from the old pueblo line. All the territory taken into the city by annexation on the south and west in 1896 and subsequently was once claimed as city land. In the Hancock survey the streets south of Pico were named after the presidents of the United States. Beginning with Washington, in regular succession followed Adams, Jefferson, Madison, Monroe, John Quincy Adams and Jackson streets; all of these, except pieces of Washington, Adams and Jefferson, that fell within the old pueblo limits, have long since disappeared from the map.

South of Boyle Heights and east of the river the rancho of San Antonio curbed the city's ambition to expand in that direction. On the north and northwest the ranchos Los Feliz and the Verdugos encroached on the city's area, and the hostile owners refused to be surveyed into the municipality. On the east, from the center of the plaza, it was two leagues to the city line. The area of the city, according to the Hancock or Hansen survey of 1855 (the survey of 1855 was really made by Henry Hansen), was a fraction less than fifty square miles — a magnificent city on paper.

The United States commission in 1856 confirmed to the city a grant of four square leagues (about twenty-seven square miles) and rejected its claim to all outside of that. After many delays, in 1875, nearly twenty years later, a United States patent was issued to the mayor and council, and then the greater Los Angeles of the early '50s shrunk to the dimensions of Gov. Felipe de Neve's pueblo of 1781 — "one league to each wind measured from the center of the plaza."

Some of the Hancock survey lots in the southwest were called city donation lots. The term originated in this way:

The city in the early years of its American period was hard pressed for funds. It was land poor. Its pueblo lands brought it no revenue. Some Napoleon of finance originated a scheme to increase the municipal income. An ordinance was passed donating a Hancock survey lot (35 acres) to any person who would put it under cultivation and make improvements to the value of $100. When the title passed to a private owner the land became subject to taxation and the city thereby received a revenue. It was a brilliant stroke of finance for the time being, but it resulted in depriving the city of some of its finest holdings. At the time the offer was made there was no wild rush of "sooners" to secure a reservation. There was no land hunger then. Every one's appetite for land was satiated or could be easily satisfied, as land was about the cheapest commodity in the country.

Later on in the '50s and early '60s the pueblo lands were disposed of at various prices, ranging from $2.50 to $7.50 per acre. At these prices most of the magnificent patrimony that the city of Los Angeles inherited from the old Spanish pueblo was frittered away. All that was left was a few tracts that were considered worthless. One of these is the tract included in Westlake Park, now the beauty spot of the city. The city council had offered the tract in vain at twenty-five cents an acre. The old-timers who had been accustomed to get a thirty-five acre lot of fertile land as a donation scorned to buy an alkaline gulch at any price and the city was compelled perforce to keep it. Another of these patches of refuse real estate that the city fathers of old left to us is the site of Elysian Park. The heights and hollows of that now attractive park could not be cultivated then for lack of a water system and nobody would take them as a gift.

The most woeful waste of the city lands considered from the viewpoint of today was in the disposal of a tract of land lying between Seventh and Ninth streets and extending from Main to Figueroa streets, known on the city map as the Huber tract. This magnificent body of land, containing about one hundred acres, was given to private parties for what seems to us the making of a very insignificant improvement — the digging of an open ditch or irrigating canal. This ditch branched off from the Zanja Madre or mother ditch near Requena or East Market street, as it is now named, then flowed down between Los Angeles and South Main streets, watering the vineyards and vegetable gardens that covered the present sites of business blocks and hotels; crossed Main street below Fourth street and flowed just south of the Union Trust sky-scraper, then zigzagged across the blocks between Spring and Olive streets to Central Park; the arid waste of which it watered and made tree-growing in it possible. Then it meandered out to the rural regions of Figueroa and Adams streets, where it irrigated the orchards and barley fields of that sparsely settled suburb. Up to 1885 the ditch was open, then it was piped and carried underground. That irrigating canal, which has long since disappeared, cost the city, figuring the land given at its present value, nearly as much as the Panama canal will cost the nation when it is completed.

It is quite the custom of some modern writers to abuse the olden-time councilmen for their lavish disposal of our city lands. It is not just to bring railing accusations against them for conditions that they could not foresee. Without water to irrigate them the pueblo lands were worthless. With irrigating facilities they could be made productive. Homes would be built on the arid wastes, population would increase and the city's exchequer, which was chronically in a state of collapse, would expand and become plethoric. To make two blades of grass grow where but one grew before is the secret of agricultural wealth. The olden-time city fathers well knew that neither the one blade nor the two blades would grow without water. Could they have foreseen that prosperity would plant houses where they planted trees and would grow skyscrapers where they grew grain, they might have done differently and escaped the wailings and the railings of posterity. In giving away city lands for public improvements the city fathers followed the policy of our national government in the disposal of the public domain.

After the completion and acceptance of Ord's survey of the city lands in 1849, lots were offered for sale. For a lot 120 feet front by 165 feet deep, located on Main, Spring, Fort or Hill streets, between First and Fifth streets, the average price was $50, or about forty cents a front foot. In the early '50s the city experienced its first boom under American domination. Readymade houses were imported from New York and Boston. Brick and corrugated iron came into use for building. The passing of the adobe age began. The city was thriving. The cattle ranches were as productive as the gold mines. A full-grown steer that a few years before was worth $2 for his hide and tallow was now worth from $30 to $40 for beef. The cow counties of the south supplied the mines with beef. The sudden acquisition of wealth from the increase in the value of their cattle engendered extravagant habits in the rancheros and their families, which later on brought financial distress to many of them.

Up to 1856 the city had been making a steady growth and was beginning to put on metropolitan airs. Then a reaction came. The rich surface placers had been worked out, and the mines were no longer yielding large returns for small expenditures of labor and capital. But the severest blow to the cow counties came from the development of the agricultural resources of the central and northern counties of the state. Hundreds of miles nearer the mines, they could supply the mining camps with products at prices with which the cow counties could not compete. The result was hard times in the south. Money in 1856-57 in Los Angeles commanded five, ten and even as high as fifteen per cent interest, compounded monthly. The unfortunates who had mortgages on their possessions at such usurious rates were on the down grade to financial ruin. To add to their misfortunes, 1856 was a dry or drought year. Thousands of cattle died of starvation, and those that survived were unmarketable. The year 1857 was but little improvement on its predecessor. Hard times continued, if, indeed, they were not intensified. This was the beginning of the end of the cattle kings. They were compelled to mortgage their lands to tide them over the hard times. The high rates of interest absorbed their income and they could not reduce the principal of their loans. From 1858 to 1861 there was a spurt of prosperity. Don Abel Stearns built the Arcadia block, on the corner of Los Angeles and Arcadia streets. This was the finest business block south of San Francisco and was said to have cost $80,000. In 1859 Juan Temple built what afterward became the court house on the plat bounded by Spring, Main, Market and Court streets. The old-timers pointed with pride to these as evidence that the city was destined to be the metropolis of the south.

During the year 1859 thirty-one brick buildings and a considerable number of wooden ones were erected in the city. This was the biggest building boom in the history of the city up to this time.

In 1860 the telegraph line between San Francisco and Los Angeles was completed, and the first message over the wires was sent by Henry Melius, the mayor of Los Angeles, at 10 o'clock p. m., October 8th, to H. F. Teschemacher, president of the board of supervisors of San Francisco. The Salt Lake trade, which began in 1855 over the old Mexican trail, now paralleled by the Salt Lake Railroad, had grown to be a very important factor in the business of Los Angeles. In one month as high as sixty wagons had been dispatched with freight for Salt Lake City. Seemingly the metropolis of the cow counties was floating on the high tide of prosperity.

In 1861 reaction set in. The Civil war divided the people. Many of the leading citizens were sympathizers with the South and some of them joined the armies of the Confederacy. The value of real estate shriveled until it was hard to tell whether there was any value in it. One oldtimer, who had loaded up with Ord survey lots, located between First and Fourth on Spring and Main streets, in the -early '50s, at the prevailing price then of $50 a lot, desiring to go east in 1861, tried in vain to dispose of his lots at the price he paid for them ten years before. Finally some of his friends clubbed together and took them off his hands. It is said that misfortunes never come singly. It did seem during the first lustrum of the '60s as if they came in droves to the city and the country around. From 1861 to 1866 the metropolis of the south was a case of arrested development. Evolution had ceased and it actually retrograded.

In the winter of 1861-62 occurred one of the greatest floods in the history of California. The rivers covered the valleys and the cattle and horses were driven to the hills, where many starved to death before the waters subsided. The city water works, which the city had been bonding itself to build, were swept away, and the inhabitants had to fall back on the Indian and the olla for their water supply. It rained almost incessantly for thirty days and the city was cut off from all communication with the outside world, except by steamer. After the deluge came the drought. During the years 1863-64 there was the smallest rainfall ever known in California. As a consequence cattle in Southern California were very nearly exterminated and the doom of the cattle kings sealed.

Smallpox was raging among the Mexicans and Indians, and they were dying so fast that it was difficult to find persons to bury them. There was a feud between the adherents of the Union and the secessionists, so bitter that a body of United States troops had to be stationed in the city to keep order. There was nothing to sell and money had become an unknown quantity to many. So impoverished were the people that no assessment for city taxes was made in 1863-64. The landed possessions of two of the richest men of the city amounting to a quarter of a million acres, were advertised for sale as the owners were unable to pay their state and county taxes, although the total of their taxes did not exceed $5,000. In 1863 an Ord survey lot on the southeast corner of Spring and Second streets, 120 feet front, sold for $37, or about thirty cents a front foot. Two thousand acres in East Los Angeles were sold in 1864 at fifty cents an acre. The purchaser, Dr. Griffen, took it under protest. He wanted to purchase eight hundred acres lying along the river for sheep pasture. As this would cut off access to the water for sheep or cattle, the city council refused to sell it unless Griffen would take also the mesa land lying back from the river.

In 1865 light began to penetrate the financial gloom that hung over the old city. The Civil war came to an end. The defenders of the Union of States and its would-be destroyers sheathed their weapons and ceased hostilities. There had been no active hostilities between them. It had been principally a war of words. The Confederate sympathizers, who were largely in the majority, were loud in their denunciations of the government and flag under which they were living and had lived all their lives. However, beyond a few arrests for outspoken disloyalty they were not harmed — a marked contrast to the way the Union men were treated in the South, where a man endangered his life whenever he uttered a word in favor of the United States government. Los Angeles furnished but one representative to the Union army — that is, one who was an actual resident of the city at the beginning of the war — Charles M. Jenkins, a member of the California battalion, which was incorporated into the Second Massachusetts Cavalry. There was a company of native Californians recruited in Los Angeles in 1864 which did service against the Indians in Arizona.

Plentiful rainfalls in 1865-66 restored confidence in Southern California, but the passing of the cattle barons had begun. There was abundant feed on the ranches, but the owners were in no condition financially to replenish their depleted herds. The growth of the city was dependent upon the prosperity of the country adjacent. Its growth was slow. Rates of interest had been reduced, but it was hard to secure a loan at less than two per cent a month. The first of the modern improvements that we now deem so necessary to our existence introduced into the city was the granting to James Walsh, May 5, 1866, the exclusive right to lay gas mains in the city. He was to expend at least $5,000 in a plant and pipes and to furnish free gas for a lamp at a few of the principal street crossings on Main street, and also for the mayor's office. The price of gas at first was $10 a thousand cubic feet. When it was reduced to $7.50 a thousand it was considered quite a reasonable price, and people clamored for more street lamps. In September, 1868, the construction of the Los Angeles & San Pedro Railroad was begun. It was completed to Wilmington, October 26, 1869. The city had bonded itself to the amount of $75,000 and the county had invested $150,000 in it. There was bitter opposition to the bonding in certain quarters, but the bonds carried by a majority of thirty-nine votes. It was contended that the railroad would destroy freighting by teams, consequently there would be no use for horses and mules and no sale for barley. The pessimists wailed in vain; the progressive citizens prevailed. The road reduced the fare from the city to steamer anchorage from $5 to $2.50, cut the price of lumber $7.50 on the thousand feet, and reduced the freight on grain $5 a ton.

The first ice factory was started in 1868. It was conducted by Martin & Beath, where the city water works building now stands, on the comer of Alameda and Marchessault streets. The capacity of the plant was a ton and a half a day. The retail price of ice was five cents a pound; wholesale rates, $4 a hundred pounds. About the same time the first soda fountain was set up by Stevens & Wood near the post office on North Spring street. The novelty of phiz for a time attracted customers, but soda water was not strenuous enough for throats accustomed to aguardiente; after the novelty wore off the sizzling liquid ceased to attract.

The first bank in Los Angeles was organized in 1868 by Alvinza Hay ward and John G. Downey under the firm name of Hayward & Co., capital $100,000. It was located in the Downey block.

The first street railroad franchise was granted June I, 1869, to R. M. Widney for a period of twenty years. The privilege was granted over the following named streets: Beginning at the junction of Main and Spring streets, thence along Spring to First, First to Fort, Fort to Fourth, Fourth to Hill, Hill to Fifth, Fifth to Olive, Olive to Sixth, Sixth to Pearl (now Figueroa). The road was completed in 1872. The next car line was built on Main street from its junction with Spring to Washington street. The motive power of the cars was the mule. Single fare, ten cents — the smallest coin in circulation in California. The car made a trip every half hour with the consent of the mule; otherwise the service might be irregular. Sometimes when the mules bucked it became necessary for the passengers to assist as motors.

The subdivision of the great ranchos into small tracts, which began in 1868, brought a migration of home-seekers to Los Angeles. They came by steamer or trecked overland. The city began to show the effect of the influx of more capital and new men. In February, 1870, the houses in the business portion of the city were numbered systematically for the first time. It was not deemed necessary to number the dwelling houses. The first city directory was compiled the same year, but was not published until 1871. The directory contained seventy pages of names. The federal census of 1870 gave the population of the city 5,614, which was an increase of 1,215 in ten years. There were no places where intoxicating liquors were sold, an average of one saloon to every fifty-five inhabitants. The assessed value of all property in the city was $2,108,061.

The railroad bond issue was a live question in 1872. The Southern Pacific Company had made an offer to build twenty-five miles north and twenty-five east from Los Angeles city of the transcontinental line that it was building up the San Joaquin valley. The Texas Pacific met this with an offer to build from San Diego (the prospective terminus of its transcontinental line) a railroad up the coast to Los Angeles, giving the county sixty miles of railroad. The Southern Pacific countered this offer by agreeing to build, in addition to the fifty miles of its previous offer, a branch to Anaheim making in all seventy-seven miles. The recompense for this liberality on the part of the railroads was that the people should vote bonds equal to five per cent of the total taxable property of the county. The bond question stirred up the people as no previous issue had done since the Civil war. The contest was a triangular one, Southern Pacific, Texas Pacific, or no railroad. Each company had its agents and advocates abroad enlightening the people on the superior merits of its individual offer, while "Taxpayer" and "Pro Bono Publico," through the newspapers, bewailed the waste of the people's money and bemoaned the increase of taxes. At the election, November 5, the Southern Pacific won.

The city reached the high tide of its prosperity during the '70s in 1874. Building was active. It was estimated that over $300,000 was expended in the erection of business houses, and fully that amount in residences.

The year 1875 was one of disasters. The great financial panic of 1873, presaged by that monetary cyclone, "Black Friday in Wall Street," had no immediate effect upon business in California.

The years 1873 and 1874 were among the most prosperous in our history. The panic reached California in September, 1875, beginning with the suspension of the Bank of California in San Francisco and the tragic death of its president, William C. Ralston. In a few days nearly every bank in California closed its doors. The two in Los Angeles, the Temple & Workman and Hellman's, closed. The latter resumed business in a few days. The former made an attempt to stem the current of its financial difficulties, failed, and went down forever, carrying with it the fortune of many an unfortunate depositor. One of the bankers, William Workman, an old and highly respected pioneer, from brooding over the failure went insane and committed suicide. Temple died a few years later, a poor man.

The hard times following the bank failures were intensified by the drought of 1877, which brought disaster to the sheep industry of Southern California. There was no business reaction during the remainder of the decade. The federal census of 1880 gave the city's population at 11,183, an increase of almost one hundred per cent in ten years. The greater part of the gain was made in the first half of the decade. Railroad connection with San Francisco and Sacramento was made in September, 1876, but it opened up no new market for Los Angeles. Times continued hard and money close. The ruling rate of interest on mortgages was one and one-half per cent per month. The adoption of the new constitution of the state in 1879 did not improve matters. The capitalists were afraid of some of its radical innovations.

CHAPTER XLI.
LOS ANGELES IN ITS SECOND CENTURY.

LOS ANGELES city rounded out the first century of its existence September 4, 1881. Its population then was estimated at 12,000. It began with 44. Its average yearly increase was 120, a slow growth as western towns grow. Its centennial celebration — a grand affair for that time — was a quaint mixture of the past and the present, a curious blending of the new with the old. In that procession, largely made up of horsemen, rode the graceful cabellero on his silver-mounted silla de montar (saddle) with jingling spurs and swingino' riata. In it, too, was the American newcomer astride of a turtle-shell saddle, knees pointing to the zenith and hand gripping the saddle-bow. In a creaking old wooden-wheeled carreta rode Benjamina, an ancient Indian lady, who was the belle of Yangna when Los Angeles was born. Fashionable coupes, newly arrived, and rumbling road wagons that had crossed the plains in '49, pieced out the long line of varied vehicles that wound through the unpaved and unsprinkled streets on that centennial day. There were orations in English, in Spanish and in French. There was feasting and rejoicing in the ancient style and in the modern. The festivities ended with a baili (ball) that was muy grande.

Through somebody's blundering, or possibly to give its first century the full measure of days, the 5th of September was celebrated instead of the 4th, the city's real birthday. Although for nearly half of its first century Los Angeles had been officially entitled to write itself a ciudad (city), yet it had not outgrown many of the characteristics of its pueblo days. When it passed its hundredth year there was not a paved street within its limits. The sidewalks were mostly graveled paths with cobble stones protruding. Everybody went to the post office for his mail. The telephone and the hello girl were unknown. Beyond the business center darkness brooded over lampless streets.

From Main street to the river, and below East Third street to the city limits was a succession of orange groves and vineyards with an occasional walnut orchard interspersed. Looking down from the western hills, which then had a few scattering houses upon them, the observer beheld stretching away to the south for miles a sea of green. Never before or since has the Angel City been so beautiful as she was in the closing years of her first century. The tourist was not much in evidence then. California on wheels had not yet made its pilgrimage of enlightenment through the eastern states; nor was there a chamber of commerce to tell the story of our wonderful products and salubrious climate. Occasionally a newspaper correspondent or a bookmaker discovered the city and wrote it up or wrote it down as the fancy seized him — patted himself appreciatively over his discovery if it pleased him, or slandered it maliciously if it did not. One of the very best descriptions ever written of Los Angeles when it was nearing the end of its first century can be found (if you can find a copy of the book) in B. F. Taylor's "Between the Gates." He visited Los Angeles in 1878. I copy a portion of his description:

"Whoever asks where Los Angeles is, to him I shall say: across a desert without wearying, beyond a mountain without climbing; where heights stand away from it, where ocean winds breathe upon it, where the gold-mounted lime-hedges border it; where the flowers catch fire with beauty; among the orange groves; beside the olive trees; where the pomegranates wear calyx crowns; where the figs of Smyrna are turning; where the bananas of Honolulu are blossoming; where the chestnuts of Italy are dropping; where Sicilian lemons are ripening; where the almond trees are shining; through that Alameda of walnuts and apricots; through this avenue of willows and poplars; in vineyards six Sabbath-days' journey across them; in the midst of a garden of thirty-six square miles — there is Los Angeles.

"The city is the product of one era of barbarism, two or three kinds of civilizations, and an interregnum, and is about as old as Washington's body-servant when he died the last time, for it is in its ninety-seventh year. You meet native Californians, wide-hatted Mexicans, now and then a Spaniard of the old blue stock, a sprinkle of Indians and the trousered man in his shirt and cue. You see the old broad-brimmed, thick-walled adobes that betray the early day. You hear somebody swearing Spanish, grumbling German, vociferating Italian, parleying in French, rattling Chinese and talking English.

"Yesterday and today are strangely blended. You stroll among thousands of vines that are ninety years old and yet in full bearing. You pass a garden just redeemed from the dust and ashes of the wilderness. You pluck an orange from a tree that was venerable when Charles the Fourth was king of Spain, and you meet a man who has sat down to wait six years for his first fruit. A drive through the old quarter of the city takes you to the heart of Mexico, with the low-eaved fronts, the windows sunk like niches in the walls, the Italic-faced old porticos, the lazy dogs dozing about in the sun. In ten minutes you are whirled between two long lines of new-made fragrance, such luxuriance of vegetation, and nothing nearer like the 'waving sword at the Eastward' of the first homestead than the slashed saber-like leaves of the banana that holds up its rich, strange, liver-colored blossoms as if it were proud of them."

"If to one city more than another, of all cities I have seen, belongs the urbs in horto of Chicago's seal, Los Angeles is the place. It is not a city in a garden, but a garden in the city. The two are interwoven like the blossoming warp and woof of a Wilton carpet. We visited the vineyard and the wine-presses of Don Mateo Keller. It is in the heart of the city, and contains one hundred and thirty-seven acres, and has two hundred and ten varieties of grapes. In the season ten thousand gallons of wine are produced daily, and there were two hundred thousand gallons ripening in the vaults."

At the close of its first century the business district of the city had traveled south as far as First street. The center of retail trade was the Baker block, and the fashionable hotel was the Pico house that looked down upon the old plaza. On the southwest corner of Spring and First streets, where the Hotel Nadeau stands, was a horse corral, and on the southwest corner of Spring and Second streets, where the Hollenbeck now stands, was another. Merchandising and manufacturing were closely associated. On the northwest corner of Main and Second streets and jutting half way across Second street was an iron foundry. On the corresponding corner of Spring and Second streets stood the old brick schoolhouse, built in 1854. On the lot just north of this stood the Mechanics' planing mill.

Lehman's Garden of Paradise, south of Third, fronting on Main street, was still a pleasure resort. Adam and Eve had been driven out of Eden and so had Lehman — ^not by a fiery sword, but by a mortgage. The cactus hedge that fenced the Spring street front of the garden was still intact, but the tree of knowledge had been cut down, and the old serpent had been scotched. It may be necessary to explain that these denizens of Eden before Adam's fall were pieces of statuary that Lehman had placed in his garden to decorate it. George Lehman, better known as "Round House George," had opened his Garden of Paradise as a pleasure resort in the early '50s. It became quite popular. The adobe round house at the Main street entrance, where the Pinney block now stands, was a famous landmark of early days. It was torn down about 1887. South of Second street. Main, Spring and Fort (now Broadway) were the principal residence streets of the city.

In 1882 the financial depression that began in 1875 with the failure of the Temple & Workman Bank, eased up a little. The Southern Pacific Railroad, building eastward, had penetrated the mining regions of Arizona and New Mexico and had opened a market for the products of Southern California. Its completion the same year gave Los Angeles direct connection with the east. The new transcontinental road, free from the deep snows in winter that often blockaded the Central road, became the popular winter route to California, and brought into Los Angeles immigrants and capitalists that were not slow to recognize the great possibilities of the country.

The Atlantic & Pacific, with connecting roads — the Atchison, Topeka & Santa Fe and California Southern — effected an entrance into Los Angeles over a leased track from San Bernardino in 1885. This gave Los Angeles another transcontinental road. In the spring of 1886 a disagreement between the roads brought on a rate war. Round-trip tickets from Missouri river points were sold as low as $15. Thousands of eastern people, taking advantage of the low rates, visited Los Angeles. They were delighted with the country, and either remained or went home to sell their possessions and return.

Real estate values went up rapidly in 1886, but in 1887 came that event that marks the turning point in the city's history — the boom. The story of the great real estate boom of 1887 is told in another chapter of this book. The boom is usually regarded by historians as an unmitigated evil — a wild craze, a speculative mania, that deprived people of their senses and wrought their financial ruin. Such a view of it exaggerates the evil done. While it had its tragic features and its comic as well, while it was the undoing of many plungers and unwise promoters, yet with all of its extravagances, its inflation of values, its unsettling of previous conditions, its bursting of bubble fortunes, the good it did far overbalanced the evil.

In a hundred years business had traveled from its first center, the old Plaza, southward to First street, a distance of about four blocks. Between 1881 and 1886 it had crossed First street on Spring and Main and in a few instances had gone below Second street. The Nadeau hotel, the most imposing structure outside of the old business section, was completed in 1883. While designed for a hotel, it was too large a building for the travel of that time. A large room on the second floor originally designed for the dining-room, was rented to the Y. M. C. A., and was the first hall of that organization in the city. Another smaller hall was leased for a justice's court, and rooms on the second and third floors were let for lawyers' and doctors' offices. The rapid development of the real estate brokerage business in 1886-87 created a great demand for offices in the district between Temple and Second streets on Spring and Main, and the enormous rents that real estate agents were willing to pay for office room in this locality virtually drove merchants to seek new locations further south. Their former storerooms were subdivided into a number of cubby-holes, each one of which rented for more than the entire room had brought before.

As an example of the rapid advance in rents caused by the demand for real estate offices, this will serve as an illustration: An old one-story wooden building on Spring street south of First, that before the boom might have brought its owner a rental of $50 per month, was subdivided into stalls after the usual method (a bar of iron between each tenant's holding) and rented at from $75 to $150 per month for a stall, prices varying as you receded from the front entrance. The rental of the building paid the landlord an income of about $1,000 a month. The building was so out of repair that the enterprising boomers who occupied it during a rainstorm were compelled to hold umbrellas over themselves and their customers while negotiating a deal in climate and corner lots.

At the beginning of the city's second century the selling price of lots on Spring street between First and Second was $50 per front foot; below Second the value decreased rapidly. In August, 1861, the lot (60x165 feet) on the northwest corner of Spring and Sixth streets sold for $1,500. or $25 per front foot. This was considered a fair price as values ranged then. Five years later, with some cheap improvements added, the lot sold for $22,000. In May, 1883, the northwest corner of Spring and Second, 120x 165 feet (on which the first school house the city owned was built in 1854), was sold by the board of education to the city for $31,000, and a new site just south of Sixth, fronting 120 feet on Spring and the same on Broadway, purchased by the board for $12,500.

The council in 1884 erected the first hall owned by the city, on the rear 60 feet of its purchase, and in 1887 sold the frontage on Spring, with a depth of 105 feet, for $120,000, an increase of over 400 per cent in three years. Such unprecedented rise in values was a source of astonishment to the old-time residents of the city, many of whom had hastened to unload their long-time holdings on the newcomers.

When the depression came in 1888 the pessimists, who had croaked dire disaster to the city, were disappointed that their prophesies proved false. The land boom of 1886-87 was followed by a building boom in 1888-89. The investors in high priced real estate were compelled to improve their property to obtain an income.

In 1884 the first cable railway, starting at Spring street, was built west over Second, Lakeshore avenue and First street to Belmont avenue. The projectors of the enterprise received a large bonus from the property holders on the western hills. It aided greatly in the settlement of the hill district, but being cheaply constructed it was frequently out of repair and was finally abandoned.

The first electric street car line was built in 1885. Its route was along Los Angeles, San Pedro and Maple avenue to Pico street, and westward on that street to the Electric Homestead tract, lying west of the old city boundary. Primarily the road was promoted to sell this tract. A common method of disposing of tracts in the early days was to build half a dozen or more cheap houses on the tract as baits or prices. Lots were sold at a uniform price, but not located; when all were sold the lots were distributed at a drawing, and the purchaser who drew a prize house paid no more for it than the man who drew a hole in the ground. The Electric Homestead and a number of other tracts were disposed of by this method.

The electric railroad was not a success. The power frequently gave out and the passengers had the choice of waiting an hour or two until enough electricity was generated to move the car, or to walk to the city. The sheriff finally levied on the rolling stock and the road for debt.

The first attempt to introduce the trolley car in Los Angeles was a failure, and the promoter, Howland, died in poverty. Howland had introduced the lighting of the city by electricity in December, 1881. Six masts, 150 feet high, were erected at different points in the city between the Plaza and Seventh street and Grand avenue and Main street. The power house was located on the corner of Banning and Alameda streets.

In 1889 work was begun on the cable railway system. A line was extended on Broadway to Seventh and west on Seventh to Westlake Park. Another line extended from Seventh on Grand avenue to Jefferson street. From First and Spring a line ran on East First to Boyle Heights, and from the same point another ran on North Spring, Upper Main and Downey avenue to East Los Angeles. A million and a half dollars were expended in tracks, power houses and machinery'. All but the tracks were discarded a few years later, when electricity was substituted for steam and the trolley for the cable. The Los Angeles Electric Railway system was begun in 1892. The first line constructed was that on West Second, Olive, First and other streets to Westlake Park. The people on the line of the road gave a subsidy of $50,000 to the promoters. The traction (or Hook) system was begun in 1895.

The horse car disappeared from the city streets in the last decade of the 19th century, and was relegated to the category of the carreta and the caballo de silla (saddle horse), the motors of travel in old pueblo days. The bob car and the mule held the right of way on Main street the longest of any of the principal streets. They were pushed off by the trolley in 1895.

In February, 1892, Messrs. Doheny and Connon, prospecting for petroleum, dug two wells with pick and shovel on West State street, in the resident portion of the city. At the depth of 150 feet oil was found. From this small beginning a profitable industry has grown up. The oil belt extends diagonally across the northwestern part of the city. The total number of wells drilled within the city limits up to June, 1900, was 1,300, and the yield of these from the beginning of the oil development was estimated at 7.000,000 barrels, worth in round numbers about $6,000,000.

The oil industry reached its maximum in 1901. Over-production and the Standard Oil octopus caused a rapid decline in prices. From $1 a barrel in 1900 the price steadily declined until in 1904 it reached fifteen cents a barrel. Drilling new wells within the city practically ceased in 1903, and the unused derricks began to disappear.

When the oil industry was at high tide in 1899-1900, it was forced by a certain class of promoters to take on some of the wildcat characteristics of the great real estate boom of 1887. For a time it was no uncommon feat to incorporate a half dozen oil companies in a day. The capital stock of these companies ran up into the millions, sometimes the amount paid in by the promoters reached as high as $10. The man on the outside was the fellow who put up the money to get inside — "to be let in on the ground floor" was a favorite catch phrase then. It was not necessary to own oil lands to incorporate a company. A promise of a lease of a few acres of a pasture field or a mountain canon was sufficient. The profit to the promoters came from selling stocks, not oil. During the height of the oil boom stocks could be bought at all prices, from a cent a share up. Stocks in a new company would be advertised at five cents a share, in a short time advanced to ten cents, then raised to fifteen cents, and when buyers began to lag the last call was sounded. "At the last stroke of the clock at midnight next Saturday the stock of the Grizzly Bear Oil Development Company will be advanced to twenty-five cents a share. Oil sand has been struck in the company's wells and all unsold stock will be withdrawn from the market in a few days." This "call of the wild" (cat promoter) hurried the halting, and there was a rush for the stock. Strange to say the clock of these promoters never struck twelve on Saturday night!

One company of enterprising promoters, to satisfy a crying need of the times— cheap stock — organized a company with a capital of $5,000,000 and placed its stock on the market at a cent a share. The stock advanced to two cents a share, and might have gone higher had not the boom burst and the company been forced to suspend — the sale of stock, their only asset. The oil stock mania gradually subsided. Beautifully lithographed certificates of stock were the only returns that many an investor could show for "very hard cash" invested.

Another of the forgotten enterprises of the closing years of the nineteenth century was the Belgian hare industry. An enterprising magazine writer made the discovery that the meat of the Belgian hare as an article of food was superior to beef or mutton and could be produced at a minimum of cost. This "back yard industry," as it was called, could be launched on a very small capital. A coop with a Belgian hare buck and doe and you were ready for business. The rapidity with which the mania spread was equaled by the rapidity with which the hares multiplied. It was a rare thing at the height of the epidemic to find a back yard that was not decorated with a rabbitry. While the ostensible purpose of the industry was to produce a food product, the fad soon took the form of producing fancy stock at fabulous prices. Kings, lords, dukes, queens and princesses with their wonderful pedigrees pushed the plebeian Belgian out of business, or rather the pedigree maker converted the pleb into an aristocrat. A king with the red foot and peculiar markings on the back, sure signs of an aristocratic lineage, was rated at $1,000, and the queens and princesses ranged in value all the way from $25 to $500 each. Exactly what these high-priced hares were good for, except to sell to some one who had been seized with an attack of the craze, no one seemed able to find out, or rather cared to find out. "When the supply exceeds the demand," queried the pessimist, "what then?" "Oh! that never can be; all the world wants haxes and Southern California is the only place where they can be grown to perfection." The craze increased with every report of big profits from small beginnings. But there came a time when it was all supply and no demand. It was found that as an article of food the flesh of the most aristocratic of the red-footed gentry was not up to the standard of the despised California jack-rabbit.

319

Then came a scramble to get out of the business, but few of the operators did without loss. The lords, the dukes and the duchesses died, but not of old age, and the tenantless rabbitries were converted into kindling wood or chicken coops. History has kept alive for three centuries the story of the tulip mania of Holland, when a rare bulb sold for 13,000 florins and stolid Dutch merchants traded ships' cargoes for choice collections of tulip tubers that were of no utility and scant beauty. The Belgian hare boom of Southern California is forgotten, although in volume it was greater than the tulip craze of Holland. How much capital was invested in it it is impossible to say. Some of the wholesale rabbitries were incorporated with capitals ranging from $50,000 to $100,000. Experts made frequent trips to Europe for fancy stock. A magazine was published in the interest of the industry, and at its height from ten to twelve columns of liners in the Sunday dailies told those interested where they could find the highest rank of Belgian aristocrats. There were experts in hare heraldry, who made good incomes by writing pedigrees for would-be aristocrats. Many of their pedigrees were works of art — the art of lying.

During the closing decade of the nineteenth century there was but little advance in the price of real estate outside of the choice business streets; prices in 1900 were lower than in 1887. The city had doubled in population and business had increased, but many of the property holders were staggering along under mortgages, the legacies of the great boom. These were the optimists who had implicit faith in the future of the city. The great financial depression that had spread over the United States in the middle years of the last decade of the century had been intensified in Southern California by a series of dry or drought years. It was not until the first year of the new century that light began to break through the financial gloom.

H. E. Huntington bought a controlling interest in the Los Angeles Electric Railway and began the building of a system of suburban or interurban electric railways to the different cities and towns contiguous to Los Angeles. The road to Long Beach was completed in 1902, to Monrovia in 1903, and to Whittier the same year. The seven-story Huntington building, corner of Sixth and Main, the entrepot of all Huntington interurban lines, was completed in 1903. These improvements, together with the extension of new street car lines in the city, stimulated the real estate market and brought about a rapid advance in values. Lots on South Main street held at $100 a front foot in 1900 sold five years later at $1,500, and frontage on South Hill street valued at $200 a front foot in 1901 sold in 1906 at $2,500. Real estate contiguous to the business district, but still residence property, had advanced in value in five years from one thousand to twelve hundred per cent.

The completion of the San Pedro, Los Angeles & Salt Lake Railroad in March, 1905, gave Los Angeles its fourth transcontinental line. The discovery of gold and silver mines in southern Nevada has made Los Angeles a mining center both for supplies and stocks. An idea of its rapid growth in buildings, wealth and population may be obtained from the number and amount of the building permits, the city assessments and the school marshal's returns:

Year	No. of Permits	Valuation
1901	2,730	$ 4,099,198
1902	4,655	8,981,974

1903	6,398	13,175,446
1904	7,064	13,409,061
1905	9,543	15,482,067
1906	9,408	18,273,318

City Assessments—Increase for each year:

Year	Value	Increase for the Year
1901	$70,562,307	$4,962,387
1902	86,410,735	15,854,428
1903	109,223,823	23,507,088
1904	126,126,563	16,202,740
1905	156,661,566	30,535,003
1906	205,767,729	49,106,163

CHAPTER XLII THE PASSING OF THE RANCHO

At the time of the conquest of California by the Americans the greater part of the arable lands west of the Coast range between San Diego and San Francisco was held in large tracts known as ranchos. These were devoted by their owners, the rancheros, to the raising of cattle for their hides and tallow — the only commodities produced that would bear shipment to distant markets.

The rancheros were not all of Spanish or Mexican nativity, among them were Americans, English, Scotch, French, and a few representatives of other European nations. These men had become citizens of Mexico by naturalization, married into Spanish families and had obtained land grants on the same terms as the native Californians. They had learned the language, embraced the religion and adopted the customs of the country. The rancho and the vaquero were Californian of the Mexican era. The cattle range and the cowboy were adjuncts of the far west of a later American period. The romance of the former had departed before the advent of the latter.

The era of the rancho as a distinctive feature of Californian colonization industry began with the rise of Mexican domination in California. While the great ranchos are spoken of as Spanish grants, but very few of them were granted while California was under the rule of Spain. The San Rafael rancho, lying on the left bank of the Los Angeles river and extending to the Arroyo Seco, was granted by Gov. Pedro Fages, October 20, 1784. The San Pedro rancho, lying along the ocean and the estuary of San Pedro bay, Col. J. J. Warner claims, was granted the same year. The Santiago de Santa Ana rancho was granted in 1810. These are all Spanish grants made by Spanish governors and among the oldest grants in California.

As the Indian population at the missions decreased the mission lands not in use were granted to settlers, but it was not until secularization of the missions returned to the public domain the vast landed possessions held by these establishments in trust for their Indian converts, that the rancho era really began.

After secularization it was easy to obtain a grant of land. The individual seeking it applied to the local official of the district in which the land was located. If on examination it was found the land was vacant and the applicant had the means to stock it, his application was sent to the governor for his approval. If found correct, the governor confirmed the grant and issued an expediente or official title. The largest area that could be granted in one expediente was eleven square leagues, the smallest one league (a Spanish league contains 4444.4 acres). There was no limit, however, to the amount a ranchero could acquire by purchase.

To obtain judicial possession of a grant of land, application was made to the alcalde of the district, who, with two witnesses and a riata fifty varas in length, would go out on horseback and measure off the tract. The survey, if it could be called such, was begun by throwing up a pile of stones or earth as an initial point, and planting a cross thereon. No compass directions were noted and a line was run by sighting to some natural landmark. This loose and indefinite method of establishing boundary lines opened a Pandora box of evils for the unfortunate landowners later on.

It cost but little to stock a range, cattle multiplied rapidly and in a few years, with but little exertion on his part and almost no expenditure of money, the ranchero found himself the owner of vast herds of cattle — a veritable cattle baron. It required no continuous brain fag — no nerve-destroying worry, no scheming to outwit a competitor, no promotion of a trust to become rich in this lotus land of ease, in the halcyon days of the cattle barons. Given thousands of acres of fertile land, an army of retainers, a continually increasing band of cattle and a caballada (band) of horses, the baron who ruled over all this led a life of ease with dignity. The annual matanza was his harvest. The hides of the slaughtered cattle were dried and packed and the arrobas of tallow stored in caves to await the coming of the hide droghers with their department stores of merchandise and Yankee notions to barter. The rancheros devoted a few of their myriads of acres to the growing of grain, fruit and vegetables for their own use, but produced none for market because there was no market for such. The Indians did the work and took their pay in products of the soil and a scanty supply of clothing. The cattle barons built no palaces — their abodes were commodious, but not imposing — but stored away in trunks, chests and drawers in some of these adobe houses, to be worn on state occasions, were silks and satins and costly jewelry that a queen might envy. Alfred Robinson tells of a dress-suit that Tomas Yorba. the owner of the great Santiago rancho of 62,000 acres, used to wear on festal occasions. It cost over $1,000 and yet the manor of this feudal baron had an earthen floor. His daughter had one hundred and fifty dress patterns of the finest silk and satin, and jewelry to match. It might be added that the fashion changed about once in fifty years and the accumulated finery of one generation descended to the next. A man might wear his grandfather's hat and the grand-daughter might wear the bridal robes of her grandmother and still be in the fashion.

Bancroft, in his "California Pastoral," says of the Californians:

"As for houses, the climate was mild and the men were lazy. Opening their eyes in the morning they saw the sun; they breathed the fresh air, and listened to the song of the birds; mounting their steeds, they rode forth in the enjoyment of healthful exercise; they tended their herds, held intercourse with each other and ran up a fair credit with heaven. How many among the statesmen, among the professional and business men and artisans of our present high civilization can say as much? It was their business to live, to do nothing but exist; and they did it well."

The discovery of gold and the mad rush to the mines in '49 and the early '50s for a time increased the wealth and power of the cattle barons. Their great ranchos were still intact. The demand for meat, in the mines and towns that sprang into existence after the discovery of gold, could be supplied only from the vast herds of the cow counties.

From the coming of the hide droghers down to the rush of the gold-seekers the price of cattle had not changed materially. Two to four dollars for a full-grown steer was the usual rate of exchange. The overwhelming tide of Argonauts that flooded California immediately after the discovery of gold upset all previous standards of value, and inflated the price of all the products of the ranchos. The standing price of cattle in hide-droghing days was increased a thousand per cent by the influx of gold-seekers. Full-grown steers in the early '50s sold at prices ranging from $30 to $40 each, and mustangs that had no marketable value in the olden time were elevated in price at least to the dignity of thoroughbreds. The ranchero who had cattle on a thousand hills, or even a thousand cattle on a hill, had a source of revenue more certain and more profitable than a gold mine. Cattle buyers from the mines came over the Tehachapi mountains, or down the coast in steamers, bringing with them sacks of gold; and golden twenties and octagon-shaped fifty dollar slugs became more plentiful in the old pueblo of Los Angeles than silver pesos had been in the days of the padres.

This sudden accumulation of riches turned the heads of the frugal rancheros and they spent with the prodigality of princes. General Vallejo, one of the cattle barons of Central California, said in those early days he never thought of tipping the boy who held his horse with less than an ounce of gold, equivalent to $16. The rancheros had always been accustomed to card-playing, but bets in the olden days were at most a few pesos or a few horses or cattle; with the sudden accession of wealth gambling became a passion and fortunes were lost at a sitting. One extravagance of the native Californian in the olden time was rich dressing — with the golden days of '49 this passion was increased a thousand-fold, and not alone was the passion for costly dress increased, but the taste for costly viands as well. The simple wines of their own make palled on their taste and the costly imported wines of France alone satisfied. Cattle ranges were more productive and more profitable than gold mines. Why save? — spend while you have it — mañana (tomorrow) more cattle to sell, more money to spend. Come easy, go easy.

But a change was coming — slowly, but surely. The first knell in the doom of the cattle barons had been sounded, but they heard it not. Each year less drovers came over the Tehachapi and the price of cattle was steadily falling. Poco tiempo — by and by — prices will go up again, said the ranchero. Unknowingly he was facing those problems that have been the bane of the producer since the dawn of civilization — cost of transportation and excess of production.*

In 1849 and the early '50s Argonauts were in such mad haste to reach California before all the gold was dug out of its hills and gulches that they thought of no other industry but gold digging. But after an experience with pick and pan, often disastrous, many of them sought other vocations.

At the time of Marshall's discovery of gold the great valleys of the San Joaquin and Sacramento were uninhabited except by Indians. Great bands of elk, droves of wild horses and herds of antelope and deer grazed upon the luxuriant grasses that covered these plains.

The speculative gringo — the nemesis of the easy-going native Californian — after figuring out the possibilities of a fortune in cattle raising in these valleys, proceeded to put his scheme into operation. In 1852 the first venture was made in driving cattle across the plains and was enlarged upon in 1853. It would seem like an exemplification of the old adage, "carrying coals to Newcastle," to bring cattle across the plains to California, where for years vast herds had been slaughtered for their hides and tallow.

In the early '50s of the last century young cattle could be bought in the western states at prices ranging from $5 to $10 each. Even if fifty per cent of a herd was lost on the journey across the plains the survivors could be sold at an advance sufficient to make a profit. The cattle brought across the plains were a vastly superior breed to the lanky, long-horned, mouse colored native bovine.

The earliest official report of the number of cattle brought into the State that I have found is for the year 1854. It is taken from the Los Angeles Star. It is interesting to note the various routes by which cattle as well as people came into the State in the early days. "The number of cattle brought into the State in 1854 was as follows: Via Nobles Pass, 24.025; via Beckworths Pass, 10,150; via the Gila route, 9,075; via the Sonoma Pass, 5,106; via Carson River route, 12,914; total, 61,270."

Of the total number arriving in the State, only those coming by the Gila route were brought into Southern California. Fifty thousand were thrown into the Sacramento and San Joaquin valleys and not only diminished the demand from the southern ranchos to that amount, but as these cattle were used for breeding it marked the beginning of the end of the cattle barons' prosperity.

Cattle ranges were acquired in the Sacramento and the San Joaquin valleys and along the foothills and stocked with American cattle. With the advantage of 300 to 500 miles nearer market in the mines and supplying a superior quality of beef at lower prices, the valley ranges were gradually absorbing the cattle trade and the cattle barons of the south found their source of wealth slipping away from them.

The newly-rich who have for a time reveled in wealth cannot readily return to simple living. The lush of luxuries that had come to the rancheros and their families in the flush days of gold mining when a cattle range with its herds was more profitable than a gold mine had created expensive habits that they could not or would not shake off. Money they must have and money they could have by mortgaging their ranchos. Their needs were pressing and the day of payment afar off. They had never experimented with that death gage, a mortgage. So mortgages were negotiated at ruinous rates of interest — five, ten and even fifteen per cent per month were promised. When the mortgages came due times were harder, money scarcer and prices of the products of the ranchos lower, so the only resource left was to increase the mortgages by adding the accrued interest to the original debt and giving a new lien on their lands.

A story that well illustrates this system of financiering was current among old-timers years ago. There were several versions of it. The following is as correct as can be given now:

Lemuel Carpenter, an early Californian, was the owner of the Santa Gertrudes rancho — a body of rich land covering a large portion of the Los Nietos country. Carpenter had a passion for gambling — a no uncommon form of dissipation among the rancheros. The newly imported game of faro that came with the gold rush fascinated him. Faro is a banking game in which the players play against the dealer, or banker as he is sometimes called. Fortunes were sometimes won in the days of gold, but more often lost, on the turn of a card. In miners' parlance the game was called "bucking the tiger." The name probably originated from the claw-shaped hook with which the dealer raked in his winnings. The tiger had clawed in Carpenter's last dollar, but he had discovered, or thought he had, the combination in which the cards were running and he was sure with more coin to stake he could win back his lost money and possibly break the bank, a consummation that would make him a hero in the gambling fraternity. He hunted up a local Shylock and negotiated a mortgage on his rancho for $5,000 with interest at five per cent per month, compounded monthly. Like John Oakhurst in Bret Harte's "Outcasts of

Poker Flat," Carpenter struck a streak of bad luck and he kept striking it. The faro dealer raked in his $5,000 and he could not pay the interest or principal of his mortgage. The debt soon doubled and the mortgage was again and again renewed at increased amounts until with interest compounded over and over his indebtedness amounted to $50,000; then Shylock took his pound of flesh — Carpenter's rancho — and Carpenter committed suicide. Thus the magnificent Santa Gertrudes rancho, worth today $1,000,000, was lost to its owner for the insignificant sum of $5,000, which now would scarce buy ten acres out of its twenty-five thousand. Another element that contributed towards the passing of the olden time ranchos and hastened the financial ruin of the rancheros was litigation. The careless and easy-going methods of granting lands under Mexican domination fattened many a lean and hungry lawyer under American rule. Lost expedientes, indefinite boundaries, overlapping grants and the incursion of squatters, who sometimes coolly settled upon the lands of the rancheros and held them without leave or license from the real owners — all these were fruitful sources of lawsuits.

As an illustration of indefinite boundary lines those of La Habra rancho, formerly in Los Angeles county but now in Orange county, give an excellent example and these perhaps are not the worst that could be found in the old records. "Commencing at the camino viejo (old road) and running in a right line 550 varas, more or less, distant from a small corral of tuna plants, which plants were taken as a landmark, thence in a direction west by south running along the camino viejo 18,200 varas to a point of small hills, at which place was fixed as a landmark the head of a steer; from thence east by north passing a cuchillo (waste land) 11,000 varas, terminating at a hill that is in a direct line with another hill which is much higher, and has three small oak trees upon it, at which place a small stone landmark is placed; thence north by east 2,000 varas, terminating at the right line of the small corral of tunas aforesaid, the point of beginning."

In the course of time the camino viejo was made to take a shorter cut across the valley, the corral of tunas disappeared, a coyote or some other beast carried away the steer's head, the three oaks were cut down and carted away for fire-wood, the small stone was lost, the cuchillo was reclaimed from the desert and the La Habra was left without landmarks or boundary lines. The landmarks lost, the owners of the adjoining ranchos, if so inclined, could crowd them over onto the La Habra, or its owner in the same way could increase the area of his possessions, and the expanding process in all probability would result in costly litigation.

Some of these legal contests over the ownership of ranchos were fought with persistence and bitterness, and were carried from one court to another until they reached the Supreme Court of the United States. It not infrequently happened that when the legal battle was fought to a finish all that the contestants had to show for years of litigation was a series of court decisions, from the lowest to the highest, and stacks of legal documents. The money-lenders who had furnished the sinews of war were the owners of the contested property. Litigation growing out of defective titles was the bane and curse of California for at least three decades after the conquest, and more men were killed in quarrels over the disputed ownership of lands than fell in all the battles of the conquest.

Another element that served to embarrass the cattle barons was taxations. Under Mexican rule when cattle were slaughtered for their hides and tallow there was no tax on the land and cattle. The tariff on imports and the tax on men's pleasures and vices paid the very limited cost of governing. Under American rule, although the vices were multiplied the revenue derived from fines and from licenses for saloons and gambling houses fell far short of paying the cost of governing.

The county of Los Angeles was organized by the election of county officers April 1, 1850. At that election Don Antonio Coronel was elected county assessor. As about nine-tenths of the inhabitants of the newly created county spoke and understood the Spanish language only, it was necessary to have someone who spoke their language to explain to them the new system of raising revenue inaugurated by their conquerors.

Don Antonio's first assessment was made in 1851. He prepared no roll. The assessment was made on loose sheets, which have been lost. His total valuation of property footed up $2,882,949. The assessment roll for 1852 has been preserved. It is written in Spanish and has a fanciful title page — a work of the penman's art. Don Antonio did not order a number of great leather-bound machine-ruled volumes for his assessment rolls, as is the custom now. He made his assessment roll himself, binding, ruling and all. It consists of unruled sheets of Spanish foolscap pasted into leaves over two feet long and stitched into a book of thirty pages covered with blue calico. This one book contains the entire assessment for that year, also the poll-tax list.

The following are the principal items of that assessment:

Number of acres assessed.... 1,505,180
Value of real estate $748,606
Value of improvements 301,947
Value of personal property.... 1,183.898

The land assessed, except that included in orchard and vine lands within the city limits, was the ranchos. The thirty millions of acres in the county outside of the ranchos that belonged to the public domain was not assessed. Don Antonio was economical in the use of paper and ink. He did not write out lengthy involved descriptions of the rancho giving boundaries by metes and bounds.

Here is a sample entry of Don Antonio's that, considering the large amount involved, has perhaps never been exceeded in brevity on an assessment roll:

"Eulogio De Cells— 100,000 acres— Rancho Ex-Mission San Fernando— value $12,500. Also sixty acres huerto (orchard) Angeles, value $700. Value of personal property, horses and cattle, $14,000."

The cruelty of fate that so often followed the ranchero decreed that in less than two score years the son and heir to this baronial estate should die penniless. Another entry reads: "Enrique Dalton — 45,280 acres — Santa Anita Rancho — value $10,223. also 203 acres huerto —Angeles— value $1,000. (The Santa Anita is the rancho made famous in the annals of horse racing by the late Lucky Baldwin.)

Julius Verdugo was the largest land holder in the county at the time Coronel made his assessment. He was the owner of the magnificent Rancho San Rafael containing, according to Don Antonio, 114.000 acres and assessed at $24,000. No descendant of that great cattle baron owns an acre of that vast estate now.

Don Antonio estimated the island of Santa Catalina, owned by Covarubias, to contain 95,000 acres and assessed the acreage at $6,000, about six and a quarter cents (or half a real) per acre. It was then heavily stocked with wild goats, but these were not listed as personal property. While the assessed value of the ranchos was low, almost farcical we would consider it now, when compared with present values, the personal property valuations were high. The olden-time rancheros resented this gringo innovation for raising revenue and evaded it whenever they could do so. With a cancerous mortgage eating away their possessions and a falling market, taxation bore heavily upon them.

The first board of county supervisors was elected June 14, 1852, and one of its first acts was to sit as a board of equalization. The process of equalizing by that board differed somewhat from the methods of our present board and city council. The members of that first board of supervisors equalized mainly by "augmenting," as they called it, the number of cattle and horses owned by some of the rancheros, who evidently had failed to count correctly the number of animals they owned. One ranchero had two hundred and fifty wild horses added to his band at $10 each. The supervisors added to the assessment roll over one thousand wild horses that the owners had allowed to stray away from their assessment lists. Another ranchero had a thousand cattle added to his list at $12 each, increasing his wealth $12,000, much to his disgust. But the most singular lapse of memory from the viewpoint of today was that of the land baron, who guessed eight hundred acres short of the true amount of land he owned. As it was worth only dos reales, or two bits an acre, it was not so strange that he should forget it. Today the owners of that forgotten realty would scorn an offer of $2,000 an acre — but no descendant of that ranchero of the short memory owns an acre of it now.

The cattle industry of the south — the concomitant of the great rancho — had encountered such antagonistic elements of human invention as competition, litigation, taxation and usurious rates of interest, and though crippled still survived. It was the adverse forces of nature that were to seal its doom. Deluge and drouth were to complete its final undoing.

The winter of 1855-56 heralded one of the dreaded dry years. One hundred thousand cattle starved to death in the southern coast counties during the summer and fall of 1856. That year marked the turn of the tide of prosperity in the cow counties of the south.

Wallace, editor of the Los Angeles Star, soliloquizing on affairs that year, writes: " 'Dull times,' says the trader, the mechanic, the farmer. The teeth of the cattle were so dull this year that they could not save themselves from starvation. Business is dull — duller this week than it was last — duller today than it was yesterday. The flush days are past — the days of large prices and full pockets are gone."

The year 1858 was another of the dreaded dry years. There was no great loss of cattle that year, but their impoverished condition rendered them unfit for market and the failure of any return from their herds impoverished their owners as well. The winter of 1859-60 was one of excessive rainfall. During one storm in December twelve inches fell in twenty-four hours. Many horses and cattle weakened by starvation perished from exposure. But the Noachian deluge of California floods came in the winter of 1861-62. It began raining, December 24, 1861, and continued for thirty days with but two slight interruptions. The Los

Angeles Weekly Star, in its weather report of January 4, 1862, says: "There has been one shower since our last issue, but it lasted all the time — morning, noon and night. Day in and day out it has been rain, rain, rain."

The rivers rose to an unprecedented height. The Santa Ana rivaled the Father of Waters during a spring flood. It spread out to the Coyote hills, a distance of seven miles. The Los Angeles river swept away the city water works, carried off all of Elijah Moutton's land and property, thirty acres of vineyard, orange orchard, house and all it contained. The vineyards of Dr. White, Wolfskill, Hammel and Denker, Huber and others that lined the western bank of the river were washed away.

During the long and pitiless storm thousands of cattle unhoused and unprotected perished either from hunger and cold or by miring in the quicksands of the arroyo and marshy land. After the deluge, what? The great drouth and famine years.

The successive years of excessive rainfall produced great abundance of feed and the cattle multiplied rapidly. The rancheros endeavoring to make up by numbers for the decrease in value had allowed their ranges to become heavily overstocked. From over-production and the other causes enumerated the price of cattle had steadily declined until in the winter of 1862, full grown animals were sold in Los Angeles for $2 a head, the price in the old hide drogher days of thirty years before.

The great drouth began in 1862-63, the rainfall was less than four inches, and in 1863-64 it was but little more than a trace. By the fall of 1863 all vegetation had been licked up from the sunbaked plains by the hungry herds, and cattle were dying of starvation.

As the time for the rainy season approached the rancheros anxiously scanned the heavens for signs and portents of coming storms, but none appeared. The heavens were as brass and the former and the latter rains came not. The winter passed and the hot dry summer was upon them. Cattle were dying by the hundreds every day. Herds of gaunt, skeleton-like forms moved slowly over the plains in search of food. Here and there, singly or in small groups, poor brutes, too weak to move on, stood motionless with drooping heads, slowly dying of hunger.

The loss of cattle was fearful. The plains were strewn with their sundried carcasses and along the arroyos and around the cienegas where there had been vestiges of vegetation, the ground was covered with their skeletons and the traveler for years afterwards was often startled by coming suddenly upon a veritable Golgotha— a place of skulls — the long horns standing out in defiant attitude, as if protecting the fleshless bones.

Of the vast herds of cattle and manadas of horses that roamed over the Stearns' ranchos — bodies of land aggregating 200,000 acres — when the famine years began only a pitiful remnant was left when grass again covered the sun-parched plains; and a perverse fate seemed to have decreed that the fittest should not be the survivors. The scrawniest mustang of the band survived, while the high-bred caballo perished. The remnants of the great herds that survived the famine years reveled in a luxury of abundant feed the succeeding years Nature, as if atoning for her cruelty, garlanded her Golgothas with wreaths of golden poppies and spread cerements of living green over the bleaching bones of her victims.

But what of the cattle kings of the ranchos? They were ruined, their power and possessions were gone. Day by day they had seen their herds wasting away and themselves sinking to financial ruin and poverty. The pious among them had prayed for rain, they had sought the intercession of the saints, they had performed novenas of prayer, but in vain! The rain came not. It is the will of God. Why repine! With a bravery that might be taken for stoicism and a faith that bordered on fatalism they submitted to the inevitable.

Their doom came quickly. Nearly all of the great ranchos were mortgaged. With no means to restock them, and even if the owners had possessed the means it would have been useless. The cattle industry of the south was dead and could never again be revived. Without income to pay interest or principal the mortgagees foreclosed and took possession of the desolated cattle ranges. Within five years after the famine nearly all of the encumbered ranchos had changed owners.

Looking backward from our present high standard of real estate values it seems almost farcical that the owners of the great ranchos should have lost their possessions for the trifling amounts they owed. The possession of $20,000, at the critical moment when dispossession threatened him, would have saved from bankruptcy the great cattle king who owned the ranchos Semi, Los Posos, Conejo, San Julian and Espodo, aggregating over 200,000 acres — lost on an encumbrance of ten cents an acre. Many of the best ranchos were mortgaged on the basis of twenty-five cents an acre. Figure interest at five per cent per month, the ruling rate of early days, and it is easy to see how a principality could be lost for what was a mere pittance at the beginning of the indebtedness. The loss of cattle and horses during the famine years was one of the greatest calamities that ever visited California. The assessed value of property in Los Angeles county in 1860-61 was $3,650,330, in 1864-65, $1,622,370. Over two million dollars of property was swept out of existence, a percentage of loss on the capital invested greater than that of San Francisco by the earthquake and fire of 1906. On the animals there was no insurance or salvage — the loss was total.

After the famine years the era of subdivision began. The great ranchos were cut into small farms and sold to settlers. The passing of the rancho had come. With the loss of their great land holdings the feudal barons of the cattle regime lost their political power and influence. The industry that once made them rich and powerful had, through changed sociological conditions and adverse elements of nature, been their downfall. Their passing is a tale in which "Unmerciful Disaster followed fast and followed faster."

The conditions that wrought the undoing of the cattle barons can never return, but the story of their misfortunes, and the bravery and the fortitude with which they met the decrees of fate, and the manhood with which they submitted to conditions beyond their control deserve far more merit than has been accorded them, deserve a record in the history of a land they helped to make but which misfortune wrested from them.

With the passing of the rancho passed many of the old-time customs and observances that were concomitants of the rancho. Chief among them was the rodeo. Rodeo comes from the Spanish verb rodear, to go around, to encompass. The rodeo was an annual meeting of the rancheros of certain districts at some selected place, to which their herds were driven to enable the owners to pick out the stragglers which had straggled away from their own herd to that on some contiguous rancho. These were identified by the brand. It was also the time of branding the calves. It was always held in the spring because then the calves will follow their mothers, and the mothers being branded the calves could be identified.

The rodeo was a stately and formal affair in the olden times. It was held in turns upon the ranchos of the different rancheros, beginning usually at the most southern district and moving northward. Each ranchero entertained the company when it met on his estate. Sometimes a dozen proprietors took part in a rodeo and from twenty to twenty-five thousand cattle would be gathered together. Festivities were always a part of the rodeo. The most skillful vaquero was the hero of the occasion. The skillful horsemanship and the feats performed with the riata seemed to partake more of magic or juggling than skill. The rodeo ended with a baile (ball). The jueces del campos — judges of the plains— were the officials who set the time for the rodeo and regulated proceedings at it. They settled all cases of disputed ownership. There were no juries summoned to their courts. The bench of the juez del campo was the back of a mustang, his court room the plains, his code of laws common sense ideas and a sense of justice in administering them. As there was no salary attached to the office he took his pay in honors. All this was changed under American rule.

The judges were paid salaries, their number increased, and a printed code of laws arranged for their guidance, but the salaried judge of the plains was no improvement on the codeless juez del campo who took his pay in honors.

The rancho, the rodeo and the vaquero have long since passed down and out. They are but the dimly remembered vision of a heroic age and of stalwart custom gone forever.

At the beginning of the famine years (1863) most of the great ranchos were intact. Portions of some of them had been set off to heirs or sold on foreclosure of mortgages, but no subdivisions into small farms had been made. The standard price for land in 1865, except the land with water rights and that contiguous to Los Angeles City, was twenty-five cents per acre. Four thousand acres of the northern part of San Pedro rancho was sold in 1865 to Temple & Gibson for thirty-six cents per acre. It was considered a good price.

In 1867 the Rev. G. D. Compton bought the greater portion of this tract at $5 per acre and founded the town of Compton. To induce settlers to come to his colony he offered the land in small tracts to anyone purchasing land from him within six months from the date of his purchase for the same that he had paid. Many of the old residents of the county considered the land worthless for agricultural purposes, but after one crop which proved its productiveness the land went up to $20 per acre.

The most extensive passing of the rancho that followed the famine years was the subdivision of the Stearns ranchos. These lay between the San Gabriel river and the Santa Ana and extended from the Santa Ana foothills to the sea. This body of land comprised the original ranchos of Los Coyotes, La Habra, San Juan Cajon de Santa Ana, Los Bolsas y Parrades, La Bolsa Chica and Los Alamitos. These had been bought up from time to time by Don Abel Stearns at merely nominal prices and stocked with horses and cattle. These ranchos aggregated about two hundred thousand acres of land. During the drouth years of 1863-64 nearly all of the stock on the ranchos starved to death and Stearns was reduced to the verge of bankruptcy.

In 1867 Stearns sold all these ranchos except the Alamitos to a syndicate, reserving a one eighth interest. The government form of survey was extended over them and the land was offered for sale in tracts from forty acres up at from $2 to $10 per acre on easy terms. In those days of large landed estates forty acres were considered too insignificant a holding for a man to waste his time on and the average settler spread his limited capital over as great an expanse of land as he could encompass without regard to future payment, hoping to make the land pay for itself. Many of the pioneers of the subdivision era met the fate of the cattle barons, the original owners of the ranchos; dry years, low price of products and mortgages, deprived them of their possessions.

Between 1774 and July, 1846, when the last Mexican governor was deposed by the conquest, there were sixty grants, Spanish and Mexican made, in what formerly constituted Los Angeles county. These were of various sizes, from a few acres to over a hundred thousand.

Of the vast estates held by the padres of the Mission of San Gabriel in trust for its neophytes, but a small portion was left to it after secularization. In the early years of the last century, when the mission was at the zenith of its power, it controlled more than a million acres. When the United States claims commission finished its work in California, all that was left to it was one hundred and ninety acres. The largest rancho in the county was the ex-mission of San Fernando, containing 121,619 acres and confirmed to Eulogio de Cells.

CHAPTER XLIII.
EVOLUTION OF THE ORANGE INDUSTRY

Orange growing has become one of the chief, if not the principal, agricultural industry of Southern California. The history of its development is of more than passing interest to persons even in no way connected with the industry. No other attraction that our part of the state can offer, except perhaps climate, has lured so many home seekers to Southern California as the orange. Sentiment and profit combined attract to it the capitalist as well as the man without capital but blessed with optimism and energy. It was not one of the primitive industries of the south and it was not until the beginning of the second century of California's settlement that attention began to be directed towards orange growing for profit. The subdivision of the great ranchos that followed the destruction of the cattle industry led to a number of agricultural experiments. The new owners of small fractions of the league wide grants once owned by the cattle barons sought to find some product from their newly acquired acres that would compensate them for labor and capital invested.

The first experiment tried was grain raising. The virgin soil was rich and the yield of cereals large, but machinery was expensive and labor costly and of poor quality. After harvest came the problem of transportation. The only market on the coast then was San Francisco, five hundred miles away, and there were no railroads to it from the south. Los Angeles, then, was a city of vast area, but of limited population and small commerce. A ton of barley would have demoralized its market for a month. The inhabitants pastured their horses on Spring street lots and kept dairy ranches out on Grasshopper street, now Figueroa. In the olden time cattle transported themselves to market, but grain sacks had to be carried. The farmer found after his crop was marketed that the lighterage charges, freight charge, commission, storage and other claims that ship owners, commission merchants and middlemen could trump up were as cancerous as the old-time mortgages that ate the cattle barons out of house and home. The farmer was fortunate, indeed, if after marketing his crop he did not have to mortgage his farm to pay the deficit; actually pay a penalty for cultivating his land. Then began a series of agricultural experiments to find some product that would pay the cost of production and leave a margin to the producer. One of the first of these was the seri-culture venture. To encourage silk production in California, the legislature in 1867 passed an act giving a bounty of $250 for every plantation of mulberry trees two years old and one of $300 for every 100,000 merchantable cocoons produced. This greatly encouraged the planting of trees and the production of cocoons, if it did not add to the number of yards of silk in California. In 1869 it was estimated that in Central and Southern California there were ten million mulberry trees in various stages of growth. One nursery in San Gabriel, "The Home of the Silk Worm" as its proprietor called it, advertised 700,000 trees and cuttings for sale. Two million trees were planted in and around Los Angeles. The Los Angeles News of April 11, 1869, says: "We risk nothing when we express the belief that in two years from this time the silk products of this country will amount to several million dollars."

At first the profits from the sericulture industry were large, not, however, from the manufacture of silk, but from the sale of silk worm eggs. When the industry was launched eggs sold at $10 an ounce and the worms were good layers. One sericulturist reported a net profit of $1,000 made in sixty days from the sale of eggs. Another realized $1,260 an acre in a single season. The net profits from his three acres of mulberry trees and cocoons exceeded the net profits of his neighbor's 5,000 acres of grain. With such immense returns from such small investments it is not strange that the sericulture craze became epidemic. Mulberry plantations multiplied until the bounties paid threatened the state treasury with bankruptcy. A sanguine writer in the Overland Monthly of 1869 says: "It is almost startling to think that from a calling so apparently insignificant we may be able to realize in a short time a larger sum and infinitely greater gains than from one half of all our other agricultural productions in the state."

With the increased supply the price of eggs declined until it was all supply and no demand. Then the sericulture epidemic came to a sudden stop. The worms died of starvation and the bounty-bought mulberry plantations perished from neglect. Of the millions of trees that rustled their broad leaves in the breeze not even the fittest survived. They all died.

Another agricultural experiment which promised good returns but resulted in failure was cotton growing. A number of experiments on a small scale made at different times and in different places in the state had proved that cotton could be grown in California equal in quality to the Sea Island and Tennessee upland of the Southern States, but no attempt had been made to produce it in quantity.

The Civil war had demoralized the cotton industry in the south and greatly advanced the price of raw material. The legislature of California to encourage cotton growing in the state offered premiums for a certain number of the best bales produced. About 1866-67 Don Mateo Kellar, an old resident of Los Angeles and a promoter of various enterprises, for the benefit of his home city tried the experiment of growing cotton on irrigated lands. Eighty acres of land lying north of Jefferson street and west of Figueroa, now covered with fine residences, was planted in cotton. The plants grew luxuriantly and produced abundantly. The bursting bolls whitened the field like the snows of winter in an Arctic landscape. Enthusiastic agriculturists rejoiced over the advent of a new industry and prophesied that cotton would be "King in California." Don Mateo built a gin and ginned a number of bales that took a premium, but the profits from his venture were not sufficiently great to induce him to become a cotton planter.

Col. J. L. Strong, a cotton planter from Tennessee, in 1870 secured from the Los Angeles & San Bernardino Land Company a lease of six hundred acres located near the Santa Ana river in the Gospel Swamp country, a region famous in early times for mammoth pumpkins and monster camp meetings. On this he planted a large field of cotton. The cotton grew like the fabled green bay tree and produced fabulous returns, but not in money.

On the Merced river bottoms near Snellings was a plantation of a thousand acres and in Fresno county were a number of smaller ones aggregating about five hundred acres. The California Cotton Growers & Manufacturers Association purchased ten thousand acres of land adjoining, and covering part of the present site of Bakersfield, the oil metropolis of Kern county. On account of the difficulty of obtaining seed only three hundred acres were planted the first year: a portion of this made a fine crop of excellent quality.

The association announced that it would plant 2,000 acres next year, and to encourage others to plant would furnish growers with seed and gin their cotton free. To secure laborers the members of the association imported a colony of negro cotton-field laborers from the south, built cabins for them and hired them to plant, cultivate, pick and gin the prospective crop. The colored persons discovered that they could get much better wages at other employment and deserted their employers. The cotton crop went to grass and the cotton growers went into bankruptcy.

Experiments tried in various parts of the state demonstrated beyond a doubt that cotton of the finest quality could be grown in California, but when it came to figuring profits in the business "that was another story." The negro cotton picker was not in evidence in California; the Mexican peon and the mission neophyte could pick grapes, but cotton picking was beyond their ken. White labor was too scarce and too expensive, so the coast wind did most of the picking.

For that which was gathered and baled there was no market nearer than Lowell or Liverpool — 18,000 miles away via Cape Horn. There were no railroads then in Southern California and no cotton factories on the Pacific Coast; so the cotton boll, like the silk cocoon, disappeared from the land of the afternoon, the former to reappear after a lapse of nearly fifty years as a paying industry on the reclaimed Colorado desert.

Of all the numerous experiments tried with different agricultural products none had proved a panacea for our financial ills. Our long distance from market and the consequent cost of transportation made it imperative to produce some commodity to which there could be little or no local competition when transported to and sold in an eastern market.

For nearly three quarters of a century after its settlement oranges had been grown in Southern California but not for exportation. The first oranges were produced at San Gabriel in 1805 from trees raised from seed brought from Mexico. The first grown within the limits of the pueblo of Los Angeles, according to Col. J. J. Warner, were planted in 1815. They were planted on a lot on Aliso street. They were in full bearing in 1831 when Colonel Warner came to Los Angeles. There is no record of the name of the man who planted the first tree in the pueblo. During the Mexican era some of the wealthier families had a few trees in their gardens.

Oranges were grown in the gardens of all the missions of Southern California. Edwin Bryant, a lieutenant in Fremont's Battalion, in his book "What I Saw in California," describing the Mission of San Fernando, where the battalion encamped January 11, 1847, says: "There are two extensive gardens surrounded by high walls, and a stroll through them afforded a most delightful contrast from the usually uncultivated landscape we have been traveling through for so long a time. Here were brought together most of the fruits and many of the plants of the temperate and tropical climates. Although not the season of flowers, still the roses were in bloom, oranges, lemons, figs and olives hung upon the trees and the blood-red tuna or prickly pear looked very tempting." The Mission of San Fernando was secularized in 1834. The orange and lemon trees were doubtless planted before the secularization of the mission.

William Wolfskill in 1841 planted a small grove of orange trees. Lieutenant Bryant, who visited Mr. Wolfskill, describes his vineyard. "Mr. W.'s vineyard is young and covers about forty acres of ground, the number of vines being 4,000 or 5,000. From the produce of these he told me that last year he made 180 casks of wine and the same quantity of aguardiente; a cask here is sixteen gallons. Mr. Wolfskill's vineyard is doubtless a model of its kind. It was a delightful recreation to stroll through it, and among the tropical fruit trees bordering its walks."

Wolfskill's original grove was on what are now the Southern Pacific depot grounds on Alameda street. He added to his original orchard until it covered seventy acres. But the additions were not made until long after the American occupation.

I have made an extensive search of the old records and of the reports in the early Los Angeles newspapers for statistics relating to the development of the orange industry in Los Angeles. The returns have been rather meager. The old-time editor was far more interested in state and national politics than in the local happenings of his town. A column editorial on the misdeeds and wickedness of his political opponents was much easier dished up to his readers than reports of the growth and development of the town and country where he lived.

In the early '50s there had been comparatively little attention paid to fruit raising in Los Angeles except grapes. These formed one of the chief exports from San Pedro to San Francisco.

In 1856 an increased interest began to be taken in fruit products. The Los Angeles Star of November, 1856, commenting on the report of the county assessor to the surveyor-general on the products of the county says: "Our horticulture from the decay it wore since taken out of the control of the mission padres has taken new life, and in the new hands which now preside over it are laboring to bring it back to its former luxuriance and excellence and are adding many new plants."

From the assessor's report above referred to we find there were in the county in 1856 one hundred fifty-one orange trees in full bearing and 4,200 young trees in different stages of growth. Col. J. J. Warner, in a communication published in the Los Angeles Herald in 1873, commenting on the profits of orange growing, says: "An orchard of 1,800 trees planted in 1856, between the years of 1864 and 1870, netted its owner $10,000. Another orchard of 600 trees planted the same year, when fourteen years old produced 600,000 oranges.

In 1856, according to the above report, there were only ten lemon trees in full bearing and fifty young trees. Evidently citrus growing for profit began about 1856.

The first record I have found of trees imported from foreign countries is an item in the Los Angeles Star of January 26, 1856: "Dr. Shaw has just returned from Central America with a large quantity of sweet orange trees, mangrove and coffee plants in excellent condition." There was at one time an attempt made in Los Angeles county to grow the coffee tree. A number of trees were planted, but from some cause the experiment was a failure.

Dr. Joseph Shaw was one of the pioneer nurserymen of Los Angeles who did good work in promoting the culture of semi-tropical fruits. In the Star of 1856 he advertises his nursery and gives the location "a mile and a half below the city." Its actual location was on the west side of San Pedro street between East Adams and Thirtieth street.

Major Ben C. Truman, who visited Dr. Shaw's place in 1874, thus describes it: "The thirty-five-acre lot comprising the nursery and adjacent grounds will in a few years be an orchard devoted exclusively to oranges, Sicily lemons and limes, twenty-five hundred of the two former and one thousand trees of the latter having been planted within the past year or two. At present there are in full bearing two hundred orange trees, twenty limes and twenty Sicily lemons.

"Dr. Shaw came to this part of the country about twenty years ago (he came in 1854), but did not turn his attention to semi-tropical fruit culture until several years later. When he made up his mind to do so he made a voyage to Nicaragua, and returning, brought with him seeds from oranges grown there of a superior variety. His seedlings are from fruit grown on trees raised from the Nicaragua seed and are justly renowned for their size and delicious flavor."

Major Truman says at the time of his visit there were seventy-five thousand young trees of various kinds in Dr. Shaw's nursery. "A very few years will transform this Los Angeles nursery into an estate perfect in its proportions and complete in its appointments."

This "estate" over which Major Truman grew enthusiastic and prophetic in but little more than a decade after his visit was swept by a besom of destruction. The great real estate boom of 1887 struck it. The real estate promoter cut swaths through its groves for streets and the cottony scale sucked the life out of the trees that remained. The only monument to the old pioneer horticulturist, who did much for the benefit of his city and state, is a recorded map of the subdivision of the Shaw tract in the county recorder's office.

There is a very general impression that the orange trees at San Gabriel Mission furnished the seed for the early orange groves. This is doubtless true of the small orchards planted before the conquest. After the American occupation seed was imported. Gov. J. G. Downey, in the Overland Monthly of June. 1874, says: "In the year 1853 Mathew Keller and Dr. Halsey obtained seed from Central America and the Hawaiian Islands and planted nurseries. Dr. Halsey 's nursery furnished trees for part of the Wolfskill orchard." The Hawaiian orange was larger and sweeter than the Mexican orange of the mission.

There were no doubt small shipments of oranges to San Francisco in the early '50s, but there is no record of them. The Argonauts received almost all of their scanty supply of fresh fruit from Los Angeles. This supply consisted largely of grapes. Bryant estimated the quantity of wine and aguardiente produced in California in 1847 at 1,000,000 gallons. After the discovery of gold the wine production decreased. It was more profitable to sell the grapes. The first record of the shipment of oranges that I have found was made in 1857. The oranges shipped during the season of 1857-58 amounted to 55,372 pounds, valued at $11,276, or about eight hundred boxes. This would be about $1.40 per box. The selling price in San Francisco was doubtless more than double the value given in the export report. In the export schedules, when all shipments were made by sea, oranges were mostly listed as fruit. It is impossible to ascertain the exact amount of oranges sent.

According to returns made by E. E. Hewitt, when he was superintendent of the Los Angeles & San Pedro Railroad, there were shipped from San Pedro to San Francisco during the orange season of 1871-72, 21,008 boxes of oranges. In the

337

season of 1872-73, when there was a short crop, the number of boxes shipped was only 16,582.

The assessor of Los Angeles county reports for the year of 1871-2 the total number of bearing orange trees at 34,500, and in his return for 1872-3, 34,700.

In the early days of citrus fruit culture the Mexican lime held an important place. It was a rival to the lemon. It grew on a bush that attained a height of from six to eight feet. Major Truman, describing the Shaw groves, says: "The lime trees are at all times loaded with ripe fruit and covered with blossoms, and it seemed to me that every twig had upon it limes of every size, from that of a grain of coffee to the perfected fruit. Not less than ten crops mature yearly on each of these trees. The income from each tree ranges from $50 to $7S per annum. The limes are of the Mexican variety." The trees or bushes were easily propagated and were extensively planted. Hedges of them were set out around orchards. With the increase of the trees the revenue from them decreased. In the winter of 1880 came a cold snap and a killing frost. The lime, which was more tropical than semi-tropical, disappeared from the land of the afternoon

Orange planting increased slowly. It was not until after the subdivision of the great ranchos that it began to assume the dignity of an industry. In the later '60s and early '70s Wolfskill's groves were reported to be paying at the rate of $1,000 per acre net. This reported remuneration was probably exaggerated, but it was sufficient to induce the planting of orange groves wherever suitable land with irrigating facilities could be secured.

The extraordinary profits made from oranges by Wolfskill and a few others who had bearing orchards started a boom of orange growing. Like the silk worm fad large profits were made from the sale of nursery stock. It was a very scrubby sort of tree that could be bought for $1, and a thrifty two-year-old commanded $2 or $3 at the nursery.

As it took about seventy-five trees to plant an acre it required considerable ready money to embark in the business. Many prospective orange growers, too poor to buy stock, raised their own from seed. It required two years longer to wait for returns, but with them money was more valuable than time. If oranges were apples of gold the seeds in those days were golden nuggets. The visitor to a grove might be indulged in a luscious orange, but at the same time he would be solicited "to save the seeds."

It took a seedling-orange tree eight or nine years to come into bearing. The problem of subsistence until he could realize on this investment was one of the most difficult that the prospective orange producer had to solve. The space between the rows of trees was sometimes planted or sown with some cereal that might help to tide over the long wait for returns, but this was objectionable because it retarded the growth of the trees.

The expense of constructing irrigating ditches and securing water rights was another large item that must be met. In the olden days of Mexican domination the waters of the rivers had been granted to the abutting ranches, the ill-defined riparian rights of these grants gave rise to interminable litigation. Sometimes these contests assumed a more formidable aspect than lawsuits in a court of justice. Water wars were not uncommon. Armed men stood guard over zanjas (ditches) and even fought to the death in the defense of what they conceived to be their rights.

The story of the orange groves of Southern California — of trees laden with the golden apples of Hesperides in midwinter — of groves white with bloom and the air filled with perfume in the land of sunshine, "when the bleak winds of March" made the dwellers in the Eastern communities "tremble and shiver" — like that other California tale of long ago, of golden nuggets picked up in river beds and cañons, appealed to the imagination and to the pockets of home-seekers.

Then the colony era began. Men imbued with the same purpose banded themselves together in the Eastern communities and either came themselves or sent representatives to "spy out the land." One of the first and one of the most successful of these was the Riverside colony, founded in 1870.

After experiments with the raisin grape and deciduous fruits the colonists settled upon the orange as the fittest and most profitable for their soil and location. Fortunately for them a new species of orange was introduced into the colony. In December, 1873, L. C. Tibbetts, one of the colonists, received from the Agricultural Department at Washington. D. C. two small orange trees imported from San Salvador de Bahia, Brazil (Bay of San Salvador). The fruit of these trees was seedless and of a very fine flavor. As soon as the superior quality of this orange became known there was a rush for buds from the trees to bud the seedling orange. Millions of Washington navel trees, as the orange is now called, trace their ancestry to these two little waifs that wandered over seas and continents to their western home. One of them is still living, an honored pioneer of the city of Riverside. The next was the Indiana colony, founded in 1873. Later the name was changed to Pasadena.

By the year 1885, orange growing had become the recognized industry of Southern California, and had been extended into the sheltered valleys of Central and Northern California. The great ranches lying back from the sea-coast upon which water could be had for irrigation were subdivided. Where but two decades agone, on arid, sun-burned plains cattle had died by the thousands of starvation, now groves of emerald green stretched away to the horizon's tip and the bones of the dead herds were ground into fertilizers to add more vigorous growth to the trees, and a deeper tinge to the golden fruit of the groves. It was a subject of congratulation to us that by our numerous experiments we had at last found the philosopher's stone that would transmute our baser products into gold. It was with a feeling of satisfaction that we pointed to the industry we had evolved — one that was at the same time a pleasure and a profit. But our self-complacency was to be rudely shocked by what at first appeared to be a very insignificant cause.

A few years before, T. A. Geary, a nurseryman of Los Angeles, had imported some orange trees from Australia. These were infected with the Icerya purchasi, or as it was commonly called, the cottony cushion scale. No attention, at the time, was paid to the parasite and no one dreamed of the baleful significance of the snowy flecks appearing here and there in the orchards and borne from tree to tree by the wind. The scale multiplied with wonderful rapidity and soon the leaves, branches and trunk of the tree affected were covered with a snowy mantle. The tender twigs died, the leaves turned a sickly yellow, the fruit shriveled and the tree was ruined.

Then it was that men realized the terrible character of the enemy that was taking possession of the land. Relentless in its march as the ruthless host of Attila

— The Scourge of God — it left ruin and desolation in its path. It was not alone trees of the citrus family that were attacked, but deciduous trees, vineyards, shrubbery and flowers as well. Costly experiments were tried with sprays, mixtures and emulsions, comprising every deadly poison known to chemistry and science, but no material check was put to the increase of the insect pest. Some of the experiments were effectual; they not only destroyed the Icerya, but the tree, too. It seemed as if the citrus industry, built up with so much care and large expenditure of capital, was doomed. Orange growers who had been deriving annual incomes of $500 to $1,000 an acre found themselves threatened with financial ruin — not alone their incomes, but their capital, too, suddenly was swept away.

The orange groves in and around Los Angeles were the first to succumb to the cottony plague, but it was not the Icerya alone that wrought their final undoing. The real estate promoter lent his assistance. The cottony scale and the great real estate boom of 1887 appeared almost simultaneously in Los Angeles. At that time, stretching southward from East Third street to the city limits and easterly from San Pedro street to the river, covering an area of two square miles, was a succession of orange groves, the oldest in the country. These were the first smitten. Among them was the great Wolfskill grove, the pioneer orchard, planted nearly fifty years before. The trees towered up thirty to forty feet in height and some were a foot and a half in diameter. This grove was one of the show places of Los Angeles. It had been for years an unfailing source of revenue to its owner. It was the pride of the native, the lure of the tourist and an incentive to the prospective orange grower.

The cottony scale, insignificant in size and harmless in appearance, wrought its ruin. Its productiveness destroyed, the land was divided into city lots and the trees fell before the woodman's ax and were cut into cordwood. The other groves adjoining shared the same fate. When the boom was over and the Icerya dead, all that was left to Los Angeles of its living border of green and gold was the blackened stumps of trees and the little white corner stakes of the real estate promoters. The growth of the city since has covered the site of the ruined groves with dwelling houses and factories, but the urbs in horto — a city in a garden — once the characteristic of Los Angeles, departed with her lost groves.

But the orange industry was not dead, notwithstanding the ravages of the Icerya and the wail of the pessimist. The golden apples of Hesperides had not gone to join the cotton boll and the silk cocoon in the haven of "has beens." The theory that nature always provides an antidote for every poison and a remedy for every evil within her domain proved true in this case.

There must be some parasite to prey upon the Icerya. As it had come from Australia there would be found its Nemesis. In the spring of 1888 Albert Koebele, of Los Angeles, was sent to Australia under pay and acting under instructions from the Agricultural Division of the Department of Agriculture. On arriving there he found that although at one time the white scale had been very prevalent it had almost ceased to exist. Searching for the cause, he found its extermination was due to the Vedalia Cardinalis, a small bug about the size of a grain of popcorn, but with the appetite of an alligator. In California it was commonly called the Australian lady-bug. He secured a small colony of these in Australia and passing over to New Zealand he found them in much greater numbers.

340

Several colonies were sent to Los Angeles and colonized in some of the badly infested orchards. The Vedalia increased almost as rapidly as the Icerya had done. From different distributing points hundreds of colonies were sent all over the orange-growing districts. The annihilation of the Icerya was rapid and complete. In a very short time after the Vedalia began its work all that was left of the white scale was the little cottony tuft that had aided so much in distributing it throughout the orange and lemon groves. This tuft, its winding sheet, adhered to the trees long after the Vedalia had sepulchered its body. The winds eventually whipped away these cottony flecks and the last evidence of the baleful presence of the cottony pest disappeared. With the disappearance of the white scale the Vedalia disappeared. That parasite seemed to be its natural and its only food.

After the passing of the Icerya the reclamation of the citrus groves began. Those that had not been injured by ineffectual remedies or too long neglected were redeemed and by careful nursing made productive. The groves in Los Angeles, Pasadena and Riverside that had fallen victims to the real estate promoter were beyond redemption. Unlike the Icerya, the Vedalia could not leave his winding sheet to flutter in the breeze. The orange industry once again was placed on a paying basis and it has remained there ever since, growing in importance and extent as the years go by.

In less than five decades, Southern California has been transformed from a land of cattle ranges to one of orange groves. In a third of a century the citrus industry has grown from a single carload shipment to forty-six thousand.

Sentiment as well as profit enters into the promulgation of the citrus industry. The aesthetic millionaire can afford to toy with an orange grove, not as a source of profit, but as a plaything, as a diversion, as a pleasure in creating a thing of beauty that to him will be the joy of a lifetime. The poor man who secures a few acres of wild land in the citrus belt can, by his own labor, create a source of income that will be certain and will increase as the years pass. As an imaginative writer once put it, "A man with a counterpane of a farm and six hundred orange trees can sit in the shade and draw a star preacher's salary without passing the plate."

The first carload of oranges from California was shipped to Chicago in 1877. It went via the Southern Pacific, Central and Union Pacific Railroads. The freight charges to its destination were $500. The building of the Santa Fe system and the completion of the Southern Pacific Railroad via El Paso, by increasing competition and shortening the route, have reduced freight rates. Refrigeration, icing and pre-cooling of fruit cars have greatly reduced the loss from decay in transit.

But in all the decades that have passed since that first carload of oranges was shipped out of California, the problem of transportation has been the burning question of the industry. The contention between producer and carriers has gone on through all the years, and is today as vital an issue as it was years ago.

No other industry has so many intelligent and progressive men enlisted in it. The California Fruit Growers' Exchange, an organization composed of a majority of all the fruit growers in the citrus belt, regulates the shipping and marketing of the annual crop so as to avoid ruinous competition, and divides the proceeds of the sales on an equitable basis both to the small producer and the large. It is one of the most complete and best-managed corporations in existence for the disposing of agricultural products.

CHAPTER XLIV. THE OWENS RIVER AQUEDUCT

It is a story of roseate dreams and drear realities; of schemes to outwit Jupiter Pluvius when he was withholding the aqueous downpour; of submerged dams in the river and bed rock dams in the creeks; of vast storage reservoirs that would conserve the lush rainfall of the wet year against the famine dry years; of mountain lakes that were to be tapped and of mountain streams that were to be diverted from their course and brought down into the valleys. One of the dreams of prosperity that was to be realized by a bond issue for increased water development was indulged in in 1876.

The people of the city then had the idea that the Los Angeles river and the Arroyo Seco would furnish all the water they would need both for household and irrigation purposes for years to come. Had anyone broached the scheme of bringing water from Owens river he would have been regarded as a mild sort of lunatic. There was a subterranean flow in the river and its tributaries that if brought to the surface would supply every demand and usher in an era of great prosperity. In February, 1876, an election was called by the city council and bonds to the amount of $75,000 for increasing the city's water supply for irrigation were voted. One of the city papers commenting editorially on the project said:

"This money will be used in initiating a system of irrigation which is destined not alone to supply water to serve the cultivable lands within the limits of the city, but also to reach the outside lands. If, as we are assured by the city surveyor, 17,000,000 gallons of water pass a given point above the mouth of the Arroyo Seco every twenty-four hours during the dry season, and that water can be raised by means of a submerged dam to the surface, and sent into ditches at an elevation that will enable us to establish storage reservoirs in the depressions of our adjoining hill lands, then this appropriation will inaugurate one of the most important works ever undertaken in this section.

"It will solve the irrigation problem for a very extensive district of Los Angeles county, for the system will supply water to all the lands between this city and the sea for several miles in width. It must be remembered that there are but two or three months in the year when irrigation is required here. Ordinarily the ground is moist enough everywhere up to the month of June. The surplus water of the winter can be stored to such an extent as to furnish an ample supply for the irrigating months.

"Just think of the prosperity which such a water system would inaugurate! One hundred thousand acres of land adjoining this city would be made as valuable for purposes of cultivation as are now the numberless garden spots within our city limits. The plains below the city would be turned into orange orchards and vineyards, and from here to the sea would be a stretch of country as beautiful as the Vale of Cashmere seems from Moore's description. Lands outside of the city limits, instead of selling at $30 and $40 an acre, would command from $300 to $400. The only difference in the great value now existing between the two classes of lands is the fact that inside lands are entitled to water, while those outside are not. The city is willing to assume the expense and responsibility of establishing the fact that we can irrigate all the lands to the sea out of the waters of the Los Angeles river."

A series of reservoirs were constructed, but the growth of the city absorbed both the water supply and the land it was to irrigate. The Vernon and Harmony districts, at that time outside of the city, and once covered with orange groves and deciduous fruit orchards, no longer take their water supply through zanjas. The zanjas have disappeared and so have the reservoirs and the orange groves. The city has absorbed them all.

A few years later a submerged dam was constructed in the big Tahuenga, a tributary of the Los Angeles river. At first it promised to be a success. A grand celebration was held when the work was completed. The people of the San Fernando valley turned out to celebrate the event. The waters of the Arroyo arose to the top of the dam and the hopes of the projectors arose still higher, but they were doomed to disappointment. The scheme was a failure. The waters disintegrated the bed rock on which the dam rested and the lake that had formed back of the dam disappeared in the quicksands.

When the zanjas constituted the water distributing system of the city, the olden-time citizen was not frightened by the presence of bacilli or bacteria in his drinking water and the authorities were not worried by demands for an analysis of the zanja water to discover whether there were germs in it. If there were germs in it the bacteria might find it a very unwholesome element in which to exist according to a local by the editor of the Los Angeles Star, June 16, 1855:

"The zanjas that run into different parts of the city furnish the only water that can be had conveniently to a large number of our citizens, and it is obvious to every one that they should be kept as free from filth and polluted substance as possible."

"Day after day, from sunrise till evening, groups of females from 'snowy white to sooty black' can be seen at their daily avocation of washing clothes through nearly the entire length of our water canals — and very few of them, we are informed, take any care to prevent the filthy rinsings from running back into the stream. A stranger would be very apt to suppose that our canals were built for the purpose of carrying off the garbage and foul matter that is continually accumulating within the precincts of a city instead of being the source from which a large portion of the inhabitants are supplied with water for domestic purposes."

In March, 1852, the City Council had passed an ordinance "Relative to Public Washing," which prohibited by a fine of $3 the washing of clothes in any zanja except the "water canal that runs from the Little river." Evidently the ordinance was not enforced and fines were not collected.

The Owens river project, at its inception, was regarded by many persons as but little more than an iridescent dream. There had been other projects promulgated that seemed far more feasible than this, that had failed. Would this solve the water problem of Los Angeles? Then the enormous cost of $23,000,000! If it failed it would bankrupt the city. The average intelligent citizen had a very indefinite idea where Owens river was located. It was somewhere beyond the Mojave desert at the eastern base of the Sierra Nevada mountains. The distance to it was variously estimated at from two hundred to three hundred miles. It could be reached from Los Angeles by a trip with a team across the desert (the auto was not in evidence then for long journeys), or it might be reached by rail via San Francisco, five hundred miles, then to Nevada by the Union Pacific and by narrow gauge road to the valley, a journey of one thousand miles.

Of the early history of the valley, and the story of the discovery of the river and lake very few of our citizens who grow enthusiastic over the Owens River Aqueduct, know anything, not even who Owens was for whom the river and the lake were named, although at one time he was a resident of our city.

When the project of tapping Owens river by an aqueduct and bringing its water to our city was first broached, Charles F. Lummis, then librarian of the City Library and a noted writer of California history, when asked to give some information in regard to the man for whom the river was named said: "The resources of the City Library have been exhausted but nothing has been found to give the desired information." As the years go by the question, no doubt, will recur again and again and perhaps receive the same answer.

I will digress from the general trend of my story to tell who Owens was, how the river and lake were discovered and also to give a description of the valley before the white man possessed it and of the Indians who roamed over the region desolate and drear where now the waters of the river flow peacefully down the aqueduct.

Owens river and lake were named for Richard Owens, a member of Fremont's exploring party. Fremont was fitting out for his third expedition. He was desirous of having men with him inured to the dangers and privations of frontier life. Many of his men who had been with him on his two former exploring expeditions had joined him at his rendezvous near Independence, Mo.

On the second of August, 1845, he had arrived at Bent's Fort on the Arkansas river, which was to be the point of departure on his exploring journey. .Although Fremont had with him Alexis Godey, one of his most trusted guides and Indian fighters, the expedition was not complete without Kit Carson and Dick Owens. Fremont says: "From the Fort I sent an express to Carson at a rancho, or stock farm, which with his friend Richard Owens he had established on the Cimarron, a tributary to the Arkansas river. But he had promised that in the event I should need him, he would join me. And I knew that he would not fail to come. My messenger found him busy starting the congenial work of making up a stock ranch. There was no time to be lost, and he did not hesitate. He sold everything at a sacrifice, farm and cattle; and not only came himself, hut brought his friend Owens to join the party. This was like Carson, prompt, self-sacrificing, and true. I received them both with great satisfaction.

"That Owens was a good man it is enough to say that he and Carson were friends. Cool, brave, and of good judgment; a good hunter and good shot; experienced in mountain life; he was an acquisition, and proved valuable throughout the campaign.

"Godey had proved himself during the preceding journey, which had brought out his distinguishing qualities of resolute and aggressive courage. Quick in deciding and prompt in acting he had also the French elan and their gayety of courage. I mention him here because the three men came fitly together, and because of the peculiar qualities which gave them in the highest degree efficiency for the service in which they were engaged.

"The three, under Napoleon, might have become marshals, chosen as he chose men. Carson, of great courage; quick and complete perception, taking in at a glance the advantages as well as the chances for defeat; Godey, insensible to danger, of perfect coolness land stubborn resolution; Owens, equal in courage to the others, and in coolness equal to Godey, had the coup-d'-oeil of a chess player, covering the whole field with a glance that sees the best move. His dark hazel eye was the marked feature of his face, large and flat and farsighted."

On the 27th of October, 1845, the exploring expedition had reached Walker's lake. Here it was divided into two bodies. Fremont with fifteen men started for Sutter's Fort for supplies. The main body of the explorers under command of Theodore Talbot (there were sixty men in the expedition) after remaining at the Lake two weeks to recruit their horses, under the guidance of Walker resumed their march southward. Following along the eastern base of the mountains, on the 18th of December, 1845, they reached the head of a river and following it down they came to a lake, of which Fremont later, when the two parties came together, says: "To one of the lakes I gave Owens' name." He gave the names of several of his band to rivers, creeks and lakes, but only Kern and Owens remain.

Owens was senior captain of Fremont's battalion when in 1846 it marched down the coast to assist Stockton in the Conquest of Los Angeles. When Fremont was made governor of California by Stockton, Capt. Richard Owens was given command of the battalion. During the quarrel between General Kearny and Fremont the battalion was moved to San Gabriel mission, where on the 19th of April, 1847, it was mustered out of service. Of the subsequent career of the man whose name was given to the river and lake by Fremont I know nothing. The aqueduct has made his name as familiar to Californians as that of Fremont.

Owens river valley remained almost a terra incognita for nearly two decades after Fremont's explorers passed through it. The Indians who lived on the head waters of the tributaries of the San Joaquin river and ranged over the desert to the settlements of Los Angeles county, were inveterate horse thieves. After the secularization of the missions many of the mission Indians became renegades and joined the mountain Indians. The renegades knew the country well and were expert vaqueros. They led raids upon the rancheros' bands of horses, and ran them off not for riding, but to kill them for food.

Fremont on his journey to Sutter's Fort ran into one of their strongholds where the ground for acres was whitened with the bones of the horses they had slaughtered. His party was attacked by them. Owens with his long range rifle brought down their chief. The Indians stole horses because cattle could not be driven fast enough to escape the pursuit.

Fremont says the Horse Thief Indians were far more daring and braver than those who remained in fixed villages. These horse thief tribes ranged through the country between Los Angeles and Owens River Valley. The government in 1854 established Fort Tejon at the head of the San Joaquin valley in the Tehachapi range to check the raids of these Indian horse thieves. The Sebastian Indian reservation had been established in the valley in 1853, and it was part of the duty of the soldiers of the Fort to keep them on the reservation, but they would stray away and go back to their old tricks. The depredations of these Indians caused great loss to the rancheros. The Santa Barbara Gazette in an editorial on the government control of these Indians estimates the loss of stock to the farmers of the Southern counties in the years 1850, '51, '52 and '53 at $600,000. Their raids on the rancheros' stock decreased to a considerable extent after the establishment of the Sebastian reservation.

The following account of a military expedition to Owens lake and valley made in July and August, 1859, is taken from the Los Angeles Star of August 27, 1859. The letter from a correspondent signing himself "Quis," who accompanied the expedition, is perhaps the only description extant of the valley and the Indians who inhabited it before the white man took possession of the land and killed off the Indians. I quote the account of the expedition and the correspondent's letter in full.

Expedition To Owens Lake

In consequence of the extensive depredations committed in the San Fernando valley, Lt. Col. Beall, commanding at Fort Tejon. determined to send a detachment of the First Dragoons into the Indian country, to explore its recesses, and find if the missing stock were there. The expedition has returned, having made a full and careful investigation into the affairs of the Indians— also of the general features of the country, its topography, etc.

Captain Davidson, in command of the expedition, has made a map of his explorations, and has discovered a pass through the mountains to the Salt Lake road, which will greatly shorten the distance from this point— avoid the journey over the desert, besides opening up a route on which wood, water and grass are abundant.

As the reports of the officers on such expeditions are made to the head of their respective departments, we were consequently unable to obtain any information from Captain Davidson, while in town this week, regarding his operations, further than that we may assure the public the Owens Lake Indians did not take the stock, that they are quiet, industrious, friendly, and altogether reliable. Further than this, Captain Davidson did not feel himself at liberty to disclose.

We are, however, owing to the kindness of a gentleman who accompanied the expedition, enabled to lay before the public today a very interesting letter on the subject. We have felt great interest in this expedition, and hoped to be able to lay before our readers a detailed account of its labors and discoveries, but being temporarily disappointed in our expectations the pleasure of laying the following very interesting communication before our readers is proportionately enhanced. Our correspondent has our warmest thanks for his kindness; we shall be glad to hear further from him.

Military expedition to Owens Lake — No stock in the valley — Indians peaceable and reliable — Discovery of a new route to Salt Lake. Tejon, August, 1859.

Sir: — I had the pleasure of accompanying the expedition dispatched from Fort Tejon by the commandant, Lt. Col. Beall, consisting of Company B and a detachment of Company K, First Dragoons, in command of Captain Davidson, assisted by Lieutenant Chapman, to visit the country and Indians in the vicinity of Owens lake and river. The officers and soldiers of the expedition were supplied with thirty days rations, and commenced their march on the 21st of July, with

346

instructions to proceed to the country in the vicinity of Owens Lake, and recover certain parcels of stock that had been stolen from the vicinity of Los Angeles from time to time, if found in possession of the Indians of that valley; meting out proper punishment for their offenses; making a map of the route and country, with notes of the reconnaissance. One wagon and a howitzer were the only encumbrances, in addition to the pack train, to retard their movements.

The route selected was through Walker's basin and the Kern river mines; up the south fork of Kern river, through Walker's Pass; thence along the eastern slope of the Sierra Nevada to Owens Lake. The distance from Fort Tejon to the desert, by way of Walker's Pass, is about one hundred and seventeen miles, with good camps at convenient distances, and with the exception of the ascent into Walker's basin, the road is quite good for the use of wagons. Along the edge of the desert, to the lake, with the exception of the first thirty miles, water and grass exist at convenient distances.

Arriving at the foot of the lake, we found a fine meadow of eight hundred or one thousand acres, well supplied with fine water. This constitutes the only desirable spot on the confines of the lake, as there are not five acres of grass at any one other spot on its borders.

This lake is emphatically a "saline lake," as its waters contain salts to near the point of saturation, producing a density sufficient to support the human body on its surface. From a casual examination, I am of opinion that those salts consist principally of the bi-borate of soda (borax) and the chloride of sodium (common salt). Upon the surface of this lake swam myriads of small flies, of a species with which I am not familiar, where they deposit their eggs, the larvae of which constitute an important part of the food of the Indians of that region. The constant winds from the desert drive the larvae in large quantities upon the shore of the lake, where they are easily collected by the squaws. Besides Owens (or as the Indians call it Wokopee) river, there are some four small brooks emptying their waters into the lake.

For some distance along the river, after leaving the lake, but little desirable land is found, except that supplied with water by little rivulets flowing from the mountains. Twenty-seven miles from the head of the lake is Pine creek, with a large body of meadow land and the first timber we encountered growing in the valley, save a few small cottonwoods. Beautiful streams of clear cold water come gushing fresh from the snows of the Sierras, at intervals of from one to ten miles, irrigating beautiful and fertile portions of the valley, for the following sixty-two miles from Pine creek, principal among which are Clark's and Dragoon forks, either of which supply nearly as much water, at this season of the year, as does the Kern river.

Large tracts of land are here irrigated by the natives to secure the growth of the grass seeds and grass nuts — a small tuberous root of fine taste and nutritious qualities, which grows here in abundance. Their ditches for irrigation are in some cases carried for miles, displaying as much accuracy and judgment as if laid out by an engineer, and distributing the water with great regularity over their grounds, and this, too, without the aid of a single agricultural implement. They are totally ignorant of agriculture, and depend entirely on the natural resources of the country for food and clothing. One of the greatest aqueous curiosities of the trip was a single spring, to which was given the name of "mammoth," from which runs a stream of water, with a fair current, fifteen or twenty feet wide and about two and a half feet deep.

Although from some distance below the lake we encountered the temporary abodes of the Indians, yet in no instance were the troops enabled to get sight of a single one, they having fled before our approach, as we afterwards learned, having been told that they would be killed, until we reached Pine creek, when the interpreter found a poor woman attempting to escape with her crippled child. She having been assured that the people would not be injured, soon became the means of reassuring the Indians, after which there was but little difficulty in communicating with them.

To our surprise we saw but very few horses among them, and that, too, on the upper portion of Owens river, and evidently obtained from the Walker river Indians. They informed Captain Davidson that some four or five Indians, in years past, were in the habit of stealing horses for the purpose of eating them, but esteeming it wrong, they some five years since punished some of the party with death, and the rest had died from natural causes; since when none had been stolen by their people. They told us where we could find the bones of the animals thus destroyed, and most certainly the appearances corroborated their statement, for there were no bones of more recent date than four or five years, judging from appearances.

The Wokopee or Owens river Indians appear to be both morally and physically superior to any of their race in California, for in point of probity and honesty I certainly have never met their equal, and as to their physical sanitary condition, I saw none sick or infirm save the child already alluded to — although they will number twelve hundred or fifteen hundred souls.

To illustrate their ideas of truthfulness: An Indian boy who was anxious to return with Captain Davidson, after descending the river fifty or sixty miles, encountered his elder brother, and being somewhat unwell, and perhaps a little homesick, asked his advice in regard to turning back. "Have you promised to go?" said he. "Yes." "Well, then, do not ask me; if you have promised to go, you shall go."

Whilst talking to their head men, who had assembled for that purpose, Captain Davidson informed them that so long as they were peaceful and honest, the government would protect them in the enjoyment of their rights. Their reply was, that such had always been their conduct and should ever be — that they had depended on their own unaided resources — that they had at all times treated the whites in a friendly manner, and intended to do so in the future. He further informed them, that should they become dishonest and resort to murder and robbery, they would be punished with the sword. The old captain or head man turned with a smile to the interpreter, and said: "Tell him that we fear it not, that what I have said, I have said. I have lain my heart at his feet, let him look at it."

Unsophisticated, and uncontaminated by free intercourse with whites or vicious Indians, a lack of chastity is said to be a thing almost unheard of among them. The limited opportunities for observation, certainly favored the opinion that such was the fact.

The untiring energy and industry exhibited by Captain Davidson in carrying out his instructions is certainly worthy of all commendation; and if courteous and gentlemanly conduct towards those who accompanied the expedition, and untiring attention to, and solicitude for, the well-being and comfort of the soldiers of the command, be marks of the true soldier, then the First Dragoons may well be proud of the officers of this command.

Although the primary and important object of the expedition was not achieved, yet I am of the opinion that one has been initiated, of permanent importance to the country by the labors of Captain Davidson, which is no less than establishing a direct route between Salt Lake and all parts of California — avoiding entirely the Mojave Desert, and securing to the traveler those important items to a comfortable journey — a good and direct road, and grass and water at proper distances. This Captain Davidson is of the opinion can be done, by carrying the road along the rim of the Great Basin, and entering the Wokopee or Owens Valley at its head, by a very excellent pass. In a conversation with L. Anderson, the companion of the old guide and traveler, Captain Walker, this opinion is fully confirmed. There are many and important and interesting items connected with this expedition, which I would be pleased to note, but am compelled to pass over.

QUIS.

In less than three years from the time our correspondent visited the valley this Arcadian vale of primitive contentment had become the theater of savage warfare and massacre. Gold and silver mines had been discovered in the Mona Lake and Owens Valley country and the usual "miners rush" had followed. Settlers had taken possession of the Indians' land and the red men, who a few years before had punished their own people with death for stealing from the white men, were killed for resisting the theft of their lands by the white men.

The Los Angeles Star of April 26, 1862, under the head of "Indian Depredations — Battle with the Indians — Nine lives lost," gives this among other items: "A party of citizens (sixty men), had a fight with the Indians of Owens River Valley on the 5th instant, in which they were defeated with the loss of three men killed viz — Mr. Pleasant, Mr. Morrison and Mr. Scott — the last-named sheriff of Mono county. They made good their retreat under cover of the night, going down the valley, and joined Lt. Col. Evans' command the following day.

"On the 9th instant Lt. Col. Evans' command with fifty dragoons from Fort Churchill and some thirty citizens, attacked the Indians, who were posted in a very strong position on top of a very steep hill and were repulsed with the loss of Colonel Mayfield. who commanded the company of citizens. Sergeant McKenzie of Lt. Col. Evans' command and a private, name unknown.

"Previous to the first fight the bodies of two men were found on the road near the scenes of the fight, murdered, and four men who were on the road coming south were attacked and barely escaped with their lives to Aurora, two of the party being badly wounded."

*****

"The whole of Owens valley with the different mining camps in that vicinity, together with the improvements of the settlers of the Owens valley and the valuable machinery in the mines, is entirely exposed to the attacks of the Indians. Within sixty or eighty miles of Owens lake there is an immigration of about fifty

349

large wagons — going to Aurora, Mono county, loaded with valuable goods and machinery which can reach their destination by no other road than through Owens Valley; besides these there are on the road a great many thousand head of cattle, sheep and hogs for the same destination." A military camp was established in the valley and troops stationed there until Indian depredations ceased, which they did with the extermination of the Indian.

One of the most violent earthquakes known in the history of California had its center of action a few miles from Owens lake. It occurred at two o'clock in the morning of March 26, 1872. In proportion to the population of the valley at that time the loss of life was as great as in the San Francisco earthquake. The greatest loss of life was at the town of Lone Pine, situated five miles north of Owens lake; about three-fourths of the buildings were of stone and adobe and every one of these was dashed into a heap of ruins at the first crash of the earthquake. More than sixty persons were killed or wounded, several were killed in other settlements.

The earthquake performed some queer freaks in the valley. At a point twenty-eight miles north of Lone Pine the bed of the Owens river sank, forming a lake of several hundred acres. At another point the ground sank and the river leaving its old channel made a new one about two miles west of its former channel. A row of trees stood in a straight line at right angles with the road. The earthquake moved a part of this row about sixteen feet north from where it formerly stood, thus breaking the line. The trees were not injured and continued to grow as if they had never been disturbed.

The occurrence of another such freakish earthquake in the Owens River Valley might very seriously affect our aqueduct.

I have digressed at considerable length from the story of the aqueduct. My excuse is that we are so intimately connected with the Owens valley that it is almost a part of our municipality. On the waters that will come from that valley we depend largely for our future growth and progress. In the legal contests that are on and those that will come the early history of the valley may be of value.

The Beginnings Of The Aqueduct

The inception of the project to bring the waters of Owens river to Los Angeles is due to Fred Eaton, an engineer and former mayor of Los Angeles city. Eaton had acquired landed interests in Owens River Valley. He had noted during his residence there the floods of surplus water pouring into Owens lake — a dead sea without any outlet — there to be lost by evaporation.

He had passed over the road between the valley and Los Angeles many times; his knowledge of engineering and his experience in building conduits and pipe lines while in charge of the water system of Los Angeles convinced him it would be possible to conduct the surplus waters of Owens River Valley to Los Angeles.

For years the water problem had confronted successive city councils and boards of water commissioners. Every year the solution of the problem was becoming more difficult. During the two successive dry years 1898 and 1899 the season's rainfall was respectively five and seven inches. The water famine in some parts of the city was acute. During ten days in July, 1904, the outflow from the city reservoirs exceeded the inflow by nearly four million gallons. These conditions

350

convinced the people of the city that something must be done and that very soon or the inflow of population would cease.

In 1903 Eaton outlined his project to William Mulholland, superintendent of the Los Angeles City Water System. It looked feasible to Mulholland. He knew nothing, however, of the water resources of Owens River Valley or of the country between it and Los Angeles over which a conduit must be built, and, therefore, could not figure up the expense of the undertaking. He made a trip with Eaton over the route to the valley. A hydrographic survey of the valley and its water resources convinced him that the water was there, but the most difficult problems to be solved were, can the water be piped to Los Angeles and will the people stand the great expense?

Mulholland made a careful survey of the line which he believed would be the best location on which to build the proposed aqueduct. He figured out the length, the canals, the covered conduits, the tunnels, the flumes and the siphons that would have to be constructed. He computed the cost of material, the expense of construction and the approximate expenditure to secure water rights. The total amount of $25,000,000 was appalling. Would the people of the city mortgage their homes for a project that might be a failure?

He submitted his scheme to the board of water commissioners. The board was then composed of J. M. Elliott, John J. Fay, Fred L. Baker, W. H. Sherman, and William Mead.

In April, 1905, Messrs. Elliott and Fay of the water commission. Mayor McAleer, City Attorney Mathew, City Water Superintendent Mulholland and Mr. Eaton visited Owens River Valley to examine into the water conditions existing there and if found satisfactory to recommend the purchase of the options and contracts for the land and water rights held by Eaton. Convinced that water sufficient could be secured the board of water commissioners authorized the purchase of the lands on which Eaton held options. These lands which had water rights extended along Owens river for forty miles above Owens lake. The purchase money, $700,000, was taken from the funds of the water department of the city.

Mr. Mulholland now took up the question with the Chamber of Commerce. J. O. Koepfli, then the president, took an active interest in the project. At a meeting of the chamber it was decided in conjunction with other commercial bodies to appoint a special committee to make a thorough investigation of the scheme. Messrs. H. C. Witmer, Meyer Lissner and Fred A. Hines were sent to the valley. Their report was entirely satisfactory both in regard to the quantity and quality of the water of the river.

The next move was to call an election to vote on an issue of $1,500,000 bonds for the purchase of land and water rights in the valley and to begin the preliminary work on the aqueduct. There was some opposition to the bond issue, but a report setting forth the imperative necessity for an increased water supply and indorsing the Owens river project signed by W. J. Washburn, Willis H. Booth, A. B. Cass, William D. Stephens, Jacob Baruch and Fred A. Hines, men in whom the people of the city had confidence, practically neutralized the opposition and the vote for the bonds was over ten for, to one against. This election was held September 7, 1905.

Next a consulting board of eminent engineers was employed to examine the merits and feasibility of the project. This board consisted of Frederick P. Stearns, of the Isthmian Canal Commission, John R. Freeman, expert on hydraulics, and James D. Schuyler, expert on construction of dams; all were men of wide experience and high standing as engineers.

This board in a report made December 25, 1906, fully indorsed the project as feasible and reported that a supply of at least 20,000 inches could be obtained from the city's holdings in Owens river valley.

This board estimated the entire cost, purchase of land and water right and cost of construction of the aqueduct at a fraction less than twenty-five millions dollars. One million five hundred thousand dollars in bonds had already been issued. On the 13th of June, 1907. another bond election was held to vote upon an issue of $23,000,000.. The vote for the bonds was in about the same ratio as at the former election — ten for, to one against.

Beginning with the first issue of bonds the Board of Public Works, composed at that time of James A. Anderson, Albert A. Hubbard and David K. Edwards, had control of the undertaking. The Board of Water Commissioners, who had inaugurated the work and had made the first expenditure of money, co-operated with the Board of Public Works and were consulted by that board. An advisory committee was appointed from the two boards. William Mulholland held the position of chief engineer, J. B. Lippincott, assistant chief, and W. B. Mathews was head of the legal department. There were several changes in the membership of the Board of Public Works during the progress of the aqueduct.

The preliminaries for the great undertaking had now been arranged and the money for it made available. The immensity of it might well appall the stoutest heart. Of human opposition, there was little. Only the wailings of a few pessimists and the whinings of the man-afraid-of-taxes. The horse thief Indians, who once ranged over the route from San Fernando to Owens river valley, along which it was proposed to build the aqueduct, and stole horses by the thousands and massacred travelers, had long since been sent to their celestial paradise, the happy hunting grounds — the Indian heaven.

It was the obstacles that nature had placed that confronted Commander-in-Chief Mulholland and his staff. A torrid climate at one season of the year and an arctic climate at another. .A. waterless desert, that at a moment's notice might be deluged by a cloud burst, and an arid country that produced nothing for the subsistence of man or beast. The entire length of the aqueduct from the point where the water is taken from the river about thirty-five miles above Owens Lake to the reservoir at the head of San Fernando valley is two hundred and twenty-five miles. Getting ready to begin work was one of the most important items of expense. The proposed route of the aqueduct was nearly all over government land. An act of Congress passed in June, 1906, gave the city of Los Angeles the right of way over public lands. Fifty-seven camps were organized along the line of the aqueduct. Roads had to be made to these for the transportation of material and food supplied for the men.

The cost of transportation was greatly reduced by a traffic arrangement with the Southern Pacific Railroad. That road built a broad gauge line from its main road at Mojave to connect with the narrow gauge line in Owens valley. Permanent work was begun on the aqueduct in October, 1908, and was pushed with vigor. The most difficult portion to construct was the section known as Jawbone canon. This consisted of a series of tunnels and conduits aggregating about eighteen miles. To accelerate the work premiums were offered to the squads operating the drills for the fastest work in tunnel driving. The world's record was beaten by several of the teams. Six hundred and four feet were bored in one month in Elizabeth Lake tunnel. The bonus paid in addition to the regular wages of the men increased the daily wage about thirty per cent and decreased the cost of driving per foot from ten to fifteen per cent. This bonus system resulted in some instances in the payment of individual laborers as high as $168 in one month. While this was very satisfactory to the men who received the reward, it caused disappointment and dissatisfaction to other workmen.

The feeding of the men was a big undertaking. It was let by contract to Joseph Desmond. Complaints against the quality of the food provided were numerous and investigations frequent. During the progress of the work between July, 1908, and June, 1912, there were over 210,000 different men employed. During the year 1909 the wage average per month was $64,215. The expenditures at times during the height of the work reached $600,000 per month. The magnitude of the work of building the aqueduct was not comprehended by the average citizen at the time of its construction. It was only the experienced engineer who could take it all in. S. T. Henry, associate editor of the Engineering Record, and himself an experienced engineer, spent several weeks along the line of the aqueduct watching the work and taking notes.

He says: "I do not believe that the people of this city fully appreciate the magnitude of this project. With the Panama Canal ranking first, this is the fourth largest engineering project of the day in America. It is remarkable in many ways. You have established ditch records as well as tunnel records, and I believe, if a standard of the kind could be set, you would establish records for the spirit of organization and lack of jealousy. This spirit of organization and team work is one of the most interesting features of the aqueduct work. It is this spirit that has resulted in driving so fast through the hard rock of Elizabeth Lake tunnel and laying 4,000 feet of cement ditch work every month in each division."

E. E. Meyer, government engineer of the island of Java, Dutch East Indies, who passed four days in a tour of inspection of the aqueduct, said: "I have inspected storage reservoirs and aqueducts all over the world, in fact have made a special study of that class of engineering, yet nowhere have I seen them so neatly and economically worked out as here."

Arthur P. Davis, chief engineer of the United States reclamation service and builder of the Roosevelt Dam, said: "For wisdom of plan, excellence of construction and economy of execution, the Owens River Aqueduct is one of the most ably handled works in the world.

"The city of Los Angeles is fortunate in having in charge of this great work such thoroughly wide-awake and efficient men. Mistakes have been made, of course; that naturally attends any human endeavor, but they were slight ones and quickly corrected."

Horace Ropes, a consulting engineer of Los Angeles city, and constructor of the western aqueduct of the Boston Metropolitan District, after a five days inspection trip said: "The boldness of the whole scheme impressed me, and the remarkable execution of the plans surprised me and gave me additional respect for

353

the ability of Engineer William Mulholland. Eastern engineers, if they had been called here, would have said that the project was impossible. The country is severe and the hardships appear almost insurmountable. But Mr. Mulholland and his associates have taken the bit in their mouths and built a monument to the city and to themselves.

"In my opinion the aqueduct has been constructed for a reasonable consideration. The same work done in the east would have cost a great deal more, and it will last. The work has been well done. Any person who has a knowledge of similar engineering feats will say that the project has been a wonderful success."

Notwithstanding these high opinions of the work and the economical methods of conducting it expressed by expert engineers there were criticisms of it; there were investigating committees appointed by authority and self appointed. There were voluminous reports made and published. The aqueduct question figured in political campaigns and self constituted experts from the stump denounced the project and the projectors, but Mulholland and his supporters, unmoved by the tempest in a teapot raised by the petty politicians, pursued the even tenor of their ways until the work was completed.

Wednesday, November 5, 1913, was dedicated to the celebration of the completion of the aqueduct. Thirty thousand people went up the San Fernando valley in all manner of conveyances to the mouth of the aqueduct to witness the turning on of the water.

Thursday, November 6, 1913, was devoted to the dedication of Exposition Park. Three years before Miss Mary S. Bowen, in the presence of a large assemblage, had christened the old Agricultural Park, Exposition Park, using water from Owens river brought in a bottle over desert and plains.

The corner stone of the Armory was laid with Masonic ceremonies and the fountain in the center of the sunken garden of the park that in the future will spout Owens river waters was formally dedicated by Senator John D. Works in a fitting tribute to the two great institutions which the dual celebration commemorated.

CHAPTER XLV. THE BAY OF SAN PEDRO UNDER THE RULE OF SPAIN AND MEXICO

Juan Rodriguez Cabrillo, the discoverer of California, was also the discoverer of the Bay of San Pedro. The inaccuracy of Cabrillo's reckoning of latitude throws doubt on the day of the discovery. All that we know positively is that it was some day in October, 1542, fifty years, perhaps, to a day after the discovery of America by Columbus.

Cabrillo named it Bahia de Los Humos y Fuegos — the Bay of Smokes and Fires. The land was obscured by a thick cloud of smoke by day and fires gleamed on the mountains by night. This occurred every autumn. The Indian by accident or design set fire to the long dry grass that covered the plains, and the wind carried it where it listed. The Indian was no fire fighter, and a fire once started burned until it died out for want of fuel. It is fortunate for us that Cabrillo's name for the bay did not become fixed upon it. It would have been neither convenient nor euphonious.

The next explorer who visited the bay was Sebastian Vizcaino. He paid no attention to the names that Cabrillo had given to the bays, capes and islands of the California coast. Whether he did not know the names given by Cabrillo or that he wished to obtain the honor of their discovery are questions that cannot be settled now.

Vizcaino anchored in San Diego Bay, November 10, 1602, sixty years after Cabrillo had entered it. Vizcaino named it for his flagship. Cabrillo had called it the Bay of San Miguel. After a stay of ten days, on the 20th of November, the explorers resumed their voyage up the coast. A sail of eight days against a northwest wind brought them to an island which they named Santa Catalina, for the saint's day on which they discovered it. While beating up the coast against a head wind they had put into a bay which they named the Ensenada of San Andres, the bight or inlet of Saint Andrew.

The cosmographer Cabrera Bueno discovered an error had been made in naming the bay. The 26th of November, the day they entered the bay, was the day sacred to St. Peter, bishop of Alexandria, martyred in the third century, not to St. Andrew. Bueno locates on the map of the coast that he made, the little island now known as Deadman's Island, but did not name it.

Vizcaino's explorations were made in the interest of the Philippine trade, which became an important factor in the commerce of the South Seas, as the Pacific Ocean was then called. He was sent by order of the King of Spain to discover harbors where the Manila galleons might put in for wood and water and repairs after their long voyage of two thousand leagues from Japan to the California coast. For more than a third of a century before Vizcaino's voyage the scheme of exploring the coast of California for harbors of refuge had been agitated by the viceroys and the officials of New Spain, yet nothing had come of it. Nor was anything done for more than a century later.

One hundred and sixty-seven years passed after Vizcaino's ships sailed out of San Pedro Bay before another ship's keel cut the waters of Cabrillo's Bay of Smokes and Fires. Then the mission ship San Carlos, bearing supplies for the founding of San Diego, which had missed that port and sailed up to the Santa

Barbara channel, then drifting down the coast searching for the port of its destination, cast anchor in the San Pedro Bay. Continuing its voyage, it drifted into San Diego Bay scurvy-afflicted, and ere the plague had run its course all of its crew but two had been buried at Punto de los Muertos or Dead Man's Point.

Whether the ships bringing the King's memorias (remembrances) for the Missions anchored in San Pedro Bay, I have found no record. The supplies for the Missions of San Gabriel and San Fernando doubtless were landed there. With crude and cumbersome means of transportation — the wooden-wheeled carreta — it would have been almost impossible to convey these supplies from Monterey or San Diego.

The first foreign vessels to seek the trade of California came from a nation unborn and a land unsettled when Vizcaino was exploring California's bays and harbors. These were the Yankee smugglers' crafts. The first of these vessels that appeared on the California coast was the ship Otter of Boston, commanded by Ebenezer Dorr. Dorr's ship carried six guns and a crew of twenty-six men. She anchored at Monterey October 29, 1796. Dorr had been cruising in the vicinity of Monterey for nearly a week, evidently taking the lay of the land and calculating the chances for trade in the future.

Dorr obtained a supply of wood and water on presenting a passport from General Washington signed by the Spanish consul at Charleston, South Carolina. He asked permission to land some English sailors who had secretly boarded his vessel at Port Saxon. He was refused permission. He sailed from Monterey November 6th. He landed his ten convicts on the beach at night, forcing them ashore at the pistol point. They were convicts from Botany Bay, and doubtless Dorr feared a mutiny if he kept them aboard. Governor Borica considered this a mean Yankee trick. He set the convicts at work as carpenters and blacksmiths at nineteen cents a day. They behaved so well that he would have been pleased to retain them in the country, but the fear of heresy haunted the Spaniard, and in obedience to royal orders he sent them next year to San Bias en route to Cadiz to be sent to England.

These vessels engaged in illicit trade all came to the coast well armed. The Eliza, commanded by James Rowan, which anchored in San Francisco, May 27, 1799, carried twelve guns. The Betsy put into San Diego in August, 1800. She carried ten guns. These entered the ports for supplies and for wood and water. The Spaniards were suspicious of them and granted their requests on condition that they enter no other California port.

In the early years of 1800 the smugglers became quite active. The only products of California that were of value to them were seal and otter skins. The otter skins were worth in China all the way from $30 to $100. The smugglers paid for them in goods and Yankee notions at prices ranging from $2.50 to $10. The trade was carried on in obscure ports where there were no guns and no coast guard. San Pedro Bay was one of the chief entrepots of this trade. The smuggler's craft could anchor in the lee of Santa Catalina Island watching for an opportunity when the coast was clear, then a quick run to San Pedro Bay, a rapid exchange of goods for furs and off before the guard from the pueblo could intercept trade.

The people and the padres of the missions did not consider it a very venal sin to escape duties on the necessities that the country did not produce, and which they stood in most urgent need of.

The Spanish government had undertaken to make a government monopoly of the fur trade. A royal cedulo of 1785 directed the mission padres to collect otter skins from the natives and deliver them to the royal commissioner al a fixed price. These were to be shipped to China, and it was expected that a large revenue would accrue to the royal treasury. The scheme failed and was abandoned in 1790. The padrea continued to secure skins, but instead of sending them to San Bias to the government officials at low prices, preferred to sell them where they could get the best terms. The smugglers came at an opportune time.

The Lelia Byrd was one of the pioneer American trading vessels of the Pacific coast It was the property of Capt. Richard J. Cleveland of Salem, Mass., and commanded by William Shaler. Cleveland and Shaler were fine types of the American captains of the early years of the nineteenth century, when our commerce was extended to every country on the globe.

In March, 1803, the Lelia Byrd put into San Diego to procure supplies and do legitimate trading. The comandante of the port was a conceited coxcomb of a lieutenant — who boarded their vessel with an armed escort and placed a guard on the ship and ordered them as soon as their wants were supplied to leave the port. They undertook to purchase some furs from a citizen. Two boats were sent ashore at night with goods to an appointed place, one returned with some furs. But the other with a mate and two men did not return; they had been captured while in the act of bartering with a civilian by the comandante and his escort, bound hand and foot and left under a guard on the beach. At daylight a boatload of sailors from the ship captured the guard and released the prisoners. The Spanish guard on the vessel were disarmed and sent below. The anchor was weighed and sails set. A shot from Fort Guijanos, which was on Ballast Point, where Fort Rosecrans now stands, was fired at the vessel. The Spanish guard was forced to stand on deck while their companions in the fort were bombarding the ship. Captain Shaler reserved his fire until opposite the fort, then he gave the Spaniards two broadsides, which silenced them. The guards were set on shore after passing beyond the fort. They were so rejoiced that they gave the Americans a succession of vivan los Americans, as the battered ship sailed away to Lower California.

In May, 1809, Captain Shaler visited Santa Catalina and anchored in a harbor of the island of which he supposed himself to be the discoverer. He named the harbor Port Rouissillon after a former partner. He spent six weeks in this harbor repairing his ship. Then he crossed the channel and anchored in San Pedro Bay. He secured from the pueblo of Los Angeles and the Mission San Gabriel supplies of provisions sufficient to last him twelve months. No doubt he purchased a number of otter skins. There was no government official there to interfere with trade.

The O'Cain was another of the famous fur buying vessels that haunted the California coast for several years under different commanders and different names. At first she appeared on the coast early in 1803, under command of Capt. Joseph O'Cain. She was owned in part by the Winship Brothers. O'Cain secured skins wherever he could from padres and private citizens. Keeping out of the government chitches he was said to have not only tricked the officials, but his own partners. In 1806 the O'Cain was on the coast again, under command this time of Jonathan Winship. He had entered into a contract with Baranof. director of the Russian Fur Company, to sell him all the furs he could gather upon the coast. He distributed an army of fur-hunting Aleuts with their bidarkas (skin boats) among the islands — Santa Catalina , San Clemente — and along the coast. In six months he had gathered up $60,000 of furs, which was certainly a successful stroke of business.

In 1807 Winship was back again with his Aleut hunters scattered among the islands and down the coast of Lower California. He received his supplies at San Pedro. Returning to New Archangel he sailed next year to China with a cargo valued at $136,000. These pioneers of American commerce on the coast of California were remarkably successful in evading capture. The Spanish war ships were on the lookout for them. Occasionally one came to grief.

The Mercury, commanded by Capt. George Washington Ayers, came to the coast in 1813 to engage in contraband trade. She was captured just above Santa Barbara by Nicolas Noe, captain of the Spanish ship Flora. The capture of the Mercury was a godsend to the needy officers and ragged soldiers of the presidios. One of the prizes of the capture was $16,000 in coin which was retained in California.

Noe took possession of the Mercury and cruised among the Channel islands, where a number of smuggling vessels were reported in hiding. He did not capture any. Noe left six or eight cannon at San Pedro. These were left presumably that they might be needed to protect the embarcadero in case of an Anglo-American invasion. Even at this early day there was a fear that the Americans had designs on California, and that the United States might attempt to aid the revolutionists of Mexico who were fighting to free themselves from the Spanish yoke. There is no record of what became of the cannon. Possibly the four old cannon, two of which are at the court house and two on Fort Hill, may be part of the lot left by Captain Noe at San Pedro one hundred years ago. The Mercury's guns were of American make and so are the four old cannon named above.

In 1815 Bovis Tarkanof, a Russian, and over twenty Aleuts were captured at San Pedro by Comisionado Cota and put in jail at Los Angeles. They were engaged in otter hunting. They were connected with the Russian settlement at Fort Ross on Bodega Bay. Some of these made their escape and others were converted to Catholicism and remained in the country.

Sometimes those who attempted to get the better of the smugglers by trickery came to grief and were themselves punished. In 1821 an American schooner was lying off the Malibu coast above San Pedro watching for an opportunity to trade. Antonio Birones of Los Angeles with a few companions by signals induced the captain of the schooner to send a boat load of goods ashore for trade. Birones and his associates seized the goods and arrested the men from the ship in charge of them and held them for a ransom of $1,000. Unfortunately for Birones among the goods sent ashore was a case of brandy. The guards sampled the liquor and got drunk. The prisoners made their escape.

Birones and his friends appropriated the goods but were careful to say nothing about their attempt to punish the smugglers to the authorities. Captain de la Guerra, comandante of the presidio of Santa Barbara, heard of the affair. He confiscated the goods and condemned the men concerned in the affair to pay a heavy fine towards the completion of the church of Our Lady of the Angeles at Los Angeles. Birones and Alanis, the leaders of the gang, were sentenced to six months hard labor in the pueblo chain gang.

The commerce in otter skins had fallen into decadence in California before it passed from under the domination of Spain. In 1821, the last year of Spanish rule, only two American vessels came to the coast to engage in the fur trade. The otter was being exterminated. Although otter hunting continued in an irregular manner for twenty years, later there was but little profit in it and the little fur-bearing animal that brought the first foreign commerce to California finally became extinct.

With the decadence of the otter skin industry another industry had been slowly developing and that was in the dried hides of the slaughtered cattle that covered the California plains. The long distance of California from any market limited its commerce to the articles that could be condensed into the smallest space on board a vessel. During the war for Mexican independence there had been a very limited trade between California and Peru in hides and tallow, but it was not until Mexico gained her independence that the New England shippers engaged in hide droghing on the California coast. The hide drogher was a vessel with large storage capacity. It took its name from a craft used in the West India Islands to take sugar, rum and other merchandise to the merchantmen. The hide droghers came around Cape Horn. Their cargoes on the outer voyage consisted largely of merchandise. It usually required three years to make the round voyage — dispose of their goods and secure a ship load of hides.

The ship Sachem was the pioneer hide drogher. She arrived at Monterey in 1822. In her came William Alden Gale. He had been engaged in the fur trade on the coast in earlier years. He had seen the opening for a profitable trade in hides and had induced some Boston merchants to make the venture. He found on his arrival a rival in the business in the English firm of Begg & Co., of Lima, Peru. The firm was represented by Hugh McCulloch and William E. P. Hartnell or Macala and Arnel, as the Californians called them. They entered into a contract with the friars of the missions by which Begg & Co. were to send one ship each year to touch at the different ports along the coast and take all the hides offered and at least twenty-five thousand arrobas of tallow equal to 625,000 pounds. The price fixed for hides large and small was $1 each and for tallow $2 per arroba or eight cents per pound. Those contracting with the English firm were prohibited from selling to other traders. Begg & Co. had a monopoly of the hide and tallow trade and Gale found it difficult to secure a cargo, although he offered $1.50 for hides and $4 per hundred for horns. The pueblos and rancheros had the privilege of disposing of their produce at the same price the mission padres were receiving.

Mexico after gaining her independence removed some of the most burdensome restrictions that had hampered commerce under Spanish rule, but tariff rates were still high and smuggling continued. The ports along the coast had been opened to trade, but in 1826 an order was issued by the home government that no vessel be allowed to load or unload in any other port than Monterey. A duty of forty-two and one-half per cent on goods, an anchorage tax of $10 and a tonnage rate of $2.50 per ton was levied on vessels. Relief was sought from these excessive rates in smuggling and both the people and the padres were not averse in aiding the captains of the vessels in escaping the high charges.

In January, 1828, Governor Echandia ordered that all way ports except San Pedro be closed. In July of that year San Pedro was also closed by an order which declared that all coasting trade must be done in Mexican bottoms. The increasing restrictions on commerce were burdensome on both the people and the traders and both redoubled their efforts at smuggling.

San Pedro and Santa Catalina continued to figure in illicit trade. Captain Cunningham with other masters of American trading vessels formulated a scheme of erecting buildings for a trading station on Catalina island, but Governor Echandia ordered the building removed. One Yankee captain named Lawler, sometimes appropriately written Lawless, was accustomed on coming to the coast to deposit a large portion of his cargo on some island, usually Santa Catalina, and with what was left enter some port and pay duty on the remainder on board. When these goods were sold he replenished his stock from the island cache. At one time he sailed out of San Pedro owing duty to the amount of $1,000. He was finally compelled to break up his Santa Catalina establishment, pay up his back duties and quit the coast.

As the hide and tallow trade developed, the American traders gradually got control of the commerce in hides and the Peruvians in tallow. The horns, which were a considerable item, were shipped to the United States for the manufacture of combs, one vessel from San Pedro taking 40,000 pairs. Although large quantities of country produce were shipped from San Pedro and few trading vessels coming to the coast failed to visit it, in the earlier years of Mexican rule there were no local authorities or other residents at the port. There was a sub alcalde resident at the Dominguez rancho about fifteen miles from the port. He had a limited authority over the shipping interests at the harbor.

In 1833 Antonio M. Oslo held the office of receptor of customs and resided at Los Angeles. He had charge also of the inland trade with New Mexico. In 1834, the year of the secularization of the missions, over 100,000 hides and 25,000 quintals of tallow were shipped from the port of San Pedro. The most complete and satisfactory description of hide droghing in California is contained in Dana's "Two Years Before the Mast," first published in 1840. Richard H. Dana, Jr., an undergraduate of Harvard College, with the hope of curing a weakness of his eyes by long absence from books and an open air life, shipped as a common sailor on the brig Pilgrim which sailed from Boston, August 14, 1834, on a voyage round Cape Horn to the western coast of North America. Besides his description of the country and the hide droghing commerce he gives us an insight into the customs, character and domestic life of the California people of eighty years ago. He is sometimes severe in his criticisms and inclined to view the customs of the people from a New England standpoint, but on the whole his story of the California of the cattle barons is one of the most readable and reliable that we have.

I quote his description of San Pedro, the method of landing goods and the process of loading hides on shipboard:

"Leaving Santa Barbara, we coasted along down, the country appearing level or moderately uneven, and, for the most part, sandy and treeless; until, doubling a high sandy point, we let go our anchor at a distance of three or three and a half miles from shore. It was like a vessel bound to St. Johns, Newfoundland. coming to anchor on the Grand Banks; for the shore, being low, appeared to be a greater distance than it actually was, and we thought we might as well have stayed at Santa Barbara and sent our boat down for hides. The land was of a clayey quality, and, as far as the eye could reach, entirely bare of trees and even shrubs; and there was no sign of a town, — not even a house to be seen. What brought us into such a place we could not conceive. No sooner had we come to anchor, than the slip-rope, and the other preparations for southeasters, were got ready: and there was reason enough for it, for we lay exposed to every wind that could blow, except the northerly winds, and they came over a flat country with a rake of more than a league of water. As soon as everything was snug on board, the boat was lowered, and we pulled ashore, our new officer, who had been several times in the port before, taking the place of steersman. As we drew in we found the tide low, and the rocks and stones, covered with kelp and seaweed, lying for the distance of nearly an eighth of a mile. Leaving the boat, and picking our way barefooted over these, we came to what is called the landing-place, at high water mark. The soil was, as it appeared at first, loose and clayey, and, except the stalks of the mustard plant, there was no vegetation. Just in front of the landing, and immediately over it, was a small hill, which, from its being no more than thirty or forty feet high, we had not perceived from our anchorage.

"Over this hill we saw three men coming down, dressed partly like sailors and partly like Californians, one of them having on a pair of untanned leather trousers and a red shirt. When they reached us, we found that they were Englishmen. They told us that they had belonged to a small Mexican brig which had been driven ashore here in a southeaster, and now lived in a small house just over the hill. Going up this hill with them, we saw, close behind it, a small, low building, with one room, containing a fireplace, cooking apparatus, etc., and the rest of it unfinished, and used as a place to store hides and goods. This, they told us, was built by some traders in the pueblo (a town about thirty miles in the interior, to which this was the port), and used by them as a storehouse, and also as a lodging place when they came down to trade with the vessels. These three men were employed by them to keep the house in order and to look out for the things stored there. They said that they had been there nearly a year; had nothing to do most of the time, living upon beef, hard bread and frijoles, a peculiar kind of beans, very abundant in California. The nearest house, they told us, was a rancho, or cattle-farm, about three miles off, and one of them went there, at the request of our officer, to order a horse to be sent down, with which the agent, who was on board, might go up to the pueblo.

"From one of them, who was on intelligent English sailor, I learned a good deal in a few minutes' conversation about the place, its trade, and the news from the southern ports. San Diego, he told me, was a small, snug place, having very little trade, but decidedly the best harbor on the coast, being completely land locked, and the water as smooth as a duck pond. This was the depot for all the vessels engaged in the trade; each one having a large house there, built of rough boards, in which they stowed their hides as fast as they collected them in their trips up and down the coast, and when they had procured a full cargo, spent a few weeks there taking it in, smoking ship, laying in wood and water, and making other preparations for the voyage home."

"I also learned, to my surprise, that the desolate looking place we were in furnished more hides than any other port on the coast. It was the only port for a distance of eighty miles, and about thirty miles in the interior was a fine plain country, filled with herds of cattle, in the center of which was the Pueblo de Los Angeles, — the largest town in California, — and several of the wealthiest missions; to all of which San Pedro was the seaport."

"The next day we pulled the agent ashore, and he went up to visit the pueblo and the neighboring missions; and in a few days, as the result of his labors, large ox-carts and droves of mules loaded with hides were seen coming over the flat country. We loaded our long boat with goods of all kinds, light and heavy, and pulled ashore. After landing and rolling them over the stones upon the beach, we stopped, waiting for the carts to come down the hill and take them; but the captain soon settled the matter by ordering us to carry them all up to the top, saying that that was 'California fashion.' So, what the oxen would not do, we were obliged to do. The hill was low, but steep, and the earth, being clayey and wet with the recent rains, was but bad holding ground for our feet. The heavy barrels and casks we rolled up with some difficulty, getting behind and putting our shoulders to them; now and then our feet, slipping, added to the danger of the casks rolling back upon us. But the greatest trouble was with the large boxes of sugar. These we had to place upon our oars, and lifting them up, rest the oars upon our shoulders, and creep slowly up the hill with the gait of a funeral procession. After an hour or two of hard work, we got them all up, and found the carts standing full of hides, which we had to unload, and to load the carts again with our own goods; the lazy Indians, who came down with them, squatting on their hams, looking on, doing nothing, and when we asked them to help us, only shaking their heads, or drawling out 'no quiero.'

"Having loaded the carts, we started up the Indians, who went off, one on each side of the oxen, with long sticks, sharpened at the end, to punch them with. This is one of the means of saving labor in California, — two Indians to two oxen. Now, the hides were to be got down; and for this purpose we brought the boat round to a place where the hill was steeper, and threw them off, letting them slide over the slope. Many of them lodged, and we had to let ourselves down and set them a-going again, and in this way became covered with dust, and our clothing torn. After we had the hides all down, we were obliged to take them on our heads and walk over the stones and through the water to the boat. The water and the stones together would wear out a pair of shoes a day, and as shoes were very scarce and very dear, we were compelled to go barefooted. At night we went on board, having had the hardest and most disagreeable day's work that we had yet experienced. For several days we were employed in this manner, until we had landed forty or fifty tons of goods, and brought on board about two thousand hides, when the trade began to slacken, and we were kept at work on board during the latter part of the week, either in the hold or upon the rigging."

Alfred Robinson, who came to California in 1829 and afterwards became a permanent resident of California, is less severe in his comments on San Pedro than Dana. I append his description of the harbor:

362

"The harbor of San Pedro is an extensive bay, and although not considered a safe anchorage during the winter months, when the southeast wind prevails, yet vessels frequently embark and discharge their cargoes here at all seasons of the year. The best anchorage is close under the northwest point of the bay. about three-quarters of a mile outside of a small rocky island and the same distance from the beach. There is a house at the landing place which generally serves as a landmark, in connection with the preceding location, and vessels usually, in the mild season of the year, bring this to bear W.N.W., while the point lies S.W. by S., and the island ½ E. From the month of October to the beginning of May vessels anchor at least a mile outside of these bearings, and ships are necessarily prepared for slipping their cables and getting under way, should the wind, as is often the case, chop in suddenly from the S.E. The holding ground is good, of stiff clay, in four and a half to nine fathoms.

"As we anticipated, our friends came in the morning, flocking on board from all quarters; and soon a busy scene commenced, afloat and ashore. Boats were plying to and fro — launches laden with the variety of our cargo, passing to the beach, and men, women and children crowding upon our docks, partaking in the general excitement."

In the following extract Dana describes a certain class of men found in California at that time. The ship upon which he was a sailor had come up from San Diego and anchored in San Pedro Bay:

"There was but one man in the only house here, and him I shall always remember as a good specimen of a California ranger. He had been a tailor in Philadelphia, and, getting intemperate and in debt, joined a trapping party, and went to the Columbia river, and thence down to Monterey, where he spent everything, left his party, and came to the Pueblo de los Angeles to work at his trade. Here he went dead to leeward among the pulperias, gambling rooms, etc., and came down to San Pedro to be moral by being out of temptation. He had been in the house several weeks, working hard at his trade, upon orders which he had brought with him, and talked much of his resolution, and opened his heart to us about his past life. After we had been here some time, he started off one morning in fine spirits, well dressed, to carry the clothes which he had been making to the pueblo, and saying that he would bring back his money and some fresh orders the next day. The next day came, and a week passed, and nearly a fortnight, when one day. going ashore, we saw a tall man, who looked like our friend the tailor, getting out of the back of an Indian's cart, which had just come down from the pueblo. He stood for the house, but we bore up after him; when finding that we were overhauling him, he hove-to and spoke us. Such a sight! Barefooted, with an old pair of trousers tied round his waist by a piece of green hide, a soiled cotton shirt, and a torn Indian hat; 'cleaned out' to the last real, and completely 'used up.' He confessed the whole matter; acknowledged that he was on his back; and now he had a prospect of a fit of the horrors for a week, and of being worse than useless for months. This is a specimen of the life of half of the Americans and English who are adrift along the coasts of the Pacific and its islands, — commonly called 'beach-combers.' "

Again Dana vents his spite on our beloved harbor thus: "Saturday, February 13th. Were called up at midnight to slip for a violent northeaster; for this miserable hole of San Pedro is thought unsafe in almost every wind. We went off with a flowing sheet, and hove-to under the lee of Catalina Island, where we lay three days, and then returned to our anchorage."

The vessel had gone up to Santa Barbara and returned to San Pedro. This is Dana's parting salute to the harbor of our hopes: "Two days brought us to San Pedro, and two days more (to our no small joy) gave us our last view of that place, which was universally called the hell of California, and seemed designed in every way for the wear and tear of sailors. Not even the last view could bring out one feeling of regret. No thanks, thought I, as we left the hated shores in the distance, for the hours I have walked over your stones barefooted, with hides on my head, — for the burdens I have carried up your steep muddy hill, — for the ducking in your surf; and for the long days and longer nights passed on your desolate hill, watching piles of hides, hearing the sharp bark of your eternal coyotes, and the dismal hooting of your owls."

The first shipwreck in San Pedro bay occurred Christmas eve, 1828. The brig Danube of New York with a crew of twenty-eight men dragged her anchors in a fierce southeaster and was dashed on shore a total wreck. The officers and crew were all saved. "It is an ill wind that blows nobody any good." The southeaster that wrecked the Danube was the indirect cause of the building of the first ship launched in San Pedro bay. The hull of the vessel was sold for $1,760 to Guerra and Dana of Santa Barbara (not Dana of the Pilgrim). Father Sanchez of San Gabriel Mission was an enterprising man awake to every opportunity to make money for his mission. He had long looked with disfavor on the encroachment of the Russian and American fur traders and hunters. The sea otter was being exterminated and but little profit had come to the Californians from this valued peltry.

The hull timbers and iron of the wrecked Danube furnished material that hitherto it had been impossible to secure in California. Father Sanchez had in his employ at the mission Jose Chapman. Chapman was one of Bouchard's privateers who had been captured at Ortega's rancho, as told elsewhere in this history. He was a ship carpenter, and during his residence in California had become a jack of all trades. To him was assigned the duty of getting out ship timbers in the San Gabriel mountains. These were hauled on wooden-wheeled carts, drawn by oxen, to San Pedro. The vessel was constructed on the inner bay or slough, above what was formerly known as Timm's Point. Historians differ in regard to the name of the ship. Warner calls her the "Refugio." Robinson and Bancroft the "Guadalupe." Bancroft is uncertain about the tonnage of the schooner and gives it in three different places variously at six, sixty and ninety-nine tons.

Alfred Robinson, in his "Life in California," gives the best description of the building and launching of the vessel extant. He says: "A launch was to take place at San Pedro — the second vessel ever constructed in California. She was a schooner of about sixty tons that had been entirely framed at San Gabriel and fitted for subsequent completion at San Pedro. Every piece of timber had been fitted thirty miles from the place and brought down on the beach in carts. She was called the "Guadalupe," in honor of the patron saint of Mexico, and as the affair was considered quite an important era in the history of the country, many were invited from far and near to witness it.

"Her builder was a Yankee named Chapman, who had served his apprenticeship with a Boston ship builder. He was one of a piratical cruiser that attacked Monterey, at which time he was taken prisoner, and had lived in the country ever since. From his long residence he had acquired a mongrel language, English, Spanish and Indian being so mingled in his speech that it was difficult to understand him. Although illiterate, his ingenuity and honest deportment had acquired for him the esteem of the Californians and a connection in marriage with one of the first families of the country. Father Sanchez of San Gabriel used to say. Chapman could get more work out of the Indians in his unintelligible tongue than all the major domos put together. I was present on one occasion when he wished to dispatch an Indian to the beach at San Pedro with his ox wagon, charging him to return as soon as possible. His directions ran somewhat in this manner: 'Ventura! Vamos, trae los bueyes, go down to the playa and come back as quick as you can puede.' "

Of the career of the "Guadalupe" or the "Refugio" but little is known. Warner, who came to California the year the vessel was launched, disposes of the event in a brief paragraph. He says: "In 1831, the minister at San Gabriel, Father Sanchez, aided and encouraged by William Wolfskill, Nathaniel Pryor, Richard Laughlin, Samuel Prentice and George Yount (all Americans), built a schooner at San Pedro, which was employed by the Americans named in the hunting of sea otter."

The vessel visited the channel island in search of otter. Prentice, who was one of the owners, took up his residence on Catalina Island, and died there. He was the first civilized man buried on the island. Wolfskill, being a Mexican citizen, was able to get a license; with his associates he hunted otter up and down the coast in 1832; he soon abandoned the business and became a ranchero in Los Angeles. The vessel was reported in San Francisco in 1834. She was wrecked on the Mexican coast, date not given.

San Pedro was the scene of the only case of marooning known to have occurred on the California coast.

"Marooning was a diabolical custom or invention of the pirates of the Spanish Main. The process was as simple as it was horrible. When some unfortunate individual aboard the piratical craft had incurred the hatred of the crew or the master, he was placed in a boat and rowed to some barren island or desolate coast of the main land, and forced ashore. A bottle of water and a few biscuits were thrown him, the boat rowed back to the ship, and left him to die of hunger and thirst, or to rave out his existence under the maddening heat of a tropical sun.

"In January, 1832, a small brig entered the bay of San Pedro and anchored. Next morning two passengers were landed from a boat on the barren strand. They were given two bottles of water and a few biscuit. The vessel sailed away, leaving them to their fate. There was no habitation within thirty miles of the landing. Ignorant of the country, their fate might have been that of many another victim of marooning. An Indian, searching for shells, discovered them and conducted them to the Mission San Gabriel, where they were cared for."

They were two Catholic priests — Bachelot, a Frenchman, and Short, an Irishman, who had resided for some time in the Sandwich Islands, engaged in missionary work. They were forcibly expelled by the queen regent, Kaahumau, who had recently been converted to Christianity by the Protestant missionaries. She evidently wanted but one brand of religion in her domain. Bachelot for some time officiated as priest of the Church of Our Lady of the Angeles. The queen regent being dead, in 1838 Bachelot and Short returned to the islands and were again ordered by the government to leave. On their refusal they were forcibly put on board a vessel and sent away. Bachelot died at sea.

The principal article of California commerce in the early '40s continued to be hides. All foreign ships coming to the coast were compelled to go to Monterey to have their cargoes inspected and to pay the revenue charges on their goods. The tariff rates were so excessive that all traders who came to the coast resorted to smuggling; not only the traders, but the people, were constantly watching for opportunities to evade the revenue laws.

"So large a portion of the inhabitants, both native and foreign, all classes," says Bancroft, "were engaged in contraband trade that there was slight risk of detection. Custom officers were the only ones who were at all dishonored by smuggling." The favorite method, which continued while California was under the Mexican government, was a transfer of cargo at sea. A ship would put into Monterey with a small cargo, pay the revenue and transfer her cargo to her consort at sea, and that vessel would do the trading. Another way of evading was to have a cache, or hiding place, on some island where the most of the cargo could be stored while the vessel with the least valuable part of the cargo would put into port, pass inspection by the revenue officers and then return for the remainder of its load.

Santa Catalina, on account of its nearness to the mainland and to the largest town in the territory and to the safety of ships from storms while lying on the lee side of the island, was a favorite resort for smugglers.

The revenue from customs in the last years of Mexican rule averaged about $75,000 a year. The actual revenue, could the government have collected, would have more than doubled this amount. The government had no revenue cutters or armed vessels on the coast to enforce its revenue laws. In the frequent revolutions the custom house was the bounty or reward of the successful revolutionist, and often furnished the "sinews of war" in the bloodless combats that deposed the party in power. A revolution was often cheaper than an election. Under such conditions the people could hardly be blamed for encouraging contraband trade. They could purchase smuggled goods at greatly reduced rates. Why pay a revenue to support a government that might be overturned any day?

The most important military event at San Pedro in the waning days of Mexican domination was the deportation of Governor Micheltorena and his cholo army to Mexico. After his disastrous defeat at the bloodless battle of Cahuenga (described in another chapter of this book), and his capitulation to Pic Pico and Jose Castro, February 23, 1845, he and his battalion took up their line of march to San Pedro, to be shipped out of the country. He was allowed to depart with all the military honors he could display — drums beating and flags flying — but his cholos were not allowed to march through the city. The citizens had a vivid recollection of the raids on their hen roosts and orchards, and they were willing to forego the pleasure of bidding their unwelcome guests adios. The battalion took up its line of march over the plains to the westward of the city.

It encamped on the Pales Verdes Rancho, near San Pedro, while Pio Pico and Castro were raising the money and securing a ship to deport Micheltorena and his troops out of the country. Pico and his associates made a contract with Capt. John Paty of the ship Don Quixote to take Micheltorena and his soldiers (about 200 in number) away from California. The Californians agreed to pay $11,000 for their transportation. They were to be taken to Monterey and from there to San Bias. The vessel left San Pedro March 12, 1845. One thousand dollars of the transportation money was paid Paty at the sailing of the vessel from San Pedro, $1,000 at Monterey, and Pico, Figueroa and Lugo became sureties for the payment of the balance; the funds to be taken from the receipts of customs.

This was the second occasion that the people of Los Angeles had put up money to deport refuse Mexican-born governors. In 1832, Gov. Manuel Victoria, a petty tyrant, was defeated by a southern army under Portola, Pico and Carrillo, in a battle on the plains of Cahuenga. It was not bloodless. Abila, on the patriots' side, and Pacheco of Victoria's staff, were killed and Victoria himself severely wounded. Supposing himself mortally wounded, he abdicated the governorship.

There happened to be at that time an excellent surgeon on board an English vessel lying at San Pedro. Victoria, after the battle, had been taken to the San Gabriel mission. The surgeon was sent for. He, on examining the wound, pronounced it dangerous but not necessarily fatal. Victoria, when he was able to travel, was taken to San Diego to be deported. The San Diegoans could not raise the funds to pay his fare to San Bias, so they borrowed $125 from the ayuntamiento of Los Angeles. The loan was never paid. The deportation of Mexican governors was an unprofitable industry to the good people of the angel city.

The revenue from customs in 1845 amounted to $140,000. This was the last full year of Mexican rule of California. There were sixty vessels in the California commercial fleet that year. One vessel — the Matador — paid into the treasury $67,000, the largest amount ever paid by one vessel. Most of these vessels visited San Pedro. The trade of that port had been steadily increasing despite the fact there was no custom house there, and all vessels coming to trade on the coast were compelled to enter their cargoes at Monterey.

Many whalers coming down from Alaska put into California ports for supplies; some of these carried a stock of good for trade and were adroit smugglers. These adventurous seamen of this heroic age of American shipping had thus early penetrated far up into the Northern Pacific in the pursuit of their hazardous vocation.

The first United States war vessel to enter the harbor of San Pedro was the sloop Cyane of the Pacific squadron. On October 20, 1842, Commodore Thomas Ap Catesby Jones, commanding the Pacific squadron, which consisted of five vessels, mounting one hundred and sixteen guns, captured Monterey. The French, English and American squadrons were lying in the harbor of Callao. There were rumors of war between the United States and Mexico, growing out of the proposed annexation of Texas. It was reported that Mexico had sold California to England for $7,000,000.

Admiral Thomas, commander of the English fleet, had sailed out of Callao harbor under sealed orders. Jones, suspecting his destination to be California, determined to anticipate him in the seizure of the coveted prize. After holding Monterey for forty hours he restored it to the authorities, hauled down the Stars and Stripes and raised the Mexican flag and saluted it. He had discovered his mistake. He anchored at Monterey during the remainder of the year awaiting the arrival of Governor Micheltorena. The governor with his cholo army on their march to Monterey had reached the Comulos rancho when a messenger at midnight of October 24th brought him a report of the capture of the capital. He hastily retreated to Los Angeles.

Col. J. J. Warner, who was living in Los Angeles at that time, claimed that Micheltorena began fortifying Fort Hill. His cholos did not do much digging. Stephen C. Foster, who accompanied as interpreter Col. St. George Cooke, commanding the Mormon battalion who built the fort, asserted that there was no trace of Micheltorena's fort left when Cooke began fortifying. The governor preferred to remain in Los Angeles while Commodore Jones stopped at Monterey, so the commodore had to come to Los Angeles to meet him.

With news of the restoration of Monterey, Micheltorena had grown very brave and very insolent. He wrote to the commodore in a dispatch this bombast: "Though I and my men were only one hundred and fifty leagues from you, you have thought proper to evacuate the place, to re-establish the authorities, to rehoist and properly salute the flag of my nation and to re-embark all your troops. I now answer you that we Mexicans know how to answer with arms and fire when we are addressed in terms of war."

As time passed he grew more pompous. In another dispatch he informed the commodore that "The multitude of persons now surrounding me will not be content with such satisfaction as you can give me in a single dispatch." The satisfaction, like the outrage, must be public. He insisted on a personal conference at Los Angeles "eight leagues from Jones' force at San Pedro and twelve leagues from his army at San Fernando," or if Jones feared to venture to come to Los Angeles, mistrusting the word and faith of an old soldier, then he, the general, would boldly go in person with a few officers to San Pedro.

Despite the fact that Micheltorena's terrible army was at Los Angeles, only eight leagues away, Commodore Jones ventured to come to San Pedro with one vessel only of his fleet. The frigate United States and the Dale were sent to Mazatlan.

On January 17, 1843, the sloop of war Cyane, to which Commodore Jones had transferred his broad pennant, anchored in the bay of San Pedro. About 7 p. m. a light was hoisted on shore as a signal for a boat. This was followed by a discharge of small arms to attract attention. The commodore, unaccustomed to such naval signals, sent a boat to ascertain what was wanted. The boat returned with an aide-de-camp bearing a letter of invitation to Commodore Jones and his stay to meet General Micheltorena at Los Angeles. The invitation was accepted, and on the following morning the commodore and his staff disembarked. On reaching the shore the party were agreeably surprised to find that cooks had arrived and preparations had been made to serve the visitors with a hot lunch before starting for the pueblo. The only house then at the port was a large warehouse, quadrangular in form with transverse wings — the old hide house of Dana's time enlarged. It was owned by Don Abel Stearns.

With the escort sent by the general was his six-seated barouche, drawn by three horses abreast. In the carriage was seated Major Medina, chief aide-de-camp, in full uniform. There were a number of saddle horses, some of them richly and gaudily caparisoned — -these were for the visitors. There was a retinue of outriders and a military escort of twenty-five lancers. After dinner the party started for Los Angeles, the commodore and chief officers of his staff seated in the carriage, while the others followed on horseback. Governor Micheltorena's six-seated barouche was the first four-wheeled vehicle to make the trip between the pueblo and San Pedro. It was one of the first, if not the first, carriage brought to California.

Now that the automobile has eliminated the horse as well as the barouche, it may be interesting to some of my readers to know how that carriage was propelled over the old camino between the embarcadero and the pueblo seventy years ago. I quote from a narrative written by one of the commodore's staff and published in Colonel Warner's paper. The Southern Vineyard, in 1858.

"As already said, the carriage was drawn by three horses, but these were attached to it in a manner peculiar to the Spanish people in the Americas. Harness is entirely dispensed with, save the pole and straps, which are lashed to the logger-head of the saddle of the center horse, and a single trace or tug rope leading from the pommels of the saddles of the outside horses to the fore axle-tree of the carriage. The horses are not coupled, nor in any manner attached to each other, consequently each one is governed by its own rider. In this manner the horses are urged on at the top of their power on level ground and on rising hill.

"While descending a hill the two outside horses suddenly fall to the rear of the carriage, veering out enough of the tug ropes to clear the hind wheels, when all of the power of these two horses is exerted in holding back to keep the carriage from running over the one at the pole end, which, it is clear from what has been said, cannot hold back or do more than keep out of the way of the pursuing vehicle.

"On this occasion our postilions were taken from the military escort so that the novelty of the equipage was not a little heightened by the gay dress, the painted lance with its tricolored flag fluttering in the wind and the carbine dangling on the thigh of the rider, or striking on the flank of the steed as he danced over the plain. The rate of traveling on level ground was ten or twelve miles per hour, so that a change of horses was frequently necessary, but this was effected without a moment's loss of time. The order given, a lancer from the rear would dart up to the horse he was to relieve, receive the tug rope from the previous occupant, who, wheeling out of the track, would fall in the rear, when all would be right again, the speed of the carriage being not in the least interrupted.

"Now fairly on the road, our party consisted of about forty, all told, and a more grotesque troop has seldom been seen anywhere, and never in the United States. Imagine the society of 'Odd Fellows' mounted upon odd-looking horses oddly caparisoned and no less oddly appointed, and you may form a faint idea of our triumphant entry into the City of the Angels."

The cavalcade brought up in front of Don Abel Stearns' palacio. where the commodore and his staff were entertained. Among the articles of convention presented by the governor to the commodore at the conference iv the Palacio de Don Abel was one demanding that the "United States men of war and merchant vessels at San Pedro shall salute the Mexican flag to be displayed before them by Micheltorena at noon of the next day after signing this treaty." The commodore said that he would do so upon assurance that gun for gun would be returned, that being the only condition upon which United States ships were allowed to salute foreign flags.

To this Micheltorena made reply he had no guns at San Pedro. On the following day Commodore Jones and his staff bade adieu to their entertainers, and, accompanied by their former escort and several American residents, took their departure for San Pedro. Two years later the general and his battalion fijo were shipped back to Mexico from the same port.

"What is now known as the Government Reservation on the bluff overlooking the Outer Harbor dates back to the days when that was used for a landing place. In 1827 the Mexican government made a grant of several thousand acres to the west and northwest of the harbor, known as the Rancho Palos Verdes, and from this grant the following reservation was made:

" '4th. They shall leave free on the beach at San Pedro five hundred varas square, to the four cardinal points, upon which houses may be built by persons who may obtain permission to do so; they shall not be permitted to prevent the use of water and pasture by persons engaged in traffic with oxen or horses to the Port of San Pedro.'

"This tract contains about forty-two acres, reserved for public use, but the San Gabriel Mission was allowed certain rights in a small square of about two acres in the southeasterly corner, and title was afterwards claimed by private interests to this small square. The Southern Pacific Company now claims an interest in this square, but otherwise title to the reservation passed to the federal government when California was ceded by Mexico to the United States, and the reservation is still held by the government."

CHAPTER XLVI. SAN PEDRO AFTER THE CONQUEST OF CALIFORNIA

Three hundred years had passed since that October day when Cabrillo sailed into the Bay of Smokes and Fires. In all these years it had been under the domination of the Spanish people. No change had been wrought in the contour of the great bay. It remained as nature had made it. The harbinger of a new era had come. Henceforth there were to be new methods, new customs and new men in the affairs of California. An American man-of-war cast her anchor in the bay where three years before the Cyane had anchored, but she came on a different mission. Hers was not to apologize, but to demand submission.

The conditions that impelled Commodore Jones to raise the Stars and Stripes over Monterey in 1842 impelled Commodore Sloat, who had succeeded to the command of the Pacific fleet, to raise the United States flag and take possession of Monterey in 1846.

The small Mexican army in the north retreated to Los Angeles to join the force that Governor Pico had recruited in the south. Commodore Sloat resigned and was succeeded by Commodore Stockton. Stockton determined to complete the conquest of the territory by the capture of the capital — Los Angeles.

Stockton, with three hundred marines and sailors of the Congress, his flagship, arrived at San Pedro August 6, 1846. The flag was hoisted and the troops landed to be drilled and prepared for the march to Los Angeles. The city was captured on the 13th without the firing of a shot. Pico and Castro had fled to Mexico and their army had disbanded and the soldiers returned to their homes. On the 17th of August the ship Warren, Captain Hull commanding, arrived at San Pedro with definite news that war had been declared between the United States and Mexico.

It was not until the arrival of the Warren that Stockton and Fremont knew whether they were filibustering or waging legitimate warfare.

Stockton proceeded to organize a government. He fixed the duties on foreign goods at the port of San Pedro at fifteen per cent and tonnage at fifty cents a ton. He commissioned Captain Gillespie military commander of the Southern Department, and on September 2, as he was leaving Los Angeles, he issued an order creating the office of military commander of the territory. On the 5th of September he sailed for Monterey.

Stockton's improvised government was short lived. The Angeleños promptly rebelled and compelled the military commandant and his troops to take up their line of march for San Pedro. The next event at the Bay was the arrival of the man-of-war Savannah with Mervine and his men. Their defeat at Dominguez and their retreat with their dead and wounded to their ship is told at length in another chapter of this volume.

San Pedro had suddenly become the most important port of California. During the Flores regime that continued from October 1st to January 10, 1847, a military force of the California army was kept at Temple's rancho. the Cerritos, and another was stationed at the Palos Verdes to watch the maneuvers of the Americans and report the arrival and departure of vessels.

Stockton with the Congress arrived at San Pedro the 23rd of October. The greater part of the fleet was now in the bay of San Pedro. He learned from Mervine the full account of that officer's engagement with the hitherto despised enemy. He claimed to have "taken possession and once more raised our flag at San Pedro." His stay at that port was short. The insurgents whom he estimated at eight hundred men were collected on the adjacent hills and would not permit a hoof except their own horses to be within fifty miles of San Pedro. Stockton sailed for San Diego, November 1st, in the Congress. The Savannah, Mervine's ship, was sent to Monterey to cooperate with Fremont in preparation for his march with his battalion down the coast. The Cyane, the old pioneer sloop-of-war that had been doing duty on the coast for years, joined Stockton at San Diego, and the naval array that had made San Pedro bay the center of war's alarms became once more placid and peaceful.

Some imaginative writers give Carrillo's ruse of the riderless horses that appeared and disappeared through gaps in the Palos Verdes hills as the cause of Stockton's departure. While Stockton was bombastic and given to braggadocio, he was no coward. The real reason for his transferring the theater of his military operations from San Pedro bay to that of San Diego was the bad reputation of the former for southeasters. Winter was coming on and a storm in the open roadstead might bring disaster to his fleet. He evidently gave Carrillo's riderless cavalry a few shots from his ships. The Historical Society of Southern California possesses one of the many cannon balls picked up in the hills of San Pedro.

In the final conquest of Los Angeles, San Pedro did not figure. On January 19th, Stockton and his marines embarked at San Pedro en a man-of-war for San Diego. The war was over and Fremont had been made military governor of California by Stockton. His career as governor was short and stormy. It lasted but fifty days. General Kearny did not recognize him as governor, and after he assumed the governorship he cancelled some of Fremont's appointments and revoked some of his orders. The collection of revenue at the ports was a fruitful source of trouble to the authorities. San Pedro next to Monterey was at that time the most important port on the California coast.

When Commodore Stockton, after the conquest of Los Angeles, fixed the tariff on foreign goods at San Pedro at fifteen per cent, he appointed, August 25, 1846, Don David Alexander collector of the port. The Flores' revolution following soon after, it is not probable that Don David collected much revenue. With the return of peace and a stable government the collection of revenue became an important matter; as there were no taxes levied, the cost of local government had to be paid from the duties on goods imported.

General Kearny, writing from Monterey under date of April 26, 1847, to Don David, says:

"I learn you have been appointed collector of the port and harbor master at San Pedro, which appointments are hereby confirmed to you. You will inform me what salary has been allowed you, and what amount of funds you may have received and how much on hand. You will please settle your accounts quarterly with Lieutenant Colonel Cooke at the City of the Angeles or with such officer as he may designate.

* * *

"I have received from Colonel Mason, First Dragoons, the instructions to you of March 21, signed J. C. Fremont, governor of California, by William H. Russell, secretary of state, ordering and permitting you to receive from S. Hultman 'government payment' (that is, as I understand, due bills of the paymaster and quartermaster of the late battalion of California Volunteers) in payment of his custom house duties; and I learn that you have received $1,700 of that paper bought up by Mr. H. at twenty-five or thirty per cent discount. As you have, by the act of others, been led into this mistake, what you have received from Mr. H. must be passed to your credit.

"Very respectfully,

"S. W. KEARNY,

"Brigadier General and Governor of California."

In another communication written at Los Angeles May 12, 1847, General Kearny informs Don David that "your salary for performing the duty of collector of the port and harbormaster at San Pedro will be $1,000 per year commencing from the 25th of August, 1846, the date of your appointment, the same to be paid half yearly. You report to me that you have on hand $1,731 government paper and $766 in specie. You will be allowed to retain your half year's salary ($500) from the specie; the balance with 'government paper' you will turn over to Lieutenant Davidson, First Dragoons, acting quartermaster at this place" (Los Angeles). In a subsequent communication Don David evidently asked tor an allowance for office rent. He was curtly told that was included in his salary.

The "tariff" was one of the great issues in the newly acquired territory of California, as it is and has been in the nation since the beginning of its existence. It was not tariff as a political issue that worried the Californians, but ways and methods to avoid paying duties on imports. Smuggling had been one of the chief industries of California under the Spanish and Mexican rule and it did not cease with a change of rulers. Col. R. B. Mason, the military governor, under date of November 11, 1847, writing to Adjutant-General Jones at Washington, D. C, says:

"A great deal of smuggling has been done in California and will doubtless continue, as the numerous caves, bays, etc., afford every facility for landing goods and merchandise. One or two good revenue cutters would, however, stop this almost effectually. The Commodore (Shubrick) and myself have made known that any one who would give information of goods being smuggled should have one-half of the goods seized upon such information.

"Some of the ports or points on this coast where it is customary to land goods have no military posts near them. San Pedro, for instance, is twenty-five miles from the nearest garrison."

Two companies of Colonel Stevenson's New York Volunteers were at this time stationed at Los Angeles. Some of these soldiers were of a speculative turn and not averse to outwitting the revenue officials.

Twenty of them at one time clubbed together and bought from the ship Charles at San Pedro a bill of goods consisting of two hundred and forty caps at fifty cents each, twenty-four pairs of boots at $4 per pair, sixty pairs of brogans at $2.25 per pair, one hundred and sixty shirts at $1 each, amounting to over $500. Tariff regulations allowed officers and soldiers to buy any article free of duty for their own actual individual use and consumption. Before they could get them away from the port Colonel Mason had the goods seized for duty.

In his instructions to the collector of the port he said, "Two hundred forty caps divided among twenty men would give twelve to each man. Each man did not require twelve caps for his own individual use." So after allowing two caps, six shirts, a pair of boots and two pairs of brogans to each man free of duty the soldier boys paid the tariff on the balance and their nice little speculation was spoiled.

The officers and soldiers after the war ended and while still garrisoning the post were a constant worry to Governor Mason, who was a martinet in regulations and a ' strictly honest man. A lieutenant at Santa Barbara boarded a barque and, reporting to its captain that he was a custom house officer, instructed him to sell to soldiers any amount of goods they could pay for free of duty.

Governor Mason, commenting on the account sales made to Captain Lippett's company stationed at Santa Barbara, says:

"Now it is self evident that a private soldier does not want for his own actual individual use and consumption hundreds of yards of merchandise, barrels of rum and thousands of cigars. No clubbing together to make purchases should be tolerated; each man must buy on his own account for his own use, not to be transferred to another by sale." One officer made oath that $400 of his purchase was comestibles. Governor Mason, commenting on this purchase, said: "Even if they were 'comestibles.' the amount is unreasonable and, therefore, liable to duties."

The proclamation that a treaty of peace had been declared between the United States and Mexico and that Upper California had been ceded to the United States was published by Governor Mason August 7, 1848. Orders were issued for the discharge of the New York Volunteers and all others whose periods of service ended with the war, and also that the collection of revenue as military contributions should forthwith cease.

For two years all collections at the different ports had been turned over to the quartermasters of the military posts. Lieut. J. B. Davidson, the engineer, who planned Fort Moore, was the receiver for the port of San Pedro. The discharge of the officers and soldiers left Governor Mason in a sad dilemma. He had no officers or soldiers to enforce the collection of revenue if the merchants or people should refuse or try to evade the payment of duties. He had to appoint civilian collectors and trust to their honesty and intelligence to discharge their duty. Don David W. Alexander was continued collector of San Pedro; he had proved an efficient officer.

March 3, 1849, Congress passed an act to extend the revenue laws of the United States over the territory and waters of Upper California, and create a collection district therein. San Francisco was made a port of entry, and San Diego and Monterey were made ports of delivery and another port of delivery was to be established at the junction of the Gila and Colorado rivers. San Pedro was left out, although the shipping from it exceeded any other port in the territory except San Francisco. A collector for the district was to be stationed at San Francisco on a salary of $1,500 per annum and the fees allowed by law. A deputy was allowed at each of the other ports at the magnificent salary of $1,000 per year.

James Collier of Ohio was appointed collector of customs at San Francisco. Collier was empowered to nominate his deputies. Alexander Irwin of Pennsylvania was chosen for Monterey, William Ferrell of South Carolina for San Diego and

Alexander Bradford for the junction of the Gila and Colorado. Collier started for California from Fort Leavenworth with a company of dragoons and arrived at San Francisco November 12, 1849. The party he came with had to fight Indians and four were drowned crossing the Colorado. One of the number was Captain Thorn of the dragoons. The party reached San Diego first and Collier went up to San Francisco by boat.

Writing to the United States treasurer the day after his arrival, he says:

"On my voyage to this port from San Diego I had an opportunity of visiting some of the points on the coast, which, in a commercial point of view, are of no little importance and to which your attention is solicited. One of them is San Pedro; I am fully of the opinion that more goods are landed at San Pedro than at any other point excepting only San Francisco. A large amount of smuggling is carried on at this point. It is distant from Los Angeles some twenty-five miles, and from the latter the Mexicans obtain all their goods for trade in the interior of Mexico.

"These goods are generally of a high price and rich fabric. I met several large parties of these traders on my journey to the Pacific, and in every instance I was advised by them that they purchased their goods at Los Angeles. I saw while at San Pedro (which contains but three buildings), in a warehouse, a large amount of goods from China. I have been unable to ascertain where they were entered. The collector resides at Los Angeles, and these goods, together with most if not all that have been landed, have escaped the payment of duties. I recommend that it should be made a port of delivery, and that a deputy should be stationed there."

Of the port on the Colorado, he writes: "The act of Congress making California a collection district requires the secretary of the treasury to establish a port of delivery as near as may be to the junction of the rivers Gila and Colorado at the head of the Gulf of California. The establishment of such an office I do not consider at all practicable. The Colorado will never, in my opinion, become navigable to this point. It is far off from civilization, on the borders of the great desert. The line between the United States and Mexico will not be more than two or three miles from the junction of the rivers. The valley of the Gila is utterly worthless and I would not take a deed to the whole country tomorrow. I presume that no white man could be found willing to become deputy collector where a flag would never flutter.

"I am perfectly astounded at the amount of business in this office — San Francisco. The tonnage on the 10th instant in port was 120,317 tons, of which 87,494 were American and 32,823 foreign."

If he was astounded at the amount of business, he was still more astounded at the cost of living. "Boarding without room averages $5 per day," he writes. "A small room, barely sufficient to contain a single bed, rents readily at $150 per month. Wood is $40 per cord, shingles $60 per thousand, lumber $300 and carpenters' wages from $12 to $17 per day." His little salary of $1,500 a year vanished rapidly.

His greatest worry was to secure help. "Men resort to the custom house for temporary employment and for that only. They will continue only just so long as is necessary to seek something more profitable. An instance has occurred this morning to illustrate this: I have a clerk acting as cashier, to whom I was compelled to pay (what you might regard as a high salary) $3,000 per annum. He was offered from a banking house $5,000, with the promise of a future interest, and has consequently given notice that he should leave the office."

It seemed impossible for the authorities at Washington to comprehend the condition existing in California. For half a century the compensation for revenue officials had remained unchanged. Why such extravagance in this out-of-the-world territory, California? The Secretary of the Treasury, W. M. Meredith, had given Colonel Collier these instructions on his departure for San Francisco: "Upon entering on the discharge of your duties at San Francisco should it become necessary to employ a subordinate officer or officers of the customs you may in pursuance of the second section of the compensation act of the 2nd of March, 1799, as modified by the Act of the 26th of April, 1816, employ such temporary or occasional inspectors as may be found indispensably necessary for the protection and security of the revenue to be paid when actually employed a sum not exceeding $3 per day each. In no case can the compensation for inspectors of the customs exceed $3 per day." Three dollars a day which was considered a snap in 1799 would scarce pay for a meal of victuals in the flush days of '49. Nor was it the collector alone who was in hard lines; the officers of the revenue cutters were unable to live on their meager salaries. The wages of a steward were $150 a month and those of a common seaman $100. As a result, the sailors who were receiving government pay deserted. Captain Fraser of the cutter reported he was left with three officers and no sailors and the officers were compelled to do their own washing and were in danger of starving on their meager wages.

Colonel Collier continued as the collector of the district of California until the change of administration in 1854. He was charged with being a defaulter to the amount of $700,000. Not only was he fully exonerated, but he obtained judgment against the United States for $37,000.

The charges grew out of the unprecedented conditions existing then in California. The government officials bound by tariff regulations half a century old could not understand the exigencies arising in California out of the discovery of gold and the rapid inflations of values. When it came to paying $2,400 a month for the rent of four small rooms for the collector's living apartments (whose salary was only $1,500 a year) it looked to these officials like a case of embezzlement or at least of unwarranted extravagance. Collier writing to the secretary of the treasury and quoting the exorbitant price of building, says: "These facts may startle you, but such is the true state of things. I hope, therefore, that in ordering these indispensable repairs without waiting for instructions I shall not be censured."

Nor were the chaotic conditions existing from high prices all the worry the collector had to face in establishing a collection district in the territory. The act extending the revenue laws of the United States over the territory and waters of Upper California provided that violations of these laws were to be prosecuted in the District Court of Louisiana or the Supreme Court of Oregon. A litigant in a suit had the choice of a two thousand mile trip "the plains across" to Louisiana or a thousand mile voyage up the coast to the capital of Oregon.

The change of rulers did not improve conditions at San Pedro. Under Mexican rule every ship's cargo had to be entered at Monterey, under American rule it had to be listed at San Francisco and then any article for San Pedro reshipped to that port, which greatly increased the cost.

The following memorial to Congress asking that San Pedro be made a port of entry and that a custom house be established there is the earliest effort made by the people of Los Angeles to secure improvement by the United States government for that port. A copy of this memorial was filed with the county clerk of Los Angeles county May 30, 1850 (the county had been organized in April of that year). The original draft of the memorial numerously signed was sent to Colonel Thomas H. Benton, United States senator from Missouri, to be presented to Congress. California had not been admitted to the Union and had no representatives in Congress. Senator Benton was regarded as one of the staunchest friends of the territory in Congress.

The memorial forcibly sets forth the commercial conditions existing in Southern California at that time and consequently is of great historical value:

TO THE HONORABLE MEMBERS OF THE UNITED STATES SENATE AND HOUSE OF REPRESENTATIVES IN CONGRESS ASSEMBLED.

The memorial of the undersigned inhabitants of the County of Los Angeles, State of California, respectfully represent:

"That for want of a Port of Entry within the district of country in which they reside its business and trade labor under the most serious disadvantages, its growth and settlement are materially retarded and great dissatisfaction prevails among the people.

"So numerous and aggravated are the evils which your memorialists suffer for want of a Port of Entry and a Custom House that they can but feel some little delicacy in bringing them to the notice of your Honorable body, for it is fully believed that in no section of the United States has there ever existed obstructions so serious in character to the prosperity of trade and commerce and which have been so long and so patiently endured by the same number of people as that to which your memorialists are and have been subjected.

"The conditions of the country in which your memorialists reside are peculiar and hence results a marked singularity in the state of its trade. Its proximity to the mining regions has caused it to be substantially denuded of its laboring population and hence, although strikingly agricultural in its natural features, it has for the last two years been dependent on a foreign supply for not only the greater proportion of its breadstuffs, but for even the coarser articles, such as peas, beans, oats, barley, etc. These are brought usually from some of the South American ports, taken to San Francisco and thence reshipped to San Pedro. It thus appears that not only are the people of this region compelled to obtain the more costly fabrics of manufactures at another port, but even articles of the most common consumption, at what additional cost the following facts will testify.

"The freight alone from San Francisco to San Pedro for the last two years has never been less than twice the amount of what is charged for conveying the same articles from New York to San Francisco. The expense upon a cargo of flour for sending it from the warehouse in San Francisco to San Pedro has been as high as $10.25 per barrel and has never been less than $5.75. One of your memorialists has paid for the expense of a single cargo of goods from San Francisco to San Pedro $14,000. In fine, the average additional cost upon goods purchased at San Francisco is not less than thirty per cent upon their being landed at San Pedro.

"Not alone would this entire amount be saved to your memorialists by the establishment of a Custom House at San Pedro, but many articles of trade which cannot now be procured at all at San Francisco would be brought to the former port. The people of this region are to a large extent of the Spanish race and whole cargoes of goods could be imported from Mexican ports and sold at a large advance that are never found at all in the markets of San Francisco in consequence of the population there being so essentially American in its character. "Were there a Custom House at San Pedro, cargoes of coffee and rice would be brought there from Central America; panocha (a coarse kind of sugar) from Mexico, flour from Chili and sugar from Peru, to say nothing of the enormous cost of reshipping these articles from San Francisco, which has already been alluded to, to the former place. In freight alone there would be a material reduction, for not only is the voyage some six hundred miles less, but from there not being the same inducements and facilities for desertions by his crew as at the north, a master could afford to run his vessel to San Pedro from a southern port at a much less rate than he could to San Francisco. With a bare allusion to the enormous expense of unloading and storage at San Francisco and which, of course, is included in the first cost to the purchaser at Los Angeles, and to the great lapse of time, delay and expense to the merchant of the latter place in going north to make his purchases, we pass to consider the amount of trade actual and prospective in this country: The amount of actual prove correct sales of goods landed at San Pedro for the last two years has been but little short of one million of dollars per annum. This amount was formerly much more, as it is well known that at the time of the old Missions there was more business done at the port of San Pedro than at any other port on the Pacific north of Acapulco.

"In touching upon the probable increase of trade in this section, we cannot withhold alluding to the fact that the district of country in which your memorialists reside is infinitely superior to that of any other portion of California to sustain a dense population. It contains without a doubt a larger amount of arable and irrigable land in a single body than any other portion of the state. Its soil is of the best character and is usually well watered. The climate, it is fully believed, will compare favorably for salubrity and evenness of temperature with those of the finest regions of the south of Europe. In no other part of the world will the earth yield the same variety of vegetable production as in this. Here may be found growing side by side with luxurious fields of the cereals of the north, the grape, the fig, the orange, the pomegranate, the olive, etc.. of a tropical clime. Large forests of fine timber abound in many sections. The mineral deposits, too, are numerous and valuable; salt. limestone, mineral tar. tequesquite (a natural salaratus). are found in great abundance and of the best quality. All of these natural advantages betoken a no distant day when the section of the country in which your memorialists reside will be inhabited by a populous and intelligent American community.

"Nor is it alone from the operation of these causes that a rapid increase of population is anticipated. It is well known that the mining districts of California are constantly becoming enlarged by new discoveries, already they are worked to great effect at Kings river, distant from Los Angeles but about two hundred miles; important discoveries of gold have also been made in nearer localities. On the road leading to the Great Salt Lake, gold has been found in many places, and it is

378

believed by numbers that ultimately as prolific a mining region will there be found as any within the Sacramento valley. Should these anticipations prove correct, it can be easily seen to what disadvantage the mining districts here would labor under from the increased price of goods owing to their being no Custom House at San Pedro.

"Your memorialists would now call attention of your honorable body to the fact that the port of San Pedro is the nearest commercial outlet to the large and highly flourishing community of Deseret. This is a fact but lately known even to those people themselves, party under command of Gen. C. C. Rich, one of the twelve apostles of the sect of Mormon-^ came through from the Salt Lake valley this last winter for the purpose of surveying and measuring the route leading from thence to this section; and it is from their report we learn that their foreign supplies of goods must be brought from this locality, as it is not only much nearer than to San Francisco and the road is better, but it can be traveled at all seasons of the year, while the road across the Sierra Nevadas, as is well known, cannot, as it is inaccessible at least six months out of the twelve. So well convinced are the Mormons of this fact that they have recently purchased one of the largest ranchos in this country with a view of laying out a settlement and founding a town thereon. This property they propose taking possession of in August next and they are confident in the opinion that in a few years' time they will have as large a settlement in this country as they have at the Salt Lake valley.

"Your memorialists will allude to but a single fact further in this connection; the county of Los Angeles is the great thoroughfare for two of the most important routes of travel from the Eastern States and from Mexico. Over these routes flows a throng of immigrants so numerous as almost to defy belief. Most of these would purchase more or less of their supplies from the merchants of Los Angeles did not its trade labor under so many disadvantages.

"At least ten thousand Sonoranians pass through here on their way to the mines each spring, generally returning to Mexico in the autumn. Most of these people live remote from any commercial town in their own county and would purchase largely of American manufactured goods on their return home, could goods be had here on reasonable terms.

"Your memorialists will allude to but a single further consideration upon this subject, namely, that the port of San Pedro is but about one thousand miles north of Mazatlan; at that port there are received every year large cargoes of foreign goods sent directly from Europe and selected with an especial eye to the wants of a Spanish population. Were there a Custom House at San Pedro a portion of these goods before being unloaded would be brought on to this port and sold to your memorialists not only at less than they can be obtained for in San Francisco but even in New York."

The Sonoranians, or Sonoranes, as they were sometimes called, referred to in the memorial, constituted what was known as the Sonoran migration. From the discovery of gold and for half a dozen years later, these people migrated like the wild geese, coming north in the spring and returning south in the fall. They bought liberally on their return of various commodities, but on their northern flight about their only purchases were frijoles (beans).

San Pedro was made a port of delivery in 1853. The commerce of the port increased greatly after the discovery of gold. The first steamer that visited San Pedro was the Gold Hunter, in 1849, a side-wheel vessel which ran between San Francisco and Mazatlan, touching at way ports. The next was the Ohio. These were followed by the Sea Bird, the Southerner and the Goliath. In 1853 the Sea Bird and the Southerner were running regularly three trips per month between San Francisco and San Diego, stopping at Monterey, Santa Barbara and San Pedro for passengers and freight. The Goliath was still on the line.

From 1814 to 1849, Temple and Alexander did the freighting between San Pedro and Los Angeles. Goods were carried in carts similar to the old Mexican carretas. The wheels instead of being solid were spoked and tired. Each cart was drawn by two yoke of oxen yoked by the horns, Mexican style. Freight was $1 per hundred. In 1851, D. W. Alexander purchased at Sacramento ten heavy freight wagons that had been sent in from Salt Lake by Ben Holliday, and in 1853 he purchased a whole train of fourteen wagons and one hundred and sixty-eight mules that had come through from Chihuahua, paying for the outfit $23,000. So the carretas went to join the caballadas in the commerce of San Pedro. The steamer trip to San Francisco in the early '50s was not the pleasure jaunt of the present day. First cabin fare was $55. The menu was limited in variety and not appetizing to seasick voyagers. It consisted of salt beef, hard bread, potatoes and coffee without milk or cream. The trip usually occupied about four days, depending on the amount of freight to be taken on or delivered at the way ports.

In 1852, Alexander and Banning established an "accommodation line" of stages between San Pedro and Los Angeles, carrying United States mail, the Adams and the Wells Fargo & Co. express. These stages, so their advertisement reads: "Will leave San Pedro for Los Angeles on the arrival of each steamer and at other times when there are passengers." The fare between San Pedro and Los Angeles was $10.

In 1854 the regular dispatch line of San Pedro packets was established. This line consisted of the clipper schooner Laura Bevan and the Sea Serpent. The only way port they touched at was Santa Barbara. They carried freight and passengers.

In 1854, Don Abel Stearns and Alfred Robinson built for trade between Boston and San Pedro the clipper ship Arcadia, named for Donna Arcadia, Stearns' wife. It was a vessel of eight hundred and fifty tons measurement. The Southern Californian of April 25, 1855, chronicles its arrival at San Pedro with a full cargo of merchandise only one hundred and twelve days from Boston. The Arcadia made regular trips between San Pedro and Boston. By direct shipment from the eastern cities, Johnson & Allanson, to whom most of the cargo of the Arcadia was consigned, advertised to sell merchandise cheaper than it could be sold in San Francisco.

In 1851 grapes in crates and boxes brought from twenty to twenty-five cents per pound in San Francisco and in the mines from seventy-five cents to $1 per pound. Grapes were too valuable to make wine of and wine making virtually ceased for a time. In 1854, Alexander & Banning advertised to ship from Los Angeles to steamer grapes at fifty cents per hundred pounds. The grape shipments were the largest of any commodity shipped from San Pedro. From July 1 to October 31, 1855, Alexander & Banning forwarded to San Francisco over a million pounds, valued at $156,000. The value of all other products shipped during the same time was less than $50,000. In 1857 the shipment of grapes from San Pedro amounted to 1,427,710 pounds, valued in the schedule of exports at $128,414.

Among the exports of 1857 oranges appear for the first time. The shipment amounted to 55,372 pounds, priced at $11,274. In 1859 grape shipments had decreased one-half and wine had increased from 50,000 gallons in 1855 to 280,000 in 1859. Dana, who visited Los Angeles in 1859, estimated its wine production at half a million gallons.

All of the pioneer steamships of the Southern Coast that called regularly at San Pedro in the early '50s had by 1857 found or formed new lines of trade or had gone to Davy Jones' locker. The Goliath was put on the Sacramento as a river boat. The Southerner was wrecked on the coast of Oregon. The Sea Bird became very unreliable in her flights up and down the coast and was finally withdrawn from the Southern Coast trade. The Senator was put on the lower coast line in 1856 and became a great favorite with the people. The Senator shortly after she was put on the southern route broke all previous records. She made the voyage from San Francisco to San Pedro — stopping at Santa Barbara — in thirty-six hours. The time schedule of the other vessels was from forty-eight to sixty hours. On this arrival of the Senator, Timm's stage broke all previous records, making the trip from San Pedro to Los Angeles in one hour and fifty-five minutes. The Senator and her urbane captain, T. W. Seeley, became very popular. An opposition steamer was put on the route and for a time the fare was reduced, but the opposition could not compete with the Senator and was withdrawn. The fare then between San Pedro and San Francisco was fixed at $25, which was a great reduction from what it had been a few years before ($55) and time four days.

In 1855 the imports at San Pedro were 2,465 tons, the exports were 3,849 tons. In 1856 the imports were 3,422 tons, the exports 3,959. This was the last year in the history of the port that exports exceeded the imports. In 1875 the imports were 80,548 tons, exports 14,841 tons.

CHAPTER XLVII.
EVOLUTION OF THE INNER HARBOR

For a decade after California had become legally a part of the United States there had been no change in the Bay of San Pedro. Vessels still anchored out beyond Deadman's Island, and communication between ship and shore was made by boat. Government had made no improvements. It had ordered made in 1852 what Professor Bache, Superintendent of the Coast Survey, called a "hydrographic reconnoissance of the Bay."

Professor Bache, of the Coast Survey, in a report made in 1855 says, "The Bay of San Pedro is the most important port between San Francisco and San Diego. To make this harbor easy of access to shipmasters, a survey is absolutely necessary, and instead of wasting money in surveying the islands of the coast the department should at once commence operations at the Bay of San Pedro. Why, after what is known of its importance, it should be treated with neglect is a matter which seems difficult of comprehension." We find by a report of Lieutenant Davidson made in 1855 that the coast trade of San Pedro ranked next to San Francisco at that early date. He says: "The coasting trade of San Pedro is now greater than the aggregate of all the other ports south of San Francisco. An appropriation had been made by Congress for the erection of a lighthouse, but it had been lying in the treasury unused because the government had not procured a title to land where it was to be located." The land was in a Spanish grant and the grant had not been confirmed by the claims commissioners.

In March, 1858, the citizens of Los Angeles held a public meeting and sent a petition to the Superintendent of the Coast Survey, asking that a survey of the bay be made and a lighthouse erected. The reply to the petitioners was that the government was still surveying the islands, but that surveyors were working down the coast and would eventually reach the Bay of San Pedro.

But little is known of the early history of San Pedro town or of the struggles of the pioneers of the early '50s to develop the commerce of the port. I copy the following description of San Pedro from the Los Angeles Star of May 16, 1857. It is the best description extant of the port of San Pedro when all the shipping interests were confined to the outer harbor and what is now the inner harbor was known as San Pedro slough:

"San Pedro is not a place of much pretensions in the way of houses; but the few there are occupied in the most profitable manner. At the landing of Banning & Wilson there is an extensive blacksmith shop, also a carriage manufactory, a saddlery and harness making establishment where the wagons and harness required in their extensive transportation business are manufactured and repaired. There are also extensive warehouses, stables and corrals, also a grocery, provisions and liquor store and a hotel.

"The Custom House is at this landing, the duties of which for a long time have been discharged by Deputy Collector J. F. Stevens (the collector of the district was stationed at San Diego). For the accommodation of the public a wharf has been erected on the beach, at which boats receive and land passengers and freight. A short distance from this point is Timm's Landing. A pier of considerable extent has been erected there for the shipment of merchandise; ample storage is provided in an immense warehouse; barges and boats of all kinds for conveyance of goods and passengers to and from the steamers and sailing crafts are also on hand."

In the succeeding pages I give the story of the creation of the inner harbor and the founding of new San Pedro. More than a quarter of a century before the first attempt was made to utilize the inner harbor Alfred Robinson, in describing it, outlined a plan for its development. He says:

"Due north from the place of anchorage is a narrow creek communicating with a shallow basin, operated upon by the tides, where at this time thousands of hair seal might be seen at low water, basking on the sand banks.

"The channel here when at full flood has ten feet of water over the bar; so that in moderate weather, vessels drawing nine feet can easily pass over and anchor sufficiently near the shore to discharge their cargoes without the aid of launches. With very little expense it might be made a place of anchorage for large ships, either by digging out and deepening the present channel, or by closing up another outlet to the north of the island, which would bring the whole strength of the current through one passage, and thus wash away its sandy bottom."

In 1858 the shipping interests at the bay were divided between Banning and Timm's. Banning was located at the old landing of hide droghing days. The old warehouse built by the Mission padres in the early '20s had been enlarged and a lodging house and store building erected. Timm had a warehouse at a point on the outer bay. This location for many years was known as "Timm's Point." (Don David W. Alexander, for many years Banning's partner, had been elected sheriff in 1855, and they had dissolved partnership.) Each kept stages for the transfer of passengers from the bay to Los Angeles and teams for forwarding merchandise. Passengers were transferred from a short wharf at old San Pedro to the steamer on Banning's famous steam yacht Medora.

Capt. Phineas Banning, to put a greater distance between himself and his rivals, Timm and Tomlinson, founded a new town on the inner bay, or San Pedro slough as it was then called. The ceremonies of the founding took place September 25, 1858. This town at first was known as New San Pedro, but eventually came to be called Wilmington after Banning's birthplace, Wilmington, Del. The initial ceremonies consisted in the landing of passengers and freight at the short wharf that had been built at the head of the slough. The saving of nearly five miles in distance and the avoidance of the hill to Old San Pedro gave Banning a decided advantage over his rivals. It was not his intention to abandon Old San Pedro, but fate or old Neptune decreed otherwise.

The festivities of the founding of the new town were scarcely over (the success of the undertaking had been pledged in bumpers of wine by a festive assemblage of the elite of the land), when old Neptune, as if in revenge for the attempt to escape from his domain, vented his wrath on the old landing. The Los Angeles Star of October 2, 1858, the next issue after the one that chronicled the founding of the new town, thus notes the devastation wrought by a fierce southeaster:

"The rains of the beginning of this week were accompanied with heavy winds here, but at San Pedro a regular southeaster came up, doing considerable damage to the small craft anchored in the bay. We are sorry to say that Mr. Banning's famous yacht Medora suffered from the envious winds and waves, whose swiftest course she has frequently outrun. Laying quietly at anchor, they rose in their might against her, drove her from her moorings on to the beach, where they prevailed against her and broke her up, scattering her fragments on the shore. A large barge was also broken up; another, having dragged its anchor a considerable distance, was brought to by the anchor fastening against a rock.

"The wharf at San Pedro was very much injured, a large part of the flooring having been carried away by the violence of the sea. A large quantity of lumber stored on the beach was floated off by the high tide and the violence of the storm."

After this disaster Banning directed all his energies to building up New San Pedro. The old shipping point that for nearly a century had been the commercial entrepot of Los Angeles and the embarcadero of mission days was abandoned and all of Banning's business transferred to the new port.

A local notice in the Los Angeles Star of February 5, 1859, four months after the founding of the town, says: "The place is rapidly filling up with buildings, having now all the essentials enabling it to be considered and styled a city — a grocery, hotel, blacksmith shop, etc. It will soon have a bowling alley and billiard saloon. It has also stores, offices, warehouses, workshops, corrals, all things necessary for carrying on the extensive business of Captain Banning. The county road is progressing favorably. It is much heavier work than we anticipated. The governor of the city is pushing forward the completion of the wharf for the landing of passengers, and altogether the city of Newport — that is its name up country — is a bristling, thriving, pretentious, ambitious city, which if helped along kindly will become quite a place one of these days."

A correspondent of the Star under date of February 12, 1859, asks: "Have you ever been down to New San Pedro, or Banningville, which the new town should be called, for if it ever comes to anything more than a little seaside village to Mr. Banning will the honor be due. It is by his enterprise that this new landing has been started and by his enterprise and stubborn energy that houses already sprinkle the plain."

The petition of the citizens of Los Angeles sent to the head of the Coast Survey in March, 1858, asking for a survey of the harbor and setting forth the great importance of San Pedro as a shipping point, finally brought results. The United States surveying schooner Active arrived at San Pedro June 4, 1859, and began a survey of the harbor. Captain Allen, in charge of the schooner, found from soundings on the bar sufficient depth of water at high tide for his vessel to enter the inner harbor, or lagoon, as Lieutenant Davidson called it.

The Star of September 24, 1859, says: "We understand that the survey of the harbor of San Pedro has been completed; the topography was performed by W. M. Johnson and Charles Bache; the triangulation by Capt. W. E. Greenwell, the hydrography by Captain Allen of the steamer Active. The chart is complete and has been executed with that neatness and precision requisite in work of this kind and which these gentlemen are so well qualified to perform.

"The survey extends a mile back from the shore line, reaching up to the Laguna and surrounding lands, exhibiting the heights, curves and varieties of the surface of the banks and hills with the courses of the intersecant ravines. Every curve and indentation of the coast line is accurately traced and every knoll, tree, shrub and description of vegetation covering the land within the scope of the survey marked and correctly indicated; also the houses, fences, and. in fact, everything just as it appears.

"There are thirty houses, including those in New San Pedro, exhibited on the sheet. The sheet embraces the portion of the coast extending from a point about a mile west of Point Fermin to about a mile to the eastward of the mouth of the San Gabriel river; showing an outside or extended shore line of eight miles, including Deadman's Island, touching the point of and running along outside Rattlesnake Island, exhibiting within its compass twenty miles of road and an area of fourteen square miles.

"We find the following distances shown on the sheet which may be interesting to the public. From Banning's old landing to the wharf at New San Pedro by the channel is four miles; by the road, five and one-fourth miles; from Old San Pedro to Diego Sepulveda's, by the road, two and three-fourths miles; from New Town by way of the slough to the mouth of the San Gabriel river, about two and a quarter miles." If this old chart of fifty-six years ago is still in existence a copy of it should be secured to show the numerous changes that man has wrought in the configuration of the harbor and coast line of San Pedro bay.

Southeasters, that were the dread of seamen in Dana's day, still continued to visit San Pedro. There was a fierce one December 1, 1859, but old Boreas found nothing to destroy. There were no wharves on the bay, those had been demolished in the great storm of 1858. Banning had all his boats and scows and the little Comet that had taken the place of the wrecked Medora of the year before all safely anchored up at the head of the lagoon or inner harbor and he could view 'the storm with indifference.

The freight rates from anchorage to Los Angeles in 1860 by Banning's Transfer Company would be considered excessive now. It cost $15 to freight a thousand feet of lumber to the city and fifty cents per hundred pounds to carry merchandise.

War usually retards all development, but the Civil war of 1861 to 1865 had the opposite effect on New San Pedro. The arena of hostilities was two thousand miles distant from the town. In 1861, Camp Drum was established at New San Pedro as a rendezvous for California soldiers enlisted for the Civil war.

The first camp established in Southern California was Camp Latham on La Ballona rancho, near the present site of Redondo. Several hundred soldiers were stationed there. Captain Banning, recognizing the value of a military camp in a business way, deeded the United States government twenty acres of land within the limits of New San Pedro. In September, 1861, Camp Drum was established on this land. The government built a hospital, officers' quarters, barracks, warehouses and a wharf. To bring water to the camp and town it built a ditch from a point on the river seven miles above to the barracks. Two hundred soldiers were employed on the work. An immense flume three or four miles long was constructed.

In October, 1862, the soldiers from Camp Latham were moved to Camp Drum and that post abandoned. The soldiers at Camp Latham at the September election took possession of the polls and cast over two hundred votes for the Union candidates for the legislature, defeating the Confederate sympathizers on the Democratic ticket. A great outcry was raised by the defeated candidates over the outrage and the vote of the precinct was thrown out.

Military expeditions for Utah, Arizona and New Mexico were fitted out at the camp, and at times from two to three thousand soldiers were stationed here. All supplies were hauled from New San Pedro across the desert to the various posts where soldiers were stationed.

In January, 1862, Carleton's column of two thousand troops was fitting out to march to Arizona and New Mexico. Their train was to consist of two hundred wagons and twelve hundred mules. The steamer Wright was bringing down from the north five hundred mules for the column's train. The captain, to save lighterage charges on the mules (the charges were quite heavy), undertook to run into the shore and land his mules. The vessel struck a sunken reef about half a mile from shore and he had to throw his cargo of mules overboard. One hundred and twenty of them either went to Davy Jones' locker or into the corrals of the paisanos, at least they were not present or accounted for at the round-up. Carleton's column had to delay its march until more mules could be brought down from up country. The establishment of Camp Drum greatly increased the growth and accelerated business at New San Pedro. A daily stage ran between it and Los Angeles. Pleasure parties frequently came down to visit the soldier boys. Travel by steamer was greatly increased. At one time in January, 1862, there were three steamers unloading troops and supplies in San Pedro bay.

In 1864 a post office was established at New San Pedro. The town and post office assumed the name of Wilmington, but it was a decade later before the port or landing was officially named Wilmington. The steamship companies in San Francisco sold tickets to anchorage in the harbor or bay of San Pedro. They did not agree to land passengers. The passenger was at liberty to pay $1.50 for a trip up the slough to Wilmington on one of Banning's tugs or swim ashore to Old San Pedro. The tourist on his first trip usually bestowed a liberal quantity of abuse on the steamship company for this arrangement, but he had to submit all the same.

The most tragic event in the history of the inner harbor was the explosion of the boilers of the passenger boat Milton Willis, better known as the Ada Hancock, which occurred on the 27th of April, 1863. She was heavily loaded with passengers going to the steamship Senator. Only seven escaped entirely unhurt, and among them, strange to say, was the engineer. Among the lost perhaps no one was more sincerely mourned than the commander of the Senator, Capt. T. W. Seeley.

After the end of the Civil war Camp Drum, or Drum Barracks as it was officially named in 1863, was abandoned. The buildings untenanted were going to ruin. In 1872 Congress passed an act deeding back the twenty acres to Banning and Wilson. The buildings were sold at auction in August, 1873, bringing a mere pittance of their cost. The ditch and flume to bring water to the camp, built at a large expenditure of money and labor, went to ruin, and all traces of them have disappeared. An account of the building of the Los Angeles and San Pedro railroad in 1868-69, which came to a stop at Wilmington and did not reach San Pedro for a dozen years later, and its transfer to the Southern Pacific railroad, are given in Chapter XL of this history.

The work of developing the inner harbor began in 1871. The government had made several preliminary surveys with this object in view. Congress in 1870 appropriated $200,000 for the work. The first part of the scheme was the building of a breakwater from Rattlesnake Island to Deadman's Island, a distance of 6,500 feet. Rattlesnake Island at that time was an irregular shaped strip of land about five miles long lying to the southeast between Wilmington slough and the ocean. It was not really an island, but rather a peninsula. It was only at high tide that it was cut off from the mainland. About a mile and a half from Rattlesnake Island and a quarter of a mile south of the mainland was Deadman's Island, famous in the history of San Pedro bay. It was then about a mile in circumference at its base.

Between these islands was a stretch of shoal water about a mile and a half in length through which the tide ebbed and flowed and the waves dashed in a storm. Between the mainland and Deadman's Island there was a gap or gate about a hundred and fifty feet wide. Through this gap the commerce of the inner harbor had to pass. It was only at high tide that it could do so. At the beginning of work on the breakwater there were but eighteen inches of water on the bar at low tide. There is still living in Los Angeles an old pioneer who boasts of having waded across this inlet. Through the gap between the islands the southeast gales swept with such force as to make the inner harbor unsafe for ships. These gales carried sand and silt into the estuary and filled the channel.

To close the gap between the islands would stop the inflow of sand and silt and break the force of the waves. The outflow through the narrow inlet would deepen the channel by cutting away the bar. This in brief was the plan of improvement proposed.

The first survey with the object of improving the inner harbor was made by Colonel Williamson in 1867. He recommended a breakwater of solid granite blocks. The government at that time was not making liberal appropriations for unknown harbors on the Pacific coast and this plan was abandoned as too expensive. Later a survey was made by General Alexander. His plan was a series of cribs filled with rock, but nothing came of this. Congressman Houghton in 1871 secured an appropriation for $200,000, the money to be expended under the supervision of Colonel Mendell, a government engineer. His plan was to construct a wall of wooden piles across the shallow part and a wall of rock across the deeper opening between the islands.

In June, 1871, the work of pile driving, working out from Rattlesnake Island, began. The job was let by contract to a contractor. After building a few hundred feet he failed, gave up the job and the work for several months was at a standstill.

In January, 1872, Congress made an additional appropriation of $75,000. Lieutenant Sears was given direct charge of the work under the supervision of Colonel Mendell. The work was pushed vigorously. Seven pile-drivers were kept in operation and a force of from one hundred to six hundred men was employed. The men encamped on Rattlesnake Island and that convolved island of ominous name was a lively camp.

The following description of the Wilmington breakwater, as it was called. I take from the Los Angeles Herald of October 4, 1873, which copied it from the Resources of California, a long since defunct periodical which during its existence did much toward the building up of California:

"Starting at the southwest corner of Rattlesnake Island the breakwater runs southerly to the northwest corner of Deadman's Island, a length of 6,500 feet. It is a gradual curve on an arc of an immense circle, the curve towards the southeast, the point from which the heaviest winds and breakers come. The piles are of Oregon fir; heavy iron bands are placed around these and they are connected by heavy iron rods. The material to be used for the deeper portion of the channel is huge boulders of rock; these will form a barrier against the thousands of tons of sand washed against the breakwater on the windward and tideward side.

"The wall of piles is made of heavy timbers thirty feet long and one foot square set close together and driven into the ocean. Inside of this, a second row of thick plank twelve inches wide by four inches thick is driven so as to break joints. This double trunking rises four feet above high tide. Just below the top both inside and out heavy stringers are bolted. This makes a barrier watertight and storm-proof. This work extends 3,700 feet from the original shore. Beyond this for 1,000 feet double lines of such work extend, set twelve feet apart, which being heavily ballasted below, strongly bolted through by strong iron rods and firmly planked over above, form a very strong pier.

"From the outer end of this double work to Deadman's Island, where the water is deepest and the surf the strongest, the work is to be of rock boulder, varying in weight from one to ten tons, and piled in such quantities as to make an immensely heavy sea wall. Wing dams on the outer side will be constructed to divert the current and tides from striking with full force against this sea wall. Three and one-half million feet of lumber and thirteen thousand tons of stone for rip rap work have been used so far. The timber is treated by the hydro-carbon process to preserve the wood and to prevent boring by the toredo.

"On completion of the breakwater some two million cubic yards of sand and silt that have for years been accumulating along the main channel will be dredged.

"Lieut. Clinton B. Sears, of the United States engineer corps, in charge of the work, estimated the cost of removing the sand and silt at twenty-five cents per cubic yard, or about $500,000 to clear the main channel. After dredging, vessels carrying sixteen feet can cross the bar at low tide."

Work was continued on the sea wall until it was carried to Deadman's Island. The rock for this portion of the wall was brought from Santa Catalina Island on scows carrying one hundred and twenty-five tons of rock each and making three trips a week. The boulders or blocks of rock weighed from one to ten tons. The length of wall from where the piling ended to Deadman's Island was about two thousand feet.

The rock-built stone wall was sixty feet at its base and carried to the height of the piling; at the top it was ten feet wide. Up to 1872 Congress had appropriated $425,000 for the improvement of the inner harbor. After that the appropriations dwindled down to a mere pittance. In 1876, $30,000 was allowed. In 1878 what the Los Angeles Express calls a "pitiful appropriation" of $20,000. was set down by Congress for the improvement of the Wilmington harbor.

"This," the editor says, "is a mere frittering away of the money devoted to this important work. One hundred thousand dollars, available for all the improvement, would carry the work to completion and give us a harbor in a short space of time which would accommodate a shipping fully equal to our growing maritime commerce. For less than half a million dollars the government has accomplished at Wilmington more than has been accomplished at other new harbor points with millions. It has land locked the estuary and wrested from the ocean a sheet of water capable of affording shelter and safety to a large fleet of vessels. It has cut a channel across the bar which affords now a depth of fourteen feet at ordinary high water and of seventeen feet at the spring high tides. The channel, however, is only one hundred and fifty feet wide. It should be at least three hundred feet. The depth of water in the channel before the work was commenced was less than two feet.

"Having spent half a million to accomplish the important improvement already achieved. Congress ought to be eager to carry out its work to the successful conclusion of which it is susceptible. An additional $100,000 in hand would give us in a very short time a depth of twenty-four feet in the channel at high tide and enable the engineers to widen the entrance to three hundred feet. This would give Los Angeles a better harbor than Charleston has, a far superior one to that of Galveston, and a better one than Mobile can boast of, and all for the insignificant expenditure of $600,000."

"The immense grain crops of our valleys this year will all have to be shipped abroad by way of Wilmington harbor. If vessels can be brought inside to docks, the money saved to the producers and the encouragement given to industry would be a handsome return to the government for its liberality." At this time (1878) and for several years later immense wheat crops were raised in the San Fernando valley. At one time thirteen clipper ships were anchored in San Pedro bay loading with grain for Europe.

Congress continued to dole out pitiful appropriations. In 1879, $12,000; 1880, $35,000; 1881, $33,000. In ten years from 1882 to and inclusive of 1892 the average appropriations were about $40,000 a year, about enough to keep the breakwater in repair. Even at this early day the inspector of the Southern Pacific railroad monopoly haunted the harbor. There was a fear that that monopoly might acquire frontage enough to control the harbor. Senator George Smith in the legislature of 1877-78 had introduced a bill to prevent the sale of marsh and tide lands in any of the harbors of the State. The Southern Pacific Company, which had acquired in 1874 the Los Angeles & San Pedro railroad with a terminus at Wilmington, was quietly acquiring frontage on the harbor.

It had tried to have confirmed by the surveyor general the Trichenor claim to eight hundred and eight acres of harbor frontage. As the surveyor general was friendly to the corporation it was feared that he would grant its request. In 1871, when work was begun on the breakwater. Wilmington had hopes and aspirations of becoming a maritime city. The city was incorporated and in 1872 a board of city trustees was elected. But a city government with a full corps of city officers was too heavy a burden for the little burg. The board of trustees served out their time without doing anything and quit. Under the general act ceding the frontage of harbors to incorporated cities and towns located in front of them, Wilmington claimed its harbor approaches. The claim was made that whatever power over the marsh and tide lands was acquired at that time was subsequently lost on account of the failure of the people of Wilmington to follow up their act of incorporation by continuing to elect trustees after the first election.

The question of the ownership of the harbor frontage was fought out in the courts more than forty years later. The right-of-way was granted to the Southern Pacific company to extend its road to San Pedro by the surveyor general. On the inner harbor upon the northwest bank, about a mile and a half from old San Pedro, a settlement called Linville was established in 1877. This afterwards became San

Pedro. In 1879 it had three stores, and seven families resided there. Further north was a small settlement called Fayal. These, with the town of old San Pedro, were the nucleus of the city of San Pedro. In 1881 the railroad was built from Wilmington to San Pedro; this gave an impetus to the town. The Goodall-Perkins Steamship Company had acquired twelve hundred feet frontage on the inner harbor in 1878.

The Los Angeles Express of May 1, 1880, says editorially: "The Pacific Coast Steamship Company is doing some very substantial wharf work at San Pedro. The stone abutments and the approaches are of the most endurable character and when the pier is projected to deep water, the company will have one of the finest landings on the coast. It is manifest that the steamship corporation mean soon bringing their steamers to dock in our inner harbor. When they do that, there will be no more chance to sneer at the government for the work it has done to add to our coast another accessible and secure harbor. Thus a variety of circumstances are combining to assure us of the early bringing of ship and wharf together in our harbor. The days of lighterage are rapidly drawing to a close and Los Angeles will soon enjoy the actual benefits of her harbor."

After the completion of work on the inner harbor, Capt. James J. Meyler, in an address before the Chamber of Commerce in 1891, made these statements:

"The channel has deepened, widened and straightened. Where we had depths from six to ten feet in 1871 we have now from sixteen to twenty-two feet and the depth of eighteen inches on the bar has been increased to at least fourteen feet.

"Up to the present time about 133,000 tons of stone have been placed in the breakwater and there have been excavated only about 177,000 cubic yards of material, about 58,000 cubic yards of which was stone from a ledge of rock crossing the channel at the inner bar. From rough calculation, however, I estimate that at least 2,000,000 cubic yards of material have been removed from the channel, over nine-tenths of which has been done independently of dredging or blasting, the result of construction alone — the channel scouring itself under the action of natural causes. The total number of tons of exports and imports has been increased ten-fold since 1871. The collections of the port of Wilmington since 1882 have almost paid for the government construction and work in the harbor."

CHAPTER XLVIII. THE FREE HARBOR CONTROVERSY AND THE BREAKWATER

When the Southern Pacific Railroad Company extended the Los Angeles and San Pedro railroad from Wilmington, where it had so long halted, to the strand on the inner harbor of San Pedro, it had no competitor to any seaport on the southern coast. In 1875 Senator John P. Jones and Col. R. S. Baker founded the town of Santa Monica on the Boca de Santa Monica. Senator Jones and several Los Angeles capitalists, with the design of making the new town a seaport, built a railroad — the Los Angeles & Independence — and in connection with the road a wharf extending out into the bay eighteen hundred feet. The Pacific Coast Steamship Company's boats called at it for freight and passengers coming and going.

Competition cut the excessive freight rates and fares the Southern Pacific had been charging. The hopes of the producers and consumers soared, but a blight struck their bright prospect. The Los Angeles & Independence railroad came to a halt at Los Angeles. The Southern Pacific railroad was completed from San Francisco to Los Angeles in 1876 and was being pushed eastward. The short-haul road with no connection could not compete with the longhaul and was sold in 1878 to its rival. The Southern Pacific Company continued to operate the road but allowed the wharf to fall into decay and it was eventually pulled down and the shipping transferred to San Pedro.

The next rival to San Pedro as a shipping point was Redondo, located on the southeastern corner of Santa Monica bay. The great real estate boom of 1887 had sown a plentiful crop of cities over the plains and along the sea coast. Owing to the configuration of the coast at that point it required but a short wharf to reach deep water. The salt works at the Saucel Redondo, which were extensively operated in the early '50s. had made this a shipping point, and the establishment of Camp Latham there in 1861 had brought some trade to this port. In 1888 a narrow gauge road was built to connect it with Los Angeles and a large amount of lumber was shipped in through this port. Being about twenty miles further north than San Pedro and the bulk of shipments coming from the north, it had an advantage over the old port. In 1891 the most dangerous rival to the ascendency of the Southern Pacific railroad in the monopoly of San Pedro harbor appeared in a corporation known as the Terminal Company. It was composed of St. Louis capitalists, chief among whom were R. C. Kerns and George B. Leighton. The purpose of the company was to secure terminals for a railroad on a deep water harbor that might be used by the company or transferred to some transcontinental railroad seeking an outlet to the ocean.

The first move of the company was to buy the motor roads to Pasadena and Glendale. The next was to steal a march on the Southern Pacific Company by buying that succession of worthless sand dunes known as Rattlesnake Island. When it was reported that the company paid the Dominguez heirs $250,000 for the sand bank people queried, "What can these St. Louis capitalists do with it to make it pay?" But when they constructed a railroad from Los Angeles with its terminus on deep water at East San Pedro, thus securing miles of ocean frontage on the western side of the island, Colis P. Huntington, who had succeeded Senator Stanford as president of the Southern Pacific Company, realized that he had a foeman worthy of his steel and the free harbor war was on.

Huntington decided that he would have a harbor of his own, where competition would be impossible and that the United States government would build it for him. The new port of the Southern Pacific was at the old Santa Monica cañon. The railroad was extended about two and a half miles to the canon by a cut and tunnel through the bluff to the beach. The Long Wharf, as it was called, was built out into the ocean forty-three hundred feet to five and one-half fathoms depth of water. The railroad was extended out to the end of the pier. Imports were transferred direct to the cars from ships at anchor beside the wharf and exports to ships without lighterage. The current report of the cost of the wharf was $1,000,000, which was probably thirty per cent more than it really cost. But the romance that clustered around this great work would have been rudely dispelled had some muck-raker in the halcyon days of the great wharf raked through the assessor's books to find what value the railroad company put on it for taxation. He would have found it valued at $50,000. and this value accepted by the "old guard" — the State Board of Equalization.

The Chamber of Commerce now comes into the limelight in the harbor fight. This was the new Chamber organized in 1888. The old Chamber organized in 1873 had been active in pushing forward work on the breakwater and securing appropriations for it. but had been j dead a decade before the new Chamber was born.

The first move of the Chamber was to send two of its members. Gen. Charles Forman and Thomas E. Gibbon, to Washington to secure an appropriation for deep water improvement? in the outer harbor of San Pedro. Mr. Gibbon was at that time the attorney of the Terminal Railroad Company. Senator Charles Felton, who had been appointed by the governor to fill out the unexpired term of Senator Hearst, deceased, before going to Washington had visited San Pedro and carefully examined into the need of government assistance. At the beginning of the congressional session of 1891-92 he presented the cause of San Pedro so forcibly that there seemed little doubt of a liberal appropriation being given.

The prospects of San Pedro were bright and its friends jubilant, but their hopes were blighted by a frost from Frye, of Maine. William B. Frye, senator from Maine, was then (and for years afterwards) chairman of the committee of commerce. Throughout the long and bitter contest over the free harbor he was the untiring, unreasoning enemy of San Pedro and the unwavering friend and advocate of Huntington's Santa Monica scheme. When Senator Felton presented his appeal for $250,000 to begin deep water improvements at San Pedro, Senator Frye produced a telegram from a Mr. Hood, Huntington's chief engineer, the purport of which was that the holding ground of San Pedro bay was rock and unsafe for anchorage and that piles for piers could not be driven into it.

For more than a century ships had anchored in San Pedro harbor and had ridden out fierce southeasters without discovering the rock bottom of the bay. The Southern Pacific Company itself for nearly two decades had advocated improvements at San Pedro and had pulled down Senator Jones' wharf at Santa Monica and transferred its shipping to San Pedro. Successive boards of government engineers had pronounced in favor of San Pedro as the best harbor site. All these facts counted for nothing with Huntington. He must have a harbor of his own where he owned the sea and land, where he would have no competitors: and the government must build it for him. With this object in view he used all the powerful influence of his corporation in Congress, assisted at all times and occasions by his friend Frye of Maine.

Huntington, in 1894, after the completion of the Long Wharf at Port Los Angeles, as hp called his shipping point, in an interview with the president of the Chamber of Commerce. Daniel Freeman, and Gen. Charles Forman, one of the vice-presidents, said: "Now, I propose to be frank with you people. I do not find it to my advantage to have this harbor built at San Pedro and I shall be compelled to oppose all efforts that you or others make to secure appropriations for that site: on the other hand, the Santa Monica location will suit me perfectly, and if you folks will get in and work for that you will find me on your side— and I think I have some little influence at Washington — as much as some other people perhaps." He ended the interview by saying: "Well, I don't know for sure that I can get this money for Santa Monica, I think I can; but I know d— d well that you shall never get a cent for that other place." * * *

These domineering utterances of Mr. Huntington should have caused a storm of indignation. They did incense men who were fighting for a principle, but there are in all communities men who are in all contests actuated by policy. The harbor contest divided the Chamber of Commerce and at one time it looked as if Huntington's scheme had a majority. A vote of the members was taken April 7, 1894. The vote stood "for San Pedro," 328; "for Santa Monica," 131. After that the sentiment of the Chamber crystallized on San Pedro.

The political upheaval of 1892 that put Governor Cleveland in the presidential chair for the second time and wrested from the Republican party the control of both houses of Congress, brought to the front a man who wielded a powerful influence in the Senate during the seven years of the free harbor war. Stephen M. White had come to Los Angeles in 1875 a young man just admitted to the bar. He soon gained prominence in the legal profession. He served one term in the California Senate and became the leader of his party in the Legislature. Mr. White was appointed on the Senate committee of commerce. During the first years of his term he was not able to accomplish much. The times were out of joint for expenditures on harbors. The Wilson tariff engrossed the attention of the statesmen at Washington and the financial panic that struck the country in 1893 engrossed the attention of the bankers and business men at home.

In 1895 the Free Harbor League was formed in Los Angeles. It attained a membership of about four hundred and did good work for the cause that it was organized to promote.

In 1896 two bills were reported in the lower house of Congress, one of $392,000 for the inner harbor of San Pedro, and one of $3,098,000 for the Santa Monica harbor. This scheme was engineered in the committee by Binger Herman, a congressman from Oregon. In a fit of spleen against Congressman McLachlan of Los Angeles for opposing the Santa Monica appropriation, Herman had both stricken from the bill. When the River and Harbor bill came before the Senate committee, Frye of Maine came promptly to the front with the three million appropriation for Santa Monica. Senator White secured an amendment to the bill

393

for the appointment of a board of engineers to decide which was the better harbor site, the money appropriated to go to the harbor that the engineers favored. The bill with the amendment and the $392,000 appropriation passed both houses in June, 1896, and was signed by the President. The Board of Engineers was appointed with Rear Admiral John G. Walker at its head. Four of the members reported favorable to San Pedro and one, R. P. Morgan, a civil engineer once in the employ of the Southern Pacific, came in with a report favorable to Santa Monica. His report carried no weight.

Great was the rejoicing at Los Angeles when the report of the Board of Engineers was received, but the Southern Pacific people did not join in the jubilee. The long-drawn-out acrimonious contest was ended. Now the faction fight would cease and all would work in harmony for the long-hoped-for harbor. Time passed, but no bids for the breakwater were advertised for. The people grew impatient. Investigation developed the fact that President McKinley's Secretary of War, Russell M. Alger, was delaying action apparently with the hope that Congress might again take up the harbor question and decide in favor of his friend Huntington. Appeals to Alger were met with trivial excuses or treated with indifference. After more than a year had been wasted and nothing done the President was appealed to and his secretary finally forced to advertise for bids. The apportionment for the harbor was $2,900,000. The lowest bid was from a Chicago firm, Heldmeier & Neu, for $1,303,198, the highest from a New York firm for $4,595,516. This, it was believed, was put in at Alger's request.

Another delay ensued in preparing specifications, and finally, in January, 1899, Peter W. Neu, the junior member of the firm, came to Los Angeles to take charge of the work. A few weeks after his arrival he was killed by the overturning of a tally-ho coach. The senior member, Ernest Heldmeier, then took charge of the work.

Work on the breakwater was finally begun in April, 1899. Alger had wasted two years" time by excuses and trivial objections. The dumping of the first load of rock into the bay was to be celebrated by a grand jubilee at San Pedro. April 26, 1899, was the day dedicated to the event. Thousands of people found their way to San Pedro by all manner of conveyances except the automobile, which had not yet put in an appearance. The rock was to be dumped from the boat by an electric contrivance which was to turn the boat on its side. President McKinley was to touch the button that started the electrical works in the boat, but the adverse fates that had pursued the free harbor from its inception got in their work again. The boat refused to tilt and had to be unloaded by hand. There was a feast of barbecued meats promised the visitors. The roasting was done out of doors. The coast wind peppered the meats freely with sand and the smoke-discolored viands were not attractive. The next day, April 27, was celebrated by a fiesta at Los Angeles. The building of the harbor had been begun and it would be pushed to completion. No more delays by Alger, no more obstructions by Frye. The rock was to be obtained from Santa Catalina Island at a point near the isthmus. Barges carrying from eight hundred to fourteen hundred tons were to convey it to the site of the breakwater.

But the adverse fates still pursued the great undertaking. Transportation of the material by sea proved too slow and uncertain a method of securing it. Construction was unnecessarily delayed, or at least so it was claimed. Alger could hang it up for nearly two years, but Heldmeier was allowed no days of grace and on the charge that the work was not being pushed forward fast enough his contract was cancelled by the government and bids advertised for. May 14, 1900, a few days over a year from the dumping of the first load of rock, the contract was let to the California Construction Company of San Francisco for $2,375,546.05, over a million dollars more than the former contractors were to receive. Transportation of material by barge and boat was abandoned. Rock was shipped from Daclez, in San Bernardino county, and from Chatsworth Park, over the Southern Pacific railroad. The cars were run out on trestle work on the line of the breakwater and the rock dumped from the cars.

The breakwater as originally planned began 1800 feet from Point Firmin Bluff, and extended eastward with an elbow near the middle. The gap between the shore line and the breakwater was left for the escape of silt from the harbor. During the building of the breakwater it was found that silt did not lodge in the harbor and the gap was closed. It was completed in 1910, eleven years after the first boatload of rock was dumped into the bay. The length of the breakwater is 9,250 feet, its cost $3,100,000. It is two hundred feet thick at the base and rises to an average height of sixty-four feet through the greater part of its length. It is twenty feet wide at the top.

"It extends from the shore out to the fifty-two foot contour and extends northeasterly in water varying from forty-eight to fifty-two feet deep at low tide. Up to low water it is a rubble-stone mound, the stones weighing from one hundred pounds up to fifteen to twenty tons. Two-thirds of them average more than one thousand pounds each. The superstructure, extending from low water to fourteen feet above, is laid from rectangular granite blocks, those on the ocean side weighing not less than 16,000 pounds."

"At the outer end a magnificent lighthouse has been built, rising approximately seventy feet above the water, and a flashing light of 140,000-candlepower has recently been installed."

Two decades have passed since the Long Wharf was finished and nearly a quarter of a century since the inauguration of the free harbor contest. Time and tide that wait for no man have dealt heavily with the Long Wharf, the pride of Huntington's life. No ships lie at anchor in his pristine harbor. No boats rise and fall with the tide beside his million dollar pier. Ship and rail long since ceased to come together there. Eaten by the worms, battered by the waves, deserted except by Japanese fishermen, that wonder of maritime architecture is rapidly falling to decay. Port Los Angeles is a shipless, sailless port, a port but in name — a memory — a has-been.

Of the men who were active in the great contest that gave Los Angeles its free harbor, but who have since passed away from life's activities, may be named John F. Francis, Stephen M. White, Charles Felton, Ferd K. Rule, D. C. McGarvin, R. J. Waters, W. C. Patterson, Col. S. D. Houghton and Charles Dwight Willard. Some of these lived to see the fruition of their labors, others passed away ere the work was completed. To name all who took part in the harbor contest would take more space than I can allot.

Among the earliest and most active may be named Thomas E. Gibbon, Gen. Charles Forman. Gen. Harrison Gray Otis, Major E. W. Jones, Henry T. Hazard,

William H. Workman, W. A. Spalding, Daniel Freeman, Harry Ellington Brook, J. M. Elliott, Dr. J. P. Widney, W. D. Woolwine, L. W. Blinn, W. G. Kerckhoff, James McLachlan, J. O. Koepfli, Albert M. Stephens, John T. Gaffey, and many others. The acquisition of Rattlesnake Island with its large extent of harbor frontage by the Terminal Company was without doubt the real cause that induced Huntington to transfer his interest and his influence to Santa Monica and thereby precipitate the harbor controversy.

The Terminal Company changed the uncanny name of the island to the unmeaning one of Terminal Island, a name it still bears, although the company long since disposed of its road and the island. The island was given its warning name, Isla de culebra de cascabel (Isle of the rattlesnake) on account of the great number of the genus crotalus horridas on the island in the early times. The natural increase of the reptile was occasionally augmented by immigration. The winter freshets sometimes washed the rattlers out of their lairs in the mountains and the rush of the current of the San Gabriel river brought them down to the ocean and landed them at the island. As this branch of the ophidian family is not given to navigation they remained on the island.

The Terminal railroad was transferred to a new corporation called the San Pedro, Los Angeles & Salt Lake road. The ostensible purpose of this organization was, as it was sometimes tersely put, "to unite the City of the Angels with the City of the Saints." Senator Clark of Montana was the head of and the principal financial backer of the movement. The line of the road was via Riverside, the Cajon pass and the old emigrant trail to Salt Lake City.

While it was building there were various conjectures as to what it was to be — the ocean terminal of the Union Pacific, the Denver & Rio Grande or possibly of a new transcontinental line. After many delays and disasters by flood the road was completed in 1905. It was then found that it was not a competing line. The Southern Pacific Company owned a controlling interest in it and the isle of the ophidian had passed to Huntington with all its harbor frontage. The harbor war that had been waged with virulence but without bloodshed for sever, years ended as many another war has ended! without victory to either contestant.

CHAPTER XLIX. THE PORT OF LOS ANGELES

Throughout the Spanish and Mexican regimes Los Angeles was the only municipality in California that ranked as a city. Being an inland town, it never received the notice from travelers (nearly all of whom came to the territory by sea) that San Diego and Monterey did, and consequently figured but little in the accounts of travels and voyages.

After the discovery of gold, San Francisco, but little known before, came to the front and soon became the largest city on the coast. As we have learned previously from the statement of revenue collectors and from the reports of United States Engineers Bache, Davidson and others, under American rule San Pedro held second place in the commerce of the coast, but Los Angeles, which furnished the commerce, did not receive the credit for that commerce. In reports it was credited to the local port, San Pedro, or more likely to San Diego and way ports. This practice of the steamship companies, in their reports published in the San Francisco papers, called forth a vigorous protest from the old Chamber of Commerce. In the Los Angeles Herald of October, 1873, it published a series of resolutions vigorously protesting against the San Francisco papers accrediting all freight and passengers carried on steamers from the south "to San Diego and way ports."

In their resolutions the members of the Chamber demanded that the pursers of the Pacific Mail Steamship Company's boats furnish the San Francisco papers with freight and passenger lists headed from Los Angeles "instead of San Pedro, which is merely the port where the freight and passengers are transferred to the steamer."

The protest was not heeded and San Diego and way ports were still credited with the commerce of Los Angeles. In 1873, and for years before and afterwards, all steamers anchored out beyond Deadman's Island and tickets from San Francisco to passengers bound for Los Angeles read "to anchorage at San Pedro." This often led to misunderstandings and stormy protests from passengers on their first trip down who did not know the lay of the land. I have a very distinct recollection of a heated discussion between an Irish passenger and the captain of the old Senator on which I arrived at San Pedro October 10, 1869.

Banning's little tug, the Cricket, had come alongside the steamer and the gangplank had been run out. The passengers were ordered aboard the tug and each one assessed $1.50 for the voyage up the slough to Wilmington. The Exile of Erin was very vehement in his protest against "the robbery," as he termed it.

"Yez agreed to land me ashore, and I'll stay on the boat till yez does." The captain cut the interview short with a peremptory order, "Get off my boat or I will have you thrown overboard." Muttering maledictions against the captain, the company and their system of robbery, the subdued passenger walked the plank.

In 1874 Congress changed the name of the port from San Pedro to Wilmington, "whereat there was great rejoicing at the harbor," says the Los Angeles Herald of April 10, 1874.

While this brought Wilmington to the front, it did not advertise Los Angeles as a seaport. The free harbor contest with its varying attitudes in the long-drawn-out contention between the citizens and a monopoly had emphasized the necessity of the city of Los Angeles controlling that harbor.

The most potent factor in arousing the people of Los Angeles to the necessity of owning and controlling the harbor of San Pedro was the construction of the Panama Canal. As that dream of the ages — the connecting of the Atlantic and Pacific oceans — approached realization, the people of California felt that there would be a commercial awakening all along the coast and every seaport in the State would feel it. The attempt of the French government to construct a Panama Canal scarcely caused a ripple of excitement on the Pacific coast and its failure was regarded with indifference. The people of California at that time were more interested in railroad building than in ocean commerce. When the United States government took hold of the scheme many an argonaut of '49 and the early '50s shook his head in doubt of the success of the project. He recalled the discomforts of the isthmus journey, the torrential rains, the Chagres fevers, the malaria-breeding mosquitoes, and the building of the Panama railroad with its tradition of a dead man to every tie of its fifty miles. The United States government would fail as France had done. To the man conversant with the history of the schemes of governments, kings and corporations in the centuries past to tie two oceans together and sever two continents by a canal this last attempt would result in failure, too.

In the time of Philip II of Spain it was proposed to cut a canal through the Isthmus of Panama for the passage of ships from one ocean to the other, and two French engineers were sent to examine the place with that object in view. However, they found the obstacles insuperable, and the Council of the Indies at the same time represented to the king the injuries which such a canal would occasion to the monarchy, in consequence of which his majesty decreed that no one should in future attempt or even propose such an undertaking under pain of death.

With the downfall of Spain's domination in America, the project of constructing a canal was revived. Not only governments, but private corporations and capitalists, took an interest in it and figured on the possibility of the undertaking.

Alfred Robinson, author of "Life in California," who came to the coast in 1829 and made a return trip to Boston via Panama in 1843, writing to his friend, Don Abel Stearns, of Los Angeles, says: "How pleased you would be to make a visit to your native country — your home! What a change you would find — what improvements! You will be enabled to come via Panama, or, rather, I should say, per canal. The Messrs. Baring & Co., of London, have made a contract with the 'Central Government' and in all probability the contract will be finished in five years; so at last the long-talked-of route through the isthmus will finally be accomplished."

The Baring & Company's efforts at digging an isthmus canal never materialized beyond the signing of a contract; and seventy years instead of five passed before the first ship passed through the Panama Canal.

The early years of the present century were, in Los Angeles, and indeed largely so all over the coast, years of "frenzied finance." Money was plentiful, rates of interest low and stock-jobbing schemes "thick as leaves in Valambrosa." The Owens river project had been launched. The aqueduct waters would furnish almost unlimited power. All the public utilities would pass into the possession of the city and that cherishing mother would provide light and heat and water and transportation at a modicum of monopoly rates.

Oil gushers were gushing lakes of petroleum; oil projectors were projecting on the stock market oceans of stock in companies that had millions in them; investment companies were busily investing the spare coin of the frugal worker and paying him dividends not from earnings of the company, but from his own coin.

The promise of Los Angeles becoming a great manufacturing center and also a seaport necessitated either the removal of the harbor to the city or the city to the harbor. It was possible to build the city over the twenty miles of country intervening between its southern limits and the northern limits of the inner harbor, but it might take half a century to do it and no progressive people could afford to wait that long.

The towns of Wilmington and San Pedro owned harbor frontage; to control this Los Angeles must annex these, but annexed territory must be contiguous and adjoining the city to which it was to be joined. The problem was finally solved by extending from the southern limits of the city of Wilmington and San Pedro what is known as the "shoestring strip" — a strip of land half a mile wide. The question of consolidation was solved by Wilmington by a vote of 107 to 61 at an election held August 4, 1909. The next move was to consolidate with San Pedro, which by the vote of Wilmington had become contiguous to Los Angeles. There was opposition to the consolidation. Many of the citizens of the smaller city were averse to being absorbed into the larger city. To lose their municipal identity, to surrender their hold on the harbor, to be governed virtually by a foreign power, was not complimentary to their civic pride.

The statesmen of Los Angeles visited them, pleaded with them, promised the great favors that would be showered upon them and prophesied the era of prosperity that was to come from the union. The election was held August 12, 1909, and the requisite two-thirds vote was cast in favor of consolidation, and thus the outer and the inner harbors, with the swamp lands and the tide sands — Deadman's Island, Mormon Island and more than half of the isle of the ophidian, nee Rattlesnake Island, became a part of the City of the Angels. The vote on consolidation in Los Angeles was practically unanimous. Long Beach set up a claim for the greater part of Terminal Island, but the courts decided against the claim. Wilmington had voted to bond itself to the amount of $100,000 before consolidation to deepen its harbor and at the same time raise the cit^^. For months it was a city on stilts. The houses were raised and the silt and sand from the harbor pumped onto the land. The site of a considerable portion of the city was raised from seven to nine feet, thus securing drainage and sewerage.

In 1910, bonds to the amount of $3,000,000 were voted for harbor improvements. Suits to recover the city's rights on the waterfront and to open thoroughfares to the harbor were filed. Some of these have been fought to a finish in the courts and others are still pending.

The reckless way in which the board of supervisors in early days granted harbor privileges to corporations and private individuals had caused any amount of litigation. One of the most urgent causes of consolidation was to take from the town trustees of San Pedro the power to dispose of harbor frontage. When Los

Angeles came into possession of the harbor it had free of franchises and concessions one hundred and twenty-six acres of submerged lands in the outer harbor.

Among the valuable concessions that had been given away for but little compensation or advantage to the public were the Miner, the Pacific Wharf and Storage Company, the Salt Lake and the Huntington. The most desirable sites for wharves and docks on the outer harbor were in these concessions. The one hundred and twenty-six acres that the city acquired by consolidation with San Pedro were really the refuse of the submerged lands. They were difficult of access and their development expensive.

There was one of these concessions, and one of the most valuable, upon which no development work had been done. This was the Huntington franchise. It had been granted by the city of San Pedro on condition that all dredging and filling should be done by August 5, 1910. The time passed and no attempt had been made to comply with the agreement. The city council declared the concession forfeited and took possession of the land without a contest. Thus Los Angeles secured one of the most valuable locations for docks and wharves. Among the private concessions that have been developed is the Miner fill. It has a width of eleven hundred and fifty feet and a frontage of over six thousand feet. The Southern Pacific is utilizing its concession lying north of the municipal docks. When completed it will have one of the longest wharves in the world. It is twenty-one hundred feet in length and the depth of water is sufficient to accommodate all ordinary deep-sea vessels. The Consolidated Lumber Company has established its extensive yards several miles beyond the head of the inner harbor. Its vessels unloading have the appearance at a distance of having navigated the plains — the long, narrow channel by which they come to the yards not being visible. The increase in the lumber trade during the past decade stands unparalleled in the history of any city in the world. For the calendar year of 1912 the total commerce of the port amounted to 1,867,098 tons. Of this 1,282.597 tons was lumber products and 584,501 tons merchandise. The lumber imports for several years approximated closely to a billion feet annually before the slump in building came in 1914. In the admirable history of The Free Harbor Contest written by the late Charles Dwight Willard and published in 1899, there is a picture of San Pedro deep water harbor as it will look when completed. It shows three piers extending into the outer harbor from the bluff south of Timm's Point. During the long contest for an outer harbor the prevailing idea was that the principal shipping would be from the outer harbor. The inner harbor, the Wilmington Slough of olden times, would be used for craft of light draft. Had some optimist foretold that the first merchant ship to pass through the Panama Canal, a canal that was but a dream at the beginning of the present century, would anchor in the inner harbor far up the slough, he would have been regarded as a visionary, a dreamer.

The first vessel to arrive at Los Angeles harbor from New York via the Panama Canal was the Missourian, of the American-Hawaiian line. It passed through the canal on the 15th of August, 1914, and arrived at Municipal Dock No. 1 August 28, having made the voyage from New York to Los Angeles harbor in twenty-three days. It came into the inner harbor by the main channel between Deadman's Island and the mainland. In 1871, when work began on the breakwater from Rattlesnake

Island and Deadman's Island, there were but eighteen inches of water in that channel at low tide. In successive years since then it has been deepened by dredging until now there are thirty feet on it at low tide.

The following account of the passing of the first ship through the canal becomes of historic interest. It is taken from the Associated Press dispatches of August 15, 1914: "Panama, Aug. 15. — The Panama Canal is open to the commerce of the world. Henceforth ships may pass to and fro through the great waterway which establishes a new ocean highway for trade.

"The steamship Ancon, owned by the United States War Department, with many notable people on board, today made the official passage which signalized the opening of the canal. She left Cristobal at 7 o'clock this morning and reached Balboa, on the Pacific end, at 4 o'clock this afternoon, having navigated the waterway in nine hours. "The Ancon did not anchor at Balboa, but proceeded into deep water in the Pacific beyond the fortified islands, where she anchored in the channel of the canal until her return to Balboa, when she landed her passengers. "The Ancon will remain at the Balboa docks for some time, discharging her cargo, this being the first commercial voyage made through the canal.

"The canal having been officially opened, it will be used tomorrow for the transfer of four cargo ships, which will thus shorten their routes. The private yacht Lasata, owned in Los Angeles, will be transferred to the Pacific, homeward bound.

"The trip of the Ancon was the fastest yet made by a large ocean steamer, the locking operations being quicker, owing to greater experience. The steamer went through the Gatun locks in seventy minutes, a speed never before equaled. The other lockages were equally rapid.

"Col. George W. Goethals, builder of the canal and governor of the zone, watched the operations closely and was manifestly pleased at the improved handling of the locks. He declared that even this would be made much better with time. Capt. Hugh Rodman, superintendent of transportation, who directed the trip, voiced similar sentiments.

"The decks of the Ancon were crowded with guests of the government and officials of the canal administration and the republic of Panama. The peaceful flag of the American Peace Society fluttered from the mast of the Ancon. Beneath her decks, however, were two huge pieces of artillery, which will form part of the defense of the canal.

"With the passage through the Panama Canal today of the War Department liner Ancon the great waterway becomes 'free and open to the vessels of commerce and of warships of all nations on terms of entire equality,' in accordance with the provision of the Hay-Pauncefote treaty.

"Vessels drawing not more than thirty feet of water may now make the passage. It would be possible to put the big American dreadnaughts through at any time."

The realization of the dream of centuries^ the opening of the great ocean highway between the Atlantic and the Pacific — did not awaken the authorities at Washington to the importance of the event. It was treated as mere routine business. The following press dispatch tells the story:

"Washington, Aug. 15. — The completion today of the stupendous ten years' task of the United States government at Panama was ignored by the administration here. The passing of the first large ship through the canal was treated in the light of a routine incident.

" 'Colonel Goethals had been authorized to put a ship through and open the canal today. It was assumed that he would obey his instructions and that the officials here need give no more thought to it,' said Secretary of War Garrison.

"When Colonel Goethals formally reports that he has put a ship through and that the canal is open to commerce, it is probable Secretary Garrison will send him a message of congratulation. It is expected that Colonel Goethals' report will be merely an incident in the daily routine cable dispatch from him."

Deadman's Island, that once stood out solitary and alone, a sentinel guarding the entrance to the inner bay, is slowly vanishing. Its gruesome name has already vanished. The United States government in September, 1914, changed its name to Reservation point. It is to be leveled down and the area extended to five or six acres by a fill. It will be made a Castle Garden for the detention of immigrants. Now that this historic island is to disappear from the bay a brief review of its history may be interesting to future generations.

For many years it was the cemetery of the port. Dana in his "Two Years Before the Mast" tells the story of an English sea captain who died in port and was buried on "this small, dreary looking island, the only thing which broke the surface of the bay." Dana says, "It was the only spot that impressed me with anything like a poetic interest. Then, too, the man died far from home, without a friend near him and without funeral rites, the mate (as I was told) glad to have him out of the way, hurrying him up the hill and into the ground without a word or a prayer." "The island bore its gruesome name when Dana was on the coast in 1835: how long before that time there is no record. There are several legends of how the island came by its uncanny name. Nearly fifty years ago an old Californian who had been a sailor on a hide drogher years before Dana's time gave me this version: "In the early years of the last century some fishermen found the dead body of an unknown white man on the island. There was evidence that he had reached it alive, but probably too weak to attempt the crossing of the narrow channel to the mainland, he had clung to the desolate island, vainly hoping for succor until hunger, thirst and exposure ended his existence. He was supposed to have fallen overboard at night from some smuggling craft and to have been carried in by the tide. From the finding of the body on the island the Spaniards named it Isla del Muerto — the island of the dead, or the Isle of the Corpse." The desire for brevity doubtless gave it its gruesome name. Euphony was sacrificed by the time-saving Americans.

From the most authentic records I can find, there were ten persons in all buried on the island. The lost sailor, the English sea captain, six of the Savannah's crew killed or mortally wounded at Mervine's defeat, a passenger on a Panama ship in 1851 and the last a Mrs. Parker in 1858. Mrs. Parker was the wife of Captain Parker of the schooner Laura Bevan. Once when a fierce southeaster was threatening and the harbor bar was moaning Captain Parker sailed out of San Pedro bay. His fate was that of the three fishermen as told in Charles Kingsley's beautiful poem. Nothing was ever heard of the Laura Bevan from that day to this. The ship and its crew lie at the bottom of the ocean. The captain's wife, who was stopping at the landing, was slowly dying of consumption. Her husband's fate hastened her death. Rough but kindly hands performed the last offices for her, and she was buried on

Deadman's Island. The sea has not given up its dead, but the land has. The vanishing island slowly disappearing exposed the bones of some of the dead. The bodies of all that could be found were removed — the sailors to the cemetery at the Presidio at San Francisco and the others to the local cemetery at the bay.

Rattlesnake Island lost its ominous name during the closing years of the last century. The gruesome title of Deadman has but recently vanished from the little island at the entrance to the inner harbor. Senator Frye's sneer during the Free Harbor Contest as he read from the map, "Rattlesnake Island, Deadman's Island, I should think it would scare a mariner to death to come into such a place!" has lost its significance. Senator Stanford's reply to him was prophetic: "You let us have a large enough appropriation and we will change the names to something less horrifying." Mormon Island is the only one of the three that retains its original name.

CHAPTER L,
PLAZAS. PARKS AND PLAYGROUNDS

Los Angeles city has twenty parks varying in area from 1.17 acres to 3,015 acres. The Plaza, the oldest, is one of the smallest, and Griffith Park, which came into the city by annexation, is the largest and youngest. The total area of all the parks is 3,759 acres. Their value is estimated at $10,000,000. Central Park, with an area of but 4.41 acres, is valued at $5,000,000, equal to the aggregated value of all the others. The history of the accession and development of these parks forms an interesting chapter in the annals of our city.

I shall give their history in the order of their creation.

The Plaza

In Spanish-American countries the plaza is the center of community life — the heart from which the arterial blood of the pueblo or ciudad circulates. Around the plaza are usually grouped the government buildings and the principal churches. Like the forum of old Rome it is a place where questions of state are discussed and where sometimes revolutionary plots are hatched. It is a meeting place of the people to exchange gossip and to retail the day's doings.

Los Angeles, being a town of Spanish birth, has its plaza, but its royal square has long since ceased to be the center of communal life or a political hotbed for the germinating of revolutions. When Governor Felipe de Neve, in 1781, founded the pueblo of our Lady of the Angeles his first act was to locate a plaza for the geographical center from which his town should radiate. De Neve's plaza was rectangular in form — seventy-five varas wide by one hundred in length. It was located north of the church; its southerly line very nearly coincided with what was the northerly line of West Marchessault street. On this, the cuartel, or guard house, the public granary, the government house and the capilla or chapel, fronted. In 1814, when the foundation of the Nueva Iglesia, or new church, was laid, it, too, fronted on the old Plaza; but the great flood of 1815 changed the river's channel from the eastern side of the valley to the western and the waters came up to the foundations; the location of the church was changed to higher ground— its present site. When the final location of the Nueva Iglesia had been decided upon by Governor Sola in 1818, next in importance was a plaza on which the church should front and since there was none, the evolution of a plaza from the ejidos or common land and house lots began. There were evidently some buildings on the designated area, for we find in the old records that the pueblo authorities, in 1825, ordered a house torn down that stood on the Plaza.

Previous to 1818, the trend of the pueblo's growth had been to the northward, but after the location of a site for the new church had been determined the movement to the southward began. June 21, 1821, Jose Antonio Carrillo, one of the aristocrats of the ancient pueblo regime, petitioned the Comisionado for a house lot near the "new temple which is being built for the benefit of our holy religion." A lot 40x60 varas (the present site of the Pico House or National Hotel as it is now called) was granted him. On this lot between 1821 and 1823 Carrillo built, for that time, quite an aristocratic residence, fronting it on the Plaza. It had a wing extending along the line of Main street and one running back from its eastern end to a cross wall, thus inclosing a patio or inner court. Its high gabled roof of red tiles and its white walls gave it an imposing appearance. Its spacious ballroom witnessed many a gay assemblage of the beauty and the chivalry of the pueblo.

Plaza fronts became the fashion with the pueblo aristocracy; and in the course of time the homes of the Picos, the Carrillos, the Sepulvedas, the Olveras, the Lugos, and the Abilas were clustered around the square.

There seems to have been no "piano" or plot made of the new Plaza. The building line zigzagged. A moderate deviation was not noticed, but if some one built out too far the authorities pulled down his casa. In 1838 the city authorities ordered Santiago Rubio's house demolished "to maintain the Plaza line." Santiago seems to have been fired with an ambition to outdo his neighbors in Plaza front or rather by building out to obtain three Plaza fronts, but his pride got a fall and so did his house.

When the vacant lots with Plaza fronts were all built upon, the irregular shape of what was originally intended to be a square became more noticeable. So the Ayuntamiento (Council) set to work to solve the problem of squaring the Plaza, but it proved to be as difficult a problem as squaring the circle. Commissioners were appointed and they labored faithfully to evolve plans to remedy "certain imperfections which have been allowed to creep into the form of the Plaza through carelessness; and to add to the beauty of the town by embellishing the Plaza." But like many a commission since then they encountered opposition to their laudable efforts.

Pedro Cabrera's house lot fell within the line of a street that it was proposed to open out to the westward from the Plaza. The Commissioners offered him a larger and better lot in exchange, but Pedro would none of it. He wanted a Plaza front and the new lot had none. Then the Commissioners offered him another lot and for damages the labor of the chain gang for a certain number of days. The pueblo treasury was empty — there was neither a horse nor a hide in the street fund and the prisoners' labor was all the compensation they could offer. But Pedro was inexorable. He did not propose to be sidetracked in the social scale by losing his Plaza front, so the street had to take a twist around his lot, a twist that was untwisted when the street was absorbed by the extension of Sunset Boulevard. By reducing its dimensions and by giving the lot owners who had built back the land between them and the new building line the Ayuntamiento succeeded in partially squaring the Plaza. The north, south and west lines, after squaring, were each 134 varas or about 380 feet in length and the east line 112 varas or 330 feet long. At that time Los Angeles street (or Vineyard street, as it was then called) ended at Arcadia and the principal entrance into the Plaza from the south was the Calle de Los Negros — the street of the blacks — vulgarly known in latter times as Nigger Alley.

The Old Plaza has been the scene of many a tragedy and of comedies not a few. In the stormy days of Mexican rule when revolutions and pronunciamientos were the escape valves of the pent-up patriotism of California politicians, many a time has it echoed the tread of armed men. Many a gaily-caparisoned cavalcade has ridden forth from it to do battle for the country or rather a part of it; for in most of these contests it was Californian against Californian — the patriots of the south against the rebels of the north and vice versa.

In the Civil war of 1837-38, the "Surenos" (Southerners) were defeated by the Northerners of Monterey at the bloodless battle of San Buenaventura, with a heavy loss of mustangs; and the unfortunates of the southern army who had escaped capture were compelled to foot it home to Los Angeles — an insult too grievous to be tamely borne by the proud caballeros of the south. But greater indignities were in store for them. While footsore and weary they slumbered; in the thick darkness of night — there were no street lamps in the pueblo then — Captain Espinoza, with a detachment of the northern army, stole into the sleeping town. Capturing the drowsy picket guard, he encamped on the Plaza. In the morning when the aristocrats of the Plaza fronts opened their doors they were confronted by armed men. From headquarters on the Plaza, Espinoza began a search for the concealed statesman and warriors of the pueblo; and ere the set of sun, a dozen or more of the leading men of the south were forced to begin a weary march (or ride) of 600 miles to Vallejo's bastile at Sonoma, where as prisoners of state — Alvarado's free State of Alta California — they whiled away the long summer days in durance vile.

In the revolution of 1845, from their military headquarters in the curate's house, Pico and Castro mobilized their allies on the Plaza and in command of 400 caballeros they rode forth to battle against Micheltorena's army of chicken-stealing cholos and Sutter's warriors in bronze. Victorious over Mexican and Indian on the battlefield of Cahuenga, they returned again to the Plaza to receive the plaudits of mothers, sisters, wives and sweethearts.

But the old Plaza long ago ceased to be a storm center of political disturbance. Across the plains of the Laguna came the Saxon invader and from the mesa his cannon sounded the death knell of Mexican domination in California.

The Plaza beheld its last military pageant when in 1847 Stockton's invading army, 600 strong, entered the subjugated city and marching up the Calle Principal to the stirring strains of "Yankee Doodle" and "Hail Columbia" it camped on the public square. The music of Stockton's famous brass band as it floated out on the evening air, did more, it is said, to smooth the creases out of "war's wrinkled front" than all the treaties and conciliatory proclamations of the gringo commanders.

But peace hath her pageants as well as war; and the old Plaza has been the scene of many a gay fiesta, many a brilliant civic parade, and many a solemn church procession, as well. During the Mexican era it witnessed the inauguration ceremonies of three Governors of California. The first were those of Carlos Carrillo, sometimes called the Pretender. On the 6th of December, 1837, Governor Don Carlos Carrillo, "accompanied by a magnificent cavalcade" (so an old record reads), entered the city and crossing the Plaza took the oath of office in the Juzgado or Hall of Sessions and at the head of his retinue he repaired to the church, where he listened to a solemn mass. For three nights, in honor of the occasion, the Plaza fronts were brilliantly illuminated and the big cannon on the square boomed forth the glad tidings that Los Angeles was the capital of California, and that she had a Governor of her own. Then Alvarado, the de facto Governor, came down from Monterey with his northern hordes and Carlos, the Pretender, fled to the wilds of San Diego. Later on he was captured, and a prisoner was taken back to his rancho and to his wife at San Buenaventura, where he lived happily ever afterwards. Los Angeles mourned a lost Governor and a lost capital, but she, too, was happier for the loss of both if she only could have realized it.

The next inaugural services held on the Plaza were those of Manuel Micheltorena, the last of the Mexican-born Governors of California. He took the oath of office New Year's eve, 1842, in Sanchez Hall, which until quite recently stood on the eastern side of the square. An inauguration ball, that lasted a week, followed. The Plaza fronts were again brilliantly illuminated and cannon boomed forth a glad welcome to the new Governor — cannon that but two years later sounded the trump of his doom at the battle of Cahuenga. The last Governor inaugurated was Pio Pico in 1845.

One of the most imposing of the church festivals in which the Plaza figured in the olden time was the festival of Corpus Christi. Corpus Christi is celebrated forty days after Easter; and it is intended to commemorate the ascension of the Body of Christ into Heaven. Every year, before the festival, the Plaza was swept and cleansed of rubbish, and enramadas. or booths of boughs, constructed in front of the principal houses; and altars erected. The celebration of this festival by processions on the Plaza was continued after the American occupation — indeed, down to within the past thirty-five years. From the Weekly Star of June 5, 1858, I extract the following description of the celebration of that year:

"Immediately after Pontifical Vespers, which were held in the church at 4 p. m., a solemn procession was formed which made the circuit of the Plaza, stopping at the various altars which with great cost, elegance and taste had been erected in front of the houses where the sacred offices of the church were solemnly performed. The order of the procession was as follows: Music — Young Ladies of the Sisters' School bearing the banner of the school, followed by the children of the school to the number of 120 in two ranks. They were elegantly dressed in white, wearing white veils and carrying baskets filled with flowers which during the procession were scattered before the Bishop and the clergy. Next came the boys of the church choir. Then twelve men bearing candles; these represented the twelve apostles. Then came Father Raho and Bishop Amat, bearing the Blessed Sacrament, supported on each side by the clergy, marching under a gorgeous canopy carried by four prominent citizens. These were followed by a long procession of men, women and children marching two and two. The procession was escorted by the California Lancers, Captain Juan Sepulveda commanding, and the Southern Rifles, Captain W. W. Twist in command.

"Very elaborate and costly preparations had been made by the citizens resident on the Plaza for the reception of the Holy Eucharist; among the most prominent of which we notice the residence of Don Jesus Dominguez, Don Ignacio Del Valle, Don Vincente Lugo and Don Augustin Olvera. These altars were elegantly designed and tastefully decorated, being ornamented with laces, silks, satins and diamonds. In front of each the procession stopped whilst sacred offices appropriate to the occasion were performed.

"Having made the circuit of the Plaza, the procession returned to the church, where the services were concluded, after which the immense assemblage dispersed, and the military escorted the young ladies of the Sisters' School on their return home."

Patroness Day or the fiesta of Our Lady of the Angels was another occasion in which the Plaza played a most important part. It is celebrated August 15th. The Mother of Christ, according to the Catholic doctrine, did not die, but was taken up into Heaven, where .she is continually adored by all the heavenly throng of angels and archangels as their queen. The following description of the celebration of that festival I take from the Star of August 22, 1857:

"At the conclusion of mass the pupils of the female school headed by their instructresses, the Sisters of Charity, came out of the church in procession bearing the image Our Lady under a canopy. They were joined by the Lancers and passing around the public square reentered the church. The appearance of the procession as it left the church and during its march was imposing. The canopy covering the representation of the angelic queen, tastefully ornamented, was borne by girls dressed in white. The girls of the school with their heads uncovered and in uniform white dresses, followed; then came the lancers, the rear of the company being brought up by a mounted division armed with lances. There was an evening procession on the Plaza. A bull-fight took place in the upper part of town in the afternoon, which was attended by a dense crowd. One hombre attempting to perform some exploits on foot which are usual at bull-fights in Lima and Mexico, was caught and tossed high in air a number of times by an infuriated bull and left for dead. A number of horses were badly gored and some killed outright. This branch of amusement was kept up for three days to the evident delight of the boys and great suffering and ruin of many a noble steed."

In the olden times, before the gringo influence had wrought changes in social customs, when the Christmas festivities broke the monotony of pueblo life and the "Pastores" (The Shepherds, a fragment of the passion play of the Middle Ages that had survived the lapse of time and crossed the wide expanse of sea and land between Europe and the western shores of the sunset sea) was played by amateur actors, often has the old Plaza resounded with shouts of mirth at the undoing of the arch fiend, Satan, by the archangel, Michael. But after the change of rulers, in the days of gold, Satan had his innings and the Plaza was given over to lawlessness, and vice ran riot on its borders. The Calle de Los Negros was as black in character as in name. For its length and opportunities it was the wickedest street on earth. Saloons, dance houses and gambling hells lined its walks and the high tide of its iniquities swept over the Plaza.

In 1854 it is said that Los Angeles averaged a homicide for each day of that year. The Plaza borders and the Calle de Los Negros were the principal battlefields where most of the victims bit the dust.

The criminal element became bold and defiant; robbers and murderers terrorized the community. Then the law-abiding citizens arose in their might and in the shape of vigilance committees and military organizations put an end to the saturnalia of crime, and to many of the criminals as well. The gallows tree on Fort Hill bore gruesome fruit and the beams over corral gates were sometimes festooned with the hangman's noose. In less than a year twenty-two criminals, bandits, murderers and thieves were hung in accordance with the law or without law, whichever was most convenient or most expeditious; and more than twice that number expatriated themselves for the country's good, and their own. After its purification by hemp, the Old Plaza became a thing of utility, and was made the distributing point for a water system. In 1857 the City Council granted Judge William G. Dryden the right to convey the water from his springs, located on the low ground southeast of where the River Station now is, "over, under and through the streets, lanes, alleys and roads of the city, and distribute it for domestic purposes."

Dryden raised the water by means of a pump propelled by a current wheel placed in the Zanja Madre into a reservoir on the Plaza, from whence it was distributed by pipes to the houses in the neighborhood. When Messrs. Griffin, Beaudry and their associates obtained the thirty years' lease of the city water works, one of the conditions of that lease was the building within a year, at a cost not to exceed $1,000, of an ornamental spring fountain on the Plaza. Another condition was the payment by the company to the city of $1,500 a year for the rent of the water works.

Juan Bernard and Patrick McFadden, who had acquired possession of the Dryden franchise and water works, disposed of their system and the old brick reservoir on the Plaza came into the possession of the City Water Company, the successors of Griffin, Beaudry, et al.

A year passed and no fountain played on the Plaza, another year waned and passed away and still the Plaza was fountainless. A third year was passing and still the unsightly debris of the old reservoir disfigured the center of the square. At a meeting of the Council, December 2, 1870, the late Judge Brunson, attorney of the City Water Company, submitted the following proposition as a settlement of what he styled "the much vexed question of the reservoir and Plaza improvements":

"The water company will remove the reservoir from the Plaza and deed all its rights and interests in and to the Plaza to the city of Los Angeles; will build a good substantial fence around said Plaza; will lay it off in ornamental walks and grounds; will erect on it an ornamental fountain at a cost not to exceed $1,000, and will surrender to the city all city water scrip (about $3,000) now held by the company; provided said city will for the considerations named above reduce the rent ($1,500 a year) now paid by the company to said city under a certain contract made July 22, 1868, to the sum of $300 per annum. Some of the Councilmen demurred to giving up $1,200 a year 'for very little return.' "

Then Judge Brunson executed one of those brilliant legal coup d'états for which he was famous. He threatened to bring suit against the city to defend the water company's rights. McFadden, one of the former owners of the reservoir, stated to the Council that the water company had no right to the Plaza except the right to use it as a reservoir site, and since the company had ceased to use the reservoir the Plaza reverted to the city. But the Council, frightened at the prospect of a lawsuit and fearful of losing the Plaza, hastened to compromise on the basis of $400 as a year's rental instead of the $1,500 specified in the original contract.

The fence was built, the walks were laid, and the ornamental fountain, too, was erected by the company, and for forty years it has spurted the crystal river water into the moss-covered basin where the gold fish play.

During the Spanish and Mexican domination in California, the Plaza was a treeless common; its surface pawed into ridges or trodden into dust by the hoofs of the numerous mustangs tethered on it or ridden over it. It had, however, its annual spring cleaning and decoration for the festival of Corpus Christi.

For a decade or more after the American occupation its appearance was unchanged. The first attempt at its improvement was made by the city authorities in 1859. It was enclosed by a picket fence, walks were laid off and some shrubbery planted. But in those days the city exchequer was in a chronic state of collapse and the improvements made were not kept up. The tethered mustangs gnawed the pickets and wandering goats nibbled the shrubbery. The Plaza gradually lapsed into its former state of dilapidation. In 1870 the City Water Company took it in hand and made the improvements named above. Its form was changed from a square to a circle.

In the five score years that have passed since the old Plaza was evolved from a chaos of ejidos and house lots, the flags of kingdoms, empires and republics have floated over it. In the beginning of its history the imperial banner of Spain waved on its borders. It was supplanted by the tri-color of the Mexican empire. Next was raised the cactus-perched eagle flag of the Mexican republic; on its downfall up rose the Stars and Stripes; and now above the ruined homes of the Dons floats in the breeze the flag of China.

Three distinct forms of civilization and several forms of savagery as well have met on its borders. The pastoral Latin with his easygoing manners and customs and mode of life long since gave way to the aggressive Saxon: and the Saxon in turn has been pushed aside by the Mongol. There have been race wars on the Plaza borders. Many of our older citizens will recall the incipient revolution of 1856, when a number of the Mexican population rose in protest against a grievous wrong done one of their people and, armed, they assembled on the Plaza with cries of down with the Americans, and "Viva Mexico!" The uprising ended with the exchange of a number of shots between the combatants, the wounding of the city marshal and the death of a horse. But the Mongolian massacre of 1871 was a more sanguinary affairs. One American was shot to death and eighteen Chinamen were either shot or hanged on that wild night of mob rule.

The Plaza offers many an object-lesson in the cosmopolitan characteristics of our population. There the civilizations and religions of the Occident and the Orient meet but do not mingle. Each maintains its own customs and beliefs and scorns those of the other. From the eastern border of the old Plaza, a heathen temple devoted to the worship of the Chinese god Joss, confronts one, on the western side of the square a Christian church dedicated to the worship of the Christian God. The little brown man of the Orient staggers along the streets of the public square weighted down by the burden he carries balanced from the end of a bamboo pole brought from his native land — burdens carried today as his ancestors bore them in ages long past; while the white man's burdens (or at least a part of them), and himself, too, are borne along by electricity and steam — motive powers which the man of the Occident has harnessed down to do his bidding. The flash of the one and the roar of the other as they "swish" their burdens past the borders of the old Plaza dissipate the romantic fantasies of its by-gone days and leave to the memory of the passerby instead only a hasty glimpse of a common meeting place of two civilizations — the one living, the other dying.

410

Central Park

There is perhaps no other great city in the United States whose inhabitants know so little of the early history of their city as do the great majority of the dwellers in Los Angeles, of theirs. This may be accounted for in part by the fact that its founders and early inhabitants were of a different nationality to that of its present citizens. No founders' or forefathers' day keeps alive the traditions and the memories of the olden time.

The present inhabitants are so intent on boosting the city and speculating in town lots that they have no time to familiarize themselves with the history of their city, ancient or modern. Space writers and sensational story mongers ignorant themselves and presuming on the general ignorance of its people in regard to the early history of their city fabricate canards and publish accounts of imaginative incidents and events that are ludicrous in their absurdities and palm these off on the public for veritable historical facts, and the credulous public gulps them down with avidity and believes them religiously.

Commenting on the opening of Central Park after it had undergone extensive repairs and improvements amounting to an expenditure of over $50,000, one of our leading daily newspapers under date of July 1, 1911, publishes the following choice bit of history:

"Central Park has been a public common since the days of King Charles II of Spain, that monarch having deeded the plot of ground to the pueblo of Los Angeles in 1781."

Our historian continues: "After the park, one of the oldest pieces of ground devoted to park purposes in America, had been given the public by King Charles II it deteriorated to such an extent that in 1870 a committee of Los Angeles citizens composed of J. M. Griffith, O. W. Childs, Andrew Glassell and P. Beaudry was appointed to improve it."

Another of our leading newspapers advocated the naming of the park for King Carlos II, its donor.

Now all this is quite romantic, but in the light of the true history of the park it is ludicrously absurd. King Charles II died in the year 1700 — sixty-nine years before the first settlement was made in California and eighty-one years before King Charles III authorized the founding of the pueblo of Los Angeles and granted it four square leagues of land from the public domain; and he, too, had been dead seventy-eight years before that rectangular piece of land — block 15 of Ord's Survey — containing about five acres — and now known as Central Park, was dedicated by the City Council "for a public square or plaza for the use and benefit of the citizens in common of said city of Los Angeles."

The following historical sketch of Central Park has been compiled from official records, and it also contains the author's reminiscences and observations of it covering a period of forty-six years.

There is a tradition which crops out periodically that the man who donated the park grounds to the city died in the poorhouse. It is true that the alleged donor, George Lehman, "Roundhouse George," died in the county hospital, but he did not donate the park site, for the very good reason that it never was his to donate.

It is one of the few pieces or parcels of the vast municipal domain known as pueblo lands that we inherited from Spain, or, to speak more in accordance with facts, that we wrested by conquest from Mexico, which has never been sold or given away. King Carlos III of Spain was the donor of the park in about the way that the president of the United States is when government land is sold or given away. Under Spanish rule in America, a pueblo was a legally organized form of settlement entitled to a tract of land (usually four square leagues) for various community uses.

The pueblo plan of colonization was used in Spanish-American countries two centuries before the time of King Carlos III. Pueblo lands were transferred by municipal authorities, not by a king. Both Westlake and Elysian parks, as well as Central Park, are parts of the pueblo lands that have never been alienated from municipal ownership.

After the conquest of California by the Americans, a portion of the pueblo lands lying between First and Twelfth streets, Main and Grasshopper (now Figueroa) streets, was subdivided into lots and blocks by Lieutenant Ord; Central Park is block 15 of Ord's Survey.

This survey was made in 1849 and a number of the lots fronting on Main, Spring and Fort streets were put on sale. The maximum price for Ord Survey lots, 120x165 feet, in the "days of '49" was $50 each. With the decadence of mining and the decreased demand for cattle — the chief product of the South — the city became a case of arrested development.

Ord's Survey lots on Main, Spring and Fort streets could be bought in the early "60s at the price of ten years before, namely, thirty to fifty cents per front foot. There was no temptation to invest in lots beyond the settled portion of the city; consequently the blocks west of Hill street remained practically intact.

There was another reason why settlers did not locate on lots on Olive and Charity (Grand avenue) streets near the base of the western hills. The Arroyo de Los Reyes, rising in the northwestern part of the city, debouched into the plain at the base of the hill on which the old Normal School stood. It crossed Olive street north of Sixth and cut a corner of? the prospective park, then it zigzagged in a deep channel through the blocks between Hill, Olive and Charity streets down to Washington street.

In the spring of the year there was considerable water in it and innumerable frogs nightly held concerts along its reedy brink. As the season advanced, millions of mosquitoes hatched in the stagnant pools of the arroyo of the kings and made night a horror to the dwellers on its banks. These appurtenances to real estate in that locality made it undesirable for first-class residences.

The Camino viejo (old road) that developed along the trail that Portola's explorers made in 1769 cut a triangle off the corner of block 15 at Olive and Fifth streets. This old road made nearly a century and a half ago, of which North Spring street is the last remnant, cut diagonally across the blocks between First and Third, Spring and Broadway. It crossed Hill street at Fourth, and Olive at Fifth. It passed out of the old pueblo limits near Ninth street, where it forked, one branch leading to the Cahuenga Pass and the other to the brea beds on the Rancho La Brea, where the inhabitants of the old pueblo obtained their roofing material (crude asphaltum).

412

For nearly a century after the founding of the pueblo of Los Angeles this road was the camino real or main traveled road leading westward out of town. More than sixty years ago the court of sessions decreed it as one of the six caminos reales that led out of the old pueblo.

For years after Ord made his survey the people ignored his streets and came into town across lots. Thirty years ago, at the gate entrance to the park at the corner of Sixth and Olive and also at the entrance at Fifth and Hill, there were large signs that read "Heavy teams are forbidden to cross the park," but as there was no guard to prevent and no penalty to enforce, heavy teams and light, horseman and footman took the short cut into town through the park. |

The setting apart of block 15 for a park dates I back nearly fifty years. In 1866 the City Council passed an ordinance "disposing of certain lots at public auction and reserving others for a public square." Section III of this ordinance reads as follows:

"Lots from Nos. 1 to 10 in block 15 of Ord's Survey of said city are hereby set aside for the use of said city and the residents thereof as a public square, and the same is hereby declared to be a public square or plaza for the use and benefit of the citizens in common of said city, remaining under the control of the mayor and council of said city."

The ordinance was approved and signed December 11, 1866, by C. Aguilar, mayor. Cristobal Aguilar was the last Spanish-American mayor of Los Angeles.

Four years passed and still the public square was a treeless and grassless common. Times were hard and money was scarce, but there were public spirited citizens then as now, who were willing to devote their time and money to the improvement of the city. Early in 1870 a public meeting was called to discuss the question of improving the public square. It was decided to raise by subscription funds sufficient to fence it.

In those days the mustang and the bovine were free to roam where fancy or feed attracted them, and the first preliminary was to fence them out. There was no law to compel their owners to fence them in.

At that meeting the square was named Los Angeles Park and it was decided to petition the council to dedicate it for a park and authorized a committee appointed at that meeting to improve it. The following ordinance was passed by the council.

"Section 1. Whereas the block bounded as follows: On the east by Hill, south by Sixth, west by Olive and north by Fifth street, has been reserved for some public purpose, and whereas an association of gentlemen have subscribed funds for the purpose of fencing and ornamenting the aforesaid block of which the following gentlemen are the executive committee, J. M. Griffith, O. W. Childs, A. Glassell, J. S. Griffin, J. G. Downey and P. Beaudry, be it ordained by these presents, do we ordain that the above-named association be allowed to fence in and ornament with fruit and forest trees the aforesaid block, and be it also ordained that the aforesaid block be declared a public place forever for the enjoyment of the community in general." The ordinance was passed November 17, 1870.

The committee secured and expended $600 in fencing and improving the park. This did not complete the work. Evidently some had wearied in well doing.

February, 1872, the committee reported to the council that a number of the subscribers had failed to pay their subscriptions and that work on the park had

413

been suspended. The committee recommended that the council vote $1,000 to complete the fence and plant trees. The request was granted and May 28, 1872, a sub-committee consisting of Workman, Beaudry and Macy, reported the fence completed at a cost of $685. The balance of the appropriation would be used in painting the fence and other improvements, but the committee advised that no more work be done on the park at expense to the city.

It is said that George Lehman, "Roundhouse George," planted the first trees in the park and carried water in oil cans to irrigate them. He was one of a committee to collect subscriptions. From his activity in improving the park came the tradition that he donated it to the city.

Besides the Garden of Paradise, a suburban pleasure resort just south of Third street and extending from Main through to Spring street, on which was located the roundhouse, he owned the southwest corner of Spring and Sixth street. On this lot back from the street until quite a recent date stood an old brick house on the front of which was painted, "Georgetown, 1859." That suburb of the city then was known as Georgetown.

There was no lawn planted in the park for a number of years after it was enclosed. The water was not piped that far down. An open ditch supplied the park with water. This ditch branched off from the Zanja Madre, or mother ditch, near Requena street (East Market) then flowed down between Los Angeles and South Main streets, irrigating the vineyards and vegetable gardens that covered the present sites of business blocks and hotels; it crossed Main street below Fourth street, and passed just south of the Hibernian skyscraper, then zigzagged across the blocks from Spring to Hill streets, entering the park at the southwest corner of Hill and Fifth street, and running along its Fifth and Olive street fronts, it passed out of the park, at Sixth and Olive streets. Then it meandered out to the rural regions of Figueroa and Adams streets. Up to 1885 this ditch was an open channel, then it was piped and carried underground across the business streets.

In the fifty years of its existence the park has had a number of different names. It was first known as the public square; later St. Vincent Park, Los Angeles Park and Sixth Street Park. On some of the old city maps it is marked "plaza."

When the city began to develop other parks further out, it was officially named Central Park. The first plan of the park was diagonal walks or rather drives along the lines where the present bricked walks are. When the old fence was pulled down and the ditch filled, the park grounds were laid out in serpentine walks, lawns planted, and a bandstand built.

The last transformation of the park took place in 1911-12. The serpentine walks were changed to diagonals. The bandstand was removed, many of the trees taken out and the park grounds enclosed by a low cement wall or curbing. This transformation cost about $50,000 and is intended to be permanent. The park has ceased to be the forum of the disaffected and has become a place of rest and quiet for visitors.

About twenty-five years ago a bond election was called to erect a library building in the park. The believers in the tradition of Roundhouse George's reversionary donation of the Park; the windjammers who at that time infested it in great numbers, and wailed over the robbery of the poor man of a public forum in which to air his grievances; and the men-afraid-of-taxes all combined and defeated the bond issue, and our library is still a wanderer and a homeless waif.

Elysian Park

Elysian Park, which contains 532 acres, is the second largest park owned by the city. It is part of the pueblo lands that we acquired by conquest from Mexico. When successive city councils were giving away, for small compensation, the vast domain that was donated to the pueblo at its founding, the lands that form Elysian Park were considered worthless and the councilmen could find no one to take them off their hands. So these refuse lands remained in the city's possession.

As the city grew larger and its landed possessions decreased, some one conceived the idea of making a park of its refuse lands. The lands that constitute the park were set apart for that purpose in 1886. Buena Vista street was extended to the river and trails built over the prospective park lands. In 1896, when the financial stringency following the boom was the most pressing and hundreds of men were out of employment, the business men of the city raised by subscription $20,000 with which to give employment to the unemployed and at the same time to improve the park. The men were paid $1 a day for their labor, and as the cost of living was much less than it is now, this enabled them to keep the wolf from the door.

One rabid reformer who prided himself as being the champion of the down-trodden workingman mortgaged his little homestead and began recruiting a Coxey army to march on to Washington. He tried to induce the laborers on the park to strike for higher wages and failing in this he persuaded a few of them to join his army. The great majority, however, preferred to stick to their job. He and his deluded followers set out on their march to Washington. They marched boldly through the Cajon Pass, but the dreary outlook of desert beyond halted them. Two hundred miles between saloons struck terror into their hearts and they retreated to civilization and saloons. The workers who remained built the Fremont road and the Fremont gate or entrance to the park.

A tunnel was at one time constructed along the bluff overhanging the river. It was intended to convey water from a hill reservoir to the Zanja Madre (mother ditch) which meandered at the base of the hills that border the Southern Pacific Railroad's freight yards. Through defective construction or bad engineering or both the tunnel failed to subserve the purpose for which it was built. It cost the city a considerable sum of money. The father of the project was Bernard Cohen, councilman and a promoter, who did much to develop the resources of the city. The Southern Pacific railroad was recently given a strip of land from the point of the bluff at the bridge crossing in exchange for a strip of land widening North Broadway. The cutting away of the face of the bluff eradicated all traces of Cohen's tunnel.

Portola's explorers, the first white men who trod the soil of Los Angeles, crossed the river near this point or bluff. They encamped on the river August 2, 1769. Father Crespi in his diary says, "After traveling for about a league and a half through an opening found between two low hills we came to a rather wide cañada having a great many Cottonwood and sycamore trees. Through it ran a beautiful river toward the north northeast, and curving around the point of a cliff it takes a direction to the south. Toward the north northeast we saw another river bed which must have been a great overflow, but we found it dry. This arm unites with the river and its great floods during the rainy season are clearly demonstrated by the many uprooted trees scattered along the banks. We stopped not very far from this river to which we gave the name of Porciuncula. Here during the evening and night we experienced three consecutive earthquakes." (The dry river is the Arroyo Seco.) "At half past six August 3rd," continues Father Crespi, "we set out and forded the Porciuncula river where it leaves the mountains to enter into the plain." The entrance into Elysian Park should have been named Portola's gate instead of Fremont's gate and not only the gate but the whole park should have been named for the first explorer. Portola Park is as euphonious as Elysian. It would have some historical significance which Elysian has not.

The cliff and the mountains which Father Crespi notes in his diary are part of the park and with the river (which Portola's Expedition discovered) are the only landmarks noted by the explorers in their march across the site of the future city of Los Angeles.

Echo Park

Echo park, containing thirty acres, is another park evolved from the city's refuse lands. In 1868 the city council contracted with the Los Angeles Canal & Reservoir Company, a corporation, with a capital of $200,000, of which George Hansen was president and J. J. Warner, secretary, to construct a system of reservoirs and canals in the northwestern part of the city. The reservoirs were to be filled by water from the river conducted in a canal. A dam, twenty feet high, was built across a canon near the head of the Arroyo de Los Reyes and a ditch following the canon of this arroyo down to Pearl street, now Figueroa, was constructed. This zanja in later years was known as the Woolen Mill ditch.

Los Angeles had an ambition to become a manufacturing city. The water brought down by the ditch could be used for power to propel machinery and for irrigation. The ditch was extended down to the southern part of the city. For this improvement the company was to receive several thousand acres of hill land in the northwest part of the city. In 1873 a woolen mill was built on the line of this ditch near Figueroa and Fifth streets, and for a decade or so manufactured a fair quality of blankets. Then it was turned into an ice factory. Competition froze it out. The Woolen Mill ditch disappeared before the march of improvement and all the city has left for its leagues of land is a pond or reservoir now known as Echo Lake. The other reservoirs that appear on the old maps as reservoirs 1, 2, and 3 were never completed. The land surrounding reservoir No. 4 (Echo Lake) was converted into a park and the land below the dam — about four and one half acres — belonging to the city was converted into a children's playground. Echo Lake is the largest body of water in any of the parks. It is a favorite boating resort and a few deluded fishermen occasionally angle for carp in its turbed waters.

Eastlake Park

For many years there had been a dispute between the Mission padres of San Gabriel and the pobladores of Los Angeles in regard to the boundary line between the mission lands and those of the pueblo. The Mission padres claimed a large slice off the northeastern corner of the pueblo or rather the Rosa de Castella rancho was floated down on to the pueblo. As the land was hilly and waterless the dispute never became acute.

When the United States claims commission was adjudicating disputed land claims Ancilito Lestrades presented a claim for the rancho under a grant purporting to be from Governor Victoria given in 1831. The commission in 1855 rejected Lestrades' claim. The Hancock survey made in 1853 had not been extended over this disputed territory. The land inside the city's boundaries became public land. In the famine year of 1864 when cattle, sheep and horses were starving to death on account of no feed, Dr. J. S. Griffin applied to purchase a strip of moist land contiguous to the river from the city council. The members of the council were too shrewd to be caught by such a proposition. They required Dr. Griffin to buy about two thousand acres of mesa land lying back from the river in addition to the tract he had asked for. He secured the land at fifty cents an acre and was not enthusiastic over his purchase.

In 1874, when the Southern Pacific Railroad was projecting its line through Los Angeles, among its demands for a bonus was fifty acres for shops. The citizens, recognizing the great benefit that railroad shops employing a large number of men would be to the city, purchased a body of land containing fifty acres along the projected line of the railroad from Dr. J. S. Griffin, paying $200 per acre for it. This was included in the $600,000 subsidy given the railroad for building its line through the county of Los Angeles. The road was built through to its eastern terminus, but no shops materialized. Time passed — years lengthened into decades — but no shops were built. The people grew impatient. Forbearance had ceased to be a virtue. In 1889, when Henry Hazard was mayor, backed by the city council and the people, he made an insistent demand on the railroad company to build the shops or deed the land back to the city.

The company finally deeded it to the city for a park. It was at first called East Los Angeles Park, but when Westlake Park became an attractive resort it was named Eastlake, which was considered shorter and more euphonious than its original name. A menagerie was located in it, but was afterwards moved to Griffith Park.

Westlake Park

Westlake Park, like Elysian, was evolved from refuse pueblo land. In early days the city council could find no one who would buy it at any price. It was formerly designated as Lot 1, Block 25 of Hancock's Survey of the Pueblo lands. It contains thirty-five acres.

In 1865 the city's finances were at a low ebb. The famine years of 1863-64 had destroyed the cattle by the thousands. In the fall of 1864, all of Don Abel Stearns ranches and city property were advertised for sale on a judgment for delinquent taxes and he was the richest man in the city.

To raise funds the council offered a number of the best blocks of the Hancock survey for sale at auction. The uniform price for the best lands was $10 an acre, a price that scarce would buy a square foot in some of them now. In the course of the sale the auctioneer and his patrons came to the site of the future park. It was a most unpromising piece of real estate. In the center of it was a basin or pond which during the rainy season filled with water. During the dry season this evaporated. The bottom of the lake then was covered with a thick coating of alkali, giving it the appearance of having had a snow storm.

Noyes, the old-time auctioneer, undertook to sell it. "Who will give me $10 an acre for Lot 1?" No response. "Who will give $9, $8, $7, $6? He ran the gamut to $1. No response. "Who will give me two-bits?" No answer. Its absolute worthlessness saved it to the city and to future generations for a breathing place. It was then beyond the settled portion of the city. In 1886-7 a number of the Hancock thirty-five-acre lots were subdivided into town lots. Population began to drift out into the western part of the city. In 1887 William H. Workman was mayor of the city. A number of the leading men of that section who had bought land for subdivision came to Mayor Workman with a proposition to give $5,000 towards converting Lot 1 into a park if the city council would give a similar amount. The proposition was accepted and the money expended on developing the park. Work has gone steadily on year after year until the refuse land of fifty years ago that no one would invest twenty-five cents an acre in, has been made one of the most attractive spots in the city.

Hollenbeck Park

Hollenbeck Park is the gift of Mrs. Hollenbeck and Hon. William H. Workman. Mrs. Hollenbeck gave eight acres of the land and Mr. Workman gave sixteen. It is a favorite resort for picnic parties and is the only park of any size east of the river.

Exposition Park

Exposition Park is a part of the Pueblo lands granted to Los Angeles by the Diputacion or Departmental Assembly of California in 1834, when the Pueblo's area was extended to sixteen square leagues. No survey of these lands was made during Mexican domination.

In 1853 Henry Hancock was given a contract to survey thirty-seven thousand acres of these lands lying south of Pico street and west of the old Pueblo limits and divide them into thirty-five-acre lots. The United States claims commission in 1855 rejected the city's claim to all lands lying beyond the original pueblo lines. The lands outside became government land and the government survey was extended over them. The streets beginning with Washington and running parallel with that street in the annexed area were named for the presidents. Adams, Jefferson, Madison, Monroe, John Quincy Adams and Jackson exhausted the territory and Old Hickory's street collided with the boundaries of the rancho Los Cuervos. When this land became government land it was bought up by settlers. The original

418

Agricultural Park is the North West quarter of Section 7, Township 2, Range 13, San Bernardino Meridian. In 1872 James Thompson sold it to a syndicate, the purchase price being $6,000. July 3, 1872, this syndicate deeded the land to a corporation known as the Southern District Agricultural Society.

The intention of the members of this society was to conduct a fair on the plan that fairs were then conducted in the eastern states — the exhibition of prize pigs, poultry, cattle, sheep and other farm products — the show enlivened by an occasional mildly conducted horse race. The times were not auspicious for the venture. The days when a cattle baron could bet a thousand head of cattle on the speed of a favorite mustang were long past. The barons had neither cattle nor coin to bet and the newcomers, who had acquired their lands, were but little better off financially.

The Fairs did not pay and the Park fell into disrepute. There was an attempt at one time to convert it into a corida de toros for bull fighting. The Los Angeles Journal of October, 1879, describes one of these exhibitions:

"The bull was lassoed and thrown and his horns sawed off so close to his head that they bled. When he regained his feet he made it lively for the toreadors, knocked one down and very nearly trampled the life out of him; his other tormentors took to the top of the fence. This bull had too much fight in him. He was turned out and two milder ones run in. They were more interested in fighting the flies than the toreadors. This was the last attempt to revive bull fighting, the national amusement of Spain and Mexico, in Los Angeles."

The incorporators of the society were unable to pay the interest on the mortgage or the principal when it came due. It was foreclosed in 1879 and the property sold July, 1880, on a writ of execution for $9,190 — the interest and cost of foreclosure having nearly doubled the original debt. The ruling rate of interest at that time was fifteen per cent per annum.

May 20, 1880, the Sixth District Agricultural Association was formed and a Board of Directors appointed by the governor of the state, W. E. Hollenbeck was made president of the Board and William Niles secretary. The Board of Directors and a number of public-spirited citizens combined to redeem the property and convert it into fair grounds. They laid off a portion of it on the east, south and west fronts in building lots. One hundred and thirty of these were sold at $100 each and sufficient funds were received from the sale to pay off the indebtedness. The deed was made to the Board of Directors of the Sixth District Agricultural Association, "to hold in one piece or divide as they may elect the property known as Agricultural Park."

William Niles, the secretary, prepared the deed to transfer the property to the Sixth District Agricultural Association. He inserted a clause in it providing that it should be used for a period of twenty-five years for Agricultural Expositions or Fairs and after that it was to revert to the stockholders, of which there were about one hundred. This action of Niles was disclaimed by all the stockholders except Niles, his brother and Fairchild.

In 1883 action was begun in the superior court to set aside this deed, all the grantees except the above named three being plaintiffs. Judgment was rendered in favor of the plaintiffs.

In 1895 new complications arose in the legal status of the Park. John Lynch was speaker of the Assembly. He secured the enactment of a law providing that fair grounds could be managed by a board of directors elected by the stockholders of the grounds. This virtually took the management of agricultural expositions out of state control. The capital stock of the new association, which was named Agricultural District Number Six, was divided into one hundred and thirty shares of $100 each and transfer of the property made to the new association.

Litigation and the change of owners and managers had a demoralizing influence on the Park and it had again lost its character and fallen into disreputable habits. The grounds were leased to "Col." I. D. Black and were devoted to horse racing, rabbit coursing and various gambling games. Jack rabbits were trapped and kept in cages. On Sundays these were turned loose with a pack of hounds after them and a pack of boys and men after the hounds. The yelping of the hounds and the yelling of the boys made Sunday a day of horror to the neighborhood.

Hon. William M. Bowen, a prominent lawyer living in that section of the city, was teaching a class of boys in the Sunday School of the University Methodist Church. In the spring of 1899 he noted a falling off in the attendance of his class. Examining into the cause he found it was due to the orgies in Agricultural Park. He set himself the herculean task of cleaning the Park of its undesirable tenants. The Park at that time was beyond the city limits, and the city ordinances could not be enforced against the transgressors. An attempt had been made in 1896 to annex it to the city, but the sporting element voted it down. In June, 1899, a second election was held, and although bitterly fought by the race track crowd, the district in which the Park was located was annexed.

Mr. Bowen was elected to the council and was successful in securing the abatement of the objectionable amusements at the Park. To prevent it from retrograding into disreputable habits he set to work to raise money to purchase it for a city park. When about $25,000 had been subscribed he received a hint from the late J. S. Slauson that it might be well to examine into the title and find out who were the real owners.

An investigation of the title led to litigation, which carried to the supreme court, resulted in that court deciding the act of 1895 unconstitutional and void and restoring the Park to the state and its control passed to the reorganized Board of Directors of the Sixth District Agricultural Association.

The property having come to the state with a clear title, the question arose what can be done with it. A plan was evolved to erect a Museum and Exposition building. The state leased the property jointly to the city and county for park and exposition purposes for fifty years. The county supervisors agreed to expend $150,000 on the erection of a Museum of History, Science and Art, the city $100,000 on beautifying the grounds and the state to appropriate $250,000 towards the Exposition buildings. It has also appropriated a similar amount for an armory.

The first movement towards the erection of buildings in the Park was made in January, 1910, by the Historical Society of Southern California. The president. Dr. George F. Bovard, and the secretary, J. M. Guinn, met with William M. Bowen in Dr. Bovard's office. Mr. Bowen presented a rough sketch of the proposed Museum building.

It was decided to invite the Southern California Academy of Science, the Fine Arts League and the southern branch of the Cooper Ornithological Society to unite with the Historical Society to interview the Board of Supervisors and ask that Board to appropriate funds sufficient to build and furnish a building for the collections of these societies. The secretary of the Historical Society, J. M. Guinn. was instructed to communicate with the officers of these societies and to ask them to assist in securing an appropriation.

February 14, 1910, Dr. George F. Bovard and J. M. Guinn, who had been elected on the Board of Governors of the proposed Museum Building, William M. Bowen and representatives of the Academy of Science and of the Art League met with the Board of Supervisors. The Supervisors assured the representatives of the different societies that money sufficient to build and fit up a suitable building would be appropriated.

William M. Bowen presented the outline of a plan for the government of the building. "The building and the exhibits in it will be under the management of a Board of Governors apportioned as follows: Two from the Historical Society; two from the Academy of Science; two from the Fine Arts League; one from the Cooper Ornithological Society; one at large and the Chairman of the Board of Supervisors." The plan was adopted. The following-named persons constituted the board: At large, William M. Bowen; Historical Society, Dr. George F. Bovard and J. M. Guinn; Academy of Science, Dr. A. Davidson and William A. Spalding; The Fine Arts League, Mrs. William H. Housh and T. E. Gibbon; Cooper Ornithological Society, Howard Robertson; Board of Supervisors, the chairman, C. J. Nellis. William M. Bowen was elected president and Howard Robertson secretary of the Board of Governors.

Monday, July 11, 1910, the following-named members of the Board of Governors of the Museum of History, Science and Art assembled at Agricultural Park to break ground for the erection of a building: William M. Bowen, president of the Board of Governors; C. J. Nellis, chairman of the Board of Supervisors; J. M. Guinn, secretary of the Historical Society of Southern California; W. A. Spalding of the Southern California Academy of Science; Howard Robertson of the Cooper Ornithological Society, and Mrs. W. H. Housh, president of the Fine Arts League.

The corner stones of the Museum of History, Science and Art, and also of the Exposition Building were laid by the Masonic fraternity, December 17, 1910. At the time of laying the corner stones of the Museum and Exposition Building Miss Mary S. Bowen, daughter of William M. Bowen, christened the grounds Exposition Park, using water brought from the head of Owens River Aqueduct.

Sunset Park

Sunset Park, containing ten acres, was donated to the city by Mrs. Shatto. It is located in an aristocratic district and although small in area is one of the most valuable of our parks from a financial standard, and is a very attractive resort.

Griffith Park

Griffith Park, containing 3,015 acres and claimed to be the largest public park in the world, was donated to the city by Col. Griffith J. Griffith. At the time it was donated it was outside of the city, but by the annexation of East Hollywood and Ivanhoe, February 27, 1910, the limits of the city were extended to include it.

The menagerie has been moved from Eastlake Park to Griffith Park. Mount Hollywood, in the park, is the most elevated land within the city. Its elevation is 1,647 feet.

South Park

South Park was bought by the city. It was purchased in 1898 by the issue of bonds voted that year. The amount of the bonds was $10,000.

The area of the park is eighteen and one-half acres. Its money value is estimated at $175,000.

Sycamore Grove

Sycamore Grove was purchased by the city for a park. In Pueblo days before Los Angeles owned a park it was a favorite place for holding picnics. The Arroyo Seco in 1914 cut away several acres of its area. It contains twenty acres.

There are a number of small parks in the city which have but little history. Several of these are less than an acre in area. The total acreage of the city parks is 3,983 acres.

Playgrounds

The city maintains a system of playgrounds. There are eight of these, varying in size from the sixty one hundredths of an acre to forty-three acres. They are as follows: Violet, Echo, Recreation, Slauson, Hazard, Downey, Exposition, Solano. In addition a summer camp and a bath house are maintained. The total acreage of all the playgrounds is 69.70 acres. The value of the land is estimated at $175,000; the improvements, buildings, fences, etc., at $77,000; the equipment $29,767. The total monetary value of the playground property of the city is estimated by the Playground Commission at $282,465. The appropriation made by the City Council for the maintenance of the playgrounds amounts to about $60,000 per year.

CHAPTER LI. EXPANSION OF THE CITY BY ANNEXATION AND CONSOLIDATION

For more than a century after Governor Felipe de Neve founded the little Pueblo of Los Angeles, with but one slight addition its boundaries remained the same, that is "one league (Spanish) in the direction of each wind measured from the plaza center." Its area reduced to our measurement was 27.7 square miles.

The Department Assembly or Diputacion with a desire to expand the limits of the prospective city and capital, in 1834, gave it an area of sixteen square leagues or "two leagues measured in the direction of each of the four winds." This gave the pueblo a domain of 111.1 square miles, an expansion that after a dozen enlargements by annexation and consolidation it has not yet reached.

This attempt at enlargement met with obstacles. The pueblo limits extended on the north collided with the San Rafael rancho and on the northeast with the Rosa de Castilla, one of the ranchos of the Mission San Gabriel.

On the east it extended to the rancho Laguna, on the west to the La Brea and Cienega and on the south to the Los Cuervos, but the distances from the plaza to the rancho lines were not in all cases two leagues toward each wind from the plaza center.

At the time of the conquest the municipality was holding on to its magnificent domain. The city was ten miles across from east to west and the same from north to south. It was then the largest city in area in America.

In 1853 Henry Hancock was employed by the city council to subdivide over thirty-seven thousand acres lying south of Pico street and extending two miles west by two and a half south, and as far east as the Los Angeles river into thirty-five acre lots. This was outside or beyond the pueblo area of four square leagues. He also made a survey of the four square leagues within the city limits measuring a league each way from the center of the plaza. All the lands beyond the old pueblo grants and the old survey in the city were divided into thirty-five acre lots. This is known as the Hancock survey.

When the United States claims commission began its arduous labors of confirming or rejecting Spanish and Mexican grants, the city council employed an attorney to defend its claim to its expanded area. The attorney was a politician with a pull and supposed to have influence with the political party in power. He pulled down the greater part of his munificent fee and the city lost its land. For some time after the adoption of its first charter the city had two boundaries on the south, the pueblo boundary and the charter boundary. The latter was confirmed to it in 1869 and added one and one-tenth square miles to its area, a pitiful compensation for years of litigation.

In 1875, after many delays, a United States patent signed by Gen. U. S. Grant, when he was president, was granted to the mayor and council. When Los Angeles celebrated its centennial September 4, 1881, it had increased in area just seven hundred twenty acres over its dimensions on that day one hundred years before when good Gov. Filepe de Neve planted his little colony of pobladores around the old plaza, which long ago was abandoned, and across its boundaries today whiz the automobile and electric car.

At the beginning of the great real-estate boom of 1887 population in a few places had crossed the city boundaries and planted itself beyond on town lots, but by far the greater part of the land bordering on the city outside was h.eld in small farms. What was known as Vernon, a body of land lying south of Jefferson street and extending southerly to Slauson avenue, was devoted to fruit raising — oranges, apples, peaches, pears and grapes.

During the boom a few tracts of land — small farms — lying beyond the city limits were subdivided and put on the market in town lots. With the subsidence of the boom subdivision ceased and the value of lots decreased. Some of the subdivided tracts were returned to acreage.

It was not until well along in the second decade of its second century that the city began its expansion by annexation. The first addition to the city was the annexation of Highland Park, a tract of land adjoining to and lying northeast of the city. By this annexation the area of the city was increased nine hundred and four acres. This addition was acquired by an election held in the city and the district seeking annexation, October 13, 1895. At the same election an attempt was made to take into the city Vernon, a district known as Harmony, lying south of the city and a portion of the University lying west of the city.

It was defeated by a faction fight and the men afraid of taxes. Another election was held April 2, 1896. The disaffected district was left out and the district lying along the south and western borders and an extensive tract extending along the western side of the city well up to the northern line were taken in. This was the largest annexation that had been attempted. It contained 6,517 acres — over ten square miles. The two tracts had been connected by a shoestring strip of one hundred feet wide to make them contiguous territory.

June 12, 1899, Garvanza, containing four hundred and forty acres, and University (that had refused to come in at a former election) on the same day united their destinies with the city. These two increased the city's area 1,576 acres.

With the ending of the century the city rested from its absorption of additional territory. All that was in any way compactly settled had been annexed and there was no demand from the owners of farm land to have it subjected to city taxes. The closing years of the century had been a period of financial depression. The free silver craze had demoralized finances. The Spanish war had added to the depression and two dry years in succession had reduced the farmers to the verge of bankruptcy.

With the beginning of the new century light began to break through the financial gloom that had darkened the closing years of the last. The city had grown slowly during the decade just ended. Money was plentiful and rates of interest low, but the old-time residents' experience with a real estate boom had made them cautious about venturing on new projects. It was the newcomers who began to invest. Property values advanced. Those who had been carrying mortgages since the booming days of 1887 unloaded their encumbered holdings at what they considered a good figure and were happy to be out of debt.

But when they cast about for an investment on which they could make a good turn they discovered that property values were advancing while their bank accounts had remained stationary. Then they were not happy. Great projects were being agitated. The Owens river aqueduct would be built, and that would make Los

Angeles a great manufacturing city. The Panama canal was an assured fact, and that would make Los Angeles the great seaport city of the south. The city of San Pedro controlled the outer harbor, and the city of Wilmington the inner harbor. Corporate interests entrenched by years of undisputed domination held possession of a large part of the water front of both harbors, and were scheming to get more.

The two towns were not financially able to develop the harbor to accommodate the shipping that would come when the Panama canal was completed.

The problem to be solved was how can Los Angeles get control of the harbor? It might extend its limits to those of the sea coast towns, but that would not give it control of their harbors. The only feasible plan was the consolidation of the three cities into a Greater Los Angeles, but this was barred by the fact that their territory was not contiguous to Los Angeles city. The city attorney finally solved the puzzling problem. On his advice the council called an election, and on the 26th of December, 1906, the famous shoestring strip tied Los Angeles to Wilmington and San Pedro.

The "shoestring" was a strip of land half a mile wide starting from the southern limits of the city, which were shoved down about four miles, and running in a straight line south to Gardena, where it made a right angled turn to the west of about a mile and then continued southerly to intersect the westerly lines of the sea coast cities.

The harbor cities were not pleased at the prospect of being absorbed by the inland city. The corporate interests were hostile to the union. The "shoestring" was loose. It had failed to tie the cities together. It required an enabling act to legalize consolidation, and the adverse interest could not agree upon a method. The first bill presented to the legislature of 1907 was defeated. At the session of 1909 a law was enacted which was satisfactory.

After the passage of the consolidation act a campaign of education was begun — for there were still doubters in the cities by the seaside — unbelievers who had no faith in the promises of the campaign orators who were sent to enlighten them. Opposition in the harbor cities diminished as the campaign progressed. August 4, 1909, an election was held in Wilmington. By an affirmative vote of 107 to 61 negatives, Wilmington became a part of Greater Los Angeles. On August 12th San Pedro voted on the question. The vote stood 726 for and 227 against. In Los Angeles there was scarcely any opposition.

On the 28th of August the papers legalizing consolidation were filed with the secretary of state at the capitol. By the shoestring annexation the city gained in area 11,931 acres, or 18.64 square miles. By the Wilmington consolidation 6,358 acres, equal to 9.93 square miles. San Pedro added 2,948 acres, or 4.61 square miles, to the city's area, and Los Angeles became a seaport city, or perhaps to state it more accurately, a city with a seaport.

With the approaching completion of the Owens river aqueduct a mania for annexation seemed to seize the people living in districts contiguous to Los Angeles city. The Colegrove district was the first to apply. It lay west of the western addition annexed in 1906, and extended northward beyond the northern limits of the old city. The election was held October 19, 1909. The district came in practically with no opposition from either the ins or the outs. This annexation added 5,570 acres, or 8.72 square miles, to Greater Los Angeles.

The next to apply for admission into the growing city was the city of Hollywood. It came in by consolidation at an election held January 24, 1910. The vote in Hollywood stood 409 for consolidation and 18 against. In Los Angeles 6,224 for and 373 against. Hollywood added 2,848 acres, or 4.45 square miles, to the city's area.

Following Hollywood came East Hollywood, Ivanhoe and a strip of country east of the Los Angeles city limits extending to the Tropico line. Most of this was sparsely settled, but the people had become so accustomed to annexing territory that there was no opposition from the ins. The election was held February 18, 1910. The territory brought within the city limits by this annexation was 7,112 acres, or 11.11 square miles. Included in this, however, was Griffith Park, a body of land containing 3,015 acres. This park was donated to the city by Col. Griffith J. Griffith, but lying some distance beyond the corporate limits, the city had made but little use of it. As an integral part of the city it became a valuable adjunct to our pleasure resorts.

In six months the city's area had been increased by annexation and consolidation nearly forty square miles. Then there came a lull in the annexation mania. Two years passed before any more territory was added. An attempt had been made in the fall of 1911 by what was known as the Arroyo Seco district to unite with the city. A portion of this lay west of Highland Park and Garvanza and a part east extending down the Arroyo Seco and along the eastern line of the old city. The annexation scheme was defeated by certain commuters who preferred to govern themselves. Another election was called February 9, 1912. The recalcitrant districts, Bairdstown and Belvedere, were left out and the Arroyo Seco district was taken into the city. The area annexed was 4,416 acres, or 6.9 square miles. The city by annexation and consolidation had increased its area to 107.62 square miles, a fraction less than it claimed at the time of the conquest.

At an election held May 4, 1915, 168 square miles of the San Fernando valley were annexed and four square miles of the Palms district. Through all the changes by annexation and consolidation the eastern boundary line has remained unchanged. It is where Governor Felipe de Neve would have placed it on that September morn in the year of our Lord 1781 — one league toward the east wind from the plaza where his little band of pobladores were building their tule huts.

By the various annexations and consolidations that have added to its area, Los Angeles has lost the symmetry of form it possessed in its pueblo days. With its panhandle extension to the northeast, the bulging boundary line to the west, the half mile wide by twelve miles long shoestring strip to the south that ties it to the seaside cities that have lost their individuality there is no geometric term that will describe its shape. There is no living thing with which it can be compared. The main portion of the city is approximately eight miles long north and south. There are hardly two points in its boundary lines where it is the same length and breadth. Its extreme length north and south is about thirty-two miles, its extreme width east and west is eleven miles.

The additions which followed each other rapidly in 1909 and 1910, just preceding the taking of the federal census, increased the population of the city 13,000 and added to its wealth $32,000,000. Only one foreign city — London — exceeds it in area. There are five American cities. New York, Chicago, Philadelphia,

426

New Orleans and Rochester, that include within their boundaries more square miles than Los Angeles.

While the expansion of the city's area increased its physical size among the great cities of the continent, it also added to its municipal expenses. The greatest increase was in the school department. Annexation brought in a number of antiquated school houses in various stages of dilapidation. No sooner were they within the city's limits than their patrons demanded all the modern conveniences and the teachers demanded the increased salaries paid to city teachers. All of the union high schools annexed brought with them a number of district schools that although outside of the city limits were entitled to and received the same privileges accorded to the schools within the city's boundaries.

While the city's area was increased to a little over one hundred square miles, the area of the Los Angeles City School District was enlarged to over two hundred miles. The expense of the police department was greatly increased, and also that of the street department. That department took in long stretches of country road.

The enlargement of the city was made the pretext for the formation of a new charter. A board of fifteen freeholders was elected in April, 1912, to form a new charter. After months of labor a code of basic laws was evolved by the board and submitted to the vote of the people at a special election held in January, 1913. By a vote of more than two to one against the charter the voters put the stamp of condemnation on the document. After its defeat a convocation of socialists and would-be social reformers got together and formulated a number of amendments to the existing charter.

The chief object of the amendments was to legislate out of office the city officers elected in December, 1911, and to fill their places with civic reformers. Most of the amendments carried, but one of them, minority representation, which was to affect civic regeneration, was badly beaten. By the adoption of these amendments and their approval by the legislature the time of holding the election was changed from December to June, the term of office was made two years instead of four and the salaries of all the city officers except those of the Board of Education increased. Nothing was gained by the people through the change.

CHAPTER LII. GROWTH AND DEVELOPMENT OF THE CITY BY DECADES

American cities grow erratically. Even the staid eastern cities have their booms — periods when they seem to take on the exuberance of youth and make for a limited time an unprecedented growth. We are accustomed to regard staid old Philadelphia as an example of slowness and to twit her people on their dilatory methods and antiquated customs, and yet Philadelphia in her history can show the most remarkable decade of increase in population of any city in the United States. In the decade between 1850 and 1860 its population grew from 131,000 to 580,000— an increase of over four hundred per cent in ten years. The Pacific coast cities for several decades have made the most rapid growth of any in the United States. Some of them have trebled in size between federal censuses. Los Angeles in its youth was probably one of the slowest, most unprogressive towns on the continent. The ten heads of families who built their tule huts around the old plaza north of the Church of the Angeles had no ambition to found a city. They planted their little fields, tended their herds of cattle and manadas of horses — lived out their uneventful lives, died, and are forgotten. No forefathers' day keeps alive their memories. No monument marks the last resting place of any one of them.

The little pueblo grew in a leisurely way. There were no booms in its early history. Houses were not built until there was a crying need for them and subdivisions were unknown. In the four decades that the Pueblo of Los Angeles was under Spanish domination its population increased from 44 to 650. The only public improvements made by the community during that time were the zanja madre or mother ditch, the capilla or chapel and the guard house. The Church of Our Lady of the Angels was begun in the last decade of the Spanish era. but was not completed until 1822, when California had passed from under the rule of Spain.

The awakening of the pueblo from its succession of Rip Van Winkle sleeps came with the fall of the missions. The secularization of these establishments returned to the public domain vast areas of fertile lands. Grants of these were made to settlers who had the means to stock them and cattle raising became the leading industry. This brought business to the town and it prospered and increased in population. Many of the richer rancheros had town houses where their families resided a portion of the year on account of the social advantages that urban life afforded.

In the decade between 1830 and 1840 Los Angeles made the greatest gain in population of any decade during Spanish and Mexican rule. Its population increased from 770 to 1250. In 1835, by a decree of the Mexican congress, it was made the capital of the territory and raised to the dignity of a ciudad or city. The revolutions during the decade and the capital war were drawbacks to its property, but the loss of life in the battles fought did not materially decrease its population.

The decade between 1840 and 1850 was a period of wars and rumors of wars and of war in reality. First came the capture of Monterey, October 19, 1842, by Commodore Ap Catesby Jones on the supposition that war had been declared between Mexico and the United States. Next was the overthrow of Governor

Micheltorena by Pico and Castro at the bloodless battle of Cahuenga. Pico became governor and Los Angeles the capital of the Californias. Then followed the quarrel between Pico and Castro and the marshaling of their respective armies to suppress each other. The capture of Montrey by Commodore Sloat and eventually the conquest of the territory by the Americans put an end to internicene wars between native California factions.

The pueblo's first boom under American rule came after the discovery of gold in 1848. The first effect of Marshall's discovery was to depopulate it of its able-bodied men. Many of these returned after a brief experience in the mines. They had discovered that it was easier to get gold by selling cattle and fruits to the miners than by delving among the rock or burrowing into the earth for it. The crying need of that time was houses. Houses ready framed were shipped from New York, Boston and Liverpool around the Horn and for many years supplied the need for lodging. Ord's survey, the first subdivision of the pueblo or public lands, was made in 1849. The standing price of Ord's survey lots on Main, Spring, Fort (Broadway) and Hill streets between First and Eighth was $50 for a lot 120 feet front by 165 feet in depth. This was quite a rise in value over the price of lots before the conquest. The ruling rate then was twenty-five cents per vara, about eight cents per front foot. In the decade between 1840 and 1850 the population of the city increased from 1250 to 1610. The population after the conquest was largely migratory and transitory. The tourists of that time who had come "the plains across" were not looking for climate or soil. They had no use for any soil not mixed with gold dust, so they did not stop in the metropolis of the new country.

The first years of the eighth decade (1850 to 1860) were remarkable for the extraordinary prosperity prevailing throughout Southern California. Every food product of the soil commanded a high price and a ready market. In 1856 and 1857 there was a gold rush to the Kern river mines. Much of the travel and most of the supplies passed through Los Angeles. The placer mines of the San Gabriel river and of Santa Anita creek added a new characteristic to the productions of the hitherto cow country and afforded a temporary relief to the "hard times" that were settling down on the metropolis of the cattle industry.

The year 1858 was remarkable for the number of new buildings erected. The estimate for that year is $180,000. A few of these remain. The Arcadia block on the corner of Arcadia and Los Angeles streets was built that year by Don Abel Stearns and named for his wife. Donna Arcadia. It was reported to have cost $80,000 and was regarded as the finest business block south of San Francisco. On the second floor was a hall where balls and other social functions were held. It continued to be the social assemblage room of the city down to 1885. Another building erected in 1858 and 1859 is the two-story portion of the Temple Block. The upper floor was divided into office rooms and mostly occupied by attorneys. Some of the great legal lights of the bench and bar of the state have occupied apartments in this dingy building. Devoid of architectural beauty in its youth, old age has not improved its appearance. In 1911 the city council bought it and the three-story addition to it built in 1871 on the installment plan for a city hall, agreeing to pay half a million dollars for it; the property holders of the north end of the city contributing about one-third of the purchase price.

The building designed for a market house and theater which occupied the present site of the Bullard Block was erected by Juan Temple in 1858. It was sold in 1868 to the county for a court house and used for that purpose until 1891. The county disposed of it by auction. It was sold for $100,000, which was an increase of about four hundred per cent on the original purchase price. The population of the city at the beginning of its ninth decade (1860) was 4,400, a gain in ten years of 2,790 — the largest gain in its history so far.

The decade between 1860 and 1870 was marked by disasters. At the beginning of the decade the premonitions of a war between the North and the South divided the population into antagonistic factions. There was no unanimity of action between them and no civic pride for the growth and development of the city. This condition lasted throughout the war and was continued by some of the most belligerent after its close, whose chief weapon of warfare during hostilities was that with which Samson is alleged to have slain the Philistines.

The greatest flood ever known in California occurred in the winter of 1861-62. Great damage was done by the overflow of the rivers. This was followed by the other climatic extreme, the greatest drouth ever known in the history of the state. The drouth of 1863-64 put an end to the cattle industry and financially ruined the cattle kings. The financial gloom that darkened the city and county during the decade began to lift a little near its close. This was due to immigration, attracted by cheap lands. These were the subdivisions of the great ranchos lost to their former owners on foreclosure of mortgages and put on sale by their new owners at low figures. The principal enterprise begun and completed during the decade was the building of the Los Angeles and San Pedro Railroad to Wilmington. It was completed to Wilmington October 26, 1869. The city gave $75,000 to its construction and the county $150,000. This was the first railroad built in Southern California. Another enterprise that must be credited to this decade was the completion of the telegraph to Los Angeles. The population of Los Angeles city in 1860 was 4,400; in 1870, 5,614, a gain of 1,214. This gain was made in the closing years of the decade. The assessed value of the city property in 1860 was $1,425,648; in 1870 $2,108,061, a gain of only $682,413 in ten years.

The decade between 1870 and 1880 began auspiciously. The first transcontinental railroad had been completed to San Francisco in 1869. This brought immigrants to the central part of the state and some of them drifted down into the southern counties and were pleased with the country. There was considerable building in the city. The Pico House, the most ambitious hotel in Southern California, was erected in 1871 on the site of the historic Carrillo house, the point from which Ord took his compass course when he made his plan of Los Angeles in 1849. The northern part of the Temple block was built in the same year and the Temple and Workman bank opened in it the next year.

The beginning of the decade was marked by great activity in railroad building and railroad projecting. The act authorizing what was generally known as the Texas Pacific Railroad was passed March 3, 1871. San Diego was to be its western terminus. There was great rejoicing in San Diego. Her people saw, or thought they did, a brilliant future for their city. It would become the great seaport city of the south. The trade of the Occident and the Orient would come to it. Los Angeles would become a suburb of the City of Bay and Climate. A branch road was

430

projected to Los Angeles to bring its trade to San Diego. In 1872 a railroad war or contest aroused the people of the Southern counties. The Southern Pacific company was building a road up the San Joaquin valley. Its eastern connection was uncertain. It might connect with the thirty-second parallel road or it might become a part of the Texas Pacific. To bring it via Los Angeles an offer was made to the company to vote bonds to the amount of five per cent of the taxable property of the county. In consideration of this subsidy the company was to build twenty-five miles north from Los Angeles city and twenty-five east. The Texas Pacific entered the contest with an offer to build sixty miles of its road in the county to connect Los Angeles with San Diego. The Southern Pacific Company countered this with an offer to build a branch to Anaheim and to take Los Angeles and San Pedro road as part of the bond issue. At the election held November 5, 1872, the Southern Pacific won.

The parts of the road were all united September 6, 1876, and Los Angeles had transcontinental connection with the east but by a roundabout route. The Texas Pacific was wrecked by that financial cyclone known as "Black Friday in Wall Street."

The Los Angeles and Independence Railroad was another road of this era. It was intended to connect the mining regions in the Owens river country with tide water at Santa Monica. It was completed to Los Angeles and was operated for a few years when it was purchased by the Southern Pacific Company and became part of that system.

The decade between 1870 and 1880 was a colony founding era. Riverside was the first of the colonies founded. The San Gabriel Orange Grove Association which eventuated in Pasadena came next. The American Colony which founded Long Beach came near the end of the decade.

A financial crisis in 1875 closed nearly all the banks in the state for a time. Some of them never reopened. Among these was the Temple and Workman bank of Los Angeles. It carried down with it the fortune of many an unfortunate who had trusted to the good name of the bankers, who were supposed to control its destinies but who had unwisely trusted its management to subordinates. The drouth of 1877 wrought havoc with the sheep industry that had taken the place of the cattle industry killed by the drouth of 1863-64. Of improvements, the Baker block, the most imposing structure hitherto erected in the city, was completed in 1878 on the site of the Palacio de Don Abel as Abel Stearns' residence was called. The federal census of 1880 gave the city's population 11,183, an increase of 5,569 in ten years — a gain of almost one hundred per cent. The assessed valuation of the property in the city in 1870 was $2,108,061; in 1880 it was $6,871,913. Considering the financial reverses that had occurred during the decade this was a good showing.

At the beginning of her tenth decade (1880 to 1890) Los Angeles was still clinging to many of her old customs and methods of living and doing business. The streets were unpaved and in the rainy season almost impassable. The sidewalks were of boards or gravel. The street cars were still propelled by horses or mules, car fare ten cents a ride. There was no free mail delivery. The retail stores kept open from seven in the morning to ten at night and to twelve on Saturday night. The smallest coin in circulation was the "bit," ten cents. The fire alarm was three shots

431

in quick succession and three more if the engine did not arrive. The business streets were lighted with gas, but the greater part of the residence portion was shrouded in darkness.

The telephone was unknown and electricity unused for light or power. All transcontinental railroad travel and traffic came via San Francisco. The Pico House was the aristocratic hotel of the city, the St. Charles the next in order. The Baker block was the center of the fashionable retail trade and best office building in the city. The decade was one of transitions — the passing of the old and the ushering in of the new. The completion of the Southern Pacific Railroad to its eastern connection brought immigrants direct to Southern California. In December, 1881, the city was lighted by electricity. Seven masts one hundred and fifty feet high were erected at different points and ' the light diffused from the globes was supposed to be sufficient to light the city.

The Nadeau, the first business building of any size south of First street, was built in 1882. It towered above its surroundings. The only two-story building in the block was the brick school house on the northwest corner of Spring and Second streets. The tourist had only to a very limited extent found Los Angeles. The Nadeau was too large to be devoted entirely to hotel purposes and a number of the rooms were rented for offices. The Y. M. C. A. began business in it and a justice's court was held in it. The cause that effected the most rapid transition from the old to the new was the real estate boom of 1886 and 1887 fully described in Chapter XXXVIII of this volume.

The completion of the Santa Fe Railroad system, competition between the railroads, low fares and a plethora of money in the middle west poured in an army of speculators. A speculative mania prevailed. New towns were created and the older cities and towns expanded into the surrounding country. The horse car was superseded by the cable car and the first attempt was made to establish an electric line, but it was not a success.

A building boom accompanied the real estate speculations. The business district spread over into Broadway and its movement southward on Main and Spring streets was accelerated. The population of the city increased from 11,183 to 50,395, a growth unprecedented by any other city on the coast. Property values increased from $6,871,913 to $46,997,160— an accumulation of wealth as unparalleled as its increase in population.

The closing decade of the century (1890 to 1900) was a period of business depression and financial gloom. The reaction had come from the extravagances of the previous decade. "Hard times" prevailed not only in Los Angeles, but throughout the United States. The people had been living beyond their incomes and mortgaging the future for the pleasure of the present.

A financial panic in 1893 closed every bank in the city except two; all except two in time resumed business. Money was almost immune from borrowers. The millionaires of the boom who had loaded themselves with unproductive realty saw the values of their possessions shrivel day by day until there was nothing on which to plaster a mortgage. The depression of the decade was further increased by two successive dry years, 1897 and 1898. The rainfall was respectively 7.18 and 5.53 inches. Two drouth years drove the farmers on the dry lands to the verge of bankruptcy. The wail of the free-silver advocates over the demonetization of the white metal and their portents of the financial ills that would come upon the country if their wailings were unheeded deepened the despondency. Notwithstanding the dolor that darkened the decade there was a spirit of optimism and confidence in the city's future that did much to bring about a reaction.

The Spanish war had but little effect on the city. The Seventh California Regiment made up from the southern part of the state contained three companies from the city. It did not leave the state. A battery of light artillery under command of Capt. J. D. Fredericks raised in Los Angeles county did service in the Philippines.

Despite the hard times several important public improvements were made. The court house was completed in 1891. The Los Angeles High School was finished and occupied the same year. An outfall sewer to the ocean was constructed and several of the business streets paved. Electric car lines were substituted for the cable cars. The first cable line had been built up Second street and over Bunker Hill out to Belmont avenue. It was abandoned after a few years of unsatisfactory service. The first electric line extended up Second to Olive, north on Olive to First, thence on First and other streets to Westlake Park.

Oil discoveries were made within the city limits. The oil development extended a line of derricks diagonally across the city from Buena Arista street (now North Broadway) to Westlake Park. While the oil industry helped those who owned property in the district it retarded the development of property adjoining the belt and was a potent factor in accelerating the growth of the city to the southward.

The population of the city increased during the decade from 50,395 to 102,479 and the assessed value of city property from $46,476,713 to $64,915,326.

CHAPTER LIII.
TWENTIETH CENTURY LOS ANGELES

The beginning of the twentieth century found many of the older residents of the city who had speculated in town lots and unproductive acreage still struggling to throw off the incubus of debt that had weighed them down for a decade or more. The financial depression was slowly lifting. Rates of interest had fallen from eight and ten per cent per annum to five and six. Business had drifted but little to the southward in the preceding ten years. Several of the large retail houses remained on North Spring street. The wholesale district extended along Los Angeles street from the Plaza to Second street. All the banks with one exception — the Farmers and Merchants National — were still north of Fourth street.

Although times were improving there was but little speculation in real estate. Remembering the fate of many a promoter who had plunged in the booming days of 1887 those who ventured on subdivisions in 1900 did so with extreme caution. There might be a reaction and they had found that unproductive real estate with a mortgage attachment was about as dangerous as a dynamite bomb with a time fuse. The awakening came largely through new men, some to the manor born and some with eastern capital that they were not afraid to invest. Thus new blood was injected into the sluggish arteries of trade and speculation. New enterprises were inaugurated. Beginning about 1902 and increasing in volume until 1914 the two leading characteristics of the development of Los Angeles were the subdivision of acreage into town lots and the erection of business blocks and residences.

The first sky scraper was built in 1902. It is now known as the Hibernian building and is located on the southeast corner of Fourth and Spring streets. It reached an altitude of fourteen stories. The city council later put a limit on the ambition of builders, restricting them to twelve stories. Previous to the erection of the Hibernian or Braly building as it was called when it was built, the highest building in the city was but seven stories. Property values on the business streets were low. Twenty-five hundred dollars per front foot was paid for the site of the Braly building. This was regarded at that time as a very high price.

The erection of the Pacific Electric building, southeast corner of Main and Sixth streets, in 1902, and the inauguration of a system of interurban electric railways by Henry E. Huntington, connecting the beach and interior towns with their terminal, the Pacific Electric building, accelerated the drift of business to the southward. Among the earlier large buildings erected within the sky scraper area might be named the Herman W. Hellman building and the Angelus Hotel on the northeast and southwest corners respectively of Spring and Fourth streets. These were followed by the Hotel Alexandria, the Story, the Central, the Security and the Hamburger buildings. This last on Eighth and extending through from Broadway to Hill street was the furthest venture south in the earlier stages of the southward migration.

The rapid movement southward alarmed the property holders in the northern portion of the city. The post office had been moved from the government building on the southeast corner of Winston and Main streets to Grand avenue and Seventh street preparatory to erecting a larger building on the old site. When the government officials undertook to purchase additional ground they were blocked by the high prices asked. With the expectation that a new building was to be erected on the old site the post office building was partially demolished and after the attempt to secure more land failed the half demolished building stood for several years a monument to the government's parsimony or to the property holders' greed.

The property holders in the northern part of the city saw or thought they saw an opportunity to check the southern trend of business and possibly recuperate their lost prestige. They raised by subscription $200,000 and bought the historic Downey block at the junction of Temple, Spring and Main streets and donated it to the United States government for the site of a Federal building. The leisurely way in which the general government makes improvements consumed four years from inception to finish of the building. The building was completed and dedicated October 15, 1910. After wandering for sixty years from the Plaza to Seventh street and from Main to Grand avenue, the post office returned to its old mooring. Across the street from its present location in 1849 Col. John O. Mieeler established his wash tub free mail delivery.

In the meantime the business district of the city had been drifting southward with increasing speed. Again the northern property holders assessed themselves to aid the city authorities in securing a new site for a city hall. An eastern expert had planned a scheme for a civic center where all the public buildings, City, County and Federal, would be grouped together. The county was building the Hall of Records — a million and a half dollar building — the Federal building was approaching completion; to carry out the iridescent dream of the eastern expert to create a civic center, the city council bought the site of the Temple block, a flat-iron shaped piece of ground at the junction of Spring and Main streets, agreeing to pay for it half a million dollars on the installment plan, the property holders in that part of the city contributing $175,000. The purchase was made in 1910. Nearly a quarter million dollars of taxpayers' money has been invested in this venture. Five years have passed but no city hall towers on the site.

Among the later large business buildings built may be named the Title Insurance building, the Title Guarantee, the Van Nuys. the San Fernando, the Alexandria Annex, the Union Oil, the New Rosslyn, the Los Angeles Investment, the Merchants National, the Higgins, Washington, Citizens National and Robert Marsh & Co.'s building — corner Ninth and Main, the furthest south that any large office building so far has been erected.

While the business district of the city was moving southward and westward the residence district was expanding from its old center towards all points of the compass. Subdivision after subdivision was thrown onto the market until it seemed as if there would be no land left for farming between the city and the sea, or between the city and the mountains. Investment companies, building associations, home makers, home builders and corporations of various kinds limited and unlimited were organized to furnish lots and houses to the houseless and lotless. The bungalow boom began in the early years of the present century. Houses were sold on the installment plan, the purchaser agreeing to pay $10, $20 or $30 a month according to the amount of his savings from his income. It might take ten years to pay for his home, but hope and the persuasion of the real estate agent buoyed him up to make the venture.

The Los Angeles Investment Company was one of the most extensive and most daring adventurers during the subdivision boom. Starting with a small venture it advanced rapidly in placing lots and houses on the market. Its stock advanced from $1 per share to $4.50. Its managers in their ambitious project for expanding their business and the city at the same time, overreached themselves. They purchased from the Baldwin heirs 3126 acres of the La Cienega rancho, agreeing to pay $6,252,815, about $2,000 per acre. The price was exorbitant; expert real estate dealers valued it at about one-half the purchase price. Over speculation and depression in the real estate market brought a disaster to the company. Its stock went down to about fifty per cent of its par value and the end is not yet.

The prosperity of the city was materially increased by the completion of the Salt Lake Railroad in 1905. This gave Los Angeles its fourth transcontinental railroad. After its completion an exchange of visits was arranged between the Commercial Club of Salt Lake city and the Chamber of Commerce of Los Angeles. These visits were productive of amicable business and social relations between the two cities. Preceding and following for a short time the completion of the Salt Lake Railroad there was near the line of that road in western Nevada a mining boom that took on some of the characteristics of a mining rush in "the days of '49." One of these was the peculiar nomenclature of the mining camps and towns. Goldfield had an attractive sound to the prospector that seemed prophetic of the presence in abundance of the precious metal. Bullfrog and Tidewater were doubtless named by the rule of contraries.

The names helped to disguise the absence of the aqueous fluid in the desert regions in which they were located, while Searchlight and Skidoo might be applied respectively to a doubtful mine or an undesirable miner. Another characteristic similar to "the days of old," "the days of gold" was the rapid growth of the towns. Goldfield, the metropolis of a district, boasted at one time of a floating population of 20,000. Most of this floated away, leaving a residence population of possibly one-fourth of that number.

After the bursting of the boom in 1888-89 the values of real estate were utterly demoralized. It was not what property was worth that fixed the price nor yet what the seller asked, but what will a buyer, if one can be found, give. The reaction was greatest in what is now the most valuable business property. A few examples will show the depreciation that followed the boom of 1887 and also will illustrate the great advance since 1900. A lot adjoining the Mercantile Place property on the east side of Broadway held at $500 a front foot in 1887 was offered in 1893 at $250 a foot and no takers.

The present site of the Consolidated Realty building was bought by the First Congregational church in 1887 for $52,000. After putting a building on it and holding it for eighteen years the church people sold it in 1905 for $75,000. In 1908 it was resold for $350,000 and eight months later the Consolidated Realty Company bought it, paying $450,000. The northeast corner of Eighth and Broadway bought in 1900 for $27,500, in 1906 sold for $300,000, and in 1911 was sold for $400,000. Among the remarkable rises in value the lot on the northeast corner of Spring and Sixth streets is a good illustration. It was bought in 1882 for $2,300, in 1912 it was

436

sold for $1,000.000. The lot on the northwest corner of Spring and Sixth streets, 60x165 feet, was sold in July, 1881, for $1,500, now worth probably half a million dollars. The property known as Mercantile Place, 120 feet front on Spring street and the same on Broadway, between Fifth and Sixth streets, was bought by the Board of Education in May, 1883, for $12,500. It was not considered a bargain; some three months before it had been bought by the seller for $9,000. It is now valued at $1,500,000. H. E. Huntington in 1902 bought the block bounded by Main, Spring , Eleventh and Twelfth streets for $250,000; in 1913 he sold it for $3,000,000; it was subdivided and resold at an advance.

Among the legends of accidental purchases that have made fortunes for the buyer this one passes current. A resident of Spring street in the late '70s owned a cow with a crumpled horn that he was accustomed to stake out to feed on the sites of future skyscrapers. The cow was in the habit of breaking her tether and invading his neighbors' gardens. This caused unpleasantness. So to keep peace in the community he bought the lot on the southeast corner of Broadway and Eighth street, paying $600 for it, and built a corral for the cow. The cow ceased troubling the neighbors and eventually passed into beef steaks, but the lot remained in the family and is worth today probably $400,000, all due to the predatory habits of that cow. Another legend of the days of cheap lots is that of an old pioneer who traded a lot on Broadway near Fourth street to a tailor for a dress suit. As the price of the lot goes up he marks up the price of that ancient suit. It has already reached a quarter million dollars and is still going up.

Among the names of the benefactors who aided the city in the days of her poverty and the era of cheap lots should stand out in bold relief that of Jacob Weixel. In 1875 he donated to the city for a school site two Ord survey lots with a frontage of 240 feet on Grand avenue between Seventh and Eighth streets. Weixel owned a large amount of property in that neighborhood. Adversity overwhelmed the prospective millionaire. He lost all his property and died in poverty. The school department still owns the lots. At the price property across Grand avenue opposite these lots sold for recently Weixel's donation to the city is worth $750,000, but the donor sleeps unwept, unhonored and unsung in a nameless grave.

While the beginning of the oil industry of Los Angeles dates back into the decades of the nineteenth century, it was not until the closing year of the first decade of the present century that the oil gusher came into the history of the industry. While the gusher was the product of other fields, Los Angeles men and Los Angeles capital were largely instrumental in the development of the country where the great gushers were struck.

During the year 1910 a dozen wells that might be classed as gushers were developed in the Sunset-Midway field of Kern county. A history of the performance of some of these gushers will be interesting in the future when the gushers have become a thing of the long past.

The first of these that passed the line of a flowing well into that of a gusher was the Mays well located on Section 20, 21, 22 in the southern portion of the Midway field. It came in March 6, 1910, and began its performance with spouting oil and gas at a terrific rate, drenching the adjoining country with a rain of oil. Then it choked itself and for a week was quiet, when it began again with renewed vigor, wrecked the derrick and blackened the sands for miles around with oil spray. After several months of alternate spouting and resting it settled down to a moderately producing well.

The world champion gusher was the Lakeview, which came in March 14, 1910. It is located on Section 25, 12, 24 in the Sunset-Midway district. It was ushered in with a great rush of gas followed by a flood of oil estimated at 18,000 barrels in twenty-four hours. After twenty-four hours of steady gushing it stopped for a brief space of time. Then a torrent of rocks and sand was shot out of it, demolishing the top of the derrick and sending the drillers scurrying for their lives.

The following extract from a description of the great gusher written by Wallace Morgan is taken from the Los Angeles Times of January 1, 1911:

"Oil rained on everything for miles around as the breeze carried the spray from the gusher. The Union Oil Company's new camp, just built on a near-by hill, was abandoned, and the neat, green cottages were soon a funeral black. Other wells drilling in the neighborhood were left unfinished, fires were put out in all the boiler plants within the radius that the gas from the Lakeview reached. Hundreds of men and teams were rushed to the scene to dig ditches, build dams across gulleys, and scrape reservoirs in the earth to catch and hold the oil. The sand that the well threw out built a mound fifteen or twenty feet high all about the derrick, burying the engine house. Gradually the derrick was torn to pieces by the rushing column of oil, and sections of the inner casing of the well, worn as thin as a knife blade, were hurled out. The question of whether the casing would all be worn out by the cutting of the sand and the well become a great crater in the ground became a very serious one.

"The Union Oil Company's engineers tackled the job of harnessing the great well with faint hope of success. An hour's work in the suffocating gas and drenching rain of oil about the gusher cost S4 or $5 and upwards, and men did not seek the jobs at that price. The first futile device for smothering the well was a great wooden hood made of timbers a foot and more in thickness. But the stream of oil ate its way through the wood and went on playing the biggest and blackest fountain the world ever saw. Every train to Sunset bore sightseers, and a line of guards was placed in a great circle about the well to prevent the possibility of any accidental ignition of the gas.

"Finally after some months of effort, when the well was largely cleared of sand and the upward force of the oil was less, an embankment was built about the gusher with sacks of sand and earth to a height of twenty or thirty feet, thus confining the oil over the mouth of the well and forming a cushion against which the big black geyser could beat. By that time every vestige of the derrick was gone, and the well looked like an inky fountain, playing in an inky pool.

"Meantime, down on the flat a half mile and further away, lakes of oil were accumulating. By September, 5,000,000 barrels of oil had been stored in these makeshift reservoirs. The seepage was great, and the evaporation was greater, and the danger of accidental fire turning the whole into a flood of flame to go further down the valley was the greatest anxiety of all.

"At one time the Lakeview output reached 68,000 barrels per day, twice the capacity of the greatest oil pipe line on the coast. There was no such thing as properly caring for the oil. During the months of September and October the Producers' Transportation Company's pipe line to the coast was placed almost exclusively at the service of Lakeview oil, and pumps and pipe lines installed by the Union were set to work forcing the oil from the temporary reservoirs on the flat to two new reservoirs built in the edge of the hills. These reservoirs, dug in a canyon and protected with earth and concrete dams and artificial waterways cut through the hill above them, will hold 5,000,000 barrels of oil. The well is still flowing 10,000 to 12,000 barrels of oil per day after nine months of steady work, and it seems not unlikely that the total product of the great well may reach 10,000,000 barrels.

"While the Lakeview gusher is abundantly worthy of a place in history as a natural wonder, an engineering problem and a source of wealth that might make Midas envy, its story is not complete without the human interest features that attach to it and to the men who are associated with it. The land on which the gusher is located was taken up as an oil placer mining claim by Julius Fried, J. M. Dunn and Parker Barrett. Fried began life as a cashier of a country bank, became a stock broker and went broke, turned to developing oil lands and drifted to the Sunset field. Dunn was a cowboy in Texas, a bridge-carpenter in Missouri and then a rig builder in the California oil fields. Barrett was successive stock raiser, a carpenter, a fireman, a locomotive engineer, a timber framer in the mines of Shasta county, and finally, like Dunn, a rig builder in the Sunset oil field. All of them together did not have money enough to develop the land they had located, and Fried, with Charles Off, R. D. Wade, E. F. Dunlap and others, formed the Lakeview Oil Company and took a lease from the locators.

"It cost the Lakeview stockholders $70,000 to drill down 1900 feet, and there they found themselves with a dry hole, at the end of their resources. Less than 100 feet deeper was the first pay oil sand, but they did not know it, and the Maricopa flat was only prospective oil land then. Under these circumstances a majority of the stock was sold to the Union Oil Company, and the latter undertook the completion of the well. The first oil sand was reached and cased off, and the drill sent down to explore the deeper strata. The well had been sunk past the 2200 mark with no result, and the directors ordered the drilling stopped and the casing perforated at the upper oil stratum. The order was delayed or the drillers did not obey it promptly, and the drill, going down a few feet farther, uncovered the great gusher sand — uncovered it only, for the well was never sunk more than a few feet into the sand." The Lakeview has continued to gush intermittently up to the present time.

What has been called the "Crime of the century" was committed about one o'clock on the morning of October 1, 1910. The building of the Los Angeles Times was destroyed by a bomb placed in an alleyway and discharged by a clockwork mechanism. The explosion wrecked the building and damaged several adjoining. Fire instantly followed the explosion and swept through the building with incredible speed. Some of the employees escaped onto the roofs of adjoining houses, others by jumping out of windows and others down elevator shafts. Twenty lost their lives either in the building or from injuries in trying to escape from it.

At the time of the destruction of the Times building unsuccessful attempts were made to destroy the residences of Gen. H. G. Otis, president and manager of the Times corporation, and that of F. J. Zeehandelaar, secretary of the Merchants and

Manufacturers Association. The mayor of the city offered a reward of $10,000 for the detection and arrest of the dynamiters. The board of supervisors offered $5,000, and later the legislature offered $10,000. A stick of dynamite found at the Zeehandelaar residence was identified as having been manufactured at Giant, a place on the bay of San Francisco. Early on the morning of December 25, 1910, the Llewellyn Iron Works were dynamited and a portion of the building destroyed.

The stick of dynamite found at Zeehandelaar's residence gave a clew which, followed up by the famous detective William J. Burns, resulted in the arrest, April 23, 1911, in Detroit of J. B. McNamara and Ortie E. McManigal, where they had gone to dynamite structures on which non-union workmen were employed, and of J. J. McNamara, secretary-treasurer of the International Bridge and Structural Iron Workers Association, at the headquarters of the Association in Indianapolis.

The men were hurried across the continent and lodged in the Los Angeles county jail. McManigal made a full confession, implicating his two associates in a number of dynamite plots. The summer was spent in gathering evidence. The trial began October 11, 1911. Clarence Darrow, a Chicago lawyer, was chief counsel for the defense, and District Attorney J. D. Fredericks, and Joseph Ford assistant, conducted the prosecution. Superior Judge Walter Bordwell presided. There were a number of sensational episodes in the case. After eight weeks spent in trying to secure a jury, the trial came to a dramatic ending. A secret service agent in the employ of the defense was detected in an attempt to bribe a prospective juror.

The evidence against the accused was so strong that the lawyers for the defense induced the McNamaras to change their plea of not guilty to guilty in hopes of clemency from the judge. This they did. J. J. McNamara was sentenced to fifteen years' imprisonment in San Quentin for complicity in dynamiting the Llewellyn Iron Works, and J. B. McNamara to life imprisonment in the same prison for the murder of Charles Haggerty, one of the Times employees. McManigal remained in jail for two years or more, when he was released, but his place of concealment was kept secret.

At the close of the first decade of the present century the population of the city was 319,198; about 13,000 of the increase was due to annexation of contiguous property and to consolidation with Hollywood, Wilmington and San Pedro. The estimated population July 1, 1914, was 550.000.

The tabulation of the assessed valuations of the city and county property in Chapter XXXVII brings them down to and including the fiscal year of 1906-07.

The following continues them to and including the fiscal year of 1914-15.

City Valuation.	County Valuation.
1907-08....$267,120.304	1907-08'...$384.051.740
1908-09.... 263,570,272	1908-09.... 407,172,330
1909-10.... 270,801,517	1909-10.... 593,861,497
1910-11.... 332,507,474	1910-11.... 521,400,559
1911-12.... 391,341,212	1911-12.... 607,182,761
1912-13.... 443,362,844	1912-13.... 720.110,668
1913-14.... 481,483,342	1913-14.... 804,046,374
1914-15-... 508,247,113	1914-15.... 849,991,598

The per cent of increase in the assessed valuation of the county is a more correct index of growth than that of the city. The area of the county remains the same, while that of the city has been increased by annexation.

Bank Clearance

The following table gives the Los Angeles bank clearings beginning with 1900 and continuing to and including 1914. It will be noted in this table and in the tabulation of the amount spent in building that there was a marked falling off in business in 1908. In the latter part of that year there was a temporary financial panic. The banks paid their deposits in scrip for several months, reserving their coin and currency against a run should one come. It did not come:

1900 $113,766,378	1908 $ 481,831,177
1901 143.170,307	1909 630,620,123
1902 225,917,730	1910 811.387,487
1903 288,527,582	1911 922,914,526
1904 332,715,240	1912 1,168.941,700
1905 419.953,039	1913 1,211,167.980
1906 549,648,223	1914 1,145,167,110
1907 628,170,919	

Building Permits

The building record of Los Angeles during the present century has kept pace with the rapid advance of real estate values. The value of the permits granted in 1900 was $2,517,060. This was about the yearly average for the preceding six years.

The number of permits granted each year beginning with 1901 and their valuation, and continuing to 1907, is given earlier in this volume.

The following table, beginning with 1907, continues the record to the close of 1914:

Year.	Number.	Valuation.
1907	7.584	$13,275,943
1908	7,373	9,934,298
1909	8,571	13,260,713
1910	10,738	21,684,100
1911	12,408	23,004,185
1912	16,453	31,366,357
1913	16,442	31,641,923
1914	10,108	17,500,000

Record Of The Rainfall

The season's rainfall as reported by the officer in charge of the United States Weather Bureau up to September 1, 1906, is given on page 430 of this volume.

The following table gives it by seasons to September 1, 1914:

441

Seasons.	Inches.
September 1, 1906, to September, 1907	19.25
September 1, 1907, to September. 1908	11.80
September 1, 1908, to September, 1909	19.10
September 1, 1909, to September, 1910	12.67
September 1, 1910, to September, 1911	17.81
September 1, 1911, to September, 1912	11.60
September 1, 1912, to September, 1913	13.42
September 1, 1913, to September, 1914	22.66

The extension of the city over a large area has necessitated a widely extended car service. The facilities for local transportation exceed that of cities with a larger population. The last horse car line ceased operation about the close of the last century. The cable car went out of business a little later, and was succeeded by the electric car. The latest innovation of means for local transportation is the motor coach. These came in July, 1914, and were introduced by a public parade of the coaches. They were of the omnibus build with a deck and a winding stairway to climb up to it. They made regular trips to the beach towns, competing with the cars and slightly reducing the fare. The run of the auto coach was short.

The innovation did not pay. The auto conch was succeeded by another innovation that threatens to stay with us — the "jitney bus." These are automobiles of varying dates of construction and various conditions of dilapidation. The jitneys so far are largely independent ventures, the owners in many cases operating their own conveyances, acting both as conductor and motorman. These conveyances are operated on the densely populated streets at a nickel a ride.

Although the jitneys have been in operation only a few months, they have multiplied to such an extent as to decrease the revenue of some of the street car lines so that part of the cars have been taken off these routes and employees discharged. Another effect of this innovation has been to congest travel on the business streets and endanger life. Unlike most innovations, the jitney originated on the Pacific coast and has traveled eastward, but in what city or town it came to the front first is uncertain, and the origin of the outlandish name is unknown. Whether the "jitney" has come to stay or is only transitory is an unsolved problem at this time.

The public schools of the city have kept pace with the growth of the city. The total enrollment in 1900 was 20,497. Total amount expended on the schools was $451,438. Paid for teachers' salaries, $367,886. The number of teachers employed was 501. There were at that time but five school houses outside of the original city limits. These had been brought into the city by annexation of adjacent territory in 189596-97. There was but one high school in 1900, the Los Angeles High. The Polytechnic High was opened in 1905, the Manual Arts in 1909. By annexation and consolidation in 1909-10-12 the Los Angeles city school district gained a High School in each of the following named towns: San Pedro, Wilmington, Gardena and Hollywood. The enlargement of the area of the district, also, brought in forty district schools. Some of these were outside of the city limits but within the High School districts annexed.

442

The total number of elementary schools in the district is 152. Of these ten are classed as special and ten as intermediate. The total enrollment in all the schools for the school year ending June 30, 1914, was 87,309. The total expenditure for all the schools was $3,931,865. Amount paid for teachers' salaries was $2,941,674. The total number of teachers employed was 2380. The members of the Board of Education at that time were Mrs. R. L. Craig, J. H. Bean, R. E. Blight, H. W. Frank, J. M. Guinn. Joseph Scott and J. J. Steadman; of these Joseph Scott, H. W. Frank and J. M. Guinn served ten consecutive years. The superintendents at that time were: J. H. Francis, superintendent; J. B. Monlux, deputy superintendent; M. C. Bettinger, first assistant; Melville Dozier, second assistant; Grant Karr, third assistant, and Mrs. Susan M. Dorsey, fourth assistant.

San Diego Panama California Exposition

The two events occurring this year (1915) that will stand out most prominently in the future history of California are the Panama California Exposition at San Diego and the Panama-Pacific International Exposition at San Francisco. The first opened with the ringing in of the New Year at midnight January 1, 1915, when President Wilson at Washington touched the electric button turning on all the lights of the Exposition. This was accompanied by the ringing of bells, the tooting of horns and the booming of cannon, ushering in at the same time the year 1915 and the Exposition, which will continue throughout the year.

One of the most attractive features of the midnight display was an electric piece representing the mingling of the waters of the Atlantic and the Pacific Oceans in the Panama Canal. President Wilson was represented at the opening of the Exposition by his son-in-law, Hon. William G. McAdoo and Mrs. McAdoo. The buildings are of the Mission type of architecture and busts of distinguished persons of the Spanish era are set in the facade of the California building.

One of the peculiar features of the San Diego Exposition is the "Painted Desert." It is a reproduction of an Indian village in the Southwest. Indian houses built of native material brought from Arizona and New Mexico represent Indian architecture of centuries past; and a colony of Indians from New Mexico illustrates life in their pueblos present and past.

The Panama Pacific Exposition At San Francisco

The Panama Pacific International Exposition was opened at San Francisco at noon, February 20, 1915. The day had been declared a legal holiday by Governor Johnson. For five years the people of San Francisco had been looking forward to this great event, and as the time approached for its opening their enthusiasm grew intense. The morning of the opening day was ushered in by every imaginable variety of noise — toots, whoops, booms and roars. At six o'clock in the morning horns, sirens, whistles, bells, telephones — everything that could add to the din was turned loose.

To provide conveyance for all to the Exposition grounds was impossible, so it was decided that all who were physically able would walk. By nine o'clock the greatest crowd that ever assembled in the history of the city had gathered in Van

443

Ness avenue. This avenue along which the people marched to the exposition grounds was decked with the Exposition colors and American flags. The open spaces of the Exposition grounds were jammed with people when President Wilson, at Washington, touched the electric button and promptly at noon, February 20, 1915, the great Exposition opened. Then the big guns of the forts boomed; the water in the fountains flowed; the engines in the Palace of Machinery began to move, and three hundred thousand waiting people with bared heads sang "The Star Spangled Banner." The great Exposition was formally opened.

California is prepared to exhibit to the world the achievements of years of work, of energy, of push and of enterprise. The Exposition does not belong to San Francisco, but to the whole state.

Printed in Great Britain
by Amazon

82476746R00261